Prepublication praise for

IN PURSUIT OF PEACE

There can hardly be a better person to record and analyze the history of Israel's peace movement than Mordechai Bar-On, who combines a rigorous academic discipline with first-hand experience and knowledge of the movement from the inside. This is a grand tour-de-force and a first rate analysis of the movement. His treatment of the subject is well documented, comprehensive, engaging, and lucid—the best resource on the subject so far.

—Shulamit Aloni,
Israeli minister of culture, science and communication

In an engaging and simple style, Bar-On relates the trials and tribulations of the "peaceniks" of Israel, who struggled against many odds and reached out to their counterparts among the Palestinians, who were ready to stand up and hold hands together. This study is a conclusive and creative analysis of the Israelis peace forces; it certainly invites the recording of the parallel forces of the Palestinian side.

—Faisal Husseini,
Palestinian leader in charge of the Jerusalem portfolio

The endeavors of the Israeli peace movement, their collisions and collusions, are the main theme of this brilliant book. The fact that they were proven right is the more reason to have their arduous and persistent exertions documented—for which difficult task none is more competent and better equipped than the learned and distinguished author.

—Chaim Cohen,
retired Israeli Supreme Court justice

Bar-On's book is full of fascinating, little-known details, enriching a sweeping historical synthesis of the whole course of the Israeli-Arab conflict since the 1930s. Bar-On has a unique way of looking at the history through the eyes of peace pioneers and activists, without overstating their roles. An extraordinarily balanced treatment of the subject.

—Samuel W. Lewis,
former U.S. ambassador to Israel

In Pursuit of
PEACE

A History
of the
Israeli
Peace
Movement

MORDECHAI BAR-ON

UNITED STATES INSTITUTE OF PEACE PRESS
Washington, D.C.

United States Institute of Peace
1550 M Street, N.W.
Washington, D.C. 20005

First published 1996

Printed in the United States of America

The paper used in this publication meets the minimum requirements of American National Standard for Information Sciences—Permanence of Paper for Printed Library Materials, ANSI Z39.48-1984.

Library of Congress Cataloging-in-Publication Data
Bar-On, Mordechai, 1928–
    In pursuit of peace: a history of the Israeli peace movement / Mordechai Bar-On.
       p. cm.
    Includes bibliographical references and index.
    ISBN 1-878379-54-2 (hardback). —ISBN 1-878379-53-4 (pbk.)
    1. Peace movements—Israel—History. 2. Jewish-Arab relations—1949– 3. Israel—Politics and government. I. Title.
DS119.7.B2832 1996
956.9405—dc20
                                    96-4787
                                        CIP

For my daughters
Einat, Tal, and Hilla
who were there too

Contents

Foreword

The title of this book neatly encapsulates its twofold aim: to cover the history of the Israeli peace movement, and to demonstrate that it is very much a work in progress—the pursuit of a peace that is by no means assured.

In this fascinating work, Mordechai Bar-On traces the evolution of the Israeli peace movement over a period of no less than forty-five years, from the birth of the Jewish state to the signing of the Declaration of Principles by the Israeli prime minister and PLO chairman in 1993. While the first two decades of this period were relatively quiet in terms of peace activism, thereafter an increasing number and variety of groups appeared on the Israeli political scene urging their fellow countrymen and women to come to some peaceful accommodation with the Palestinians and neighboring Arab states. Bar-On, himself a prominent activist as well as a former senior army officer and member of the Knesset, presents intimate portraits of the impressively diverse range of groups and individuals involved in this peace movement: soldiers, statesmen, professors, poets, diplomats, journalists.

This volume is much more than a narrowly focused examination of a protest movement, however. Bar-On's chief objective, to be sure, is to detail and explore the dynamics, character, and development of the Israeli peace groups, and he fulfills this objective masterfully, providing the most readable and best-researched account of the Israeli peace movement available in English. But he accomplishes much more than this. With an even-handedness remarkable for one so deeply enmeshed in public debate on peace and security issues, Bar-On portrays the sweep of Israel's shifting ethnic, ideological, and political tides, which at times buoyed up the peace activists, but at other times threatened to overwhelm them.

Furthermore, he presents an impressive historical synthesis of the entire course of the Israeli-Arab conflict. Capturing the way in which diplomatic and political developments influenced the agendas and activities of the peace groups, the action switches back and forth between street politics and high diplomacy, between mass demonstrations in Tel Aviv and maneuvering and negotiations in Washington, Cairo, Amman, New York, Tunis, and Oslo. The galvanizing shock of war, terrorism, and civil unrest is likewise conveyed, with fascinating analyses given of the course and consequences of the Six Day War, the October War, the Lebanon war, and the Intifada. The fate of the territories occupied in 1967 and of the Palestinian people—the issue that most preoccupied and animated the peace activists—appropriately receives much attention.

This work is certainly a history, but the issues it discusses are very much alive today. In the conclusion, written after the assassination of Prime Minister Yitzhak Rabin in November 1995 and before the bombings of February and March 1996, Bar-On notes that the story of the Israeli peace movement, like that of the Middle East peace process, is far from complete. In part because of the efforts of groups such as Peace Now, Yesh Gvul, and the Women in Black, Israelis and Palestinians are edging toward implementation of an agreement that would have been almost unimaginable only a few years ago. But continued progress in the peace process is by no means assured, and Israeli society is deeply riven with disagreement on how best to assure the country's security. This awareness of the uncertain future of the process begun in Madrid and Oslo—and, indeed, of the fact that peace can never be secured once and for all, and must instead be cultivated constantly—prompted our choice of title, that of a quest as yet unfulfilled.

The wide purview of this study covers many themes of continuing interest to the United States Institute of Peace: conflict and reconciliation in the Middle East; the ability of nongovernmental organizations to build support for nonviolent solutions to long-standing disputes; the role of track-two diplomacy in bringing longtime political adversaries into dialogue; the interrelationships among domestic, regional, and international actors and events; and the lessons of successful efforts to manage conflicts. Among its other achievements, this work stands as an impressive case study of the strengths and limitations of nongovernmental organizations in effecting some degree of reconciliation in highly charged national and regional climates, and in helping to bring about remarkable shifts in the attitudes of political leaders and the conduct of national policy.

The Institute of Peace has long had an interest in Middle East issues, and has addressed them through numerous grants, fellowships, workshops, and publications. Notable among the latter are *Making Peace Among Arabs and Israelis: Lessons from Fifty Years of Negotiating Experience,* by Kenneth W. Stein and Samuel W. Lewis; *Arms Control and Confidence Building in the Middle East,* edited by Alan Platt; and *Palestinians, Refugees, and the Middle East Peace Process,* by Don Peretz.

A former Institute peace fellow and grantee, Mordechai Bar-On has written a book that advances the Institute's congressionally mandated task of furthering knowledge about peacemaking and conflict resolution. *In Pursuit of Peace* may be read for its account of the struggles of a diverse and determined cast of Israeli peace activists; for its insights into the dynamics of protest groups and democratic processes; for its exploration of half a century of Israeli-Arab conflict; for its analysis of the interrelationships among national, regional, and international politics; and for the sheer enjoyment of reading a dramatic and meaningful tale well told. For whatever reason, it deserves to be read, and we are pleased to publish it.

Richard H. Solomon, President
United States Institute of Peace

Acknowledgments

During the academic year of 1992–93 I had the good fortune to be selected as a Jennings Randolph Peace Fellow at the United States Institute of Peace in Washington, D.C. My project was to research and write a book on the history of the Israeli peace movement. Although I completed some of the research before I arrived in Washington, most of the writing was done under the auspices of the Institute. My year in Washington was wonderful due in large part to the supportive environment at the Institute. By sharing their thoughts and ideas with me, the other peace fellows, their research assistants, and the Institute staff helped to create an intellectual environment beneficial to this study.

Although I cannot mention all the kind people I met at the Institute, I would like them to know how much I appreciated their help and friendship. I would particularly like to thank Michael Lund, who was the director of the Jennings Randolph Fellowship Program, and Barbara Cullicott, the program administrator. Joseph Klaits was not only my program officer but also a friend and colleague who provided me with useful comments and suggestions on earlier versions of the manuscript. Nigel Quinney of the Publications Department gave my project special attention, offered many important comments that helped me avoid a number of pitfalls, and at the end trimmed and fine-tuned the manuscript. After completing my fellowship year in Washington, I received an additional grant from the Institute that allowed me to continue working for another year in Jerusalem. I would like to express my gratitude to the staff of the Grants Program at the Institute.

My partner in producing this study was Joseph Helman, my research assistant from 1992 until 1995. Joe played a vital role in the research and bibliographic components of this study. He provided me with valuable advice throughout the course of the project, and his comments and suggestions enriched every aspect of the study. He also edited the entire manuscript and transformed my "Hebrew English" into proper English. Additionally, he compiled the bibliography. This book could not have been completed without his friendly contribution.

The Ben Zvi Institute in Jerusalem became my new academic home upon my return to Israel. The last four chapters were completed under its auspices, and I want to thank Tzvi Tzameret and other members of the staff for their help.

Many members of the peace movement provided me with interviews that helped guide me throughout the study. Some also gave me access to their private archives, which yielded a wealth of information. Although all of them are mentioned in the relevant notes, I want to thank them again for their generous assistance. Special mention is deserved by Janet Aviad, who encouraged and assisted me in numerous ways.

Last but not least, I would like to thank the hundreds of friends and colleagues whom I met over the years as a result of my own activity in the peace movement. These sensitive, intelligent, and energetic young people (most of them around the age of my daughters) were active in the movement before I joined. They always gave me great hope for a brighter future. By dedicating this study to my daughters, I want to thank them all for who and what they are.

Introduction

The Focus

In the Six Day War of June 1967, Israeli forces defeated the combined armies of Egypt, Syria, and Jordan, in the process conquering substantial areas and doubling the size of the territory under Israel's control. In the lyrics of a Hebrew folk song that became popular during the war, a soldier returning from the battle tells his young daughter, "I promise you, my little girl, that this will be the last war." This expressed the sentiment shared by many Israelis during the euphoric weeks that followed the stunning victory of 1967. However, this was not to be the last war. Over the course of almost thirty years since, Israel has fought three more major wars, suffered scores of guerrilla attacks, and confronted in the occupied territories a popular uprising known as the Intifada.[1]

During the decade that followed the 1967 war, Israel was governed by parliamentary coalitions dominated by the Labor Party. In principle Labor supported the "Land for Peace" formula as incorporated in United Nations Security Council Resolution 242, which refers to an Israeli withdrawal from "territories occupied in the war" in exchange for peace. This famous resolution became the departure point for subsequent negotiations.

During this same period a strong grass-roots peace movement appeared in Israel, and a dialogue with Israel's enemies gradually became part of the political landscape. A peace treaty between Israel and Egypt was achieved by the government of Menachem Begin in 1979, dramatically altering the terms of the Arab-Israeli conflict. The psychological barriers to peace began to erode as the treaty demonstrated that peace could, in fact, be achieved between bitter adversaries on terms acceptable to both. In the short term, however, the Egyptian-Israeli Peace Treaty did little to alter the core conflict between the Palestinians and Israelis and failed to induce any of the other Arab states to end their belligerency toward Israel.

Twenty-seven years after the Six Day War a cautious experiment in Israeli-Palestinian reconciliation began. On September 13, 1993, the Israeli prime minister and the chairman of the Palestine Liberation Organization signed a Declaration of Principles, and Israeli troops began to withdraw from Gaza and Jericho. After numerous delays, serious negotiations began between Israel and its Arab neighbors. In a festive ceremony near Aqaba in October 1994, Israel and Jordan signed a peace treaty and ended the state of war that had existed between them since 1948. Although yet to bear fruit, negotiations between Israel and another neighbor, Syria, are continuing. Meanwhile, despite bloody opposition and political uncertainty, the Israeli-Palestinian experiment moves forward, with negotiations on an ultimate settlement scheduled to begin in May 1996.

As one watches old adversaries take these long-overdue steps toward peace, a difficult question presents itself: Could reconciliation have been achieved earlier? Why did it take more than a quarter century after the Six Day War, and tremendous costs in human and economic terms on all sides, before the parties began to talk seriously about peace?

Obviously, numerous factors contributed to the success or failure of the various peace initiatives undertaken over the years. For many years the Palestinian national movement adhered to radical positions, insisting on the elimination of Zionism and the Jewish state. Over time the views of many Palestine Liberation Organization leaders moderated as they recognized that although it may have been satisfying to speak of Israel's destruction through Palestinian armed struggle, this strategy was unlikely to prove successful. The United States was involved in the peace process, but not always with the necessary resolve and consistency. Superpower rivalry in the Middle East made Israel and the Arab states valuable Cold War clients, but at times it was the clients who guided the regional policies of their patrons rather than the converse. The Arab states, especially Egypt, had to restore their national dignity following the 1967 defeat before they could feel confident enough to begin the process of reconciliation. From 1977 to 1992 successive Israeli governments were either headed by or included the Likud party. Many within the Likud were committed to maintaining Israel's control over the occupied territories, which they viewed as parts of the historical Greater Land of Israel. Finally, the Palestinians needed the psychological and moral victory provided by the Intifada.

The object of this book is not to pass judgment on who was most or least responsible for blocking the road to peace, nor is it to present a history of the conflict or to describe the evolving peace process. The subject of this study is more limited, and centers on an examination of what is generically referred to as Israel's peace movement, its development, and the role it played in Israel's pursuit of peace. Domestic, regional, and international factors and events are incorporated into the study only as they relate to the efforts and reactions of the peace movement. Such events are examined from the perspective of the political and psychological environment within which the peace movement operated.

This does not mean that the conditions that developed were created exclusively by the individuals and groups mentioned in this study. The history of Israeli peace politics and diplomacy is primarily a story of governmental and parliamentary decision making, and this requires a separate study. However, as we try to demonstrate, the peace movement constituted a salient factor that influenced the political process.

The reader will recognize two constants that were present throughout the history of the peace movement: differences of opinion, and organizational fragmentation. This study describes a variety of peace groups and their leaders, who at times held divergent and even conflicting opinions and sometimes pursued very different strategies. However, focusing on the controversies that frequently occurred within the movement may distort the broader picture. Despite the debates that sometimes divided the movement, a unity of purpose and vision of a common goal prevailed. This study attempts to describe and explain these dynamics.

Bias and Objectivity

This book was written by an Israeli who was personally involved in many of the events described in it. In 1968, after serving for twenty years in the Israeli Defense Forces, I was elected to head the Youth Department of the World Zionist Organization. In this position my responsibilities included working with Jewish youth who subscribed to a very broad range of political and ideological perspectives. This responsibility demanded objectivity in my decision making and required that (as also during my years of military service) I restrain the public expression of my personal political views.

When I retired in 1978 and began to pursue academic interests, I felt free to express my own political and ideological convictions. My two eldest daughters, Einat and Tal, were already active in Peace Now, having joined the relatively new but large and influential peace group at its inception. I soon joined them and have been an active member ever since. When I entered the movement I was considerably older than the average activist. Although I did not participate in its day-to-day activities, I regularly attended the street demonstrations and accepted special assignments the movement's leaders asked me to undertake. Consequently, I was present at many of the events described in this study and occasionally played a leading role in them. I was also one of the founders of the International Center for Peace in the Middle East and participated in many dialogues with Palestinian leaders. Throughout this period I actively engaged in the seemingly endless political and ideological debates within Israeli society and within the peace movement itself.

As an insider who participated in many of the events described in this study, I recognize the potential dangers of bias and subjectivity. However, these must be weighed against the advantages of intimate knowledge and understanding of the issues here addressed. In approaching this study I recognized that I could not—and therefore did not attempt to—anesthetize my sympathies with those individuals and groups who like myself sought to promote peace between Arabs (especially the Palestinians) and Israelis. However, I have tried to be fair to all parties and to describe personalities and events as objectively as possible. The reader may judge whether I have succeeded. One bias that I freely admit is my devout belief that it is a vital national interest—and a moral obligation—for Israel to resolve the hundred-year conflict with its Arab neighbors.

Clearly, this study is one-sided in another way too. It tells the story primarily from the Israeli perspective. To tell the story in its entirety, another study is necessary, one that will describe and analyze the pursuit of peace inside the Palestinian national movement. Such a study, I believe, will be better undertaken by a Palestinian. The story I tell here, though it occasionally touches on the "other side," concentrates on the Israeli side and thus remains incomplete.

Some Methodological Considerations

The organization of this book is mainly chronological. The first chapter is dedicated to a few "peaceniks" who were active in the 1950s and 1960s and examines why no significant peace movement existed in the first two decades of Israeli statehood. The story becomes more detailed after the 1967 war. The flow of the narrative is interrupted at times to discuss specific factors in Israeli politics and society that influenced the peace movement. The study ends on September 13, 1993, with the signing of the Declaration of Principles on the White House lawn. This ceremony was followed by negotiations between Israel and the Palestine Liberation Organization concerning Israel's withdrawal from the Gaza Strip and Jericho, and the transfer of authority over parts of the West Bank to Palestinian self-rule. However, though the peace movement certainly did not cease its activities in September 1993, these events are beyond the scope of this study, and I offer only a few tentative reflections on the future of the peace process and peace movement in conclusion.

The account given here of the activities of the peace movement is (as the endnotes testify) based heavily on primary sources. The movement conducted itself with little secrecy. In fact, with its leaders always eager to attract media attention, the movement considered transparency to be a great advantage. I had full access to the archives and personal files of groups and individuals associated with the movement. Additionally, I conducted many interviews, which provided me with valuable information and insight. (Details are given in the bibliography.)

Those parts of the narrative that deal with international developments are based chiefly on press reports, memoirs, and various secondary sources. Most of these events have been discussed and analyzed at length elsewhere; for the purposes of this study these developments are relevant only in terms of how they were perceived and acted on by Israeli peace activists.

Many of the commentaries available on the peace movement are in the form of newspaper and magazine reports and articles. Only a small amount of academic research has been undertaken and published so far.[2] I hope the original contribution of this study is to be found in its scope, in terms of both the time frame and the number of groups examined. Perhaps the descriptions, explanations, and analysis offered here will provide the reader with a better understanding of the forces that shaped public opinion and eventually made it possible for leaders such as Begin, Rabin, and Peres to travel the road to peace.

*　　*　　*

This is essentially the story of how a limited number of Israelis over the past three decades perceived their situation and its effects on the future of their state and how, despite the prevailing consensus to the contrary, they unequivocally advocated political and territorial compromise in pursuit of peace. They took upon themselves the task of persuading their fellow Israelis to accept their perceptions and prescriptions. This study recounts how a group of dedicated men and women tried to construct peace in the minds of many.

In
Pursuit
of
PEACE

1

Zero-Sum
The First Two Decades

During the first two decades after the birth of the State of Israel, many attempts were made at mediation between the Arab states and Israel. How and when peace might be achieved were much debated by Israelis, Arabs, and the international community. From time to time certain political forces within Israel challenged governmental policy regarding the Arab-Israeli conflict. Some initiatives were suggested and undertaken by parliamentary factions, others by private and extraparliamentary groups. In this chapter three initiatives are discussed in some detail. In two cases, journalists used their publications to argue for the possibility of a peaceful solution to the conflict. Another initiative was begun by an employee of the World Jewish Congress, who tried to make use of his special contacts with Arabs around the Mediterranean.

However, despite the growing tensions between Israel and its neighbors, what one might generically refer to as "peace forces" were neither significant in scope nor influential in results in the Israeli body politic at the time. The price Israel was asked to pay for peace was viewed by most Israelis as too high to be seriously considered, and the bellicose rhetoric that emanated from Arab capitals made peace sound unattainable to most Israelis. In short, subjective and objective barriers made conciliation between Jews and Arabs impossible. In the Middle East of the 1950s and 1960s, belligerency prevailed.

The Painful Legacy of the 1948 War

From the Jewish perspective, the Arab-Israeli war of 1948 was undeniably a war of expansion. The newly created State of Israel had two objectives in this war: first, to defend itself and the Jewish community in Palestine against the attempts of the Palestinian Arabs (and later the regular armies of neighboring Arab states) to prevent the establishment of the Jewish state; and second, to expand the territorial area of Jewish sovereignty in which future immigrants would be settled. For their part, the Arabs attempted not only to undo the United Nations General Assembly resolution of November 29, 1947 (which partitioned Palestine into two separate states, one Jewish and one Arab), but also to erase the events of the previous five decades during which the Zionists had succeeded in building a formidable national existence.[1] A day after the UN resolution was adopted, Palestinian irregular forces tried to stifle its implementation by launching an intensive guerrilla campaign. Although helped by volunteers from the neighboring Arab states, the Palestinians were unable to stop the establishment of the Jewish state, which was declared in Tel Aviv on May 15, 1948. An invasion by the regular armies of five Arab states followed shortly thereafter, but did not fare much better.[2]

During the fall and early winter of 1948 the new Israeli army launched a number of military counteroffensives and managed to further expand the territorial base of the Jewish state. In addition to the 5,600 square miles allocated to it by the UN partition resolution, Israel gained control over an additional 2,500 square miles of territory that would have been part of the Arab state proposed by the resolution.[3] Toward the end of the war Prime Minister David Ben-Gurion concluded that the conquest of too much land could become a liability for Israel. He believed that if Israel overreached itself and tried to hold on to too large a part of Palestine, especially if that land was inhabited by many Arabs, the resulting backlash could endanger Israeli control of the territories already acquired. Consequently, toward the end of the war he restrained his generals and ordered the retreat of advanced forces in a few battle zones, thus sacrificing additional territorial gains.[4] "Israel needs now more people, not more land," was a theme often sounded by Ben-Gurion in those days.[5]

Ben-Gurion rose through the ranks of the Jewish labor movement in Palestine during the period of British rule (1918–48) and by the late 1940s had become the uncontested leader of the Zionist movement. Since late 1946 he had been responsible for the security and defense of the Jewish community and settlements in Palestine, and was the chief architect of Israel's political and military victory in its 1948 War of Independence. He was the natural choice to be the first prime minister of the State of Israel. Except for a brief hiatus in 1954, Ben-Gurion also held the defense portfolio until his final retirement in June 1963. In these capacities he, more than anyone, shaped Israel's defense and foreign policies, which were proactive and even aggressive for much of the period. However, by late 1949 it seemed to Ben-Gurion and a majority of the Israeli public that the armistice agreements concluded under UN mediation earlier in the year had established the practical and permanent borders of the state, as well as the peace necessary for the state to begin to grow.[6] The absorption of hundreds of thousands of Jewish immigrants during the early 1950s, the need for rapid economic development, and the establishment of modern public services became Israel's priorities.

When in the fall of 1949 Ben-Gurion presented his government to the first Knesset for approval, he declared that the pursuit of peace was one of his primary goals.[7] Moshe Sharett, Israel's first minister for foreign affairs, remembered the prevailing mood in those early days: "We, all of us, lived with the hope that peace was around the corner. We believed that the Arab world accepted the verdict [of the war]. We all thought that peace would be established and crystallized more and more."[8]

In December 1948 the UN General Assembly nominated the Palestine Conciliation Commission in the hope of translating the armistice agreements into stable and lasting peace treaties. Abba Eban, the Israeli representative to the United Nations, told the Security Council that "there is an organic link between these armistice agreements and the peace settlement which is now being sought under the auspices of the General Assembly through its Conciliation Commission . . . the armistice is envisaged not as an end in itself but as a transition to permanent peace."[9]

However, it quickly became apparent that this hope was to be shattered by the complex realities of the Arab-Israeli conflict. The Arabs would not accept the outcome of the war; in fact, they were unwilling to soften their resolve to try again to undo the creation of Israel, which they viewed as a blatant historical injustice. They were adamant in their determination to keep their belligerence against the "Zionist invasion" alive and active. It was also clear that Israel was not prepared to pay the price for peace that would have been required at that time, even by the most moderate Arabs. Israel was ready neither to give up significant portions of the territories it had gained in the war, nor to allow a significant number of Palestinian refugees to return to their homes in what was now the State of Israel. For the Arabs, the presence of close to three-quarters of a million Palestinian refugees in shanty camps throughout the neighboring countries served as not only a permanent reminder of their military and political failure but also a symbol of injustice and evil.[10]

During the 1950s and 1960s several diplomatic and semiofficial efforts at mediation were made between Israel and Arab states.[11] These efforts produced few if any results. Some observers accused Israel of intransigence and aggressiveness during that period, while others blamed the Arabs for clinging to their desire to destroy Israel as soon as they were militarily able to do so.[12] Nevertheless, while opportunities were missed by both sides,[13] the accumulated experience of the nineteen years between 1948 and 1967 suggests that underlying political and strategic conditions made reconciliation impossible during this period.[14]

The Arabs had little incentive to make peace with Israel because they had little reason to abandon the hope that in time they would be able to defeat Israel militarily. The 1948 defeat was rationalized, particularly in Egypt, as another symptom of the corruption of the old regimes. Repeated pronouncements from Arab capitals suggested the intention to resume the armed conflict as soon as the military and political circumstances were ripe. To be sure, no evidence has been found to date that would indicate that a "second round" was in the immediate plans of the Arab leaders. By the same token, there were certainly no Arab leaders who seriously recommended making peace with what they considered to be the criminal Zionist intrusion in their midst.

President Gamal Abdul Nasser often claimed that the Israeli raid on an Egyptian army post in the Gaza Strip on February 28, 1955, made him painfully aware of the danger that Israel posed to his country and the Arab world at large.[15] In his perception of his role as the most prominent Arab leader, Nasser elevated the confrontation with Israel to become a main theme of his leadership. Speaking before the Egyptian People's Council on the occasion of the fifth anniversary of his revolution, Nasser outlined his desire "to build in Egypt a great nation" in order to "prohibit Israel from fixing its foundations on the holy and pure land it has torn away from us."[16]

Robert Anderson, a special envoy of President Eisenhower, was sent to the Middle East on a secret mission early in 1956 to mediate between

Nasser and Ben-Gurion. When Anderson pressed the Egyptian leader to meet Israeli leaders face-to-face, Nasser recalled the fate of King Abdullah of Jordan, who had been assassinated five years earlier, apparently as punishment for his decision to enter into negotiations with Israel. The Egyptian leader said that he feared for his life, and argued that the Arab world was not ready for such direct negotiations.[17] This was certainly true, and Nasser himself had little incentive to risk his populist leadership position, not least because Israel did not seem to him to be capable of seriously threatening Egypt's national interests.

For its part, Israel equivocated on the subject of serious negotiations. During the discussions held by the Palestine Conciliation Commission in Lausanne in 1949 it became clear to the Israeli representatives that if the Arabs were ready for a deal, their minimal conditions would be the return of most Palestinian refugees to territories held by Israel and the return of all Israeli-occupied territories not allotted to the Jews by the 1947 UN Partition Resolution.[18] Meeting these terms would have meant that Israel, with close to 1 million Jews at the time, would have had to absorb nearly 750,000 Palestinian Arabs, who could soon become the majority in the state, thus ending the Zionist enterprise. During the 1950s and 1960s the main territorial demands of the Arabs focused on the Negev, the arid area south of Be'er Sheva stretching down to Eilat on the Gulf of Aqaba. Israel was not prepared to cede control of the Negev, as to have done so would have cut Israel's access to the Red Sea, Asia, and Africa and taken away much of its land reserves.[19]

There was agreement in principle on this position even between Ben-Gurion and Sharett. As we shall see later, Foreign Minister Sharett was sometimes inclined to take more moderate positions than his prime minister. But during the Lausanne discussions, when the heavy price Israel was required to pay for peace became apparent, Sharett said in a staff briefing, "Formal peace with the Arab States is not a vital necessity for us," later adding that "of course we want peace, but we cannot run, we must walk slowly."[20] The perception of the overwhelming majority of Israelis during the first two decades was that a second round of war with the Arabs was inevitable. This unshakable popular conviction was based not only on the political logic of the situation, but also on the flood of bellicose declarations by Arab leaders that seemed entirely to rule out Israel's ever reaching true conciliation with them. Arab rhetoric was the more convincing because of the repeated infiltrations and attacks of Arab guerrillas, often with the acquiescence and blessing of Arab governments.

Consequently, resources that were not consumed by Israel's efforts toward economic development and the absorption of immigrants were dedicated to defense. Discussions of peace and reconciliation during this period were considered by most Israelis to be idle chatter.[21]

Early Parliamentary Peace Alternatives

In such an atmosphere it was highly unlikely that a serious peace movement could develop. Nevertheless, the hope for peace and the efforts to keep this hope politically alive continued among small factions in Israeli politics. The small Israeli Communist Party was certainly the most outspoken of these groups. This party was still committed to its traditional anti-Zionist stand and was loyal to Soviet ideology and political strategy, which from the last days of Stalin (and more so under Khrushchev after the watershed Czech-Egyptian arms sale of 1955) became outspokenly pro-Arab in its orientation.[22] By this time Israel had already cast its lot with the West, as evidenced by its support in 1950 for the Western position regarding UN resolutions on Korea.[23] The Soviets worsened their standing in Israeli public opinion when, in the Security Council, they supported the closing of the Suez Canal to Israeli navigation and endorsed the Syrian demand that Israel refrain from diverting water from the Jordan River in 1953 and 1954.[24] The Soviets also consistently supported the Arab demand that Israel retreat to the UN partition lines and allow all Palestinian refugees who so desired to return to their homes. The positions taken by the Israeli communists reflected these views and therefore had no impact on Israeli public opinion beyond the party's own constituency. Adhering to Marxist-Leninist doctrine, the Israeli communists insisted on an antinationalist posture, hailing "people's fraternity" and declaring themselves an Arab-Jewish party, but managed to attract very few Jews to their ranks. Their constituency mainly came from Israel's Arab minority, which saw this party more as a means of expressing their national aspirations and grievances than of promoting world revolution. For all practical purposes the Israeli Communist Party evolved during these years into being the most significant political expression and representation of the Palestinian Arab minority of Israel.

The United Labor Party (Mapam) was by contrast avowedly Zionist. Indeed, it was originally a Zionist-socialist movement based primarily on two of the most successful kibbutz groups, Hakibbutz Ha'artzi and Hakibbutz Hameuchad, that combined socialist ideology with an ardent belief in the gathering of all Jews in their ancestral land and the achievement of a just society through collective farms and industries. Before the creation of the State of Israel, some of the political groups that later formed Mapam had advocated a binational state in which Jews and Arabs would live side by side. Although it tried to attract Israeli Arabs to its ranks, Mapam was primarily a Jewish party. As such it was fundamentally loyal to the Zionist project. However, it continued to maintain a dovish posture toward the Arab-Israeli conflict and advocated compromise and reconciliation. This tendency was especially marked after the secession in 1952 of Achdut Ha'avodah (The Union of Labor), which was based primarily on the Hakibbutz Hameuchad and adopted a hard line on security issues.

Mapam joined the government coalition in November 1955, but often voted in the minority against taking aggressive action toward the Arab states. For example, Mapam was the only coalition party that voted against the launching of the Sinai campaign in October 1956. This campaign came as a result of growing tensions with Egypt during 1955 and 1956 and the massive arms deal Nasser concluded with the Soviet Union, which threatened to undermine Israel's deterrent posture.[25] Ben-Gurion eventually decided on this military adventure after a secret agreement was made that coordinated an Israeli attack with British and French plans to invade Egypt, destroy Nasser, and resume international control over the Suez Canal.[26] Mapam's leadership objected to this campaign for two reasons: they did not believe that a military initiative would solve the security problems facing Israel, and they did not wish Israel to be involved in a colonialist plot. Nevertheless, instead of resigning they decided to remain in the government because the nation was at war. The party announced that it would share the collective responsibility for the government's decisions along with all other coalition members.[27]

Late in 1949, leaders of Mapam and the Israeli Communist Party, together with some independent intellectuals, formed the Israeli Peace Committee (IPC). The IPC was officially a branch of the World Peace Council, a seemingly neutral but actually pro-Soviet and anti-American international front founded in Paris in the fall of 1949. Although the IPC was constituted as an independent, nonpartisan movement based on personal affiliation, it remained in essence a coalition of its two founding parties.[28]

In the first few years of its existence, the IPC scored some impressive achievements. Three times it circulated public petitions, which as many as 30 to 40 percent of Israeli adults signed.[29] A number of public gatherings were well attended. These successes, however, owed much to the

IPC's avoidance of the thorny issues of the Arab-Israeli conflict. Instead, the IPC operated on the basis of messages formulated by the World Peace Council that addressed broad international topics (such as the banning of nuclear weapons, opposition to the rearming of Germany, and calls for neutrality in the Cold War) that were less controversial in Israel.

The appeal of the IPC began to fade in 1953 and diminished significantly in the wake of the Soviet Union's adoption of an unmistakably pro-Arab position after the death of Stalin. As the World Peace Council and many of its branches around the world embraced anti-Israeli positions after the 1956 Suez War, the IPC splintered. Its activities dwindled to the occasional publication of proclamations that met with public and media indifference and the half-hearted participation of a nucleus of semiprofessional members who remained active in international gatherings—gatherings that increasingly tended to end in harsh criticism of Israel and Zionism.

The IPC can hardly be considered a genuine Israeli peace movement because most of its activities concerned issues with little relevance to the problems that preoccupied Israelis. Whenever the committee did deal with local issues, its own internecine controversies undermined the impact of its messages on the larger public, which by and large considered the IPC to be little more than a poorly disguised tool of the Soviet Union.

Mapam was not the only party that sometimes felt ill at ease with the aggressive policies of Ben-Gurion. The small Progressive Liberal Party, as well as some members of the National Religious Party, voted against Ben-Gurion's proposals at times. However, neither Mapam nor the other parties could offer serious alternatives for peace during those years. None was prepared to recommend concessions on the issues of territory or refugees—both of which were regarded by the Arabs as prerequisites for negotiation. Their differences with Ben-Gurion were chiefly tactical and did not amount to an alternative policy direction on the outstanding issues between Israel and its enemies.[30]

Ben-Gurion versus Sharett

Ben-Gurion's main challenger on foreign policy matters during the early 1950s came from within the ranks of the ruling Labor Party.[31] Moshe Sharett, who not only served as foreign minister but also replaced Ben-Gurion as prime minister during the latter's yearlong temporary retirement in 1954, deeply disagreed with Ben-Gurion on the management of the Arab-Israeli conflict. Whereas Ben-Gurion believed that Israel would have to encounter another round of wars and would occasionally have to demonstrate its power for the purposes of deterrence, Sharett believed that moderation and restraint could de-escalate the conflict and possibly bring about similar restraint on the Arab side.[32]

But the gap between these two leaders was not as wide as it seemed at the time. There were many indications that Ben-Gurion did not believe he could resolve the conflict by imposing a solution on the Arabs. In December 1955, in front of the officers of Israel's High Command, Ben-Gurion defended his government's decision not to launch a preemptive attack on the Egyptian forces in the Sinai. This idea was widely supported among the Israeli security establishment in the fall of 1955, particularly after the announcement of the Egyptian-Soviet arms deal. "No war can end all wars," Ben-Gurion told his officers, arguing that even if a preemptive strike succeeded, Israel would still have to encounter more wars in the future.[33]

On the issue of territories and refugees Sharett was as adamant as Ben-Gurion. For example, he told the Labor Party's Political Committee, "We are obliged to make it clear to the [U.S.] administration that no territorial change can be spoken of, no violation of our sovereignty, no return of refugees."[34] On many occasions Sharett made clear his conviction that peace between the Arab states and Israel could be concluded only between "the Arab states as they are and Israel as it is."[35]

To be sure, Sharett was often disturbed by Ben-Gurion's security policies. For instance, after a long consultation on the preparations required to confront an expected Egyptian attack in April 1956, he wrote, "All those cumbersome preparations for the big catastrophe are unfounded, and will vanish like smoke when no war will erupt." He felt himself "caught up by the feeling of irreality of the entire discussion."[36] Perhaps many of these misgivings were little more than matters of style and temperament. Neither Ben-Gurion nor Sharett believed that peace was attainable under the existing circumstances, and both considered that the conflict must therefore be managed as well as possible. Sharett, Mapam, and the other moderates could at most present a pious conviction that by refraining from aggravating the conflict through aggressive initiatives, Israel might lay the foundation for reconciliation sometime in the remote and unforeseeable future. However, since no progress toward peace could be demonstrated, Sharett was unable to generate much political support for his views. There was little opposition when Ben-Gurion decided to dispense with Sharett's services in June 1956.[37]

The Palestinian Factor

In the years between 1949 and 1967 the Middle East conflict was considered by most observers to be primarily a struggle between Israel and its neighboring Arab states. During much of this period the Palestinians were not present as an independent political force. Nevertheless, as they had before the War of Independence, some Israelis continued to view the clash between Zionism and the nascent Palestinian national movement as the main cause of the bitter strife. The first Zionist leader who realized that the Zionist venture in Palestine would inevitably lead to a head-on collision with the national movement of the Palestinian Arabs was Ze'ev Jabotinsky, the leader of the extreme right-wing Revisionist Party.[38] Jabotinsky had recognized the idiosyncrasies of Palestinian identity early on. In a July 1921 speech at the Zionist General Council, and later in two articles he published in the Russian-language Zionist magazine *Rasswiet* in 1923 and 1924, he discussed his belief that the Palestinian Arabs are not a part of the larger Arab world but a people with a particular identity, collective memory, and intrinsic connection to the land of Palestine. "They look upon Palestine with the same instinctive love and true fervor that any Aztec looked upon Mexico or any Sioux looked upon his prairie," he wrote. Therefore, even if the Zionists were able to convince the Arabs of Baghdad and Mecca that Palestine is a territory of marginal significance, "Palestine will still remain for the Palestinians not a borderland, but their birthplace, the center and basis of their own national existence."[39]

Jabotinsky concluded that two possible options existed: "Zionist colonization, even the most restricted, must either be terminated or carried out in defiance of the will of the native population. This colonization can, therefore, continue and develop only under the protection of a force independent of the local population." Choosing the latter option, he advocated the creation of an "Iron Wall" behind which the Zionist project would proceed until the time arrived when the Palestinians realized the irreversibility of this venture and ended their struggle.[40]

This idea was vehemently rejected at the time (and for another two decades) by all mainstream Zionists. It was difficult for most Zionists to accept that the fulfillment of the Zionist dream could be achieved only by force. The recognition of the Palestinians as a unique national entity could not be reconciled with the belief that the Jews have the right to exercise sovereignty in the land of Palestine. The solution to this dilemma was to view the Palestinians as part of the larger Arab nation, which had room enough to accommodate Palestinian national aspirations. The Zionist establishment, led by David Ben-Gurion and Chaim Weizmann, criticized Jabotinsky for exacerbating tensions and endangering the support of Great Britain. The studiously ambivalent (and perhaps hypocritical) mainstream Zionist strategy proved to be more successful than Jabotinsky's realpolitik. By blurring the intrinsic contradiction between Jewish and Arab interests, the mainstream Zionists gained time and managed to increase the Jewish population in Palestine from 100,000 in 1923 to 650,000 in 1948.

In the 1920s, and especially the 1930s, anti-Zionist consciousness rapidly grew among the Palestinian Arabs under the leadership of the mufti of Jerusalem, al-Hajj Amin al-Husayni, though strong pan-Arab undercurrents at the time helped delay the development of a proactive Palestinian nationalist movement.[41] The collaboration of al-Husayni with Hitler's Germany during World War II, coupled with his virulent anti-British posture, damaged the Palestinian cause. This also led to the collusion between Great Britain, Abdullah (the emir of TransJordan), and the Jewish Agency to bring about the creation of the Hashemite Kingdom of Jordan, which was to control the West Bank from 1948 to 1967.[42] The presence of the Kingdom of Jordan on both sides of the Jordan River relieved the Israeli leadership of the need to confront the fact that Zionism clashed not only with the local segment of the Arab nation but also with the growing reality of a specifically Palestinian national movement.[43]

For a brief time during 1948 Sharett and his colleagues in the Israeli foreign ministry considered the potential advantages of helping the Palestinians create their own state in accordance with UN Resolution 181, thus abandoning the "Hashemite Option."[44] However, the absolute refusal of the Palestinian leadership to make any compromise with the Zionists made this "Palestinian Option" unrealistic. The consequences of the 1948 war, when local Palestinian forces were decimated by the new Israeli army, and hundreds of thousands of Palestinians fled their homes and became refugees, further hardened Palestinian resolve against a negotiated settlement with the Zionists. This, combined with the military conquest of the West Bank by Jordanian forces, crippled Palestinian national aspirations for nearly two decades. The Hashemite king, a ruler most Palestinians considered a foreigner, now spoke for them in the absence of a genuine representative of their own. In desperation they turned to the pan-Arab ideals represented by Nasser.[45]

Between 1949 and 1967 few Middle East observers, and few even among the Arabs themselves, saw the Palestinian issue as particularly salient. Many saw the Palestinian entity and the refugee problem primarily as propaganda tools used by the Arab states in their struggles with Israel and one another. For their part, the Palestinians were split between supporting the Hashemite regime or Nasser's pan-Arab nationalism. In most international forums the Palestinian problem was presented more as a humanitarian issue of refugees than as a political question involving national rights, and many Palestinian groups were often viewed as little more than pawns in the intra-Arab "cold war."[46]

Despite occasional incidents along the armistice frontiers, Israel was satisfied with the status quo on its eastern front and wanted to see the regime of the young King Hussein continue along with his control over most of the Palestinians. In August 1958 Golda Meir, then minister of foreign affairs, told her British counterpart Selwyn Lloyd, "We all pray three times a day for King Hussein's safety and success."[47]

Uri Avneri and the Semitic Action

Considering this state of affairs it was rather odd to hear an outspoken Israeli voice calling for greater attention to the Palestinians. Such a voice belonged to Uri Avneri, for many years the controversial owner and editor of *Ha'olam Ha'zeh* (This World), a weekly magazine that offered a strange combination of radical political editorials, socialite gossip, and mild pornography. After 1948 Avneri was perhaps the first to articulate the need to recognize the Palestinian Arabs as a unique people and to cooperate with them. He defined his political philosophy in simple terms: "I believe the Palestinian people have the same rights as I have. I have the right to live in a state of my own, under my own flag, to hold my own passport, to elect my own government, good, bad, or very bad. The Palestinians must have the right to live in their own state, under their own flag, to hold their own passport, to elect their own government—hopefully a good one."[48] Earlier than most, Avneri recognized the rights of the Palestinians to self-determination and realized that they were the people with whom Israel would eventually have to make peace.

Born in Vienna, Avneri emigrated to Palestine with his parents in the late 1930s to escape Nazi persecution. As a teenager he joined the Irgun (a right-wing underground military organization influenced by Jabotinsky's doctrine) to fight against the British in Palestine. Like many other Jews at the time he adamantly opposed the partition plan. Unlike others who opposed it out of territorial and strategic considerations, Avneri opposed it for demographic and moral reasons. While the main Zionist opposition to the partition plan came from the maximalists who did not want anything less than all of Palestine for the Jewish state, Avneri wanted to share the land with the Palestinians.

In October 1947, shortly before the United Nations passed the partition plan, Avneri formed a short-lived group that he named the Young Palestine Association. The group called on the Zionist leadership to adopt a policy that would aspire to create "the unity of the Semitic Sphere."[49] Avneri was initially influenced by the Hebrew poet Yonatan Ratosh and his "Young Hebrews," who were later referred to as the "Canaanites." Ratosh envisioned an alliance of all minorities of the Middle East aimed at resisting Sunni Arab hegemony, and advocated a strong Jewish state on both sides of the Jordan River.[50] Avneri, however, came to believe that the "Hebrew Nation" that was evolving in Palestine would be able to persuade the predominantly Sunni Arab Palestinian nation to jointly create a bilingual and bicultural state. This union, he predicted, could then form the nucleus of a progressive "Semitic Alliance" that would control the Fertile Crescent from the Euphrates River to the Suez Canal in a federal arrangement modeled on the United States or Soviet Union. In later years Avneri admitted that he "believed in the importance of nationalism in the life of people, but also believed in transnationalism."[51] In retrospect his "Semitic Action," as he called it, was naive and inappropriate for the times. What remains important is that his approach was based not only on the recognition of a Palestinian Arab entity, but also on legitimization of their national rights. Avneri's views were based on the assumption that the Jews and Arabs of Palestine were destined to coexist on the same land whether they liked it or not.

Avneri also regularly criticized the aggressive defense policies of Ben-Gurion. He maintained that the prime minister did not believe in peace and thus led Israel down avenues where peace was unattainable. "Everybody knows that the management of war requires precise military planning and the mobilization of all forces in an overall military effort," Avneri wrote in 1954, "but most people think that peace manages itself, and there is no need to do anything for it, no planning, no mobilization of forces. Nothing is further away from the truth—peace must be prepared with the same amount of imagination and momentum as wars are managed."[52]

Shortly after the 1948 war, in which he fought the Egyptians as a noncommissioned officer in the famous Givati brigade, Avneri bought a defunct small weekly magazine, *Tesha Ba'Erev*. After renaming it *Ha'olam Ha'zeh*, he used the magazine to propagate his political ideas and to criticize the Israeli establishment. For example, in the wake of the December 1955 anti-Western riots in Jordan, in which the Palestinians played an important part, Avneri published a number of editorials in which he supported the "Palestinian Liberation Movement." Avneri believed this movement would eventually cooperate with Israel in the establishment of a common homeland for Jews and Arabs.[53]

After the Sinai Campaign of 1956 Avneri joined forces with Nathan Yellin-Mor, the leader of the Stern Gang during the 1940s.[54] Yellin-Mor, who had resurfaced in Israeli politics on the far left, worked with Avneri to reestablish his Semitic Action. Avneri called for the establishment of the "Union of Jordan"—a federation of the Jewish state and the state to be created with the help of Israel by the "free efforts of the Palestinians who will take into their hands their own fate and . . . eject the foreign and despised [Hashemite] ruler."[55]

Many of Avneri's articles of that period reflected a deep sense of frustration at the partitioning of "Eretz Yisrael" (The Land of Israel). The land was "destined by historical heritage, feelings, culture, geographical realities, economic necessities, and military conditions to be the homeland of the Hebrew people," he wrote in the mid-1950s. "We want the integrity of the land, the dressing of the bleeding wounds in the body of our homeland."[56] This may be a reflection of the indoctrination he received in his early days in the Irgun, which was commanded at the time by Menachem Begin and was under the spiritual influence of Jabotinsky. However, while Avneri often used the same language employed by advocates of "Eretz Yisrael Ha'shleima" (Greater Israel—the territorially maximalist version of Eretz Yisrael, according to which the Jewish state should encompass the entire historical land of Israel), he never thought in terms of dispossessing the Palestinian Arabs. On the contrary, for him the integrity of the land required recognition of, and cooperation with, the other nation that inhabited the land.

Avneri possessed at the time a rather naive and paternalistic outlook vis-à-vis the Palestinians. "Hebrew Israel," he wrote, "will be inevitably the senior sister [in the Union of Jordan]. The million residents of its

Arab part, who still live on a much lower level, will be good partners." His vision of the future included "an Arab regime which will sympathize with Israel, a progressive anti-feudal regime."[57] In later years this naïveté disappeared from his views. What remained was his steadfast recognition of the Palestinians as a distinct nation. His efforts to orient Israel's conceptions of peace toward a cooperative venture with the Arab residents of the land, coupled with his support for the political rights of the Palestinian community, established his credibility with many Palestinian nationalists and helped him, after the 1967 war, to formulate a more realistic approach to a negotiated settlement. Avneri, however, did not enjoy similar acceptance among Israeli Jews. Prior to the 1967 war his voice remained solitary and most Israelis did not take his pleas seriously. A party he formed in the 1960s managed to win two Knesset seats in the 1965 elections, but most observers attributed this success to his popularity as an outspoken critic of the political establishment rather than as support for his Semitic crusade.

New Outlook

Unlike Avneri, Simcha Flapan was not a lone wolf. He was a second-tier leader of Mapam and well established in the kibbutz movement. Although he identified with the left wing of his party, especially in regard to the Arab-Israeli conflict, he enjoyed the full support of his colleagues and served in a number of formal roles within the party. Like his colleagues he strongly opposed the 1947 partition plan and preferred the establishment of a binational state in the whole of Palestine. But unlike many others, he never abandoned this idea. He believed that such a state could have been established had it not been for Ben-Gurion's misguided decisions in 1948.[58]

Flapan dedicated most of his energies to reaching out to moderate and leftist leaders from the intellectual elites of the Arab states and Israeli Arabs.[59] In undertaking this task he saw himself as continuing the legacy of Martin Buber, the world-renowned philosopher and theologian who came to Palestine at the end of the 1930s to become a professor at the Hebrew University in Jerusalem and join Brit Shalom (Peace Alliance), a group that, in the 1920s and 1930s, advocated restraint of the Zionist project and full cooperation with the Arabs.[60]

Buber, along with a dozen or so of his colleagues, remained active throughout the first decade of the State of Israel's existence. Most members of the group that was reconstituted in 1943 as Ihud (Union—a reference to the hope for unity between Jews and Arabs) were veteran professors of the Hebrew University who had immigrated to Palestine in the 1920s and 1930s, bringing with them from Europe (and from Germany in particular) more or less pacifist philosophies. During the 1950s, the group congregated around a highly intellectual magazine called *Ner* (Candle).[61] But the group, which during the 1948 war actively opposed the creation of a Jewish state, had almost no following and was considered by the public at large to be a clique of theoreticians detached from society and reality. Even Mapam and the younger generation around Avneri distanced themselves from Ihud.

Flapan was part of a group that went to see the octogenarian Buber in 1958. The old sage told them: "We have to start a dialogue with the Arabs. For a dialogue two persons are required, but sometimes one is enough, if only the other is ready to listen. . . . the time has come for the people of the Middle East to acquire a new outlook."[62] Encouraged by the hope that the "other side will listen," Flapan and his colleagues founded a monthly journal that they called *New Outlook*. The magazine was published in English to reach the widest possible audience and was dedicated to the "clarification of problems concerning peace and cooperation among all the peoples of the Middle East . . . to reflect those aspirations and accomplishments . . . that are common to all the peoples and countries of the area and could, given the elimination of friction and animosities, flourish and produce ever greater abundance of well-being and happiness."[63]

New Outlook soon reached Arab capitals, and through it wide circles of Arab intellectuals were exposed to a voice of peace and conciliation coming from behind "enemy lines." Flapan, the chief editor, viewed the journal as a potential catalyst for further dialogue between Arabs and Israelis. Its readership extended beyond the Middle East and included left-wing political circles in Europe and the United States.

Over the years Flapan managed to develop a vast network of contacts with European communists and other left-wing anticolonial activists. Henri Curiel was an Egyptian communist, a Jew who escaped persecution in Egypt and settled in Paris after World War II, where he associated with many Third World revolutionaries.[64] Through Curiel, Flapan was able to communicate with many Arab leaders, especially those on the left. Flapan tried to nurture these contacts as best he could, primarily through frequent meetings in Europe. Most of these radicals were either in exile or in opposition to the regimes of their native countries, and the meetings rarely led to more meaningful contacts with the Arab mainstream.

Flapan enjoyed greater success among Israeli Arabs. In January 1963 he convened a conference in (Jewish) Tel Aviv and (Arab) Nazareth called "New Paths to Peace." Most of the participants were Israeli Arabs and left-wing Jews. Flapan managed to secure the attendance of a few prominent Americans and Europeans, as well as a few individuals from Israel's political center and right.[65] Shortly before the Six Day War Flapan organized a tour in Egypt and Israel for Jean-Paul Sartre and Simone de Beauvoir in cooperation with the Egyptian progressive journal *El Talia*. After his visit to the Middle East, Sartre prodded both sides on the possibility of initiating a direct dialogue. Unfortunately, the outbreak of the 1967 war reinforced the popular belief that the protagonists were not yet ready for reconciliation.[66]

La Pira and the Florence Conferences

Flapan also participated in the only public conferences that involved face-to-face encounters between prominent Arab leaders and Israeli officials. In 1958, 1960, and 1961 Giorgio La Pira, the mayor of Florence, convened seemingly innocuous conferences called "Congrès Méditerranéen de la Culture" (Congress on Mediterranean Culture). The behind-the-scenes initiator of these meetings was Joseph Goldin, an Israeli who later became better known as Joe Golan. At the time Golan had joined the staff of the World Jewish Congress at the request of its president Nahum Goldmann.[67] Golan was fluent in Arabic and had lived for many years in Damascus and Alexandria, and was well acquainted with Middle Eastern affairs. Goldmann asked Golan to create a Middle East desk at the World Jewish Congress to deal primarily with the welfare of Jews who still remained in Arab countries and with their emigration to Israel and elsewhere.

While a student in Paris, Golan had made useful contacts with North African émigrés who were leading the struggle against French colonialism in the region. These contacts were important for the World Jewish Congress because hundreds of thousands of Jews still lived in Morocco, Algeria, and Tunisia. In 1955 Golan also secretly visited the Egyptian embassy in Paris and met with Colonel Sarwat Okasha, who was a colleague of Nasser and a member of the Officer's Revolutionary Council that had staged the Cairo coup in July 1952. They discussed the question of whether

Goldmann, who was at the time also the president of the World Zionist Organization, should be invited to visit Cairo to meet with Egyptian leaders. The idea was eventually shelved because of the international storm caused by Nasser's nationalization of the Suez Canal in July 1956. For its part, the Israeli government did not support the proposed trip for two reasons: a lack of confidence in Goldmann and concern that Nasser might try to use him to drive a wedge between Israel and world Jewry.[68]

Golan continued to cultivate his North African contacts. By the end of the 1950s such key figures from the recently liberated Morocco as Alal Alfassi and Mehdi Ben Barka were frequent guests at Golan's home, which he moved to Rome to escape the scrutiny of the French security services.

In 1957 Golan approached Giorgio La Pira, the mayor of Florence and an internationally renowned progressive Catholic leader, and encouraged him to convene a conference to deal with the "Culture of the Mediterranean."[69] It soon became obvious that despite its seemingly neutral title the conference had strong political undercurrents and would not limit itself to cultural affairs. This broader character accorded with Golan's objective of increasing the involvement of Israel and world Jewry in the unfolding independence of Mediterranean and African nations. He hoped this would help safeguard the Jewish populations and interests in these countries while also helping to pave the way for Israel's integration into the region.

The first conference met in September 1958 and was attended by several prominent figures from the Arab world as well as a few representatives of the Israeli establishment. Egypt approved the participation of a few intellectuals, with only "one limitation . . . the avoidance of any political debate."[70] Israel's representatives included members of leftist groups, nonpartisan academics, and a few notable officials including Maurice Fisher (Israel's ambassador to Italy) and Reuven Barakat (a member of the Knesset and head of the Department for International Affairs of the general union of workers, the Histadrut). The most prominent Israeli in attendance was Reuven Shiloah, a senior member of the Israeli foreign service and the founder of Israel's central intelligence agency, Mossad.

The conference, held in the Palazzo Vecchio in Florence, was somewhat overshadowed by the recent rise to power of Charles de Gaulle and the efforts of the French army to quell the revolt in Algeria. North African politics seemed to take precedence over other Mediterranean issues, and even the Egyptian and Lebanese delegates were more interested in discussing the politics of Algeria than those of Palestine.

Rustum Bastuni, an Israeli Arab, was the only Palestinian invited to attend the conference. No Palestinians came from either Jordan or the Palestinian diaspora,[71] chiefly because there were no serious and credible Palestinian organizations at that time. Yasser Arafat's Palestinian armed struggle movement (Fatah) began to take shape in 1957 but did not become a coherent and active body until the next decade; and Ahmad Shuqairi's Palestinian Liberation Organization was not created until 1964. Nevertheless, for the Israelis this was a rare opportunity to meet Arab leaders and intellectuals.[72] *New Outlook* viewed the conference as offering hope: "At this stage in Middle East affairs, this represents progress in comparison with the boycotts of the past, and indicates the line to be taken in the future."[73]

Israeli officials did not attend the second conference, which took place in the summer of 1960. The venerable Martin Buber attended, however, and the Israeli government announced that the philosopher should be viewed as the official delegate of the State of Israel. He quickly became the center of attention and, as a result of his imposing presence, the Arab-Israeli issue became much more prominent. Buber spoke of Palestine as a land of two nations and called for coexistence and a serious attempt to overcome mutual hatred.[74]

The second Florence conference was a great success in terms of its intellectual level and the conciliatory atmosphere it engendered. But "in order to avoid past difficulties, general topics and philosophical-cultural-economic questions were chosen, keeping as far away from politics as possible."[75] One of the conference's significant results was that the Israeli press reported widely on the fraternization between the Egyptian and Israeli delegates.[76] Ben-Gurion sent Mayor La Pira a personal note and assured him that the "desire most cherished in Israel is peace."[77]

Israel's Ministry of Foreign Affairs was becoming increasingly concerned with Joe Golan's independent activities. Shortly after the third (and last) Florence conference Golan had to terminate his activities on behalf of the World Jewish Congress and as secretary-general of the Congrès Méditerranéen.[78] Secret talks between Algerian rebels (led by the Front de Libération National—FLN) and French plenipotentiaries were well under way by that time, and with Algerian independence on the horizon, the fate of the Jewish community in Algeria became a growing concern. At Goldmann's direction, Golan went to FLN headquarters in Tunisia to meet some of his old contacts and to lobby them to recognize the Jews as if they were French nationals, even though Jews lived in Algeria centuries before the arrival of the French. Such a recognition would enable Jews to choose either to remain in the country and receive the new state's citizenship or to leave and retain their French papers. The FLN leaders responded by discreetly recommending to Golan that the Jews hasten to leave the country due to the potential for widespread anti-Jewish riots.[79]

In March 1962 Golan sent an urgent message (using an FLN courier) to the chief rabbi of Algeria, and the exodus of Algeria's Jews began. Golan was expelled from France when the French secret service caught wind of his actions. When he returned to Tel Aviv, his Israeli passport was confiscated under the orders of Golda Meir. A brief public storm erupted that attracted the attention of the Knesset and media, and Golan was allowed to retrieve his papers.[80] Frustrated and embittered, Golan eventually redirected his energies toward business and never returned to political life.

The Iron Wall—Peace Impossible

Avneri, Flapan, and Golan were not the only Israelis who dreamed of peace and tried to promote it, but they represented the most consistent and sustained efforts to actually achieve peace during the first two decades of the State of Israel's existence. Their frustrated attempts to reach out to the other side exemplified the underlying alienation between Arabs and Israelis. The perception on both sides was that peace required extremely painful concessions that would yield few gains. Furthermore, the prevailing condition of "no war, no peace" that resulted from the 1949 armistice agreements did not seem to be an unbearable price for either side to pay.[81]

In a conflict in which vital interests are at stake, as in the Arab-Israeli conflict, the transformation of a zero-sum game into a positive outcome occurs only when both sides recognize that the costs of continued conflict are greater than the price each will pay for a settlement. During the 1950s and 1960s, both Arabs and Israelis were far from this recognition, and the political, strategic, and psychological environments were not conducive to such a change in perception. The price the Arabs would have had to pay was recognition and acceptance of the Jewish state and agreement that at least some of the territories Israel had gained in the 1948 war would remain in Israeli hands. Consequently, some of the Palestinian refugees would have had to be absorbed in neighboring Arab states. All these requirements were unacceptable.

Furthermore, the Arabs did not consider the costs of another war too high a price in pursuit of their objectives and in defense of their dignity.

The defeats of 1948 were rationalized and the new revolutionary regimes in Egypt, Syria, and (somewhat later) Iraq had no reason to believe that they would not eventually be able to translate their overwhelming demographic and economic advantages over Israel into military superiority.[82] Moreover, the condition of "no war, no peace" did not exact a heavy price from Egypt and Syria. Most of the border skirmishes took place far from Egypt's population centers (in the Gaza Strip and the desert borders of the Sinai Peninsula), and did not significantly threaten Egyptian interests. Despite the conquest of the Sinai by Israeli forces in 1956, Nasser portrayed the Sinai-Suez War as a great victory for himself, with Egypt having survived invasion by the armies of France and Great Britain.[83] Syria felt safe behind its reinforced fortifications on the Golan Heights, literally looking down at Israeli settlements in the valley below. Jordan and Lebanon were more vulnerable but were too weak politically either to influence regional Arab politics or to pursue independent courses.

Prospects for peace were further hampered because of the Arab nations' shared sense of wounded pride after the Zionist victory in Palestine. Arab humiliation was aggravated by Israeli military retaliations along the armistice frontiers throughout this period. In May 1967, when Nasser ordered the UN Emergency Force (UNEF) out of Egypt, closed the Straits of Aqaba to Israeli navigation, banned Israeli overflights, and deployed his army in the northern Sinai, he described these actions as the first steps to eradicating the "shame of 1956" and promised soon thereafter to eradicate the "shame of 1948."[84]

For its part, Israel likewise did not consider peace its highest priority and certainly was not ready to pay the price even the most moderate Arabs required. For the overwhelming majority of Israeli Jews, relinquishing the Negev or allowing hundreds of thousands of Palestinian refugees to return seemed tantamount to suicide and was viewed as totally unacceptable. In addition, Israelis were treated to daily litanies of hatred and indignation on Arab radio and were all too aware of deadly incursions by Arab guerrillas. In this context, the conciliation efforts of Flapan, Golan, and others did not seem to offer Israelis serious prospects of a genuine and lasting peace.

During the first two decades of their state's existence, Israelis regarded peace as desirable but beyond reach. Jabotinsky's perception of Israel's relationship with its neighbors accurately described Israel's situation in the Middle East after 1948. His Iron Wall prophecy was to a large extent realized through Israeli policies in the 1950s and 1960s, as Ben-Gurion focused the state's resources on developing the ability to defend the new political, demographic, and territorial circumstances created by the 1948 war.

The Sinai Campaign of October 1956 brought about a respite in Arab belligerency toward Israel, at the same time increasing Arab resentment of Israel's aggressive posture. Nasser's decision on October 31, 1956, to redeploy his army from Sinai to Egypt's heartland to counter the French and British invasion forestalled a full-scale confrontation between the Egyptian and Israeli forces and left him with little reason to suspect the Israeli military was more than a match for his own. With his prestige boosted by the political victory salvaged from the military defeat of that war, Nasser used the following decade to champion his vision of Arab unity but was careful not to provoke Israel before he was sure he was ready for another round.

Despite Nasser's self-restraint, the Arab-Israeli conflict heated up again after a series of incidents in 1964 and 1965. The first such incident surrounded Israel's plan to build a National Water Carrier to channel water from the Sea of Galilee in the north to irrigate the arid south. A Syrian attempt to divert the headwaters of the Jordan River from flowing into the Sea of Galilee was checked by an Israeli military response.

Tensions were further heightened by another development. On January 4, 1965, Arafat's Fatah launched its first guerrilla incursion into Israel. The National Water Carrier was the target of a mine placed not far from the Sea of Galilee. The explosion caused minimal damage, but the attack carried significant symbolic value. It marked the beginning of the "armed struggle" against Israel.[85] Between 1965 and 1966 Palestinian guerrillas infiltrated Israel seventy-six times, causing thirty deaths.[86] While these operations were not significant from a military point of view, they exacted a psychological toll on Israel by demonstrating that their Iron Wall was not impenetrable. Fatah's actions also represented the emergence of the Palestinians as an independent factor in the region's political and strategic calculus. Because most of these attacks were launched from Syria and Lebanon and were committed with the blessing and support of the Syrian regime, they also contributed to the spiral of conflict that led to the next Arab-Israeli war. The 1967 Six Day War, and its military and political results, contributed to a renewed pursuit of peace and the recognition by growing numbers of Israelis that peace must be viewed as a national priority.[87]

2

The Debate over Peace Options in the Labor Party, 1967–70

From Anxiety to Euphoria

The June 1967 war resulted in the defeat of three major Arab armies by Israeli forces in less then one hundred hours, and the conquest of the West Bank from Jordan, the Golan Heights from Syria, and the Gaza Strip and Sinai Peninsula from Egypt. This dramatically changed the terms of the Arab-Israeli conflict.[1] In the wake of the victory the entire nation was swept by exhilaration and a genuine sense of salvation. But as odd as it may seem in light of the enormity of the victory, during the three weeks just before the war (a time that came to be known as the "waiting period") Israelis had become acutely fearful for the survival of the Jewish state. Many viewed Israel's situation in catastrophic terms not unlike the Holocaust.

After the war a group of young kibbutz members recorded a series of revealing interviews and discussions about the war, later published as a book titled *Chats of Combatants*. In one interview two brothers, both combat battalion commanders, spoke of their war experience with their father, Matityahu Shelem, a prominent figure in the field of Hebrew folk culture. The father spoke of his feelings and thoughts during the waiting period. "I used to think a lot about the concentration camps, about what might happen, about almost anything that a sick imagination could devise, and about all the things I'd seen down through the years: the [Arab] riots in 1929, and the riots in 1936. . . . I went backwards in my thoughts, to the time before I came to Palestine, way back to my childhood. . . . I often had the occasion to discuss the gas chambers."[2]

Moshe Shamir, a famous Israeli novelist, wrote in his diary of fear and doomsday expectations at the time: "The air around is not assured for us. We have to secure it every day anew. This is true only for our people, of all people on the surface of the earth."[3]

Three factors help explain this widespread fear among Israelis. First, the enduring national trauma of the Holocaust, which thousands of Israelis personally experienced, has always played a central role in the political, cultural, and psychological socialization of all Israeli Jews. The main lesson most Jews derive from the Holocaust was that because such an event happened once it could happen again.[4] The second factor was the enormity of weaponry and forces amassed during the later part of May 1967 along three of Israel's borders, coupled with the pronouncements by Arab leaders of the Jewish state's imminent destruction.[5] Third, there was a widespread sense of political isolation, which grew out of the failure of the United Nations and U.S. President Lyndon Johnson to soften Egypt's aggressive posture.

It was therefore understandable that the nation breathed a collective sigh of relief when the news arrived on the morning of June 6 that the Egyptian air force was destroyed. By the end of the six days the combined forces of Egypt, Jordan, and Syria had been decimated. Israelis by the hundreds of thousands began to swarm into the newly conquered territories to see the stunning victory for themselves. Their fears of just a week earlier turned into national euphoria.[6]

But beyond this collective sense of relief and salvation, two seemingly contradictory emotions engulfed the nation. The first was joy at the return to "Eretz Ha'avot" (The Land of Our Fathers).[7] The second was a sense of hope and expectation that an end to the Arab-Israeli conflict was near. An illustration of this contradiction took place on June 9 when two men, friends and officers on active duty, met by coincidence at the Tomb of Rachel near Bethlehem shortly after the Israeli Defense Forces (IDF) entered the Arab town. They embraced with great emotion and kissed each other's cheeks, which were flushed with tears of joy. One of these men was Moshe Shamir, who later became a founder and leader of the Movement for Greater Israel and the right-wing Techiya party. The other, the author of this book, was at the time the chief education officer of the IDF and later became a leading activist of Peace Now and the left-wing Movement for Citizens' Rights and Peace (known as Ratz). In their younger years they were both members of a Marxist kibbutz movement. Later they were both members of the Knesset, though on opposite sides of the political spectrum. But on this June morning, at the grave of the most beloved of the ancestral Israelite mothers, they were unified by a sense of joy. The Tomb of Rachel symbolized for both the renewed connection with the part of the land from which they had been barred for nineteen years by Jordanian rule. More than the coastal plain, the hills of Samaria and Judea preserved the memories of the Bible and embodied much of Jewish identity and history. Yet at the same time their embrace expressed their intense desire and hope that "this will be the last war," and that peace would soon come.[8]

A few days after the war an Israeli folk singer recorded a song with the refrain, "O Mother Rachel, we shall never go away again from the fields of Bethlehem!" These words, and their historical significance, touched the hearts even of those who were ready from the outset to relinquish those fields if they could be traded for peace. And whereas others, such as Moshe Shamir, believed from the outset that Israel must keep the territories, they also believed in the urgency and possibility of peace. In late June 1967 Shamir wrote in his diary, "Just as the military victory was this time greater than any preceding victory, likewise will be our dedication to peace . . . you may speak of retreat as much as you want, from a full and total peace there will be no retreat this time."[9]

For Israel, the conquest of the new territories seemed to present new possibilities for peace. The results of the war significantly improved Israel's bargaining position with regard to a "territory for peace" settlement. But it also awakened dormant aspirations among many Israelis for the acquisition of the entire area of historic Eretz Yisrael. Meanwhile, the new territories afforded the Israeli defense establishment the illusion of greatly enhanced security through the new lines of defense, which were farther from Israel's population centers. For the first time, Israeli military planners were able to reconsider the previous strategic doctrine of preemption and to develop a national defense strategy based on relative territorial depth and the containment of enemy initiatives.[10]

Within two weeks of the stunning victory the government of Israel passed two significant resolutions concerning the newly conquered territories. At first these resolutions seemed to lead in contrary directions. However, it soon became clear that both (one by design, the other by default) led to the same political conclusion—the establishment of a new status quo in the Middle East with Israel in control of the entire area that the Jews refer to as Eretz Yisrael and the Arabs call Palestine.

On June 27, 1967, by a unanimous vote in the cabinet and a near-unanimous Knesset vote, the government of Israel annexed Arab East Jerusalem, which had been controlled by Jordan since 1948. The holy city (with expanded boundaries) was unified as the "eternal capital of the State of Israel."[11] This unilateral act was violently rejected by the Arab world and to this day has not been recognized by any other government.[12] The overwhelming majority of Israeli and diaspora Jews viewed the unification of Jerusalem under Jewish sovereignty as a divine act of historic justice and the answer to the prayers of their fathers and forefathers, who for more than two millennia had prayed three times every day, "And to Jerusalem, thy city, return in mercy, and dwell therein as thou hast spoken."[13]

The second resolution had been adopted a week earlier, far away from the public eye. On June 19 the government of Israel decided by a majority vote to send a message to the United States, to be passed on to the relevant Arab governments, in which Israel expressed its readiness to return the entire Sinai Peninsula to Egypt and the Golan Heights to Syria. In return these states were expected to conclude a formal peace treaty with Israel, assure freedom of passage to Israeli navigation through the Suez Canal and the Straits of Tiran, and allow the unimpeded flow of water from the Jordan River sources. The Gaza Strip and the West Bank were not specifically mentioned in the diplomatic note, but it was understood that these areas, excluding Jerusalem, were negotiable.[14]

Israel was ruled at this time by a Government of National Unity, which had been formed a few days before the outbreak of hostilities in expectation of the approaching national emergency. For the first time the government of Israel included Menachem Begin and his right-wing Gahal party.[15] Begin voted against the decision concerning the return of territories but did not resign from the government. On June 27 Prime Minister Levi Eshkol made a formal declaration to the press, saying, "Our hand is extended in peace to all who are ready for peace."[16] No territorial conditions were mentioned. The only conditions Israel demanded were direct and unmediated negotiations, no return to the armistice regime, full and unequivocal peace, and a solution to the refugee prob-lem. The operative part of the declaration, however, was that "so long as our neighbors . . . persist in their policy of belligerence . . . we will not relinquish the areas that are now under our control."[17]

At this point the Arab-Israeli conflict was far from being "ripe for reso-lution."[18] Nevertheless, the majority of cabinet ministers (and a clear majority of the public) believed that peace was around the corner.[19] During the summer of 1967 the leadership of the dominant Labor Party, especially Prime Minister Eshkol, Minister of Treasury Pinhas Sapir, and Minister of Foreign Affairs Abba Eban, were ready to explore the possi-bilities of trading peace for territory.[20] Even Moshe Dayan, the military hero and political hard-liner, was said to have remarked that he was "waiting for a telephone call from King Hussein" to discuss the modali-ties of peace.[21] But the telephone did not ring and soon the euphoria faded to a sober realization that peace was far down the road. Worse, what lay ahead was another war.

Attrition—War Once More

The cease-fire along the Suez Canal lasted less than three weeks. By the beginning of July there were skirmishes in the northern section near the town of Port Fouad, and during the rest of July and early August the canal frontline increasingly turned into a battle zone.[22] At the interven-tion of the UN Security Council another temporary cease-fire was achieved. Despite this the fighting resumed on October 21 when Egyp-tian boats carrying Soviet missiles sank the Israeli destroyer *Eilat*. In retaliation Israel destroyed oil refineries and other installations in the town of Suez at the southern tip of the canal. This led to the evacuation of the Egyptian residents of the towns and villages along the Suez Ca-nal, which by this time had fully become a war zone.[23]

The War of Attrition lasted intermittently for almost three years.[24] The war was part of a strategy in which President Nasser, who had risen like a phoenix from the ashes of his military defeat, used a belligerent posture against Israel to support his continued claim to leadership of the Arabs. Nasser could not accept the Israeli proposal of June 19, which offered the return of Sinai in exchange for his acquiescence on the Pal-estinian issue and which allowed Israel to hold on to Jerusalem and parts of the West Bank and Gaza, without losing all claim to leadership in the Arab world.[25] In his view, the only path open for him was to launch a war of attrition in which he hoped to wear down Israel politically, economically, and psychologically.[26] Although he recognized that his army could not match Israel's, and despite Soviet advice to the contrary, he believed that he must resume the fighting (albeit in a limited way) as soon as his generals were ready.[27] He adopted the plans devised by the new minister of war, General Mahmoud Fawzi, to conduct the war in three consecutive phases: the defensive phase of "steady resistance," the phase of "active deterrence," and lastly the phase of "liberation."[28]

This strategy led to the declaration at the Khartoum summit meeting of Arab leaders on September 1, which affirmed the Arab world's commitment to the "three noes": no peace with Israel, no recognition of Israel, and no negotiation with the Jewish state. The declaration also spoke of "upholding of the rights of the Palestinian people to their land."[29] Mohamed Heikal, editor of the Cairo daily *al-Ahram* and a close confidant of Nasser, summarized this intransigent posture succinctly: "No peaceful solution exists. Most probably it never existed in the past. . . . In the Arab-Israeli conflict the two sides cannot even sit together at the negotiating table, and cannot sign a common document. There are many reasons for that and the first is that any negotiation held while Israel occupies Arab land will amount to dictation of conditions; every document which may be arrived at in this way will amount to total surrender."[30]

A congruent development, though under very different conditions, took place on the East Bank of the Jordan. After an aborted attempt to raise a popular armed uprising inside the West Bank and Gaza Strip during the summer and fall of 1967, Fatah and other Palestinian groups established themselves in Jordan and South Lebanon and initiated their own war of attrition.[31] From makeshift bases on the hills east of the Jordan, Palestinian guerrillas frequently attempted to cross the river and pass through the West Bank en route to their targets in Israel. They often made use of the many caves along the eastern slopes of the West Bank to hide and store weapons. More sporadic (but often more successful and painful for the Israelis) were the attacks perpetrated by clandestine groups within Israel that survived the massive "mopping up" operation conducted by the IDF and the Shin Bet (a Hebrew acronym for Sherut Bitachon, the Security Service) during the early months of the occupation. These groups planted delayed-action bombs in Jewish cafeterias, supermarkets, bus stops, and other public places. Mortar and Katyusha rockets were also lobbed from across the Jordan onto Israeli towns and villages situated close to the cease-fire lines.

Israel launched a massive campaign to seal off the routes used by the Palestinians to cross the river and to track down guerrilla fighters who managed to infiltrate Israel. The IDF responded to the attacks with artillery and aerial bombardments of Jordanian and Palestinian targets on the East Bank. Occasionally the IDF crossed the river in ground assaults on the guerrilla bases.[32] An important episode took place on March 21, 1968, when an Israeli commando brigade supported by armor, artillery, and aircraft attacked Fatah's command post at Karameh. The Palestinians put up a gallant fight but were overwhelmed by the Israeli forces. They surrendered their base after some 120 of their fighters were killed.

The battle of Karameh became an important symbol of Palestinian resistance. Despite overwhelming Israeli military superiority, the Palestinian fighters stood up to the Israeli Goliath. Many observers view this battle as Fatah's greatest moment of glory.[33] In his memoirs Abu Iyad remarks that the name "Karameh" means "honor" in Arabic, and that in the eyes of the Palestinians their fighters in Karameh successfully defended the honor of their nation.[34] In the aftermath of Karameh, Fatah recruitment stations and training bases swelled with thousands of new recruits.[35] By the spring of 1968 the Jordanian border from the Sea of Galilee in the north to the Dead Sea in the south became an active battleground.

Politically and ideologically the Palestinian national movement underwent a process of radicalization after 1967. During the nineteen years (1948-67) of Jordanian rule over the majority of the Palestinians on both sides of the Jordan, loyalty to and an interest in the preservation of the Hashemite Kingdom developed, especially among the upper and middle classes. After the Six Day War, however, it became increasingly clear that King Hussein could not be relied upon to save the Palestinians from Israeli occupation. The Palestinian guerrillas represented a new sense of defiance and gradually gained the loyalty of their people. Moreover, Egypt's humiliating defeat in the 1967 war disabused Palestinians of the previously widely held notion that their liberation was tied to Nasser's pan-Arabist vision. The ideological soil was now fertile for the new brand of Palestinian nationalism espoused by Yasser Arafat and his colleagues in Fatah. Even the diehard pan-Arabist marxist George Habash and his colleagues from the pan-Arab Nationalist Party (Qawmiyyun al-Arab) felt obliged to reconsider their exclusive involvement in pan-Arab politics and joined the Palestinian armed struggle.[36]

Israel's shocking victory in the June 1967 war brought about a sober realization among many Arabs that Israel could not be destroyed by conventional military means.[37] But for the Palestinians, Israel's conquest of the West Bank and the Gaza Strip meant that the entire land of Palestine, along with an additional one and a half million Palestinians, had been brought under Israeli control. This led them to view their struggle not only in terms of the destruction of Israel, but also as a war of liberation from a colonial occupation (though whether an occupation of the West Bank and Gaza only or of the entire land of Palestine remained unspecified). The popular concept of a Palestinian nation now included those who lived in the territory west of the Jordan River and refugees who lived elsewhere but aspired to return. This undermined the claim of the Hashemite regime to represent the entire Palestinian people and led to a growing acceptance in the Arab world as well as the international community of the Palestinian demand for political self-determination.[38] For the Palestinians the Six Day War brought more suffering but also a decisive stimulus to take their fate into their own hands. After the defeat they could no longer rely on the Arab states for their salvation, and their armed struggle gained a new and more credible status.[39]

The new prominence of the Palestinian guerrillas, and of Fatah in particular, inexorably led to the takeover of the Palestine Liberation Organization (PLO) by Yasser Arafat in the late 1960s. The PLO, which since its establishment in 1964 had largely functioned to serve the interests of the Arab states—and of Nasser's Egypt in particular—became under Arafat's leadership an independent body that gathered together within its framework a great variety of Palestinian groups. The PLO came to represent the collective will of the Palestinian people to pursue their national struggle for independence and retrieval of their homeland.[40]

A public expression of the new radical trend of the PLO was the revision of the Palestine National Charter, which was originally drafted in 1965 by the PLO's first chairman, Ahmad Shuqairi.[41] Advocates of armed struggle successfully pressed for the inclusion in the charter of such phrases as "armed struggle is the only way to liberate Palestine," "the Palestine Arab people assert . . . their right to normal life in Palestine, and to exercise their right to self-determination and sovereignty over it," and "[the PLO] aims at the liquidation of Zionism in Palestine." These changes made it clear that no compromise could be reached with what the Arabs referred to as the "Zionist Entity." The question of the return of territories occupied in the war was made moot by demands for an end to Israel's existence and the establishment of the State of Palestine in its place.[42]

To underline their extreme ideological posture, Palestinian guerrillas began a series of indiscriminate attacks against Israeli and Jewish targets around the world, with aircraft traveling to and from Israel being particularly hard hit.[43] In retrospect, this phase of belligerency seems to have been vital to the development of Palestinian nationalism and its unique identity. The emergence of the Palestinians as independent actors in the Middle East political arena required a period in which a new leadership, a sense of dignity and defiance, and new institutions of self-governance had to emerge. The élan necessary for the mobilization of the masses, and the cohesion necessary under the adverse circumstances of the Israeli occupation, international skepticism, and the duplicity of the Arab states, could be achieved only by dramatic acts of self-assertion and a radical, uncompromising ideology. From the Israeli perspective this helped to undermine any belief in the feasibility of a negotiated settlement in the wake of the Six Day War. In light of growing Palestinian belligerence and intransigence, the demands of Israeli peaceniks for a conciliatory and concessionary policy on the part of their government sounded naive to most other Israelis.

Israel's Shifting Policy

Facing Arab intransigence and renewed violence, Israel began in the fall of 1967 to move away from its earlier attitude of "waiting for a telephone call." Peace seemed now more remote than ever, and Israel found itself stuck with the territories. The optimism and diplomatic flexibility of the early months evolved into a firm resolve not to relinquish the spoils of the war. And, as was often remarked between 1968 and 1970, even if Israel were to try to open a dialogue with the Arabs, "there is nobody to talk to anyhow."

The hardening of Israeli attitudes was noticeable in the changing tenor of the prime minister's position. Eshkol sought to resist political pressures in three areas: a unilateral withdrawal by Israel, the return to the conditions that prevailed before the 1967 war, and UN interference. The prime minister stated Israel's refusal to discuss details of a possible settlement before direct negotiations were agreed upon. Responding to the Khartoum resolutions, Eshkol declared that "in view of this [intransigent] posture of the Arab states, Israel will continue to fully maintain the situation which prevailed under the cease-fire agreements [of June 12] and will fortify its hold according to the vital needs of its security and development."[44] In the realities of the Middle East at the end of 1967, these words signaled a deadlock.

At first the attention of Israeli leaders was focused primarily on the demand for a basic change in the overall attitude of the Arabs toward

Israel. A formal peace treaty was a sine qua non for any Israeli retreat from conquered territories. Remembering the tremendous pressure exerted on Israel to withdraw from the territories occupied during the Sinai Campaign of 1956, the Israeli government assumed initially that neither the United Nations nor even the United States would indefinitely tolerate Israel's occupation of the territories. However, it gradually became clear that international conditions had changed since 1956 and that no effective pressure was forthcoming. Whatever formulations the American administration suggested, it would not repeat its demands of 1957 and pressure Israel to withdraw unilaterally from any territory unless the Arabs were ready to significantly rethink their attitudes. This virtually amounted to a mandate from the United States for Israel to keep the territories as long as the Arabs maintained an inflexible posture.[45]

On June 19, 1967, the same day that the government of Israel agreed to trade most of the occupied territories for peace, President Johnson outlined U.S. policy on the Arab-Israeli conflict. The policy was based on five principles. It required that each nation in the area accept the right of others to exist, and that each respect the political independence and territorial integrity of other nations. Further, it said that justice must be accorded the refugees, that the parties must agree upon limitations to their arms race, and that they respect one another's maritime rights.[46] There was no demand for unilateral Israeli withdrawal. To the contrary, the president clearly stated that "a return to the situation of June 4, 1967, will not bring peace," and although "boundaries cannot and should not reflect the weight of conquest . . . there must be secure and there must be recognized borders." "Certainly troops must be withdrawn," Johnson added, but he clearly regarded such a withdrawal as linked to the acceptance of the other five principles.

Israel's leaders must have been relieved by the U.S. president's position. This sense of relief grew on November 22, 1967, when the UN Security Council adopted the famous Resolution 242. This resolution declared the "inadmissibility of the acquisition of territory by war" and provided for the "withdrawal of Israeli armed forces from territories occupied in the recent conflict." But it linked these provisions with "the need to work for a just and lasting peace," and required the "termination of all claims or states of belligerency and respect for and acknowledgement of the sovereignty, territorial integrity and political independence of every State in the area and their right to live in peace within secure and recognized boundaries free of threats or acts of force."[47]

Much has been written about this resolution. Most interpretations have failed to recognize the simple fact that in view of the reluctance of the Arab states to cease their belligerency and conclude a peace agreement with Israel, the net effect of this resolution was that Israel was permitted to hold on to the occupied territories. By its own terms, the resolution precluded any effective UN pressure to bring about the end to the occupation. Oddly, Menachem Begin and his colleagues on the right rejected the resolution and eventually resigned from the unity government to protest the government's acceptance of its terms. Begin failed to understand that the principles incorporated in this resolution in effect sanctioned the continuation of the Israeli occupation, rather than requiring withdrawal.[48] Together with Arab rejectionism, U.S. policies and UN resolutions in the fall of 1967 facilitated the hardening of Israel's diplomatic posture. They also rendered the resolution of the Israeli government of June 19 obsolete.

Nonetheless, the rigidity that started to prevail in Israel's policies in the fall of 1967 can be explained only partially by Arab intransigence and the absence of international pressure. It should be recalled that Israel was governed during this period by a Government of National Unity that included Begin's Gahal party. Begin, the ideological disciple of Jabotinsky, was uncompromisingly committed to an Eretz Yisrael that stretched from the desert to the sea. While in the National Unity Government he was constantly vigilant against any territorial compromise and opposed even the conditional and tentative use of the term "withdrawal." Although the Labor-dominated unity government was not dependent on Begin and his colleagues to survive a vote of no confidence in the Knesset, the government managed to last for more than three years because there were no compelling challenges to the new status quo and because it was thought desirable to leave the government intact for as long as possible. As long as the Arabs were not ready for a compromise, Israel "decided not to decide." This was a safe way to facilitate the continuation of the National Unity Government.

But this too is only a partial explanation. Within the Labor Party itself factions existed that supported the decision not to decide, mainly because they could not agree on a policy. But the decision "not to decide" did not mean "not to act." In the meantime those within the government who favored Jewish settlement of the territories devoted themselves to creating "facts on the ground" that would entrench Israel's presence in the territories.

Creating facts on the ground was very much part of the Zionist tradition. The creation of an impressive demographic and economic Jewish presence in Palestine and the survival of the Jewish state since 1948 both reflected and encouraged a belief that dreams could be realized only by constant activity. Collective human will—more particularly, collective Zionist will—was regarded as irresistible. As expressed in one of Theodor Herzl's most popular sayings—one that every Israeli child still learns— *Wenn ihr wollt ist es kein Maerchen* (If you want it, it is not a fairy tale). This mind-set gave to Israeli political culture a clear preference for action over inaction and infused Israeli politics with an overriding sense of activism.

Furthermore, the thought that Zionism might have already achieved its maximum attainable goals was foreign to most Israelis, from both the right and the left. Indeed, loyalty to the full realization of Zionism's goals had become a measurement of loyalty to the entire Zionist project. Those who doubted the validity of the maximalist interpretation of the Zionist idea—especially in terms of immigration of Jews to Israel and of settlement of the land ("the blooming of the desert")—were regarded not merely as wrong but as nonbelievers. The Six Day War was hardly over before new settlements were established in the occupied territories.

The War of Attrition caused the Israeli army to construct reinforced bunkers, electrified barbed wire fences, and wide mine fields along the Suez Canal and other fronts. Quasi-civilian rural settlements were constructed in these areas, based on the popular but outdated assumption that the presence of civilian settlements bolstered local security. Thus began the Israeli settlement of the Golan Heights, the Jordan Valley, and in the Etzion area on the hills of Judea. To emphasize their historic rights to the land of their forefathers, Israelis introduced a word previously unused in the Zionist vocabulary. The Hebrew term *hityashvut* (settlement) was replaced by the word *hitnachalut,* which was used in the Old Testament to designate the settling of the Israelite tribes in the land promised to them by God in the time of Joshua and the Judges. With every new settlement the path toward compromise and a solution to the conflict became more difficult.

Galili and Dayan—Competition in Intransigence

It is impossible to assert with certainty if a more consistent and active peace policy by Israel in the months after the war could have brought about a change in the course of events in the Arab-Israeli conflict. Nevertheless, it is important to explain why the Labor Party (which ruled the country for a decade after the war and repeatedly declared its willingness to trade territory for peace) did not pursue peace more vigorously.

The hardening of Israel's position was a departure from the traditional policies pursued by the veteran Labor Party elite and was contrary to the convictions of such influential leaders as Pinhas Sapir, Abba Eban, Pinhas Lavon, and Zalman Aran. These four, and some younger ministers, shared dovish tendencies. Sapir, who was considered the most powerful political figure in his party and in the country, was convinced that continued Israeli control over the Palestinians would be a disaster,[49] and predicted that the occupation would inevitably lead to the annexation of the occupied territories. "This is madness," argued Sapir. "We shall entangle ourselves in a morass with no exit. . . . Why do we need another piece of a mountain on which Arabs sit and look upon us with envy and hatred?"[50] Somewhat later Sapir said, "If we continue to hold the territories, at the end they will hold us."[51] And on another occasion he remarked, "We should not be like a child who ties himself to a tree and then cries that the tree does not let him go."[52]

By the end of 1967 these veteran leaders, led by Sapir, exercised full control over the party and held the most important positions in the government. Why then did they fail to impose their political will on it? Why did they allow an uncompromising policy to gain the upper hand in the party they effectively controlled?

Arab rejectionism was certainly part of the answer, but so were the complex political dynamics of the Labor Party. By the fall of 1967 this veteran group of leaders was confronted by two new political factions within the party and by a younger generation of leaders who did not share the veterans' ideological convictions.

Back in 1965 Ben-Gurion had seceded from the Labor Party and formed a new party known as Rafi (its full name was Rishimat Poalei Yisrael—the Israel Workers' List). He succeeded in attracting some of the activist leaders of the younger generation, including Shimon Peres and Moshe Dayan, who at the time advocated a hard line in foreign policy and security affairs. To counter this loss Eshkol and Sapir decided to facilitate the return of Achdut Ha'avodah, which had seceded from the Labor Party in the 1940s. Achdut Ha'avodah was led by Itzhak Tabenkin, an old colleague and foe of Ben-Gurion, who had long been committed to the collective and agricultural settlement of the land, both as a way to create a new society and as a way to establish the civilian infrastructure for defense.

In 1965 the aging Tabenkin was still the main source of ideological inspiration for Achdut Ha'avodah, but the political operative of this group was his longtime confidant and successor Yisrael Galili, who had served as the political head of the Haganah (the underground military organization of the Jewish Agency) prior to the creation of the state. General Yigal Allon was another follower of Tabenkin and like Galili held an important government position in 1967. These two relatively young personalities, and some lesser figures of this faction, were seen by the veteran Labor leadership in the mid-1960s as a counterforce against those who had defected with Ben-Gurion.

However, in May 1967 during the tense waiting period before the war broke out, Prime Minister Eshkol was persuaded to form the Government of National Unity. Under heavy popular pressure he was compelled to appoint General Moshe Dayan of the Rafi faction as minister of defense. This paved the way for the return of most Rafi members to the Labor Party. A year after the war the Labor Party reunited and included both former secessionist groups.[53]

As a result of these developments within the party, Eshkol found himself in an unenviable position in the months after the Six Day War. He was confronted with a rejectionist Arab posture on the one side and, on the other, by members of his own party who advocated a hard line vis-à-vis the Arabs and an expansionist policy in the new territories.[54] By tradition, voting in the Israeli cabinet is secret, so it is impossible to know with certainty who voted on June 19 in favor of the decision to offer Egypt and Syria the Sinai and Golan respectively. It is very likely that the ideological maximalist Galili and the pessimistic pragmatist Dayan could not support such an offer, and certainly Begin vigorously opposed it.

Tabenkin and his followers had vehemently opposed the partition of Palestine in 1947 and tried to push Ben-Gurion to conquer the entire land during the 1948 war.[55] The outcome of that war did not satisfy them. In the 1950s Tabenkin recommended expanding the territory under Israeli control. In 1951 he prophesied that "the land will eventually be unified and completed since partition is not tenable and presents a continuous danger to the very existence and practical independence of the country."[56]

Sixteen years later Tabenkin felt that his predictions had been proven accurate. He maintained his expansionist sentiments. "The aim of the entire Zionist endeavor was and remains the entire Land of Israel, with its natural and ancient boundaries—from the Mediterranean to the desert, from Mount Lebanon to the Red Sea—this is the renewed patrimony of the majority of the Jewish people."[57]

Yisrael Galili had a more cautious style but was no less dedicated to his teacher's doctrine. In response to a critical letter the prominent Israeli historian Jacob Talmon published in 1969, Galili wrote that "the Arabs of Palestine neither crystallized nor defined themselves as a separate national unit . . . and do not constitute a subject for a separate state." He continued, "We have never acquiesced morally to the closure of parts of our land to Jewish settlement . . . our new settlements were planted on the ground by permission of a title we received from God many years ago."[58]

Moshe Dayan was less sentimental, more sophisticated, and unconventional by nature. As minister of defense he was in charge of the administration of the occupied territories and was responsible for translating policy into the day-to-day practice of government. This involved the administration of more than a million and a half Palestinians living under Israeli jurisdiction. Unlike Tabenkin and Galili, who had only little experience with Arabs, Dayan had grown up on a farm alongside Arab and Bedouin farmers with whom he alternately socialized and fought. Dayan spoke Arabic fluently and possessed a good understanding of Arab aspirations and thought, and he felt a genuine compassion for the Palestinians and their plight. At the annual convention of the Israeli Student Union held in Tel Aviv on October 16, 1968, Dayan told his audience: "We must make a supreme effort to listen to the inhabitants of the [occupied] territories. We must listen to them, get close to them, meet with them, and create with them a human touch." To illustrate his point he read a moving nationalist poem written by a Palestinian poet, Fadwa Tuqan. In the poem Tuqan refers to Israel as "the bird of sin, which flew in and defiled Jerusalem; a diabolic bird, cursed and hated even by the devil himself."[59]

Defying loud public criticism Dayan invited Tuqan to his home. To those who criticized him, he responded, "[Tuqan] is now a national poetess of the Arab-Palestinian public, and I think that it is incumbent upon us to try to find out what this public thinks, what they feel, with what they can live, and against what they will fight."[60] "I know well," he said, "that in this stage the contact will be one-sided. But even if the understanding will be unilateral we have to continue listening to them, hoping that one day they will listen to us too."[61] Interestingly, these words are similar to those that Martin Buber had used when he spoke to the founders of *New Outlook* ten years earlier.

Despite these compassionate sentiments Dayan was a staunch protagonist of territorial expansion. "I do not think that our destiny, the destiny of our generation, is to leave the Arabs open options," he said. "I think that the task put on us in this generation is to find proper solutions for the future of the Land of Israel."[62] In one of Dayan's most revealing lectures, he alluded to his own thoughts on the current political situation through a review of the ideological development of Arthur Rupin, a relatively obscure Zionist leader during the 1920s and 1930s.[63] In the mid-1930s, Rupin, who had earlier favored the establishment of a binational state in Palestine, abandoned his belief in the possibility of persuading the Arabs to cooperate with Zionism, yet refused to give up his Zionist convictions. He concluded therefore that "we are destined to live in a situation of permanent war with the Arabs, and cannot escape the necessity of blood sacrifices . . . if we want to continue our work in the Land of Israel, in contradiction to the Arab will." This was written in 1936, in the early stages of the Great Palestinian Revolt.[64] Thirteen years after Jabotinsky wrote of the need to erect an Iron Wall, Rupin came to a similar conclusion. Peace will be possible, argued Rupin, only when the Arabs are forced to realize that "they are not called upon to grant us something we do not already have, but to recognize reality as it is. Only the weight of the facts will eventually bring about the relaxation of the tensions." More than thirty years later Dayan acknowledged that the facts created by Zionism over three generations had not resulted in a relaxation of tensions; Dayan had to agree with Rupin and Jabotinsky that his generation, and perhaps generations to come, were destined to live in a continuous war with the Arabs.

Dayan's attitudes in the years after the Six Day War were influenced by two factors: his pessimism as to the readiness of the Arabs to compromise with Israel and end the conflict, and his strong attachment to the land of the Bible.[65] In a eulogy to the forty-eight defenders of the Jewish Quarter of Old Jerusalem, who died in battle in 1948 and were reburied in August 1967 in a state ceremony, he said: "We did not betray your dream, nor did we forget your legacy. We returned to the mountains, the cradle of our people, to our patrimony, the land of the Judges, to the fortress of David's Kingdom, we returned to Hebron and Shchem, to Beit Lehem, to Anatot [the village of the prophet Jeremiah], to Jericho and the passages of the Jordan River." He added, "We know that to give life to Jerusalem we have to place our soldiers and armor on the hills of Shchem and at the entrances to the bridges of the Jordan."[66]

Dayan's strange mixture of pragmatic realism and poetic nostalgia resulted in policies that were often inconsistent and contradictory but in fact helped entrench Israeli control over the occupied territories and impeded efforts to test new peace opportunities. It is difficult to discern what solution Dayan envisioned from the many formulations he offered during his almost seven years as minister of defense. The general impression one gets is that Dayan did not believe that any solution was possible in the first place.[67] Dayan adopted a strategy of "maximum coexistence within a conflict."[68] This meant that Israel would brandish a stick over the heads of the terrorists and hold out a carrot for those who were ready to live peacefully under Israeli rule.[69]

Dayan's day-to-day policies in the occupied territories[70] were on the whole open-minded and humane. He tried to allow the Palestinians maximum freedom of movement, public expression, and uninhibited contacts with the Arab world and with other Palestinians in Jordan and elsewhere. The "open bridges" policy was not only a technical decision to allow the flow of merchandise and people across the Jordan, but also an all-encompassing attitude on his part. As General Shlomo Gazit, who coordinated Israeli government administration of the occupied territories from 1967 to 1974, has noted, Dayan hated quislings and preferred to deal with genuine Palestinian representatives without regard to their political and emotional dispositions.[71]

The most notable element of this policy was the permission given to Palestinians who lived outside the territories to visit their relatives and friends in the territories. This led, in the summer of 1968 (during the War of Attrition along the Jordan River), to visits by 12,500 people. This number grew consistently and eventually reached more than 150,000 per year. The policy was criticized by some at the time as compromising Israel's security. Dayan argued that the Palestinians in the territories "are an integral part of the Arab world and are connected to the Arab people around us. . . . I do not believe that we can create a national separation between them and the other Arabs."[72]

The net result of these attitudes was that no meaningful peace initiative could be undertaken by the Labor-led governments between 1967 and 1973. Whatever the motivation of their colleagues from Rafi and Achdut Ha'avodah, Eshkol, Sapir, and the other veterans of Mapai found themselves squeezed by Tabenkin's Zionist maximalism on the one side and the ambivalent pragmatism of Dayan on the other.

Allon—Spurious Compromise

Quite early in the debate over the future of the territories another disciple of Tabenkin tried his hand at what he considered to be a fair compromise. Yigal Allon was a war hero in 1948 and was considered by many an important military strategist.[73] He was a candidate for the post of minister of defense in May 1967, but lost to Dayan. Nevertheless, in 1967 he was an important member of the cabinet. Allon strongly believed in the Jews' claim to the entire land of their forefathers. He was an advocate of rural settlement as the chief means of creating facts on the ground and as an important component of national defense. Like Dayan he was raised alongside the Arabs, spoke their language, and was familiar with their ways. After the end of the war Allon advocated a territorial compromise but insisted that this should be done not on the basis of "giving up our historical claims to these territories, but despite our right to hold on to them. It should be done in order to achieve another historic achievement, not less important—peace."[74]

There was one important difference between Allon and the other members of the government. Allon was opposed to the decision not to decide. "The fact that the Israeli government does not take a position," he argued, "does not mean that positions are not taken in other power centers, both friendly to Israel and not friendly."[75] He wanted to preempt the formulation of other plans that might be dangerous from the Israeli perspective. Allon felt that an explicit Israeli peace plan would help abate Arab suspicions that Israel wanted not peace, but the annexation of all the territories. Allon also argued that a clear plan with regard to the territories would allow Israel to start a rational settlement program in those areas that would eventually remain part of Israel.

To delineate "what kind of peace [Israel] desires, and in which ways it must and can be achieved," Allon presented a plan to the government on July 26, 1967. The plan, which became known as the Allon Plan, was never formally adopted but became a de facto guideline for future Labor Party policy. It is symbolized today by a road that bears his name and runs parallel to the Jordan along the eastern slopes of the West Bank mountain ridge.[76] The Allon Plan proposed to annex a ten- to fifteen-kilometer-wide belt along the Jordan with a connecting corridor from the northern tip of the Dead Sea to Jerusalem, the entire unpopulated Judean desert east of Hebron, and the Gaza Strip. He also suggested settling these areas intensively and undertaking massive construction in East Jerusalem.[77] He proposed allowing the Palestinians in the rest of the area to establish an "Autonomous Arab Region" to be connected to Israel economically, culturally, technologically, and militarily. Allon later included in his proposal a plan for the resettlement of the Palestinian refugees under Israeli control in the West Bank and Sinai. He also included in the areas to be annexed Sharm al-Sheikh (at the southern-most tip of the Sinai), a bulge into the Sinai just south of the Gaza Strip (known later as "Pitchat Rafiah"—the Rafah Wedge), and a strip of land along the Gulf of Eilat to connect the two enclaves.

Allon left the future of the areas in which the Palestinians would have autonomy open-ended. He was ready to consider the possibility of re-uniting this region with Jordan, but also did not exclude the possibility of gradually developing it into a Palestinian state.[78] In 1972 Allon explained that "the future map is based on the following: the moral basis—the his-toric rights of the people of Israel [meaning the Jews] to the land of Israel; the geostrategic basis—defensible borders; the national basis—demo-graphically a Jewish state, including an Arab minority which will enjoy full civil rights."[79] Allon, somewhat naively, believed that the Palestin-ians, and perhaps Jordan, would accept his plan. He was surprised that both totally rejected it, though at the time he was not overly concerned because he advocated unilateral implementation. From 1967 to 1973 the Allon Plan served as a blueprint for substantial settlement activities on the Golan, along the Jordan River, and in the Rafah Wedge. During their tenures as chairmen of the powerful ministerial committee on settlement, both Allon and Galili attempted de facto implementation of the Allon Plan.

Shortly before he died in February 1969, Prime Minister Eshkol gave an interview in which he offered a view of an acceptable settlement that was much harder than the one he had given eighteen months earlier. He said that Israel would never give up the Golan Heights and would demand a physical presence in the Straits of Tiran. Despite this, some of his other formulations reflected his moderate nature and the mood of the more flex-ible wing of the Labor government. "I can pledge my word to Nasser," Eshkol declared, "that greater Israel never has been and never will be our policy. We are flexible on everything . . . we don't want any part of the West Bank which is settled by the Arabs."[80] This interview caused considerable public uproar among the hawkish elements within his own party and in the ranks of Likud, which was still a member of the National Unity Government.

Despite the hawks' protests, the fact remains that Eshkol, like the nation as a whole, had hardened his stance since 1967. Hopes for peace had given way to the sober realization that peace was still far away. Views of what compromises Israel should be willing to make had nar-rowed. New peace initiatives failed to materialize and the desire to keep the territories became more popular. Golda Meir, who succeeded Eshkol, remembered the disillusionment in her memoirs. "The so-called fruits of victory turned into ashes before they could ripen, and the lovely dream of immediate peace faded away."[81]

When Eshkol died on February 26, 1969, Sapir (the king-maker of his party) wanted to avoid a succession struggle between Dayan and Allon. He also sought to keep the power in the hands of the older guard of Labor leaders. He called on the ailing seventy-year-old Golda Meir (who had retired a few months earlier) to accept the premiership.[82] She agreed, but to his dismay she proved to be no less hawkish than both Galili and Dayan. Golda (in Israel, she was always referred to by her first name) remained faithful to the basic formulation of her party that "the price [for withdrawal] would be peace, permanent peace, peace by treaty based on agreed and secure borders."[83] Golda's implementation of this policy meant not only taking no initiatives but also refusing to try any other formulation—as she herself remarked in her memoirs, "intransigence was to become my middle name."[84]

3

Professors for Peace

Lova Eliav Discovers the Palestinians

The Labor Party's decision not to decide anything with regard to the occupied territories invited pressure from both hawks and doves. The expansionists on the right heard Labor's leaders saying that they were ready to trade territories for peace if the Arabs were ready to end the conflict, thus raising the possibility that some accommodation might be reached that would imperil the hope of establishing Greater Israel. The doves on the Israeli left, ready for a compromise, accused the government of failing to undertake genuine initiatives to encourage the Arabs to change their belligerent posture. They also asked the government to avoid any measures that might make a future settlement more difficult. For the hawks the decision not to decide appeared as wavering from the eventual annexation of the territories occupied in 1967, while for the doves it sounded like a covert plan for creeping annexation.

It was natural that the peace activists, who even before the 1967 war saw the Arab-Israeli conflict in a very different light than most Israelis, viewed the conquest of the West Bank and the Gaza Strip as presenting a new opportunity for seeking peace. They tried to reach out to the Palestinians who had come under Israeli rule, and proposed bargaining the territories in exchange for peace. On June 9, before the end of the war, Uri Avneri wrote to Prime Minister Eshkol and pleaded with him to establish a Palestinian state in the recently occupied territories and to conclude a peace treaty with it: "In order to make peace with the Arabs Israel must take one step back. It means to give up assets acquired in the last round."[1] A few days later Avneri again pressed his argument: "Now, Mr. Prime Minister, all our thoughts must be dedicated to the achievement of permanent peace, which will assure the State of Israel independence, security, and development for generations to come. Wisdom of statesmen is now required to reap the harvest of the seeds which were sown by the blood of the soldiers."[2] But most Israelis equated the notion of a Palestinian nation with little more than occasional acts of terror perpetrated at the behest of various Arab states and a refugee problem manipulated for utmost pathos by Arab states seeking to promote their own intra-Arab rivalries and embarrass Israel.

An outspoken and dissenting voice from within the Labor Party itself belonged to Arie Eliav. Known by his Russian nickname "Lova," Eliav was a member of the Knesset (MK) and a deputy to the minister of trade and industry at the time of the Six Day War. In the latter capacity he was responsible for economic programs in Israel's development towns, which had been established to accommodate the Jewish immigrants who flooded the country in the 1950s and 1960s. Despite his relative youth, Eliav had already built a colorful and impressive career.

After serving in the British army during World War II, Eliav served in the Haganah, commanding a ship that transported illegal immigrants and broke the British naval blockade of Palestine. During the 1948 war he served as a lieutenant colonel in the Israeli navy, and in the 1956 Sinai campaign he commanded the operation that rescued the Jewish community of Port Said. During the 1950s he coordinated the construction of Arad (a new town overlooking the Dead Sea) and the Lachish project (a regional settlement plan for new immigrants established around the new town of Kiryat Gat). In the late 1950s Eliav served as a diplomat in the Soviet Union, where he maintained contacts with many of the Soviet Jewish communities struggling for survival under communism. In the early 1960s he headed a special Israeli mission to Iran. The mission's purpose was to assist in the reconstruction of the Kazvin province, which had been devastated by an earthquake. In 1966 he was sent on a secret mission to Kurdistan in northern Iraq to represent Israel in talks with Mustafa Barazani, the Kurdish rebel leader who was fighting the Iraqis and had asked Israel for technical assistance and military expertise. His adroit execution of these missions gave Eliav the reputation of an effective operative who could be called upon for intricate and often dangerous assignments. This reputation helped pave his way to the senior ranks of the Labor Party.[3]

Soon after the 1967 war Eliav resigned his post as deputy minister and received the permission of Eshkol and Dayan to spend half a year exploring the new territories with the explicit intention of "learning the problems of the Arabs of the territories."[4] At the end of the six months, in a meeting with Eshkol, Eliav reported that he had "discovered in the territories an evolving Palestinian nation with all the trappings which make for a national movement and a people." This national evolution, he added, constitutes "the main problem of our own life and existence as Zionists and as Jews, and we must consider how to solve this problem." He recommended undertaking a massive economic development plan as part of a broad effort to reduce the plight of the Palestinian refugees who now lived under Israeli rule. Citing the expertise he had acquired in Arad, Lachish, and Kazvin, Eliav asked to be appointed to head such a project.[5]

Eshkol sent Eliav to discuss his ideas with Dayan, who as minister of defense was in charge of the territories, and Golda Meir, then party secretary. Dayan was lukewarm toward the plan and did not encourage Eliav. Golda was openly negative: "What Palestinian people? Where is there an evolving nation? What are you talking about?" As for Eliav's plans for economic development for the Palestinian refugees, she quoted a biblical passage: "The poor of your own town must have precedence. We have enough troubles within ourselves."[6]

A discouraged Eliav agreed, for the time being, to accept Eshkol's suggestion to drop the matter. However, Eliav did not give up entirely. In November 1968 he published a booklet in Hebrew in which he reviewed basic Zionist ideals in light of the struggle with the Arabs. "During the struggle," he wrote, "the nucleus of a Palestinian Arab nation, a twin to the Jewish people in the Land of Israel, started to appear. It may well be that such a nation did not exist fifty, thirty, or even twenty years ago . . . but it is the ironic paradox of fate and history that Zionism itself contributed to the creation of this Palestinian nation. We have to view the existence of a Palestinian nation as an evolving fact."[7] Eliav proposed that Israel unequivocally declare that if the Arabs were ready for peace, Israel would be ready to relinquish territory. "The Arab people must know that we shall never suppress the right of the Palestinians for self-determination."[8]

A few thousand copies of Eliav's brochure were distributed. Golda, who became prime minister after Eshkol's death in February 1969, must have overlooked this publication or dismissed it as insignificant, for she did not object to Eliav's election to succeed her as party secretary in January 1970. Eliav remained committed to his ideas and refused to be coopted by his new status. The position of secretary general of the Labor Party was a senior post in the Israeli power elite, and Eliav used this podium to fight for his agenda. Soon after his election he said in an interview with *Time* that "the first thing we have to do . . . is to recognize that the Palestinian Arabs exist as an infant nation . . . the sooner we do it the better it will be for us, for them, and for eventual peace. . . . The solution has to be that two states can live equally together."[9] These ideas were incompatible with the position taken by the prime minister, who refused to accept that there existed a distinct Palestinian people and nationality separate from the broader Arab world. Eliav found himself isolated in several Labor debates over the future of the occupied territories. Leaders such as Pinhas Sapir and other colleagues who were known generally to share Eliav's views rarely voiced their support for his outlook in public. "I started to move away from the heart of the party consensus to which I had belonged all my adult life," Eliav later commented.[10]

Eliav came to doubt whether Golda, who still felt more comfortable in English than in Hebrew, read his brochure. However, he had no doubt that the interview in *Time* had caught her attention. Within a few days of its publication Golda suggested to Eliav that he disclaim the controversial statements. Eliav's adamant refusal ended their long-standing friendly relationship. Eliav promised to run the party's affairs through the difficult period of internal elections and a planned party convention without inappropriately advocating his views. He resigned immediately after the end of the convention in May 1971.[11]

The Rehovot Group

Labor's decision not to decide and Golda's reluctance to pursue any peace initiatives stifled even plans that were much less ambitious than those advocated by Eliav. During 1968 a group of scientists from the Weizmann Institute in Rehovot met with a small group of government officials to discuss the human and economic dimensions of the occupation. On July 13, 1968, they presented to the government an informal document that became known as the Rehovot Group Plan.[12] The paper cautiously refrained from discussing the political future of the territories, and focused instead on a proposal to launch a massive development program aimed at elevating the standard of living of the Palestinians now under Israeli control. The group believed that the implementation of the plan not only would ease tensions and reduce the problem of unemployment but also might "turn the territories into a model of a progressive and orderly regime, and . . . lead to a positive meeting point based on peaceful and constructive relations between Israel and its neighbors." It was assumed that funding for the plan could come from international monetary sources, private investors, and the Israeli authorities.[13]

The Rehovot Plan was shelved and was never seriously discussed by the Israeli government, which shared the public's growing disbelief in the possibility of reaching a peaceful settlement. Whereas in the summer of 1967 close to 50 percent of Israelis believed that the Arabs were interested in peace, by the end of that year fewer than 15 percent did so. The number continued to dwindle, reaching its lowest level of 8 percent in the summer of 1970.[14]

The Movement for the Greater Land of Israel

Whether for strategic reasons or because of their emotional attachment to the idea of Greater Israel, hawks without and within the Labor Party quickly organized a lobby against withdrawal from the territories. Nathan Alterman, a prominent poet, and Moshe Shamir, the novelist, led this effort.[15] They held preliminary discussions with a few veteran leaders from the Israeli right, the most prominent of whom were Uri Zvi Greenberg, a flamboyant poet, and Israel Eldad, a publicist. Both Greenberg and Eldad had been leaders of the Stern Gang before the establishment of the state and were longtime advocates of Zionist maximalism. Many of the participants in this new initiative were members of the Labor Party and followers of Itzhak Tabenkin, who called for the settlement of an additional two million Jews "from the mountains of Lebanon to Sinai, from the sea unto the desert."[16]

On October 31, 1967, in a festive public meeting held in Tel Aviv, the Movement for the Greater Land of Israel was officially founded.[17] Conference chairman Alterman delivered the opening remarks: "The territories are a natural part of the continuous essence of the Jewish past and its future. . . . We must create a counterpressure which is still lacking, the pressure of the Jewish people who say that they will never give up, who say that it is impossible to tear this land from them." Shamir added, "Now I met again my real Land of Israel, the correct Land of Israel, the land with its natural and obvious borders." He called for "a full and resolute struggle to make the present borders into the unavoidable and permanent borders of the State of Israel."[18] A few hours earlier Israeli newspapers had appeared containing a manifesto in which the new movement declared, "We do not have the license to give up the Land of Israel any more than to give up the State of Israel." The manifesto was signed by fifty-seven prominent Israelis, including military figures, members of the business community, rabbis, writers, and academics. The group included some disciples of Jabotinsky and leaders of the National Religious Party, but most came from the ranks of the Labor Party.[19]

Professors on the Alert—Peace and Security

In the summer of 1967 Jacob Talmon, a prominent historian of eighteenth- and nineteenth-century European ideas, was engaged in a heated public debate with Albert Hourani, a well-known Oxford historian of the Middle East.[20] Hourani presented the Arab interpretation of the conflict, which in his opinion was rooted in the expansionist nature of Zionism. Hourani supported the "moderate" Arab demands for the return of the Palestinian refugees to their homes and the retreat of Israel to the 1947 UN partition plan lines.

Talmon defended Israel's decision to preempt an Arab attack by launching the Six Day War. He presented a harsh critique of the Arabs whose "sense of grievance blinded them to the historic rights, the background of tragedy behind the Jewish aspirations, the ardor and idealism motivating them, and the constructive achievements resulting from them."[21] However, in articles intended more for the Israeli public he also stated that "it does not behoove the victor to mock the vanquished and to trample under his feet the fallen foe." Talmon defined the Arab-Israeli conflict as "a clash of rights," and supported the government's position, which demanded an end to the "state of half peace, half war," arguing that "in view of the permanent danger of erupting into total war, there is no alternative to total peace." This formulation still echoed the established Israeli line, which opposed any interim measures.[22] Sixteen months later Talmon published a letter to Yisrael Galili, then minister of information. Talmon harshly criticized official policies and called on Golda's government "to recognize the right of the neighboring people [the Palestinians] to live their own life, and to remain a separate unit or rejoin Jordan." He urged the government to stop waiting and take the initiative, especially with regard to the Palestinian issue.[23]

Another historian, Yehoshua Arieli, joined in the debate and published a series of articles in *Davar* (the official newspaper of the Labor movement) in which he warned against the corrupting effect the occupation would have on the democratic fiber of Israeli society.[24] Unlike Talmon, Arieli was a veteran of public struggles and sought to sustain the public debate.[25]

Some months earlier Gadi Yatziv, a sociologist from the Hebrew University, was about to end his military reserve duty and used his last days of service to initiate contacts with Palestinians in the West Bank. Upon returning to Jerusalem, Yatziv met with some like-minded colleagues and issued a bold public statement: "Security—Yes! Peace—Yes! Annexation—No!" "We were not pacifists," Yatziv later explained, "nor was it a continuation of the moralistic Zionist minimalism of Martin Buber. We were seriously concerned about the future security of Israel."[26]

These academics and others tried at this point to organize in response to the establishment of the Movement for the Greater Land of Israel, which had managed to recruit an impressive roster of intellectuals.[27] The mood of the country seemed to be sliding to the right and the professors felt an obligation to try to stem the tide.[28] A further impetus was provided during the Passover holiday on April 12, 1968, when a group of extreme right-wing orthodox activists squatted in a hotel in the midst of the Arab town of al-Khalil (known to Jews as Hebron), with the declared intention of reestablishing the Jewish community of this ancient holy site. (The Jewish patriarchs are buried in Hebron, and a Jewish community had existed for centuries there until massacred by Palestinian nationalists in 1929.) The leader of the settlers, Rabbi Moshe Levinger, a staunch advocate of Greater Israel, demanded permission from the government to establish a yeshiva in Hebron.

The government was divided on the issue. Dayan feared an increase of tensions in the area and opposed the request. Allon supported it on the grounds that the Allon Plan did not exclude Jewish settlement anywhere in the land and had advocated the annexation of the Judean desert just east of Hebron. With the government unable to decide on a coherent policy, no decision to remove the squatters was made and they remained on the site.[29]

These developments spurred the dovish academics to take action. At a July 1, 1968, conference in Tel Aviv, they established the Movement for Peace and Security. The movement's charter demanded that the government "declare unequivocally that the State of Israel does not intend to annex territories, and adopts the principle of evacuating administered territories as a result of a peace agreement based upon agreed and secure boundaries."[30]

Much of the early activity of the Movement for Peace and Security involved publishing opinions and analyses.[31] The movement had two main branches, one in Jerusalem, which was more philosophical in orientation, and one in Tel Aviv, which was more political. Some Mapam leaders joined and *New Outlook* offered its pages to the movement for the purpose of distributing its ideas abroad.[32] However, the intensification of the War of Attrition at the beginning of 1969 presented the group with mounting difficulties in their attempt to gain support. In light of the Arabs' refusal to negotiate with Israel, the members of the movement found it difficult to convince broader sections of the public that the enactment of their recommendations would make any noticeable difference to Israeli-Arab relations.

Most of the movement's activists were politically and ideologically part of the Israeli mainstream, not radicals or leftists who could be easily disregarded as being beyond the pale of Israeli society. Many of them were members of mainstream parties and were seen as loyal Zionists, and they hoped to attract other mainstream Israelis and to have some influence with the Labor Party's elite. They constantly feared suffering the same kind of marginalization that befell Buber, Avneri, Flapan, and Golan in the 1950s and 1960s. However, the absence of a serious response from the Arab side frustrated the movement's best efforts well into the 1970s. Yigal Eilam, a historian of Zionism and one of the movement's founders, expressed his reservations to a colleague: "It is clear that the principle of negotiations [with the Arabs] cannot be the key to the solution, simply since the situation is that the Arab states are not ready to enter any negotiations. This turns the entire discourse and the expectations for negotiations unrealistic and may jet us out of the picture."[33]

For the next two decades Israeli peaceniks constantly had to remind the public that they were as concerned about Israeli security as were their rivals on the right, and that they were fully aware of the evils perpetrated by Israel's enemies and sensitive to the suffering of their victims. The very name "Peace and Security" was meant to serve as a reminder that one aspiration need not necessarily come at the expense of the other. Almost every public declaration that the movement issued during the War of Attrition and the years of intensive Palestinian terrorism tried to underline the point. A 1969 declaration, for instance, said plainly, "We firmly denounce the violation of the cease-fire agreement by the military forces of the Arab states and the activities of the terrorist organizations."[34]

Most of Peace and Security's positions were critical of the National Unity Government, and in particular its decision not to decide.[35] The movement argued that the attempt to maintain the facade of national unity "prohibits the government from issuing clear initiatives for a dialogue with the Arabs, and does not permit the assertion of a clear political line."[36] For its part, the movement presented five main demands: that the Israeli government clearly declare that it would not try to annex any of the territories, keeping them only against the time they might be traded for a genuine peace; that the government refrain from allowing any civilian settlement of the territories; that it create and implement initiatives to resolve the problem of Palestinian refugees; that it state its readiness to allow Arab inhabitants of the territories to participate in the peace process; and, not least, that it initiate the development of an honest and consistent peace plan and vigorously pursue its goals.[37]

Yehoshua Arieli, who was the most active academic in the group, summarized its positions in a June 1969 speech: "We must seek peace in every possible way and refrain from taking roads which may prevent us from achieving peace. Continued occupation creates a situation which must inevitably corrupt the image of the society which gave meaning to our entire life."[38]

Between March 27 and 30, 1969, *New Outlook* in cooperation with Peace and Security convened an international symposium called "Inevitable War or Initiatives for Peace." Most of the Israeli participants were movement activists, but an impressive group of foreign intellectuals also attended.[39] One of the issues addressed was the political character of the Palestinian problem. For the first time mainstream Israelis identified the clash between the Jewish and Arab peoples of Palestine as "the very heart of the conflict." As the introduction to the published proceedings of the symposium states, "The continued anomaly of the Palestinians as a politically homeless people breeds the desperation and the terrorism leading to an ever more dangerous escalation of the Israeli-Arab conflict and presenting a permanent threat to peace." Despite these pronouncements the conference was limited in its impact because the Arab side was not present and much of the talk amounted to a series of monologues. The hope was expressed that "the time will not be too far when we can hold another symposium of this kind in which all the parties involved will participate."[40]

It was, however, to be a very long time before that hope was realized. Eighteen years later, in collaboration with the Palestinian journal *al-Fajr,* *New Outlook* convened another symposium, this time with the participation of many Palestinians, including official delegates of the PLO.[41]

Stepping Up Activities

By the end of 1969 internal as well as external developments caused Peace and Security to step up its activities. During the summer of 1969 the Labor Party was preparing for the Knesset elections scheduled for the end of October. A heated controversy erupted when Moshe Dayan threatened to quit and form a new party if Labor did not adopt a hard-line stance on the territories. Given Dayan's popularity, his departure could have spelled defeat for Labor and led to the forging of a coalition between him and Menachem Begin.[42]

Dayan demanded that the terms "territorial compromise" and "retreat" not be mentioned in the party's platform and that there be no reference to UN Resolution 242. A compromise formula was adopted that stated that it was not yet time to identify the final borders. But in an "Oral Doctrine" (*Torah Shebealpeh*) that was formally agreed upon, it was unofficially announced that the Labor government would insist that even if peace were achieved Israel would not relinquish the Golan Heights, the Gaza Strip, Sharm al-Sheikh, and a strip of land leading to it along the Gulf of Eilat. Furthermore, the Jordan River should remain the "security border" of Israel. The precise meaning of "security border" was intentionally left vague. It also was decided that Israel would unilaterally implement a plan to settle those areas that were ultimately to be included in Israel. This Oral Doctrine was formulated by Yisrael Galili and Dayan with the consent of Golda Meir. It signaled a hardening of the party's line.

At the same time the War of Attrition was causing hundreds of casualties and eroding public morale. Growing public disillusionment with the Labor leadership was reflected in the 1969 Knesset elections, which resulted in an overall loss of seven seats in the parliamentary representation of the Labor bloc. Most of the votes lost by the Labor Party went to smaller parties, mainly on the right.[43] In light of the mounting international pressure on Israel to retreat from the territories, Golda felt obliged to form another Government of National Unity with Likud and Menachem Begin, thereby ensuring that the new government would be adamant in its opposition to territorial compromise.[44]

One of the first decisions the new government made was to reject the Rogers Plan. Basing his plan on Israel's decision of June 19, 1967, William Rogers, the U.S. secretary of state, proposed a full Israeli retreat to the prewar borders in the Sinai and Golan and a minor adjustment of the border with Jordan. Jerusalem would remain unified but controlled jointly by Israel and Jordan. Also, in consideration of Israel's security concerns, some demilitarized areas would be created on all sides. In line with UN Resolution 242 all these arrangements would be contingent on the agreement of the Arab states to conclude peace with Israel.[45] This plan was to be negotiated by Gunnar Jarring, a Swedish diplomat whom UN Secretary-General U Thant enlisted to serve as a special diplomatic envoy and mediate on behalf of the UN Security Council. On December 22 Israel announced publicly that it would not enter into negotiations on the basis of the Rogers Plan.[46]

In the run-up to and aftermath of the elections the Movement for Peace and Security issued critical appraisals of the government's policies. At the end of September 1969 the movement published a critique of the Oral Doctrine, calling it "an indication that Israel's leadership [has removed] itself from the pursuit of peace." The critique continued: "The transfer from a state of war to a state of peace is often dependent on the initiative of one side, his power of persuasion, and his persistence in looking for ways which will allay the tension and pave the way to conciliation and negotiations. . . . We must undertake such an initiative and make peace our highest priority."[47]

The movement denounced the National Unity Government for moving "the State of Israel further away from the ability to offer solutions to the crisis in which we find ourselves." Although Peace and Security, like the government, viewed the Rogers Plan as too risky for Israel, the movement criticized the government's unqualified rejection of the plan and called on the government "to declare its unequivocal readiness to accept [Resolution 242] in its entirety as a basis for a peace settlement."[48] As before, however, Peace and Security had little impact beyond the few thousand Israelis sympathetic to its aims.

In the spring of 1970 a political storm arose around the question of the future of the Jewish settlement in Hebron. Rabbi Levinger and his settlers, who had remained in temporary lodgings within the confines of a military base during the previous two years, were pushing for governmental approval to build permanent residences for themselves and future settlers. Deputy Prime Minister Allon favored the proposal and advised the settlers to build the new Jewish town of Kiryat Arba (the biblical name of Hebron) on a hill at the eastern approaches to the Arab town. This way they could be included in the Jewish territory outlined in his Allon Plan. On March 9, 1970, Allon announced in the Knesset that the government would decide on the matter within two weeks.[49]

The Labor alliance was divided on the issue. The Movement for Peace and Security mobilized about 150 prominent academics, artists, businessmen, and politicians to publish yet another appeal. It called on the government to reject Allon's proposal because such a move "would be interpreted by all as a step towards the annexation of the administered territories . . . and would create facts which would block the road to conciliation."[50] Once again, this protest was in vain. The pro-settlement forces were exercising increasing political influence, and the tenacity of Levinger and his associates proved insurmountable. Kiryat Arba became a fact and within a few years its population grew to 5,000 settlers.

For many in the peace camp this again demonstrated that the decision not to decide was untenable and that in practice it amounted to expansionism because little was being done to impede further settlement. On the issue of settlement the government was clearly ambivalent, but this ambivalence served well the interests of the right wingers, who were actively pursuing their agenda. Peace advocates demanded that the government adopt a policy that would prohibit settlement activity. But the decision not to decide was in fact a decision not to take such initiatives.

A month later another crisis erupted. Through intermediaries, including a special envoy he sent to Paris, Nasser explored the idea of extending an invitation to Nahum Goldmann (still president of the World Zionist Organization and the World Jewish Congress) to come to Egypt and present his ideas on the possibility for reconciliation.[51] Egypt's one condition was that the mission be authorized by the Israeli government. Golda, who never trusted Goldmann, suspected that Nasser's gambit was intended to drive a wedge between Israel and world Jewry by having Goldmann convey or even endorse proposals that the Israeli government would inevitably turn down. She brought the issue to the cabinet, which refused to endorse the trip, justifying its decision with the argument that Nasser's proposal was an attempt to circumvent Israel's demand for direct, unmediated negotiations.[52]

The Goldmann affair occurred at the height of the War of Attrition when Israeli newspapers carried daily pictures of casualties and the general mood of the country was somber.[53] That mood became yet darker when fifty-eight high school seniors who were about to begin their military service wrote an open letter to the prime minister in which they questioned the decision not to sanction Goldmann's mission. "Until now we believed that we must serve three years and be ready to fight because there is no other choice," the seniors wrote. "This affair has proven that when there is a choice, even a slight one, it is ignored. We and many others are therefore wondering how can we fight in a permanent, futureless war, while our government's policy is to ignore any chance for peace."[54]

This letter was unprecedented and alarming because it touched on a highly sensitive nerve in Israeli society. Israelis had long assumed that their young people were motivated to serve in the military from the conviction that Israel had no alternative but to defend itself in a hostile environment. This readiness to bear arms was considered an important national asset, one that now seemed to be endangered. Amid the national debate stirred by the letter and the refusal to authorize Goldmann's trip, the Movement for Peace and Security was emboldened to take more dramatic steps. Instead of relying, as usual, on the publication of analyses and appeals, the movement placed prominent advertisements in the media exclaiming, "Enough! Enough with the excuses! There is an opportunity for contact with the enemy! Let Goldmann try! The government's refusal is a betrayal of the chance for peace!"[55] For the advocates of an aggressive peace policy the Goldmann affair served as a litmus test, not because they were convinced that Goldmann would be able to bring peace, but because it represented an opportunity with no security risks. No real damage would have been caused if Goldmann had been allowed to try. But the refusal of Golda's cabinet was clear proof in the activists' eyes that peace was not the highest priority for Israel's political leadership.

This episode was followed by a mass protest in front of the prime minister's office in Jerusalem on April 8, 1970. At the end of the demonstration some of the more extreme participants clashed with the police, much to the dismay of the more cautious and law-abiding leaders of the movement.[56] The issue of what tactics the protesters should employ was to become a perennial source of tension within Israel's peace movement. Occasionally, in order to present a broader front, the mainstream Zionist majority in the peace movement was tempted to cooperate with non-Zionist elements on the Israeli left. For their part, the leftist groups often tried to piggyback on mainstream demonstrations even when not specifically invited to participate. The confrontational tactics that the radical left employed embarrassed the moderates and enabled the adversaries of the peace movement to label the entire movement anti-Zionist and radical.

The April demonstration near the prime minister's office had been planned to include all factions opposed to the unity government and its policies. It included members of the New Communist List (Rakach—a group that had seceded from the Israeli Communist Party and had primarily an Arab constituency), as well as a few members of Matzpen (a small, ultra-left group that advocated the abandonment of Zionism in favor of a "socialist republic of all its citizens").[57] These radical groups tried their best to make their participation known to the public in an effort to gain exposure. But the mainstream members of the peace movement hurried to divest themselves of these embarrassing partners and publicly denounced the clashes with the police.[58]

End of Attrition

During the winter of 1970 Israel's casualties along the Suez Canal mounted and the government decided to escalate its reprisals with bombing raids deep inside Egypt, penetrating as far as the outskirts of Cairo. In response Nasser called on the Soviets to increase their military involvement. The Soviets provided Egypt with the latest surface-to-air missiles (SAMs) operated by Soviet technicians and dispatched Soviet pilots to fly Egyptian MiG-21 combat aircraft on defensive missions over Egyptian airspace.[59] In response to the Soviet intervention and growing concern at the possibility of further escalation, the United States renewed its efforts to achieve a cease-fire. In cooperation with the Soviet ambassador to Washington, Secretary Rogers issued a new initiative—the Rogers Plan II—on June 16. This initiative called on the parties to declare a cease-fire for ninety days in order to allow Ambassador Jarring to renew his mediation efforts.[60]

The Soviet SAMs significantly limited the effectiveness of the Israeli air force along the canal and caused a higher rate of aircraft attrition. Despite a dramatic encounter that ended in the downing of five Soviet pilots (flying Egyptian MiGs) with no casualties to the Israelis, the IDF high command and the majority in the Israeli government realized that the War of Attrition could not be won. Added to this recognition was concern over potential further entanglement with the Soviets. The Egyptians were eager to capitalize on the relative advantage they had gained through Soviet intervention, notwithstanding some opposition from within Egypt and the rest of the Arab world. On July 23 Nasser announced Egypt's acceptance of the latest Rogers initiative.[61]

Despite opposition from Likud, Golda announced Israel's acceptance of the Rogers Plan II on July 31.[62] The American initiative provided for a cease-fire and a standstill agreement, which required both sides to maintain the military status quo. The Egyptians took immediate advantage of the cease-fire, violating the standstill agreement (which came into effect at midnight August 7) by advancing their ground-to-air missiles to positions closer to the Suez Canal. This extended their air defense umbrella twenty kilometers further to the east of the canal. This was a significant alteration of the status quo at Israel's expense. The Israeli defense establishment immediately recognized the strategic and tactical implications of the Egyptian move. Defense minister Dayan declared in the Knesset that Israel "ought not to, and cannot . . . ignore the fact that . . . this moving forward of these [missile] sites [has] considerable military significance."[63] In response to this violation Israel suspended its participation in the Jarring talks.[64]

In the following weeks two unconnected events led to a significant reconfiguration of the Arab-Israeli conflict. In the second half of September full-scale conflict broke out between the Palestinian guerrillas in Jordan and the Jordanian military, with the Palestinians suffering major losses and, eventually, being ejected from the Hashemite Kingdom.[65] Then, on September 27, 1970, a day after he had brokered a cease-fire between King Hussein and Yasser Arafat, President Nasser died of a sudden heart attack. He was replaced by his vice president, Anwar Sadat, who was initially viewed as a transitional figure.

During the summer of 1970 the Movement for Peace and Security was engaged in trying to push the Israeli government to accept the American peace proposal or to propose a peace initiative of its own. The movement continued to publish newspaper advertisements warning of the danger of a settlement imposed by outside powers, and maintaining that "the negation of initiatives which cannot be accepted is not enough. [The government] must clearly articulate counter-proposals based on Security Council Resolution 242. . . . An effort must be made to renew the mediation mission of Dr. Gunnar Jarring, and to enable the implementation of a limited and well-supervised cease-fire agreement which will not be exploited by the Egyptians to the detriment of Israel."[66]

This cautious formulation was characteristic of the group. Such leaders of Peace and Security such as Arieli and Yatziv were close enough to governmental circles to appreciate the complicated considerations confronting Israeli decision makers. Thus they were fully aware of the disadvantages of the Rogers initiatives to Israel's vital interests. They were also aware of the dangers of Egypt's exploitation of the cease-fire agreement to improve its military deployment along the canal. Their efforts were primarily directed at what they perceived to be the government's lethargy regarding new peace initiatives.

The Movement for Peace and Security defined its role on three levels: as a counterforce to the growing extraparliamentary activities of the Israeli right; as a direct lobby to try to influence the government's policies; and as an educational and informational tool to influence public opinion. With the bitter experience of the thousand days of the War of Attrition leading many Israelis toward acceptance of arguments for retaining all the territories, the movement tried to shift public opinion in the opposite direction: "If we had followed the advice [of those who opposed the cease-fire agreement] we would have not only missed yet another opportunity for a peace settlement, but would also have found ourselves in a direct military confrontation with the Soviet Union; losing vital sources of military and economic aid from the United States . . . and strengthening the hands of the terrorists."[67] Despite their avoidance of moral appeals and their focus on specific security concerns, these arguments had little or no effect beyond the circle of believers. Attempts to persuade the government did not fare much better. The deadlock over the territories that froze the Labor Party in the late 1960s did not provide many opportunities for creative solutions. As for the prime minister, Golda was too resolute in her views to be susceptible to persuasion.

By the end of 1970, under heavy U.S. pressure, Israel agreed to resume its participation in the Jarring talks.[68] During February 1971 Jarring questioned Egyptian leaders to see if they were prepared to enter into a peace agreement with Israel and to terminate the state of belligerency. At the same time Jarring asked Israel if it was ready to withdraw its forces from occupied Egyptian territory to the former international boundary, provided arrangements were made to create demilitarized zones in the Sinai, and freedom of navigation in the Straits of Tiran and Suez Canal was assured.

The Egyptian response, while essentially positive, was unsatisfactory. Although Egypt was ready to terminate the state of belligerency and satisfy all of the mediator's substantive demands, it agreed to enter into a peace agreement with Israel only if the Palestinian question was resolved and Israel withdrew from *all* occupied territories. On its side, Israel was ready to negotiate a bilateral agreement with Egypt without giving any assurances with respect to other aspects of the mediator's questions. Furthermore, Israel did not agree to declare its readiness to withdraw from all of Sinai, and certainly did not agree to retreat from the Gaza Strip. Instead, the government restated its readiness to retreat to "secure and recognized borders."[69]

Partial and Interim Agreements

The cease-fire agreement along the Suez Canal introduced a new approach to the negotiations. For the first time the possibility of an interim settlement was proposed and was seriously entertained by Israel, Egypt, and the United States. Labor MK Gad Ya'acobi proposed to stabilize the Israeli-Egyptian standoff along the canal by a partial retreat of Israeli forces in the Sinai, the establishment of a demilitarized zone along both sides of the canal, opening the canal for international navigation, and the return of the Egyptian refugees to the canal zone followed by economic redevelopment.[70]

From the end of the Six Day War, Israeli policy had been based on a rigid demand that any settlement that included Israeli retreat from occupied territories be part of an explicit, comprehensive, and final peace settlement. Israel's previous experiences with partial and inexplicit arrangements—for example, the 1949 armistice agreements and the "understandings" after the Sinai Campaign of 1956—had created a deep sense of distrust of any settlement short of a full, public, and formal peace treaty. The disappointments that Golda Meir experienced at the United Nations as Israel's minister for foreign affairs back in May 1957 had left a lasting impression on her. Israeli policy was guided by a determination not to repeat the mistakes of 1949—armistice agreements without peace—or the mistakes of 1957—some hocus-pocus in the United Nations and a nebulous undertaking by the United States without as much as a piece of paper. "This time, after the third war, Israel was stubborn in her resolve not to agree to any arrangement which fell short of full peace and was not based on formal peace treaties."[71]

After June 1967 the American administration too had supported the idea that a settlement must be comprehensive. By the end of 1970 the likelihood of a comprehensive settlement seemed remote, however. Meanwhile, the danger of renewed violence was real enough to warrant a new attempt at stabilizing the situation along the cease-fire lines, even if only through partial and interim agreements.

During a private visit to the United States during September 1970, Ya'acobi held discussions with senior State Department officials and with

Henry Kissinger (at the time President Nixon's national security adviser) regarding stabilizing the situation along the Suez by opening the canal to navigation.[72] Initially the State Department was cool to the idea, and the Pentagon was adamantly opposed on the grounds that opening the canal would serve Soviet interests by shortening Soviet lines of communications to the Far East. Golda also rebuffed Ya'acobi's private initiative in a meeting of the Political Committee of the Labor Alliance. Yitzhak Rabin, then Israel's ambassador to Washington, too expressed some misgivings.[73] Despite this opposition, by October Moshe Dayan had begun to speak about a new proposal to replace the Rogers formula and the Jarring talks, which were bogged down.[74] Sadat ultimately took the initiative and announced his willingness to open the canal to international navigation in return for a partial retreat of Israeli forces in the Sinai.[75]

During much of 1971 American officials undertook intensive diplomatic efforts to reach an interim agreement based on Dayan's and Sadat's openings. But the gap between the parties was too wide and the efforts failed.[76] The details of these tedious negotiations generally remained secret. Those that leaked to the press, and the pieces of information reported to the Knesset by the prime minister or other senior cabinet members, were often intricate and confusing. Uncertain of what, if any, progress was being made, the peace movement found it difficult to critique government action. Even when they felt the negotiations were not producing results, the peace activists could only claim that "we live today with the feeling that the government of Israel did not yet exhaust all options open to her to start negotiations with Egypt and prevent the danger of a renewed war."[77]

On December 25, 1971, an independent group of prominent lawyers and academics close to the Peace and Security circles wrote a letter to the prime minister in which they called on the government to "check once more its declared positions and come up with proposals which without risking the security of Israel may provide a realistic basis for negotiations with Egypt."[78] In her characteristic response Golda adamantly denied the allegation that Israel had not explored all political avenues that might lead to negotiations with Egypt and asserted that her government had "indeed come up with proposals, which . . . could have served as a basis for such negotiations."[79] This exchange attracted considerable media attention, particularly after Golda, with much fanfare, received a delegation from the Movement for the Greater Land of Israel. This gesture stood in stark contrast to Golda's refusal to meet with the "peace professors." A spokesman for the peace movement expressed his frustration to the media:

"It seems that those who agree with the government's policy are listened to, while those who do not agree are ignored."[80]

The Road to Another War

An important factor that contributed to the inability to move toward an interim settlement was the sense of complacency and self-assuredness that characterized the mood of Israel's public and its leadership during 1972 and 1973. Occasionally Dayan and others warned of the possibility of another war,[81] but on the whole the defense establishment considered the probability of renewed fighting as fairly low. Notwithstanding his own forebodings, Dayan, like many others, was convinced that Israeli forces could repel an Arab attack without much difficulty,[82] and projected—with his tone as much as his words—a sense of security and great confidence. In a speech at the annual gathering of paratrooper veterans he said, "Until recently I was not sure, but now I believe that we have arrived at the zenith of the return to Zion."[83]

Egyptian president Anwar Sadat announced in 1971 that this would be the "Year of Decision," alluding to the threat of another war. Yet nothing of the sort happened—despite a similar announcement the next year. To the contrary, in July 1972 Sadat expelled thousands of Soviet technicians and military advisers. This action appeared to confirm Israel's belief that a war was unlikely; after all, few Israelis thought the Egyptian army could sustain a serious military effort without the help of the Soviets.[84] Yet Sadat continued to rattle his sword, declaring that he was ready to sacrifice two million Egyptians to retrieve his nation's dignity. Israel's political and military leadership did not take him seriously. "We are convinced," Golda stated, "that an offensive initiative by the Egyptians will bring them defeat and deep disappointment."[85] And in a more pugnacious mood she declared: "The Egyptians know well that war will not bring them any advantage. If Sadat speaks of sacrificing one million or two or three, this may indeed happen!"[86]

Dayan's primary motive for supporting the interim agreement along the Suez Canal was to further reduce the probability of war. However, he was not prepared to fight for his opinions. He often said, "If Golda does not support my position, I don't either."[87] Apparently Dayan did not perceive another war as a major danger for Israel and felt secure behind the heavy fortifications along the Bar-Lev Line (named after the chief of staff under whose command the line was designed) and under the umbrella of the Israeli air force. Moreover, in the summer of 1973 Dayan plunged into a heated campaign in which he wanted to make sure that the "return to Zion" materialized through an aggressive settlement policy.

Elections for the Ninth Knesset were scheduled for October 1973. During the summer the Labor Party was busy preparing its political platform once more. Dayan demanded that Labor adopt an ambitious settlement plan in the occupied territories, especially on the Golan, in the Jordan Valley, and in particular in the Rafah Wedge southwest of the Gaza Strip. He envisaged the construction of a deep-water harbor and a large town in Yamit, on the shores of the Mediterranean halfway between the Gaza Strip and the Egyptian town of El Arish. Characteristically, the main objection to Dayan's plans came from Minister of Finance Pinhas Sapir, who objected on economic rather than political grounds. But once again Galili worked out a compromise document that carried his name and mollified Dayan for the time being.[88]

The Seagull—Eliav's Solitary Crusade

Back in 1969, while Lova Eliav was still party secretary, a new "circle" had been organized within the party by a group of young intellectuals who wanted to strengthen Eliav's hand. In the late 1950s, the writer and historian Yigal Eilam had led a nonpartisan student list at the Hebrew University in Jerusalem that won a majority in the student council elections. "We had an acute political awareness but no particular partisan loyalty," explained Dan Bitan, Eilam's colleague during the university years. "We wanted to cut off student life from party interests."[89] They created a Students' Parliament for public debates and founded a student magazine, The Ass's Mouth, which Eilam edited.[90]

In 1966 Eilam together with Tzvi Kesse, a former kibbutz member whom Eilam met during the struggles against Ben-Gurion in the 1960s, and other young intellectuals began to organize an independent think tank that sought to reformulate Zionist ideology. They dreamed of building a Jewish senate in which Israelis and diaspora Jews would jointly discuss issues of common interest to world Jewry.[91] The group planned a founding convention for July 1967. However, the Six Day War split the group between a right-wing faction, which joined the Movement for the Greater Land of Israel, and the leftists who viewed Eliav as their leader.

To help Eliav in his struggles within the Labor Party, Eilam and his colleagues joined the party and with Eliav's blessing formed the Circle for the Study of Social and Political Affairs (Hachug Lelibung). They were immediately recognized as the Peace and Security branch within the party, because they advocated withdrawal from the occupied territories. The group distributed pamphlets, lobbied party leaders, and conducted debates in party branches throughout the country. But in the early 1970s after Eliav left the secretariat they felt increasingly alienated from the party's mainstream and gradually distanced themselves.

After resigning in May 1971 as party secretary, Eliav spent a year in seclusion writing his magnum opus. As if in a trance he worked day and night.[92] "It was like fire in my bones," Eliav remembered. "I felt with all my fibers the compulsion to tell the public that which was in my heart." The result was a political and ideological credo, *Eretz Ha'tzvi* (The Land of the Hart).[93] The term "Land of the Hart" had long been used in Jewish tradition as a poetic name for the Land of Israel. "This was indeed the way I wanted to see my land," explained Eliav.[94]

The book was perhaps overambitious in its scope and at times naive, but its position with regard to the Arab-Israeli conflict was courageous. It clearly opposed the majority perspective within the Labor Party.

> The Palestinian aspect of the problem is the most delicate, the most tragic, and the gloomiest of all. It appears to be insoluble but it also carries the greatest potential for peace. The question of our relations with the Palestinian Arabs occupies first place in the broad question of our relations with the Arab world as a whole. Therein lies the key to the resolution of the struggle over the land.

Responding to his own rhetorical question as to the right of the Palestinian people to define themselves as a unique nation, Eliav wrote:

> We [Zionists] struggled for the right of self-determination of Jews and succeeded. How can we deny this right to others then, to people who wish to see themselves as a nation? The Palestinian nation has a history of its own, special memories of its own, wars, sacrifices, sufferings, and heroes of its own, poetic and literary expression of its own. The Six Day War intensified the Palestinian Arab identity.[95]

Eliav's prescription was clear. Israel must unequivocally declare its readiness to return most of the West Bank and the Gaza Strip in order to allow the Palestinians to create an independent and sovereign state of their own on both sides of the Jordan River. "There is room in the land of the Twelve Tribes for the State of Israel and a Palestinian-Jordanian state. In exchange for a full and permanent peace we will waive implementing part of our historical rights in this Arab state."[96]

The book, published in the summer of 1972, was met with enthusiasm by some and ridicule by many. Golda Meir asked, "What happened to Lova? Maybe he needs medical treatment?" while pointing to her head as if to suggest he was out of his mind.[97] But Eliav, who remained a member of the Labor Party until the middle of 1974, did not give up easily. He sought to propagate his ideas through a nationwide lecture tour. But his sense of isolation from the party was now complete. "The complacency, self-righteousness and the overwhelming conviction that 'we are right in everything' were like plaster which sealed off every opening for new thoughts."[98]

When the Galili Document was debated in the party, Eliav distributed an alternative platform to the general public in the form of a petition. This was an unprecedented act and one which was considered inappropriate by the party leadership. When the Galili Document came to a vote in the party Secretariat (a body much smaller than the Central Committee and with less statutory power), Eliav accused the leadership of steamrolling the decision. In a brief speech he claimed that members of the Secretariat were frightened to voice their honest opinions and demanded that the decision be transferred to the Central Committee: "Many in this room, and across the party, in its chapters, in the towns and villages, are now sitting and secretly crying over this document." As a voice for all these secret opponents he proclaimed, "Never, for any price and in any forum shall I vote for this document." It was a courageous gesture but had little effect. When it came to the vote Eliav's was the only hand raised in opposition; all other seventy-nine members approved the document. "I remained in glorious isolation," remembered Eliav.[99]

A few days before the 1973 war, Eliav wrote a poem in which he imagined himself a seagull hovering above a ship that is heading toward a cliff. The seagull tries unsuccessfully to arouse the attention of the ship's navigator and captain who are blind to the oncoming danger because they "are drunk with the wine of their glory, and the liquor of their greatness, self-assured in their position." Night falls on the ship and "the seagull circles around crying into the night."[100]

*   *   *

The Movement for Peace and Security continued to operate during 1972 and 1973, but much of the wind was taken out of its sails. The center of its activities moved to Tel Aviv and came under the heavy-handed influence of politicians from the left wing of Mapam who were better able to dedicate the time and energy needed to orchestrate the movement's operations than were the professors from the Hebrew University in Jerusalem. The group's activities soon became routine and lost their initial momentum. Despite occasional conferences and publications, the movement faded gradually into the background of the political landscape.

Peace and Security was the first peace group in Israel worthy of the term "movement," because it managed to mobilize people outside the small circle of activists who had pursued peace during the 1950s and 1960s. Though still led by a handful of prominent intellectuals, Peace and Security did represent a significant minority of Israelis who were deeply disturbed by the government's policies and the entrenchment of the Israeli occupation. Its failure to make a greater impact was not due to any lack of clarity, courage, or energy on the part of its leaders, but to the prevailing political environment. The raging controversies within the ruling party, the continuation of warfare along the new border, the rising tide of Palestinian terrorism, and, most especially, the profound complacency that swamped large sections of the Israeli public and leadership effectively drowned out the warnings that the peace movement tried to sound throughout the Israeli body politic.

4

The October War and the End of Labor Supremacy, 1973–77

The October War—A Defeat in Victory

The tranquility of the Israeli public was abruptly shattered on October 6, 1973. It was Yom Kippur (the Day of Atonement), the holiest day of the year for Jews, spent by most Israelis in prayer and reflection at daylong religious services. At 2:00 p.m. air raid sirens disrupted the solemnity of the day. Soon military trucks hurried through the empty streets, transporting reserve soldiers to their preassigned assembly points—particularly strange because traditionally on Yom Kippur there is little or no vehicular traffic. The sight and sounds of cars and trucks racing through the streets left no doubt in the mind of the astounded public that Israel was at war for the fifth time in its twenty-five-year existence. Israelis immediately turned to their radios for information—again a departure from the norm, because radio transmissions are normally suspended on Yom Kippur. What they heard was the military spokesman announcing, "Today, at about

1400 hours, Egyptian and Syrian forces opened an attack in the Sinai and the Golan Heights."[1]

The attack came as a surprise to the Israeli defense establishment. Although Egyptian and Syrian plans for such an attack had been known to Israeli military intelligence for some time, nobody took them very seriously. When threatening signals were detected a few days before the attack, the Intelligence Branch of the IDF disregarded them as indicating only a "low probability" of a limited attack. Less than twelve hours before the attack Israeli intelligence received definitive indications of the impending attack. "My greatest surprise in this war," General Yitzhak Hofi, the commander of the Northern Command, admitted later, "was the fact that it actually erupted."[2]

The failure of Israeli intelligence to provide adequate warning was not the only obstacle that had to be overcome; two other strategic setbacks awaited Israel. The IDF launched a counteroffensive along the Suez Canal on October 9 as soon as enough reserve armor units were deployed at the front. However, Israeli forces were unable to dislodge the two Egyptian armies that had crossed the canal two days earlier from their hold on the east bank. The IDF commanders had taken into consideration the possibility of an Egyptian attempt to cross the canal but were confident that they could repel such an invasion within forty-eight hours. They were unprepared for the combined effect of heavy artillery barrages and the dense deployment of Soviet ground-to-air missiles along the canal. Other tactical problems for Israel included the effective use of thousands of antiarmor missiles by the Egyptian infantry and the sheer number of forces that participated in the crossing.[3]

The worst surprise, however, became apparent only much later, and to many Israelis it remains a puzzle. The October War demonstrated that Israel could lose a war even when it prevailed militarily. The surprises and setbacks the Israeli forces had to cope with during the first days of the war cast a shadow of doubt and disappointment among civilians and soldiers alike. The loss of more than 3,000 Israeli soldiers, four times the losses of the Six Day War, shocked and profoundly disturbed Israelis. This psychological earthquake was felt not only in the military, but throughout Israeli society. While some argue that the October War ended in a draw, a purely operational analysis shows the Israeli military won more battles than did their Egyptian—and certainly their Syrian—counterparts. On the Suez front Israel was unable to dislodge the Egyptians from the east side of the canal but managed to cross westward and reach a point only sixty miles east of Cairo, encircling and besieging the Egyptian Third Army. On the Golan Heights, Israel reversed all of Syria's initial gains and advanced to a point forty miles west of Damascus. Egyptian and Syrian losses in terms of men and materiel were far heavier than the losses suffered by Israel.

Nevertheless, the prevailing mood in Israel at the end of the war was that of a defeated nation. The deep penetration west of the canal by the Israeli forces could be heralded as an operational victory but could not be seen as a decisive strategic victory or translated into political gains. On the contrary, the fact that the Egyptians remained entrenched on the east side of the canal, albeit only with the assistance of the great powers,[4] demonstrated to Israel that its heavy losses had produced no real gains. The Egyptians were the beneficiaries, not only strategically but also politically. If Sadat's objective was to alter the military and political status quo that had prevailed since 1967, his tactical defeat was a strategic victory.

A Delayed Reaction—The December 1973 Elections

The gradual decline of the predominance of the center-left bloc in Israeli politics had already begun before the 1967 war. It initially arose from the schism that divided the Labor Party in the early 1960s and caused a steep decline in its electoral appeal. From a peak of 51.4 percent of the popular vote in the 1959 Knesset elections, the Labor coalition gained only 43.3 percent in 1965. It recovered only slightly to 46.2 percent in 1969 in the wake of the victory in the Six Day War. The reunification of the Labor Party with its secessionist partners and a new alignment with Mapam did not help matters much.

The growing popular disillusionment with the Labor government and its ineffective response to the problems confronting the nation became evident in the period preceding the October War. Whereas 92 percent of Jewish respondents agreed with government policies in June 1967, only 54 percent did so in October and November 1972. By March 1974 the figure was just 27 percent.[5]

It is difficult to say with certainty whether the electorate's growing dissatisfaction with the Labor Party was primarily due to the security and foreign policies it adopted prior to the October War. Other factors such as a growing aversion toward the party's bureaucratic style of governing and its internal power struggles likely had some effect as well.[6] Most observers believe that at least a partial explanation may be found in the measurable shift of public opinion to the right and the general toughening of the attitude of a majority of Israelis toward the Arabs.[7] The further decline in support for Labor at the end of 1973 was unquestionably influenced by the trauma of the October War.[8]

Until about 1973 most of Israel's lively, at times very intense, political participation had been party-affiliated. Political initiatives by individuals outside of the established parties rarely occurred during Israel's first two decades.[9] After the disasters of the October War, and the public perception of the failure of the government and military establishment to foresee the dangers and respond appropriately, Israeli public desire for change gave rise to new initiatives in the form of political movements outside the channels of party politics. In a survey conducted a month before the war, 47 percent of the respondents expressed a desire to influence government policies. In response to the same question in a survey taken two months later, the positive response jumped to 65 percent.[10]

The Knesset elections held at the end of December 1973, however, came too soon after the trauma to fully reflect this change. The 1973 elections had originally been scheduled for the end of October, but the war forced a postponement until December. Despite considerable debate the parties' lists of candidates, which had been sealed (as required by law) before the war, were not permitted to be reopened to allow the addition of new candidates.[11] It was too early for the public to fully digest the war's trauma, particularly because the fighting did not fully stop during the disengagement negotiations and many of the reserve soldiers had not yet returned home.[12] A portion of the electorate was ready to express its loss of faith in Labor's ability to govern, but many voters apparently hesitated to change horses before the crisis was resolved. Labor's representation in the Knesset declined from fifty-six to fifty-one seats—a decline from 46.2 percent to 39.6 percent of the popular vote. Menachem Begin and the right-wing opposition received 31 percent of the vote and for the first time posed a serious challenge to Labor's dominance.[13] But for the time being Labor remained the only party that could form a coalition.[14] Golda Meir and Moshe Dayan remained the prime minister and minister of defense respectively.[15]

Frustrated and angry, some segments of the public resorted to independent and dramatic ways to express their disdain for the business-as-usual approach of the Labor-led government. With the customary channels of party politics, especially within the Labor Party, seeming to be blocked, the accumulated anger and energy sought out new means of expression. During the winter of 1974 Israel witnessed its first large-scale antigovernment street protests focused entirely on security issues and foreign affairs. The brunt of the public's outrage was directed against Moshe Dayan. More than anyone, he epitomized the spirit of overconfidence and complacency that had prevailed in the country during the early 1970s.[16] Where once his charismatic image and reassuring presence had inspired a near-blind confidence in his leadership, now he seemed like a hero who had fallen from grace.[17]

"Our Israel"—Street Protests, Winter and Spring 1974

Soon after he was released from reserve duties on February 1, 1974, Motti Ashkenazi, an unassuming reserve officer in his early thirties who had gallantly commanded the defense of the only fortified position along the Suez Canal that did not fall into Egyptian hands during the war, began a solitary protest vigil in front of the prime minister's office in Jerusalem. He demanded Dayan's resignation and the establishment of an inquiry to examine the military mismanagement of the war. Soon other people joined Ashkenazi's vigil, and within a few days various groups began protesting in other locations. The protestors and the media spoke in terms of the "Great Blunder."[18] By the end of the first week more than 5,000 sympathizers had signed a petition demanding the dismissal of Dayan on the grounds that he was "the person who undertook this responsibility as a political mandate and must discharge it."[19] The issue was not one of personal guilt but of ministerial responsibility.

The rapid growth of the protest movement fed on a deep malaise that the war and the unresolved political and security problems fueled among many Israelis. Polls indicated a sharp decline in almost every indicator of public morale. For example, the number of people who said that their mood was "almost always good" or "mostly good" declined from an average of 45 percent before the war to an all-time low of 16 percent by November 1973.[20] Many Israelis who said that they were "almost never or never" worried also lost their composure for a while, their numbers dropping from 60 percent to below 30 percent shortly after the Yom Kippur War.[21]

Street demonstrations were not a new feature on the Israeli political landscape. During the 1950s members of the Israeli Communist Party, Mapam, and other left-wing and pro-Soviet groups had occasionally demonstrated in the streets against the pro-Western orientation of Ben-Gurion's government.[22] Early in that same decade ultra-orthodox religious groups had led violent demonstrations in Jerusalem and elsewhere to protest the violation of religious laws, such as the strict observance of the Sabbath and the prohibition of mixed gender bathing in public swimming pools.[23] In July 1959 violent protests occurred when the police shot and wounded a young immigrant from Morocco in the economically depressed Wadi Salib quarter in Haifa. These demonstrations expressed a strong dissatisfaction on the part of new immigrants from Middle Eastern countries with the government's and society's apparent lack of concern for their socioeconomic plight.[24] The imbalance in the distribution of economic and social resources between the Ashkenazi and Mizrachi communities was a constant source of unrest in the 1960s, erupting into violent demonstrations and other illegal actions in the spring of 1971 when a group of young Moroccan residents of Musrara, a slum area of Jerusalem, organized themselves under the name "Black Panthers."[25]

Although some of these events tested the limits of legality, none came so close to challenging the system itself as did the demonstrations initiated by Motti Ashkenazi in February 1974.[26] Observers interpreted Ashkenazi's demonstrations as reflecting a desire on the part of many Israelis to "reconstruct their own worldview by recharting the normative and cognitive chaos which the war inflicted on them."[27]

During the winter and spring of 1974 Golda and Dayan tried to hold on to their positions while the number and size of the demonstrations continued to grow. Entire reserve units reported to the tent Motti Ashkenazi erected in front of the prime minister's office. On February 27 a large group of paratroopers who had been the first to cross the Suez Canal during the war demonstrated silently before the Knesset under a banner that read "We Are Here!"[28] A number of large demonstrations were organized in Tel Aviv, Haifa, and Jerusalem, attended by crowds that numbered in the thousands. Some agitated parents of soldiers killed in the war pelted Dayan with tomatoes, spat at him, and called him a murderer.[29]

Ashkenazi's movement named itself "Yisrael Shelanu—Hatnua Letmura" (Our Israel—The Movement for Change). This name was chosen because it signified the unwavering patriotism of the members despite their bitter criticism of the government, and to point out that their primary motivation was their love for the state and their desire to guard it against corruption.[30] As he came out from a meeting with Dayan, Ashkenazi said to a journalist, "It seems that in the State of Israel there is 'they' and 'we.' 'We' are the people who underwent a traumatic experience and feel that we cannot continue to live in the way we used to live in the past, while 'they' live on a different planet and manage [the state's] affairs as if it was their private estate."[31]

The movement's goals soon broadened to include reforming the electoral system, abolishing the nominating committees for political positions, requiring internal party elections, limiting the terms of political positions, and strengthening public control over the bureaucracy.[32] As Ashkenazi put it, "We are trying to break the walls of the Israeli bureaucracy and cause a small crack in the self-defense edifice the Israeli leaders have erected around themselves."[33] By mid-March 1974 the movement had reached its peak; more than 25 percent of persons polled answered that they would vote for a unified list of all protest groups if new elections were held.[34]

Although the movement advocated sweeping reforms in the political structure, it was not a revolutionary movement per se.[35] Throughout its brief existence Our Israel insisted on legal behavior, and every demonstration ended with the singing of the national anthem.[36] The activists regarded participation in the movement as representing steadfast loyalty to the original goals of Zionism.[37] Despite its extraparliamentary nature, its tactics sought to influence and reform the power structure rather than replace it with an alternative system based on a different ideology.[38] Perhaps this can be explained at least partially by the fact that most protesters were upper-middle-class and well-educated people with a substantial stake in the existing society. Of the core leadership of the 1974 movement, 84 percent held at least one academic degree; all were of Ashkenazi origin.[39]

An official inquiry commission, headed by Supreme Court Chief Justice Shimon Agranat, was established on November 18, 1973, to investigate the intelligence failures and poor military preparedness for the war. It submitted its preliminary report on April 2, 1974. Unclassified parts of the report, including the commission's specific recommendations with regard to personal responsibilities, were immediately made public. The chief of the General Staff, General David Elazar; the chief of military intelligence, General Eli Zeira; the commander of the Southern Command, General Shmuel Gonen (better known as Gorodish, which was his name until he Hebraized it); and a few other officers of lesser rank were harshly censured and summarily relieved of their duties. As to ministerial responsibility, the commission interpreted its mandate narrowly and decided to pass judgment only on those directly responsible. The report stated, "We did not consider it our duty to pass judgment on what may be implied by the parliamentary responsibility [of ministers]," so Dayan and Golda escaped the commission's scrutiny and censure.[40]

The conclusions of the Agranat Commission further enraged the public and triggered new and intensified protests. After all, it was precisely the acknowledgment of ministerial responsibility that Motti Ashkenazi and his colleagues had demanded of Dayan from the outset. During April more demonstrations and assemblies took place throughout the country. Representatives of the different groups convened to coordinate their tactics and planned a major demonstration to take place in Jerusalem on Independence Day.[41]

Golda preempted the protests. On April 10, only one month after she had formed her new cabinet, she told the party leadership, "It is beyond my strength to continue to carry this burden." She begged her colleagues not to try to dissuade her from resigning. "It will not help," she said. "My political career is over."[42]

According to Israeli law the resignation of the prime minister entails the resignation of the entire cabinet. It was clear that the career of Moshe Dayan as minister of defense was also over. During the war, and immediately thereafter, Dayan had offered Golda his resignation three times; she did not accept. Out of concern for the integrity of the party she had decided to renominate Dayan as minister of defense when she formed the new coalition. The party was weakened to such a degree that Dayan, even with his own political problems, could have rallied those within the party who remained loyal to him and toppled the government. Golda also felt a sense of gratitude to Dayan, who throughout her tenure had remained unwaveringly loyal to her. She probably also felt that they shared much of the responsibility for what had happened and that she could not simply dump him without eventually being held accountable as well. However, now she was no longer at the helm and no longer capable of defending Dayan.[43]

The protest movement that Motti Ashkenazi started proved ephemeral. As soon as Golda's and Dayan's resignations were made public, the momentum of the demonstrations subsided. During April 1974 the group focused on a critique of the Agranat Commission's report, but by May the number of active members had declined substantially.

The October War formally ended on May 31 when Syria and Israel signed a disengagement agreement that included a stipulation providing for an unlimited cease-fire agreement.[44] By then Israel had a new Labor government. Yitzhak Rabin took over from Golda, Shimon Peres replaced Dayan as minister of defense, and Mordechai Gur was named chief of the General Staff. With the war finally over, the reserve soldiers returned home and a tired citizenry was eager to resume some normalcy after seven months of internal and external turmoil. The protest movement soon found it difficult to organize vigils and other activities. Fewer than fifty people attended the convention to officially charter Our Israel. As one observer pointed out, "The founding convention . . . [was] the funeral ceremony of the protest movement."[45]

The Protest Legacy

Our Israel was not a peace movement and, unlike such movements, refrained from taking a position on substantive issues pertaining to security and foreign affairs. As such it managed to attract a larger following, including not only those who felt the blunders of the Yom Kippur War were primarily connected with the government's failure to pursue peace more vigorously, but also those who attributed those blunders to the mishandling of the national defense.[46] According to Dayan's recollection of his only encounter with Motti Ashkenazi, the young captain preached to him only about the strategic mismanagement of the Six Day War. Ashkenazi argued that the war had been a failure because the IDF had failed to penetrate deeper into Syrian territory and remain permanently in the Druze Mountains, "thereby denying territorial contiguity between Jordan and Syria." Ashkenazi also argued that on the southern front Israel should have crossed the canal and "compelled [Egypt] to sign a peace treaty with us"[47]—hardly a dovish point of view.

Very few of the leaders of the 1974 protest movement surfaced again three years later among the different peace groups that were established after President Sadat's visit to Israel in 1977. For the most part they faded from the political landscape. Nevertheless, Motti Ashkenazi and his colleagues left an important legacy to the Israeli peace movement. The sense that politics is too serious a business to leave entirely to politicians; the recognition that single-issue groups can influence the system; the belief in the value and influence of public demonstrations: all became guiding principles in the activities of the peace groups that followed later.

A study conducted in 1982 reported a dramatic rise in the number of extraparliamentary political activities from a low of 23 events per year in 1957 to a high of 241 in 1979. Mass protests became almost endemic in Israeli political culture after the October War.[48] Clearly, the demonstrations of 1974 acted as a catalyst for this phenomenon, born of dissatisfaction with the incumbent leadership and frustration at the inability either to reform or to replace it from within.

No less frustrating was the impression conveyed by the leadership that it had not learned anything from the traumatic experience. Ten days after the drama along the Golan and Suez, the Knesset went into a marathon session in which almost all members voiced their opinions on the recent events. These sessions were broadcast live on Israeli television. The scene in the Knesset resembled a farce in which everyone argued that if only his advice had been followed, disaster could have been averted. It was commonly said that "we all are to be blamed," but it seemed that if in fact all were responsible, no single individual was willing to be held accountable.[49]

In an emergency meeting of the Central Committee of the Labor Party held before the elections in early December, Prime Minister Golda Meir said that the entire government and primarily the prime minister should be held responsible for successes as well as failures. She said she was profoundly affected by Israel's human and materiel losses in the war and vowed that such a surprise would never recur.[50] However, while she apparently was honestly and deeply upset by the debacle, her attitude toward the conflict in general remained unchanged. In her remarks before the Central Committee she explained that she "did not believe that . . . our policy has to be blamed for the fact that we did not arrive at peace. . . . If we are to do justice in our judgment we must state that we were ready for all compromise proposals, while the Arabs rejected them." She restated her adamant denial of the rights of the Palestinians. "Don't they really have another place?" she asked, and refused to rescind the Galili Document.[51]

The public, however, was less wedded to the policies of the past. Growing disenchantment with the government and its policies was fueled by the Israeli media, the members of which felt themselves partly responsible for contributing to the national sense of complacency before the war. It seemed that most journalists now seized every opportunity to criticize the government and provide coverage to every opposition group within Israeli society. The protest groups soon discovered how hungry the media, especially the electronic media, were for visual images of political controversy and opposition—indeed, the efficient use of the media was another important lesson that the later peace activists (as well as their opponents on the right) learned and successfully applied.

On the issue of peace and how to achieve it, the 1974 protest movement did not take a unified position. But the public began to understand that the decision not to decide taken after the 1967 war was the worst of all possible paths. Some argued for active reconciliation with the Arabs while others moved in the opposite direction—outright annexation of the territories through intensive Jewish settlement of the land.

Gush Emunim and the Advent of Messianic Nationalism

In February 1974, while Our Israel was still fully active, a small group of young members of the National Religious Party (NRP) convened a meeting in Kibbutz Kfar Etzion.[52] The outcome of this meeting was the formation within the NRP of a new faction, which later seceded and became an independent settlement movement. The founders called the new organization "Gush Emunim" (Bloc of the Faithful).[53] This seemingly modest initiative had an immediate effect on the political landscape in Israel.[54]

Most observers trace Gush Emunim's origins to the struggle that the Zionist sections of the orthodox religious community had to wage simultaneously on two fronts. On the one side they had to confront the old anti-Zionist ultra-orthodoxy, against whose criticism the Zionists had to rationalize their collaboration with the secular majority in the Zionist mainstream. On the other side they had to assert their unique identity as a religious movement within the broader Zionist enterprise, in which for many years they had played only a marginal role. Their constant advocacy of observant Judaism to the secular majority caused them to maintain a rather defensive posture during Israel's early years.[55]

The tension between the Zionist religious orthodoxy and the anti-Zionist ultra-orthodoxy gave birth in the 1920s and 1930s to the mystical doctrine of Rabbi Avraham Hacohen Kook. Kook was a disciple of the Maimonidean teachings that messianic redemption would come not through supernatural events but through human acts. According to this doctrine, Zionist activity, whether performed by believers or unwittingly by secular pioneers, is the indication of what Kook called *atchalta de geula* (the beginning of redemption). Consequently, it is incumbent upon the faithful to take an active part in the materialization of the Zionist dream, shoulder to shoulder with the secular Zionists.[56]

The venerable rabbi died in 1935 and his legacy included a small religious school named after him, Yeshivat Merkaz Ha'rav. After his death the yeshiva suffered a long period of decline but was eventually revived in the 1950s by his son, Rabbi Tzvi Yehuda Hacohen Kook. Kook continued his father's educational mission with less sophistication and spiritual depth but with greater zeal. He taught that the establishment of Israel, and the successes of the Israeli army in 1948 and 1956, were proof that the Messianic

Era had already begun. This conferred holiness on the state and its army, as well as upon everyone who was contributing to the success of this messianic project. Kook the son maintained that the holiness of Eretz Yisrael, including the parts that were not yet under Jewish sovereignty, derived from a divine promise from which people could not disassociate themselves. The conquest of the unredeemed parts must eventually be accomplished.

During the 1950s and 1960s a generation of well-educated people graduated from the elite network of schools that the Zionist orthodox religious community had developed over the years. Most of these modern yet devout youngsters were also graduates of Bnei Akiva, the religious youth movement that combined religious devotion with a pioneering zeal characteristic of all Zionist youth movements at the time. The male members of the modern orthodox Zionist group wore knitted skullcaps, which became their identifying symbol, distinguishing them as it did from secular Israeli men who do not cover their heads at all, as well as from the anti-Zionist ultra-orthodox—the "Black Hats"—who cover their black skullcaps with black hats.[57]

Unlike their anti-Zionist ultra-orthodox counterparts, the "Knitted Skullcaps" served in the military, but often in separate units that combined military service with religious studies.[58] The women from this group frequently claimed an exemption from military service on religious grounds but undertook another form of civilian national service. When the option of fulfilling their Zionist mission by joining a religious kibbutz became less attractive during the 1960s, these young religious Zionists found a new mentor in Rabbi Tzvi Yehuda.[59] Many opted to spend more years in the Yeshivat Merkaz Ha'Rav to study Torah and listen to the rabbi's sermons, which inculcated a strong sense of mission and purpose.

To these devout students the victory of June 1967 and the conquest of the entire Land of Israel west of the Jordan River were clear signs of divine intervention and proof that the Messianic Era had arrived.[60] Rabbi Tzvi Yehuda told his students, "We are already in the middle of redemption . . . the Kingdom of Israel is being built again . . . this is the revelation of the heavenly kingdom."[61] Shortly after the war he issued a religious edict that has become known as the "Lo Taguru" (Do Not Be Afraid) Declaration. In it, the rabbi asserted unequivocally, "This entire land is definitely ours, and no part of it can be handed to others; it is a legacy we inherited from our Fathers."[62]

To preserve this inheritance the Jews, like the Israelites in biblical times, had to inherit the land physically through the act of settlement. It was not surprising that the first attempts at settling Judea and Samaria were undertaken by two disciples of Rabbi Tzvi Yehuda: Rabbi Moshe Levinger in Hebron and Hannan Porat in Kfar Etzion. Before the October War the Labor government supported settlement in the occupied territories only on a selective basis. Roughly along the lines of the Allon Plan, new settlements were initiated and approved on the Golan Heights, along the Jordan River, and in the Rafah Wedge. The heartland of the West Bank was to be held in escrow and eventually exchanged for peace. Permission to settle the Gush Etzion area was given, albeit reluctantly, because of the sentimental value attached to the Jewish settlements that had been destroyed in 1948. Permission to settle Hebron was slow to come and was eventually granted only for the eastern slopes of the Arab town, which could be added to the land reserved for Israel by the Allon Plan.[63]

During the first few years after the Six Day War, Rabbi Tzvi Yehuda and his followers were dissatisfied with this selective settlement policy but were not yet ready to challenge the government. When the October War broke out, a group of Rabbi Levinger's students from Hebron were already talking about the need to settle in or near Nablus, the largest Arab town in the West Bank. They gave their group the biblical name "Elon Moreh."

The students of Merkaz Ha'Rav did not see the results of the Yom Kippur War as a setback to their messianic expectations. To the contrary, the war provided additional proof of their just mission. In Jewish eschatology the advent of the Messiah must be preceded by a period of great agony and a major war against the enemies of the Messiah. The agony of Yom Kippur was interpreted as ominous—the ultimate sign that the redemption was at hand.[64] The malaise that was so apparent among the secular public; the discrediting of the Labor government; the pressure exerted on Israel by Henry Kissinger to make territorial concessions along the Suez and in the Golan; and the general weakness of the government during these negotiations: all these elements combined to alarm the youthful disciples of Rabbi Tzvi Yehuda but also to stiffen their resolve to take unilateral action to reverse the mood of defeatism.

The immediate question for the young Zionist orthodox was whether and under what conditions the NRP should join the new coalition that Golda Meir tried to form after the December 1973 elections. The old guard of the NRP saw a golden opportunity to extract further concessions with regard to religious affairs legislation from the weakened Labor Party. But the younger members of the NRP, whose agenda now extended far beyond religious affairs, were disturbed by this bargaining and argued that their party should not join the new government unless Begin's Likud party also joined, thus ensuring—so they believed—aggressive settlement policies. The NRP's decision to join the coalition led Gush Emunim to conclude that its activities should not be limited to the framework of the coalition agreements. The members of Gush Emunim announced that their movement was nonpartisan and that its leaders were now free to be active in various parties and parliamentary factions.[65]

On June 6, 1974, the aging Rabbi Tzvi Yehuda Kook joined his students in their first symbolic settlement.[66] They tried to set up tents in Havara, an Arab village south of Nablus, but were repelled and dispersed by the Israeli army. Although they did not succeed in establishing a lasting settlement on this occasion, they successfully used the media to raise awareness that a new and important political phenomenon had entered the Israeli political scene.

The period from spring 1974 to fall 1977 was a heady one for Gush Emunim, which disengaged itself from the NRP in early 1974 and launched its own independent settlement effort. During this period three new settlements were established: Ofra, to the north of Ramallah; Maale Adumin, on the road from Jerusalem to Jericho; and Kaddum, near Nablus.[67] It was soon apparent that the few hundred zealots of Gush Emunim had the courage, dedication, stamina, and skill to act not only symbolically but also in a fashion that would have a permanent impact on Israel's demographic and political landscape. In the past two decades the settlement effort begun by Gush Emunim has brought the Jewish population of the West Bank to well over 120,000.

During the spring of 1974 U.S. Secretary of State Henry Kissinger was shuttling between Jerusalem and Damascus in an effort to conclude a disengagement agreement on the Golan Heights. This was to include the return of Qunaitra, the central town in the Golan, to Syrian control. On May 12 a small group of settlers squatted in a military bunker at the outskirts of the ruined Syrian town and pronounced the creation of a new settlement, which they called "Keshet" (Arrow) after the Hebrew translation of Qunaitra's Arabic root. Initially, this amounted to little more than a symbolic and apparently short-lived gesture against the return of the town to the Syrians. But Gush Emunim soon came to the assistance of the original group, and after some hesitation the Rabin government recognized and relocated the new settlement to a spot not far from the original bunker. While the settlers could not prevent the return of Qunaitra to Syrian hands, they were able to achieve their objective of establishing a new settlement very close to the new demarcation lines.[68]

Gush Emunim sought to exploit personal and ideological rifts within the Labor Party. The Elon Moreh group made five attempts to settle around Nablus without government authorization. Each time the army dispersed them. However, their media exposure and popular support grew from one event to the next, as did the number of supporters who joined in the demonstrations and squatting activities. The forcible removal of the settlers by soldiers became increasingly embarrassing. A prolonged demonstration near the Roman ruins of Sebastia, north of Nablus, ended on December 7, 1975, during the Jewish holiday of Hanukkah, when Prime Minister Rabin succumbed to the pressure and authorized the establishment of Kaddum, ostensibly a new military base but in effect a Gush Emunim settlement.[69] Its members' deep ideological conviction and readiness for personal sacrifice made Gush Emunim popular among wide circles and even earned the admiration of its political opponents. At the time it seemed that these young and devoted Knitted Skullcaps were the only ones who knew exactly what they wanted and that they were ready to do everything in their power to achieve it.

In demographic terms, however, all these events did not amount to much during the first three years after the October War. By the beginning of 1977 fewer then 4,000 Jews lived in the West Bank (excluding East Jerusalem) in four settlements.[70] Nevertheless, the symbolic and psychological effects of their presence were remarkable. These were days of confusion and frustration in Israeli society.[71] Kissinger had forced Israel to retreat not only from the additional territories it had conquered west of the Suez Canal and east of Qunaitra during the October War, but also from some of the land it had captured in 1967. This was exacted without any tangible reciprocal concessions on the part of the Arabs beyond their agreement to maintain stable cease-fire arrangements.[72]

Yitzhak Rabin, the hero of the 1967 war, was not personally tainted by the October War and the Agranat Commission's report, because he had not held any formal position after completing his assignment as Israel's ambassador to Washington shortly before the war. This qualified him to replace Golda Meir as prime minister in April 1974. However, it soon became clear that his leadership within the Labor Party, as well as his image among the general public, suffered greatly from the internecine fights among Labor's leadership. The long-standing rivalry between Rabin and Shimon Peres (who served as minister of defense after he lost his bid for the party leadership by a narrow margin) was well known and continued to damage both their images. Also, the new government seemed incapable of effective leadership,

and accusations of improper and even criminal misconduct by Labor officials further eroded the public's confidence in the party and its leaders.[73]

Fighting from Within: Stifled Partisan and Parliamentary Peace Efforts

Not all of Labor's electoral losses in the 1973 elections went to the right.
Shulamit Aloni, until this point a little-known lawyer who quarreled with
Golda Meir on civil rights, women's status, and the application of religious laws, defected from the Labor Party before the war and formed a
new party, formally called the Movement for Citizens' Rights but better
known by its nickname "Ratz." To the surprise of many, her party won
three seats in the Eighth Knesset. Ratz was not initially outspoken on
peace issues and at that time was centrist-liberal in character.[74]

Uri Avneri lost his Knesset seat after an eight-year tenure, but Moked,
a small party clearly to the left of Labor both on social and peace issues,
won one seat.[75] Moked was an odd mixture of old-time communists who
had become disillusioned with the Soviet Union and young activists who
were influenced by the New Left in the West.[76] This group tended to be
critical of both Western capitalism and Soviet communism. They resented
the fact that Mapam, which otherwise would have served as their political home, had joined the Labor Party in a parliamentary bloc. What unified these groups more than anything else was their belief that there was
an urgent need and a real opportunity to make peace with the Arabs.

Israeli Arabs were also experiencing a political transformation, with
traditional family and clan loyalties giving way to a growing sense of
Palestinian national identity. In the 1950s and 1960s the Labor Party had
been able to capitalize on traditional clan loyalties by placing docile Arab
notables on Labor-backed election lists. After they were elected to the
Knesset their loyalty to the Labor Party was maintained by the distribution of government resources through the patronage system. However,
these old methods were becoming outdated and ineffective. The young
Arab generation was growing more politically aware and active, and renewed contacts with the Palestinians in the occupied territories contributed to a growing sense of national identification. The New Communist
List (Rakach) was the political embodiment of this new identification.
Rakach won close to 50 percent of the Arab vote in 1973, occupied four
seats in the Knesset, and became the main voice of Israeli Arabs.[77]

The fragmentation of the peace forces reduced their potential electoral
strength, especially given the nature of the Israeli electoral system, which

apportions Knesset seats according to the number of votes received by each party that wins at least 1 percent of the votes cast. The peace vote was split among a large number of parties on the left, many of which narrowly failed to reach the numerical threshold of votes for a Knesset seat. Many votes were thus in effect wasted.[78] Even including Aloni's party as part of the evolving parliamentary peace caucus, the entire group totaled only four members of Knesset, plus the four communists.

Another disappointment to the Israeli peace camp was that the Labor Party itself did not produce any significant peace faction within its ranks despite the lessons that should have been learned from the Yom Kippur War.[79] Pinhas Sapir resigned from the Knesset, and thus the cabinet, and assumed the less prominent role of chairman of the Jewish Agency until his death a short time later. Avraham Ofer, minister of housing and a dove on security matters, was implicated in criminal activities and committed suicide. Lova Eliav was reelected to the Knesset on the Labor list, but soon became disgusted with his party's policies and defected from its parliamentary caucus and established his own faction.

A Failed Attempt at Unity

The electoral weakness the peace movement experienced as a result of its fragmentation and its inability to break out of its marginality led many activists to attempt to unify the forces.[80] For a while it seemed as if they might succeed. Lova Eliav, Shulamit Aloni, and a few members of the Study Circle who left the Labor Party and continued their activities independently, along with some veterans from Our Israel, formed a new, though short-lived, coalition called "Ya'ad" (Destiny). "Ya'ad began on the left foot," recalled Danny Yakobson, one of the founders of the Study Circle and later a professor of labor studies at Tel Aviv University. A clash of personalities and differences in political attitudes hampered the group. Although both Aloni and Eliav originally came from the Labor Party, Aloni was more interested in civil rights issues, while Eliav focused more on the Palestinian issue. Also, both had strong personalities and found it difficult to work with each other. Both could have gained prominence in the Labor Party if they had been willing to compromise their values and ideas. If they were unprepared to make compromises for the Labor Party, they felt even less inclined to make such compromises for each other. Ya'ad disbanded after only eight months, the final crisis involving an initiative undertaken by Eliav without adequate consultation.

In December 1975 Lova Eliav, Uri Avneri, Simcha Flapan, and other peace activists from Mapam and Moked founded the Israeli Council for Israel-Palestine Peace.[81] Early in 1976 the council published a charter that stated:

> This country is the home of two peoples—the people of Israel and the Palestinian people. The historic conflict between these two peoples over this land, which is dear to both, lies at the bottom of the Arab-Jewish conflict. The only road to peace is in the coexistence of two sovereign states, each one with a distinct national identity: the State of Israel for the Jewish people and a state for the Arab-Palestinian people which will serve as an expression of their right of self-determination in the political framework of their choosing.[82]

Shulamit Aloni and her colleagues from Ratz were not so keen on the Palestinian orientation. Most preferred the "Jordanian Option," the official Labor position, which offered to return territories to the Hashemite Kingdom from which they had been taken, rather than to the Palestinians. According to this perspective Jordan represented a more reliable and stable partner for peace. Aloni thus disagreed with the Council for Israel-Palestine Peace in principle and was subsequently excluded from its deliberations.

Lova Eliav moved further to the left and along with Uri Avneri formed a new party named "Sheli" (a Hebrew acronym meaning Peace for Israel), which campaigned in the 1977 Knesset elections. Sheli adopted, by and large, the position of the Council for Israel-Palestine Peace, which viewed the Palestinian problem as the heart of the Arab-Israeli conflict and contended that Israel could achieve a genuine reconciliation only by granting the Palestinians self-determination in a Palestinian state alongside Israel.

Neither Sheli nor the Council for Israel-Palestine Peace had a significant impact at the time. The Palestinian flag, which was included in the council's emblem, was perceived by almost all Jews as the flag of the terrorist PLO. For Israelis it symbolized the indiscriminate terror perpetrated against Israeli and Jewish targets around the world by groups such as Black September, the Popular Front for the Liberation of Palestine (PFLP) led by George Habash, and the Democratic Front for the Liberation of Palestine (DFLP) led by Nayif Hawatmeh. Spectacular terrorist acts included the attack on civilians at Lod Airport in Tel Aviv in May 1972 by members of the Japanese Red Army Faction operating on behalf of the Palestinians, and Black September's massacre of Israeli athletes at the Munich Olympic Games in September 1972. On April 11, 1974, a squad of the PFLP assaulted an apartment building in the northern town of Kiryat Shmonah and killed eighteen civilians, including eight children, before they themselves were killed.[83] A month later, on May 15, a band of DFLP guerrillas occupied a school in Ma'alot and killed twenty-one children during an IDF rescue attempt.[84] At the end of March 1975 a Fatah squad landed on the beach at Tel Aviv and occupied a hotel in the center of the city, holding a number of hostages for two days. When Israeli paratroopers stormed the hotel all the guerrillas were killed, as were three Israeli soldiers (including the commanding colonel) and three hostages.[85] These were only some of the more spectacular attacks. Dozens of other attacks also took place between 1974 and 1977.

The growing recognition accorded the PLO by the United Nations increased Israeli anger and resentment toward the world body. On November 10, 1975, the UN General Assembly accorded the PLO observer status as "the representative of the Palestinian people to participate in all efforts, deliberations and conferences on the Middle East," and to "secure the invitation of the PLO to participate in all other efforts for peace."[86] The General Assembly also recognized the "inalienable rights [of the Palestinian people], including the right of self-determination, and their inalienable right to return to their homes and property from which they have been displaced and uprooted."[87] The resolution that followed incensed Israelis even more. The UN General Assembly reiterated its condemnation of "the unholy alliance between South African racism and Zionism" and called for the "elimination of colonialism and neocolonialism, foreign occupation, Zionism, Apartheid and racial discrimination in all its forms."[88] A defiant speech to the General Assembly by Israel's ambassador, Chaim Herzog, expressed Israeli outrage toward the United Nations and the PLO, which manipulated the organization through its relationships with the Arab states, Soviet client states, and the rest of the Third World. Israelis strongly supported Herzog's statement that "the issue is not Israel or Zionism. The issue is the continued existence of the organization [the United Nations] which has been dragged to its lowest point of discredit by a coalition of despotism and racists."[89]

In so heated an atmosphere, few Israelis noticed that Fatah's leadership was actually beginning to move, albeit slowly and ambivalently, toward a political compromise with Israel. That the Twelfth Palestine National Council in July 1974 declared its intention to establish an "independent and fighting sovereignty . . . on every part of Palestinian land to be liberated" did not sound any better to Israeli ears than the previous doctrine espoused by PLO leaders, which favored the establishment of a "secular democratic state" in the entire land of Palestine. Only a handful of Arabists specializing

in the Palestinian national movement were able to interpret the new formulations as implying an initial agreement on the part of Arafat and his
colleagues to the establishment of a Palestinian state *alongside* Israel, not
instead of it.[90]

Time and again peace activists had publicly to denounce Palestinian
acts of terror, while also reminding their Israeli audience that peace has to
be made between enemies rather than friends—and that therefore, despite the atrocities, Israel had no choice but to recognize the Palestinians
and their political representative, the PLO. But the peaceniks' denuncia-
tions of terror, as well as their recommendations, usually fell on the deaf
ears of angry Israelis who were unable to conceive of a compromise with,
or recognition of, the terrorist PLO. Members of Sheli and the Council for
Israel-Palestine Peace were branded as traitors, defeatists, or at best naive. As the country's mood shifted noticeably to the right, the already weak
peace forces appeared more and more to be unrealistic dreamers.

Emda

Yael Yishai, a professor at Haifa University, has referred to the years from
1973 to 1977 in the history of the Israeli peace movement as the "long
hibernation." "The peace option was once again promoted by the characteristic though hardly effective strategy of sending open letters to the
press and regular publications."[91] However, one of the impressive achievements of the peace activists during those lean years was the publication
of a monthly magazine called *Emda* (this word has a double meaning in
Hebrew; a trench and a position or an attitude).[92] The first issue was
published in October 1974 and was edited by Menachem Brinker, a teacher
at the Hebrew University of Jerusalem, and Niva Lanir, one of the founders
of Siah (the Israeli New Left).[93] Brinker did not take part in the activities
of the Israel-Palestine Council. "I did not oppose it, but I thought it was
premature and too presumptuous," he explained. "The main effort, I believed, was to be invested in educating the Israeli public."[94] His belief
that a magazine would educate the Israeli public might have been presumptuous too, because *Emda* primarily preached to the converted. But
it had a substantial impact inside the peace movement in terms of policy
articulation, value clarification, and contribution to the broader national
intellectual discourse.[95]

At its peak the magazine regularly sold 3,500 copies—not an insignificant number for this type of publication in Israel. It avoided being
identified with one particular party or group, its high quality attracting

writers and intellectuals from the Israeli left, the center of the Labor Party, and even Rakach. "We were convinced that the 'dovish space' was wider than the parliamentary deployment indicated," Brinker recalled. "Our magazine served as a forum for this entire space. With us it could express itself without any partisan constraints."[96] *Emda* expressed a spectrum of opinions but emphasized the unifying elements within the peace movement. It also served as a tool for nurturing contacts with intellectuals abroad, including Palestinians.[97] The first reports of human rights abuses in the occupied territories also appeared in a special section edited by Ruth Gabison, a professor of law in Jerusalem and one of the founders of the Association of Civil Rights in Israel.[98] Perhaps the most important function of *Emda* in that era of hibernation was to serve as a reminder that the peace option was not dead.

The End of Labor Rule

When Yitzhak Rabin presented his cabinet for Knesset approval on June 3, 1974, Henry Kissinger's "step-by-step" diplomacy was well under way. The outgoing government, still headed by Golda Meir, signed disengagement agreements with Egypt and Syria after hard bargaining. Israeli forces retreated to a line fifteen miles east of the Suez Canal and returned some narrow slices of the Golan Heights, including the ruins of Qunaitra, to the Syrians.[99]

Most of the diplomatic activities in the Middle East during 1974–77 occurred under the umbrella of the so-called Geneva Conference. UN Security Council Resolutions 338 and 339 ordered a cease-fire and the beginning of peace negotiations at the end of the October War. In addition to ordering an end to the fighting, Resolution 338 (adopted on October 22, 1973) called on the parties "to start immediately the implementation of Security Council Resolution 242 and start negotiations . . . under appropriate auspices aimed at establishing a just and durable peace in the Middle East."[100] To facilitate these negotiations, Kissinger and his Soviet counterparts agreed to convene an international conference in Geneva, to serve as a permanent forum for multilateral meetings under UN auspices. This forum was intended to "provide the symbolic umbrella under which various diplomatic moves might be made."[101]

On December 21, 1973, the first session of the conference was convened, cochaired by Kissinger and the Soviet Minister of Foreign Affairs Andrei Gromyko. In attendance were the foreign ministers of Egypt, Jordan, and Israel.[102] The conference provided an opportunity for public statements, but Kissinger preferred to continue the practical negotiations through bilateral talks under the auspices of his own shuttle diplomacy.

The Israeli government disliked the Geneva formula, fearing that the Arab states would gang up and be supported by the Soviets, which could isolate Israel, particularly if the United States employed an "even-handed" approach. Consequently, Israel demanded unmediated face-to-face negotiations with each of the Arab states. Ultimately, the conference was never reconvened because the disengagement agreements were concluded in direct talks mediated by Kissinger. Reconvening the conference remained a possibility for the next three years, however, and became a regular threat used by the superpowers, and especially the United States, against Israel whenever it was accused of "intransigence." This caused many Israelis to take a negative view of the credibility of the peace process overall.

Kissinger viewed the first two disengagement agreements as first steps on the road to a general settlement. He did not give Rabin much of a respite, and at the beginning of 1975 began to push for a second disengagement agreement with Egypt. He supported the Egyptians' demand for Israel to retreat behind the Mitla and Gidi passes (some thirty miles further east of existing lines) and to return the oil wells of Abu Rudeis.[103]

Rabin initially resisted the Egyptian demands and insisted that the quid pro quo be a formal end of belligerency. Following a threat by President Ford and Secretary Kissinger to conduct a "reassessment" of U.S.-Israeli relations, Rabin was compelled to agree to the withdrawal without receiving a commitment by Egypt to disavow its claim to a state of war with Israel.[104] Egypt agreed only to allow the passage of goods destined for Israel through the Suez Canal.[105] Reluctantly, on September 1, 1975, Rabin signed the agreement and ordered the retreat of Israeli forces from the Sinai passes.[106] To induce Israel to accept the deal Kissinger had had to make certain commitments on behalf of the United States, most significantly a promise "not to recognize or negotiate with the Palestine Liberation Organization as long as the PLO does not recognize Israel's right to exist and does not accept Security Council Resolutions 242 and 338."[107]

Kissinger was less successful with regard to a disengagement agreement with Jordan.[108] In the summer of 1974 King Hussein conducted a rearguard operation against the growing influence of the PLO inside the occupied territories as well as in the Arab world at large. Fearing that the PLO would receive a mandate to exclusively represent the Palestinians in the upcoming Arab summit in Rabat, the king sought to preempt this possibility by securing some initial territorial concessions from Israel.[109] Israel, however, refused to make such concessions because they either contradicted the essence of the Allon Plan, which remained Rabin's blueprint for an eventual Israeli retreat,[110] or imperiled his promise to the NRP not to agree to any withdrawal from the West Bank without first holding Knesset elections or at least bringing the issue to a referendum. Rabin's coalition majority was narrow, and he was unwilling to rely on Arab votes in the Knesset for his government's survival. Consequently, he felt that he did not have a mandate to accept the king's overtures.[111]

Rabin's courtship of the NRP was unsuccessful, and its nearly thirty-year coalition with the Labor Party soon came to an end. Under the influence of Gush Emunim, the NRP, which until 1967 adhered to a moderate line on security and foreign policy issues, had become ideologically closer to Likud. As the 1977 elections approached, the NRP looked for ways to demonstrate its independence from Labor. The opportunity presented itself on a Friday afternoon in December 1976. The Israeli Air Force had invited government officials and other dignitaries to a ceremony at an air base in the south of the country, on the occasion of the arrival of the first F-15 fighter planes procured from the United States. The planes arrived later than expected and many of the participants had to travel back to their homes after sundown, thus violating religious law. Consequently, the NRP proposed a Knesset vote of no confidence in the government. The government withstood the no confidence vote, but Rabin fired the rebellious NRP ministers and resigned soon after to pave the way for new elections, which were advanced to May from the scheduled date of October. After thirty years in opposition, Menachem Begin emerged as the winner in this election. His Likud party would remain in power for the fifteen years that followed.

5

Shalom Achshav— Peace Now

Peace Feelers

Menachem Begin's first days in office confirmed the peace activists' worst fears. On his return from the president's house, where he had received the mandate to form the new government, Begin went to the home of Rabbi Tzvi Yehuda Kook to receive his blessing.[1] Shortly after his coalition was confirmed by the Knesset, Begin visited the Gush Emunim settlers in Kaddum, the Jewish settlement west of Nablus, whose unauthorized establishment in 1976 had led to a prolonged struggle with the previous Labor government.[2] He was accompanied by Ariel Sharon (popularly known as Arik), whom Begin had just nominated minister of agriculture. Sharon was a general with a splendid military record—among his other achievements he had commanded the crossing of the Suez Canal in the 1973 war—and extremely hawkish temperament and convictions. Begin declared with pride and determination that under his government there would be "many more Elon Morehs"[3] and that "Samaria and Judea are an inalienable part of Israel."[4]

These gestures were not surprising. They reflected the ideology Begin had espoused for decades and the political platform he had promised to implement if his party won the elections. "Whoever is ready to hand over Judea and Samaria to foreign rule," he cautioned, "will lay the foundations for a Palestinian state. . . . The borders between Israel and Egypt should be delineated *inside* Sinai, and the border with Syria should be drawn *on* the Golan Heights."[5]

The nomination of Moshe Dayan as minister of foreign affairs was a significant and surprising move by the new prime minister. Dayan had been reelected to the Knesset on the Labor list and then defected and joined the Likud government. While defections from parliamentary factions were not unknown, a jump from the senior ranks of Labor to a senior position in Likud was unprecedented. Leaders of the Labor Party were furious and vented their indignation in a heated parliamentary debate. Dayan did not participate in the debate because he was already abroad, secretly negotiating with top Egyptian officials. Within less than two years these negotiations would lead Begin to conclude a peace treaty with the strongest and most populous Arab state.[6]

Despite his aggressive image, Begin's main concern from the time he became prime minister was avoiding another war,[7] and even though tensions with Egypt and Syria had been significantly reduced by the two disengagement agreements between them and Israel, it was clear that the Arabs would not accept these arrangements as permanent. Unless progress were made on the road to peace another bloody war might prove inevitable.[8]

Probes were sent in different directions and resulted in a secret meeting in early September 1977 between Moshe Dayan and Muhamed Hasan al-Tuhami, the deputy to the Egyptian prime minister. Although Dayan and al-Tuhami parted not much closer to bridging the divide between Israeli and Egyptian positions, President Anwar Sadat decided to take matters into his own hands. Sadat, who had gained respect and prestige among his people by what they perceived as a daring and successful defiance of Israel along the Suez Canal in 1973, was aware of Begin's desire to meet him face-to-face and discuss the possibility of reconciliation.[9] Al-Tuhami may well have told Sadat that Israel seemed prepared to agree to return the entire Sinai in exchange for full peace.[10] Whatever the case, Sadat clearly felt that a dramatic gesture was required to create a sense of urgency in the minds of all the parties involved. He also became concerned upon receiving the news that President Jimmy Carter was seeking to revive the U.S.- and Soviet-sponsored Geneva Conference, while Sadat's Arab partners (especially Syria and the PLO) dragged their feet and confused the process with all kinds of preconditions. Wary of a renewed Soviet role, Sadat sought to block this route.[11]

On November 9, 1977, Sadat surprised everybody when he departed from a prepared speech he was delivering in the Egyptian National Assembly and said that he was prepared "to go to the end of the world if it would prevent the killing or even wounding of one of my soldiers or officers. Israel will probably be surprised to hear me saying now, I shall be ready to visit them, in their home, in their Knesset, in order to argue with them. I do not have time to waste."[12]

Begin was surprised indeed. Despite earlier invitations he had sent to President Sadat to come to Israel, Begin spent four days considering Sadat's bold move. On November 13 he extended a formal invitation to the Egyptian president "to come to Jerusalem in order to hold discussions about a permanent peace between Israel and Egypt."[13]

The Impact of Sadat's Visit

Sadat landed at Lod Airport on the evening of November 19.[14] He spent three days in Israel, but during that time only a limited amount of negotiation took place. The centerpiece of the visit was Sadat's speech to the Knesset,[15] in which he repeated his unqualified demand that Israel retreat from all the territories it had conquered in 1967 and grant the Palestinians the right of self-determination.[16] He believed that his gesture of visiting Jerusalem was in itself a big sacrifice entailing considerable risks, and he looked to Israel to reciprocate by relinquishing the territories.

When Begin rose to respond to Sadat's speech he reiterated Israel's requirements for "secure borders"—a well-known euphemism for rejection of retreat to the pre-1967 borders. He also clearly rejected the creation of a Palestinian state. Perhaps in their private meetings Begin confirmed Sadat's earlier impression that Israel was ready to return the Sinai Peninsula to Egypt in exchange for full peace. But the exact meaning and details of full peace, as well as the disposition of Israeli settlements and air bases in Sinai, apparently were not discussed in any detail.[17]

In Dayan's pessimistic opinion it was clear that the Israeli and Egyptian positions were still far apart.[18] Nevertheless, the overall mood in Israel was one of exhilaration. Sadat's festive declaration of "No more war! No more bloodshed!" resounded in Israeli ears. Tens of thousands of Israelis came out to greet Sadat when his motorcade passed through the streets of Jerusalem and Tel Aviv.[19] In the minds of many it seemed that Israel would never be the same again. "There could be no retreat from the track Sadat and Begin started to pave in this glamorous encounter."[20] Sadat's visit to Jerusalem was not only a revolution in Middle Eastern politics but also an upheaval in the consciousness of Israelis. Thirty years of bitter strife and animosity had left deep doubts among many Israelis as to whether peace was a genuine possibility. The sight of the most prominent Arab leader addressing the Knesset and announcing his keen desire for peace challenged the long-held convictions of most Israelis about Arab intransigence. Simply stated, Sadat created the belief that peace was possible.

But the only practical result of the Jerusalem discussions was an agreement to continue to explore avenues toward a possible peace agreement in further meetings at the ministerial level and through committees of experts. And Sadat soon came under heavy attack from all quarters of the Arab world, not least because of their suspicions that he had negotiated a separate peace treaty for Egypt. He urged Israel to speed up the negotiations in order to dispel this impression among his neighbors—but this was precisely what the Israeli leadership wanted to avoid. For their part, the Israeli leaders were concerned that linking Israeli-Egyptian negotiations to those with other Arab states and the Palestinians would permanently stall the progress that was actually being made, without opening up hope for more.

At first the lingering excitement over the Jerusalem visit concealed this stumbling block. Only Dayan remained openly skeptical, telling Egyptian foreign minister Boutros Boutros-Ghali that Egyptian insistence on linkage to a solution for the Palestinian problem would lead the whole venture to a dead end.[21] And indeed, it was only a few weeks later that these obstacles seriously threatened the process that Sadat's trip had launched.

The Peace Process Goes Sour

Although Sadat and Begin agreed to continue the process that had begun in Jerusalem, no specific format was established. Sadat wanted to capitalize on the momentum he had gained by his visit to Israel. Encouraged by the enthusiastic welcome he received on his return to Egypt, he convened a conference in Cairo to which he invited Israel, the United States, the United Nations, and the Arab states.[22] In the event, however, none of the other Arab states attended, and the discussions only reiterated the areas of disagreement.

In the meantime Begin rushed to Washington to deliver a detailed Israeli peace plan to the American president. His plan included the idea of granting autonomy to the Palestinians—an idea never before advanced by the Israeli leader.[23] President Carter was impressed, and, though he did not endorse it, he considered the plan constructive and a good basis for further discussions. Carter telephoned Sadat and recommended that he invite Begin to Egypt to listen to the prime minister's new plan.[24]

Sadat met Begin (who was accompanied by Dayan, among others) at Isma'iliyya on the Suez Canal on December 25, 1977. This meeting did not yield any breakthrough, however, and the only decision reached was the establishment of two committees—one political, one military—to work out the details of an agreement. On matters of substance the two leaders could not go beyond the now customary expressions of their honest desire for peace and mutual lectures about each nation's history and unique situation. The only novelty of Begin's proposals was his suggestion to postpone the negotiations on the ultimate solution to the Palestinian problem while providing the Palestinians with an interim arrangement for limited self-rule. Sadat had no use for a complicated and detailed plan and sought instead a general statement of principles that would signal to the Palestinians, and the rest of the Arab world, that his initiative was not conceived as a separate Egyptian peace with Israel.

Dayan's grim face upon his return from Isma'iliyya conveyed the sense of a deadlock. The euphoria of November gave way to a growing suspicion that Begin and his hawkish cabinet were unable to rise to the opportunity and might let the chance for peace slip away. This impression was strengthened in mid-January when the Cairo meeting of the military committee produced no tangible results.[25] The political committee, which convened in Jerusalem on January 15 in the presence of U.S. Secretary of State Cyrus Vance, quickly fell into a crisis. Israeli lawyers and American diplomats were in the midst of an attempt to reach an acceptable compromise formula when President Sadat, apparently angered by Ariel Sharon's decision to order preparations for the establishment of new settlements in the Sinai, instructed his mission to return to Cairo immediately.[26] This dramatic and surprising move was seen by many as the end of Sadat's initiative and the failure of the peace talks.

A Letter from the Officers

A grim mood cast a pall on the streets of Israel. Some veterans of the 1973 protest movement and other peace activists met with a number of reserve officers who had fought in the October War, and asked themselves how they could help save the peace process from being extinguished. Some of them had previously been involved with a group of Jerusalem students who called themselves "Hatnua Le Tzionut Aheret" (the Movement for a Different Zionism), but had been unable to spark a real movement. (A similar group had also been meeting in Tel Aviv.) Anxiety that the opportunity for peace might be squandered united these different groups.

Begin was preparing to depart on yet another trip to Washington in an attempt to salvage his relations with President Carter, who now seemed to lean to the Egyptian side.[27] The group of young reserve officers decided to dispatch an urgent letter to the prime minister, expressing their deep conviction that he should explore all possibilities for compromise.[28] This group initially included a number of women, but it was decided that to achieve the maximum effect they would present themselves as "combat veterans."

Yuval Neria, an armor commander who had earned the highest Medal of Valor for his bravery during the 1973 war, explained, "We decided that the Prime Minister would find it hard to ignore a letter written by combat officers who had proven their worth in action and had already made a contribution to Israeli society."[29] Within a few hours of the letter's completion, 348 reserve officers and noncommissioned officers signed it and forwarded it to the prime minister on March 7, 1978. Widely published in the daily newspapers, the letter read:

> This letter is sent to you by Israeli citizens who serve as soldiers and officers in reserve units. We write the following sentences to you with a heavy heart, but in these days, when for the first time new horizons of peace and cooperation in the region are opening before us, we consider it our duty to call on you to avoid taking steps which may be deplored by the coming generations.
>
> We write to you with profound anxiety. A government that prefers the establishment of the State of Israel in the borders of a Greater Israel above the establishment of peace through good neighborly relations, instills in us many doubts. A government that prefers the establishment of settlements beyond the 'Green Line' [the pre-1967 borders] to the elimination of the historical quarrel and the establishment of normal relations in our region, will awaken in us questions as to the justice of our cause. A government policy which will continue the domination over millions of Arabs may damage the democratic and Jewish character of the state and make it difficult for us to identify with the path taken by the State of Israel. We are aware of the security requirements of the State of Israel and of the difficulties facing the road to peace, but we know that true security will be achieved only when peace will come. The strength of the Israeli Defense Forces lies in the identification of its citizen-soldiers with the posture of the state.
>
> We call on you to choose the road of peace and strengthen thereby our belief in the justice of our path.[30]

That so many young combat officers publicly questioned the "justice of our cause" was a serious matter for Begin and his government. Until then the assumption was that, notwithstanding the political debates that raged in the country, no one doubted that the army was a vital defense force in which Israelis should willingly serve in the common defense effort. The letter sent by the high school seniors to Golda Meir in 1970 had used similar language, but these were youngsters who had not yet served their country in the military.[31] For more than three hundred reserve soldiers who had fought in the bloody Yom Kippur War, many of whom were still serving as reserve soldiers in elite fighting units, to write such a letter was something quite different.

A Movement Is Born

The letter struck a raw nerve. A significant part of Israeli society already had doubts concerning the government's handling of the peace talks. This anxiety needed only a spark to be ignited into widespread demonstrations. "They lit a match which ignited a huge flame. Despondence met with despondence and was turned into a large wave of energy."[32] Within a few hours of the letter's publication, the newspapers, the Broadcasting Authority, and the homes of the letter's signatories were flooded with telephone calls. Hundreds of people wanted to add their names to the letter and asked what they could do to help. The young and inexperienced reserve officers were both surprised and overwhelmed. Most shied away from public attention, and when they were asked to send a spokesperson to appear in a television news program nobody volunteered. They eventually selected one and imposed the mission on him "because he was a handsome combat pilot."[33] At this point the new movement's core of activists numbered only a few dozen young men and women. They had not planned anything except writing the letter. Now they were encouraged by the letter's enthusiastic reception and sought to capitalize on the momentum they had unwittingly created. As they considered their next move they discovered that other groups in Tel Aviv, Haifa, and some of the kibbutzim were already holding meetings and considering political demonstrations. They began to coordinate their activities to mobilize further support for the "Officers' Letter." Within a week they collected a few thousand new signatures. The officers were surprised to find themselves at the center of a rapidly growing protest movement—a movement that was soon to evolve into Peace Now.[34]

The new movement did not possess a clearly defined and permanent group of leaders. There were, however, some personalities who played prominent roles. It is impossible to give details of all those men and women, numbering perhaps a few dozen, who formed the core of the new group, but a few examples may help to suggest their backgrounds and talents.

Naftali Raz, an energetic professional youth worker from Jerusalem, was more a manager than an ideologue. He had a keen ability to attract the media's attention and a creative approach to public relations, and his military experience helped him in coordinating the movement's projects.[35]

Orly Lubin, at the time a communications student at Tel Aviv University, was an eloquent debater with radical convictions who had been raised in an intellectual, upper-middle-class household. Lubin became one of the pillars of the Tel Aviv forum and often served as the voice of the left wing within the movement.

Avshalom (Abu) Vilan, a second-generation kibbutznik from Negba in the south, became the liaison between Peace Now and the kibbutz movement. This connection was very important because kibbutzim provided the movement not only with many volunteers, but also with equipment and other material assistance. Vilan's greatest attribute was his fiery sense of conviction; he was often asked to speak at demonstrations.

Janet Aviad, though she joined the movement somewhat later, became a central figure. An American-born sociologist, she taught at the Hebrew University and wrote on religion in Israel and in particular on the ideological roots of Gush Emunim. Aviad's devotion, insight, trustworthiness, and organizational skills made her indispensable and she soon held the position of treasurer, one of the two official positions in the movement.

Yossi Ben-Artzi was a young teacher of social and historical geography of the Land of Israel at the University of Haifa. He was a veteran of the 1973 protest movement and one of the founders of the centrist party Shinui (Change). In many ways Ben-Artzi played the role of the movement's right-wing guidepost, often cautioning against excessive radicalism.

Shulamit Hareven, a prominent novelist and essayist, was somewhat older than most of the activists. She provided not only her personal prestige but also her pen, coining many of the movement's slogans and catchwords, as well as writing numerous articles over the years articulating the movement's positions.[36]

Tzali Reshef, then a young lawyer in Jerusalem, occupied the second official position as the movement's spokesperson. His legal training was also beneficial whenever litigation proved necessary. His ability to clearly articulate ideas made him a leading voice in the movement's decision making, and his charismatic personality made him a natural speaker at many of the movement's public events. If one person came to epitomize Peace Now, it was Tzali Reshef.[37]

Throughout March and April the informal leadership of the nascent movement began preparations for its first demonstration. Events, however, conspired to delay this public debut. On the afternoon of March 11, eleven PLO guerrillas landed on an isolated beach between Haifa and Tel Aviv. They killed an American woman who was photographing seabirds and then proceeded to the main coastal highway, where they hijacked a bus full of Israeli families returning from vacation. A second bus was hijacked and its passengers crammed into the first vehicle, which then headed south. When the police managed to stop the bus a few miles north of Tel Aviv a massacre ensued. Most of the hijackers were killed, but not before they managed to set fire to the bus and kill thirty-five Israelis. Seventy-one others were wounded.[38] Minister of Defense Ezer Weizman, who hurried back from meetings in Washington, wrote, "The peace process, which was anyhow hanging between life and death, was now perishing in the flames of the burning bus."[39]

The "officers'" reaction to this event reflected a feature that became a permanent characteristic of the movement. They tried to be sensitive to variations in the public's mood. They did not believe that the bloody attack on the highway should lessen their dedication to the advancement of the peace process. On the contrary, it served as a grim reminder why peace should become the nation's highest priority. Nevertheless, they did not feel that their demonstration was appropriate at the moment when so many people were bereaved and while the nation was engulfed by anger and frustration. They decided to postpone their demonstration until a more stable atmosphere prevailed.

A few days later Israel launched a major counteroffensive against Palestinian strongholds in southern Lebanon. Israeli forces conquered the southern part of that country up to the Litani River, excluding the town of Tyre. The IDF held this area for a few days and then retreated after dismantling several Palestinian military strongholds. The Palestinian guerrillas suffered some losses, but most managed to escape to the north.[40] The UN Security Council established UNIFIL (United Nations Interim Forces in Lebanon), a new peacekeeping force, which was installed in south Lebanon to act as a buffer between the warring parties.[41]

Operation Litani, and the passage of time, assuaged Israeli outrage at the coastal highway attack. Begin and Dayan went to Washington once more to meet with Carter and his team. The apparent failure of this encounter reminded Israelis of the impasse that had provoked the Officers' Letter.[42] When the founders of the new movement felt that the pursuit of peace had returned to the center of public interest, they resumed their preparations for a major demonstration. By the end of March more than 10,000 people had signed the Officers' Letter, and on March 30, 1978, a small rehearsal demonstration took place in front of the prime minister's residence in Jerusalem. This became a standard technique for the peace movement: heat the atmosphere with a number of small activities, arouse public interest, and mobilize sympathizers for the big act. In preparing for the larger demonstration, scores of volunteers spent nights in makeshift offices painting on cardboard and linens the slogans to be hoisted. This was not just a question of physical labor; it was an opportunity to express in brief phrases the ideas and convictions of the nascent movement. "Peace Is Better than Another Piece of Land!", "The Lives of Sons Are Better than the Graves of Fathers!", and "Mr. Begin, We Are Worried!" were among those that were used.[43]

David Tartakover, a commercial artist, printed in bold letters the simple slogan "Peace Now." These words conveyed in the most direct way the overwhelming sense of urgency much of the general public felt at that time. The media henceforth referred to this group as the "Peace Now Movement." The activists liked the name and adopted Tartakover's graphic design as their permanent logo.[44]

Peace Now's first large-scale demonstration took place on April 1, 1978, in front of the Tel Aviv Town Hall. The participation of some 40,000 demonstrators was unexpected and made it one of Israel's largest political demonstrations to that point. Ten Knesset members attended, including some from the Labor Party. A letter of encouragement from Saul Bellow, signed by thirty-seven Jewish-American intellectuals, was read from the stage. Encouraged by this success, the organizers announced the founding of a nonpartisan movement dedicated to pressuring the government to proceed vigorously toward peace.[45]

An Unstructured Structure

The main innovation Peace Now introduced to Israel's political landscape was that, without creating a permanent machinery, and despite having no paid staff, it succeeded for many years in maintaining its identity and sustaining a significant political presence.[46] Peace Now never tried to become a registered membership organization, yet at various times it measured its popular strength by asking participants in its activities to register on a presence list or sign a petition. The mailing list that was developed as a result was the only "membership list." At the movement's peak of strength, more than 200,000 people expressed their identification with its goals.[47] The largest demonstrations Peace Now organized attracted more than 100,000 participants.[48]

Yet these figures do not properly convey the nature and size of the constituency. Peace Now was made up of three concentric circles. The inner circle was comprised of "activists" who participated and planned the group's activities. During the movement's formative years (1978–83) this group numbered some 500, mostly well-educated middle- and upper-middle-class Israelis, in their mid- to late twenties, born to parents of European or American origin. The second circle was made up of "loyal participants" who attended all Peace Now demonstrations. This circle often included between 5,000 and 6,000 people, and while due to its size it was naturally more heterogeneous, it shared a similar profile to the inner circle. The third and largest circle was made up of "sympathizers"—people who occasionally joined demonstrations or signed petitions. The number of this group varied, largely depending on the prevailing political and psychological environment and the level of public energy generated.[49] This concentric circle structure was not deliberately planned and remained fluid, expanding and contracting with the tides of public opinion. The boundaries between the concentric circles were vague, and people moved from one level of activity to another as their interest and circumstances warranted.

The number of participants also depended greatly on the different types of activities the movement undertook. Small vigils, parlor meetings, or meetings in public halls with limited seating capacity needed only a few hundred protesters.[50] These activities usually drew on the inner circle of activists. Street demonstrations in the confined spaces of Jerusalem's squares, in the occupied territories, or along major intercity roads would be considered a failure if fewer than 2,000 to 3,000 people participated. These required the mobilization of most of the loyal participants. The major demonstrations, which customarily took place in the large squares of Tel Aviv, required at least 15,000 to 20,000 participants to convey an impression of success. Such demonstrations would be undertaken only when the movement was convinced that there was enough support among the sympathizers. While small- and medium-sized activities were usually advertised by a well-organized telephone network, the larger demonstrations required expensive advertisements in the newspapers.

Often many months passed during which, whether by design or neglect, no major demonstrations took place. But the inner circle always continued to be active in other ways. The most active group was in Jerusalem. There were also strong groups of activists in Tel Aviv, Haifa, and Beer Sheva, and the kibbutz movement could always be relied upon to provide material and financial assistance as well as a few busloads of participants. In the main chapters of the movement, meetings were held every two or three weeks to consult, plan, or prepare activities. A national steering committee known as the "Upper Forum" (*Forum-Al* in Hebrew) held consultations at least once a month. This committee formed the practical leadership of the movement, but no extensive formal leadership was recognized. Though necessity required the services of a treasurer and a spokesperson (the latter was the only person authorized to make statements on behalf of the movement), anyone could participate in a steering committee meeting and influence its decisions.

This also explains why decisions were never made by a formal vote. In most cases the group acted only on the basis of consensus. Most of the movement's activities required both the support of the loyal participants and considerable organizational effort by volunteers, and such people could be mobilized only if they were keenly enthusiastic and convinced of the advisability and potential effectiveness of a particular activity. A simple majority vote could not achieve this. Lengthy debates and negotiations to reach consensus and fine-tune plans of action were needed to generate the energy and conviction necessary for each activity. Significant minorities could prevent the movement from taking an action they strongly opposed.

Occasionally a gathering of a few hundred activists would be convened for a full day of deliberations; however, no decisions were made on these occasions. They were meant only to get a sense of the prevailing mood and to facilitate an exchange of views on the movement's general direction. These large meetings usually took place at the Ga'ash kibbutz north of Tel Aviv and were known in the movement as the "Ga'ash Meetings."

The grass-roots membership was able to significantly influence decisions taken by the movement as a whole. Ideas generated by one or more participants were taken up and discussed by groups of activists in the main chapter meetings, and, if they gained support, referred to the Upper Forum for further consideration. Sometimes a specific proposal or issue would be referred back to the chapters for further deliberation. When consensus was reached in support of a proposal, a committee would be formed or assigned to begin detailed planning for implementation.

A number of permanent committees were established, including the Operations Committee, which was responsible for planning all public actions, and the Committee on Public Affairs, which was charged with formulating the movement's public statements.[51] The process of decision making was facilitated by access to good, up-to-date information. With many of its activists involved in national politics, employed in governmental institutions, or otherwise well connected politically, and with many young journalists sympathetic to the movement, Peace Now did not lack for expertise in national and international affairs.

A Movement of Slogans

From the outset Peace Now was a conglomeration of people with different, sometimes contradictory, opinions on various issues other than the issue of peace. Some were ardent socialists; others were free market capitalists. Some were religious, but most were secular. Some believed that only a radical change in the electoral system could save Israeli democracy, while many disagreed. In light of such diversity the unity within the movement was maintained by keeping Peace Now a single-issue movement. The activists always resisted the temptation to become another political party, which would necessarily have had to address a wide range of issues.

A divergence of opinion existed even on matters concerning the Arab-Israeli conflict. Some activists believed that only by negotiating with the Palestinians could a solution be found, while others advocated the Jordanian Option. Some were convinced that peace could be achieved only by a retreat from all the territories, including Jerusalem, whereas others contended that a territorial compromise could be achieved with Jerusalem remaining in Israeli hands. Some were convinced that the PLO was a terrorist organization that had to be fought, others that Israel should recognize the PLO as the only legitimate representatives of the Palestinians.

The only way to avoid intramovement conflict was to base Peace Now's activity on a limited set of tenets to which all supporters could subscribe. These included the following:

- Peace is the highest priority facing Israel and Zionism today.
- The security of Israel depends on peace, not on territories.
- The government should reach peace with Egypt based on the principle of "territories for peace" as determined by UN Resolution 242.
- Israel should stop all settlements in the occupied territories. Settlements are an impediment to peace and push the Arabs away from the negotiating table.
- Israel and Zionism cannot be based on the domination and suppression of another nation. The occupation corrupts the occupier.[52]

Attempts to go into greater detail on specific policies would have caused unnecessary friction and dissent. This was undesirable because the movement's main goal was to reach the media and influence public opinion to believe in peace in principle, not to elaborate the precise outlines of a peace settlement. This was perhaps one of the important differences between Peace Now and its predecessor, the Movement for Peace and Security. Peace and Security was directed, at least at the beginning, by professors who articulated their positions through lengthy and sophisticated essays. In comparison, Peace Now devoted many of its meetings to devising clever short phrases and slogans appropriate for a specific occasion. These slogans reflected the inclusive, nonideological, and pragmatic direction of the movement. Peace Now was essentially a movement of slogans, but this was the way the activists, otherwise sophisticated people, preferred it. This was perhaps also the main secret of its success.[53]

One activist described the movement as "a slow-moving train allowing people to get off at different ideological stops,"[54] and indeed one of its strengths was that it allowed people to join or rejoin at different points. This facilitated the coexistence of people from different political, ideological, economic, and religious backgrounds.

The movement's leaders were skillful in maintaining the group's legitimacy within the Israeli body politic. Attempts by the extreme right to brand Peace Now as traitors and beyond the pale failed; the movement's image as a group of loyal Zionists and patriotic Israelis was left untarnished.[55] At worst Peace Now could be criticized as naive, mistaken, or misled, but never as disloyal. The activists made sure that numerous Israeli flags were present at all events and that they always concluded with the singing of the national anthem.[56] Some radical ideologues could be found within the movement, but as veterans of other protest activities they knew that while an uncompromising position might make them feel good, it would inevitably marginalize the movement to the fringes of Israeli politics. They had learned the important lesson that in politics it is not enough to be right; one must also be influential.

On the Road

On April 21, 1978, representatives of Peace Now held a meeting with Prime Minister Begin at their request. The results of the meeting were disappointing. The group urged Begin to freeze the settlements in the occupied territories and to show maximum flexibility in negotiations with the Egyptians. The prime minister listened to them with fatherly patience but was unmoved. "It was a dialogue of the deaf," said Tzali Reshef.[57] But that such a meeting had taken place at all was indicative of the nonpartisan attitude the movement adopted during the first phase of its development. It was clear at this juncture that peace with Egypt could be concluded only by Begin; any hope for a change of government was futile. Therefore, Peace Now, later labeled anti-Begin and anti-Likud, tried to avoid unduly attacking the government. Though publicly critical of Begin's handling of the negotiations, Peace Now still hoped to lobby and influence Begin himself.

The movement viewed itself as a pressure group, and lobbying was an important feature of its activities. During the spring and summer of 1978 activists met with senior politicians in the government and the opposition, including Deputy Prime Minister Yigal Yadin (the retired-general-turned-archaeologist who led the short-lived political party Dash). They even went to see the aging Golda Meir, who did not express great enthusiasm for their message. The only significant leader who refused to meet with them was Moshe Dayan, who never had much patience for peaceniks.

Many Peace Now activists had a good sense for public relations. They always sought media coverage, primarily television reporting. Protests in Israel are noticed largely to the degree that their message is carried on the nine o'clock news, which 2 million Israelis faithfully watch every evening. Peace Now's Operations Committee was responsible for inventing all kinds of media gimmicks. For example, less than a month after the first big demonstration in Tel Aviv, the movement organized a human chain along the road that passes through the Judean Hills on the way to Jerusalem. More than 60,000 people had signed the Officers' Letter by this time, and a copy was passed from hand to hand all the way to the prime minister's office. This time Begin refused to accept it.[58]

The human chain highlighted another characteristic of the movement. Most participants came out with their children and were able to exchange joyful greetings with friends who passed in their cars on their way to or from Jerusalem. Even the occasional encounter with individuals who stopped their cars to argue was handled in a friendly manner. The entire event looked more like a picnic or a festival than an angry protest. In later years political animosity cast a shadow on Peace Now demonstrations, and it became increasingly difficult to maintain the friendly, peaceful, and often joyous atmosphere that had characterized its earlier activities.

Deadlock

During April and May 1978 Begin's government grappled with growing pressure from President Carter, who had become convinced that the Israelis were procrastinating and who had little liking for the Israeli prime minister.[59] In an understatement Carter remembered that "at that time . . . relations with Israel were not very good."[60]

The next meeting between Israelis and Egyptians took place on July 18, 1978, at Leeds Castle, England. The Israeli delegation was headed by Moshe Dayan. Ibrahim Kamel, who had replaced Ismail Fahmy as Egypt's foreign minister after the latter resigned in protest at Sadat's peace initiative, was the senior Egyptian representative. The American delegation was led by Secretary of State Cyrus Vance.[61]

The Egyptians were prepared to drop their demand for a preliminary joint statement of principle, and started to discuss details and modalities of a solution to the impasse. Nevertheless, the gap was still very wide, and neither Dayan nor Kamel had the authority to go beyond his specific instructions.[62] In a memorandum handed to Secretary Vance, Dayan reiterated that Israel would not agree to withdraw to the pre-1967 borders in Judea, Samaria, and Gaza, and would object to the establishment of any Arab sovereignty in these territories. However, Israel was ready to consider some kind of territorial compromise, perhaps along the lines of the Allon Plan, *if* the Arabs offered one. It seems that Begin had agreed to this formula in order to reduce international pressure on Israel, and perhaps because he was convinced that the Arabs would not make the offer.[63]

At about the same time, under heavy pressure from almost all Arab countries, Sadat announced that no further negotiations would take place. He demanded that the Israeli military delegation, which had been stationed in Cairo since the meeting in Isma'iliyya eight months earlier, return to Israel. This was a disappointing development, because for many Israelis the permanent presence of this delegation in Cairo had symbolized a thread of hope.[64] During this time Ezer Weizman managed to gain Sadat's personal friendship. Weizman believed that President Sadat was genuine in his desire for peace, and publicly advocated a more flexible attitude on Israel's part. However, most of the other cabinet members did not take Weizman seriously, which frustrated and angered him. On one occasion he saw a poster in the prime minister's office that applauded the imminent peace. Angrily, Weizman tore the poster off the wall and exclaimed, "I am not so sure that the government really wants peace!" This incident strengthened the suspicions and skepticism of the Israeli peace movement.[65] It soon became clear that only another face-to-face meeting between the heads of state could overcome the stalemate. At the beginning of August Secretary Vance traveled to the Middle East once again. His mission was to invite Begin and Sadat to Camp David, the U.S. president's retreat in Maryland, in early September.[66]

A Dovecote in Samaria

Peace Now continued its activities throughout the summer of 1978. By the end of May the number of signatures on the Officers' Letter surpassed 100,000. The movement held eight large town hall meetings across the country in which the activists explained their approach in greater detail than was possible through demonstrations, posters, or newspaper headlines.

On Saturday, June 10, 1978, three hundred booths were erected at highway junctions and beaches and other recreation centers across the country. Pamphlets were distributed and more signatures secured. In several places structures made of straw blocks and empty barrels were erected, with large posters attached to them to attract the attention of passing cars and the media. The message of peace reached hundreds of thousands of Israelis who went out for a day in the sun. Some were angered by this display, but many others easily identified with the spirit of the message. The success of this operation—called "Shabbat Shalom" (Sabbath of Peace)—was indicative of the large constituency the movement had built during the few weeks of its existence.

The Israeli media in general, and television news in particular, liked the new phenomenon because it provided them with arresting visual images. The Operations Committee was adept at manipulating this media interest.

For example, when Dayan reported to the Knesset on his negotiations at Leeds Castle, a few dozen activists occupied the Knesset's visitor galleries. During the proceedings they simultaneously exposed Peace Now shirts. They had quietly notified Israeli television of their intended display, which ensured they would receive media coverage before being escorted out of the hall for violating Knesset regulations.[67] On June 26, 5,000 demonstrators encircled the prime minister's office in a human chain with hundreds of signs that read, "Begin! Compromise or Resign!" Typically, the Hebrew version was a play on words— *"Begin! Hitpasher o Hitpater!"*

The Struggle over Settlements

Begin's supporters and the more extreme right wing did not completely surrender the street initiatives to groups on the left. Likud operatives tried to organize a grass-roots countermovement, which did stage a few demonstrations, but its partisan origin was quickly exposed and it soon dissolved. Gush Emunim was also active in the streets, but mainly focused its propaganda against the concessions members suspected Begin was prepared to make. In December 1978 Gush Emunim, along with members of the Movement for Greater Israel, demonstrated against Begin's autonomy plan.[68] Zvi Shiloah, who had defected from Labor in the late 1960s and joined the Likud Central Committee, resigned in protest and organized a vigil outside the prime minister's office.[69]

The main challenge to the peace process came from inside the government. Sharon took Begin's promise to build "many more Elon Morehs" literally. Soon after taking office as minister of agriculture Sharon approved a Gush Emunim plan to create twelve new settlements in the West Bank near or around deserted Jordanian military camps.[70]

Begin initially hesitated, and wary of American protests, dragged his feet for a while. But he could not long oppose a plan that his own party had promised to implement if elected. Under heavy pressure from Sharon, he finally approved the secret establishment of five new settlements. At the beginning of August 1978, Peace Now received news of the imminent operation from sympathetic journalists, who were barred from publishing the information by the military censor. There was little doubt that such a move, undertaken with the acquiescence of the government, would torpedo the already fragile peace process. Peace Now decided to expose the plot. During the night of August 5, activists placed large posters with the names and locations of the planned settlements on the streets of Israeli cities and towns. This move forced the government to take action and the settlement operation was called off.[71]

A few days later the movement undertook another symbolic demonstration against the settlers. Yet another settlement had been created, this one disguised as an "archaeological expedition" to excavate Shiloh, the site of the Israelite Tabernacle in the days of the Judges. Peace Now decided to expose this fiction in a colorful manner. Igal Tumarkin, a noted Israeli sculptor, designed a dovecote and, under the guise of installing electrical devices, activists built and erected the symbolic monument at the entrance to the settlement. Peace Now was pleased by this successful gesture. They managed to fool the settlers, attract media attention, and force the government to accept responsibility for its actions. However, the dovecote at Shiloh exposed an inherent weakness of Peace Now. Within two days the demonstration was over, but the settlement remained. Fifteen years later Shiloh is a flourishing village, while the dovecote is nothing more than a memory in the minds of a handful of activists who enjoyed the few hours they spent staging a clever protest in Samaria.

By their very nature Peace Now activities were transient phenomena, whereas Gush Emunim created permanent facts on the ground. With regard to the settlements Peace Now advocated a negative policy of what *not* to do, whereas Gush Emunim undertook positive activities and created new concrete realities. Members of Gush Emunim were engaged in a project that involved their entire lives. Their objective was not a temporary protest but a total commitment to an ideology of divine redemption that called upon them to change the reality in and on the land in Judea and Samaria. In contrast, members of Peace Now, by the very nature of their purpose, came and went largely depending on the issue and environment of the moment, and at the end of the day they all returned home. Hence, in terms of the personal conviction and commitment of its members, Peace Now was the weaker party.

In the summer of 1978, however, Peace Now was conscious chiefly of its growing strength. Indeed, the movement reached its first political peak toward the end of that summer. Begin's aides were aware that, though the movement worked hard to preserve its nonpartisan nature, it had subversive potential, and they sought to discredit it in the public mind. For example, MK Roni Milo, a senior supporter of Begin, floated a rumor that he had received from reliable sources information that Peace Now was subsidized by the CIA.[72]

Camp David

In his remarks to advisers in preparation for the meeting with Begin and Sadat at Camp David, U.S. President Jimmy Carter observed, "Compromises will be mandatory. Without them, no progress can be expected. Flexibility will be the essence of our hope."[73] What might come out of the Camp David Summit and the parameters of the negotiations were unclear even to members of the Israeli delegation, let alone the Israeli public.[74] Therefore, Peace Now attempted to soften Menachem Begin's heart as much as possible, and to push him to make whatever concessions were necessary to ensure that this dramatic effort would not fail. While the Peace Now plea lacked specifics it conveyed a strong desire to see him bring back a peace agreement.

On September 2, 1978, the day before the Israeli delegation departed for Washington, Peace Now organized a farewell demonstration in Tel Aviv. The public mood was conducive to such an event. There was little controversy over the gathering's intent, which implied support for Begin not only as Israel's prime minister but also as Israel's best hope for successfully concluding the negotiations. Over 100,000 citizens marched in a procession from the Tel Aviv Museum to the Kings of Israel Square in front of the town hall. Posters read, "Mr. Begin, Go in Peace and Return with Peace!" Delegations from the Jewish diaspora participated, calling on Begin "to utter one great word, Yes!"[75] In a letter Begin sent to the prominent Israeli author Amos Oz months later, Begin remarked that while at Camp David he could not stop thinking of the 100,000 citizens who had beseeched him to return home with a peace agreement. Moshe Arens, a confidant of Begin who later served as Israel's ambassador to Washington and minister of defense, and who opposed the Camp David Accords and subsequent peace treaty, blamed Peace Now for pushing Begin to make unnecessary concessions.[76] Whatever the impact of this huge demonstration on subsequent events, it certainly surpassed the expectations of the organizers and placed Peace Now, for a brief period, at the center of the national consensus.

The details of the negotiations at Camp David have been adequately recorded by others.[77] It will suffice here to make two general comments. First, notwithstanding the rationalizations Sadat and Begin later made, one thing stands out. They each made one painful concession that had previously been unthinkable and had blocked the negotiations up to that point. Begin accepted the withdrawal of Israel from the entire Sinai Peninsula. This "up-to-the-last-inch" concession required relinquishing the airfields that Israel had built, as well as the dismantling of the town of Yamit and a dozen other villages in Sinai. For his part, Sadat withdrew his demand for a simultaneous solution to the Palestinian question. Despite his continued commitment to the rights of the Palestinians, Sadat in essence concluded a separate peace with Israel.[78]

Second, it seems certain that both Sadat and Begin made these painful concessions at least in part due to a misconception. Both believed that future progress would be guided by the precise wording of the Camp David agreement. Sadat believed that Israel's commitment to recognize "the legitimate rights of the Palestinian people and their just requirements" included the creation of a transitional regime in the West Bank and Gaza based on "full autonomy," which would lead to open negotiations "to determine the final status of the West Bank and Gaza."[79] He thus honestly believed that these accords fulfilled his obligation to the Palestinians and paved the way for their deliverance from Israeli occupation. For his part, Begin had the illusion that by establishing a formal veto power concerning the fate of the territories he could assure future Israeli control over them for the long run. Both Sadat's and Begin's beliefs proved unfounded. Both thought they had achieved their objectives without paying in Palestinian currency; both turned out to be wrong.

The Camp David Accords and the subsequent peace treaty created a paradox for the peace movement. After ten years of struggle the peace movement watched with amazement as the prime minister it most vociferously opposed achieved the first dramatic breakthrough in the Arab-Israeli conflict, and concluded peace with the strongest and most populous Arab nation.[80]

Flowers for a Victor

This was indeed the great achievement of Menachem Begin, and Peace Now gladly acknowledged it. On September 22 Begin was welcomed at Lod Airport and at the entrance to Jerusalem by members of Peace Now with thousands of flowers and signs reading, "We Are All with You on the Road to Peace!" Many in the movement thought that their role had ended, but within a few weeks it became clear that their relief was premature.

The Camp David Accords provided only a "Framework for an Agreement," the details of which remained to be worked out by the parties. General Avraham Tamir, who led the Israeli military team, observed that the Palestinian issue left many unanswered questions, "since the basis which was put to it [in the Accords] was thin and nebulous."[81] When the Israeli and Egyptian delegations met at Blair House in Washington on October 12 to work out the details, many of the problems that had tormented the negotiators before Camp David reappeared, and by the beginning of November an impasse had again been reached. The military and territorial issues concerning the Israeli withdrawal from the Sinai were not especially problematic.[82] The primary difficulty arose from conflicting interpretations of the Palestinian issue and around the linkage the Egyptians sought to maintain between the Palestinian question and the normalization of relations between Egypt and Israel.[83]

Another point of contention that added tension to Carter and Begin's relationship involved the resumption of new settlements in the occupied territories. Carter believed that during the negotiations at Camp David, Begin had agreed to freeze new settlements throughout the negotiations, whereas Begin understood that this freeze was limited to three months only.[84]

Details of the negotiations in Washington and the exact cause of the deadlock were unknown to the public at the time, but the stalemate gave cause for renewed concern within Peace Now. For a few months the movement limited itself to low-key activities. At first the peace activists praised the autonomy plan and tried to convince the Palestinian leadership, which had condemned it, that it was the beginning of an open-ended process that would not limit their pursuit of Palestinian independence. But the subsequent publication of a more detailed plan for Palestinian "self-rule" by the government indicated that Begin sought to foreclose such options.

When the deadlock between Washington and Jerusalem had become evident, Peace Now gathered its circle of activists for consultation. On December 5, 1978, the activists unanimously concluded that the movement's role had not ended, and they decided to shift the focus of their activities from the negotiations with Egypt to the Palestinian problem. The demand for direct negotiations with the Palestinians and the struggle against new settlements were now the group's primary objectives.

The movement planned nightly torch parades under the slogan "Shed Light on Peace" but postponed them when the negotiations seemed to be regaining momentum. This last-minute cancellation highlighted another feature of Peace Now's methods. Mass demonstrations required a high degree of dissatisfaction among potential participants. Once events significantly reduced the level of energy among sympathizers, a demonstration could fail and even become counterproductive. The leadership routinely sought to measure the willingness of sympathizers to take to the streets, and preferred to err on the side of caution. The complexity and fluidity of the negotiations in Washington did not provide the movement with clear opportunities for successful large-scale street activity.[85]

During the winter of 1979 negotiations dragged on intermittently. Carter feared a complete breakdown of the talks and decided "to arrive on the shore before the storm broke out."[86] He met with Begin in Washington, and the United States and Israel finally arrived at some understandings. Even so, a trip by Carter to the Middle East was still necessary to achieve a final agreement. On March 10, 1979, Carter arrived in Israel, where he was welcomed simultaneously by opposing demonstrations in Jerusalem. Peace Now greeted him warmly while Gush Emunim shouted "Carter Go Home!"[87] Carter gave a speech at the Knesset, which was received politely out of respect for the visiting dignitary. The same was not the case for the speeches delivered by Begin and opposition leader Shimon Peres, which were constantly disrupted by hecklers from the extreme right and left. "It was not the Knesset's finest hour," observed Dayan.[88] Nonetheless, Carter's visit brought the hard bargaining to an end. Final proposals were drafted and Begin brought them to the Knesset for approval.

Peace Now decided to lobby Knesset members from different parties in an effort to gain their support for the proposed peace agreement (a method the activists would often use in the future) but discovered it was hardly necessary. Despite harsh criticism regarding the way the negotiations had been handled by the government and reservations over some details of the agreement, the Labor Party voted in favor and the treaty was ratified by an overwhelming majority of ninety-five to eighteen. In a rare departure from parliamentary norms, Knesset members from Labor and Likud were informed by their respective party leaderships that they could vote according to their conscience and that party discipline should not be a factor. Most of the "no" votes and some abstentions came from the ranks of Begin's own Likud. Yitzhak Shamir, who became Israel's prime minister five years later, opposed the agreement but chose to abstain in consideration of his special position as Speaker of the Knesset.[89]

On March 26, 1979, sixteen months after Sadat's visit to Jerusalem, the Egyptian-Israeli Peace Treaty was signed in a ceremony on the south lawn of the White House. A few days later Sadat invited Begin to Cairo, a visit the Israeli prime minister had coveted for some time. Begin was ecstatic. In a telephone call from Cairo to Washington he expressed his jubilation. "The people of Egypt opened their hearts to me," he told Carter. "I went into the crowd which was crying, 'We like you, we love you!'"[90] This reception was well deserved but turned out to be the last time Begin would enjoy such a welcome. The hard work of implementing the treaty remained ahead. The retreat of Israeli forces and the normalization of bilateral relations proceeded as planned, but negotiations over legitimate Palestinian rights soon reached a new impasse.

Peace Now versus Gush Emunim

Within Israel the issue of settlements now took center stage. Gush Emunim and Sharon's rejectionist wing within Likud decided to use further settlements to stall the negotiations, or at least to make sure that no concessions with regard to the West Bank and Gaza would be made.

The settlement efforts during 1979 were based only partly on official government decisions, as Begin sought to avoid further aggravating his relationship with President Carter. Some of the activities were illegal, though it was clear that Sharon was privy to these endeavors and supported them in one way or another.

At the beginning of January 1979 the Elon Moreh group, which during Labor's tenure had tried to settle a number of times in and around Nablus, squatted on land confiscated from Palestinian farmers from the village of Rugeib, a few miles east of Nablus. Peace Now voiced its objection and looked for an opportunity to confront the settlers. The main showdown took place in Rugeib on June 9 and 10. More than 4,000 peaceniks blocked the dirt road leading to the new settlement and refused to clear the way until Ezer Weizman came and heard their grievances. At eight the next morning Weizman arrived by helicopter. Tzali Reshef, Peace Now's spokesman, explained to Weizman that building a civilian settlement on land confiscated from Arab farmers was illegal. Weizman halted work on the settlement and promised to bring the matter up for consideration before the cabinet; the demonstrators kept their word and cleared the road.[91] Before leaving the area they lit a "Torch of Sanity," which was brought to the Knesset Plaza a few days later while the issue was being debated inside. In another demonstration attended by 25,000 participants in Tel Aviv on June 16, 1979, a ceremony reminiscent of the lighting of the Olympic flame took place in which a large torch in the center of the rally was lit by the torch carried from Rugeib by Peace Now youths.[92]

The struggle over Rugeib eventually progressed to the Supreme Court. Peace Now helped the Palestinian farmers present a formal petition challenging the legality of the confiscation of their land for civil purposes. General Chaim Bar-Lev, the former chief of staff, testified that the new settlement had no particular security significance. The government called on other military experts to challenge Bar-Lev's testimony. The settlers, however, viewed this case as a struggle over principles and voluntarily admitted that their motivation for settling the confiscated area had nothing to do with security considerations. They claimed in court that the historic rights of the Jewish people justified their actions, which therefore should be recognized as legitimate. After hearing this testimony the Supreme Court declared the confiscation of the land null and void.

The government tried to circumvent the Court's order, arguing that the settlers remained only on a few patches of land that did not legally belong to the farmers. The attempt to ignore the Supreme Court's decision generated considerable criticism from several quarters. On January 5, 1980, Peace Now again blocked the road to the settlement. This time the protesters brought heavy equipment and welding tools, and blocked the road with large concrete blocks and chained themselves to the blocks and trucks. They unknowingly trapped Ariel Sharon (who happened to be visiting the site with guests) inside the settlement for three hours. For Peace Now this was a symbolic victory because Sharon, more than anyone, epitomized the despised settlement policies of the Likud government.[93] Eventually the government relented, adhered to the Court's decision, and removed the settlers from Rugeib. This was a Pyrrhic victory for Peace Now, however, because the settlers were immediately resettled on a hill a few miles to the north, this time on government land.

Peace Now versus Menachem Begin

As 1979 dragged on it became clear that negotiations on the portion of the peace treaty that dealt with the Palestinians led to a dead end. As laid out in the agreement, an Israeli-Egyptian Commission was established to negotiate the implementation of the autonomy plan. The Egyptians agreed to begin the discussions even though the Jordanians and

Palestinians who were invited to participate declined to do so. Joseph Burg, the minister of interior from the NRP, was selected by Begin to head the Israeli delegation.[94] Burg was considered a moderate, but under the influence of Gush Emunim his party now took a position on the territories to the right of Begin himself. Begin chose Burg over Moshe Dayan, the more logical choice, because the prime minister wanted to appease the hawks inside his own party and to assure them that he had no intention of yielding Israel's control over the territories.[95] These negotiations soon became deadlocked, with the Israeli proposals being far from satisfactory to the Egyptians, let alone the Palestinians.[96] It surprised few when Moshe Dayan resigned from the cabinet in frustration.

Dayan's resignation was soon followed by Weizman's. These resignations clearly signaled that Begin's government was unwilling to relinquish control over the West Bank and Gaza Strip. To some observers it appeared that Begin was regretting the concessions he had made at Camp David and had decided to return to his original plan—namely, to gain a free hand in the West Bank and Gaza as the price for his total retreat from Sinai. In a cabinet meeting on May 3, 1979, in which he presented his narrow interpretation of the autonomy plan, he declared, "I shall not allow my old age to shame my youth. I was born a son of the Land of Israel and I shall remain that until my last day. This government was formed in order to guard the Land of Israel."[97]

To most peace activists it became evident that Begin was unwilling to translate the initial breakthrough into a comprehensive peace settlement, and certainly would not reach a negotiated agreement with the Palestinians. In a demonstration held in June 1980 the peace activists set up a giant hourglass to symbolize that time for peace was running out. After listing the government's shortcomings and the dangers they posed for the nation, a flyer distributed by the movement concluded, "Every day this government continues to rule is another day of danger, loss of hope, moral corruption and national malaise. . . . Let us together advance the elections! Let us say to this government: Your way is not our way! Go home!"[98] The peace movement was now explicitly pitted against the incumbent government.

6

Consolidation, 1980-81

Marching On

During 1980 and the early months of 1981 Peace Now experienced a period of relative stagnation. Unlike political parties, which have changing agendas and address numerous issues, Peace Now (like many other protest movements) was essentially reactive in nature, its activities being undertaken in response to particular events and government decisions. Consequently, the prevailing political environment and public mood were important variables in generating participation in Peace Now activities.

Compared with the dramatic events of 1978 and 1979, the political environment at the outset of the 1980s seemed rather bleak and the future uncertain. The autonomy talks dragged on in Alexandria and Herzliyyah (north of Tel Aviv), but the gaps between the Egyptian and Israeli positions seemed to be widening. With Dayan and Weizman having resigned, Begin was freed from the moderating influence of the two former generals. His policies and gestures conveyed the message that he had no intention of relinquishing Israeli control of the West Bank, Gaza Strip, or the Golan Heights.[1]

This intransigent position was shared by a majority in the Knesset, which in July 1980 passed a Basic Law affirming Israel's claim to Jerusalem as the "sole and indivisible capital of Israel."[2] This act, condemned by the international community, was initiated by MK Geula Cohen, who had previously defected from Likud to form a new party, Tehiya (Renaissance), which strongly opposed the peace treaty with Egypt. In December 1981 Likud introduced a resolution in the Knesset that resulted in the formal annexation of the Golan Heights.[3] In another largely symbolic move the cabinet decided to move the prime minister's office to the Arab side of East Jerusalem.[4] Peace Now denounced these unnecessary moves, but because they were little more than dramatic gestures the movement was unable to generate widespread public protest.

The government's actions also angered the Reagan administration, which publicly opposed the unilateral Israeli decisions. The United States suspended the Memorandum of Understanding on strategic cooperation, which Secretary of Defense Caspar Weinberger had reluctantly signed with Israel only a few weeks earlier. Some financial transactions were also frozen. Although the American moves did not amount to serious pressure on Israel, Begin was incensed, and in a public tirade announced that Israel was not a "banana republic" of the United States.[5]

But Ronald Reagan was deeply committed to the security of the Jewish state and considered Israel "a major strategic asset of America."[6] His administration's main concern was American-Soviet rivalry in the region, especially after the fall of the Shah in 1978 and the Soviet invasion of Afghanistan in December 1979.[7] Moreover, the administration opposed the creation of a Palestinian state, and the breakdown of the autonomy talks did not lead to American pressure on Israel of the degree exerted by President Carter a year earlier. Begin's intransigent policies seemed to meet with American indifference.[8]

Sadat, on the other hand, grew increasingly indignant over the pace and substance of the negotiations and vented his feelings by sending Begin strongly worded appeals, particularly on the issue of Jerusalem. Negotiations on the future status of Jerusalem held special importance for Sadat in view of his growing isolation in the Arab and Islamic world, and his personal attachment to the holy shrines as a devout Muslim. However, beyond sending these letters there was little Sadat could do lest he jeopardize the scheduled withdrawal of Israeli forces from the Sinai and risk a collapse of his peace initiative. By the end of 1980 the autonomy talks had been suspended; they were not resumed until a decade later.[9]

During 1980–81 Peace Now developed a strong inner circle of a few hundred devoted activists who were convinced that the peace treaty with Egypt would lose much of its value if it could not be broadened into

a comprehensive Middle East peace agreement. At this stage the movement adopted a long-term approach and tried to recruit new members,
especially young people who had recently completed their military service. Peace Now also tried to attract young Israelis before they entered
their military service. Youth groups were established in a number of
high schools. In May 1980 a large youth rally was held in a Tel Aviv park.
In December a bicycle marathon from Tel Dan in the north to Eilat in the
south was organized by these new young activists, who distributed the
movement's pamphlets and carried its banner along their six-day route.[10]

Early in Peace Now's development it became evident that a large measure of ethnic, social, and economic homogeneity existed throughout the
movement. Most members were well-educated, well-off Ashkenazim—
and their personal closeness was cemented by their similar life histories.
Most of the activists' parents had been born in Israel, or had come to the
country as idealistic pioneers before the establishment of the state. The
activists themselves generally shared a common experience in one of the
country's socialist youth movements during the late 1950s and 1960s,
had typically spent a few years in a kibbutz, and had served in the Israeli
Defense Forces and were veterans of at least one of the wars since 1967.
Many knew one another from their days at university, where they had
often participated in left-of-center political groups. Many had also been
involved in the protests after the 1973 war. As a result of these similar
experiences and backgrounds the core of Peace Now looked and sounded
very much alike.[11]

Peace Now's right-wing opponents also had their similarities. Most
were young Mizrachim—Jews of North African and Middle Eastern de-
scent—from poorer neighborhoods, who were alienated from the socialist, Zionist legacy shared by most Peace Now activists. Although Peace
Now sought to diversify its membership, there were a number of obstacles to including the Mizrachim, not least because they were likely to
be Likud supporters with a hawkish outlook.[12] The movement took the
strategic decision to attract Mizrachim by developing ad hoc coalitions
with groups rather than by attempting direct recruitment of individuals,
who often felt uncomfortable at movement meetings amid a cadre of
Ashkenazi intellectuals. Greater success was achieved when Mizrachi
groups were approached and invited to participate as self-organized
groups. This allowed Mizrachim to assert themselves as equals.

The Jerusalem-based Black Panthers were natural allies, having been
associated with left-wing radicals since the early 1970s, when young
Moroccans in the Musrara area had formed the group to protest social

inequalities.[13] Peace Now and the Black Panthers jointly organized a demonstration intended to raise awareness of social justice as a national priority and an alternative to the expensive settlement efforts in the occupied territories. The demand to stop wasting the nation's limited resources on new settlements in the territories and to redirect them to economically depressed areas inside the Green Line was used to establish a relationship between social and economic justice and peace issues.[14] The connection between Peace Now and the Black Panthers was short-lived, however, because of the collapse of the latter movement.

Peace Now's reputation spread quickly throughout the Jewish diaspora. Left-wing Zionist youth movements and student groups in Europe and the United States contacted activists in Israel and requested more information. Invitations for Peace Now representatives to come and explain the movement's objectives arrived from different Jewish communities. Initially the propriety of political advocacy abroad was debated within the movement, with some activists considering it improper to wash Israel's dirty laundry on foreign soil. However, since the international media had already amply reported on the internal controversies in Israeli politics, Peace Now decided that there seemed no good reason why the debate should not also be waged by Jews abroad. Furthermore, this practice conformed with previous Zionist norms. Other political parties and factions had always advertised their agendas and solicited financial support from Jews in the diaspora.

The first organized opportunity to meet with sympathetic Jews abroad came when *New Outlook* convened a conference in Washington, D.C., in October 1979. This was the first attempt to reach out to North American Jews in an effort to put peace issues on the agenda of American Jewry. Peace Now's small delegation attracted considerable attention. After the meeting the group proceeded to Montreal, where it participated in the General Assembly of the Council of Jewish Federations.[15] In a special session, attended by a few hundred Jewish community leaders, the Peace Now delegation explained the nature and aims of the movement. Chapters of "Friends of Peace Now" were soon established around the world, and raised badly needed financial support that helped defray the growing expenses of the movement's intensified activities.[16]

Peace Now and the Palestinians

Peace Now's activities in opposition to the Gush Emunim settlers were often conducted in or near Arab villages or towns in the West Bank.

This inevitably led to contacts between the peace activists and Palestinians in the occupied territories, and a dialogue soon began. On May 21, 1980, several dozen Peace Now activists went to the town of Beit Sahour (east of Bethlehem) to visit the home of a Palestinian, a retired officer in the Jordanian army, whom the Israeli military governor had ordered temporarily deported to Jericho in response to a violent riot in which the Palestinian's son had participated. In another case a group went to Hebron to protest the repeated harassment by the settlers of Kiryat Arba of an old Palestinian widow whose house, in the eyes of the settlers, was situated too close to their settlement's fences. Peace Now activists soon established a relationship with some of the Palestinian leaders of Hebron, including the deposed mayor Abd el Nabi Natshe.[17]

Such dialogues were often initiated by individual activists prior to receiving formal approval from the peace movement. Thus, for example, a group of Jewish peaceniks from Jerusalem and a group of Palestinians from Beit Sahour organized weekly meetings held alternatively in Palestinian and Jewish homes. These informal initiatives, which continued for years and led to the development of close friendships between Palestinians and Israelis, were welcomed by Peace Now. Early in the 1980s, though, the movement began to develop more formal relationships with a group of Palestinian leaders who were soon to gain national stature. The Israeli activists invited some of the Palestinians to participate in a public dialogue intended to expose the Israeli public to the existence of moderate Palestinian opinion in the occupied territories. The movement also organized Palestinian mayors and other public figures in West Bank and Gaza towns to help educate the Palestinian public about the political and psychological constraints with which even moderate Israelis were grappling.[18]

Despite this ongoing dialogue the movement was careful to distance itself from acts of violence perpetrated by Palestinians and from those who supported such methods. For example, Peace Now publicly denounced Bassam Shak'a, the nationalist mayor of Nablus, when he praised and endorsed acts of terror.[19] Peace Now carefully defined its role in this regard as listening to the "enemy" and interpreting its views to Israelis in the hope that this would assist in eventual conciliation.[20]

An important difference of opinion that led to a heated debate between Peace Now and its Palestinian interlocutors centered on the form and sequence of negotiations laid out in the peace treaty with Egypt. Despite a growing disillusionment with the autonomy talks, the idea of beginning the Israeli-Palestinian peace process with an interim phase of self-rule seemed to Peace Now a wise approach. The Palestinians, however, would have nothing of it and stood at the forefront of opposition to Sadat and his initiative. The adamant criticism and widespread Arab condemnation of Sadat were viewed as a critical mistake by Peace Now, which believed that autonomy, if honestly implemented, could open new options for broader self-determination later.

Back in 1976 Rabin's government had permitted the Palestinians to hold municipal elections in the occupied territories. In 1978 the new mayors, most of whom were supporters of the PLO and its different factions,[21] established the Committee for National Guidance, which soon became the de facto representation of the PLO inside the occupied territories.[22] During 1980 and 1981, they were instrumental in mobilizing Palestinian public opinion against the Egyptian-Israeli Peace Treaty. All this did not deter Peace Now from pursuing contacts with even the most extreme nationalist leaders. If Israeli authorities viewed these mayors as the representatives of their constituencies, why should the movement not deal with them similarly?

The attitudes of peace activists toward the PLO, and contacts with PLO representatives outside the occupied territories, was another contentious matter. Peace Now adopted the position that as long as the PLO did not officially recognize Israel, and continued to undertake and support acts of terror, Israelis should refrain from dealing directly with it. This position grew out of the concern shared by many Peace Now activists of being marginalized within Israeli public opinion—as indeed happened to the Israel-Palestine Council when it maintained contacts with PLO representatives throughout this period.[23]

This issue caused the most serious internal crisis the movement had yet faced, nearly crippling it. Early in October 1980 two central figures in Peace Now, Dedi Zucker and Yael Tamir, traveled to Europe on behalf of the movement.[24] During a brief stay in Vienna they went beyond their mandate and secretly met with Issam Sartawi, the PLO official responsible for contacts with Israelis. Sartawi had previously held numerous meetings with Israelis from the Avneri-Eliav circle, and there was nothing extraordinary about such an encounter. However, the clandestine meeting with an official of the PLO by official representatives of Peace Now violated movement policy. Moreover, Zucker and Tamir had neither consulted with their colleagues nor received prior permission for such a meeting. There were several heated verbal exchanges and calls for the censure and removal of Zucker and Tamir, but no formal action was ultimately taken because the two resigned and terminated their involvement with Peace Now.[25]

A number of other core activists also left the movement, apparently from displeasure at the changes that had occurred in its character as it had grown. Omri Padan, an economics student and a veteran of the most elite combat unit of the IDF, resigned from his post as the movement's first spokesperson, claiming he no longer found himself at home in Peace Now, which he felt had lost the intimacy of the founding group. A number of other active members including Yuval Neria and Amos Arieli (the son of Yehoshua Arieli, the leader of Peace and Security in the late 1960s) also expressed a sense of alienation.[26] Although these were major blows to the movement's leadership, the base of activists was strong enough to enable Peace Now to overcome the crisis, and the remaining leadership managed to close ranks and continue the struggle.

By the end of 1980 Peace Now had become a recognizable voice on the Israeli political stage. In the eyes of many people on the right, it was seen as a nuisance and as a negative influence in Israeli politics. A few even went so far as to accuse the activists of treason. A growing number of people on the left, however, viewed the movement sympathetically; the number of active members grew; and the movement solidified. At the end of October 1980, a few weeks after the crisis over the meeting with Sartawi subsided, the movement held a conference in the Nation's Hall in Jerusalem, which attracted more than 2,000 participants. The conference's theme was "Zionism Now!"—a challenge to Gush Emunim's claim that it alone adhered to genuine Zionism.[27]

Thirty Minutes from Tel Aviv—Settlements on the Open Market

Although Peace Now continued its struggle against Gush Emunim and the settlement movement, nowhere were its practical limitations more obvious. The settlers had full policy support from the Begin government, and small groups were now scattered throughout the hills of Judea and Samaria in makeshift caravan camps or temporary wooden huts. Rabbi Moshe Levinger, who in 1968 had squatted in the Arab town of Hebron and eventually established the new Jewish town of Kiryat Arba on its outskirts, now sought to settle in the heart of Arab Hebron, near the tombs of the Patriarchs, where in 1929 the Jewish community had been massacred by Arabs.

A group of women from Kiryat Arba, led by Mrs. Levinger, squatted in a house known as the Hadassah Building, which had been owned by Jews before the 1929 massacre. On September 17, 1979, a group of religious orthodox activists from Peace Now went to Hebron to demonstrate against the plan to build a new yeshiva on the site of the old synagogue in the Arab market. Despite the demonstrations the yeshiva was built. A few months later six of its students were murdered in the streets of Hebron. Peace Now denounced the murders as "another tragedy . . . in the bloody cycle in which terrorists and hooligans dictate the turn of events."[28]

With little publicity, Ariel Sharon, who was in charge of the Land Authority as well as agriculture minister in Begin's first cabinet, opened the occupied territories to private entrepreneurs, offering them generous subsidies as incentives. Israelis who were prepared to relocate to new towns and villages that were being constructed throughout the occupied territories were tempted with cheap land and government funding of all infrastructure costs. Advertisements depicted affordable luxury villas with beautiful landscapes "only 30 minutes from Tel Aviv." Sharon's scheme was to settle the West Bank with Jews who would be willing to commute to the industrial and commercial centers of Israel while living in modern and spacious housing across the Green Line. The deals on land and housing afforded those who were prepared to resettle better conditions than they could ever dream of enjoying in their squalid and congested old neighborhoods.[29] Sharon's clever strategy could attract more people than could Gush Emunim's messianic crusade. And while Peace Now could confront Gush Emunim on ideological and legal grounds, it was far more difficult to persuade families who were motivated not by ideology or religion but by the desire to dramatically improve their quality of life.

Within a few years the Jewish population of Judea and Samaria quadrupled.[30] To secure enough land, Sharon confiscated large areas under the formal ownership of the Jordanian monarch or with no clear evidence of ownership. Lands were often sequestered in cases where the resident Arabs, though they had lived and worked on the plots for generations, could not easily document their ownership rights. By 1982 more than 40 percent of the West Bank lands had been secured by the military authorities for Jewish use.[31]

Intransigence with Impunity

Begin now seemed determined to limit peace with Egypt to a mere bilateral agreement that would include a full withdrawal from the Sinai but have no bearing on Israel's control over the remaining occupied territories.

Israel meticulously fulfilled its obligations under the treaty, handing back the last of the Sinai in April 1982, but Begin's government pursued its relations with the other Arab states and the Palestinians as it saw fit.

Egypt also honored its end of the agreement. It exchanged ambassadors with Israel, opened the borders, and normalized relations.[32] Although very few Egyptians visited Israel and almost no commercial relations developed, Israeli ships now passed freely through the Suez Canal, and the ability to visit the pyramids and other ancient sites gave many Israelis a tangible sense of the dramatic change the peace with Egypt had brought.

There was, however, no progress on the Palestinian issue. Sadat symbolically expressed his displeasure with Begin when he refused to go to Oslo to receive the Nobel Peace Prize jointly awarded to him and Begin.[33]

On October 6, 1981, while reviewing a military parade at the commemoration of the crossing of the Suez Canal during the War of Ramadan—the October 1973 war—Sadat was cut down by assassins' bullets. Though the assassination probably had more to do with domestic controversies than with Sadat's Israel policy,[34] many were reminded of the fate of Jordan's King Abdullah, who had been murdered thirty years earlier for his collaboration with the Zionists. As the dust settled and events returned to normal, Israel was relieved to discover that despite the tragedy the new Egyptian regime headed by Hosni Mubarak was stable and adhered to the peace treaty.

The 1981 Elections

Elections to the Tenth Knesset were scheduled for June 30, 1981. Polls taken late in 1979 indicated a sharp decline in the popularity of Begin and Likud[35]—a decline that had less to do with peace and security issues than with domestic problems. Mismanagement of the economy and other internal issues laid at the door of Likud made the return of Labor to power a much stronger possibility as the summer of 1981 approached. However, while the Labor Party grew increasingly complacent about its prospects at the forthcoming elections, the fear that they would have to return to the opposition after only four years in power instilled fresh vigor and determination in Begin and his supporters.

Likud conducted a campaign marked by an aggressiveness and stridency of a degree previously unknown in Israeli politics. A police spokesman noted that "there hasn't been an election campaign in Israel as violent as the present one."[36] Much of the campaign turned into a personality contest between Menachem Begin and Labor leader Shimon Peres. The battle between Likud and Labor polarized Mizrachim (especially of Moroccan origin, who overwhelmingly supported Begin) and Labor supporters. To many observers the chant "Begin is the King of Israel!" frequently heard at Likud campaign rallies had a distinct North African accent.

At a February 1981 meeting Peace Now considered its strategy for the campaign. An overwhelming majority rejected the idea of forming a new party that would campaign on the peace agenda. Nor did most activists support the idea of identifying exclusively with one of the dovish parties, partly because to do so would have damaged Peace Now's nonpartisan base, and partly because the choice was far from clear. Several existing small parties could identify with the positions adopted by Peace Now, among them Shulamit Aloni's Ratz, Amnon Rubinstein's Shinui, and the left-wing coalition of Sheli. Significant parts of the Labor Alignment, including Mapam and dovish Laborites, also identified with Peace Now's positions though not always openly with the movement itself. Aloni, eager to attract the nonaffiliated followers of Peace Now, changed her party's name by adding the word "Peace" and invited Dedi Zucker and Yael Tamir to join its list of candidates.[37]

Many Peace Now activists wished to remain loyal to their longtime party affiliations. The remaining unaffiliated activists created a committee that drafted a position statement dealing with issues pertaining to the Arab-Israeli conflict. They circulated this to the different parties, attempting to persuade them to incorporate it into their election platforms. Ratz, Sheli, and Shinui readily accepted the statement, but the Labor Party had to be pushed.

Circle 77

In August 1977, in response to Labor's election defeat, a group of teachers and graduate students from the Hebrew University in Jerusalem had joined the Labor Party and sought to reform the party from within. They called themselves "Chug Avoda 77" (the 77 Working Circle).[38] In a letter to Shimon Peres they explained that they sought "to create a national working circle" that would "endeavor to refresh the Labor Party and its ideological path." They envisaged three primary courses of action: refining the party's ideology, public campaigning, and reforming the party's structure. They also supported "territorial compromise in the Sinai, the Golan, the West Bank and Gaza," and pledged to achieve "a constructive partnership between the intelligentsia . . . and other strata [of the party's membership] such as farmers, laborers and youth." They would also "assist in the building of a new leadership for the party which will reflect its new image."[39]

Peres had replaced Yitzhak Rabin as prime minister in the final days of the Labor regime.[40] Unable to rescue the party from its 1977 defeat, Peres saw his main tasks as the renewal and reform of the party and promised to lead it to victory in 1981. He must have been pleased to receive the letter from Circle 77, which coincided with his own aspirations "to assure that the year 1977 will turn out to be a turning point which will lead to a renaissance in the organizational and ideological makeup of the Labor Party . . . and will pave the way to the recapturing of its hegemony in the state and the Israeli society."[41] He invited a few of the leaders from Circle 77 to join the party's Central Committee, and two were even appointed observers to the powerful Central Bureau (Halishka).[42]

Circle 77 shared similar views with Peace Now activists on peace and security issues but pursued a broader agenda.[43] The young academics of Circle 77 published numerous papers on such diverse issues as the future of the powerful Israeli trade union Histadrut, the question of the separation of religion and state, and the method for selecting party candidates to the Knesset. "We did not have large troops," Amnon Sella remembered, "but we had a lot of prestige and heavy qualitative weight." However, in the final analysis, Circle 77 was undercut by the Labor Party's politicos and defeated on all levels. Its candidate for the Knesset did not make it to a "safe" slot, and even in the fight for secondary positions on the local level—such as the position of the party secretary in Jerusalem—its candidate was easily defeated by a coalition of party apparatchiks. In these matters, long-standing personal and political loyalties took precedence over other considerations.

As the elections drew nearer, Circle 77 lobbied for a more dovish party platform. Similarly motivated, a group of a few hundred Peace Now activists demonstrated outside the hall where security issues were being debated and called on the party leadership to adopt an unambivalent peace policy.[44] Unfortunately, "the overriding concern of the party leaders [was] the manipulative semblance of unity and avoidance of rift, rather than the honest groping with the real stuff and substance of politics."[45] Neither those who fought inside nor those who shouted outside managed to soften the Labor Party's platform on issues concerning the Arab-Israeli conflict. The party continued to adhere to the Jordanian Option and the so-called territorial compromise, even though King Hussein continued to refrain from committing himself to any compromise along the lines envisaged in the Allon Plan. It seemed as if the Labor leadership could conceive of an agreement with the Palestinians only within the framework of a Palestinian-Jordanian political entity, which very few Palestinians would accept.[46]

Anyone But Likud!

As the election campaign heated up, many Peace Now activists participated in partisan struggles within their respective parties, and those who remained outside of party frameworks sought other means of participation. A trend developed among left-wing activists to vote for the Labor Party rather than to dilute their collective strength by distributing their votes among the smaller parties on the left.[47] The slogan "Anyone But Likud!" became popular within the peace movement. Some of the smaller leftist parties later claimed that this slogan cost them many votes because it was interpreted by their constituents as implying "Vote Labor!"

As election day approached Begin rose to meet the occasion.[48] He campaigned as aggressively as if he was still in the opposition fighting against the Labor establishment.[49] Out of desperation he allowed his new minister of finance, Yoram Aridor, to run an "elections economy" in which he expended scarce resources to bring about a temporary increase in the standard of living of many Israelis. The most visible result of Aridor's ploy was a proliferation of relatively inexpensive color televisions.[50]

Begin, who had personally assumed the minister of defense portfolio after Weizman's resignation, took a hard line as tensions rose on Israel's northern border with Lebanon. On April 28, 1981, an Israeli aircraft shot down two Syrian helicopters over the town of Zahle. This triggered a crisis when Syria responded by introducing Soviet-made surface-to-air missiles into the Bekaa Valley.[51] On June 7, 1981, three weeks before the elections, Israel attacked and destroyed Iraq's Osirak nuclear reactor.[52] Begin justified the attack as self-defense and argued that he had saved Israel from another Holocaust. The daring and tactically impressive air strike provided Begin with a resurgence of domestic popularity.[53]

The election results produced a virtual draw, with an impressive showing for Labor but not enough to oust Likud. Labor gained fifteen seats, rising from thirty-two to forty-seven MKs. But Likud also increased its representation, from forty-three to forty-eight seats, mostly from heavily Mizrachi areas.[54] The smaller parties on the left virtually disappeared—Aloni's Ratz party returning only one member, Shinui two, and Sheli not gaining enough votes to qualify for even one seat. Likud remained the largest faction in the Knesset, and only Begin was strong enough to form a coalition, which he did with the help of other right-wing and religious parties.[55]

In his new cabinet, Begin appointed Ariel Sharon minister of defense and Yitzhak Shamir minister of foreign affairs; both opposed the peace treaty with Egypt. Peace with Egypt had become a fact of life but generated little hope for a comprehensive peace.[56]

Ariel Sharon, the Palestinians, and the PLO

A sense of frustration overtook the peace movement, and for more than six months during the second half of 1981 Peace Now remained inactive. The movement's offices were deserted and meetings were rarely convened. Most of the activists now viewed the movement in nostalgic terms rather than as part of an ongoing crusade. Considering the pace of Sharon's settlement policy, it seemed there would be little to struggle for by the time the next elections arrived.

With Egypt neutralized as a strategic threat, Sharon set his mind to ending—or at least reducing—the PLO's influence in Palestinian politics. This led to the pursuit of two objectives, the first military and the second political. The first was to eliminate the numerous bases that various Palestinian guerrilla factions had established in Lebanon after their 1970 expulsion from Jordan. The second objective was to counter the growing popularity of the PLO inside the occupied territories, where it had made impressive progress in politically mobilizing large numbers of Palestinians.

Some Israelis criticized the Labor governments, and especially Dayan, for their policies in the territories, which had, in the critics' opinion, weakened the pro-Hashemite elements in the Palestinian community and paved the way for the PLO's gains.[57] Shortly before the 1981 elections Menachem Milson, an Israeli expert on early Islamic literature and philosophy, published an article in which he argued that the inroads made by the PLO had been assisted by Israel's ignorance of the use of patronage in Arab politics.[58] Milson was not a Likud supporter and actually seemed to be an advocate of the Jordanian Option supported by the Labor Party.[59] His chief criticism of the policies implemented by Labor leaders in the occupied territories during the 1970s was that, by not seeking to restrict PLO activities in the territories, they had unwittingly aided the development of a rejectionist Palestinian attitude opposed to any peace proposal, including peace with Egypt. He emphasized the need for a political compromise that only Jordan and moderate Palestinians were capable of, but which could not be achieved as long as the PLO maintained its grip over the Palestinians, either by patronage or intimidation.

It is unclear whether Sharon understood the intricacies of Milson's views or was merely interested in his prognosis. "This situation," Milson wrote, "was not inevitable, and is not irreversible." There are ways, he argued, "to free the population of the territories from the grip of the PLO."[60] As minister of defense by the end of 1981, Sharon asked Milson to implement his ideas on the ground. Sharon's first act was to separate the military aspects of the occupation from civilian matters. A new civil administration was created and Milson was named its head on November 1, 1981.[61]

Milson implemented his policies in the territories with the help of Mustafa Dudin, a Palestinian who three years earlier had founded the Village League in Hebron. The league's objectives were "the resolution of local disputes among villages, . . . [and] the encouragement of rural cooperatives, social and charitable societies which will work for the benefit of all villages."[62] Milson believed that the urban centers were already contaminated by PLO propaganda but that the rural population—70 percent of the Palestinian population in the occupied territories—might be more easily freed from the PLO's grip. He invited Dudin to expand his Village League and create chapters in other villages across the West Bank.

The military component of this policy, which included the suppression of pro-PLO elements, did not come under Milson's authority, but inevitably intensified the cycle of violence. Palestinian mayors refused to cooperate with the new civil administration and boycotted Milson. Merchants went on strike, students clashed with the Israeli military and police, and Dudin's office in Hebron was attacked.[63] Within the first two months of the new regime sixteen Palestinians were killed. Several leaders of the Village League, and Palestinians who publicly expressed support for the Egyptian-Israeli Peace Treaty, were assassinated by PLO agents.[64]

By the later part of 1981 Peace Now was in deep hibernation. However, many activists viewed the deterioration of the situation in the occupied territories with growing concern and anger. At the end of November the Israeli authorities demolished three houses in Beit Sahour as a punishment to the families of students implicated in stone-throwing and firebomb attacks on soldiers. Responding to the action, which seemed to them disproportionately harsh, some fifty Israelis traveled from Jerusalem to Beit Sahour to demonstrate their sympathy with the affected families and their opposition to the extreme measures. This spontaneous initiative was the first sign of Peace Now's reawakening.[65]

The Battle of Yamit

According to the terms of the Egyptian-Israeli Peace Treaty, the final retreat of Israeli forces from Sinai was scheduled to take place on April 26, 1982.[66] This required the evacuation of a number of Israeli settlements on the soon-to-be Egyptian side of the Rafah Wedge, including the small town of Yamit. Many of the settlers were prepared to leave the homes they had built, and had negotiated with the government on the amount of compensation they would receive. Some of the more politically oriented settlers, especially a group of Gush Emunim loyalists headed by Rabbi Israel Ariel, planned to resist the transfer of the area to Egypt.

In January 1982 a group of Gush Emunim leaders, along with some extremists from the Yamit area, formed the Movement to Stop the Withdrawal from Sinai.[67] They were assisted by Geula Cohen's Tehiya Party and by followers of Meir Kahane, the explicitly racist American-born rabbi who founded the Jewish Defense League in Brooklyn in the late 1960s and immigrated to Israel in the early 1970s. The movement's first act was to send a group of settlers to construct a new settlement in the area despite the imminent withdrawal date. As the evacuation drew nearer, they called on their supporters to go to Yamit and squat in houses that had already been deserted by their previous occupants. The three Knesset members from Tehiya moved to Yamit to lead the battle.

In light of these developments, Peace Now's dormant call-up system was reactivated. On January 21, 1982, a few hundred veterans and some new volunteers met at Kibbutz Ga'ash to outline a strategy for the movement's revival. It quickly became clear that it was undesirable to devote time and energy to protesting against the settlers in Yamit, because for a change it was the settlers who were confronting the Begin government. Even Sharon, whose sympathy for the settlers' objectives was well known, had to oppose their schemes, because as minister of defense he was responsible for the implementation of the final withdrawal of the Israeli forces. Thus, Peace Now decided to concentrate its efforts on the West Bank and Gaza Strip and on relations with the Palestinians.

On March 23, 1982, four senior reserve officers who had recently been responsible for implementing Sharon's policies in the occupied territories appeared (after their release from reserve duty) at a public meeting organized by Peace Now in Jerusalem. The media reported their statements concerning atrocities committed as a consequence of Sharon's oppressive methods. They blamed the defense minister for corrupting young Israeli soldiers by ordering them to clash with unarmed civilians. A few days later the movement took to the streets. Close to 100,000 demonstrators marched in Tel Aviv to protest Sharon's "iron fist" policy. This again demonstrated that when circumstances warranted, and there was adequate popular support, the movement could mobilize the masses. It also demonstrated the value of the often mundane work the core group of activists concentrated on during less intense periods, which served to keep the name and network of Peace Now alive and allowed it to call on mass support when crises arose. The dedication of the inner circle of activists made this remarkable comeback possible after Peace Now's long period of stagnation. It also strengthened the resolve of the activists to preserve the movement as a permanent feature of Israeli politics.

In the middle of April Sharon sealed the Yamit area and barred entry to civilians. Despite this the Movement to Stop the Withdrawal continued to send hundreds of youngsters to infiltrate the area. This led to repeated confrontations with the army—a politically painful state of affairs for Begin's government. Inside Yamit about a thousand zealots fortified themselves in bunkers, on water towers, and on rooftops and defied repeated orders to leave the town. Sharon was left with no choice but to order the army to forcibly evacuate the remaining resisters. Scenes of physical confrontation were televised daily and Israelis witnessed the unprecedented spectacle of soldiers clashing with Jewish civilians—a profoundly disturbing sight for many Israelis, even though there were no serious casualties.

After all the civilians were removed from the area, and apparently without consulting the government, Sharon ordered the razing of all the buildings in Yamit and the neighboring villages.[68] Many viewed this as an attempt by Sharon to create a scene of such devastation as to make Israelis recoil from the idea of a similar retreat from the West Bank and Gaza. The hysteria that surrounded the evacuation of Yamit transmitted a sense of insecurity throughout the ranks of Gush Emunim. "What impressed settler activists about the events of April 1982 was not how secure they saw the future of Israel's presence in Judea, Samaria and Gaza to be, but how tenuous; not how difficult it was for a government to resist the pressure exerted by the settler lobby, but how easy; not how traumatic was the shock of withdrawal for Israelis, but how rapidly it could be assimilated and forgotten."[69]

In a largely meaningless gesture, Prime Minister Begin solemnly declared to the Knesset that his government would not sign another treaty that included withdrawal from any territory in Eretz Yisrael or the removal of Jewish settlements.[70] To demonstrate his commitment to the settling of Judea and Samaria, Sharon approved the establishment of a number of new settlements in the West Bank on Independence Day, May 28, 1982. Although the peace movement had abstained from involvement in the drama of Yamit, it sent activists to Judea and Samaria to demonstrate against the new settlements. In an effort to preempt Peace Now demonstrators Sharon ordered the territories closed. Despite this the demonstrators managed to gain access to the area and disrupt the ceremonies at some of the new settlements. A few hundred peaceniks experienced the effects of tear gas for the first time when the IDF blocked their entrance to a settlement near Hebron. Palestinians from the outskirts of Hebron, who had experienced this suffocating feeling many times before, gave the demonstrators onion peels and drinks to help alleviate the effects of the gas.[71]

Sharon's acts conformed with the apparent rationale of Begin's strategy—to pay a high price in Sinai to free his hands in the West Bank and the Gaza Strip. The new settlements symbolized Begin's commitment that the retreat from the Sinai would not be repeated elsewhere. Peace Now strongly disagreed with this rationale. The peaceniks did not believe that Israel would receive carte blanche in the West Bank as a result of its substantial concessions to Egypt. On the contrary, they felt that peace with Egypt could be jeopardized by intransigence in the other areas. With the withdrawal from Sinai completed, the next act of the drama was now quickly unfolding not in the hills of Judea and Samaria but in the mountain ranges to Israel's north.

7

War in the Land of Cedars
The Fragmentation of the Peace Movement

Hit the Snake's Head, Not Its Tail

A de facto political and military alliance between Israel and Lebanon's Maronite Christians evolved amid the civil war in Lebanon, reaching a peak early in 1976.[1] The relationship developed on two levels. One level involved clandestine contacts between Israeli officials and the leaders of the Maronite community. Their meetings took place mostly in Christian East Beirut and on Mount Lebanon, an area that during the late 1970s effectively became a sovereign enclave controlled by the Phalange militia, the most important faction of the Lebanese Forces.[2]

The second level developed just across Israel's northern border. Major Sa'd Haddad, a Lebanese army officer who was initially sent by his superiors to protect the Christian and Shi'a villages in the south, became in the mid-1970s for all practical purposes an extension of the Israeli army. After being cut off from the Lebanese army in the north, and facing the immediate dangers posed by the Palestinian forces deployed around the Christian enclaves in the south, he sought to fulfill his mission by establishing a relationship with the Israeli military deployed a few miles to the south.

Israel began to view Major Haddad as a surrogate, and supplied his troops with weapons and training. As the civil war continued in the north, and the Lebanese Army ceased to exist as an effective and unified force, Haddad declared the establishment of a separate military entity, which he called the South Lebanon Army (SLA).[3] Shimon Peres, then Israel's minister of defense, named the international border between Israel and the small Haddad-controlled region in southeastern Lebanon the "Good Fence." It was opened for human and commercial traffic in both directions.[4]

In the past the Maronites had constituted the largest single confessional group in Lebanon. However, between 1945 and 1975 the Maronites gradually lost power and influence to the Druse, the Sunni Muslims, and the Shi'a community, which was increasing in size and strength.[5] Added to this mixture was the growing Palestinian population concentrated in refugee camps throughout the country since 1948. The Palestinians possessed formidable and largely autonomous militias. The strength of the Palestinian guerrillas increased significantly after the PLO established a new base of operations against Israel in south Lebanon in the wake of its expulsion from Jordan in 1970.[6] By 1975 the Maronites were involved in a bitter civil war against the Palestinians and other Muslim militias, and turned to Israel for help.

During Yitzhak Rabin's first tenure as prime minister, between 1974 and 1977, Israel was cautious, limiting its assistance to the Maronites to the provision of materiel and training. "We shall help you to help yourselves," Rabin told former Lebanese president Camille Chamoun in a secret meeting.[7] Seeing an opportunity to advance its own struggle against the Palestinian guerrillas, Israel transferred small arms and ammunition to the Maronites; Israeli intelligence officers frequently visited the Maronites, and some were even permanently stationed in Lebanon; and Lebanese Christians received training at Israeli military bases and wore Israeli-made uniforms.[8]

The first Likud government, with Ezer Weizman as minister of defense, continued this cautious approach and refrained from direct intervention.[9] Direct involvement was judged even more unwise after the Syrian army joined the Lebanese conflict in 1976. By 1977 Damascus controlled large areas in Lebanon, especially in the Bekaa Valley on the eastern slopes of Mount Lebanon. This created a potential second front for Israel in the event of a war with Syria. However, the Syrians adhered to unofficial "red line" agreements with Israel, according to which each side made known what actions by the other side would be viewed as unacceptable and could result in war.

With the Lebanese state effectively defunct and the country divided into clearly demarcated zones of influence, the PLO could conduct operations from a semiautonomous region in south Lebanon that had a contiguous border with Israel. Israeli retaliatory military actions against Palestinian bases in south Lebanon became more complicated as the possibility of a war with Syria became a central consideration. For their part, the Maronites were eager to pull Israel into the Lebanese imbroglio as a counterbalance to Syria; the Maronites recognized that as long as Syria controlled large areas of their country they would not be able to reestablish their dominant position.

Toward the end of 1979 Begin increased Israel's involvement in Lebanon by promising Camille Chamoun and Bashir Gemayel that he would order the Israeli Air Force into action against the Syrians if they conducted aerial attacks against the Maronites. In a show of force on July 8, 1978, two Israeli Kfir jets overflew Beirut, "breaking the sound barrier and sending sonic booms crashing through the city, shattering windows and daunting faint hearts."[10]

The Israeli defense establishment had its view of the Lebanon situation radically altered after Ariel Sharon was appointed minister of defense in Begin's second government, following the 1981 elections. Sharon believed that PLO dominance among the Palestinians could and should be reduced or even eliminated. Sharon reasoned that as long as the PLO had an autonomous base in south Lebanon from which it could launch guerrilla operations and influence the Palestinians, attempts to undercut its position in the occupied territories would fail. The elimination of the PLO presence in Lebanon, Sharon argued, would thus help facilitate the implementation of Begin's autonomy plan envisaged in Camp David, and turn it into a permanent settlement of the Palestinian issue with Israel maintaining control of the West Bank and Gaza Strip.

By the early 1980s the PLO had established quasi sovereignty in and around most of the refugee camps south of Beirut and around Tripoli in the north. Even their Lebanese allies wondered if the Palestinians were not trying to carve an alternative homeland for themselves in Lebanon.[11] An elaborate system of Palestinian social, medical, cultural, and administrative services replaced the now-defunct bureaucracy of the Lebanese government in the refugee camps. New offices filled with Palestinian bureaucrats became increasingly visible, particularly around the Fakhani neighborhood south of downtown Beirut, where most Palestinian organizations were headquartered.[12]

The expansion of the Palestinians' political autonomy in Lebanon was naturally followed by the enhancement of their military capabilities. The PLO transformed itself from bands of guerrilla units into a force that looked more like a regular army. For the first time the PLO incorporated heavy (albeit mostly outdated) equipment into its frontline units. Older models of Soviet tanks, field artillery, antiaircraft guns, and mobile Katyusha rocket launchers were now part of the PLO arsenal.[13] While these weapons could have an impact on the internecine fighting in Lebanon, they were no match for the Israeli army in combat. Nevertheless, they provided the PLO with a significant nuisance capability.

Fierce exchanges of artillery, mortar, and Katyusha shells between the PLO and the IDF along Israel's northern border in summer 1981 presented Israeli military strategists with a new dilemma. Previously Israel had retaliated for Palestinian guerrilla raids and terrorist attacks abroad by artillery shelling and aerial attacks against Palestinian bases in Lebanon. The PLO's new military capability enabled it to respond to Israeli attacks in kind. While Israeli artillery and aerial attacks wreaked havoc on villages and refugee camps in south Lebanon, they could not stop the Palestinian retaliatory shelling, which caused much damage and considerable panic among Israeli civilians in the north.

After extensive negotiations President Reagan's special envoy, Philip Habib, mediated a cease-fire agreement between Israel and the PLO in July 1981.[14] The quasi recognition of the PLO by Israel implied by this agreement reflected the political and military progress made by the PLO during the previous decade. Israeli military planners recognized that if fighting resumed, a major land operation to remove the PLO from south Lebanon and destroy its military capability would be necessary. The traditional means of retaliation now seemed to be ineffective.[15] Additionally, Sharon became convinced that if the goal were to eliminate the PLO as a military and political force, its headquarters in Fakhani had to be destroyed as well.[16]

For Sharon, Israel's intensified relationship with the Maronites and the new dilemma presented by PLO's military buildup converged. By the fall of 1981 he seemed determined to undertake the military assault code-named Operation Big Pines. Operation Big Pines was designed to invade Lebanon, destroy PLO positions in south Lebanon, advance north to Beirut, converge with the Lebanese forces along the Beirut-Damascus highway, and eventually push the Syrians out of the country.[17] The political outcome of this operation was designed to facilitate the election of Bashir Gemayel as president of Lebanon; he would in turn conclude a peace treaty with Israel.[18] Sharon must have been impressed by Gemayel, who objected to a more limited Israeli war plan aimed only at putting Israel's northern settlements beyond the range of Palestinian artillery. Gemayel insisted, "You must hit the snake on its head, not on its tail!"[19]

Peace for Galilee

Sharon eagerly awaited the opportunity to launch Operation Big Pines. Because the plan did not yet have adequate support within the government, he sought to provoke a situation that would make the invasion of Lebanon inevitable. Toward this end, he believed that repeated air strikes on Palestinian targets in Lebanon would eventually provoke the PLO into retaliating by shelling northern Israel. The government would then be forced to take action and launch a ground assault into Lebanon.

During the winter and spring of 1982 the PLO carefully abided by the terms of the cease-fire agreement mediated by Habib the previous summer, presumably fearful of an Israeli ground invasion of southern Lebanon.[20] When, on April 21, 1982, an Israeli soldier was killed by a land mine north of the Israeli border in the zone controlled by Major Haddad, the cabinet finally acceded to Sharon's pressure and authorized a few limited air strikes, but the PLO abstained from any military response. On May 13 the cabinet again ordered air strikes and the PLO returned fire this time, but the shelling was inaccurate and caused only minor damage. In comparison to its destructive shelling the previous summer, the PLO seemed to be doing its best to miss.[21]

Individuals both within and outside the government advised Begin against taking rash steps. Many used the media to openly criticize the plan to invade Lebanon, which by this time had become a well-publicized and highly controversial secret. Labor Party leaders objected to sending the Israeli army to undertake a largely political task for which there was no national consensus. While they agreed with Likud that the presence of Palestinian forces in the areas contiguous to Israel represented a genuine security problem, Labor leaders believed that the involvement of Israeli forces further to the north (especially around Beirut and the Beirut-Damascus highway) was designed more to serve Maronite interests than to satisfy legitimate Israeli security requirements.[22]

Peace Now, of course, adamantly opposed such schemes. On May 16, 1981, at the height of the intensive artillery exchanges in the north, Peace Now had organized a demonstration against the increasing likelihood of a war in Lebanon. But in the spring of 1982 Peace Now discovered that it was difficult to mobilize people against a plan that Begin regularly denied existed.

The fact that the plan addressed, at least partially, a genuine national security concern also made the protest harder to sell to the general public.[23]

For its part, the Reagan administration warned Israel against unilateral action in Lebanon, but the language used by U.S. Secretary of State Alexander Haig was ambiguous. In February 1982 Begin sent General Yehoshua Saguy, the chief of military intelligence, to solicit American understanding if Israel decided to invade Lebanon. Haig responded with the requirement that "there be a major, internationally recognized provocation."[24] Sharon himself went to Washington in May 1982 and met with Haig.[25] The secretary of state reiterated what he had told General Saguy, adding that if Israel was obliged to attack Lebanon it should act swiftly and precisely. Sharon apparently emerged from this meeting with the impression that an adequate provocation was all that was required.[26] A letter sent by Haig to Begin a few days later did little to dispel the Israeli leaders' impression that the United States would not be averse to an Israeli offensive in Lebanon.[27]

The Palestinian provocation came on June 3, 1982, when a gunman from the Abu Nidal group, a renegade Palestinian faction, shot and severely wounded Shlomo Argov, the Israeli ambassador to London. This attack caused outrage among Israelis, who on the whole do not differentiate between the various Palestinian factions. This attack gave Sharon the opportunity to successfully press for a resolution in the cabinet to begin massive air strikes against targets in Lebanon. This time, despite the likely Israeli response, Arafat ordered massive shelling of towns and villages throughout northern Israel.

Sharon had found the "major, internationally recognized provocation" he wanted, and he received a green light from the cabinet to launch an offensive now named "Operation Peace for the Galilee." A mobilization of reserve military units was under way. Government ministers and Labor leaders were summoned to a special briefing and told that the offensive would be limited to a "cleaning up" operation against the PLO in an area forty kilometers north of the border. Furthermore, they were told that strict orders had been issued not to engage the Syrians.[28] With these assurances, the Labor Party gave its endorsement to the assault.[29]

The Committee against the War in Lebanon

The plan to invade Lebanon was well known to Peace Now activists by the winter of 1982. Some of the soldiers who had signed the Officers' Letter in 1978 had risen to become battalion commanders or held high staff positions in military reserve units. As such they were involved in military planning and preparations. Israel's security situation, and the possibility of an invasion of Lebanon, was debated within the peace movement for some time. The consensus opinion was that no justification existed for a large-scale military initiative. This view was made known to the government in a number of informal meetings, but Sharon was not going to be dissuaded.[30]

When the war began many of the movement's activists were mobilized and they often led their units into combat.[31] During the early days of the war there was wide public support for the operation, including among the soldiers at the front. In light of the massive shelling of towns and villages across the upper Galilee, many Israelis felt that an operation against the Palestinian guerrillas in the southern part of Lebanon had become inevitable. Begin's assurances that the operation would involve only an area forty kilometers north of the border further solidified public support.[32]

While many Peace Now activists were aware that Sharon's ultimate design went far beyond the stated forty-kilometer limit, it was difficult to counter prevailing public opinion.[33] There was also the widely shared feeling that, during a period of active hostilities, soldiers are due full public support, and that second-guessing the military is unseemly, at the least. This can be explained by the unwavering loyalty of the overwhelming majority of Israelis to the security of Israel in general and the IDF in particular. Because almost all Israelis pass through the ranks of the IDF they are aware of the importance of doing nothing that might undermine the effectiveness and discipline of the IDF while it is engaged in combat. Therefore, during the first days of the war, Peace Now activists at the front sent urgent messages back to their friends in Israel requesting that they not undertake any actions "as long as soldiers are still being killed in battle."[34]

Despite these requests some activists critical of Peace Now's hesitance refused to accept the plea for restraint and within a few days had initiated a petition against the war and collected several thousand signatures. They also organized a demonstration in Tel Aviv under the slogan, "*Dai!*" (Enough!). This ad hoc group, which called itself the Committee against the War in Lebanon, made it clear that it was independent of Peace Now and did not speak on behalf of any other organization.[35]

Many of the individuals who formed the committee were not new to the Israeli political scene. The nucleus included members of the old Communist Party, Siah (the Israeli New Left), and other independent intellectuals. In the early 1970s this group had congregated around an English-language publication called *Israleft*, which translated articles from the Hebrew press and sent them to politicians and intellectuals on the European and American left. Aware of their marginality in the Israeli political scene, the members of this group did not presume to build a mass movement. Instead they preferred to create informal committees around specific issues and exert influence among the Israeli left and within the broader peace movement.[36] The "committee" format allowed for coalition building with other more or less formal groups, and it kept the group transitory in nature and thus always able to focus on a timely issue.[37]

Members of these committees often participated in Peace Now demonstrations as well, but took a more radical position on most issues. By the mid-1970s they had advocated the opening of a dialogue with the PLO and the establishment of a Palestinian state alongside Israel. Some activists even accepted the demands of the Palestinian left to create a "democratic secular state" for both Jews and Arabs on the basis of civil equality. "The gap between us and Peace Now was ideological," recalled Judy Blank, a central figure in the committees whose house was frequently used for meetings between Israeli and Palestinian intellectuals. "Peace Now activists were close to the Israeli establishment and wanted to influence it from the inside. We came from the critical margin. The difference was not social, since most of both groups came from the intellectual upper-middle class. The difference could be described by the German idiom *Sitz in Leben* [position in life]. Most of us went to Peace Now demonstrations, but this was not enough for us. . . . Also the Israeli Arabs, who did not feel at home with the emphatically patriotic atmosphere of Peace Now, preferred to be active in the 'committees.' We were able to mobilize many Israeli Arabs, which made our demonstrations look more massive."[38]

Most of the demonstrations organized by these informal committees of the 1970s attracted far fewer participants than did those staged by Peace Now. But at the beginning of the war in Lebanon, when Peace Now dragged its feet, the Committee against the War in Lebanon drew many Peace Now sympathizers to a demonstration of 30,000 people in the main square in Tel Aviv. This turnout was a surprise also to the committee members themselves, and showed that Peace Now was not the only game in town. It reflected a fragmentation within the peace movement and demonstrated that the calls for peace were often spoken with different voices.

What Do We Kill For? What Are We Being Killed For?

Sharon's thinly veiled secret soon became known to all. Troops landed from the sea in the area of Damour, halfway between Saida and Beirut, during the early hours of the operation. This was far north of the forty-kilometer limit Begin had used to justify the operation. While this particular assault could be seen as a necessary tactical maneuver, the arrival of Israeli paratroopers and forward armor units at the outskirts of Beirut on the fifth day of the war left little doubt as to what Sharon and Chief of Staff Raphael Eitan had in mind.[39] On the eighth day of the fighting, June 13, contrary to government decisions and Sharon's own assurances to the cabinet, forward units joined up with the forces of Bashir Gemayel in Ba'abda, near the presidential palace above West Beirut.

By this time fighting with the Syrians had approached the level of a full-scale war. Cease-fire agreements mediated by Philip Habib were repeatedly broken. Apprehension increased among Israeli government ministers as a growing number realized that Sharon was misleading and manipulating them into approving his private war plans through piecemeal requests that incrementally changed the strategic situation and led the ministers to authorize actions they had originally opposed.[40] One minister told Sharon with sarcastic humor, "Arik, perhaps you'll be good enough to tell us what you're going to ask us to approve the day after tomorrow so that you can secure what you're going to ask us to approve tomorrow."[41]

The cabinet, and to a growing degree the military, faced a moral and political dilemma. There was a growing realization that Sharon and Eitan had deceived the leadership and the nation and were dragging Israel into a war it had not bargained for. Peace Now activists serving at the front reported to their friends back in Israel about the shocking discrepancies between what they had heard Sharon, Eitan, and military spokesmen state on the radio and what they had seen with their own eyes.[42] Israelis also became aware of the great damage done to their country's image in international public opinion by extensive television reporting of the atrocious scenes caused by a war in such a densely populated area.[43]

At long last Peace Now decided to launch a large public protest. Ten days after the beginning of the fighting, the movement published a declaration in the major newspapers, demanding an immediate end to the war, and asking, "What are we killing for? What are we being killed for?"[44] As the war continued and the siege of Beirut deepened, Peace Now organized a major demonstration in Tel Aviv on June 26. Twenty days into the war, popular opposition had become strong enough to draw more than 100,000 angry and frustrated demonstrators into the streets.[45]

Despite Peace Now's reawakening, some activists did not forget its hesitation and procrastination at the beginning of the war. In their eyes, Peace Now had lost much of its moral authority, and they decided that in the future they would act alone if Peace Now did not play a more active role.[46] By the end of June Peace Now found itself under fire from both sides. The left criticized it for its inactivity at the beginning of the war, and the right accused it of "stabbing Israel in the back."[47] Likud and other Sharon supporters countered Peace Now's demonstration with an even larger gathering at the same venue on July 17. Yasser Arafat praised the Peace Now demonstration from his bunker in Beirut, thus making it easy for Sharon and his supporters to label the activists collaborators and question their loyalty to the state.

Yesh Gvul

Conscientious objectors and draft resisters were a rare phenomenon during Israel's first three decades.[48] The few cases that did occur generally involved philosophical pacifists who objected to war in itself, and did not necessarily pass judgment on the specific political circumstances or merits of a particular war.[49] Most Israelis, however, agreed that the wars Israel had to fight were wars of national defense dictated by their country's enemies and fought for lack of an alternative. Furthermore, memories of the Holocaust fueled a desire to be militarily strong and act decisively.[50] Consequently, draft resistance remained a largely unknown phenomenon. The political and moral divisions cut through Israel by the war in Lebanon, however, brought the limits of obedience into question for the first time. The shock this war caused within Israeli society, especially among its intellectual elite, was psychological and moral as well as political.

Sharon's manipulation of information had undermined a foundation of Israeli civic obedience. The deceptions perpetrated on the government and the people by protagonists of the war, followed by the absence of parliamentary accountability, led Israelis of all political persuasions to ask in what instances citizens can or should resist orders.[51] The use of the army for the pursuit of questionable political objectives eroded the previously unquestioned obedience to military orders.

Selective refusal by some to participate in military duties, based on political and moral considerations, had begun among Peace Now activists in the spring of 1981. Ishai Menuchin, a reserve company commander, Yehuda Meltzer, a philosophy teacher at Tel Aviv University, and others sent a letter to the prime minister (who at that time also served as defense minister) requesting that they not be sent to serve in the occupied territories when mobilized for their annual reserve duties. Peace Now did not agree to officially sanction the letter, and the issue became a source of heated discussions within the movement when the war in Lebanon began.[52]

A few days after the war began, and its false pretenses and high costs became clearer, a letter was sent to Sharon regarding service in Lebanon. As with the earlier letter to the prime minister, it was formulated as a request rather than a demand or a unilateral notice of refusal to serve. The letter stated:

> We, officers and soldiers in reserve service, appeal to you not to send us to Lebanon, since we can endure no more! We killed too many and too many of us were killed in this war. We conquered too much, we blew up and destroyed too much. What for? It is now clear that by means of this war you are trying to solve the Palestinian problem militarily, but there is no military solution to the problem of a nation. You are trying to impose a new order on the ruins of Lebanon, to spill our blood and the blood of others in favor of the Phalange. We did not join the Israel Defense Forces for this purpose. You lied to us! You spoke of a 40-kilometer line, but you actually intended to reach a line 40 kilometers from Damascus and to enter Beirut. Again the vicious circle of occupation-resistance-suppression is awaiting us. Instead of peace to the Galilee you have brought about a war, the end of which may not yet be seen. This war, these lies, this occupation has no national consent! Bring the soldiers back home! We took an oath to defend the peace and security of the State of Israel. We remain loyal to this oath. Therefore, we appeal to you to enable us to serve our reserve duty inside the boundaries of the State of Israel, not on the soil of Lebanon.[53]

During the first two weeks of the fighting in Lebanon a few hundred soldiers signed the petition, but no one actually refused mobilization orders. However, when a cease-fire was declared (despite the fact that the siege of Beirut and the heavy shelling of the Palestinian camps in West Beirut continued), the request was replaced by a blunt refusal, and soldiers began going to military jails for refusing service in Lebanon.[54]

A new group, Yesh Gvul, organized to support those who refused to serve in Lebanon. The Hebrew term *yesh gvul* has two meanings: "there is a limit" and "there is a border." The name was chosen because it referred both to the principle of obedience and to the refusal to serve for any reason other than in defense of the borders of the State of Israel.

Yesh Gvul never became a mass movement. During the first year of the IDF's encampment around Beirut some 100 soldiers refused orders to go north, and about 2,000 others signed a petition to show their support for the group's aims.[55] The symbolic impact of the new phenomenon was significant. A retired general observed, "The main achievement of disobedience was that the government understood, at long last, that success in war is not measured only by its tangible results but also in what was left of it in the consciousness of the people."[56] "The shatter-ing of the traditional norms of Israel's political culture," wrote another observer, "triggered to a large degree the need for renewal of political symbols." The relatively small number who actually refused did not matter greatly because "in order to undermine the validity of certain codes of political communication it is often enough to deny publicly the existence of an unquestionable consensus and its validity. Even a tiny minority may subvert the status of such codes, and their total common acceptability, which are so vital for the very existence of any communi-cative code."[57] The intense media coverage given over the years to this handful of "refusers" also testified to their symbolic impact.

A heated debate on the issue of draft refusal took place within the peace movement, for Yesh Gvul presented a challenge to the movement's customary mode of operation. Unlike the "committees," which had ex-plicitly positioned themselves to the left politically and ideologically, Yesh Gvul did not differ greatly from Peace Now in its political orientations. Moreover, many of the refusers were Peace Now activists.[58] Their ac-tions, however, challenged the self-restraint that Peace Now had im-posed on its selection of tactics and methods of protest.

Traditionally Peace Now had refrained from blatantly confrontational tactics. At times activists approached the limits of legality, but as a rule did not transgress them.[59] The argument for showing restraint was that once Peace Now had broken the law it would not only move outside the national mainstream but also legitimize law breaking by its opponents on the right, who might have benefited more than the left from such tac-tics.[60] Yesh Gvul challenged these assumptions and in the process risked implicating Peace Now, which was obliged to defend itself and publicly distance itself from those who crossed the boundaries of legality. Yet Peace Now sought to do this without delegitimizing the refusers. The refusers' right to resist orders that they felt they could no longer obey, and their readiness to pay the associated price, had to be upheld. The Nuremberg trials in 1945–46 had established the principle that a moral limit to obedi-ence did indeed exist, and the Eichmann trial in Jerusalem itself was a living memory for many Israelis. The controversy surrounded the ques-tion of at what point this limit was reached. "Philosophically there cer-tainly is a limit to obedience, and circumstances may be created in which we too may decide to disobey," declared a Peace Now spokesman in an attempt to clarify the movement's position vis-à-vis Yesh Gvul. "Despite its bitter critique of the invasion of Lebanon, Peace Now does not think that this limit has been reached. Yesh Gvul is not our rival. In many ways they are a piece of our flesh and bones. Sharon and Begin have to be blamed for creating the circumstances which have pushed some people to feel that they have reached the limit. Individuals may have the right to resist orders they feel they cannot live with, as long as they are ready to pay the price. But as a movement, as a collective, Peace Now is not ready to adopt disobedience as its official line."[61]

A Brigade Commander Quits

During June and July 1982 the fighting on the outskirts of Beirut and on the Beirut-Damascus highway continued intermittently. By the end of June battles with Syrian forces erupted in Bhamdun, east of Beirut, and in the area north of Lake Qar'un near the Syrian border. Israeli casualties grew daily, and despite military censorship the people back home became aware of the havoc the war had wrought over vast areas of southern Lebanon. Yet at this stage even the war's critics recognized the strategic gains that were being achieved by removing the PLO from its bases in southern Lebanon, and the potential gain that could be achieved by ousting the PLO from Beirut.[62] Yitzhak Rabin referred to the situation Sharon and Begin had dragged Israel into as a *plonter* (a Yiddish word for a knot that is difficult to untangle), but even he recognized that now that the IDF had "arrived at the outskirts of Beirut and put a siege on it in order to force out the guerrillas, the inability to achieve this aim will practically amount to a political and psychological defeat for Israel." He advised against an assault on West Beirut but supported other measures such as "tightening the siege by cutting from time to time the water and electricity supply."[63] U.S. Secretary of State Haig favored a solution that would "ultimately see all foreign forces out of Lebanon," and made it clear that he desired the PLO's departure from Beirut.[64]

Arafat attempted to negotiate the best deal possible for the PLO. He was ready to relinquish his position in the besieged city contingent upon a number of preliminary conditions, not the least of which was his demand that the Palestinian militias be permitted to leave with their weapons, and only after the Israeli forces retreated five kilometers and relieved the siege.[65]

For Sharon and Eitan, humiliation of the PLO was the name of the game. Their ultimate objective being to deal a death blow to the PLO as a military and political factor in the Middle East, Sharon and Eitan preferred a direct assault on the city and tightened the siege on West Beirut through constant shelling and other measures.[66] Negotiations for the PLO's departure, and the search for Arab states that would accept the evacuated guerrillas, were conducted by American envoy Habib.[67] Sharon, convinced that the PLO was attempting to play for time and to avoid having to relinquish its bases in Beirut, readied for a ground attack on the southern part of West Beirut, where most of the Palestinian guerrillas and civilians were concentrated. Toward the end of July IDF commanders were instructed to prepare for an imminent attack. These orders were received with growing unease. The local commanders estimated that an attack on West Beirut would result in a high number of IDF casualties as well as casualties among Palestinian and Lebanese civilians. Many did not consider the cost worthwhile.[68]

Upon receiving the order to prepare for the attack, Colonel Eli Geva, a commander of an armor brigade, asked to be relieved of his command. He said he could not give orders to his soldiers that would entail "the killing of entire families."[69] This was an unprecedented event in IDF history. Chief of Staff Eitan tried to portray the case as an isolated event and personal matter for Colonel Geva, but it was clear to the public and within the ranks of the IDF that the colonel was merely the first to step forward. He represented the growing doubts of many soldiers regarding the moral justification and political wisdom of the entire war. "It seemed to many of the soldiers stationed on the heights around Beirut that the IDF's self-image as a defensive force was being demolished along with entire neighborhoods in Beirut. . . . The IDF's sense of moral propriety was being overwhelmed by an unqualified dependence on force."[70]

Begin could no longer deny the war's broader political objectives, and began to employ a different approach. In a lecture to the graduates of the Staff and Command College in August, while the siege of Beirut was still being waged, he argued that "there is no precept to fight only wars of no choice. . . . To the contrary, a free nation, which hates war, loves peace, and cares for its security must create conditions in which the choice will remain in its hands. And if a war must be waged, it should not be a war of last resort."[71]

The Hebrew term *milchemet ein breira*—literally, "a war without a choice," and essentially comparable to "a war of last resort"—implies that Israel should use its military forces only when there is no other option, or when refraining from the use of force might threaten Israel's security. "Our philosophy," said Yitzhak Rabin, "is that the destiny of the Israeli Army should be, as its name implies, only defensive. . . . This dictates the conclusion that IDF should not be employed in a self-initiated offensive operation which is not directly connected to the security needs of Israel."[72]

Unlike the concept of "just war," which can be defined according to widely understood criteria, the notion of "a war without a choice" is essentially subjective. General Aharon Yariv, a former cabinet minister and head of military intelligence, observed that after six wars in less than four decades, "the people of Israel wanted to be convinced that the threat to the security of the state was real and immediate enough not to leave another choice but to fight."[73] The national consensus that had supported the removal of the PLO's capability to harass northern Israel splintered when the IDF pushed deep into Lebanon. "Public protest and disagreement were triggered not in response to the decision to start a war to secure the peace of the Galilee," Yariv concluded, "but in response to the unrevealed goals the architects of the operation have set for themselves, and in response to the crooked way the war was managed and the dishonesty perpetrated on the public and on the cabinet. . . . These corroded the sense of justice a large part of the public had at the beginning."[74]

Parents against Silence

The initial support within the IDF for the war's objectives rapidly eroded among a growing number of soldiers, even those on the front lines. Soon after the first soldiers were released from duty and returned to Israel their anger and opposition became public. At the beginning of July two soldiers who had returned from the front decided that they could not keep silent anymore and organized a vigil across from the prime minister's office in Jerusalem. Soon other soldiers joined them under the name "Soldiers against Silence," calling for Sharon's dismissal as minister of defense and for an immediate end to the war. They expressed their anger at the misleading reporting by the IDF spokesmen and what they viewed as the immorality of IDF's continued presence in Lebanon. "We entered the war clean and come out of it soiled in blood spilled in vain," said one soldier who spoke in the first large rally the new group held.[75]

At about the same time, and initially independently of the soldiers' initiative, a few mothers of soldiers who were fighting in Lebanon also spoke out. Among them was Naomi Bentsur, a communications consultant and the wife of a senior Israeli diplomat. She recalled:

> My son was a tank driver in an armor unit which was first to penetrate Lebanon and first to arrive on the Beirut-Damascus highway. When my son

came for a few hours' leave from Lebanon he told me that they had received from the outset an order to drive their tanks as long as there was fuel. This meant by far more than forty kilometers. I felt betrayed. They took my son and then lied to us about the purpose of all that. I felt thoroughly depressed. He did not know why and where he was sent to fight. We took our son to the railway station to bid him farewell and pictures I had seen of the First World War came to my mind. This was not like previous wars Israel had to fight. I called a few of my friends whose children were also in Lebanon and we decided to protest. We remembered the dictum "When truth is silent, silence is a lie," and decided to call our group "Parents against Silence." We never thought at the outset that we would have to struggle so long, but eventually we continued our activities for three years, until the final retreat.[76]

Their first demonstration took place in front of the prime minister's office less than three weeks after the beginning of the war.[77] During the planning the organizers discovered parents in other cities and town who were fashioning similar initiatives. Shoshana Shmueli, a history teacher from Tel Aviv, organized a vigil near the Ministry of Defense and published a letter criticizing the government's actions. The various groups decided to unite their efforts.

Massacre

Early in August 1982, as relations between Israel and the United States became increasingly strained,[78] Israel intensified its shelling and aerial bombardment of West Beirut. Sensing that his bargaining position had weakened, Arafat dropped his demand that Israeli forces retreat before the evacuation of PLO forces began. However, he insisted that an international force supervise the evacuation in which PLO forces would be permitted to leave with their personal weapons. He also sought guarantees for the safety of the Palestinians remaining in the refugee camps.[79] During the course of these negotiations the Americans made arrangements with several Middle Eastern countries to accept departing PLO guerrillas.[80] On August 21 an international peacekeeping force was deployed in West Beirut and around the harbor, and seventy days after the Israeli invasion the first PLO contingent left Beirut by ship bound for Cyprus.[81] During the following two weeks 8,856 Palestinian guerrillas and 6,062 Syrian soldiers who were also trapped in West Beirut departed either by sea or overland to Syria.[82] The international media were on hand to televise the evacuation, and despite the obvious military defeat the PLO had suffered at the hands of Israel, the PLO fighters departed Beirut in an atmosphere of victorious celebration. An observer noted,

"The 60,000 shells and countless bombs that had rained down on Beirut had not buried the PLO."[83]

Israeli forces continued to encircle West Beirut after the evacuation but did not enter that part of the city. On September 1, ten days after the last Palestinian fighter left, the multinational peacekeeping force also departed. West Beirut remained a no-man's-land where different Lebanese militias, including some residual Palestinians, continued to provide security for their respective communities.[84]

After several delays Lebanon's parliament convened and elected Bashir Gemayel, the commander of the Maronite Lebanese Forces, as president. Sharon must have viewed this as the successful culmination of Operation Big Pines and a vindication of his strategy. In any event, he had little time to relish his victory, for Gemayel was killed on September 14 in a bomb attack carried out by a Syrian agent at the Phalange's Ashrafieh headquarters where Bashir regularly held meetings.[85]

Upon receiving this news Sharon ordered Israeli forces to enter West Beirut and seize the main road junctions, but to refrain from entering the Palestinian refugee camps.[86] An IDF spokesman announced that the action sought "to prevent possible serious events and to assure calm."[87] What the spokesman did not disclose to the public was that Sharon and Chief of Staff Eitan had encouraged the Phalange militia to enter the Palestinian refugee camps to "cleanse" them of the Palestinian guerrillas who remained after the evacuation.[88] During the prolonged siege of Beirut, when the Palestinian guerrillas were still in the city, Sharon and Eitan had repeatedly urged Gemayel to take a more active role in the fighting. The Phalange, however, considered that it needed to save its forces for future battles, and relied on the IDF. Now that the Palestinians in the refugee camps were practically defenseless after the PLO evacuation—and now with a murder to avenge—the Phalange agreed to move in.[89]

During the 36 hours from the evening of September 16 to the morning of September 18 the Phalangists perpetrated a massacre of civilians, including women and children, in the Sabra and Shatila refugee camps. There were early indications available to Israeli officers stationed in the vicinity of the camps that a massacre was under way. Nevertheless, the local commanders did not issue orders to stop the advance of the Phalange into the camps until the afternoon of Friday, September 17.[90] By the evening of September 16, if not much earlier, both Sharon and Eitan knew that a bloodbath was under way, although the scope of the massacre was not yet clear. In a further meeting between the commanders of the Phalange and Eitan it was agreed that the Phalange would leave the camps by Saturday morning, September 18.[91]

After the Phalange exited the camps the Red Cross and journalists entered and discovered a macabre scene. Some six hundred to eight hundred civilians, including at least five dozen women and children, had been killed and their bodies strewn through the streets.[92] Although it soon became evident that the massacre was perpetrated by the Phalange with no direct involvement of Israeli soldiers, it was also clear that Israel could not dissociate itself from its responsibility for what had occurred, nor could it deny that it was at some level guilty of complicity.[93]

Furor

Horror and outrage characterized the response of the international community to the scenes of brutality in the camps.[94] A similar reaction was felt among a large portion of the Israeli public. Brigadier General Amram Mitzna voiced unprecedented public criticism of the minister of defense, charging that Sharon had lost the confidence of the army. Mitzna asked to be relieved of his duties for the duration of the IDF's involvement in Lebanon. Many other high-ranking officers of the General Staff also voiced harsh criticism of Sharon and Eitan. Even the Israeli president, Yitzhak Navon, in an office that customarily does not intervene in politically controversial issues, demanded the appointment of a commission of inquiry.[95] Begin called a special meeting of the cabinet and expressed sadness at the acts perpetrated by the Phalange on the civilian population "at a point far away from the Israeli positions." He went on to say that any attempt to attach responsibility for the human tragedy to Israeli forces is "a blood libel against the Jewish state and its government, and should be rejected in disgust."[96] Many Israelis, however, thought very differently.

The public's anger went beyond the immediate event in the camps. The massacre at Sabra and Shatila was viewed by many Israelis as the last in a series of deceptions and manipulations that had led Israel into the Lebanese morass. Calls for the government's resignation were now being voiced by growing segments of the Israeli polity.

On the evening on September 19, as the news from Beirut began to reach the Israeli public, a crowd of 3,000 spontaneously gathered outside the prime minister's residence in Tel Aviv. The demonstrators demanded an independent investigation of the events in Sabra and Shatila and the resignations of those directly and indirectly responsible for the atrocity. Due to the spontaneous nature of the demonstration—it lacked an official permit—the police declared the gathering illegal and employed tear gas to disperse the protesters.[97]

As public outrage continued to mount, the leaders of Peace Now felt they should take large-scale action. They approached the leaders of the Labor Party and several kibbutz movements and proposed a joint demonstration. On September 25, 1982, the largest demonstration ever to take place in Israel assembled in the Kings of Israel Square in Tel Aviv. More than 250,000 boisterous demonstrators (about 6 percent of Israel's Jewish population) packed the large square.[98] They listened to speeches by the most prominent political and spiritual leaders from the center and left of Israeli politics. Placards carried an assortment of demands of the government: "The People Demand Your Resignation!" "Get Out of Beirut Now!" "The Blood of All Children Is the Same!" and "Call an Inquiry Committee for the Massacre in Beirut!"

This demonstration was the all-time peak of Peace Now's activities. It brought together a cross section of the Israeli public to demonstrate not just against the atrocities committed in the refugee camps of Beirut, but against the entire Lebanese fiasco. However, despite growing opposition to the war, significant segments of the population continued to support Sharon and Eitan throughout the Lebanon episode and were angered by the blame attached to Sharon for the massacre. Sharon publicly criticized Peace Now and the Labor Party for encouraging the PLO to remain in Beirut, and claimed that they had prevented Israel from destroying the PLO once and for all.[99]

Whether he was impressed by the Peace Now demonstration or by some of his own ministers who suggested they might resign if a commission of inquiry was not established, Begin yielded. He seemed perplexed and apparently did not understand the uproar when "goyim kill goyim."[100] As required by Israeli law, the government asked the chief justice to nominate a commission to investigate "all the facts and factors related to the atrocious actions perpetrated by a unit of the Lebanese Forces against the civilian population of the Sabra and Shatila camps."[101]

In the wake of these events the IDF vacated West Beirut on September 21 and entrenched itself a few miles to the south. The multinational peacekeeping forces now returned to replace the IDF and to maintain order and defend the civilian population.[102] For Israel, however, the war in the Land of Cedars was not yet over. The international forces, particularly the Americans, who sought to return stability to Lebanon, would experience their own tragedies before they departed Beirut.

8

Peace and Ethnicity

The Reagan Initiative

The war in Lebanon presented the Reagan administration with an opportunity to make a new attempt to resuscitate the peace process, frozen since the Israeli-Egyptian autonomy negotiations were suspended by President Sadat shortly before his assassination. With the PLO uprooted from Beirut and in political and military disarray, it appeared that the political climate might be favorable to a negotiated settlement.[1]

On September 1, 1982, the day after the PLO completed its evacuation from Beirut, President Reagan announced his "Fresh Start" initiative for peace in the Middle East.[2] The initiative used the Camp David Accords as a point of departure, and suggested the election of a representative body in the West Bank and Gaza to provide the Palestinians with self-rule for five years as part of an interim arrangement. The Fresh Start initiative departed from the Camp David Accords in a few important ways. For the first time the United States expressed its own view concerning a possible compromise. It called for a freeze on Jewish settlements in the occupied territories during a transition period of five years. While it objected to a Palestinian state, it favored the principle of "land for peace," which entailed a significant retreat by Israel from the occupied territories. According to the initiative, the Palestinians should enjoy self-rule "in association with Jordan, and Jerusalem should remain a united city but its final status should be negotiated."[3]

The recently appointed secretary of state, George Shultz, played an important role in the initiative. "The Arab-Israeli peace process . . . ," he later observed, "was a casualty of the Israeli invasion of Lebanon. The wounds would be fatal unless we planned for peace while the war still raged."[4] From the outset Shultz viewed the need to solve the Palestinian problem as central to peace in the region.[5] At the same time the "acceptance of Palestinian self-determination or PLO recognition of some sort," or any other political bonus to Yasser Arafat for his agreement to leave Beirut, was out of the question. In Shultz's view, the key to the solution was held by King Hussein of Jordan.[6]

The Israeli prime minister immediately rejected the Fresh Start initiative.[7] U.S. Ambassador to Israel Samuel Lewis, who informed Menachem Begin of the plan shortly before the president announced it, reported back to the State Department that the prime minister "reacted to the initiative with shock and outrage conveyed in a calm, steely manner."[8] Within twenty-four hours the Begin government issued a communiqué that stated that the Fresh Start initiative "entirely contradicts the Camp David Accords," and that "the Government of Israel has resolved that on the basis of these positions it will not enter into any negotiations with any party."[9]

On September 8 the Knesset debated the American initiative. Supporters of the government's decision to reject the plan pointed to the grave dangers that would be posed by a Palestinian state, which in their opinion would be the inevitable outcome of the Reagan initiative. Labor leaders continued to advocate the Jordanian Option and argued that the PLO's defeat in Beirut created a new opportunity to bring King Hussein back into the peace process.[10]

The stormy Knesset session was accompanied by a Peace Now demonstration of some 5,000 protesters held in the plaza in front of the Knesset. In principle, Peace Now supported Reagan's initiative for focusing attention once more on the Palestinians as a people and on the problems that had resulted from the prolonged Israeli occupation. At a minimum, the movement expected the Israeli government to discuss the merits of the plan as a possible catalyst for the peace process rather than to summarily reject the initiative. Tzali Reshef, the movement's spokesman, told the demonstrators, "The Israeli-Palestinian conflict will not be decided in Lebanon. Furthermore, the Palestinian problem is essentially a Jewish problem, and can be solved only through direct treatment of the questions related to the national existence of the Palestinians in a way that will be acceptable to both parties."[11]

A Martyr

The various activities of the peace movement against the war in Lebanon during summer and fall 1982 angered supporters of the government and of Ariel Sharon, especially those among the Mizrachi community, many of whom nurtured strong anti-Arab sentiments.[12] They were particularly angered by the way Israel, rather than the Phalange alone, was blamed both at home and abroad for the events at Sabra and Shatila.

The Lebanon war had brought about a significant change in the image of the ethnic composition of the IDF. By 1982 Mizrachim comprised a larger share of the officer corps and the elite fighting units than in previous wars. Whereas the prototypical fighting soldier of previous wars had been the Ashkenazi kibbutznik, the war in Lebanon was seen as being to a large degree fought primarily by young Mizrachi soldiers and officers. Many of them were second- or third-generation Israelis who had been educated and socialized in the Israeli educational system. They were proud that after thirty years of social submersion they had finally achieved an honorable place in the army, the most important institution in Israeli society. Perhaps this development may have been an added factor that mobilized Mizrachi support for the war. In contrast, Ashkenazi kibbutzniks demonstrated against the war, as if trying to deprive Mizrachim of their newfound status by challenging the wisdom of this fight.[13]

The Kahan Commission, which was appointed to investigate Israel's role in the Sabra and Shatila massacre, recommended the dismissal of Sharon as minister of defense. The commission found that the prime minister, the defense minister, and a number of senior IDF officers had "indirect responsibility" for what had occurred. Spontaneous demonstrations by Sharon's supporters called on the prime minister to disregard the commission's recommendations and keep Sharon in office.[14]

Peace Now responded by organizing a large demonstration to demand Sharon's dismissal. On the night of February 10, 1983, about 10,000 demonstrators gathered at Zion Square in the center of Jerusalem. They carried placards and torches, and had to pass through neighborhoods heavily populated by Mizrachim on their way to the prime minister's office, where the cabinet was deciding Sharon's fate. Incidents of violence between the demonstrators and pro-Sharon forces (mostly Mizrachim) occurred along the route. Some of this violence was witnessed by Shulamit Hareven:

> As the demonstration started up the street from Zion Square it became evident that this time it was not just a regular clash of opinions, or the usual violence at the fringes. Even before Peace Now demonstrators arrived, organized groups of strongmen waited for them all along the route. They charged the demonstration in coordinated assaults and attempted to push a wedge between the demonstrators in order to disrupt the march. They were shouting, booing, spitting and hitting, hitting hard and frequently. The police were apparently unprepared for such a level of violence. Here and there we noticed a lone policeman fighting back the strongmen. . . . The march progressed slowly, amidst incessant beatings without respite. Stones were now being thrown as well. Somebody threw a burning cigarette in the face of Amiram, a chemistry professor. Anat, from a distant kibbutz, got a severe beating. Someone snatched a torch from the hands of Tala, an artist from the Israel Museum, and tried to push it into her face. . . . The marchers held back, they did not react. The strongest feeling here today was that the streets were on the threshold of a civil war which must be prevented at all costs. I saw Yarom, Zohar, Emile and Amos, all reserve paratroopers, create a chain of hands to form a human wall against the intruders, a thin wall in front of the violent intruders. All this to allow the demonstration to go on, indeed to allow Israel's democracy to go on.[15]

The worst was yet to come. By the time the march arrived at the prime minister's office a counterdemonstration awaited them, which voiced the now-familiar chant, "Arik [Sharon], King of Israel!" More fistfights broke out, but Peace Now managed to conclude its demonstration as planned. Chana Maron, the first lady of the Israeli theater who had lost a leg in a terrorist attack at the Zurich airport a few years earlier, offered a moving speech. As always, the "Song for Peace" and the national anthem were sung and the crowd started to disperse. Most of the crowd had already left the area, but the demonstration's organizers remained behind to collect debris. Suddenly, a hand grenade was thrown into their midst from a nearby wooded area. Emil Gruenzweig, a Ph.D. candidate at Hebrew University and one of the movement's founders, was hit by the explosion and died within minutes. Several others were wounded and rushed to hospitals, where a few thugs awaited them and tried to assault them even as they were being rushed into the emergency rooms for treatment.[16]

Gruenzweig's murder was a shock not only to the members of Peace Now but also to the public at large. Even during the period before the creation of the State of Israel, when internecine factional strife was commonplace within the Jewish community, political killings among Jews were extremely rare.[17] The attacker's identity was unknown at the time and it was unclear whether he had acted alone or on behalf of a group.[18] While it was possible to believe that the murder had been the spontaneous act of a crazy individual, it was difficult not to associate the attack with the violence that had preceded it in the streets of Jerusalem.

Thousands attended Gruenzweig's funeral, including many supporters of the government who wanted to demonstrate their abhorrence of the use of violence in political disputes. The media focused a considerable amount of attention on the growing ethnic dimension of the political strife. Although the peace movement did not publicly suggest that their support for Begin and Sharon necessarily implied that Mizrachim were more violent in their expression of political opinion, it was a widely held belief throughout the movement.[19]

"I Have No Sister," an article by left-wing journalist Amnon Dankner published a few days after the shocking events at the Peace Now demonstration, contributed to the tense atmosphere. Dankner was enraged by the behavior of the right-wing demonstrators both before and after Gruenzweig's death. In his anger he declared, "Those people who hit the wounded of Peace Now in hospital are not my brothers! The people who extinguished burning cigarettes on the faces of the demonstrators in Jerusalem last Thursday are not my brothers! Those who cursed me and spat on my face, who threatened my life and called me a traitor until their eyes bulged and their veins exploded in rage—these are not my brothers. Full stop." Dankner's message was clear. He expressed the prevailing feeling that the Mizrachim had perpetrated a violent attack against the peace movement that made civil dialogue impossible.[20] By the winter of 1983 it had become increasingly difficult to overlook the ethnic component of the bitter national divide.

The Ethnic Factor

It has been in the nature of Israel's development that it has been settled in waves, from the Zionist immigration to Palestine in the late nineteenth century to the present day. Most of the Mizrachi population immigrated after the establishment of the state in 1948, with the first two decades of statehood bringing some 700,000 Jews from Asia and Africa to Israel.[21] Where the Ashkenazim had constituted 78 percent of Israel's Jewish population in 1949, by 1968 the Mizrachim had achieved numerical parity, and soon thereafter became the majority group.[22]

The absorption of these immigrants was a painful process in a number of ways. The limited financial resources of the new state during the height of the Mizrachi immigration led to long periods of substandard housing, unemployment, and inadequate social services. These immigrants also suffered from an identity crisis. Israeli society, politics, economy, and culture had been shaped by the earlier immigrants who primarily came from eastern and central Europe, and who had little understanding of the more traditional cultures of the new immigrants from the Middle East.[23]

Perhaps the thrill of finally arriving in Israel, coupled with David Ben-Gurion's charisma, at first mitigated the socioeconomic and cultural deprivation experienced by the older generation of Mizrachim. However, when the younger generation reached maturity and were called upon to share the burden of military service, feelings of frustration began to surface.[24] Although many eventually shared in the nation's improving standard of living, the economic gap between the Ashkenazi and Mizrachi communities remained wide, especially among Mizrachim in the new development towns and the economically depressed suburbs of the large cities.[25]

For the generation of Mizrachim educated and socialized in the 1960s and 1970s, Menachem Begin's political style and the tenor of opposition in his rhetoric seemed to express their own status as perpetually outside of the establishment. For them a vote for Likud was a way to express their disenchantment with the old Ashkenazi Labor elite. Despite his Polish origin and distinctly European mannerisms, Begin managed to project the image of a traditional Jew for whom religion and tradition were an important source of identity.

Likud (and its forerunner, Herut) regularly attracted a significant element of the disgruntled Mizrachi community.[26] Repeated polls asked respondents to choose between the two major parties. The number of Mizrachi Jews who chose Labor declined steadily from a high of 79 percent in September 1969 to 43 percent in December 1973 and 33 percent in June 1977.[27] Because the Mizrachi community accounted for approximately 50 percent of the electorate in those years, the support by two-thirds of this community gave Likud a sizeable electoral base.

In the 1977 elections Likud won a majority of the votes in poorer neighborhoods of the large cities, which were heavily inhabited by Mizrachim.[28] In the 1981 elections Likud's gains came from a shift in the voting pattern of the Mizrachi community, coupled with their increased representation in the electorate. But the ethnic factor played an important role in 1981 not only because of the quantitative significance, but also because it was visible in the heated public atmosphere that surrounded the campaign. According to analysts Michal Shamir and Asher Arian, "In 1981 the ethnic issue became interwoven in the election campaign as it has never been before. Ethnic polarization and the high degree of competitiveness combined to produce political intolerance and violence targeted mostly toward the [Labor] Alignment. This violence was perceived as based on ethnic identification."[29] Despite the fact that the Labor list of candidates included more Mizrachim in "safe" places than did the Likud list, and though the senior leaderships of both parties were overwhelmingly Ashkenazi, in the popular mind Likud was identified with the Mizrachim while Labor was seen as predominantly Ashkenazi.

Did the Mizrachim support Menachem Begin because of a disposition toward a more hawkish posture and maximalist version of Zionism, or was their support a result of their personal admiration for Begin and his rhetoric on issues other than the Arab-Israeli conflict? A precise answer to this question may never be found, and both hypotheses probably have some validity.[30] Throughout the 1970s polls found a strong correlation between hawkish postures and ethnic origin.[31] In a poll conducted in 1971, 54 percent of Ashkenazim were ready to return at least some parts of the West Bank to Arab sovereignty, while only 31 percent of Mizrachim were willing to consider such a territorial compromise. The gap narrowed somewhat when Israeli-born respondents of the two communities were compared, but was still significant—67 percent of the Mizrachim were against any concessions versus 52 percent of the Ashkenazim.[32]

By the late 1970s and early 1980s the hawkish tendencies of the Mizrachim were clearly identifiable. They opposed territorial concessions and supported an aggressive policy toward the Arabs. A 1984 poll showed that 64 percent of Israeli-born Mizrachim favored outright annexation of the occupied territories, while 53 percent of Israeli-born Ashkenazim favored territorial compromise.[33]

Roots of Prejudice

Many moderates among the Mizrachim resented the stereotype of Mizrachi Jews as "Arab haters," an image that was often attributed to their history and cultural background.[34] Their resentment was fueled by what they saw as contemptuous Ashkenazi dismissals of Mizrachi culture and identity as essentially primitive.[35] Some Mizrachi leaders tried to explain their group's attitudes toward the Arabs as a product of the past policies of Israeli governments. They pointed out that the government had repeatedly placed Mizrachi immigrants in the front lines of the confrontation with the Arabs, both economically and geographically.

It has also been suggested that during Israel's formative years Mizrachi Jews experienced what sociologist Ofira Seliktar calls "alienated identification." Mizrachim were alienated from many social norms and from the dominant culture, formed by the Ashkenazi elite, which often expressed contempt for the cultural practices of Mizrachi immigrants. The dominant Ashkenazi culture expected them to "desocialize," to abandon their native cultural identity, before they could successfully "resocialize."[36] Desocialization required a "retreat from some of [the immigrant's] past personal achievement as a precondition for his future advancement on the social ladder of modernity."[37] Despite the prejudices experienced by Mizrachim during the integration process, their alienation did not lead them to reject the prevailing dominant ideology and the symbols of the state. On the contrary, the new immigrants were eager to identify themselves with the basic goals of Zionism and thus achieve some measure of social and cultural legitimacy. As such they became what Seliktar referred to as "alienated identifiers." They adopted an extreme version of Zionism even as they were struggling against the current political and cultural elite. "Oriental alienated identifiers," Seliktar suggested, "could vent their frustration against Labor without undermining their commitment to the state" by attaching themselves to the nationalistic counterculture that Menachem Begin symbolized.[38]

On the whole, religiously observant Mizrachim follow a more flexible set of religious norms than the stricter Ashkenazi orthodoxy. However, their adherence to their tradition is not comparatively weaker. On the contrary, Mizrachi religious traditions are more biblical, sentimental, and expressive. Their attachment to holy sites (of which there are many in the occupied territories) makes the concept of the Holy Land an important factor in their political orientations. This aspect of the political-cultural values of Mizrachim may also help explain their attachment to Menachem Begin on a more general level. Begin espoused an ideology that, contrary to the secular Zionists from the left, claimed that Judaism was an inseparable combination of religion and nationalism. This ideological approach appealed to Mizrachim, as did Begin's frequent references to traditional Jewish metaphors and symbols.

Repeated surveys indicated a significant correlation between levels of education and political attitudes, especially with regard to the Arab-Israeli conflict. For example, a 1972 study found that 40 to 45 percent of Israelis with fewer than twelve years of education thought that "a more aggressive policy toward the Arab countries is desirable." Support for this attitude declined at higher levels of education.[39]

Based on these statistics one study concluded that "the level of schooling, both for Ashkenazim and Mizrachim, is an important variable in the prediction of attitudes related to the Arab-Israeli conflict."[40] Higher learning, it is believed, exposes individuals to a wider variety of opinions, trains them in more analytical and flexible modes of thought, and enables them to relate to issues in a less emotional and more self-critical way, which leads to greater tolerance and understanding of the "other" and of the complexity of the issues.[41] According to this hypothesis the correlation between ethnic origin and hawkish posture is largely dependent on the level of education. However, because Mizrachi Jews are heavily distributed on the lower socioeconomic strata, there remains a significant correlation between ethnic origin and levels of education.[42]

The continuance of socioeconomic and educational gaps also left Mizrachim conscious of their precarious economic and social position. In the fall of 1982 the famous Israeli novelist Amos Oz published a series of interviews he held with Israelis in the wake of the Lebanon War. Oz described a meeting with a group of pro-Begin Mizrachim in the town of Beit Shemesh. A young Moroccan began to lecture Oz:

When I was a little kid, my kindergarten teacher was white and her assistant was black [meaning Mizrachi]. In school my teacher was Iraqi and the principal was Polish [meaning Ashkenazi]. On the construction site where I worked my supervisor was a redhead [an Ashkenazi characteristic]. At the clinic the doctor was Ashkenazi and the nurse was an Egyptian [Jew]. In the army we Moroccans were the corporals and the officers came from the kibbutz [an Ashkenazi-dominated institution]. All my life I have been on the bottom and you have been on top. I'll tell you what shame is. They gave us the dirty work. They gave us an education but took away our self-respect. Why did they bring my parents to Israel? Wasn't it to do your dirty work? You didn't have Arabs then, so you needed our parents to do your cleaning and be your servants and laborers. You brought our parents to be your Arabs. But now I'm a supervisor and my friend over here is a self-employed contractor. And that guy over there has a transport business. If they give back the territories the Arabs will stop coming to work, and then and there you will put us back into the dead-end jobs like before. If for no other reason we won't let you give back those territories. Look at my daughter. She works in a bank now, and every evening an Arab comes to clean the building. All you want is to dump her from the bank into some textile factory, or have her wash the floors instead of the Arab, the way my mother used to clean for you. That is why we hate you here. As long as Begin is in power my daughter is secure at the bank. If you guys come back you'll pull her down first thing.[43]

This sermon is instructive, even if it does not provide scientifically reliable evidence. The accumulated impression, which is difficult to refute, suggests that in the early 1980s the Mizrachi community arrived at a crossroads. It came of age and shed the paternalistic restraints the dominant Ashkenazi Labor regime had placed on it during the 1950s and 1960s. In this context, Mizrachi support for Menachem Begin and his nationalistic ideology served the Mizrachim well in their struggle for dignity and a proper place in Israeli society. The animosity of many Mizrachim toward the peace movement was far more than a difference of opinion regarding territorial policy. It may have been part of a broader struggle to protect the new sense of acceptance and dignity provided them by Likud's victory in 1977. Peace Now was chiefly, though not exclusively, an Ashkenazi movement that most Mizrachim detested.

East for Peace

Mizrachi members of the peace movement were profoundly troubled by Emil Gruenzweig's death. They saw the need to refute the stereotype of Mizrachim as innately chauvinist, primitive, and violent, and also to counter the nationalistic fervor that had captured much of the Mizrachi community. Consequently, they sought to persuade fellow Mizrachim to adopt a more moderate point of view. This in turn gave them what they saw as a dual responsibility: to represent the Mizrachi community within the peace movement, and to represent the peace movement within the Mizrachi community. They hoped that the establishment of a separate Mizrachi peace movement might help them achieve both objectives.

In the summer of 1983 a handful of Mizrachi peace activists established a new group that they called "East for Peace."[44] On issues related to the Arab-Israeli conflict their position was similar to Peace Now's. They sought "to encourage the peace process in the Middle East" and believed that "the physical borders of Israel shall be determined in such a way as to maintain its Jewish nature." They also aspired "to combat allegations that Oriental Jews are extremist, violent and hostile to peace; to further political consciousness of the Oriental masses . . . and to help achieve the political, economic and cultural integration of Israel in the Middle East."[45]

East for Peace's leaders believed that to attract their fellow Mizrachim away from Likud's positions they would have to advocate social justice as well as peace. According to Shlomo Elbaz, a professor of comparative literature at the Hebrew University and one of the key figures of the new movement, the Mizrachim "see themselves as victims of an oppressive political-cultural system which ran the country before 1977. The shift of the Mizrachim to the right stemmed from their social bitterness, not because they espoused a chauvinistic point of view. As products of the Middle East their natural place is with the peace camp, and the peace camp will never succeed without attracting these people back to their natural spiritual place. But that can only be achieved if we add the social dimension to our peace philosophy."[46]

Most of East for Peace's leaders had previously been Peace Now activists. During the winter and spring of 1983 the group met for a number of strategy sessions and developed a charter. Their charter was signed by prominent Mizrachi scholars, artists, and writers and was publicly announced on July 22, 1983.[47] Elbaz led this effort and continued as the group's leader in the years that followed. Born in Morocco, Elbaz had come to Israel in the 1950s during the large wave of immigration from North Africa. He lived on a kibbutz in the Negev for a few years and became active in recruiting young North African intellectuals living in France to immigrate to Israel. Through this effort he sought to increase the number of Mizrachi intellectuals in Israel and to stress the importance of education within the Mizrachi community.[48]

Like Peace Now, East for Peace was established and led primarily by intellectuals. Notable individuals in the group included Mordechai Elgrabli, Shelley Elkayam, and Ben Dror Yemini. Elgrabli, a sociologist, came to Israel in the late 1960s with a few dozen North African students, who formed a group they called "Oded" (Encourager). Elbaz became involved with this group while he was on a mission on behalf of the Jewish Agency in Paris. Several of Oded's members had become visible in Israeli politics by the 1977 elections.

Shelley Elkayam, a poet, was born in Israel to a well-established Israeli Mizrachi family and did not suffer any of the deprivations typical for Mizrachi immigrants. However, her father was very involved in the affairs of the Mizrachi community, which familiarized Shelley with the hardships these people confronted.[49]

Ben Dror Yemini, a journalist whose grandparents came to Palestine at the turn of the century from Yemen, grew up in a poorer neighborhood near downtown Tel Aviv. His father worked hard to provide a thorough religious education for his children. Despite this education Yemini abandoned his religious training and became a well-known journalist and a radical defender of Mizrachi rights.

"We were present [in all Peace Now demonstrations]," Elbaz recalled, "but our presence didn't change the stereotype. The fact remained, as it were, that all Oriental Jews were in the other [prowar] camp. . . . When the bomb at the Peace Now demonstration exploded we were right there, but a few days later the reaction in the media was terrible. As if the enemies of peace and the enemies of the peace forces were only those black faces, with foam on their lips and fire in their eyes, these riff-raffs, these Tchach-Tchachs."[50]

East for Peace enjoyed initial successes in street activities and in attracting media attention. As part of their publicity campaign, East for Peace activists released white doves in front of the prime minister's office and on another occasion chained themselves to a railing near the Knesset. Despite these colorful acts East for Peace essentially remained a small and closed group. Its members continued, however, to hold discussions among themselves and further developed their unique ideology. In 1984 they decided to add a cultural dimension to their pursuit of social justice. Israel is a part of the Middle East, they observed, but could not be accepted into the region as long as its culture and orientation were European.[51] "As long as we know who and what we are, we may use elements of other cultures, but we never should become the tail of another culture," said Shlomo Bar, a Moroccan-born singer who was active in East for Peace and who developed a distinctive artistic style based on Moroccan and other Middle Eastern cultures.[52]

East for Peace believed that the Mizrachim, culturally a part of the Middle East, could serve as a human bridge to the region. Therefore, the transformation of Israeli culture and spiritual orientation should be an essential part of the struggle for peace.[53] This effort would require reforming the educational curriculum to make Arabic a mandatory second language and to advance awareness of Middle Eastern history and culture. In this respect, East for Peace viewed its role not only as advocating peace, but also as helping to bring about the integration of Israel into the Middle East after peace was achieved.[54]

Initially the leaders of Peace Now were afraid that the newly founded Mizrachi movement would splinter and weaken the peace movement in general, but they soon discovered that particularistic groups actually strengthened the movement by appealing to a broader range of people. As a result of this diversification Peace Now became a "super-movement" of sorts, as the various splinter groups continued to participate in Peace Now demonstrations. Because there was a practical limit to the number of people who could be involved in the daily planning and organizing of activities of any given group, the fragmentation enabled a larger number of activists to become involved in the various activities undertaken by the splinter groups as well as by the super-movement—this despite the fact that the smaller groups regularly criticized the way Peace Now handled its own affairs.

East for Peace did not become the mass movement its founders hoped for, nor did it make significant progress within the Mizrachi community, which overwhelmingly continued to support Likud during the 1980s.[55] The members of East for Peace were labeled "eggheads" by other Mizrachim—socially and culturally distant from working-class Mizrachim of the poorer neighborhoods and development towns. A veteran leader of the Black Panthers described the Mizrachi peace movement as "a Moroccan salon whose members had bought a few Moroccan carpets and now sat around drinking mint tea and talking about Eastern Culture."[56] A number of Mizrachi mayors of development towns from both Labor and Likud sympathized with East for Peace, but were cognizant of the lack of support among the Mizrachi masses. "They were far from the people on the ground," commented Eli Dayan, the mayor of Ashkelon.

Shlomo Elbaz and East for Peace continued to participate in the national debate and provided an important symbol of its Mizrachi dimension and an important political alternative to the hawkish stance taken by most Mizrachim. They also actively participated in the growing dialogue with Palestinian leaders. However, Shelley Elkayam's hope that the Mizrachim would "accept us as their representatives because we are part of them" did not materialize.[57]

Paths of Peace—The Orthodox Factor

A similar dilemma confronted orthodox Jews who considered themselves part of the peace movement but otherwise identified with Israel's orthodox religious community.[58] The fact that the settlers' movement (Gush Emunim) was established and populated primarily by orthodox Jews created a strong stereotype in the public mind, which identified orthodoxy, and especially the Zionist wing of orthodoxy, with right-wing politics. There was, in truth, some basis for this stereotype. While some notable ultra-orthodox rabbis occasionally expressed dovish opinions, the majority of orthodox Jews predictably favored Israeli sovereignty over the entire Holy Land.[59] Taking the scriptures literally, they believed that God had promised this land to the Israelites and that it was not within their rights to betray the will of God. It followed that an overwhelming majority of orthodox rabbis supported expansion in the occupied territories. Both secular and religious supporters of the Israeli right wing frequently invoked Jewish religious precepts and biblical commandments to support their argument for retaining the territories.[60]

Nevertheless, many progressive orthodox Jews shared Peace Now's views and supported the peace movement. They resented the stereotype of orthodox Jews as belonging exclusively to the far right, and believed that many orthodox Israelis could be attracted away from Gush Emunim. However, to do this required using religious arguments that the orthodox would find persuasive. Peace Now, its membership and message predominantly secular, was unable to speak the language of the orthodox. Only other orthodox Jews could articulate the arguments necessary to persuade the orthodox.[61]

Back in 1975, in reaction to the creation of Gush Emunim earlier that year, a group of orthodox scholars had founded an ideological-political forum that they called "Oz ve Shalom" (Strength and Peace).[62] Some of the group's founders were veteran orthodox politicians who had sat in the Knesset as MKs of the National Religious Party. The group also included biblical scholar Uri Simon, a professor at the religious Bar-Ilan University and a senior member of the peace movement. They were supported by such prominent rabbis from the Jewish diaspora as the Chief Rabbi of the United Kingdom, Lord Rabbi Immanuel Jakobovits. The group announced that it had been founded "in response to the exclusivist territorial ideology of other religious groups, notably Gush Emunim. Our educational materials . . . are intended to convey another vision of religious Zionism."[63] While Oz ve Shalom gained a high level of prestige, its activities were mainly limited to intellectual exercises such as publishing articles and convening conferences. Its message was that genuine Torah values gave precedence to "peace, justice, and the sanctity of every human life."[64]

After the invasion of Lebanon and the massacres at Sabra and Shatila, some of the younger members of Oz ve Shalom, and other religious men and women previously active in the peace movement, decided to increase their involvement. Among them were Avi Ravitzky, a teacher of medieval Jewish philosophy at Hebrew University in Jerusalem,[65]

Yehzkiel Landau, the information secretary for Oz ve Shalom, and Moshe Halbertal, a promising young philosopher and the son-in-law of the famous Rabbi David Hartman. They organized public prayers during the ten-day period between Rosh Hashanah and Yom Kippur—the time known in Jewish tradition as the Days of Repentance. Many orthodox soldiers who had fought in Lebanon attended the prayer sessions, which received the blessing of Rabbi Yehuda Amital and Rabbi Aharon Lichtenstein, the directors of Yeshiva Har Etzion, based near Kfar Etzion in an occupied region south of Bethlehem. In January 1983 they established a group that they named "Netivot Shalom" (Paths of Peace), "to arouse new thoughts concerning the issues on the [national] agenda: The Land of Israel, peace, the sanctity of life, moral considerations in time of war, and a Jewish critique of the direction of government policy."[66]

Peace Now welcomed the establishment of Netivot Shalom because it attracted a constituency that the larger, secular movement had been unable to reach.[67] The concern that the religious peace movement would attract secular followers away from Peace Now was marginal. Netivot Shalom used Jewish symbols and metaphors that were largely alien to secular Israelis.[68] For example, their activities were usually linked to a significant religious date or event such as fasting during Ta'anit Esther, which no secular Israeli would observe, or sitting in a *succat shalom* (tabernacle of peace).[69] Also, most Peace Now demonstrations were planned for the Sabbath (Saturday), partly because this was the only time most Israelis were able to attend, and partly because it allowed the demonstration to be reported on the popular Saturday evening television news, which begins immediately after the end of the Sabbath. For orthodox Jews, however, participation in such demonstrations would have meant desecrating the Sabbath.

Initially there was some duplication between the two orthodox movements but in 1984 they merged under the name "Oz ve Shalom/Netivot Shalom." Oz ve Shalom, which continued some activities under its own name, acted as the movement's ideological compass.[70] The new movement's statement of principle declared its adherence to the tenets of religious Zionism and stated that the "attachment to the Land of Israel is of fundamental importance to our faith and outlook." However, it also maintained that "peace is a religious and moral value and is an essential goal in both individual and public life. . . . God found no better way to bless Israel than with peace." Between the love of the land and the love of peace a fateful choice has to be made—and because "we are commanded to make the sanctity of human life, peace and respect for all people, the highest priority," so the choice must be for peace. "With all the pain and sacrifice inherent in the decision, we must agree to a territorial compromise." The statement of principle concluded that "true Zionism strives not only for redemption of the land, but also for the redemption of the people within the land."[71] Rabbi Aharon Lichtenstein summarized this approach saying, "It is not that we love Eretz Yisrael [the Land of Israel] less, but that we love Am Israel [the Nation of Israel] more."[72]

Concerned about their image within the orthodox community, the founders of Netivot Shalom attempted to dissociate themselves from Peace Now. They hoped that by keeping their distance from the secular peace movement they would improve their chances for success among the orthodox. They felt that an image of their group as "Peace Now with skullcaps" would be a sure recipe for failure.[73] Despite these efforts, the movement's success was limited. At its peak it had about 1,500 dues-paying members, and an estimated 1,500 additional supporters.[74]

The movement's founders had also hoped to attract young orthodox Mizrachim. Mizrachi Chief Rabbi Ovadia Yosef often expressed opinions similar to those held by Oz ve Shalom/Netivot Shalom. For example, he believed that "it is permitted to return parts of the Land of Israel in order to achieve this goal [of peace] since nothing is more important than saving lives."[75] In fall 1986 and again in 1987 Oz ve Shalom/Netivot Shalom organized a *succat shalom* in collaboration with East for Peace, but the results were unimpressive. The religious peace movement, much like the secular movement, remained essentially a middle- and upper-middle-class Ashkenazi movement. Like East for Peace, the religious peace movement's main contribution was largely symbolic and psychological. It helped counter the hawkish stereotype of Israeli orthodoxy. Its alternative interpretations of religious obligations also contributed to a lively debate within orthodox circles.

East for Peace and Oz ve Shalom/Netivot Shalom contributed to the broader peace movement by addressing previously untapped constituencies. In both cases the stereotypes they sought to dispel were not entirely untrue, for the majority of Mizrachim and the majority of orthodox Jews did indeed tend to support hawkish ideologies and policies. However, they managed to demonstrate that being Mizrachi or orthodox did not automatically make one a hawk. They also encouraged those members of the Mizrachi and orthodox communities who held dovish attitudes by showing them that they were not entirely alone and by raising the hope that, in the future, perhaps their numbers and influence would grow.

9

Under the Shadow of National Unity, 1984–87

Wasted Blessing

The war in Lebanon led to a proliferation of Israeli peace groups. In the wake of the war, though Peace Now remained by far the largest group, it was joined by a dozen or so other organizations, some short-lived, others that enjoyed greater longevity. During most of 1983 and the first half of 1984 the different groups of the peace movement focused largely on two objectives: opposing the government's settlement policy in the West Bank, and increasing public pressure on the government to withdraw from the quagmire in Lebanon. The first of these had become particularly salient when, following the expiration of the three-month freeze promised President Carter at Camp David, Menachem Begin had accelerated new settlement activities in the West Bank.[1]

Peace Now could do little to stop these officially sanctioned settlements, which it continued to view as major obstacles to peace. The movement, however, never decided its activities solely by a calculation of their practical short-term results; their long-term psychological impact was also important. Thus, demonstrations against the settlement policy continued even though most public attention was focused on the situation in Lebanon.

On November 27, 1982, three simultaneous demonstrations took place. The first was in the center of Hebron, where Jewish settlers had begun to encroach on the area densely populated by the town's Arab inhabitants.[2] The second and third occurred in the two newly established settlements of Nofim and Shavei Shomron, not far from the Green Line in the Samaria region. Makeshift monuments were erected with bronze plaques inscribed with the biblical phrase, "Seek peace, and pursue it." Eight weeks later, on the stormy winter night of January 14, 1983, a few thousand Peace Now demonstrators "conquered" the new town of Efrat, south of Bethlehem. This settlement was not yet inhabited but was approaching completion. The demonstrators welded a makeshift sculpture across the road and draped it in a giant cloth placard that read, "Do Not Block the Road to Peace!" The value of this otherwise successful demonstration was lessened by a few hotheaded participants who caused some damage to the buildings—an action that Peace Now disavowed as contradicting its policy of acting within the law.[3]

A much less equivocal success came a few months later, during celebrations for the thirty-fifth Independence Day, on April 18, 1983. The government had announced that the main event of the day would be the transfer of a military post overlooking the heavily populated Arab West Bank town of Nablus (Shchem in Hebrew) into the hands of civilian settlers. According to the Bible, Shchem is situated in a valley between the Mountain of Curse (Har Haklala in Hebrew) and the Mountain of Blessing (Har Habracha). The new settlement was to be established on top of the latter hill and to be named "Bracha" (Blessing). It was clear that this step would be interpreted by the Palestinians as a provocative act, likely to exacerbate tension and perhaps lead to violence. The government's decision to highlight this essentially partisan and controversial act on Independence Day, a day supposed to symbolize and generate national unity, angered Peace Now.

The Central Forum decided that at a minimum the movement should seek to disrupt the festivities. A huge tent was erected on the main highway to Nablus at the junction of the road leading to Bracha. Giant placards were posted, facing in all directions and carrying the slogan "Bracha Levatala" (A Wasted Blessing). The symbolic significance of this event, and the considerable media attention it received, prompted the settlers to attempt to organize a counterdemonstration. However, the Peace Now demonstrators far outnumbered the settlers and their sympathizers. Deputy Prime Minister David Levy, who arrived by helicopter to participate in the ceremony, managed to avoid the angry protesters but was forced to swiftly conclude the ceremony and depart. Peace Now's demonstration did not prevent the establishment of another Jewish village in the midst of the Arab area, but the celebrations of Independence Day were disrupted and the controversial settlement policy was again publicly challenged. The historian Shaul Friedlander and the lyricist Chaim Hefer, who that day received the prestigious Israel Prize, participated in the demonstration and went to the prize-giving ceremony directly from the "battlefield."

Out of the Quagmire

By the end of November 1982 it became clear that the Israeli army would remain entrenched in Lebanon at least through the winter and possibly beyond.[4] The cost to Israel in human and economic resources was mounting. The different Lebanese militias, while continuing to fight each other, had by now turned against the Israelis. Even the Shi'as in the south, who had at first welcomed the Israelis for freeing them from the harsh hand of the Palestinian guerrillas, now turned against their liberators. A small group of Shi'a fanatics inspired and supported by Iran organized themselves under the name "Hizbullah" (The Party of God) and launched repeated attacks against Israeli forces.[5]

Reserve soldiers who had already fought in the Lebanon War were being recalled and sent to Lebanon for the second, even the third time. An increasing number refused to serve because they regarded the continued presence of the IDF in Lebanon as immoral, unnecessary, and counterproductive. By the middle of 1983 the number of refusers had surpassed one hundred. Ruth Linn, a psychologist who studied the motivations of those who refused to serve in Lebanon, found that most who resisted did so only after receiving their second or third call-up orders, when the prospect of returning yet again to participate in a campaign that seemed cruel and futile finally overcame their reluctance to disobey orders. "After two months of fighting, with a break of four days, I came back home and there was another call-up notice waiting for me. This time to Ansar (a detention camp in Lebanon built to jail Palestinian and Lebanese prisoners). I knew I had reached my red line, my moral limit."[6]

The Likud government was unwilling to cut Israel's losses and withdraw, as to do so would have amounted to an admission that the

Lebanese adventure was a costly mistake. Instead it attempted to cajole from the Lebanese government—now headed by Amin Gemayel, who had succeeded his murdered brother—what would essentially have amounted to a peace treaty that included a plan for the normalization of relations between Lebanon and Israel.

The Reagan administration also seemed to believe at this stage that a political agreement between Israel and Lebanon was achievable. It gave its blessing to negotiations between the parties, which began on December 27, 1982, in the Lebanese town of Khalde, not far from the Beirut airport. The negotiations alternated between Khalde and Kiryat Shmonah in northern Israel (and later Netanya, north of Tel Aviv). Morris Draper, who had assisted Philip Habib in earlier mediation efforts, participated in the negotiations on behalf of the U.S. State Department.[7]

The negotiations dragged on for five months, stalling repeatedly as a result of the Lebanese government's concern over domestic and foreign opposition to the negotiations.[8] It required the personal intervention of Secretary of State George Shultz to bring the negotiations to an apparently successful conclusion, and an agreement was reached on May 17, 1983.[9] Ultimately, very little came out of the entire effort because despite the formal approval of the Lebanese Parliament, President Amin Gemayel failed to ratify the agreement, and eventually abrogated it under heavy Syrian pressure less than a year later on March 5, 1984.[10]

The IDF's continued substantial presence deep inside Lebanon was viewed by a growing number of Israelis as both pointless and too costly. On Saturday, June 4, 1983, a year after the invasion of Lebanon, Peace Now organized a symbolic weeklong march from Rosh Hanikra, in northern Israel near the Lebanese border, to the center of Tel Aviv, where a huge demonstration was held. The marchers followed a preplanned route along the coast and stopped in communities along the way to organize demonstrations in public squares. They spent the nights in the woods or in public parks near main road junctions where they held public discussions. Sympathizers joined the march en route, and the crowd of a few hundred who had started in Rosh Hanikra had grown to several thousand by the time it reached Tel Aviv a week later. One hundred thousand people participated in the large demonstration at the now traditional location in front of the municipal building. The main demand heard above all others was "Get Out of Lebanon!"[11]

By this time Peace Now was five years old, yet no permanent structure had been established. All activities were performed by volunteers. Funds raised in Israel, and from sympathizers in the United States and Europe, were spent on preparing and publishing materials such as newspaper advertisements, leaflets, posters, and other forms of communication. An impressive amount of experience and expertise had been accumulated, as demonstrated by the success of the logistically complex march to Tel Aviv. Most of the smaller peace groups also participated in the march. Peace Now had become a national symbol for the various elements of the peace movement.

At this stage the group called Parents against Silence intensified its activities against the war.[12] "During the many months of the negotiations in Khalde and Kiryat Shmonah we stopped our activities," Naomi Bentsur recalled. "We had an illusion that the war would come to an end shortly, but we were fooled. We lost precious time. But when the so-called peace talks came to nought we decided to come out once more with a clear message: Bring our boys home!"[13]

Parents against Silence organized a continuous vigil near the prime minister's residence in Jerusalem, and a larger demonstration near his office during the weekly Sunday cabinet meeting. Demonstrations were also organized in front of the defense minister's office in Tel Aviv. Parents against Silence lobbied heavily in the Knesset, meeting with all members except Ariel Sharon, whom the group held responsible for the Lebanese fiasco. Additionally, 100,000 parents signed a petition to end the costly presence of the IDF in Lebanon. A delegation of parents also went to see Menachem Begin:

> We composed our delegation with great care [Naomi Bentsur recalled]. It included men and women: a member of a kibbutz from the border with Lebanon; a Holocaust survivor; a veteran member of Begin's party, and a man who was born in Kiryat Shmonah [the shelling of which had initiated the war]. Begin listened to us intensely and did not utter a word, but I felt that our words fell on his head like bombshells. He only said at the end that he could not stop the Israeli involvement in Lebanon right away, but his personal assistant told us later that he was deeply moved and that our meeting with him had a great impact.[14]

In February 1983 Moshe Arens, Israel's ambassador to Washington, had replaced Ariel Sharon as minister of defense. Sharon was dismissed according to the recommendations of the Kahan Commission, but remained in the government as a minister without portfolio. Chief of Staff Raphael Eitan ended his appointed term and was replaced by General Moshe Levi. Arens and Levi were far less enthusiastic about Israel's involvement in Lebanon's internal struggles, particularly in light of Amin Gemayel's reluctance to endorse the treaty signed on May 17, 1983. Consequently, they felt that Israeli forces should be withdrawn from their northern positions along the Beirut-Damascus highway. In August 1983 they received the government's permission to withdraw southward to a line along the Awali River just north of the town of Saida.

For the peace movement this was too little, too late. The new deployment still left the IDF with the task of dealing with nearly half a million angry Palestinians in refugee camps near Saida and Tyre. Compounding this problem were the nearly 500,000 Shi'a in the area and the various Shi'a militias who found southern Lebanon an area hospitable for guerrilla warfare.[15]

Elections Once More

In August 1983 Begin shocked the public when he unexpectedly announced his resignation. Begin never elaborated on the reasons for his departure; he only told his colleagues in the cabinet, "I can go on no more!"[16] Speculation naturally followed Begin's announcement. The prime minister had been in poor health for some time and suffered from a heart condition that may have weakened him to the point where he felt incapable of continuing to meet the demands of his office. The death of his beloved wife Aliza, who had been his loyal companion for half a century, grieved him and certainly added to his depression. Some observers also attributed his decision to the failure of the Lebanese adventure and the resulting deaths of so many young Israelis, a toll that weighed heavily on his conscience.[17] Begin lived in seclusion for another eight years in his Jerusalem apartment and never made any public appearances again.[18]

Yitzhak Shamir, the minister of foreign affairs, replaced Begin as prime minister. Although he did not significantly alter his predecessor's basic policies, Shamir's grey style and Aren's soft-spoken demeanor were in marked contrast to the acid, polemical rhetoric of Begin and Sharon. Shamir presented his government to the Knesset on October 10, 1983.[19] In addition to mounting casualties from attacks on Israeli forces in Lebanon[20] the new government had to confront an economic crisis marked by hyperinflation, depletion of foreign currency reserves, and diminished consumer confidence in the banking system. The replacement of the minister of finance brought no relief, and by the beginning of 1984 it seemed clear that Shamir's government would not complete its full term. In March 1984 it collapsed when one of the smaller coalition parties voted with the opposition for early elections.

Around this time polls suggested that the Labor Party had a good chance of defeating the Likud in the approaching elections. Consequently, many peace activists directed their energies away from extraparliamentary activities and toward achieving a Labor victory. Peace Now employed the same strategy it had used in the 1981 elections. A committee drafted an eight-point platform and presented it for endorsement to all center and left-of-center parties. The movement then recommended that its followers vote for the party of their choice, taking into consideration the conformity of this party's political platform with the eight points articulated by Peace Now.[21] The following tenets appeared on the platform:

- The goals of Zionism, as the liberation movement of the Jewish people, cannot be fulfilled so long as Israel continues to occupy the Palestinian people in the West Bank and the Gaza Strip.

- The suppression of one nation by another is not only immoral but also corrupts the society of the occupier and weakens its security in the long run. Peace on the eastern border is therefore vital.

- Peace must be based on the partition of the Land of Israel. Israel must recognize the right of the Palestinians to a national existence as much as the Arabs, including the Palestinians, must recognize the same right for the Jews.

- Israel must undertake to negotiate with representatives of the Palestinians who accept negotiations as the only way for reconciliation. Jordan should be invited to join the negotiations. Autonomy should not be used as an instrument for de facto annexation of territories and for blocking peace agreements in the future.

- Further settlements in the occupied territories must be frozen, and the freed resources spent to solve problems of poverty and deprivation inside Israel. Except for strictly security considerations, the Palestinians in the occupied territories should be constrained in no way, and should be free to control their own lives through their own institutions.

- Israel should extricate itself from the Lebanese quagmire, set a timetable for the retreat of its forces, establish a friendly regime in the "security belt" north of its border, and reestablish a regime of "red line" agreements with Syria.

- In light of the declared policies of the Likud, joining a coalition led by this party should be excluded.

- A law should be enacted for indemnification of victims of violence perpetrated against legal political demonstrations, including those who were wounded in the demonstration in which Emil Gruenzweig was killed.[22]

Three parties—Mapam, Shinui, and Ratz—unequivocally endorsed this platform. The Labor Party announced that it had some reservations regarding details and wording but accepted the overall spirit of the document. Many Peace Now activists supported these parties in their campaigns, and some appeared on their lists as candidates for Knesset seats—a situation that did not, as it had in 1981, engender any ill feeling inside Peace Now. Indeed, several people who were active in the movement gained seats in the Eleventh Knesset.[23]

The results of the elections were inconclusive. Likud lost a few seats and Labor gained a few, but neither party was able by itself to form a stable coalition. The most noticeable shift in seats involved the strengthening of the extreme right and extreme left.[24] After lengthy but unsuccessful bargaining by Likud and Labor to form coalitions with the smaller parties, they decided to jointly form a National Unity Government. The governing agreement called for a rotation of the prime ministership between Shimon Peres and Yitzhak Shamir, with Peres serving as prime minster for the first twenty-five months, while Shamir served as minister of foreign affairs. Labor received the Ministry of Defense, which went to Yitzhak Rabin, and Likud the Ministry of Finance, to be headed by Yitzhak Modai. Of the smaller parties, only the orthodox joined the coalition, while the fringe parties on the right and left remained in opposition. A complex and cumbersome agreement between the two major parties, coupled with mutual veto power for both, assured a virtual deadlock on any controversial policy decisions.[25]

The Jewish Underground

Despite their preoccupation with partisan politics during the election campaign, Peace Now activists continued with a range of activities. These included educational programs, activities with Mizrachim in poorer neighborhoods, and efforts against settlements in the occupied territories. Creativity was not lacking. A group from a poor area of Jerusalem constructed a mock settlement at the outskirts of their neighborhood, declaring that the only way to get the government's attention was to establish a new settlement. They erected a few tents and makeshift huts and demanded that the government provide them with funding just as it did for Gush Emunim settlements.

The discovery of a Jewish underground terrorist organization in spring 1984 shifted public attention away from Lebanon and back to the occupied territories. During the previous few years a number of attacks had been perpetrated against Palestinians in the occupied territories by unidentified assailants.[26] On June 3, 1981, bombs were planted in the cars of Bassam Shak'a, the mayor of Nablus, and Karim Khalaf, the mayor of Ramallah, both supporters of the PLO. The bombs permanently maimed both mayors.[27] In July 1983, in retaliation for the murder of a Jewish student in the streets of Hebron, an armed group burst into the Islamic College firing automatic rifles. The attack killed three Palestinian students and wounded thirty-three others.[28]

The Shin Bet quietly investigated these incidents, and in April 1984 uncovered a ring of settlers and members of Gush Emunim who had organized themselves into a clandestine vigilante group to fight the growing influence of the Palestinian national movement. Their terror plots included bombing mosques on the Temple Mount in Jerusalem.

The group was apprehended after members had placed bombs on a number of Arab buses. The bombs were timed to explode when the buses were packed full of passengers returning to their homes in the occupied territories.[29] After their trials and convictions the members of what came to be known as the "Jewish Underground" were sentenced to various prison terms. These trials exposed the sharp political polarization that had existed since the war in Lebanon. Gush Emunim attempted to distance itself from the Jewish underground, but that was difficult because some of the terrorist ringleaders were also part of the senior leadership of Gush Emunim. The settlers did not hide their sympathy for their friends in prison. For the peace movement this was proof of the veracity of its warning that the occupation would inevitably corrupt the occupier as well as the occupied.[30]

Enter Kahane

The 1984 elections did not bring about any radical political changes, but one outcome that attracted considerable attention was Rabbi Meir Kahane's election to the Knesset. After previously unsuccessful attempts to win a Knesset seat, Kahane managed to gain enough votes for a seat. Reflecting the growing polarization of the electorate, he received 25,000 votes in 1984, up from 5,000 in the previous two elections.[31] His campaign introduced a new element into Israeli politics: an explicitly racist platform.[32]

Meir Kahane was born to an orthodox family in New York City. In the late 1960s he founded the Jewish Defense League (JDL), which was involved in antiblack vigilante activities in Jewish neighborhoods of New York. The JDL also demonstrated, sometimes violently, for the right of Soviet Jews to emigrate to Israel.[33] In 1971 Kahane immigrated to Israel and established a small party called "Kach" (Thus). The name was taken from "*Rak Kach*" (Only Thus), which was the slogan of the Irgun underground movement before 1948. Kach's logo was a fist raised on the background of a yellow Star of David, similar to the yellow star used by the Nazis to identify Jews.[34]

The first groups Kahane attacked with his rhetoric and provocative visits to their homes were Christian missionaries operating in Israel and the Black Hebrews, a small sect of African-Americans who had settled in the southern town of Dimona. Both of these groups were easy targets for Kahane but too marginal to attract much attention. However, he soon discovered the Palestinians, both in the occupied territories as well as within the Green Line.[35] In April 1973 Kahane was indicted for mailing thousands of letters to Israeli Arabs urging them to leave Israel. The letters included offers to purchase their property and help them emigrate to the United States.[36]

Kahane believed that Arabs did not belong in the Holy Land and should be induced to leave, or be expelled if necessary. His propaganda was replete with racism and antidemocratic polemics. Despite his proclivity for dramatic manipulation of the media, during the late 1970s very few Israelis took Kahane seriously. But the dissatisfaction of the extreme right with the results of the Lebanese adventure, coupled with Begin's departure from the political arena, enabled Kahane to gain popularity among some dissatisfied right-wing voters in the early 1980s.[37]

Kahane's election to the Knesset, and his increased legitimacy as a result of this victory, caused alarm not only among liberals but even among some members of Likud. The minister of education, Zevulun Hammer, a leader of the National Religious Party and supporter of Gush Emunim, established within his ministry a special department for the enhancement of democratic values among the young. In addition, a number of MKs from different parties launched a parliamentary initiative to pass an antiracism law.[38]

During 1985 and 1986 many antiracist activities were organized by concerned citizens throughout the country. Antiracist groups appeared wherever Kahane and his followers organized public activities. These counterprotests sometimes led to fistfights. On one occasion Kahane announced that he would arrive at the Arab town of Umm al-Fahm to propose to its inhabitants that they "peacefully" leave the country. At the designated hour 5,000 Jews joined with the local Arabs and blocked his entrance to the town. Later some of these groups organized a national coalition under the name "Ma'ane" (An Answer—also an acronym for The General Coalition against Racism) and coordinated anti-Kahane activities across Israel.[39]

Many efforts to improve relations between Israeli Jews and Israeli Arabs had been undertaken during the previous decade. A number of educational institutions had long-standing coexistence projects that created opportunities for Jewish and Arab youths to meet one another and reduce their mutual alienation and mistrust. In light of the threat posed by Kahane these activities proliferated and intensified.

Many examples of this work can be cited. For example, Givat Haviva, the adult education center of one of the kibbutz movements, started a project called "Children Teaching Children," in which for one year Jewish and Arab junior high school students met weekly in small groups to teach one another their respective languages. Another creative effort was the village called "Neve Shalom/Wahat Al Salaam" (The Oasis of Peace). This village, on the road from Tel Aviv to Jerusalem, was established jointly by Jews and Arabs to demonstrate their ability to coexist peacefully. A "School of Peace" was founded there in which Jewish and Arab high school students discussed mutual stereotypes, prejudices, and their concerns in a relaxed atmosphere.[40] Re'ut (Friendship), a youth movement that emphasizes Arab-Jewish coexistence, was also established during this period and organized hikes, camping trips, family visits, and community projects involving young Israeli Arabs and Jews. Beit Hagafen (The House of the Vine), a community center located on a junction connecting Jewish and Arab neighborhoods in the city of Haifa, developed an impressive array of mixed social and cultural activities.[41]

Many of these groups and institutions saw themselves as making a significant contribution to peace, which was true insofar as the reduction of hatred and stereotyping of Israeli Arabs by Israeli Jews helped to create a better psychological environment for peacemaking.[42] However, these antiracist efforts tended to overlook the fact that the problems confronted by Israeli Arabs are significantly different from the problems of the Palestinians in the occupied territories. In essence, the problem confronting the Palestinians who are Israeli citizens is one of integration and *civil* rights, while the essence of the problem facing the occupied Palestinians is of separation and basic *human* rights.[43] To do justice for Israeli Arabs one must pursue a civil society in which all people live as equals and share the same civil liberties. However, the Palestinians in the occupied territories do not wish to share sovereignty and a civil society with the Jews. Instead, they speak of political rights based on the principle of self-determination.

This inattention to the differences between Israeli Arabs and Palestinians has also left its mark on historical understanding of the peace movement during the 1980s. Many commentators mistakenly assert that four or five dozen peacemaking organizations were active in Israel during the decade. In fact, most of these should properly be defined as co-existence groups working to improve relations between Israeli Arab and Jewish citizens. The number of groups that actually dealt with peace issues never exceeded one dozen, although there was an overlap of people active in the two areas.

Kahane and Peace Now

Similar to its attitude toward other issues on the periphery of the peace process, Peace Now initially participated in but did not officially sponsor Arab-Jewish coexistence programs or demonstrations targeting Kahane and his racism. Individual members of the movement often played a central role in these activities, and Peace Now's mobilization and recruitment network was used to help generate participation in such events as the anti-Kahane rally in Umm al-Fahm, but the movement as a whole did not consider them part of its mandate. However, when Kahane and Kach became increasingly active in the occupied territories as well as Israel, Peace Now began to view them as a serious threat and came to the conclusion that well-organized and consistent opposition was necessary. Whether in response to pressure from the activists, or because little progress was envisioned in the peace process at the time, in 1984 Peace Now and other peace groups began to devote a greater amount of their resources to the struggle against racism.

In December of that year, Labor MK Muhamed Darawshe announced his intention to fly to Amman to meet with Yasser Arafat. Although his plan did not materialize for technical reasons, the "Young Guard" of the Likud announced their intention to visit Darawshe's village, Iksal, in the lower Galilee to demonstrate against him. Peace Now took the initiative and arrived in the village in time to block the right-wing demonstrators, and in doing so created a sense of fraternity with the Arab inhabitants.[44]

During spring and summer 1985 a new wave of terror against Israelis was unleashed both inside Israel and abroad. On two occasions Jewish hikers were murdered in forests not far from Israeli towns, and a number of Israeli soldiers were kidnapped while hitchhiking and murdered.[45] Outside of Israel, three Israeli tourists were murdered on their boat at the marina in Larnaka, Cyprus, on September 25.[46] On October 7 the cruise ship *Achille Lauro* was hijacked in international waters by Palestinian guerrillas. Leon Klinghoffer, an American Jew confined to a wheelchair, was cruelly thrown overboard and drowned.[47] On December 27 simultaneous attacks on the El Al ticket counters in the Rome and Vienna airports were carried out by the Abu Nidal terrorist group. Eighteen people were killed and 104 wounded, mostly non-Israelis.[48]

These attacks caused considerable anguish among Israelis, and erased much of the progress made by the antiracist groups. In a poll conducted in the summer of 1985, 9 percent of the Israeli electorate declared that they would vote for Kahane. Observers attributed this groundswell of support to a show of anger against the Palestinians rather than to admiration for Kahane. Nevertheless, deep concern spread among the ranks of the Israeli left.

Naftali Raz, the energetic "operations officer" of Peace Now, and a few other activists decided to take a longer look at the issue of racism. At the beginning of 1986 they established an educational institution to nurture democratic values among young Israelis. The institute was dedicated to the memory of Emil Gruenzweig and was named "Adam" (Human). The institute offered seminars on democracy and tolerance to Israeli high school students, and trained a network of discussion leaders who provided their services to schools and youth groups throughout the country. Adam was not formally attached to Peace Now, although most of the staff came from the peace movement.[49]

Out of Lebanon—At Long Last

Peace Now's agenda expanded not only because of Kahane's electoral gains and his brand of racism. By the end of 1985 the peace movement was plagued with apathy—apathy born, ironically, of the growing feeling that the new government might succeed at making peace without the peace movement doing anything.

Shimon Peres, who had become prime minister in September 1984, welcomed Reagan's 1982 Fresh Start initiative as a good point of departure. From 1967 onward, the Labor Party had been wed more or less to the Jordanian Option, which accepted a return of occupied territories only within the context of an Israeli-Jordanian peace agreement. The Reagan initiative was also based on a Jordanian orientation. Not unlike the Labor Party, the Reagan administration opposed the creation of a separate Palestinian state, and until December 1988 refused to hold official, direct talks with the PLO. According to both the Labor and the U.S. formulas, peace had to be made with Jordan, not with the Palestinians as a separate political entity.

When Peres became prime minister he outlined three main objectives he hoped to achieve during his tenure: completion of the IDF's withdrawal from Lebanon, restoration of the ailing economy, and the achievement of an understanding with King Hussein regarding the modalities for a serious peace process.[50] Peres also strove to improve relations with Egypt, and renewed the Israeli-Moroccan connection during a low-key but public visit to King Hassan in July 1986—like Rabin in the 1970s, Peres believed that King Hassan might be able to help bring other Arab states to the negotiating table.[51]

Of Peres's objectives, the only one for which he could rely on the cooperation of his Likud partners in the National Unity Government was economic rehabilitation.[52] As far as the withdrawal from Lebanon was concerned, it was still difficult for Likud leaders to accept the futility of their war and admit it publicly by supporting an unconditional withdrawal (in a Knesset vote) without at least some formal security guarantees from the Lebanese government.[53] Despite this a few Likud ministers who had expressed reservations about the war from the start—most notably David Levy, the Moroccan-born construction-worker-turned-politician who became Begin's deputy prime minister and was popular among Likud's Mizrachi voters—gave Peres the necessary votes to withdraw Israeli forces from the Awali River.

Israel gave up on the Maronites, its erstwhile allies in Lebanon, and closed its informal legation in Beirut. The IDF proceeded unilaterally to establish a so-called security belt, which stretched ten miles north of the international border. The security belt was to be controlled by the South Lebanon Army (SLA), supplied and trained by Israel and commanded since the death of Major Haddad by General Antoine Lahad, a retired Lebanese army officer. The IDF continued to patrol the area and occasionally moved additional forces into the area to support the SLA whenever it came under heavy attack by Hizbullah and other militias.

Despite the IDF's continued involvement in the security belt, the withdrawal from the Awali River virtually ended Ariel Sharon's Lebanese adventure. In May 1985 the last units came home and Israel returned, by and large, to the geographic positions it had held before 1982. At the beginning of June 1985 the members of Parents against Silence held their last public meeting and announced the end of their activities and the disbanding of the movement.[54] The war in Lebanon was over, and Israel was back to square one. For the peace movement, one of its most important struggles had come to a successful end.

Exit Hussein

Although Washington agreed with Peres that King Hussein was central to the peace process, the Jordanian monarch himself seemed unlikely to take any unilateral steps.[55] At the Rabat Arab summit in 1974 the mandate to speak for the Palestinians had been formally taken from the king and given to the PLO. Furthermore, over the years the Palestinian population in the occupied territories, and certainly in the Palestinian diaspora, had developed a strong allegiance to the PLO, which they saw as a symbol of Palestinian national aspirations.[56] Although the PLO had been weakened by its political and military defeats in Lebanon (first in South Lebanon and in Beirut by the IDF and then in Tripoli by renegade Palestinian factions supported by Syria), its consent was still necessary to any deal on the Palestinian issue.[57]

Too weak politically to initiate formal negotiations with Israel,[58] King Hussein demanded that any negotiations start with and be sanctioned by an international conference in which other Arab states, and perhaps the PLO, would also participate. Peres kept his channels to the king open, and agreed in principle to participate in such an international conference.[59]

Long and difficult negotiations between Arafat and King Hussein yielded the Amman Agreement on February 11, 1985, which provided for a "special relationship between the Jordanian and Palestinian peoples" based on the right of the Palestinian people to self-determination and on an agreement to become the "confederated Arab states of Jordan and Palestine" once the retreat of Israeli forces from the West Bank was secured.[60] According to this agreement, the peace process would be conducted under the auspices of an international conference in which PLO representatives would constitute part of a joint Jordanian-Palestinian delegation. The most significant phrase in the document was the definition of its purpose to achieve "total withdrawal [of Israel] from the territories occupied in 1967 in exchange for a comprehensive peace as established in United Nations and Security Council Resolutions."[61] Though UN Resolution 242 (to which the PLO had initially vehemently objected) was not specifically mentioned, this statement amounted to a reversal of traditional PLO policy. Arafat essentially agreed to the partition of Palestine and to the creation of the State of Palestine, which would be confederated with Jordan alongside Israel.[62] However, as soon as the Amman Agreement reached the PLO's Executive Committee, a number of qualifications and amendments were added that were unacceptable to the king, let alone the Americans and Israelis.[63]

As it turned out, the entire Jordanian venture was ultimately scuttled by rejectionist elements within the PLO. During 1986 Arafat struggled to create unity in the ranks of the PLO, but this meant he had to abandon his tentative alliance with the king.[64] Hussein was infuriated by what he considered to be the volatility and lack of credibility of the PLO leadership. On February 19, 1986, he announced in parliament his disengagement from negotiations with Arafat and suspended the Amman Agreement signed a year earlier. The king subsequently proposed a five-year economic plan for the rehabilitation of the West Bank in an attempt to regain his influence with the Palestinians in the occupied territories.[65] This was too little and too late, as the loyalty of the West Bankers to the PLO could not be reversed.

For their part, Israeli leaders failed to recognize or accept the loyalty of the Palestinians in the occupied territories to the PLO as an irreversible political reality. But the PLO too was not yet ready to recognize Israel unequivocally, a necessary first step for any direct negotiations even in the eyes of Israeli doves.[66] The recent wave of terror, Arafat's equivocation, and the intransigence of many PLO factions made it difficult for Peace Now's leaders to formulate their positions in bolder terms. Few in the movement were ready to speak in terms of the inevitability of future Palestinian independence and of the need to negotiate with the PLO. For the time being this advocacy was left to the more radical but less influential "committees" (like the Committee against the War in Lebanon) and the Arab-dominated Communist Party and the Progressive List for Peace.[67]

A heated debate surrounded the 1986 publication of an updated version of Peace Now's basic position paper. Some members demanded the inclusion of a phrase supporting the "recognition of the right of the Palestinians to self-determination," but others argued that this implied the recognition of the Palestinians' right to sovereignty. The compromise formula reached was "recognition of the right of the Palestinians to a national existence." Around this time Shimon Peres completed his term as prime minister under the National Unity Government agreement and was replaced by Yitzhak Shamir. Whatever hope there had been for a breakthrough during Peres's tenure quickly faded, and in summer 1986 the prospects for peace appeared remote.

The International Center for Peace in the Middle East

During his tenure as prime minister Shimon Peres increased his popularity among Israelis, many of whom had previously viewed him as a politician of questionable integrity.[68] However, this improved stature did not provide him with the ability to mobilize even his own party to support bolder peace proposals. By the end of 1984 it was evident that the main efforts of the peace movement should be directed toward encouraging Peres to undertake more ambitious initiatives. This task, however, became increasingly difficult because the details of many of the government's efforts were concealed from public view, and those efforts that were known were too complex to be dealt with by the rather simplistic methods of the peace movement. The new political circumstances made it difficult for the extraparliamentary groups to play an effective role using their traditional tactics and activities. Additionally, the IDF's withdrawal from Lebanon dramatically reduced the public's energy for protest.

Although its leaders were drawn mostly from the intelligentsia, Peace Now's forte as a protest movement was its ability to mobilize mass participation in public demonstrations. Successful demonstrations depended less on subtlety than on simplification; slogans had to be simple and unambiguous, not intellectually sophisticated. Lacking a permanent staff and consistent funding, the movement did not have the resources for complex research and political analysis. These tasks, together with participation in the parliamentary process, were left to a smaller body, the International Center for Peace in the Middle East, which sought to create political coalitions among the dovish elements in the Labor Party and elsewhere on the left.

Since its establishment in 1958, *New Outlook* had built a solid base of contributors and supporters among progressive Jews (and some non-Jews) in Europe and North America. It also had an impressive record in organizing international symposia and conferences, as well as in maintaining dialogues with Arab intellectuals. Despite this, *New Outlook* essentially remained just another left-wing journal with little political influence. In 1977, triggered by Likud's election victory, editor Simcha Flapan and some of his colleagues began an effort to establish an Arab-Jewish center for peace research. This initiative was somewhat modified after the second Likud victory in 1981 when the same group established the International Center for Peace in the Middle East (ICPME).[69] David Shaham, a veteran journalist and writer who was a member of the editorial board of *New Outlook*, organized the new institution together with Willy Gafni, a fund-raising specialist who had many contacts with Palestinians in the occupied territories, and Arie Ya'ari, a political scientist from a Mapam kibbutz.

The notion of creating an academic research center was soon discarded in favor of forming an institution that would combine policy planning with peace advocacy. ICPME sought to influence Israeli politics and policies through symposia and conferences, research publications, and a permanent parliamentary forum in which MKs from different parties could work together.[70]

ICPME received the blessing of prominent international leaders, including the former French prime minister Pierre Mendès-France, former German chancellor Willy Brandt, Chancellor Bruno Kreisky of Austria, and Nahum Goldmann, the veteran president of the World Jewish Congress. It also received the cooperation of some key Palestinian leaders from the occupied territories such as Rashad Shawwa and Elias Freij, the mayors of Gaza and Bethlehem respectively, and pro-PLO journalists Ziyad Abu-Zayyad and Hanna Siniora. The new center was inaugurated during a "world conference" held in Tel Aviv on December 15–17, 1982.[71]

People participated in the activities of the center on an individual basis, not as representatives of the political organizations to which they belonged, but the fact that MKs and senior members of political parties devoted their time and energy to ICPME gave the center prominence and a measure of influence. The honorary president was retired chief justice of the Israeli Supreme Court, Chaim Cohen; the chairman of the board was Abba Eban, the former Israeli foreign minister who was now a Labor MK and chairman of the powerful Knesset Committee on Defense and Foreign Affairs. Other senior members of the Labor Party such as Chaim Tzadok, who had served as minister of justice in previous Labor governments, were active in the center's daily affairs. Figures from the peace movement, including Lova Eliav, Galia Golan (a political science professor and a central figure in Peace Now), and Mattiyahu (Matti) Peled (a retired general who became a professor of modern Arabic literature at Tel Aviv University, and in 1984 entered the Knesset as an MK for the Progressive List for Peace), used the center as neutral ground on which they held meetings and strategy sessions. Israeli Arabs also participated in the center's activities, among them several Arab leaders who later became MKs. These included trade union activists Nawaf Masalha and Walid Sadek, and intellectuals Majid al-Hajj and Sami Mar'i from Haifa University.

Another important asset of ICPME was its numerous supporters abroad. These included prominent Jewish leaders such as Rita Hauser, a lawyer from New York; Stanley Sheinbaum, a businessman from Los Angeles; André Wormser, a banker from Paris; David Susskind, a community leader from Brussels; and Hanneke Gelderblom, a senator from the Netherlands.

In many ways ICPME shared a common philosophy and policy advocacy with Peace Now, but differed in its structure, function, and method of operation. The center did not aspire to operate in the streets; instead it chose to direct its activities more toward the political elites. In contrast, Peace Now had neither the capability nor the desire to sustain long-term efforts. It chose to be flexible and able to respond quickly to an agenda that changed as issues and events unfolded. As such the two organizations were very different in their nature but essentially complementary.[72]

The center's three most important achievements in its first few years were the progress made in dialogues with Palestinian leaders (discussed in greater detail in the following chapter); the creation of the Arab-Jewish Educators Council, a body that brought together Jewish and Arab educators in an effort to improve the quality of education in Arab towns and villages and promote coexistence initiatives; and the creation of a parliamentary peace caucus in the Knesset—the "MKs Forum," as it was called by the center.[73]

In the Tenth Knesset (1981–84) twenty-eight members from various parties met regularly to discuss parliamentary strategy in the quest for peace, and other relevant issues.[74] Despite the fact that no binding decisions were reached, this forum became an important element of the peace movement in the early 1980s. The participation of prominent MKs from the Labor Party gave this group added significance, though this advantage was undermined when Labor joined the National Unity Government. The blessing of a broad political base, which characterized ICPME at the beginning, ultimately became its main weakness; fearful of disrupting the unity in its ranks, ICPME declined to undertake more daring initiatives and gradually lost its originality and currency.

Lethargy

By spring 1986 a growing sense of futility and apathy permeated the rank and file of the fragmented peace movement. The establishment of the National Unity Government had led to an increase in tension between the doves in the Labor Party and those in other parties who opted to remain in opposition. Mapam, which ran in the 1984 elections under a joint slate with the Labor Alignment, gained six seats in the Eleventh

Knesset as a result of a prearranged deal with Labor. However, Mapam left the alignment and formed an independent faction when Peres decided to join the Likud in the unity government.

Yossi Sarid, a skillful parliamentarian and longtime member of the Labor Party who had supported the cause of peace since his days as the closest lieutenant of Pinhas Sapir, defected from Labor to join Shulamit Aloni's Ratz, which won three seats in the 1984 elections. The ten MKs (six from Mapam and four from Ratz) were joined by the two members from the Progressive List for Peace and formed a majority in the ICPME parliamentary peace caucus. But there was little meaning to the caucus without the participation of the Labor doves, who provided the vital link with the political establishment and the government. These Labor MKs were reluctant to take radical positions that might embarrass Peres within the party or the coalition.[75] Under such circumstances the parliamentary peace caucus was rendered largely irrelevant. It met infrequently and nothing practical came of the few meetings that were held.

Circumstances outside Israel were no more encouraging for the peace movement. During 1986 it became clear that the conditions vital for advancing the peace process were being decided neither in Jerusalem nor Washington but in Amman and Tunis. The Palestinian-Jordanian controversy and the debate within the Palestinian community could hardly be influenced by the Israeli peace forces. King Hussein's announcement of his suspension of the dialogue with the PLO was a day of joy for rejectionists on both sides of the conflict but a day of mourning for those who believed that the pursuit of peace was not an act of charity by one side to the other but a necessity for the continued existence of both sides.[76]

The momentum of new settlements in the occupied territories had slowed somewhat after 1984 for economic reasons, but by 1986 was still progressing at an alarming rate. In the report of the West Bank Data Project (a research project financed by the Ford Foundation to monitor changes in land tenure, demography, and patterns of Jewish settlement in the West Bank), the historian and journalist Meron Benvenisti concluded that the settlement process had become irreversible and that any attempt to repartition the land would be futile.[77] The peace movement did not accept Benvenisti's conclusions and a heated internal debate followed,[78] but peace activists, however reluctantly, had to acknowledge the accuracy of Benvenisti's factual description. Despite their long and bitter fight against the settlement movement, they had to recognize that they had essentially been defeated as the number of settlements increased from year to year. MK Geula Cohen of the right-wing Techiya Party used to tease the left by recalling the Russian folk expression, "The dogs are barking but the caravan goes on."

Although replaced in September 1986 as prime minister by Yitzhak Shamir, Shimon Peres did not stop trying to breathe life into the peace process. In his new role as minister for foreign affairs he met secretly with King Hussein in London and in April 1987 agreed upon a formulation for a process that would start with an international conference and lead to a series of bilateral negotiations.[79] Shamir and his Likud colleagues were furious with Peres, not only because they objected to an international conference, but also because they had not been consulted in advance. In reality they had little to worry about because Peres was obliged to present any agreements he had reached to the cabinet for approval, and there was no chance that he would gain the votes necessary to proceed with his gambit. The London formula remained a curious episode in the search for peace, and the peace movement soon recognized that there would be little hope for any significant progress in the peace process during Shamir's two-year tenure as premier of the National Unity Government.

Around the end of 1986 Peace Now (and most of the other peace groups) entered a long period of hibernation. The biweekly meetings of the various forums ceased. The large cellar in the German Colony in Jerusalem, where Peace Now activists regularly met, was deserted. The rented offices in Haifa, Tel Aviv, and Beer Sheva were closed for lack of users and money. The movement's call-up network fell dormant as well. Beyond small, informal gatherings in homes and in the library at the Van Leer Institute (where a number of academics often met for coffee),[80] discussion subsided; no formal meetings were convened for more than six months. Many had the impression that the movement had faded into obscurity. The media, which had previously carried the movement's announcements as if they represented significant political events, lost interest. Activists started to wonder whether the movement's mission had ended, or whether despite past successes the movement had finally been defeated by the sad realities of the absence of peace and the continuing occupation. In the movement's circles an atmosphere of despair and fatigue prevailed.

My Brothers the Collaborators

June 6, 1987, marked twenty years of Israeli occupation of the West Bank and Gaza Strip. Hundreds of thousands of young Palestinians could not remember a time before Israeli soldiers patrolled their towns and villages. Nor could hundreds of thousands of young Israelis recall an Israel before the conquest of the territories, a time when Israelis were denied access to the Western Wall in East Jerusalem and other symbols of their ancient history. Perhaps worst of all, neither Palestinians nor Israelis could clearly envisage an end to the prevailing situation.

Two young scholars from Tel Aviv University, Adi Ofir and Hannan Hever, had been influenced by the work of structuralist and neomarxist thinkers, especially French philosopher Michel Foucault's analysis of the relationships among culture, human discourse, and the structure of power relations in society.[81] Foucault demonstrated how people are coopted into a suppressive system by the language and culture they share with the suppressors.[82] Ofir, a philosopher, and Hever, a literature teacher, had been active in the peace movement for ten years. They had met through Ilana Hammerman, a literary critic and editor and a member of radical peace groups. The three decided to take a fresh look at the Israeli peace movement and did not like what they found. The peace movement, they argued, had become an integral part of the suppressive apparatus of occupation.

> A smooth dialogue had developed unwittingly between the protest movements [Hever recalled], which overtly opposed the occupation, and the occupation authorities. Both collaborated unwittingly in the continued oppression of the Palestinians. The protesters protested and nothing changed, since in fact both sides were partners in the suppressive process. Both performed their distinctive roles in a grand power game in which the Israelis totally dominated the Palestinians. The government could occasionally even draw pride from the fact that amidst the suppression "nice" Israelis protest. All along clear lines were drawn which could not be trespassed. Peace Now [activists] always insisted on operating within the framework of Israeli law, and took pains to define themselves as being part of the Zionist camp, but this law and this camp were the framework and tools of oppression.[83]

The occupation, Ofir, Hammerman, and Hever maintained, was not merely a military or a political reality, but a "total situation" to which every aspect of life was subordinated—day-to-day behavior, psychological phenomena, and human discourse. The only way out was by "total resistance" and identification with the oppressed. "We decided that the time had come to speak as occupiers who identify with the occupied. We must go beyond the overriding consensus, to stretch the line as much as possible, and have no qualms about identifying with the occupied morally and ideologically."[84]

These were radical thoughts indeed, but to the frustrated peace activists in the spring of 1987 they sounded like a clear bell. They were tired of running after the settlers on the hills of Judea and Samaria and the streets of Jerusalem and Tel Aviv without being able to stop the occupation, only to go home with the illusion that they had done their duty. Some of the most dedicated members of the peace groups sought a new way to intervene more effectively and were attracted by these new and vigorous ideas.

> We wanted to provide not only new practical alternative ways but to introduce a totally new way of looking at our situation. . . . We decided to expand the refusal into the total span of human life; into the economy (through boycotting products of the settlers) and in education (by organizing parents to refuse participation of their children in chauvinist activities in school). . . . We also felt that we must begin to act on the borders of legality, and be ready to trespass it and pay the price.[85]

In the June edition of *Politica*, a progressive Hebrew political and literary magazine, Ofir published a letter addressed to "My Brothers the Collaborators"—his friends from the peace movement who had, in his opinion, become "collaborators in spite of themselves, teeth-clenching collaborators, collaborators with an agonized conscience."[86] "I decided to refuse," he wrote, "[and despite] the despair which is gnawing us from inside we still possess the power to say to them [the authorities] No! This No! is our power, this No! is almost the only thing left to say, the only thing which ought to be said. This No! is our obligation and the best of our capability." Noting that evil has many faces and very often goes unnoticed, Ofir declared: "This evil, my conscience-agonized brothers, you produce. This oppression you serve, my teeth-clenching brothers, as small screws in a large machine, with some leeway for demonstrations, for protests, and for futile attempts at persuasion."

Declaring his own intention to resist evil, he called on

> every man who is sick and tired of the occupation, every woman who has had enough, all those who have the courage to say that the time has come, to rise and throw their No! in the face of the nation, each man according to his ability, each woman in her own way. Let them say, at long last by deed, by actual deeds, in a way which will cause pain—that the road taken [by Israel] is not the road they are ready to share.

The article made a strong impression within the peace movement. While some were angered by the hard-hitting self-critique, many felt that there was a painful truth in it. Within a few weeks a new group organized around Ofir, Hever, and Hammerman.

The 21st Year

At the beginning of October 1987 a small group of intellectuals met at the Van Leer Institute in Jerusalem and decided to form a new movement. They

hoped that after twenty years of reluctant conformity and tacit collaboration the next year might bring a change, at least in terms of their own posture vis-à-vis the occupation. They called themselves "The 21st Year," and
published a charter that they invited others to sign. The charter stated:

> The occupation is not only a deplorable situation affecting the lives of the
> Palestinians, it has an equally pernicious effect on the very political and
> spiritual substance of Israeli society. The occupation has become an insidi-
> ous fact of our lives. . . . It is among and within us. . . . Expressions of
> protest against the occupation are circumscribed by the national consen-
> sus; protests do not transgress the boundaries deemed permissible by the
> occupation regime. The Israeli conscience . . . implicitly collaborates with
> the occupation. The presence of the occupation is total. Our struggle against
> the occupation must therefore also be total. We shall resolutely refuse to
> collaborate with the system of occupation in all of its manifestations. Re-
> fusal is the only morally and politically sound form of participation in Is-
> raeli society during the occupation. Refusal is . . . a source of hope for our
> moral integrity as Israelis.

The declaration detailed some of the methods of resistance to be offered by the new movement, such as boycotting national celebrations
held in the occupied territories; refusing to expose children to educational curricula that sanctioned the occupation; and exposing and boycotting institutions that denied their Palestinian employees human dignity and decent working conditions.[87]

In the beginning the new movement developed in much the same
way as Peace Now had in its early days. Some 1,500 people signed their
names to the new charter but only a few hundred became active. Decisions were made by an informal forum of those who were active. Committees were established to run different projects, and anyone who
wanted to participate in a project could join the relevant planning committee. Most decisions were made on an ad hoc basis.

Nurit Shleifman, a scholar of Russian history, and Rachel Freudental,
an expert in German literature, both founders of the new group, explained:

> We considered the possibility of forming a formal leadership group, but
> rejected this idea and continued to work in the spontaneous way in which
> we began. Membership in the movement meant only one thing, activity in
> its projects. . . . Most of us were active in Peace Now early on but we came
> to doubt the effectiveness of street demonstrations, and Peace Now did
> not provide us with a framework for active involvement and ongoing prac-
> tical activity. The gap between our discourse and the cruel reality of the
> occupation bothered us for quite some time. We were looking for a more
> radical framework. The "committees" were more confrontational than Peace
> Now, but we could not live with the alienation from Israeli society which
> they represented. The 21st Year provided us with the combination of radi-
> calism within our Israeli identity.[88]

The 21st Year raised once more the dilemma that had preoccupied the Israeli peace movement from the outset. From an Israeli perspective, does one oppose the occupation because of its power to corrupt the occupier and the damage it does to Israel's national interests, or is one motivated primarily by outrage at the moral injustice being perpetrated on the occupied Palestinians? Is the dilemma pragmatic or moral? To what extent can one identify with a Zionism in which the Israeli right wing adheres to policies from which the peace movement clearly wants to dissociate itself?

A couple of members of the more extreme groups went so far as to join the young Palestinians in stoning Israeli soldiers, but such an approach was not only suicidal for any peace group but also an emotional impossibility for the overwhelming majority of those groups. One cannot stop being what one is so long as one continues to be a part of society. Adi Ofir spoke to this condition:

> We deal with disengagement, not desertion. We try to challenge, not to revolt. It is still a kind of [Israeli] partnership. . . . Refusal is essentially a blatant provocation against the majority, and a commitment to a moral minority community which gives you backing and confirms your act, but it is ipso facto an expression of responsibility to the community at large. . . .The refusal draws the line, but contrary to acts of desertion and self-imposed exile it draws the line from within. This is the line beyond which no agreement is possible, not only with this or that policy, but with the entire system. . . . This is a line which if crossed will make us either exiles or rebels.[89]

Various attempts were made to apply the basic philosophy of the group, such as a boycott of merchandise produced by Jewish settlers in the occupied territories, but these had little effect. Organizers considered distributing lists of such products in supermarkets but ultimately rejected the idea because it would have meant breaking the law, which the activists were reluctant to do.

The 21st Year supported the refusers from Yesh Gvul in a more public and outspoken manner than did Peace Now. The new movement recognized the refusal to serve in the occupied territories as one mode of legitimate resistance open to its members.[90]

In December 1987, when the 21st Year was but a couple of months old, the Intifada erupted, creating new circumstances that presented an even harsher challenge for the peace movement. Young Palestinians refused to continue to accept the status quo that had been created by the Six Day War and that had prevailed for twenty years. In doing so they confronted Israel with a new moral dilemma.

10

The Israeli-Palestinian Dialogue

The Children of Abraham

At this point, we must pause in the flow of our narrative and turn back to review the antecedents of one of the most important activities of the Israeli peace groups—the promotion of Israeli-Palestinian dialogue. Though contacts between the two peoples grew more intense and politically more significant in the 1970s and 1980s, such dialogue had, of course, been under way for many decades. Indeed, from the beginning of the Zionist project in Palestine it became clear that a constant feature of the relations between Palestinian Arabs and Jews would be that enmity and friendship would exist side by side. The geographical pattern of Zionist settlement throughout the country brought Jews and Arabs into close proximity. At times this led to violent confrontations; at other times relations were warm and even intimate. As early as the 1920s, despite the rapid intensification of the political and military strife between the two national movements, contact and dialogue between Jews and Arabs became an intrinsic part of the conflict. Interactions varied from commercial transactions and political debates to personal visits to Arab and Jewish homes.[1]

During the 1930s and 1940s the World Zionist Organization established a special department to develop and monitor political contacts with Palestinian Arabs and other individuals throughout the Arab world.[2] After 1948, however, these contacts became increasingly difficult to maintain and were usually conducted in secret.[3] Contacts with Palestinians who became citizens of Israel were readily available but of little political consequence, Israeli Arabs having little or no influence in the rest of the Arab world, and the Palestinians as a whole playing only a minor role in Middle Eastern politics before 1967.[4] Consequently, Israeli efforts between the War of Independence and the Six Day War focused primarily on developing contacts that could lead to negotiations with the Arab states.[5]

Among the many changes wrought by the Six Day War was a dramatic alteration in the circumstances that shaped Israeli contacts with Arab "enemies," and in particular with the Palestinians. The fact that they now governed the largest segment of the Palestinian people made it relatively easy for Israelis, both officials and private individuals, to meet and discuss issues with Palestinian leaders in the occupied territories. Convenient access to the Palestinian diaspora and the Arab world was also maintained through the "open bridges" across the Jordan River.

Private contacts between Arabs and Israelis were viewed as more acceptable after 1967 than before. In 1974 Amos Elon, a prominent Israeli writer, and Sana Hassan, an Egyptian woman from a well-known Cairo family who at the time was a student at Harvard, published a book recounting their dialogues during a series of personal encounters that took place in the United States. They hoped that the dialogue would serve as a signal to their respective nations that peace was a genuine possibility.[6] The dialogue and the book became a cause célèbre. In 1976, more than a year before Sadat came to Jerusalem, Hassan accepted Elon's invitation to visit Israel. But Egyptian society was not yet ready for such a bold gesture, and Hassan suffered harsh private and official recriminations and her passport was revoked for some time.[7]

During the late 1960s and early 1970s many official and unofficial contacts took place with Palestinians in the occupied territories. However, the increasing prominence of the PLO and its guerrilla activities made contact between Israelis and Palestinian diaspora leaders more difficult. Israeli rejection of the PLO as a potential partner for peace and growing anger at its terrorist activities made contacts with PLO representatives appear to the Israeli public to be both legally and morally offensive.

During the 1970s the PLO, for its part, was not ready for an official dialogue with Israel. The Palestine National Charter rejected any compromise with the Jewish state, and advocated an armed struggle for the removal of the "Zionist Entity" and the creation of a "secular democratic state in Palestine."[8] As late as March 1977 the Palestine National Council reaffirmed that only contacts with "progressive and democratic forces in Israel, struggling against Zionism as a doctrine and in practice," were permissible.[9] Consequently, the PLO initially would meet only with Israelis who were outspoken anti-Zionists and opposed to the existence of the Jewish state. Some Israelis of the ultraleft Matzpen groups who resided in London and elsewhere in Europe maintained contacts with the PLO early on. Most of these ultraleft Jews and Israelis advocated various Trotskyite or Maoist doctrines and considered Judaism nothing more than an archaic religion.[10] For them Zionism was just another repressive colonialist movement, and thus they supported the dismemberment of Israel.[11]

The contacts the PLO maintained with these marginal Jewish and Israeli elements were not meant to prepare the ground for reconciliation or to encourage a better understanding of the other side. They served instead to confirm misperceptions and to solidify the PLO's rejectionist attitudes. Only a handful of Palestinian leaders tried to reach a broader Israeli audience.[12]

Abie Nathan—The Voice of Peace

Born in Iran and raised in India, Abie Nathan came to Israel at the age of twenty-one after serving as a fighter pilot in the Indian Royal Air Force during World War II. During the 1948 war he served in the Israeli Air Force, and during the 1950s he was a captain for El Al. In the 1960s he opened a popular restaurant and an art gallery, and became a favorite of the bohemian circles in Tel Aviv.[13]

On February 28, 1966, Nathan caused an international event when he flew his private plane (which he renamed "Shalom One" for the occasion) to Port Said as a gesture to promote the idea of peace. This was a daring if futile act, for the possibility of reconciliation hardly existed in the years before the Six Day War. Furthermore, the enmity of the Egyptian regime toward Israel at the time could easily have cost Nathan his life. Despite the risks he managed to land safely but failed to meet any Egyptian officials and was promptly returned to Israel.

Nathan's daring act violated the Israeli law prohibiting unauthorized visits to an enemy country. His gesture generated a significant amount of popular sympathy, however, and the fact that he neither caused nor intended to cause any damage to Israel's security persuaded the government not to prosecute. The considerable media attention Nathan received gave him the status of a champion of peace, and for a while it seemed that he was even able to mobilize a certain constituency. On October 28, 1966, he led a few hundred supporters in a peace march from Tel Aviv to Jerusalem. Shortly after the Six Day War, on July 28, 1967, Nathan again flew to Port Said. This once again created a media spectacle but little else. However, this time upon his return to Israel he was charged with violating the law and chose to spend forty days in jail.[14]

In the early 1970s Nathan directed his resources to a new idea; he raised enough money to buy a 570-ton freighter, which he converted into a floating radio station. In March 1973 the "Peace Ship," with a crew of volunteers from many countries, anchored in international waters off the coast of Israel. He named his new radio station "The Voice of Peace" and began broadcasting a mixture of music and conversation.[15]

The Peace Ship stayed on the air (with a few intermissions) for more than twenty years, and visited a number of Middle Eastern ports. Nathan regularly made symbolic gestures of peace; in October 1975, for example, he attempted to enter the Suez Canal with a cargo of thousands of flowers for the people of Egypt. As usual his gimmick failed. However, in Israel (especially along its Mediterranean coast) his music and message gained enough popularity to enable the effort to remain financially afloat.

In the late 1980s Nathan turned his attention to openly challenging the law enacted by the Knesset in 1986 that specifically prohibited contacts with the PLO.[16] In September 1988 Nathan went to Tunis to meet with Yasser Arafat.[17] After his return he was charged by the police. In further gestures of defiance he met with Arafat two more times, once in Strasbourg and once in Geneva, while awaiting his trial on the original charge. Nathan was sentenced to six months in prison.

As soon as he was released in March 1990 Nathan again traveled to Tunis and met with Arafat and other PLO officials. This time he was sent to jail for eighteen months.[18] On May 8, 1991, he began a hunger strike in jail to protest the law and his imprisonment. The government received appeals for clemency from the media, politicians, and intellectuals, but Nathan refused the government's demand that he express regret and promise not to violate the law again (as required by law in the case of pardons). His fast lasted for forty days and his absolute commitment to his ideals won the sympathy of many. Ultimately, President Ezer Weizman, who knew Nathan well from the days of his service in the Israeli Air Force more than forty years earlier, intervened and reduced Nathan's sentence. He was released on March 30, 1993, after 173 days behind bars.

Abie Nathan has always been essentially a lone crusader, unable to organize or sustain a movement. In the big picture of the Israeli peace movement he has had little impact or influence, but he has endeared himself to many by his courage and flair for the outrageous.

Said Hammami

By 1973 Yasser Arafat must have begun to doubt the usefulness of continuing a dialogue exclusively with anti-Zionist Jews and decided to float a trial balloon. He was not authorized by the PLO leadership to stray from the official "secular democratic state" policy that prohibited contact with any Israelis other than anti-Zionists. Nevertheless, he authorized one of his lieutenants to publicly depart from the party line. On November 16, 1973, the London *Times* published an article by Said Hammami, the PLO representative in Great Britain, in which for the first time a PLO official spoke of a "Palestinian state in the West Bank and the Gaza Strip," and raised the possibility of "emptying and closing down of the refugee camps, thereby drawing out the poison at the heart of the Arab-Israeli enmity."[19] In another article published a few weeks later he called for mutual recognition. "The Israeli Jews and the Palestinian Arabs should recognize one another as a people, with all the rights to which a people is entitled."[20] This amounted to the recognition of the right of the Jews to a state of their own, a position that would later be known as the "two states solution."

Hammami's articles made little impression in Israel[21] but caught the eye of Uri Avneri, who had advocated a similar formula for more than two decades. Avneri sought a meeting with Hammami, and after repeated delays the meeting took place in a London hotel on January 27, 1975.[22] The encounter had a significant impact on Avneri who, despite his detailed knowledge of the Arab-Israeli conflict, had only a limited understanding of the intricacies of Palestinian politics. Over the course of the conversation, Hammami taught Avneri to better understand the internal conflicts and tensions inside the Palestinian camp that would have to be taken into account as part of a realistic peace process.[23]

Two months after this first encounter Hammami delivered a speech to the National Liberal Club in London in which he advocated the establishment of a Palestinian state alongside Israel. He discussed the need to conduct "a continuous and developing dialogue with any elements within Israel who were prepared to meet and talk with Palestinians regarding the form of a mutually acceptable coexistence which might in time develop between the two peoples." Hammami was still constrained by the official PLO line, but tried to get around it by suggesting that the dream of creating a "secular democratic state" in Palestine should become a long-term aspiration to be achieved only by persuasion and with the consent of both Israelis and Palestinians.[24]

Two Flags Crossed

Hammami's speech received little notice among Israelis, but Avneri and some of his colleagues decided to create a group that "could act instead of the establishment, and respond in some way to the growing signs of moderation in the ranks of the PLO, thus providing our counterparts with the ammunition they need in their battle to win the confidence of their people."[25] In early June 1975 Avneri, Amos Kenan (a prominent Israeli satirist and writer), and Yossi Amitai (an Arabist and at the time the secretary of a kibbutz in the south) published a manifesto for the founding of an organization to be called the Israeli Council for Israel-Palestine Peace.[26]

Other individuals, closer to the mainstream of Israeli politics, also became aware of the urgent need for a dialogue with the Palestinians. Among them were Lova Eliav, at that time an MK for the short-lived Ya'ad Party; Meir Pail, a retired colonel with a long military career, including an assignment as commander of the IDF's officer's school, and an MK from the left-wing Moked faction; Ya'acov Arnon, the former director general of the Ministry of Treasury and a confidant of Levi Eshkol and Pinhas Sapir; David Shaham, the former editor of the Labor Party's ideological magazine *Ot* and later an editor of *New Outlook* and director of ICPME; and most significantly, Matti Peled, a retired general who became a professor of modern Arabic literature at Tel Aviv University. Both Peled and Eliav enjoyed good access to the senior ranks of the Labor Party, including Prime Minister Yitzhak Rabin.[27]

Peled, who was well versed in Arabic publications, recognized a subtle but significant shift in the PLO's position. While Said Hammami argued for recognition of Israel and the establishment of the Palestinian state alongside Israel, other writers were similarly advocating recognition of Israel and the need to open a diplomatic track in addition to the armed struggle. One such writer was Sabri Jiryis, an Israeli-Arab who had emigrated in the late 1960s after the Palestinian nationalist party he created—El Ard (The Land)—was outlawed by the Israeli authorities and who later became the head of the Israeli desk at PLO headquarters in Beirut. For voicing these "heresies," Jiryis was kidnapped by members of the PFLP and was released only after the forceful intervention of Yasser Arafat. "These events," remembered Peled, "unleashed a storm among Palestinians and it became clear to me that an important upheaval was taking place inside the PLO that required a courageous response on the part of Israelis."[28]

In December 1975 all these forward-looking activists convened at the Tel Aviv Theater Club. They decided to organize a nonpartisan council that would advocate a formal dialogue with the PLO based on mutual recognition of the right of self-determination for both Israel and the Palestinians. They adopted the name of Avneri's group—the Israeli Council for Israel-Palestine Peace. The prominent Sephardi leader Elie Eliachar was elected honorary president and Matti Peled was elected chairman.[29]

More than a hundred well-known Israelis, including writers, journalists, artists, and academics, signed the new council's manifesto. The council adopted two crossed flags as its emblem: the Israeli flag, and a flag of black, white, and green stripes joined by a red triangle, which during World War I had been carried by the Arab rebels who opposed Ottoman rule, and which in the 1920s had been adopted by the Palestinians as their national banner. In the 1970s this flag became the recognized symbol of the Palestinian national movement and was customarily referred to by Israelis as the "PLO flag." For many Israelis the flag was more of a red rag.[30]

Issam Sartawi

The next step was mediated by Henri Curiel, who during the 1950s and 1960s had liaised with different Third World liberation movements on behalf of the Israeli left.[31] During the 1970s Curiel surrounded himself with a small circle of Jewish communists from Egypt and other Arab counties, and maintained contacts with political circles in the newly independent North African states. He subsequently began to reach out also to Palestinians.[32]

Dani Amit, a professor of physics from Hebrew University, also maintained contacts with PLO delegates in Europe during the mid-1970s. As a graduate student at Amherst University in the 1960s Amit had met many Palestinians and other individuals from the Third World, as well as individuals from the American left. He gradually became more critical of Israel's policies vis-à-vis the Arab-Israeli conflict, and upon returning to Jerusalem shortly after the Six Day War he joined an obscure group called the Committee for Just Peace. He soon discovered that this group was actually a front for the New Communist Party, and began to seek new and independent contacts with Palestinians in the occupied territories and in the Palestinian diaspora.[33]

During 1975–76 Amit spent a sabbatical year in Paris and became acquainted with the Curiel circle, who introduced him to Said Hammami. Amit and Hammami conversed frequently. "For Hammami I was a step beyond his previous contacts with the anti-Zionists," Amit recalled. Amit tried to interest some of his colleagues at Hebrew University in meeting with Hammami but had little success. In the spring of 1976 he and Hammami began to plan a major Israeli-Palestinian conference; Beirut, however, was not prepared to endorse the idea.

At about the same time, Arafat sent Issam Sartawi to Paris to take charge of contacts with Israelis. Sartawi had advocated opening a dialogue with mainstream Israelis for some time. He was an American-trained heart surgeon who had begun his career in the PLO as the leader of a small guerrilla faction that had been involved in some skirmishes with the IDF. Later, Sartawi joined Arafat's Fatah faction and served as an emissary on different diplomatic missions.

Sartawi met Curiel in Paris and Curiel introduced him to Amit, who suggested that Sartawi meet with someone from the Israeli Council for Israel-Palestine Peace. Upon his return to Israel, Amit contacted Matti Peled.[34]

Peled met Sartawi for the first time in the house of one of Curiel's group in Paris. "I wanted to clarify the areas of agreement between Sartawi and the positions of our council and found little divergence," Peled later recalled. After a good dinner the mood warmed up and Sartawi joked, "I just want another good fight with the Israelis to show you that we can give a good fight." "I told him we should do it on a football field and he seemed to be delighted with my response since he later repeated this story many times."[35]

The ground was now prepared for a larger meeting, which took place a few weeks later in Rambouillet, in a villa that belonged to one of Curiel's friends. The Israeli delegation included Matti Peled, Lova Eliav, Ya'akov Arnon, and Meir Pail. Sartawi was accompanied by Sabri Jiryis and an aide, Razi Khouri. Sartawi told the Israelis that his mission had been personally authorized by Arafat, but the meetings were supposed to remain secret. If information about the meetings were made public, they had to be seen as a private initiative of the participants.[36] Early in the discussions it became clear that the historical and moral aspects of the conflict had to be avoided because those issues invariably caused emotional and acrimonious exchanges, and both sides agreed to concentrate on the current situation and prospects for reconciliation. Sartawi insisted that the meet-ings remain secret because public knowledge of his contacts with Israelis could place him in great danger. Consequently, Sartawi declined an Israeli offer to release a joint statement at the end of the meeting.[37]

This presented a problem for the Israelis because once they reported back to their colleagues in the council they could not assure absolute secrecy. They also felt that public knowledge of a successful Israeli-Pales-tinian dialogue was an important step on the road to reconciliation.[38] To compensate for the lack of public exposure, the Israelis proposed to give the event some international recognition by recruiting a few notable indi-viduals who could later testify to the historical breakthrough in which high-level officials of the PLO met with pro-Zionist Israelis. Sartawi agreed and joined Matti Peled and Lova Eliav on a late night visit to Pierre Mendès-France in his vacation home in the south of France. Mendès-France, a Jew who had served as the prime minister of France in the mid-1950s, presiding over France's withdrawal from Indo-China, Tunisia, and Mo-rocco, enjoyed a reputation as a staunch advocate of peace.

With a joint declaration being out of the question, Sartawi agreed to make an unequivocal statement in the presence of Mendès-France to the effect that an agreement should be reached between Israel and the Pales-tinians on the basis of the 1967 borders, with some mutually acceptable modifications. He also stated that such an agreement should bring an absolute end to the conflict between the two national movements, at which time the Palestinians would have no further territorial claims against Israel. These were far-reaching declarations from the mouth of a Pales-tinian who claimed that his mission was authorized by Arafat.[39]

The Israelis reported the results of their meetings to Prime Minister Rabin and several ministers and MKs. Rabin permitted the continuation of the dialogue but remained "cold and almost indifferent."[40] Issam Sartawi reported to Arafat in Beirut, where he incurred the wrath of many within the PLO's leadership, especially Faruq Qaddumi, who was in charge of the PLO's foreign relations. Despite the opposition of Qaddumi and oth-ers, Arafat agreed to continue the dialogue. Eventually, Hammami (in London) was sidestepped and Sartawi became the chief liaison with the Israelis during the later part of the 1970s and early 1980s.[41]

Despite Sartawi's insistence that the dialogue remain secret, a rela-tively large number of people knew of the meetings, and inevitably ac-counts eventually leaked out and were reported in considerable detail in the Israeli media.[42] This public exposure triggered a storm in both

Israeli and Palestinian circles. The Israeli government felt obliged to publicly distance itself from the initiative,[43] and the Israeli media was full of criticism of the dialogue effort.[44]

Sartawi did not fare much better. When, on January 1, 1977, Sartawi consented to Matti Peled's request for a published statement that would not include any substantive element, but would only confirm an ongoing dialogue and affirm that a range of understandings had been achieved,[45] Faruq Qaddumi publicly denied any PLO involvement in the affair. Arafat, who according to Sartawi had personally authorized him to enter into the dialogue, remained silent.[46]

Meetings between Sartawi and members of the council continued intermittently for the next six years and the number of his Israeli acquaintances grew. Yet, despite these efforts, no significant change occurred in the prevailing attitudes in either the Palestinian or Israeli communities. The Israeli establishment continued to refuse to accept the PLO as a potential interlocutor. Indeed, at that time even Peace Now chose not to open lines of communication with the PLO, and censured its members Dedi Zucker and Yael Tamir for their unauthorized meeting with Sartawi.[47] On the other side, the PLO continued to use terrorism as part of its armed struggle, placing conciliation beyond reach for the time being.

On April 10, 1983, Issam Sartawi was murdered in a hotel in Abulfeira, Portugal, where he was attending the Socialist International convention. Before departing for Portugal, Sartawi had announced his intention to meet with Shimon Peres, the head of the Labor Party. This announcement exposed his agenda and itinerary and possibly precipitated his assassination.[48] The assassination was carried out by Abu Nidal, a terror group not associated with the PLO. Abu Nidal maintained that Sartawi's contact with Israeli Zionists amounted to a betrayal of the Palestinian dream to fight until Israel was destroyed. It is still unclear whether Sartawi's efforts managed to influence the PLO to accept the notion that conciliation could be achieved based upon mutual recognition and compromise. However, there can be little doubt that his meetings and discussions with the Israelis opened the door for future dialogue efforts and made conciliation thinkable.[49]

The Israeli Council for Israel-Palestine Peace remained a rather esoteric group in Israeli politics, especially after Likud's victory in the 1977 elections. For Likud, recognition of the Palestinians as a nation with political rights and acceptance of the PLO as a representative of such national aspirations were anathema. Likud leaders belittled the value of serious dialogues with Palestinians and regularly objected to such initiatives undertaken by the Israeli peace movement.

Despite such criticism and numerous setbacks, the meetings and dialogues Peled, Avneri, Eliav, and others held with Palestinians did have a significant, long-term impact. Avneri identified three main achievements that resulted from this dialogue. First, it provided both sides an important opportunity for learning. "We learned more about the sensitivities and sensibilities of the Palestinians and could better appreciate what course of action had a chance to succeed." It also contributed to a greater sense of realism among PLO moderates. Second, a process of mutual persuasion was set in train. "It helped to close gaps which at the beginning seemed to be unbridgeable." Third, it made each side more accustomed to seeing the human side of the other. "We managed to break the perception that to meet the enemy is a treasonous activity."[50] One observer of Palestinian politics commented, "The dialogue with Israeli democratic forces amounted for the Palestinians to recognizing, step by step, the national reality of Israel. It was no longer a matter of seeing them join the PLO's struggle [as previously had been the case with contacts with anti-Zionist Israelis]; it was a matter of jointly hammering out the principles of an understanding. It was a decisive step towards recognition of the binational reality existing in Palestine."[51]

Interactive Problem Solving

In the late 1970s and early 1980s contacts between Israelis and Palestinians proliferated on many levels. International peace organizations such as the American Friends Service Committee, which had been involved in mediation efforts in the Middle East since the early 1950s, increased their efforts to facilitate Israeli-Arab encounters.[52] Interest in conflict resolution and mediation increased significantly within the international academic community, and the Arab-Israeli conflict served as a useful case study for testing assumptions and hypotheses. Seminars, retreats, and workshops in which Israelis and Arabs (including Palestinians associated with the PLO) participated were held in a number of universities in the West. A pioneer in these endeavors was Herbert Kelman, a prominent social psychologist from Harvard University. Inspired by two earlier conflict resolution workshops that addressed other international conflicts, Kelman organized a workshop in which Israelis and Arabs, along with a few American scholars, met to discuss the Middle

East conflict.[53] The underlying idea was to use "clinical [psychological] procedures to promote change and collaborative problem-solving among conflicting parties . . . generating feedback to national and international decision making."[54] Kelman's assistant, Stephen Cohen, observed that "the most difficult problem of such workshops has been to assure some transfer of training from the isolated workshop setting to the highly charged political atmosphere of the conflict itself." Therefore "the ideal participant would be one who has access to, or is an unofficial member of, top leadership and decision making groups."[55]

Securing the participation of such figures was not easy given that in most cases the leaders of both sides questioned the value of such experiments. However, the fact that the experiment was directed by American academics helped Kelman and Cohen persuade some mainstream Arabs and Jews to participate. Kelman and Cohen, both American Jews, also recruited three Arab-American scholars to give the experiment greater balance and assure greater objectivity.[56] During the 1970s they traveled throughout the Middle East conducting workshops, interviews, and lectures. Most of the meetings were conducted on a private and confidential basis, and the names of the participants were not made public in the hope that this would contribute to more candid discussions.[57]

Kelman did conduct some public meetings in the presence of larger audiences. In 1984 he brought together five MKs and five Palestinians publicly associated with the PLO. He also recruited Phillip Mattar of the Institute for Palestine Studies to cochair the meeting.[58] Such groups were sometimes able to draft a mutually acceptable document that delineated the principles on which reconciliation might be achieved, but the documents were not usually made public.[59] In one case, MK Yossi Sarid (then a member of the Labor Party) and Afif Safiyah (later the PLO representative in London) published side-by-side op-ed pieces in the *New York Times* in which they articulated the general agreements achieved in the workshop.[60]

Over the years Kelman's initiatives established direct and intimate contact between a few dozen Israelis and Palestinians, many of whom were leading figures in their respective communities.[61] However, he was less successful in this effort during the seven years of Likud rule (1977–84), when he had only limited access to Israeli governing circles. On the Palestinian side, he was also not successful in his attempts to reach out to the hard-line factions of the PLO, which repeatedly declined his invitations. These failures were hardly surprising, for the workshops' two underlying assumptions were equal status for both sides and the necessity of compromise, neither of which was acceptable at the time to the Israeli right and to many hard-line Palestinians in the mainstream of the PLO.[62]

Kelman's efforts, along with those of others who initiated similar contacts, helped to develop among both Israelis and Palestinians "cadres of individuals who have acquired experience in communicating with the other side and the conviction that such communication can be fruitful."[63]

A Season for Dialogues

During the early 1980s interest in a negotiated settlement gained momentum on both sides of the conflict. The peace treaty with Egypt had demonstrated that reconciliation was not beyond reach. Furthermore, it led the Egyptians to try to overcome their political isolation in the Arab world by expanding the peace they had reached with Israel. Egyptian officials often helped bring Israelis and Palestinians together for informal discussions.

Eastern European governments also tried to facilitate informal negotiations, often through the Israeli Communist Party or other communist parties in western Europe. Nongovernmental organizations affiliated with the United Nations held annual conferences in which Israeli peaceniks exchanged views with Arabs and Palestinians.[64]

Two incidents in particular illustrate the nature of these multiple contacts. In spring 1983, shortly after Arafat and the PLO were expelled from Tripoli by the Syrian army, a group of Israelis from ICPME were invited to Budapest by the Hungarian peace movement. Accidentally or not, Arafat's deputy, Salah Khalaf (better known by his nom de guerre, Abu Iyad), was also in Budapest. The Hungarian hosts suggested an informal meeting over dinner. Several of the Israelis already had experience with such encounters and did not hesitate. One who did hesitate was Chana Zemer, a central figure in the Labor Party and the editor-in-chief of its daily newspaper *Davar*. For Zemer a meeting with the man known to Israelis as the organizer of the Black September terror squads (which had murdered the Israeli athletes at the Munich Olympics in 1972) was not easy. Eventually Zemer agreed to participate in the discussion, though she refused to shake hands with the man who was deeply involved in several violent attacks on Jews and Israelis. "I will talk to you as my enemy," Zemer told the Palestinian. Despite this the discussion was surprisingly friendly and instructive.

The second illustration draws on a personal experience. About a year later Ron Young, the representative of the American Friends Service

Committee in Amman, invited me to participate in a tour of the United States along with Muhammad Milhem, the former mayor of Halhoul, a Palestinian town in the Judean hills. In 1981 Milhem had been accused of inciting his people and deported to Jordan in response to the murder of six Jewish yeshiva students in Hebron. The tour was designed to expose the possibilities of dialogue and peacemaking to the American public.

To ascertain that the tour would not result in mutual recriminations Milhem and I exchanged letters in which we outlined our views of the possible modalities of peacemaking and our motivations for undertaking the tour. We agreed that a two states solution was the best way to end the conflict.[65] I was prepared to recognize the right of the Palestinians to self-determination while Milhem expressed his recognition of Israel's right to exist. We agreed to avoid futile debates on past grievances and promised to advocate future relations between Israelis and Palestinians based on equality and friendship.[66]

The tour was an ordeal for both of us. We both experienced harsh criticism from our respective communities. Small groups of supporters of Meir Kahane and other right-wing Jewish-American groups tried to disrupt the meetings by heckling inside the auditoriums or demonstrating outside. Members of extremist Palestinian groups distributed leaflets with personal slurs against Milhem and threatened his life. Our relationship was also a dynamic process with ups and downs. Occasionally, when one of us slipped into emotional recriminations against the other side, the other would also resort to the almost automatic tendency to defend his own side. Despite these occasional transgressions, the purpose of the dialogue was largely achieved. It demonstrated that a civilized dialogue could be developed between enemies and conditions for reconciliation created.[67]

Meeting Arafat

The various meetings between Israelis and PLO officials culminated in a dramatic meeting between representatives of the Israeli Council for Israel-Palestine Peace and Yasser Arafat in his headquarters in Tunis on January 18, 1983.[68] This was an important vindication of Issam Sartawi, at least among some of his critics within the PLO, and something of a breakthrough in light of the PLO's previously unwavering opposition to negotiating with Zionists. The event was widely reported in the international media, and a communiqué was published simultaneously in Tunis and Tel Aviv in which Arafat expressed his appreciation "for the role of the Israeli peace forces and their struggle for a just and lasting peace."[69] However, other than this symbolic statement nothing more substantive was announced.

Israeli public opinion by and large failed to appreciate the importance of this gesture by the head of the PLO. For most Israelis the episode appeared to be an insignificant ploy by Arafat, who, it appeared, had taken advantage of naive Israelis to score propaganda points.[70] This negative assessment seemed to be confirmed three weeks later in Algiers at the sixteenth session of the Palestine National Council (PNC), when Arafat was bitterly criticized by radical elements in his own movement for violating the 1977 decision not to meet with Israelis unless they opposed Zionism. The PNC explicitly reiterated its prohibition of meetings with Zionist Israelis.[71]

The next meeting between members of the Israeli Council for Israel-Palestine Peace and Arafat came on August 31, 1983, this time in Geneva during a special UN conference on Palestine. Matti Peled and Uri Avneri were invited and again met with Arafat. This meeting was brief, Arafat having promised the Swiss government that he would leave Geneva promptly after delivering his speech to the assembly. However, it lasted long enough for photographers to capture Arafat embracing the two Israelis.[72]

The meeting was counterproductive in terms of its effect on Israeli public opinion. The Geneva conference, and the speech Arafat delivered just moments before he embraced Peled and Avneri, were replete with vitriolic anti-Israeli rhetoric. Even those in the Israeli peace camp who advocated recognition of the PLO found it necessary to denounce the event.[73]

Peled, Avneri, and Arnon met Arafat once more, in a secret meeting on April 21, 1984, in Tunis.[74] Arafat was preoccupied at the time with the situation in Syria, the divisions within his organization, and challenges to his leadership. This meeting proved to be of little consequence, though Peled claimed that it "helped break the Israeli stereotype of Arafat as a monster."[75]

Outlaw the Dialogues

By 1985 the frequency of meetings between Israelis and Palestinians (including officials of the PLO) increased, and the number of Israelis who recognized that Israel would eventually have to deal with the PLO steadily rose.[76] This was a source of concern among Likud leaders and other right-wing Knesset factions, which consequently sought to prohibit such meetings through legislation.

The Labor Party, which in the summer of 1984 had joined Likud in the National Unity Government, had its own political concerns. In view of the growing popularity and public acceptance of Meir Kahane's Kach party, Labor demanded that its Likud partners support legislation that would outlaw racist political parties. It was hoped that such a law could be employed to prevent Kahane from being reelected to the Knesset in the next elections. After considerable bargaining Likud struck a deal with Labor to support such legislation if Labor supported legislation that would make unauthorized meetings with PLO representatives a criminal offense. With most Labor MKs opposing dialogues with the PLO anyway, Labor accepted the deal. On August 5, 1986, the Knesset passed the two laws, and meetings with members of the PLO now became punishable by three years in prison.[77] The law exempted journalists in the conduct of their work and academics participating in international conferences. It also implied that nonacademic international conferences in which Israelis did not establish direct contact with PLO members were exempt.

The peace movement now faced a new dilemma. Some advocated opposing the new law by ignoring it, even if this meant facing criminal prosecution. Others argued that the letter of the law should be obeyed while they sought loopholes that would allow them to continue their dialogues with Palestinians without violating the law. Peace Now, which itself had had reservations about meeting with the PLO without prior assurances of tangible results, including mutual public recognition and an end to terror attacks, decided to concentrate on dialogues with Palestinian leaders inside the occupied territories.[78]

Mizrachi peace activists were the first to challenge the new law. The PLO, misperceiving the role Mizrachim play in Israeli society, had sought contacts with Israel's Mizrachi population for some time. Many within the PLO looked upon Mizrachim as "Arabs of the Jewish faith" who could agree with the PLO view that "Judaism, being a religion, is not an independent nationality."[79] The erroneous conclusion drawn from this flawed assumption was that Mizrachim would naturally support the creation of a "secular democratic unified Palestine." In this scheme, Mizrachim could become "Palestinians of the Jewish faith" if they were born in Palestine. Otherwise they would be induced to return to the Arab countries from where they had emigrated.[80]

In reality, even radical Mizrachi critics of the Israeli establishment never shared any such common interests with the PLO. The majority of the Mizrachi community tended to support the rightwing in Israeli politics, for whom the PLO remained the main enemy, and even those Mizrachim on the left who nurtured grievances against the Ashkenazi elite never aspired to undermine the Zionist ideal of a Jewish state in Israel. Nevertheless, many Mizrachim in the peace camp believed that because of their familiarity with Arab society and culture they might serve as a bridge to the Arab Middle East. They saw it as their obligation to encourage and participate in dialogues with the PLO.

Latif Dori, an Iraqi-born member of Mapam's Central Committee and head of its Arab Affairs Department, was among those who favored challenging the new law head on. On January 26, 1986, Dori and several other Mizrachi peace activists had founded the Committee for Israeli-Palestinian Dialogue.[81] The committee was designed to be an umbrella organization and included members of East for Peace and other Mizrachi peace groups. The new group published a declaration of principles signed by prominent Mizrachi individuals who resolved to resist "the criminal generalization which depicts all these oriental communities as Arab-haters." They declared that "Israelis of oriental origin possess the ability and the desire to build a bridge between the Arab world and Israeli society, and to renew the centuries-old tradition of cultural partnership as a step towards our integration in the region."[82]

Hanna Siniora, the editor of the Palestinian pro-PLO newspaper *al-Fajr,* welcomed the new committee and in July published its declaration in both the Arabic and English editions of the newspaper.[83] As soon as the law barring contact with the PLO was enacted, Dori, Siniora, and Shlomo Elbaz (of East for Peace) convened a press conference in which they asserted that "no power in the world can prevent the dialogue between the Israeli and Palestinian peace seekers which will continue at all times in all places." Dori also stated that he was prepared to pay the price for his actions.[84]

The opportunity to test his determination arrived in November 1986. After complicated preparations, a well-publicized meeting with several prominent members of the PLO Executive Committee was held in Constinesti, Romania, on the Black Sea. The Palestinian delegation was headed by General Abd al-Razzak Yahya, the former commander of the Palestinian Liberation Army. More than a hundred international journalists were present to cover the event.[85]

The meeting provoked significant opposition. The Israeli attorney general announced that the participants would be arrested upon their return to Israel. Even Mapam's leadership denounced the initiative and temporarily suspended Dori's membership in the party. Many Mizrachim who had originally planned to attend the meeting changed their minds at the last minute as a result of internal dissent and several demonstrations organized by right-wing elements at Ben-Gurion Airport.[86]

The conference itself was a disappointment. It lasted only ninety minutes, no substantive discussions took place, and the Palestinians offered no signs of moderating their position. Nevertheless, this nonevent became a cause célèbre in Israel because it represented the first clear challenge to the new law. The meeting received considerable media coverage in Israel, and some right-wing members of the Knesset demanded a police investigation.

Upon returning to Israel, Dori and three of his colleagues were arrested and charged with criminal offenses.[87] The court sentenced the group to six months in jail plus a one-year suspended prison term and a small fine. The verdict was appealed to the relevant district court, where the judge, though he seemed to feel that the charges were not morally justified, followed the letter of the law and upheld the verdict of the lower court. The group appealed once again, this time to the Supreme Court. The case dragged on for several years until rendered moot by the repeal of the law by the Rabin government in 1993.[88]

Abie Nathan, Latif Dori, and some others confronted the law directly. Others in the peace camp used a different and less dramatic approach, but one that also helped to render the law little more than a farce.

It soon became clear that the police and the state attorney did not like enforcing the law, and with the exception of cases involving demonstrative defiance (which left little room for discretion) they preferred to avoid prosecution.[89] With the help of individuals and organizations in Europe and the United States, Israeli activists organized many meetings under academic auspices in which blatantly public contacts were avoided. The rules of the game were simple. A third party served as the chairperson of the meeting and the Israelis addressed themselves to the neutral chairperson, thus avoiding "direct contact" with the PLO representative.[90] Members of the Knesset also continued to meet with PLO representatives, invoking their parliamentary immunity to shield themselves from criminal prosecution for activities undertaken in the conduct of their political work.[91]

The New Palestinians

Another way to circumvent the law was by expanding the existing dialogues with the Palestinians inside the occupied territories who identified themselves with the PLO. The Likud governments did not alter the policy enunciated by Moshe Dayan in the early 1970s, which held that as long as a Palestinian did not engage in acts of terror or public incitement he or she was entitled to his or her personal opinions. In effect this permitted Palestinians in the territories to openly identify with the PLO, which many chose to do.

By the early 1980s Peace Now (which agreed to meet officially with the PLO only much later) supported the idea of nurturing contacts with pro-PLO Palestinians in the occupied territories. A new generation of Palestinian leaders was emerging as many of the older leaders were deported, died, or lost the support of their constituencies. Younger people like Ziyad Abu-Zayyad, Hanan Ashrawi, Ghassan al-Khatib, and Faisal Husseini gradually replaced the previous leadership, which had included Rashad Shawwa, Karim Khalaf, and Bassam Shak'a.[92] Most of the peace groups on the Israeli side maintained contacts with these new leaders and tried to persuade Israelis that these Palestinians could be partners in negotiations.[93] For Peace Now this became an important source of activity during the period of the National Unity Government, in which the prevailing political environment undermined Peace Now's ability to organize large public demonstrations. As one observer commented, "Peace Now's resurrection followed from its ability to establish a working relationship with a number of West Bank and Gaza Strip leaders."[94]

Meetings between the leaders of Peace Now and the younger Palestinian leadership began to resemble a semiformal committee that convened frequently to exchange information and opinions and to plan joint activities that would assist in breaking the wall of enmity between their respective nations. The Palestinians preferred to hold these meetings in one of the Palestinian research institutes in East Jerusalem or in neutral territory such as the American Colony Hotel or the Notre Dame Hotel.[95]

After Issam Sartawi's murder in 1983 a growing number of second-tier PLO officials reached out to Israelis. To many within the PLO it became evident that armed struggle alone would not achieve their national aspirations and that some mutual compromise was necessary. They also began to understand that their future was inextricably tied to Israeli public opinion, which had to shift toward favoring some kind of accommodation before any Israeli government would try to reach a compromise. Despite its security problems, Israel was plainly not going to be forced by terror or other violent means to relinquish any part of the territories it had occupied in 1967. Consequently, in the second half of the 1980s the

Palestinians sought to make contact with Israelis closer to the political center and even to the right of the center.

The new Palestinian leadership met frequently with members of ICPME, and became regular participants in its annual conferences. This enabled them to meet many individuals associated with the Labor Party, such as Abba Eban, MK Ora Namir, MK Chaim Ramon, and former Justice Minister Chaim Tzadok.[96] By 1987 at least one of the sessions of ICPME's International Board of Trustees Conference was convened in the American Colony Hotel in the Arab side of Jerusalem to accommodate the Palestinian leaders.

Much of this activity, however, remained within limited elite circles of the Palestinian and Israeli communities and did not reach the broader public. The Palestinian masses came into contact with Israelis on a totally different plane. More than 100,000 Palestinian workers commuted every morning from their squalid camps and villages to work as cheap labor in Israel. In the occupied territories, almost all the Israelis the Palestinians encountered were either soldiers or settlers. For most young Palestinians, the Israeli was either a parsimonious employer or an oppressive occupier.

As the peacemakers on both sides sought a way to change the situation through dialogue and informal diplomacy, anger and desperation were growing in the refugee camps in the West Bank and Gaza Strip. The new generation of Palestinians who were born into the misery of occupation hardly noticed the efforts of the new generation of Palestinian leaders. They also became skeptical of the PLO's ability to deliver them from their poverty and indignity. Beneath the hopeful dialogues the cauldron of frustration was reaching its boiling point.

11

Intifada
The Palestinian Uprising, 1987–88

Sticks and Stones

On the outskirts of Gaza on the afternoon of December 8, 1987, a truck driven by an Israeli crashed into a car full of Palestinian laborers returning home from a day of work on the other side of the Green Line. Four Palestinians were killed and several others wounded.[1] Other than the unfortunate loss of life there was nothing particularly noteworthy about this accident. However, it served as the spark that ignited the anger, frustration, and humiliation that had mounted among the Palestinians in the occupied territories during the previous two decades. A rumor quickly spread through Gaza that the death of the four Palestinians was no accident but a cold-blooded murder perpetrated by an Israeli whose brother had been stabbed in Gaza's main market two days earlier.

As the mourners returned home from the Palestinians' funerals that evening, the IDF outpost inside the Jabalya camp near the town of Gaza was attacked by stone-throwing Palestinians. The spontaneous demonstration continued well into the night and quickly spread throughout the camp. Most of the camp's roads and alleys were blocked by the residents, who erected makeshift barricades. By morning it became evident that this riot was not going to be easily contained. Within three days the rioting had spread throughout the Gaza Strip and into parts of the West Bank as well. Caught off guard, the poorly prepared Israeli soldiers fired their weapons into the crowds to extricate themselves from the increasingly daring Palestinians, who lobbed barrages of stones and occasional firebombs.[2] Palestinian casualties mounted by the hour, and the international media recorded brutal scenes of soldiers beating and shooting at Palestinians. By the end of the tenth day of escalating violence it was clear that a massive Palestinian uprising was under way. The Arab media referred to the uprising as an *Intifada*—literally meaning a "shake-up"—suggesting a dramatic departure from the status quo.[3]

The Intifada came as a surprise to all groups involved—the Israeli authorities, the PLO, the local Palestinian leadership, even the young Palestinians who were responsible for it all. The PLO leadership had suffered repeated setbacks in the preceding months, and failed at first to take command of the events, which were now clearly beyond its control. This can be attributed partly to the fact that the uprising not only came as a response to the humiliation of the Israeli occupation, but also reflected the disillusionment the Palestinian masses felt toward the ineffectiveness of the PLO itself, particularly its inability to deliver them from their misery.[4]

The masses of young Palestinians who took to the streets did so without any preconceived plan or long-term objectives. They were driven by the momentum of their anger and frustration, seemingly without concern for the broader meaning or impact of their actions. They soon discovered that the Intifada provided them with a significant psychological and political victory, at least in terms of winning the support of international public opinion and restoring their own dignity. The initial media successes of the uprising served to fuel its growth and helped it gain overwhelming support within the Palestinian community and the rest of the Arab world.[5]

For Israel the Intifada caused a rapid and significant change in the operational environment in the occupied territories.[6] The IDF was now responsible not only for defending its own troops and other Israelis from Palestinian violence, but also for preventing (or at least minimizing) violence against Palestinians by Israelis. Israeli soldiers had to encounter "frenzied people taunting [them] and daring them to shoot while they stood rooted to the spot in defiance."[7] Despite the fact that the Palestinians' weapons (mostly stones and firebombs) had the capability to injure and kill, for the most part they were not weapons meant to inflict casualties so much as to provoke a response. The defiant young Palestinians seemed to be sending a message that, even if they were too weak to kill their occupiers, they could compel the soldiers to kill them and create martyrs for the cause. The high number of casualties in the early phases of the Intifada demonstrated the willingness of the Palestinians to sustain heavy losses, including women and children. Daily images of Palestinian suffering and Israeli brutality catapulted the Intifada to the center of world attention.

The disorganized policies and insensitive public statements of Defense Minister Yitzhak Rabin during the early phases of the Intifada indicated the Israeli authorities' lack of understanding of the significance of this latest chapter in their struggle with the Palestinians. Initially, Rabin viewed the Intifada as a passing event. Upon his return from a trip to the United States three weeks after the outbreak of violence, Rabin seemed to believe the Intifada was already waning, declaring that "the disturbances will not happen again, even if we have to use massive force."[8] While he recognized the need for political negotiations, he was resolved to pacify the territories by force.[9]

During the first two years of the Intifada 600 Palestinians were killed and 8,500 wounded by Israeli forces.[10] Concerned by the growing number of fatalities, Rabin sought to contain the uprising while reducing the use of lethal force. Consequently, he ordered his troops to stop shooting and to start beating the rioters instead. "More force, less shooting," he told the Knesset Defense and Foreign Affairs Committee.[11] The fatality rate declined for a while, but beatings and "breaking bones" (as Rabin was reported to have ordered) produced more disturbing media images than did shooting from afar. Scenes of Israeli soldiers beating unarmed Palestinians provided invaluable ammunition for the Palestinians' propaganda war, further damaging Israel's image abroad and shaking public conscience at home.[12] Some soldiers seemed to believe that the prevailing chaos provided them with a license to use force as they saw fit, and there were many instances of excessive use of force. For other soldiers, however, the situation raised moral dilemmas concerning the limits of obedience and the legality of the orders they received from their superiors.[13]

Within three months of the Intifada's eruption, there was no doubting that the Israeli-Palestinian conflict had entered a new and radically different phase. The traditional concept of "armed struggle" with occasional terror attacks on Israeli or Jewish targets, sporadic strikes, demonstrations, and clashes with the Israeli occupation forces was supplanted by a new mode of resistance. This included a sustained effort to challenge the occupation through daily acts of defiance and civil disobedience, and by refusing to cooperate in the occupation as docile partners with no control over their destiny.[14] "It was not a revolt," said one Palestinian leader, "it was a new way of life, a new mode of existence."[15] A commercial strike went on for months, and roads were regularly blocked with burning tires and other obstacles.[16] Palestinian flags were repeatedly hoisted on houses, electric lines, and minarets, and political graffiti covered every inch of visible wall space. The walls of cities, villages, and refugee camps were pasted with defiant slogans in the red, green, and black of the Palestinian flag. Arab citizens communicated with the Israeli civil administration only when unavoidable. Social and other services provided through independent networks of citizens' initiatives—which had grown by leaps and bounds in the occupied territories since the collapse of such services in Lebanon after 1982—were now strengthened, and helped Palestinians avoid using the services provided by the occupation authorities.[17]

Enough with the Occupation!

By the beginning of 1988 many Israelis began to accept that the new situation with the Palestinians could not be resolved through military means. The Intifada was a psychological and political phenomenon and an outgrowth of the Israeli occupation, and only a political settlement that included an end of the occupation would bring about an end of the Intifada. This conclusion was rejected by the Israeli right, but Chief of Staff Dan Shomron and other high-ranking officers publicly expressed their belief that "the IDF cannot handle the root of the matter, since the solution of the Israeli-Palestinian conflict requires a political, not a military, solution."[18]

The peace movement was now faced with a dilemma. It could focus exclusively on protesting the occupation and demand that the government initiate a process that would lead to the withdrawal of Israeli forces from the occupied territories. But though this approach was morally and intellectually appealing, it failed to address the short-term issue of Israel's immediate response to the Intifada. Opinion was also divided as to if and how the peace movement should address the handling of the uprising by the IDF and other security forces. Among other issues, this raised the question of whether it was appropriate for the movement to publicly criticize the IDF's conduct in the territories. Some within the peace movement believed that if they debated the modes and means of the occupation they might be accused of tacitly acquiescing to it.

Members of the more radical wing of the movement were not particularly concerned with these nuances. As had been the pattern in the past, they created a new "committee" and took to the streets under a new banner, *"Dai Lakibush!"* (Enough with the Occupation!). The solution they advocated was quite simple—"two states for two peoples!" They were also unambiguous in declaring that Israel's negotiating partner should be the PLO, as the sole legitimate representative of the Palestinian people.

Michel Warschawski (better known to his friends as Mikado) had emigrated to Israel during the 1968 student revolt in France. While in France he had been associated with marxist groups, and after his arrival in Jerusalem he joined Matzpen, the small far-left anti-Zionist group. In addition to his participation in the usual debates over ideology and doctrine, Mikado became active on the left-wing fringes of the peace movement. During the late 1970s and early 1980s he was active in the various "committees," his personal integrity and intelligence earning respect not only among his Jewish friends but also within the Palestinian community.[19] During the war in Lebanon Mikado served two jail terms for refusing to report for his military reserve duties.

During the first years of the National Unity Government (1984–86), when the peace movement was at a low point, Warschawski, along with some of his colleagues from Matzpen and the Communist Party, formed a new committee. They opposed the self-declared "iron fist" policy inspired by Defense Minister Yitzhak Rabin. The unique feature of this committee was that it was a joint venture with several Palestinian leaders, including Faisal Husseini, Sari Nusseibeh, and Mubarak Awad.[20] Warschawski recalled that "for the first time Husseini and his friends understood that at least in Jerusalem they could and should use protest methods which the Israeli system considered legitimate, and transcend the struggle against the Israelis by trying to persuade them."

On behalf of the group, the Jews on the committee would apply for and receive a police permit to hold a demonstration; however, 80 to 90 percent of the participants would be Palestinians. Using this ploy Palestinians could hold demonstrations in Jerusalem without breaking the law.[21] The police soon recognized this trick and denied permission for a large demonstration planned on the occasion of the fifth anniversary of the Sabra and Shatila massacre. The police claimed that the Palestinian organizers were agents of the PLO.[22] A few days later Faisal Husseini was placed under administrative arrest, and his Arab Studies Society at Orient House in East Jerusalem, where the committee had its headquarters, was ordered closed.

Husseini's arrest helped Mikado and his colleagues awaken dormant activists from the earlier committees. As they prepared for a demonstration to demand Husseini's release, the Intifada erupted and "Dai Lakibush" was born. According to Warschawski:

> We managed to mobilize all the groups and parties on the left of Mapam, Ratz, and Peace Now. But for us the initial support of the Communist Party was most important. They provided us with the backing of a stable organization and many reserve units. We could always trust that a few busloads of their followers, mainly Israeli Arabs, would attend our activities.[23]

Many of Dai Lakibush's followers were Israeli Arabs who had gained a new sense of dignity and preferred to be referred to as "Palestinian citizens of Israel," rather than as "occupied Palestinians." The renewed contact since 1967 between Israeli Arabs and the Palestinians in the occupied territories had contributed to a growing awareness of their dual identity as Palestinians and as citizens of Israel, and the Intifada intensified their identification with their Palestinian brethren.[24] Mikado explained:

> The Intifada compelled us to make a sharp choice. Either you identified with the Intifada or else you were on the side of the suppressors. There was no third way for us. The option to remain critical of the occupation without becoming part of the uprising was closed. . . . In view of this total clash with the entire Palestinian population, all the arguments used by the peace movement, stressing the need to end the occupation primarily as an Israeli interest, lost their moral standing. The only argument left for us was the injustice being done to the Palestinians.[25]

For some Jewish followers of Dai Lakibush this posture was sometimes difficult to maintain. In any prolonged national conflict there is a tendency to close ranks with one's own ethnic group, particularly in turbulent times such as the early months of the Intifada. Supporting the "other side," even if only morally, thus presented a dilemma. However, many, even within the more moderate peace groups, attempted to address the new circumstances created by the Intifada frontally.

The Markers of the Breach

Established shortly before the outbreak of the Intifada, the 21st Year was presented with new challenges and opportunities by the uprising. Early in 1988 Adi Ofir, one of the group's founders, received his orders to report for reserve duty in the occupied territories. He refused and was sentenced to nineteen days in prison. In an exchange of letters with Yitzhak Rabin, Ofir accused Rabin of ordering excessive measures against the Palestinians. "My refusal," Ofir added, "is an attempt to stick a spike on the slippery road between democracy and another regime." Rabin responded, "Political controversies in a democratic regime have their forums: the Knesset, the ballot, but not the military service."[26] On his release Ofir proudly declared, "We are the markers of the breach in the society. We are the pioneers, the avant garde within the occupation."[27]

The 21st Year undertook other peace activities as well. The most successful of these was the project known as "Edei Kibush" (Witnesses of Occupation). Rabin's harsh anti-Intifada policy led some Palestinians to invite Israelis to witness their suffering. Nurit Shleifman, who was active in this project, recalled:

> We would receive a call from a mother whose son had been arrested the previous night, from a family whose house had been blown up, or from a village in which a clash with the army had left a number of people dead or wounded. We would then hire an Arab taxi [because it was dangerous to travel into the territories with Israeli license plates] and send out a team to investigate the claims and report back. We were often accompanied by a journalist. We collected testimonies from the local inhabitants and prepared a detailed report. We always managed to report our findings to the media in one way or another.[28]

There was a good measure of naiveté in this operation because the "witnesses" were not trained investigators, often did not know the precise context and circumstances of the event they were investigating, and were sometimes taken in by Palestinian propaganda. Despite this, the compassion they showed toward the Arab population, and the protest they directed toward the Israeli authorities, were perhaps more important than the details. The group's reports also helped to produce a more balanced flow of information in light of the stonewalling of the Israeli media about what was happening in the territories.

Within the 21st Year a schism developed between those who personally participated in the investigations and came to identify with the suffering they witnessed and those who learned about events mostly through the Israeli media and thus tended to take the Israeli perspective. According to Shleifman:

> Once you go into the area you cannot avoid a certain level of identification with the other. You cannot look at the Palestinians only as an instrument for your political struggle. You cannot look at them only as an object of the oppression which you denounce. They are after all and foremost subjects. You meet human suffering and you cannot maintain your exclusive orientation on the Israeli side of the tragedy. You must cross a crucial line. You cannot speak about the Palestinians without speaking to them and together

with them. You are no longer only an Israeli who comes to visit; you become in a certain way also an occupied Palestinian.[29]

This division was especially noticeable over what came to be known
as the "Beita Affair." Beita is a small Palestinian village five miles east of
the main highway that runs from Ramallah to Nablus along the Samarian
hills. During the Passover holiday in the spring of 1988 a group of youngsters from several nearby Jewish settlements set out on a hike. They
came upon a couple of Arab shepherds and a confrontation ensued. In
response, the adults who were acting as an armed escort for the young
hikers entered Beita and went on a shooting rampage. When the gun-
fire ceased one Jewish girl and two Palestinians were dead.[30] The Jewish girl's death, though probably caused by shots fired by one of the
Jewish escorts, provoked an uproar among the settlers, who demanded
retribution. The following day the army destroyed thirteen houses and
placed Beita under curfew without any investigation.[31]

These precipitous acts enraged the entire peace movement. The most
extreme members of the 21st Year (mostly those who had acted as "witnesses") organized themselves as the "Beita Committee" and recommended
several dramatic actions. They proposed that the movement organize a
march to Beita to express solidarity with the villagers, even if this resulted
in a violent confrontation with the army. The steering committee rejected
this proposal, arguing that the 21st Year was created to influence the Israeli
public, and that a confrontation with the IDF would be counterproductive.
The "witnesses" argued that it was impossible to promote peace if the Palestinians were approached only as objects. Hannan Hever observed that
"we were convinced that there were interests common to us and to the
occupied people which loomed larger then the common Israeli interest."[32]

The organizers of the Edei Kibush project noticed that many of their colleagues shied away from going into the territories. "At first we thought people
were afraid of the Intifada, but soon we understood that people were afraid
to cross a certain boundary. They were afraid that it would bring them to
view the entire conflict from the perspective of the Palestinians."[33] This exposed a growing schism between those in the movement who viewed their
activities as primarily an outgrowth of Israel's self-interest (in promoting
the country's long-term security, countering the corrupting effect of the occupation on Israeli society, and so forth) and those who were motivated by
moral considerations, compassion, and solidarity with the occupied Palestinians. As time passed it became clearer that playing the role of the "markers of the breach" (as defined by Adi Ofir) was not an easy undertaking.

The ideological division inside the movement soon resurfaced. Early in 1989 a large group from the 21st Year went to Qalqilya (a Palestinian town near the Green Line in the central section of the West Bank) to demonstrate against a violent and destructive assault conducted by Jewish settlers the previous day. The protesters were unaware that the army had closed the area earlier in the morning. The group was stopped at a military roadblock and ordered to leave the area. Some of the protesters proceeded to leave, because they objected to the prospect of a confrontation with the IDF. However, a group of twenty-seven protesters headed by Adi Ofir and Ilana Hammerman circumvented the roadblock and entered the town through the surrounding fields. They were apprehended by the IDF, charged with illegally entering a closed area, and accused of inciting Palestinians in the town.

This occurred on a Friday and the judge refused to release the protesters on bail—as was customary in such cases—and ordered that they remain incarcerated through the Sabbath (Saturday). On Sunday the judge extended their detention for an additional five days. Eighteen women were sent to a women's prison in the north, and the nine men were dispersed to various prisons. This decision received a considerable amount of media attention, and Knesset members intervened on behalf of the accused. By the middle of the week the protesters had been indicted and released on bail.[34]

For some of the activists this was a traumatic experience, while for others it served as a source of pride and strength. This latter group demanded that the movement undertake even more radical activities. It was widely assumed that the court would impose suspended minimal prison terms with the understanding that any further illegal activities would activate the suspended sentences. For the first time the movement faced the possibility that a substantial price would be paid by some members for their activities. While some were ready to pay it, others hesitated or refused outright.

> During the court proceedings [Hannan Hever remembered] our spirit was high and in the name of 150 people who came to show solidarity with their colleagues I declared "We are all Qalqilians!" I received an ovation, but this was misleading. The prison experience eventually brought some people to the realization that they were not ready to pay the price.[35]

This debate soon reached an impasse. A secretariat was formed to review further activities, but it convened only a couple of times and no decisions could be reached. The movement soon stagnated. "We came too close to the fire," Hever recalled. "We had to distance ourselves, and most of us found our way back to Peace Now, which under the new circumstances became relevant again."[36]

Net Refusal

When the IDF withdrew from its positions in central Lebanon in May 1985, Yesh Gvul (the movement of military service refusers) seemed to have reached the end of its road.[37] Other than a few marginal activities, it had exercised little influence between 1985 and 1987. Perhaps its most significant contribution was the publication of a book, *The Limits of Obedience*, which sparked a lively debate in the media concerning moral and political principles.[38]

The Intifada breathed new life into Yesh Gvul. On December 24, 1987, just two weeks after the start of the uprising, Yesh Gvul released a statement announcing that more than one hundred reserve soldiers had already notified the IDF that they intended to refuse orders to "participate in the killing and brutal suppression." In the name of the movement they declared that they "could no longer share the burden of responsibility for this moral and political deterioration."[39] Shortly thereafter the first refusers were arrested. On January 16, 1988, the movement organized a demonstration near the Erez checkpoint (near the Gaza Strip) to symbolize the line they refused to cross.[40] By the end of February activists began distributing a "Service Brochure" to soldiers serving in the territories, calling on them to disobey illegal orders.[41]

During the 1960s the IDF had distributed to its recruits a pamphlet that contained Justice Benyamin Halevy's verdict in the notorious Kfar Kassem massacre case. Halevy stated that soldiers have an obligation to disobey orders that are blatantly illegal and may be seen as such "like a black flag."[42] Rabin's directive to "break bones" rather than to shoot to kill, and other harsh measures being used by the IDF in an effort to suppress the Intifada, accorded special urgency to questions concerning the legality of orders. The IDF attempted to address this sensitive moral and operational subject and issued a number of vague directives that left a considerable amount of discretion to the soldiers confronting the Intifada. A few cases of excessive uses of force were brought to trial, but the problem continued to haunt the soldiers and left the public confused.[43]

Despite the fact that the IDF itself struggled with this problem, the fact that private citizens were calling on soldiers to disobey orders was considered unacceptable by the authorities. The state attorney general, Yosef

Harish, requested that the police conduct an investigation into the activities of Yesh Gvul. This triggered harsh criticism from the left.[44] Ishai Menuchin, a central figure in Yesh Gvul, accused Harish of "an exercise in intimidation in order to neutralize an essential debate on the most burning issues facing Israel."[45] Additionally, in an effort to limit the scope of the refusal, the Executive Committee of the Israeli Broadcasting Authority decided to refrain from reporting on the refusers' demonstrations—a decision protested by several prominent journalists and public figures.[46]

By the end of 1989 more than 150 soldiers had gone to jail for refusing to serve in the territories; some of them served more than one prison term.[47] Menuchin claimed that more than 2,000 soldiers either refused or requested not to serve in suppressing the Intifada and were subsequently dismissed by their commanders. Some spoke of "grey refusal" in which thousands of soldiers found ways to avoid serving in the territories without directly refusing their orders. Because the IDF had an adequate supply of soldiers to meet its needs, it often chose to turn a blind eye to this phenomenon.[48]

Yesh Gvul believed that its protest had significance far beyond the circle of refusers, as the debate concerning the limits of obedience spread throughout the peace movement. In their response to the police investigation of Yesh Gvul, the various peace groups spoke with one voice, issuing a joint announcement that declared, "We hold different opinions on the questions of the limits of obedience and the right to refuse, but the conviction that public protest in its varied forms is the soul of democracy unifies us all."[49] However, members of Peace Now, Mapam, and Ratz continued to express their objection to acts of military disobedience and draft refusal. When he asked the minister of police about the investigation of Yesh Gvul, MK Haim Oron of Mapam began by stating, "I do not share the road taken by Yesh Gvul. I think that their call to refuse service in Israel today is a political mistake."[50]

This debate came to a head in July 1990 because of a dispute within the ranks of Ratz. Ornan Yekutieli, a senior representative of the party on the Jerusalem Municipal Council, along with forty-three other Ratz members, published a statement of solidarity with a colleague who had refused to serve and had been sent to jail. Yossi Sarid strongly opposed this action, arguing that the statement could have been interpreted as the party's endorsement of the act of refusal.[51]

A heated session of the party's executive committee followed, at the end of which the committee endorsed a resolution offered by MK Shulamit Aloni, the party's founder and senior leader. The resolution declared that the party "opposed any refusal to serve in the territories or any encouragement of such refusal. . . . [but expresses] its understanding of those willing to pay the price for their conscientious objection."[52]

The leaders of Yesh Gvul criticized the position taken by Ratz, Mapam, and Peace Now as hypocritical. It was inconceivable to Yesh Gvul that these groups could oppose the methods being employed in suppressing the Intifada while encouraging their members to obey their orders as reservists in the territories. This position was cynically characterized with the phrase, "They shoot and weep."[53]

Criticism was also directed specifically against Peace Now, which according to the refusers had drawn the wrong conclusions from the situation and had been coopted by the suppressive system. In essence this was a controversy over defining "red lines"—lines beyond which civil disobedience becomes inevitable. Nobody on the left denied that red lines existed in principle. But Peace Now did not believe these lines had yet been reached, despite the terrible situation that prevailed in the territories, and insisted that as long as the democratic process was maintained, opposition had to adhere to legal methods. Dissatisfied with this position, some Peace Now members became active in Yesh Gvul.

Don't Rub It In

From the beginning of the Intifada, Peace Now had decided that sporadic demonstrations targeted only against the occupation itself would not be an adequate form of protest. In addition to organizing street demonstrations that condemned the overall political situation, the movement began to question the specific methods used by the authorities in response to the new situation. Peace Now publicly criticized measures taken to suppress the Intifada as unnecessary, inhumane, and ineffective. This was consistent with the approach typical of most Peace Now members, who conscientiously remained within the mainstream of society and were wary of doing anything that might marginalize themselves or their activities. Rejecting Adi Ofir's claim that to address the details of the occupation is to participate in it, they argued that the daily actions of Israeli soldiers in the occupied territories were of no less concern than the eventual solution to the conflict, which could take a long time to achieve and which did not absolve the movement from addressing other controversial issues.

The year 1988 witnessed the third peak in Peace Now's history. During the first six months of the Intifada, Peace Now organized scores of street demonstrations, public conferences, panel discussions, vigils, and other forms of public protest in which more than 200,000 people participated.[54] In 1985 a journalist had described the movement as "a dead horse." But in January 1988, after three years of lethargy, Peace Now demonstrators reappeared in front of the Tel Aviv town hall, prompting another journalist to comment, "The horse is not dead, rather like a phoenix it came back to the familiar plaza."[55]

A significant part of Peace Now's constituency were either members or supporters of the Labor Party. Even these people felt uncomfortable with the fact that Rabin, as minister of defense in the National Unity Government, had direct responsibility for the management of the security forces and their response to the Intifada. Rabin soon became a chief target of Peace Now's criticism.

At the beginning of January 1988 the Palestinians in the territories formed a clandestine leadership group called the Unified Leadership of the Uprising (UNLU), which coordinated the Intifada on behalf of the PLO.[56] It distributed leaflets calling for the intensification of the uprising, and gave specific orders and guidelines directing the activities of the Palestinian population.[57] In "Leaflet Number One" the UNLU ordered a three-day general strike of all shops, transportation, and businesses for January 11 through 13. The leaflet included a warning against anyone who might dare to violate the edict.

These business strikes became a central feature of the Intifada. Eventually the security services ignored the strikes, but initially they were concerned that successful strikes would give Intifada leaders a symbolic victory and strengthen their influence over the Palestinian masses. Therefore, the IDF was instructed to coerce the merchants to open their stores, and if they refused, to break the shops open by force. As should have been obvious, UNLU threats, coupled with overwhelming Palestinian support for the uprising, were more powerful than the measures taken by the security forces, and Israeli efforts to curtail the strikes proved futile. All the Israeli actions achieved was to increase anger and tension, which led to further casualties and in turn fueled the Intifada.

Other examples of the IDF's confrontational approach involved its response to the display of Palestinian flags and the daubing of political graffiti—activities that the young Palestinians (the "Intifada Children") considered significant acts of defiance, demonstrating their readiness to challenge the Israeli soldiers. Once again the Israeli authorities decided that to ignore the flags and graffiti would provide a victory to the Intifada, and Israeli soldiers spent a significant amount of time covering the graffiti with black paint and coercing the Palestinians to remove their flags. This often led to violent confrontations, with young Palestinians trying to foil the soldiers' efforts by throwing stones or firebombs at them. This test of wills usually produced additional casualties; and shortly after the Israeli soldiers left the scene, the flags and graffiti always reappeared.

These counterproductive tactics by the IDF called for some response from the peace movement. A Peace Now delegation requested an audience with Yitzhak Rabin and tried to persuade him against continuing these measures. Rabin listened politely but refused to change his orders.[58] The movement reacted by organizing yet another demonstration, this one held in Jerusalem on February 13, 1988, and dedicated to the memory of Emil Gruenzweig, the Peace Now activist murdered five years earlier. Characteristically, the notice announcing the demonstration focused on Israeli interests rather than on the plight of the Palestinians. "We demand that we, the people of Israel, be freed from the territories which have conquered us!"[59] For the first time at a Peace Now event, Israeli soldiers were encouraged to disobey illegal orders—the call to do so coming from two MKs, Ran Cohen of Ratz and Yair Tzaban of Mapam. For the first time too, a Palestinian leader from the occupied territories spoke at a Peace Now rally. Hanna Siniora, of the Jerusalem-based pro-PLO newspaper *al-Fajr*, told the crowd that the Intifada "is not directed against the State of Israel but against Israel's occupation of the West Bank. . . . The Palestinian people recognize the right of Israel to exist. It is now up to Israel to recognize the right of the Palestinians to self-determination."[60]

Back to Diplomacy

During 1986 and 1987 U.S. Secretary of State George Shultz attempted to salvage the peace process and, contrary to his erstwhile opposition, was willing to consider convening an international conference in coordination with the Soviets. Prime Minister Shamir opposed such a move, however, and thus stalled any further progress.[61] In February 1988, two months after the outbreak of the Intifada, Shultz undertook a fresh diplomatic initiative that he described as "a new blend of substance and procedure."[62]

Between February and June 1988 Secretary Shultz made four visits to the Middle East. The main feature of his new initiative was to explore the chances for an interim or transitional arrangement modeled on the Camp David autonomy principle. The negotiations on the final status of the occupied territories would begin within a short time of the implementation of the interim arrangement. Another feature was that the new Palestinian leadership that had emerged during the Intifada would be recognized as a full partner alongside the Jordanians in the proposed negotiations.

Shamir adamantly opposed King Hussein's demand to hold at least a ceremonial opening to the process with an international conference, and continued to insist that the PLO not be a partner in the process. In view of Shamir's opposition to the international conference, Hussein's procrastination, and Syrian president Assad's opposition to an interim arrangement, the new initiative produced few tangible results. Hussein appeared eager to play a role in the process, but could not afford to lead such an effort himself. The king's influence with the Palestinians had waned further during the Intifada, and he could no longer claim to speak on their behalf. Furthermore, the Palestinians refused to proceed without the full participation of the PLO. By the spring of 1988, after its initial confusion at the beginning of the Intifada, the PLO had managed to reestablish its leadership role and directed many of the activities associated with the Intifada.[63]

Peace Now publicly supported Shultz's diplomatic efforts and, without endorsing the details of the plan, urged all sides to enter into negotiations. On February 27, 1988, the day before Shultz returned to Jerusalem from visits to Amman and Damascus, Peace Now organized a supportive demonstration in Jerusalem. Placards read "Speed Up the Peace Process!" and speakers claimed that they represented the majority of Israelis in their demand to proceed with negotiations.[64]

On March 12 Peace Now organized another major demonstration in the familiar plaza in Tel Aviv. Close to 100,000 participants packed into the square. Their purpose was to bid farewell to Yitzhak Shamir, who was on his way to Washington, and to "demand that the prime minster say 'Yes!' to the peace initiative, 'Yes!' to the principle of peace in exchange for territories, and 'Yes!' to peace."[65] Amir Peretz, the Moroccan-born mayor of Shderot, a southern town inhabited primarily by Mizrachi immigrants, said, "Shamir, peace is stronger than you, take advantage of it. Enter the history books as Menachem Begin did!" Tzali Reshef, voicing Peace Now's criticism of the Palestinian refusal to negotiate with Schultz, declared, "We call on the Palestinian leadership to be worthy of the peace process."[66]

Palestinian leaders in the occupied territories were initially surprised at the success and persistence of the uprising. Much of what happened in the streets was initiated and coordinated by local "popular committees." But the Palestinian leadership that traditionally represented the PLO in the territories, and with whom Peace Now and other Israeli peace groups had developed close relations over the years, attempted to give the Intifada some coherent political direction. In January 1988 Faisal Husseini, Hanan Ashrawi, Ziyad Abu-Zayyad, Abd el Nabi Natshe, and more than a dozen others formulated a document of "Fourteen Points." The members of the group were careful not to present themselves as partners to any negotiations or as an alternative to the PLO. Their demands were limited to specific grievances concerning the daily lives of Palestinians in the occupied territories.[67]

The content of the document was of little significance, for there was little chance that the Israeli authorities would be persuaded to alter their policies. However, the fact that a group of leaders who enjoyed public standing and prestige within the Palestinian community had united to produce such a petition was significant.

The "Fourteen Points" were presented to Peace Now and to some members of the peace caucus in the Knesset. Although these were not the first discussions between Peace Now and Palestinians from this group, this meeting established an institutional precedent and created a forum for further discussions and coordination of activities. In response Peace Now addressed a letter to the Palestinian community in which the movement recognized the significant achievements of the uprising, but argued that they could not be maintained "unless they are translated into the language of reconciliation and compromise, so that the political process can begin as soon as possible."[68]

Meetings between Peace Now and the group of Palestinian leaders became routine and created an effective channel of communication for both sides. However, the Palestinians recognized that the contacts Peace Now maintained with many Labor and leftist members of Knesset were limited in terms of access to the Israeli political establishment. Policy decisions concerning peace and security remained in the hands of Shamir and his Likud colleagues. Consequently, the Palestinians sought an avenue through which they could reach the Likud leadership.

Coming from the Right

Moshe Amirav was among the younger generation of up-and-coming Likud leaders. Amirav's political socialization occurred in Betar, the Revisionist Zionist youth movement formed by Ze'ev Jabotinsky. After his military service he attended university, where he became the chairman of the Israeli Student Union as a representative of Likud. As part of the young elite in his party, Amirav's career was assured during the decade of Likud's political dominance after 1977.

Amirav, however, subscribed to an unconventional interpretation of Jabotinsky's teachings. He believed that the founder of his movement was essentially a liberal who, if given the circumstances of the 1980s, would have sought reconciliation with the Palestinians and granted far greater autonomy than Begin had offered as part of the Camp David Accords. While Amirav was committed in principle to the integrity of the historic Land of Israel, he envisioned it in terms of greater equality between Arabs and Jews. He vehemently opposed the Jordanian Option advocated by the Labor Party, because he believed that it would inevitably lead to a repartition of the land. He therefore maintained that Israel was obliged to orient its peace effort toward the Palestinians, with whom an undivided land could be shared in a confederation between Jewish and Arab political entities.[69]

During the mid-1980s David Ish-Shalom, an activist of a Mizrachi peace group, participated in dialogues with Palestinian leaders in Jerusalem and abroad and developed a friendly relationship with Faisal Husseini and Sari Nusseibeh. These Palestinian leaders, having heard from Ish-Shalom of Amirav's views, agreed to meet the young Likud leader. On July 4, 1987, Nusseibeh visited Amirav in his home in Ein Karem.[70]

Some of Amirav's ideas were more appealing to the Palestinians than were some of the solutions proposed by the peace camp. Like Amirav, the Palestinians preferred a formula that would not require the repartition of Palestine. They had unenthusiastically accepted the "two states solution" because it appeared to be the only compromise the Jews might eventually accept. However, the unified "secular democratic state" formula had been energetically advocated by the Palestinian mainstream for many years.[71]

At their meeting Nusseibeh suggested that Amirav meet with Faisal Husseini, and Amirav said he would seek the participation of several of his Likud colleagues who were in more senior positions and closer to the prime minister than himself.[72] Amirav informed some of his Likud colleagues of his encounter with Nusseibeh. These included Dan Meridor (later minister of justice) and Ehud Olmert (later mayor of Jerusalem), both MKs and confidants of Yitzhak Shamir. Throughout July and August 1987, Amirav continued to meet with Nusseibeh and Husseini and suggested that a formula "which is less than a separate state but more than autonomy" might prove acceptable to Shamir. He reminded his interlocutors that at this stage he had no mandate to speak on behalf of anyone but himself, but the Palestinians seemed to believe he represented a direct channel to Shamir.[73]

Amirav had little prior experience in dialogues with Palestinians, and was unfamiliar with some of the nuances of these dialogues and the exact meaning and implications of certain formulas. "You request a special status for Jews in the territories you will retreat from," Husseini told him, "and likewise I request a special status in Haifa and Jaffa for the Palestinians." Amirav agreed and was even willing to recognize symbolically the right of the Palestinian refugees to the houses they had abandoned in 1948, which was an unacceptable position for most Israelis. By this point he had already dramatically departed from his own party's positions.[74]

Shamir, who apparently had knowledge of Amirav's meetings early on, did not stop him, but advised caution and warned against publicity. On July 30 Ehud Olmert met Nusseibeh at Amirav's home for an exchange of views. But Amirav went a step further and drafted a "Document of Principles" together with his Palestinian partners, to be presented to Shamir and Arafat. The language used in this document exceeded the positions that even Peace Now was willing to support at this stage: "The national rights of self-determination of both peoples in this country are inalienable. . . . The PLO is the sole and legitimate representative of the Palestinian people."

This was heresy enough for Shamir. But the document went still further and discussed the implementation of a peace process during which "international guarantees required for the final settlement" would be explored. Furthermore, during the interim phase the "Palestinian entity [would locate its] administrative capital in the Arab parts of Jerusalem [and would] adopt various national attributes, such as currency, a flag, a national hymn, an independent broadcasting system, and the authority to issue identity cards and travel documents."[75]

Unsurprisingly, Arafat immediately embraced the document and invited Amirav to meet with him in Geneva. This turn of events led to an angry outburst by Shamir. He summoned Amirav to his office and ordered him to cease all contacts with the Palestinians. A few days later Husseini was placed under administrative detention. Amirav, still a member of Likud's Central Committee, complied with Shamir's orders, but Ish-Shalom went to Geneva with MK Charlie Biton of the Israeli Communist Party and presented Arafat with the document on September 6, 1987. On their return, to protest Husseini's arrest and Shamir's handling of the matter, Biton and

Ish-Shalom released the "Document of Principles" to the media and described the entire episode that had led to this turn of events.[76]

Under heavy pressure Amirav wrote a letter of apology to his Likud colleagues, but continued to propagate his views. Shamir felt the need to distance himself and his party from accusations of contacts with the PLO. Amirav was publicly denounced, forbidden to publicly represent the party, and had his membership in all party representative bodies terminated.[77] Although not expelled from the party, Amirav chose to leave and in a symbolic gesture tore up his membership card in front of the media.[78] "I am glad to quit the bunker in which Shamir has entrenched himself," Amirav told the journalists, and called on his former Likud colleagues to oust Shamir.[79]

Ironically, the cautious approach preferred by Peace Now was vindicated by Amirav's experience. Amirav's good intentions were undermined, perhaps, by his political naiveté. In prolonged national conflicts prenegotiation dialogues are not simply a matter of formulating documents and exchanging views, but serve as important tools for building constituencies in support of reconciliation. Politically exiled by his own party, Amirav could accomplish little. Although he was frequently invited by the Israeli left to participate in conferences and dialogues[80] and briefly held formal positions within the peace movement,[81] and although he was able to increase his contacts with the Palestinians in the years that followed, Amirav was unable to consolidate his early successes and remained a loner without a significant constituency.

A Plethora of Protest Groups

The Intifada triggered a proliferation of groups and factions within the peace movement. Some formed as a result of dissatisfaction with Peace Now's cautious posture, while others claimed they could make a unique contribution within the broader movement.[82]

In January 1988 Dov Jeremiah—a former colonel in the IDF and an expert on Israeli Arab issues who had participated in coexistence activities since the early 1950s—and a group of Arabs and Jews from the Galilee in northern Israel launched an initiative they called "Red Line."[83] In February, emulating Peace Now, Red Line, along with several other small groups, organized a march from Rosh Hanikra on the Lebanese border to Jerusalem to protest the occupation. They stopped in communities along the way and organized public gatherings. They also organized a Peace Festival in Tel Aviv that attracted thousands of participants.

In March 1988 students and faculty at Tel Aviv University organized a new group called "Ad Kan" (Up to Here), which held a number of conferences in which Palestinians from the territories described the suppressive measures employed by the IDF. In one such gathering Muhamed Sha`ban, a lawyer from Gaza, participated and was arrested immediately thereafter. To express their solidarity with the detained lawyer, a group of professors and students organized a protest vigil in front of Rabin's home, which was close to the campus, and visited Sha`ban's family in Gaza amid a violent confrontation that was taking place outside the lawyer's house.[84]

But groups such as Red Line and Ad Kan lacked the human and financial resources to mount a sustained effort. To some degree they duplicated the activities of existing groups, and many of their followers were already active in the more established groups. Consequently, most of them soon faded from the scene. Other groups, such as the Committee of Jewish and Arab Creative Writers, enjoyed somewhat greater longevity and success. The committee was established before the beginning of the Intifada, but became politically active in the early months of 1988. In addition to the dialogue these writers maintained among themselves, they also organized public conferences and published joint statements in which they called for the establishment of a Palestinian state alongside Israel.[85]

In December 1988 several rabbis from Israel's burgeoning Reform and Conservative movements established the Rabbinic Human Rights Watch, a group that offered its moral and spiritual support to the ongoing struggles against human rights abuses in the territories, and to the struggle for peace and reconciliation.[86] A substantial number of mental health professionals expressed their concerns for the negative long-term effects the Intifada might have on both young Israelis and young Palestinians. In June 1988 they founded an association called "Imut" (a Hebrew acronym for Mental Health Workers for the Advancement of Peace), and sponsored a conference entitled the "Psychological Implications of the Uprising in the Territories."[87] In June 1989 they organized a second conference called "Psychological Barriers to Peace," which included panel discussions on such themes as "The Psychology of Dehumanization and Victimization," "Abuse and Racism," and "The Impact of Emotional Stress on the Individual and the Group."[88]

Health care services in the occupied territories were inadequate and the casualties produced by the Intifada strained the already limited resources.[89] Many Israeli physicians, regardless of their political beliefs, felt an obligation to offer a helping hand. In late 1988 the Association of Israeli-Palestinian

Physicians for Human Rights was established. The group provided medical services in cases where the facilities in the territories were inadequate. Additionally, they monitored medical care in military prisons and regularly questioned the authorities about the treatment of detained Palestinians.[90]

Perhaps the most surprising initiative came from a group of high-ranking reserve officers, which included 34 major generals, 86 brigadier generals, and 115 colonels. They were joined by more than 200 economists, ex-diplomats, and academic experts in international politics and Middle Eastern affairs to form the Council for Peace and Security in April 1988. The first chairman of the council was General Aharon Yariv, who had served as the chief of military intelligence during the 1967 war.[91] The council defined its objectives as "advocating the position that peace is essential for Israel's security, disputing the belief that the territories are essential for Israel's security, and convincing the public that security depends on the IDF, not on territories."[92]

Coming from the highest ranks of the military and academia, these "peace generals" received considerable media attention for their activities. Most were not members of a particular party, but sympathized with the Labor Party and its foreign affairs and defense policies. Likud tried to assemble its own cadre of generals, but both in numbers and prestige they failed to match the "peace generals." Perhaps the council's most important contribution was that it demonstrated that an increasing number of mainstream Israelis (in this case, individuals who had been responsible for national security) now viewed the occupied territories as a liability and an obstacle to peace, rather than as a vital element of Israel's security.

Five years after Parents against Silence had protested the aims and conduct of the war in Lebanon, many parents—particularly mothers—similarly agonized about Israel's response to the Intifada. They were concerned that their children were unnecessarily charged with the morally corrupting task of suppressing a revolt in which the use of violence was a calculated strategy rather than a last resort.[93]

In December 1988 these mothers organized a group they called "Horim Neged Shkhika" (Parents against Erosion), which was a slight variation of the name of the earlier group "Horim Neged Shtika" (Parents against Silence).[94] The new name reflected their belief that the war against the Intifada was eroding the morality of their sons. More than 2,000 parents sent letters to Defense Minister Rabin to express their "anguish over the situation our children find themselves in." They maintained that "the IDF's policies in the territories make immoral behavior inevitable," and demanded that the government and IDF "institute policies that will not force the army to act in ways that are immoral, but policies that will allow us to be proud of the IDF, and not ashamed of it."[95]

Rabin was moved by the parents' sincerity and sent a reply to each of those who wrote to him. He reiterated his conviction that a solution to the situation could be achieved only through negotiations. At the same time, he took exception to the parents' concern for the immoral behavior of the soldiers. "The IDF's soldiers are in my opinion, the most moral, fair, and conscientious soldiers one can find in any army in the entire world," he wrote. On the whole, they "wage, with grinding teeth and total discipline under restraining and lawful orders, a war against fathomless hatred." The group was not satisfied with the letter and managed to receive a personal audience with Rabin, but nothing concrete came out of that meeting.[96]

The group focused on legal issues, in one instance petitioning the IDF's attorney general to indict a colonel who was implicated in abuses of Palestinians by soldiers under his command.[97] They also published various pamphlets and a set of guidelines called "Legal Instructions for the Soldier: What Is Permitted? What Is Forbidden?"; the latter was based on a military judge's verdict in a case involving soldiers who had tortured a Palestinian youth.[98] Although Parents against Erosion did not remain on the scene for long, the group made an important contribution to the public's awareness of the moral dilemmas involved in responding to the Intifada. At one of the group's public meetings a reserve captain said, "Eighteen-year-olds ask me if it is frightening to serve in the territories. I tell them the greatest fear is of myself—what I could become—and what I could be drawn into."[99]

Women in Black

Perhaps the most striking element within the Israeli peace movement during the Intifada was the group known as the "Women in Black." Despite the fact that Peace Now's origin could be traced to a letter written by a group of male officers, women had always formed the majority among the movement's activists. They also played a prominent role in most of the other peace groups, and led most of the activities of the 21st Year. In many ways the Intifada contributed to "the predominance of women participating in political activism."[100] The Arab-Israeli conflict was no longer a war between men fought on distant battlefields but a clash in which entire populations, including women and children, were deeply involved.

In January 1988 a group of women affiliated with groups to the left of Peace Now organized a women's vigil in the center of Jerusalem. Impressed by the Madres de la Plaza del Mayo in Buenos Aires, they dressed in black and stood quietly for an hour holding cardboard signs in Hebrew and English that read "End the Occupation!"[101] Within a short time other women joined the vigil, which now took place every Friday at noon at a busy intersection in Jerusalem. This day, hour, and place were carefully chosen, the women's mournful silence contrasting profoundly with the frenetic atmosphere as thousands of people rushed around Jerusalem in preparation for the Sabbath, which begins at sunset. The demonstration was an obvious departure from the usual sights and sounds one expected to encounter at this time and place.

The group was politically and ideologically diverse. Many of the women were also involved with other peace groups in which disagreements often occurred concerning objectives and strategy. However, the Women in Black put controversy aside for the sake of their unique statement, and the only slogan they permitted during their years of activity was "End the Occupation!"

This phenomenon soon spread throughout the country, with vigils being organized in Tel Aviv and Haifa and at several major road junctions. On one Friday as many as thirty vigils were held.[102] Men were invited to join the vigils only on special occasions, as the organizers wanted the protests to remain distinctly female. In addition to protesting Israel's policy toward the Intifada, the Women in Black also sought "to introduce a uniquely feminine voice into the [customary] all-male discourse [on security affairs], a voice that would not be subsumed by the male voice on the one hand, and would not allow for exclusion of women from this crucial discourse."[103]

The women's black attire served as a powerful metaphor, suggesting mourning mothers or widows. It triggered an angry response from the Israeli right. Male passersby and men who turned up just to taunt the protesters often became almost hysterical. As the women stood solemnly and quietly they were bombarded with "intense verbal abuse, mostly sexual in nature."[104] Gila Svirsky, a feminist activist, recalled that "the verbal violence was sometimes excruciating." The women felt "exposed, naked, on the front line."[105]

Some extreme rightist groups countered the Women in Black with simultaneous protests nearby, and often led assaults upon the peace demonstrators.[106] The police intervened in such instances and upheld the right of the women to hold their silent vigil. The sight of more than a hundred women standing silently on a platform near a busy intersection every Friday afternoon became a familiar scene for many Jerusalemites.[107]

Reshet—The Women's Peace Network

Women were now organizing more activities and they soon discovered that many Palestinian women were willing to cooperate with them. One group of Israeli women, for instance, met with and were inspired by Zahira Kamal, a Palestinian feminist who was active in organizing women during the Intifada.[108]

Different groups of women addressed a variety of issues and concerns. Some women focused their attention on single issues, such as the defense of Palestinian women placed under administrative detention. "They closely monitored each case and publicized human rights abuses and gave assistance to prisoners and their families."[109] Another group of Israeli Arab and Jewish women initiated the "Peace Quilt." Several thousand women stitched a quilt that stretched two hundred meters, "depicting in drawings, writing and embroidery messages calling for peace and an end to the occupation. . . . The cloth was intended as a symbolic cover for the table around which peace negotiations would be held. It was displayed at a special ceremony held in front of the Knesset gates in June 1988."[110] Another group dealt with the issue of women (mostly with infants) threatened with expulsion from the occupied territories if they did not have the proper documents.[111]

By the end of 1988 a coalition was formed under the name "Women and Peace," which for the first time included both Jewish and Palestinian women. On December 29, 1988, an impressive "March through the Lines" was organized. Four thousand Israeli and Palestinian women joined arms and marched across the line that had divided east and west Jerusalem before 1967. The marchers called for "Two States for Two People" and the end of enmity and occupation.[112] The march proceeded without incident until just before disbanding near the Palestinian national theater (El Hakavati) in East Jerusalem. At this point two Arab women unfurled a Palestinian flag and began shouting nationalist slogans. The Israeli police responded by dispersing the remains of the gathering with tear gas.[113]

Most of these initiatives in the early months of the Intifada were organized by women on the extreme left of the Israeli political spectrum. Soon, however, the women's groups sought to expand in the direction of Israel's political and social mainstream. In June 1988 "Reshet" (Women's Peace Network) was established. In May 1989 Simone Susskind, a leader of the Belgian Jewish community who was well acquainted with the Israeli political scene, organized a conference in Brussels that attracted prominent women from Israel, the occupied territories, the United States, and Europe.[114]

The Israeli delegation suggested to their Palestinian counterparts, already working under an umbrella organization called the United Palestinian Women's Higher Council, that they establish a network for coordinating peace efforts. A steering committee was organized in which most Israeli and Palestinian women's organizations participated.[115] They published a "Call for Peace" that declared:

> We, Palestinian and Israeli women, share a vision of freedom and equality. We are joined in a common struggle against discrimination, oppression and subjugation of any type, be it on the basis of gender, religion or nationality. . . . We therefore affirm that each people has the right to live in its own state within secure and recognized boundaries, . . . the government of Israel must negotiate with the legitimate representatives of the Palestinian people, the PLO.[116]

During the later months of 1989 and much of 1990 (until the August invasion of Kuwait) Reshet organized meetings in all major Israeli cities at which Palestinian women presented their views to Israeli women. Similarly, Israeli women were invited to Palestinian homes and women's institutions. As Galit Hazan-Rokem, an anthropologist from the Hebrew University and an organizer of these encounters, later commented:

> It is easier for women to cross the lines of hatred. Even though most Israeli women served in the army, they were never involved in combat and were not likely to have served in the occupied territories on reserve duties like Israeli men frequently did. Each side felt a need to inform the other of its own fears and concerns. The Palestinian women found it difficult to realize that Israelis have genuine fears, since they were immersed in their own fears as occupied people. We too needed to understand better, in simple human terms, how it feels when your home is no longer your castle.[117]

In the Image of God

In March 1989 MK Dedi Zucker, one of the founders of Peace Now, called on a number of prominent lawyers, academics, journalists, and MKs to establish a new organization that would monitor and report human rights abuses that occurred in the course of suppressing the Intifada. They called the organization "B'tselem" (In the Image), taking their name from a passage in Genesis in which we are told that Adam and Eve were created "in the image of God."

B'tselem was perhaps the most impressive project of the Israeli peace movement. It undertook its mission under heavy attack from the right, and with significant reservations from many within the Labor Party as well. B'tselem's reports were published in Hebrew and English and frequently included ugly accounts of the behavior of Israeli security officials. Israelis both within and outside the peace movement were often disturbed by these reports. Some on the right branded B'tselem's efforts as distortions, exaggerations, and a treasonous "laundering of dirty linen in public."[118] The professional team of investigators and analysts that B'tselem recruited and trained defended the findings of their reports, which in most cases were subsequently proven to be accurate.[119]

Zehava Gal'on, the first executive director of B'tselem, recruited Bassam Eid to the organization. Eid was the son of Palestinian refugees from a village south of Tel Aviv and grew up in a refugee camp near Jerusalem. His training was in journalism, and using his vast contacts among Palestinians Eid created a network of reporters in the occupied territories who investigated media reports and complaints of human rights abuses. Investigations were thoroughly conducted and evidence checked and rechecked. Only after the investigators and a team of volunteer lawyers were convinced of the accuracy of their findings were the facts passed on to B'tselem's Information Center, where the information was compiled and edited into a final report.

B'tselem published four kinds of reports. The first were *Monthly Updates* in which specific events that had occurred during the previous month were reported—for example, house demolitions, injuries and deaths of children, deportations, and censorship of the Palestinian press. Each *Monthly Update* also provided a cumulative summary of fatalities, injuries, and the number of days on which curfews had been imposed.[120] The second type of report were *Special Case Studies*, which, for example, reported on the deaths of Palestinians during interrogation or on particular cases of abuse by Israeli soldiers. The third type were *Annual Reports*, and the fourth *Comprehensive Studies,* which examined broader subject areas.[121]

B'tselem's press conferences, which it convened whenever it released a major report, were invariably well attended by both the Israeli and international media. Indeed, B'tselem's activities almost always received extensive media coverage, and the organization was viewed by the press as a reliable source of information. One of B'tselem's leaders observed that although it is difficult to assess how much of the changes and improvements instituted by the IDF and Shin Bet [General Security Service] were the result of our work, I know for sure that, for example, our report on methods of interrogation led to the creation of two official committees, one of the IDF and one of the Ministry of Justice, which looked into the matter and issued clearer and more restraining directives to the security forces.[122]

From the outset B'tselem hoped to remain apolitical and nonpartisan. Shirley Eran, a senior member of B'tselem's staff, explained: "We always assumed that the occupation was in and of itself an abuse of human rights, inasmuch as it deprives the occupied of their basic political right to rule themselves. But we were not a protest movement and did not explicitly take a stance of denouncing the occupation. We tried to deal exclusively with specific and personal human rights."[123] Nevertheless, it was impossible to avoid the public impression that B'tselem's work clearly implied political opposition to the occupation, and the organization was seen as a part of the peace movement. At the same time, some on the radical left accused B'tselem of implicitly legitimizing the occupation by dealing only with its symptoms rather than its causes. Palestinian organizations apparently did not share this view, and regularly published B'tselem's reports in their own media.

Speak with the PLO Now!

On July 31, 1988, in the midst of the campaign for the upcoming Knesset elections, King Hussein made a dramatic and unexpected move. In a televised speech to the nation the king announced Jordan's disengagement from the West Bank, renouncing any Jordanian claim to it and stating that "it belongs to the Palestinians."[124] This move signified the demise of both the Jordanian Option and the Shultz initiative.[125] The Labor Party had to shift gears quickly, and in a joint appearance on Israeli television Peres and Rabin announced a new approach to peace. It was based on the assumption that while Israel would approach a negotiated settlement of the conflict through political rather than military means, Hussein's move meant that Jordan was no longer the central partner so far as the Palestinian question was concerned. With the demise of the Jordanian Option, Israel would have to deal with the Palestinians in the occupied territories, who would select their political representatives through elections facilitated by Israel. The statement acknowledged Jordan's continued importance to the process, because peace on Israel's eastern border would not be possible without Jordanian involvement. Finally, the revised process would follow the two-phase model established in the Camp David Accords. In an interim phase, extended autonomy or self-rule would be accorded to the Palestinians in the territories; this would be followed by the beginning of negotiations that would culminate in a final settlement between Israel and the Palestinians residing in the territories and Jordan.[126]

To some degree this was another attempt by the Labor Party's leadership to evade recognizing and negotiating with the PLO. However, since the onset of the Intifada significant changes had taken place within the PLO itself. The Intifada provided the Palestinians with a major psychological achievement, at the same time exacting a heavy price from the residents of the occupied territories. The leaders inside the territories feared that the momentum of events would dissipate before the political gains could be consolidated. They also watched, with mounting concern, the rapid growth and increasing influence of the Islamic fundamentalist movement (especially in the Gaza Strip), which threatened to undermine the leadership of the secular nationalist PLO. Consequently, they urged the PLO leadership outside the territories to undertake new political initiatives.[127]

This caused a split within the ranks of the PLO. The more radical factions advocated the escalation of the Intifada, even the use of deadlier methods. Fatah and other moderate factions sought ways to translate the achievements of the Intifada into political assets and even considered ending the armed struggle altogether.[128]

In June 1988 Arafat's senior political adviser, Bassam Abu-Sharif, published an article publicly recognizing that Israel had legitimate security requirements and that a symmetry of interests existed for both sides. He advocated direct negotiations between the PLO and Israel, and suggested that genuine peace would require political and economic cooperation between the two national entities. "Nobody," he argued, "can build his future on the ruins of the future of the other."[129]

Peace Now sought to capitalize on this significant opening and organized a public conference in the Jerusalem municipal hall on July 27, 1988, to discuss Abu-Sharif's article.[130] At the conference Faisal Husseini assured the audience that Abu-Sharif expressed the views of Arafat and the PLO mainstream. He unequivocally called for the creation of a Palestinian state "side by side with Israel."[131] Four days later Husseini was again placed under administrative detention for six months, and his Arab Studies Society at Orient House was ordered closed for a year.[132]

Peace Now was outraged by Husseini's arrest, viewing it not only as an attempt to undermine moderate Palestinians but also as part of a plan to stop the peace camp from presenting moderate Palestinians to the Israeli public. On August 6, 1988, a demonstration was held in a Tel Aviv suburb (not far from Rabin's home) under the slogan "Don't Jail Them, Speak with Them!" The demonstrators called Rabin an "obstacle to peace" and demanded his resignation. For the first time the movement employed the slogan "Talk to the PLO Now!"[133]

But the most significant political shift in the Palestinian-Israeli conflict occurred far from Jerusalem. Toward the end of 1988, a police search of Husseini's Arab Studies Society had uncovered a document containing a blueprint for the establishment of a Palestinian state. Prime Minister Shamir leaked the document to the media, apparently in the hope of demonstrating Husseini's subversive intentions, but the effect was more problematic.[134] As those long familiar with Palestinian discourse were quickly aware, the very act of imagining the establishment of a Palestinian state implied some willingness to recognize the continued existence of Israel. The document indicated that a two states solution was seriously being considered within the PLO.[135] This debate was coming to a head within the PLO, and a decision would be reached when the Palestine National Council convened that November in Algiers.

12

Time for Peace?

One Land, Two Peoples, Two States

On November 15, 1988, after a stormy session of the nineteenth meeting of the Palestine National Council in Algiers, a sweeping majority voted for a resolution declaring the establishment of the State of Palestine, with Yasser Arafat as its first president. The declaration was based on UN General Assembly Resolution 181 of November 29, 1947, which called for the partition of Palestine into two states, one Jewish and one Arab. During the previous four decades this resolution had been rejected repeatedly by the Palestinians; its formal acceptance by the most important Palestinian body was a dramatic shift in policy. While the PNC resolution implied the Palestinian demand that Israel return to its 1947 boundaries—a demand totally unacceptable to Israel—it nevertheless signified recognition of the State of Israel and the acceptance of the two states solution.[1]

From the perspective of Washington, the Algiers resolution was still too ambiguous and did not satisfy U.S. preconditions for the opening of a dialogue with the PLO.[2] "The way to deal with the issues of peace and the occupied territories is through direct negotiations," commented Secretary of State George Shultz. "Unilateral declarations have no weight."[3]

For Peace Now the PNC resolution signaled an important departure from the previous rejectionist positions held by the PLO. On November 29, two weeks after the Palestinian declaration, Peace Now convened a symposium in Jerusalem to ascertain the full meaning of the resolution and decide on the movement's response. Invited to present his interpretation, Sari Nusseibeh stated that "the Algiers resolutions are a message of peace."[4] Peace Now responded by publishing a declaration of its own that read:

> In Algiers the PLO abandoned the path of rejection and the Palestinian Charter and adopted the path of political compromise. . . . An opening for peace has emerged—we must widen it! The Government of Israel must call for direct negotiations with the PLO on the basis of mutual recognition and the cessation of violence. Only through negotiations will we know if the PLO has really adopted the path of peace as declared in Algiers. Talk peace to the PLO now![5]

Several journalists observed that the movement had come a long way since the episode in 1979 when Dedi Zucker and Yael Tamir were forced to resign after their unauthorized meeting with Issam Sartawi in Vienna. Janet Aviad responded, "We have certainly changed, but changes have occurred in the PLO as well."[6]

As in 1984, the 1988 Knesset elections resulted in a virtual draw between Labor and Likud. Another National Unity Government was formed, although this time a slight parliamentary advantage enabled Shamir to assume the premiership for four years without rotation. Under the terms of the governing agreement Yitzhak Rabin continued to serve as minister of defense, and Shamir made one of his lieutenants, Moshe Arens, minister of foreign affairs. Shimon Peres became treasury minister.[7] Shamir was adamant in his opposition to the notion that the PLO had changed anything other than its tactics. He insisted that Israel would never talk to the "terrorists."

In light of the political realities that now prevailed in Israel the peace movement recognized that progress in the peace process required greater involvement by the United States. With the recently elected administration of President George Bush about to take office, the outgoing secretary of state, Shultz, wanted to leave a clean slate that would allow his successor to begin a dialogue with the Palestinians. "I felt that cutting this Gordian knot [of U.S. relations with the PLO] would be a useful legacy for the next American administration," Shultz wrote.[8] During the summer and fall of 1988 the PLO tried to reach an understanding with the United States on the requirements for the initiation of a dialogue.

An agreement was finally achieved through the mediation of a group of American Jews who were members of the board of ICPME.[9] Led by

Los Angeles publisher Stanley Sheinbaum and New York attorney Rita Hauser (who had ties to the Republican Party), a small group met with Yasser Arafat in Stockholm on December 5–7, 1988. With the help of the Swedish foreign minister Sten Andersson, who was also engaged in the mediation efforts, the group persuaded the Palestinian leader to utter publicly the specific phrases necessary to satisfy the American requirements.[10] While the members of the group saw their contribution primarily as helping Arafat meet Shultz's demands, they also hoped this gambit would help persuade Shamir to respond with his own initiative.[11]

On December 13 Arafat delivered a speech to a special session of the UN General Assembly, which was convened in Geneva. Under heavy pressure from the PLO's extreme factions, Arafat initially remained ambiguous on several key issues. However, within a few hours of his speech several Arab and Palestinian leaders persuaded him to convene a press conference the following day to clarify his views according to the terms agreed upon in Stockholm. Before the assembled media, he unconditionally accepted UN Security Council Resolutions 242 and 338, renounced terrorism, and recognized the right of Israel to exist in peace and security.[12] In response, Secretary Shultz announced that "the United States is prepared for a substantive dialogue with PLO representatives."[13] To the Israeli peace movement these statements seemed to clear the way not only for a U.S.–PLO dialogue but also for negotiations between the PLO and Israel.

On December 24 Peace Now staged a major demonstration in the familiar plaza in Tel Aviv. The protesters were deluged by a pouring rain, but tens of thousands braved the elements. Speaker after speaker called on the government to initiate peace talks with the PLO without delay.[14] A poll published the previous day reported that 54 percent of those surveyed favored negotiations with the PLO, an unprecedented groundswell of public support for such a dialogue.[15] These developments put the ball firmly in Israel's court, while also leaving Shamir and Rabin little room for maneuver. The political status quo had witnessed a significant shift and the government would be forced to respond to the changing circumstances.

Options for Peace

During 1988 the Jaffee Center for Strategic Studies at Tel Aviv University led an effort to identify and assess Israel's different political and territorial options within the context of a negotiated settlement. Several study groups brought together Jaffee Center scholars and specialists in military strategy and Middle East politics in "an honest, painstaking and persistent effort . . . to remain impartial."[16] They identified six hypothetical options: maintenance of the status quo; Palestinian autonomy; annexation of the territories; a Palestinian state; unilateral withdrawal from Gaza; and a Jordanian-Palestinian federation to include the West Bank and the Gaza Strip.

The group worked under the assumption that severe dangers "[are] entailed in the political deadlock on the Palestinian issue. . . . The status quo bodes ill for Israel . . . the only reasonable prognosis is for worse to come."[17] The potential ramifications of each option on the various actors both within and outside the region were examined. Ultimately, none of the six options received the endorsement of the whole group. The report concluded that "under existing conditions and in their present form none of the options currently on Israel's agenda seems to offer a reasonable avenue for dealing with the West Bank and Gaza. Each of the six options examined is either not feasible or not advisable."[18]

However, the group's analysis of the Palestinian state option concluded that although it entailed substantial risks for Israel's security it was "virtually the only choice of the Palestinians, and goes further toward solving the essential conflict than any other option we analyzed."[19] Still, it did not seem feasible to the study group because the Israeli government was unlikely to attempt to implement this option unless more public support became evident. The group also observed that

> if the PLO's move toward moderation in late 1988 . . . were enhanced by a practical termination of all PLO terrorism, by annulment of the clauses in the Palestinian National Charter that reject Israel's right to exist . . . many Israelis might view the establishment of a Palestinian state as less risky than prolonged Israeli isolation and sharply reduced support from abroad.[20]

Throughout the analytical part of its report the study group sought to maintain the greatest academic objectivity. But in a separate volume, published simultaneously, it described a possible "path toward a peaceful resolution of the dispute," recommending a "gradual confidence building process" to be based on an Israeli-Palestinian agreement concluded in advance. In the group's opinion, this agreement should be negotiated between Israel and "authoritative representatives of the Palestinians. . . . Under present and immediately foreseeable circumstances only the PLO, or at the very least Palestinians identified with the PLO, meet this criterion."[21]

In the first phase of the proposed process the Palestinians would enjoy "genuine, comprehensive autonomy . . . [which should remain] open-ended." The Palestinians would have to accept "the legitimacy and permanency of a Jewish state, [renounce the] right of return [of the Palestinian refugees into Israel] and any claim to pre-1967 Israeli territory." For its part, Israel would have to cease "the establishment of any new Jewish settlements in the territories [and] forgo its control over most state lands in the territories." Perhaps the most significant point was that Israel would agree not to "negate the possibility of the eventual emergence of a Palestinian state."[22]

The six analytical options and the proposed solution were presented at a press conference. Controversy erupted immediately. Prime Minster Shamir denounced the Jaffee Center and rejected its conclusions, while Peace Now welcomed and endorsed the proposals. Labor leaders remained silent on the whole.

Although it is difficult to assess the precise impact of the Jaffee Center report on subsequent policy decisions by the Israeli government, at least some observers regard it as an important step. As one journalist wrote, "The [Jaffee Center's] research provided first-rate academic legitimization from the Israeli side to the Palestinian demand for an independent state. It presented this option for public debate, not only on an emotional and moral basis, but as a practical, logical solution."[23]

Peace in Stages

The idea that peace with the Palestinians would have to be implemented in phases had been incorporated into the Camp David Accords in 1978. Ten years later it had gained some acceptance among the leadership within the Palestinian national movement. However, it was unclear whether the Palestinians would agree to enter such a process without receiving some assurances as to its ultimate outcome.[24]

Shmuel Toledano, an old hand at Arab affairs, attempted to get the process moving with a new formula. The son of a Jerusalem Sepharadic family and fluent in Arabic, Toledano knew the Palestinians well and had befriended many in the occupied territories after 1967. In the late 1970s he had served one term in the Knesset, and in the 1980s became a freelance journalist and lecturer on Arab affairs.[25] He had not been known as an outspoken dove, but the Intifada caused him to reassess his views and he came to conclusions similar to those reached by the Jaffee Center group. However, he went one step further. He believed that in order to launch the peace process the Israeli government would have to commit itself in advance to "a specific date, after a five-year period, when Israel will vacate . . . the West Bank and Gaza and undertake not to object to the establishment of a Palestinian state in those vacated territories."[26]

Encouraged by the Jaffee Center report, and the support he received from some members of the study group, Toledano went to prominent pollster Mina Tzemach and commissioned a survey of public support for his ideas. In two polls (December 1989 and January 1990) a sampling of 1,200 Israeli Jews produced surprising results: 60 percent supported the "peace in phases" concept—18 percent answered "definitely yes" and 42 percent simply said "yes." When asked about their attitude toward a Palestinian state "if the question of the establishment of such a state were the last obstacle to peace," the level of support increased to 69 percent. Even more surprising was the fact that 53 percent of Likud voters endorsed the idea. The results of the polls received extensive media coverage. Tzemach concluded that "the substantial support for [Toledano's] plan is a product of the fear of a Palestinian state coupled with the realization that no chance exists to achieve peace without it."[27]

In light of these results Toledano and a few colleagues decided to launch a new group, and at the end of January 1991 established the Council of Peace in Stages. "There is," Toledano later explained, "a messianic minority that objects to a Palestinian state as a matter of principle, but the majority hesitates to accept it since it is motivated by fear. The new plan could allay these fears because it left ample room to test the other side's intentions and maintained an element of reversibility."[28] Faisal Husseini, and even the DFLP spokesman, gave the plan a warm reception.[29] Toledano also received the support of 100 reserve generals and colonels, 75 university professors, 16 former ambassadors, and even many on the Israeli right. The parties on the left naturally supported Toledano's initiative and 15 Labor MKs publicly endorsed it.[30] During 1990 and 1991 the Council for Peace in Stages gained considerable popular support.

Events soon overtook Toledano's group when the Israeli government agreed to negotiate with the Palestinians on the basis of a phased process, albeit without accepting that a Palestinian state would eventually be created.

Let's Reason Together

The adoption of the two states solution by the PNC in November 1988, coupled with the growing realization among many Israelis that negotiations with the PLO were inevitable and that a Palestinian state would eventually emerge, enhanced the dialogue between Israelis and Palestinians. At the same time, a growing number of scholars and research institutions began to approach the issue of Palestinian independence in practical rather than hypothetical terms. During 1989 and 1990 academic institutions and nongovernmental organizations organized dozens of international forums. A flood of books and articles examined the numerous issues associated with the establishment of a Palestinian state.[31] In Jerusalem efforts were undertaken jointly by Israelis and Palestinians. For example, Hebrew University's Harry S. Truman Research Institute for the Advancement of Peace, jointly with the Palestinian Arab Studies Society in Jerusalem, organized an Israeli-Palestinian Peace Research Project that sought "to analyze, from the perspective of Israeli and Palestinian scholars, some of the key elements of an eventual resolution of the Arab-Israeli and Palestinian-Israeli conflict." The project examined such issues as allocation of water resources, mutual security, and education for coexistence, and published more than two dozen working papers.[32]

Another notable joint Israeli-Palestinian initiative was undertaken by Gershon Baskin and Adel Yahia. Baskin had ten years' experience in education for coexistence between Jews and Arabs within Israel. In 1988 he decided to dedicate all his efforts to the promotion of peace with the Palestinians in the occupied territories. He prepared a detailed agenda of issues to be addressed in the process of reconciliation, which he published in the Arabic press. He invited Palestinian scholars to a meeting in the American Colony Hotel in East Jerusalem. There he met Adel Yahia, a history teacher at Bir Zeit University and a member of the Palestinian Communist Party, and during the early months of 1989 the two men sought and received support from Palestinian and Israeli intellectuals and political figures. They established the Israel-Palestine Center for Research and Information (IPCRI) later that year.[33]

Baskin and Ghassan Abdullah—the son of refugees from Nablus and a member of the DFLP, who later replaced Yahia as IPCRI codirector—recruited a number of prominent Israelis and Palestinians to form a board of trustees cochaired by Moshe Amirav and Hanna Siniora. IPCRI defined itself as "a think tank of Israelis and Palestinians aimed at providing concrete solutions for future public policy and planning regarding the two states solution."[34] Binational research groups regularly met at the Notre Dame Hotel, a Catholic hospice near the line dividing the Arab and Jewish sides of Jerusalem. The joint teams identified seven issues on which they would focus their attention: the future of Jerusalem; border arrangements; security arrangements for both states; allocation and development of water resources; trade and commerce; refugee settlement; and the link between the West Bank and Gaza.[35]

IPCRI also commissioned external research projects, the results of which were published and presented at conferences in Israel and abroad. One such conference, which examined the future of Jerusalem, was held there in March 1993.[36] IPCRI presented a model of shared Israeli-Palestinian rule in Jerusalem and the decentralization of municipal governance in the city.[37] A conference on security and defense issues held in Oxford in September 1992 attracted the participation of a dozen prominent individuals.[38]

IPCRI provided the opportunity for Israelis and Palestinians to meet each other and jointly seek ways to solve problems in the search for a peaceful future for both nations.[39] Baskin recalled:

> In many cases we managed to bring Israeli officials and Palestinian business people together, which later facilitated practical negotiations on different economic issues such as the opening of a Palestinian bank in the West Bank. . . . In this framework influential people from both sides could meet and discuss their ideas. When the time came for actual negotiations they could feel greater confidence in each other and begin from a better starting point. We helped them to break the ice both personally and intellectually.[40]

The Forum for Peace and Justice

The virtual draw between left and right in the 1988 Knesset elections did not conform with the polls taken during this period, which indicated a distinct increase in the number of Israelis who were ready to endorse a more moderate approach to the Arab-Israeli conflict.[41] The main reason for the outcome of the 1988 elections was the enduring loyalty of many among the Mizrachi community to Likud.[42] It became increasingly clear that if the political status quo was to be altered, a shift in the Mizrachi voting pattern away from Likud (and other parties on the right) was necessary.

ICPME directed a considerable amount of energy and resources toward this effort. Many Mizrachi peace activists consistently argued that the social and economic hardships experienced by large segments of the Mizrachi community exerted more influence on voting behavior than did other issues, including peace and security. These activists believed that if a link could be established between social and economic issues and Israel's conflict with the Arabs, some Mizrachim could be persuaded to support the peace movement.

In the late 1980s what was known as the "third generation" of Mizrachim came of age. This group was constituted of young, middle-class Mizrachim who had recently graduated from universities in Israel and abroad, and who had been exposed to American and European influences during their academic training. They were the grandchildren of Mizrachim who had immigrated to Israel, where they had had to struggle with the pains of absorption and poverty in the 1950s. One of the third generation was Yossi Dahan, a philosophy teacher in the Open University in Tel Aviv. "The Israeli left did not take its own rhetoric on cultural pluralism seriously," Dahan remembered. The leftists "spoke of tolerance but this amounted to sheer paternalism. . . . It is difficult to join those who cannot hide the fact that they look down at you. What was needed was an honest respect for the difference."[43]

At the beginning of 1989 ICPME decided to give these young Mizrachi intellectuals a chance to do it in their own way, and supported the creation of the Forum for Peace and Social Justice. Dahan explained the rationale:

> You have to activate people at the periphery, to equip them in the places where they live with the tools to change their situation and attitudes. You have to start from the problems that preoccupy these people, namely with their social and psychological needs.[44]

The forum established the Seminar for Community Leadership, which began activities at the beginning of 1990. Some 150 young Mizrachim, many of whom had held leadership positions in the army or in local affairs, organized weekly regional meetings and monthly weekend seminars. They received training in leadership skills and dealt with an array of social and political topics. A variety of perspectives toward the Arab-Israeli conflict were presented, covering the spectrum of contending opinions within the Israeli public. The participation of several Palestinians caused many participants to reconsider their prejudices. Dahan concluded that "this was a success story. . . . New action groups were organized in poor neighborhoods and development towns that fought for better living conditions and also discussed new ideas concerning the Arab-Israeli conflict."

Aggression Acted Out

During 1989 and 1990 the Intifada became almost a routine facet of life, but the violence never ceased and the casualties continued to mount.[45] "The Palestinian population is tired but the Intifada goes on," observed an

Israeli analyst. "They still have enough spiritual force to absorb the casualties and continue the confrontation."[46] Stone throwing caused minimal casualties to Israeli soldiers, but a growing number of knife and firebomb attacks[47] both within the occupied territories and in Israeli cities produced a growing number of casualties and fueled rising fear and concern among the Israeli public.[48] Despite the explicit prohibition by the Intifada leadership of the use of firearms, guns were now used with greater frequency, particularly by the Muslim fundamentalists who objected to the more moderate approach of Arafat's Fatah. There was also a dramatic increase in the number of instances in which Palestinians killed other Palestinians suspected of collaborating with the Israeli authorities.

Though suffering nowhere near the same level of casualties as the Palestinians, Israeli soldiers experienced rising frustration and fatigue. Reuven Gal, who in the early 1980s had served as the chief of psychological services for the IDF, observed that while "on the surface it seems that there is a noticeable phenomenon of adjusting to the situation, of accommodation and routinization," heightened aggressiveness was evident.[49] Gal noted that the cursing, spitting, and stone throwing by Palestinian youths caused frustration, humiliation, and duress among the soldiers, who were ill suited to deal with such an adversary. This, coupled with orders to use counterforce, led to "behavior which is natural to such situations"—soldiers acted out their frustrations and anxieties through aggression.[50] Military psychologists spoke of the wounds that were caused not by stones or firebombs but by the painful psychological experience of going into action against vehemently hostile but often unarmed people.[51] Many soldiers were embittered as a result of their service and their hatred of the Arabs intensified. Some vented their anger at the Palestinians without any moral qualms, but others experienced a painful tension between their moral values and the tasks they were ordered to perform.

Poets Will Not Write Poems

Israeli writers and poets who sympathized with the peace movement considered it their duty to describe the evolving drama and comment on its moral implications. Yet they also believed that it was impossible simply to "aestheticize" the experience. Some writers resolved this dilemma by adopting a self-consciously spartan style of writing devoid of literary embellishment, often using journalistic methods of reporting or editorial analysis.

On January 8, 1988, soon after the outbreak of the Intifada, a group of writers, poets, and artists went to Gaza. They entered the refugee camps escorted by a Palestinian journalist, and spoke with dozens of Gazans, even witnessing violent confrontations between Israeli soldiers and Palestinian youths. On their return they reported their disturbing findings in the Hebrew media.[52] Ya'ir Garbuz, a popular journalist and painter, summarized his observations: "Whoever has visited Gaza will not be able to rejoice even when a peace treaty will be signed. . . . He may feel much relief, but the guilt and shame will pursue him forever."[53] Another member of the group drew a slightly more optimistic conclusion: "In Gaza we saw the scars of the recent confrontations, the signs of the stones, the fire, the iron and the smoke. . . . But out of this great despair we found an opening for some little hope."[54] The group jointly published a statement, which declared:

> We saw in the Gaza Strip a popular rebellion led by young people and supported by the entire population. . . . The causes of the rebellion are evident: the humiliation which results from the continuous occupation; land expropriations; the permanent pressure to collaborate with the security services; the neglect and the terrible economic situation; and worst of all the lack of hope for the future. . . . All the people we spoke with aspire for a Palestinian state alongside Israel. . . . They believe that the Palestinian violence will stop immediately when Israel recognizes the PLO as a partner for negotiations. We think that the time has come to seriously consider this option.[55]

A number of attempts were made to treat the Intifada in film. To present their subject matter in its stark, disturbing reality, the producers of two films separated the audio from the visual components of their films. *The Expulsion* depicts the deportation of Palestinians to Lebanon, but the soundtrack is limited to incidental noises such as the sound of a helicopter, the whistle of a bird, and footsteps. *The Lookout* is the story of an Israeli soldier posted at a refugee camp in the West Bank. The soundtrack is limited to the music the soldier is listening to on his personal radio and the occasional exchanges he overhears on the military radio. One critic wrote, "It is as if no dialogue [concerning the situation] is at all possible. . . . The camera neutralizes all subjective dialogue with the viewer. The camera has nothing to say beyond the observed reality. This reality, not our attitudes toward it, is expressed."[56]

Ilana Hammerman, one of the founders of the 21st Year, was the editor of a series of avant garde literature called "A Different Prose."[57] In collaboration with Rolly Rosen, a young journalist, Hammerman included in her series a book titled *Poets Will Not Write Poems*,[58] which presented interviews with Israeli soldiers who had served in the territories during the Intifada, but repeatedly interrupted the text of their comments with extracts from various documents—mostly military orders and court records—and theoretical statements concerning the nature of literature.

One such insertion explained the logic of Hammerman's literary technique: "The breaking of the sequence is not designed to attract or stimulate the reader . . . it stops the flow of the fable in the middle of the unfolding events in order to compel the listener to take a position toward what transpires."[59] In a postscript Hammerman quoted a twenty-year-old soldier who believed that "poets cannot write poems about Israeli soldiers who fought the Intifada and shot at women and children." Her goal, she commented, was "to make a modest contribution to the sharpening of our sensitivities both toward literature as well as toward the reality."[60]

Progress under Duress

The opening of a dialogue between Washington and the PLO at the end of 1988, accompanied by indications from the PLO that it was prepared to negotiate a settlement, put Prime Minister Shamir on the spot.[61] Pressure to respond favorably to the PLO initiative came from a number of sources at home and abroad, and by the spring of 1989 Shamir recognized that he had to produce his own peace plan and revitalize the process that had begun at Camp David and then stalled for ten years. "The main challenge facing the new National Unity Government," Shamir later recorded, "was to prepare an Israeli peace initiative."[62]

President Bush too wanted to move the process forward, and invited Egyptian president Hosni Mubarak, King Hussein, and Prime Minister Shamir to the White House in close succession. During his visit on April 6, 1989, Shamir presented a new initiative, which, though it carried his name, more accurately reflected the thinking of his defense minister, Rabin. The initiative included four main points. First, Israel agreed to begin immediate direct negotiations, based on the Camp David Accords, with the Arab states. Second, though Israel still would not deal with the PLO, it proposed to hold general elections in the territories to select Palestinian representatives to the negotiations. Third, Israel agreed to negotiate with these representatives, with the participation of Egypt and Jordan, regarding the modalities of an interim autonomy that would allow the Palestinians to manage their own affairs. Finally, at the end of the interim period, the ultimate status of the territories would be negotiated, if the Arab states agreed to end their state of belligerency against Israel and cooperate in finding a solution to the problem of Palestinian refugees.[63]

Rabin's moderating influence was easily discernable in the Israeli initiative, but Shamir's tone in presenting it was considerably tougher.

Shamir's main concerns were to avoid opening negotiations with the PLO and to steer clear of any suggestion that the outcome of negotiations would be a Palestinian state.[64]

Although the Bush administration welcomed the plan and encouraged Shamir to move ahead and negotiate its implementation,[65] Secretary of State James Baker voiced his objections to Shamir's interpretation of the initiative.[66] In a speech to the annual convention of the America-Israel Public Affairs Committee, Baker declared that Israel must agree up front to the principle of exchanging territories for peace and "lay aside, once and for all, the unrealistic vision of a Greater Israel."[67]

Shamir was angered by these remarks, and in his memoirs recorded, "If Mr. Baker ever thought that those Israelis who are resolved not to sell any part of their land in exchange for peace would be influenced by his advice to relinquish our dream as unrealistic, he soon found out that he was wrong."[68] In response to Baker, and with Shamir's acquiescence, a group of Likud ministers headed by Ariel Sharon, who had voted against the peace initiative in the cabinet, passed a resolution in the party's central committee that effectively eviscerated the initiative. The resolution declared that the Arabs of East Jerusalem would be held ineligible to participate in the election of representatives to the negotiations; that no negotiations would begin unless the Intifada and other forms of violence were ended; that no negotiations with the PLO or "sliding toward a Palestinian state" would be permitted; and that, in the meantime, Jewish settlement of the territories would continue.[69]

It was now Secretary Baker's turn to become livid, and he accused Shamir of putting obstacles in the road to peace.[70] Despite these angry exchanges, during the summer of 1989 Baker was actively involved in efforts to start negotiations on the modalities of the proposed Palestinian elections and other aspects of Shamir's initiative. Through Egyptian mediators Baker tried to persuade the PLO to accept the elections proposal and agree to the participation of non-PLO officials in the process. However, two central issues remained unsolved: whether Palestinian residents of Jerusalem would be permitted to vote, and whether Palestinians from the diaspora would be allowed to participate in the process. These issues carried symbolic as well as political value for the Palestinians, and precisely for that reason Shamir would not compromise on them.

As the end of 1989 drew near, negotiations focused on the proposal to convene a meeting between Israeli and Palestinian delegations in Cairo. In an attempt to overcome an impasse over the composition of the Palestinian delegation, Baker prepared a five-point proposal, which included the assumption that the list of Palestinian participants would be compiled in consultation with the PLO.[71] Shamir remained adamant in his refusal to accept Palestinian residents of Jerusalem as part of the Palestinian delegation.[72]

Despite many reservations and suspicions, Peace Now publicly welcomed and supported Shamir's peace initiative. However, the movement's spokesman cautioned the prime minister not to think of his own initiative as a stopgap maneuver designed to deflect domestic and international pressure.[73] Peace Now considered the proposed elections for a Palestinian representative body the most promising element of the new initiative. The movement did not believe that such a body could replace the PLO or for that matter make decisions independent of the PLO. Nevertheless, considering the traditional refusal of Likud and Labor to negotiate with the PLO, Peace Now regarded the proposal an important step forward. Meetings between Peace Now activists and Faisal Husseini and his colleagues were now becoming a regular event, and the Israelis urged the Palestinians to take advantage of the new opportunity.

Peace Now also tried to persuade the Israeli public that Shamir's peace initiative must be pursued honestly and vigorously, and that its implementation required direct negotiations with the Palestinians.[74] In October 1989 Peace Now organized a series of well-publicized meetings with Palestinian leaders in Palestinian towns and villages inside the occupied territories in an effort to soften their position. The peace movement conveyed its firm belief that the time for compromise had arrived, and that the Palestinians should be ready to negotiate. In most cases the army blocked the peaceniks from reaching their destinations, and makeshift demonstrations were held where the activists were halted. At one such impromptu rally, Husseini told the audience, "The Palestinian peace camp has won, and now leads the PLO and the Palestinian people!" Yael Dayan, the daughter of the former minister of defense, referring to the fact that Husseini was also the child of a war hero, told the crowd, "Today I am proud to stand next to him in a peace meeting. I am sure that his children and mine will live, each in his own country, in peace."[75]

Project Majority

During the spring and summer of 1989 the group known hitherto as "American Friends of Peace Now," which for a number of years had supported Israel's peace movement with modest financial resources, was reorganized and became an independent U.S.-based sister movement under the name "Americans for Peace Now." One result of this reorganization was that its fund-raising efforts were far more consistent and successful.[76] The increased flow of revenue from abroad helped Peace Now in Israel to expand and consolidate its activities. For the first time the movement was able to employ a small number of paid staff. These included the positions of an executive director, spokesperson, parliamentary lobby coordinator, and an organizer for university faculty and students. Gavri Bar-Gil, a reserve battalion commander in the IDF and a kibbutz member who had been active in Peace Now for many years, became its first executive director. He reorganized the main offices in Tel Aviv and Jerusalem, updated the call-up lists, organized domestic fund-raising, began publishing regular newsletters, and coordinated the work of the various committees. This new arrangement gave the movement a stability and momentum that it previously had lacked.

Bar-Gil and the new professional team, with the help and guidance of the veteran volunteers, then launched "Project Majority," a campaign to recruit new supporters among young Mizrachim and students and thus enlarge the power base of the movement.[77] The campaign's modest success provided an indication that some shift, albeit highly incremental, in the political attitudes of Israelis was taking place. Most Mizrachim remained loyal to Likud, and the new chapters Peace Now established in their midst tended to remain isolated. However, the bitter acrimony of the early 1980s had apparently come to an end. While heated debates still occurred at Peace Now meetings in Mizrachi neighborhoods, the ethnic antagonism that had previously made these neighborhoods inaccessible to the activists was no longer present.

Hands around the Holy City

Peace Now's support for the recognition of the PLO during 1989 blurred many of the differences that had previously distinguished it from more radical groups like Dai Lakibush. This contributed to a greater sense of unity throughout the Israeli peace camp, and helps explain the noticeable decline of Dai Lakibush as some of its activists chose to join Peace Now.[78] Increased participation in Peace Now's street demonstrations testified to the increased vigor of the movement during that year. To mark the second anniversary of the Intifada 3,500 protesters silently marched through Jerusalem carrying pictures of the 143 children killed in the uprising. All the marchers carried the same banner, "Talk to the PLO Now!" The father of a soldier killed in a terrorist attack declared, "Enough blood has been shed. It is time for peace!"[79]

Peace Now's support for the opening of a dialogue with the PLO also contributed to improved relations between the Israeli peace movement and various European peace groups. The European peace movement historically supported Third World national liberation movements and was at the vanguard of the struggle for decolonization. It had traditionally supported the PLO and held a negative attitude toward Israel and Zionism. The Europeans viewed the Zionist project as another example of the colonial exploitation of the Palestinian people, and Israel as an expansionist and militaristic imperial power. In most cases the European peaceniks were either unwilling or unable to recognize the complex nature of the Arab-Israeli conflict.

This entrenched attitude made it difficult for members of Peace Now to reach out to European peace groups, and to the extent that such relations existed, they were noticeably strained. Consequently, before 1988 non-Zionist or anti-Zionist peace groups in Israel always had better relations with the European peace movement than did Peace Now. Even during the 1980s, as the PLO inched toward positions held by mainstream elements of the Israeli left, the European peace movement remained largely aloof. In many instances the Europeans were closer in their ideological perceptions of the conflict to such rejectionist elements within the PLO as the PFLP and the DFLP. However, once the barriers between the PLO and Peace Now fell the Europeans also began to soften their stance.

During September and October 1989 Peace Now, together with several European peace groups and the Palestinian leadership in the occupied territories, organized a joint project called "Et Shalom" (Time for Peace).[80] The project included a visit of 1,200 European peace activists, including members of European parliaments, to Israel during the last week of 1989, where they participated in a variety of educational and protest events. The climax of these events took place in Jerusalem on Saturday, December 30. Around midday 25,000 people—Israelis, Palestinians, and the European guests—lined up around the walls of the old city. Many MKs and senior Palestinian religious and nationalist leaders participated. According to a Peace Now report:

> It was a friendly demonstration and a genuine event. Peace songs and balloons, without flags and leaflets. Thousands of participants enjoyed the

warm winter sun on the green lawns surrounding the walls. . . . For the first time since the beginning of the Intifada Jerusalemites tasted the feeling of peace. For the first time in years Jews and Arabs mingled in the shadow of the ancient walls.[81]

The demonstrators joined hands at a prearranged time, forming a six-mile human chain that encircled the holy city. Several thousand balloons were released that raced skyward carrying the slogan "1990— Time for Peace." An elderly Palestinian remarked, "This is like a message to God, like a joint prayer for peace."[82] Indeed, this was a rare and impressive display of fraternity.

Despite the mood of unity the demonstration expressed, one incident marred the otherwise successful event. Overreacting to a minor provocation by a group of radical Palestinians who started to chant nationalist slogans around Herod's Gate and hoisted a nine-year-old child dressed in a military camouflage outfit above the crowd, policemen descended upon the demonstrators in a 500-meter-long area. Israelis, Palestinians, and Europeans were indiscriminately caught in the police assault. Tear gas, rubber bullets, clubs, and water cannons were employed to disperse the crowd. Sixty people, many of whom were members of an Italian delegation, had to be treated for injuries inflicted by rubber bullets and tear gas. One Italian woman lost an eye after being hit by a glass splinter.[83] The police later claimed that they had been forced to take action because a Palestinian flag had been raised, but a Peace Now investigation found no evidence to substantiate this allegation.[84] A subsequent internal police investigation led to the dismissal of the commander responsible for the area around Herod's Gate. The attorney general also conducted an independent investigation that confirmed Peace Now's version of events, and three members of the police's anti-riot squad were indicted for excessive use of force.[85]

Guarantees for a Freeze

Early in 1990 a number of international developments exacerbated the already strained U.S.-Israeli relationship, and within Israel the tenuous governing partnership between Likud and Labor was tested. With the expanded civil liberties permitted by glasnost, anti-Semitic undercurrents always close to the surface in the Soviet Union were unleashed. This increase in anti-Semitism, coupled with Mikhail Gorbachev's willingness to permit almost uninhibited emigration of Jews, led to an exodus of Soviet Jews. Many of these people would have preferred to immigrate to the United States, but immigration limitations imposed by Washington caused a flood of new immigrants to resettle in Israel, quickly overloading Israel's capacity to successfully absorb them.[86]

The Palestinians and the Arab states were alarmed by the new wave of Jewish immigration and viewed it in the context of continuing Zionist expansion. Their fears were reinforced by the incendiary statements of some right-wing politicians, who spoke of settling the newcomers in the occupied territories and thereby creating new and irreversible demographic realities.[87] Ambitious construction projects initiated by Likud in the West Bank were accelerated in anticipation of additional Soviet immigration.

Considerable financial resources were required to integrate the Soviet Jews into the Israeli economy and society and to provide them with such essentials as adequate housing, employment, and health care. Israel requested $10 billion in loan guarantees from the United States to help facilitate immigrant absorption.[88] The timing of the request was not fortuitous for Israel. The peace process was deadlocked over Shamir's refusal to accept Baker's five points. President Bush decided to link the loan guarantees to progress in the peace process, and announced that any U.S. financial support would be contingent upon the cessation of Israeli construction in the occupied territories and East Jerusalem.[89]

Washington's attempt to compel Israel to make these concessions was not well received by Shamir. In April 1990 he formally announced his rejection of Baker's five points. This in turn caused the fall of the National Unity Government, which was replaced, after considerable political squabbling and coalition bargaining, by a narrow coalition headed once more by Shamir's Likud and joined by smaller right-wing parties and the religious parties. The Labor Party moved back to the benches of the opposition.[90]

The suspension of the U.S.-PLO dialogue, which occurred in June 1990 as a result of Arafat's refusal to denounce an aborted seaborne attack on the Israeli coast by the Abu Abbas faction of the PLO, did little to improve relations between Jerusalem and Washington.[91] "The Land of Israel is not only a piece of soil, it is a sacred value," Shamir told the Knesset when he presented his new government on June 11.[92] Shamir appeared to the Israeli public as a stubborn defender of Greater Israel. Some Israelis applauded his refusal to concede in the face of mounting international pressure, whereas others felt his principled stand was causing greater harm than good to Israel's long-term interests. In any event, the peace process was stalled without much hope of renewed progress, while the construction of housing in the occupied territories proceeded without interruption.

The Settlements Watch

For Peace Now it was politically difficult to support the Bush administration's linkage between Israel's request for loan guarantees and the issue of settlements. Such a position could have been interpreted as accepting restraints on the mass influx of Soviet Jews, which all Zionists—including Peace Now—viewed as an important step in the fulfillment of their most basic goal.[93] However, Peace Now, pointing to the fact that only a small percentage of the Soviet immigrants were choosing to settle in the occupied territories, argued that the U.S. linkage was a direct result of Shamir's rejectionist policies. The accelerated pace of construction in the territories was deemed a gross misuse of resources desperately needed for the absorption of the immigrants elsewhere, as well as an unnecessary provocation that angered the Arabs and alienated the Americans, thereby endangering the entire enterprise.[94]

In a public letter on January 30, 1990, Peace Now called on Shamir to repair the damage caused to Soviet immigration by his government's policies. The movement demanded that Shamir declare that all resources designated for settlements beyond the Green Line be redirected to the construction of housing and economic infrastructure within the pre-1967 borders. The letter concluded, "If one family from the Soviet Union is denied the opportunity to escape the renewed wave of anti-Semitism, the responsibility will fall on the careless expressions and actions of the Prime Minister."[95]

Additionally, Peace Now established a group called "Settlements Watch," which monitored and publicized all settlement construction in the West Bank and the Gaza Strip. Amiram Goldblum, a chemistry professor at the Hebrew University in Jerusalem and a Peace Now spokesman, directed a team of surveyors who moved throughout the occupied territories and established contacts with Palestinians who reported any new construction they observed. The team's findings were verified and compiled into reports that were presented to the public and media.[96]

The government sought to disguise the political objectives of the increased pace of construction, and denied that Soviet immigrants were being directed specifically to the territories. In response to these claims, Peace Now exposed efforts undertaken by the settler movement (and with the government's blessing) to raise funds in the United States and elsewhere for the explicit purpose of settling Soviet Jews in Judea, Samaria, and Gaza.[97] The Settlements Watch group wrote to the prime minister that efforts to direct new immigrants to the territories were putting not only continued immigration but also the peace process "at grave risk."[98]

Members of the radical right organized symbolic acts of defiance against the American demands, and Peace Now was usually on the scene with a counterdemonstration. For example, on May 3, 1990, Gush Emunim organized a ceremony in which a couple of Torah scrolls were brought into a small ancient building near the main entrance to the Arab town of Nablus, where religious Jews believe the grave of Joseph, the son of Jacob, is located. Gush Emunim was granted permission to use this building during daylight hours for the operation of a small yeshiva—a pointed expression of Gush Emunim's intention to remain where they were.

Peace Now was initially denied access to the area by the military authorities, which also imposed a curfew on the Arab town for the occasion. Peace Now petitioned the Supreme Court, which upheld the right of Peace Now to demonstrate, but for security considerations limited the number of participants on the settlers' side to one hundred and on Peace Now's side to twenty.[99] Half a dozen MKs from both the left and the right angrily confronted each other. The right-wingers labeled the peace activists traitors, and the Russian proverb, "The dogs are barking but the caravan goes on!" could be heard repeatedly. The leftists responded by shouting their own slogans: "Settlements are an obstacle to immigration!" and "The lives of our sons are more important than the graves of the forefathers!" The army had to intervene to maintain a buffer between the opposing sides.[100]

Fire and Blood

As Peace Now intensified its activities during the spring and summer of 1990,[101] its confrontations with the radical right became increasingly acrimonious. On one occasion settlers distributed a "Letter to Peace Now" in which they labeled the peace activists "destroyers and saboteurs" and predicted that they would be remembered by the nation as an "eternal curse." The letter also quoted a passage from Isaiah: "But the wicked are like the troubled sea when it cannot rest, whose waters cast up mire and dirt."[102]

Rabbi Meir Kahane's references to violence were considerably more explicit. In a rally his Kach movement organized to extol the virtues of an Israeli who wantonly killed seven Palestinian laborers, Kahane told those present that "the central problem of Israel is not the Arabs but the treasonous leftists." Once he came to power, Kahane remarked, he would "know how to handle them."[103] His disciples, however, went beyond words. Early in June the Jerusalem office of Peace Now was torched, and Kach claimed responsibility for the act.[104] Amiram Goldblum's car was also burned, and many activists received threats to their lives and those of their families.

During these months the peace movement experienced a growing sense of frustration—a mood similar to that which had prevailed in the spring of 1978 during the Israeli-Egyptian negotiations and had contributed to the establishment of the movement. At a large demonstration on May 26, 1990, some of the speakers gave vent to this frustration and anger in their harsh criticism of the government.[105] Novelist Mair Shalev said of Yitzhak Shamir:

> This man is proud of his shield of stubbornness and the solidity of his prin-
> ciples, but he is neither an iron wall nor a brass fortification. His patriotism
> is the last refuge of a coward. . . . This man as stubborn as a cork in a bottle
> may lead us to the destruction of our third commonwealth.[106]

Amos Oz directed his criticism against "the widespread apathy which envelops us, dulls our sensitivities and blurs our human face. . . . Empires have fallen as a result of such apathy, nations were destroyed and waters turned into blood." Referring to the biblical punishment of the ancient Egyptians, he quoted a line from a famous poem by Nathan Alterman, "Since blood was in the city and the city was not shaken."[107]

The Impact of the Intifada on the Peace Process

The Intifada had a far-reaching impact on the development of the Israeli-Palestinian conflict in general and on Palestinian nationalism in particular. The momentous turn in the peace process that occurred in the years 1991–93 cannot be explained without taking into account the political and psychological influence that the acts of defiance and self-assertion by the young Palestinians during the uprising had on the parties involved.

For two decades, most Israelis had failed to recognize the full political and moral costs Israel would eventually have to pay for its occupation of the territories. The peace movement's insistence that the suppression of the Palestinian will for liberty and independence could not be sustained for long and that eventually the occupier would be corrupted often fell on deaf ears. To many Israelis, despite recurrent acts of terror and occasional acts of disobedience, the Palestinians seemed to display a docile acceptance of the occupation. The Intifada changed this perception radically.

Customary complacency was shattered as thousands of Israeli soldiers, conscripts and reservists alike, were ordered to suppress—often cruelly—unarmed civilians; as a growing de facto separation between the two peoples grew and the pre-1967 borders were effectively rees-tablished; and, above all, as the futility of the use of military force in this new situation became apparent.

The Intifada caused a sharp political and ideological polarization across Israeli society. On the one side, antidemocratic, chauvinistic, and racist elements were significantly strengthened by the outrage and frus-tration many Israelis felt as they witnessed or experienced firsthand the intensified hatred of the Palestinians. On the other side, the peace move-ment reached one of the peaks of its activity and public presence. Peace groups with a variety of agendas, tactics, and constituencies prolifer-ated. Meanwhile, Peace Now continued to serve as a common platform and could count on the participation of the full spectrum of peace groups in the large demonstrations it organized.

At the same time, the increased vigor and self-esteem the Palestinian national movement gained in the territories enabled its leaders to coop-erate more openly with the Israeli peace movement. Israeli-Palestinian dialogue and joint activities reached an unprecedented level and paved the way for greater mutual understanding—understanding that was strong enough to survive the divisions the Gulf War was soon to produce.

Despite increasing discord among the Israeli public, the Intifada drove home to growing numbers of Israelis the notion that sooner or later Israel would have to negotiate with the PLO and embark on the road to Palestinian self-determination. The rejectionist policies of Shamir and the attempt by the Israeli right to deny the very existence of a Palestin-ian nation could not hide the fact that a growing majority of Israelis had come to realize that the status quo that had prevailed during the first twenty years of the occupation had been forever shattered by the Pales-tinian resistance. A serious peace process now seemed inevitable.

13

From Sealed Rooms to Madrid

Long Live Saddam Hussein!

In the spring of 1990, shortly after the end of the bloody ten-year Iran-Iraq War, Saddam Hussein proclaimed that Iraq possessed the capability to "burn half of Israel with chemical weapons."[1] Although the Iraqi leader's threat appeared to present no immediate danger to Israel, international efforts were undertaken to calm the agitated regional atmosphere. Few doubted that Saddam would have cherished an opportunity to avenge Israel's humiliating destruction of the Iraqi Osirak nuclear reactor ten years earlier. Consequently, Saddam's threat, coupled with his ambitious efforts to develop and acquire chemical weapons and ballistic missiles with a range capable of reaching Israel, had to be taken seriously.[2]

During the summer of 1989 the relationship between Iraq and the PLO had grown closer, especially after the suspension of the dialogue between the United States and the PLO. While Egypt, looking to reintegrate itself into the Arab world following its temporary exile after Camp David, cautiously sought to attract other Arab states into the peace process, Saddam Hussein aspired to be recognized as the new champion of the pan-Arab cause, and fired bellicose threats toward Israel. Saddam's rhetoric attracted Arafat, who gradually shifted away from Egypt and toward what he perceived to be the new center of Arab rejectionism. Some PLO offices were symbolically relocated to Baghdad.[3] This political maneuvering and its effect on the peace process took on greater significance on August 2, 1990, when Iraqi forces invaded and occupied Kuwait.[4]

After the initial shock of Iraq's invasion and summary annexation of Kuwait subsided, the Arab world found itself divided on the issue of Kuwait's future. An Arab coalition headed by Egypt, Syria, and Saudi Arabia denounced the unilateral Iraqi action, and joined with the United States and its allies in political moves and military preparations aimed at compelling Iraq to withdraw from Kuwait. On the other side Libya, Sudan, and Yemen chose to ally themselves politically and diplomatically with Iraq.[5] In an attempt to gain Arab support, Saddam tried to link his actions in Kuwait with the Arab-Israeli conflict, stating repeatedly that his invasion was in support of the Palestinian cause and in opposition to American and Zionist imperialism.[6] Although his transparent ploy failed to attract Arab states away from their alliance with the West, Saddam's stock among Palestinians rose considerably.

For all practical purposes Arafat cast his lot with Saddam and the pro-Iraq coalition. This decision was influenced by popular sentiment throughout the Palestinian diaspora as well as within the occupied territories. Palestinian sympathy for Saddam was not only the result of Saddam's sabre rattling against Israel, but also a reflection of the anti-American sentiment that had long prevailed in the Palestinian community. Anger toward the United States had been further intensified by its recent suspension of the dialogue with the PLO and by what was seen as America's consistently pro-Israel posture. The fatigue and frustration felt within the Palestinian community after three years of the Intifada contributed to the embrace of an Arab leader who was prepared to stand up to the United States and Israel.[7] Across the Middle East, and especially in Amman and the occupied territories, multitudes of Palestinians poured into the streets, waving portraits of Saddam and chanting "Long Live Saddam!" and "Saddam, Deliver Us!"[8]

Count Me Out!

Arafat's support for Saddam Hussein created a deep sense of disillusionment within the Israeli peace movement. Faisal Husseini, Sari

Nusseibeh, and other Palestinian leaders with whom the Israeli peace movement had developed close relationships in the course of their efforts to demonstrate to the Israeli public that "there is someone to talk with," did little to lessen the shock. They too sympathized with the overwhelming pro-Saddam mood. On August 17, 1990, MK Yossi Sarid, an outstanding leader of the peace movement, authored a hard-hitting article in which he expressed the sentiment felt throughout the Israeli left.

> One needs a gas mask to overcome the poisonous and repellent stench emitted by the pro-Saddam position adopted by the PLO. The hugging and kissing between Yasser Arafat and Saddam Hussein are disgusting and frightening. It is not only disgusting but also a grave strategic mistake since Saddam will betray the Palestinians as soon as they are no longer of service to him. The occupation of Kuwait provided Shamir the best vindication for his annexationist policies, since he legitimated violent occupation of territories. . . . [When the crisis is over] nobody will hurry to invite the junior lackey of Saddam to the negotiating table.

As far as Sarid was concerned, "until further notice the Palestinians can count me out."[9]

A flurry of like-minded articles and speeches indicated that a significant segment of the peace movement was profoundly disturbed and confused by the Palestinian attitude. MK Elazar Granot, a central figure in Mapam, argued that the Palestinians must have succumbed to their despair, because there was no other logic in their support for Saddam. "The PLO has put its claim to represent the Palestinian people in future negotiations in question . . . since the Palestinians have proven that they are much less trustworthy partners than we thought."[10]

Yaron London, a prominent television personality, suggested that Palestinian support for Saddam raised questions concerning the Palestinian demand for self-determination, because Saddam's pan-Arab vision spoke of an Arab empire rather than a Palestinian state. "Most of them want a modern Saladin who will unify the Arab world and expel all non-Arabs from the Middle East. In the Ayyubite empire of the new Saladin from Baghdad there is no place for separate national identities"—an attitude, London reasoned, that emancipates the Israeli left from any moral obligation to the Palestinians. "Therefore, goodbye Husseini, goodbye Nusseibeh. . . . When you come back to ask for my sympathy for your 'legitimate rights' you will find that your pro-Saddam screams have deafened my ears."[11]

This sentiment was not shared by all of the peace movement's leaders. MK Amnon Rubinstein, a political centrist, also expressed regret at the Palestinian attitude and felt that the peace process had suffered a major setback. At the same time, however, he remained convinced that "when the dust settles we shall have to revive the dialogue and find a solution of peaceful separation and coexistence."[12] More radical supporters of Peace Now such as MK Dedi Zucker called for an immediate resumption of peace discussions with the Palestinians, arguing that "our basic interests demand a separate development of the two nations and the creation of a demilitarized Palestinian state alongside Israel."[13]

Indeed, Peace Now decided to maintain its dialogue with Palestinian leaders in the occupied territories despite the credibility crisis. Many peace activists believed that the anti-Palestinian hysteria prevalent in the Israeli media primarily served Likud and the other right-wing parties because it appeared to support their long-standing claim that peace was impossible in light of the fact that the Palestinians were neither trustworthy nor genuinely prepared for reconciliation. For their part, Palestinian leaders expressed disappointment with what they perceived as the patronizing attitude of Sarid and others within the peace movement. Faisal Husseini pointed to the lack of understanding by his Israeli colleagues of the frustrations of the Palestinian people, but also recognized that Israelis tend to close ranks when confronted by a military crisis.[14] Peace Now sought to mitigate the negative image the Palestinians projected to the Israeli public through a joint Palestinian-Israeli declaration, but this proved very difficult to formulate as long as the crisis was still deepening. Ultimately, Peace Now and the Palestinian leaders published separate proclamations aimed at limiting the damage caused by the existing hostile environment.[15]

On August 15, 1990, Faisal Husseini and other Palestinian leaders sent a statement to Peace Now that reiterated criticism of American intervention in the crisis and denounced Saudi and Egyptian collusion with the West. They protested against the "double standard especially apparent in terms of UN Security Council resolutions pertaining to the occupation of lands." They did, however, also state their belief in the illegitimacy "of the acquisition of land by force, and the unacceptability of resorting to military options in solving conflicts among states which may involve the occupation of sovereign states, including the Iraqi invasion of Kuwait."[16]

On August 17 Peace Now responded with an "Open Letter to the Palestinian Leaders in the Occupied Territories," which noted that "support for [Saddam] is support for the resolution of disputes between nations through force." At the same time the letter acknowledged

> the disappointment among the Palestinian people caused by the paralysis of the peace process. We are convinced, however, that a move towards

positions of confrontation distances us from a solution of the conflict and from the realization of the right of our two peoples to self-determination and peaceful coexistence. . . . We urge you . . . to convince the Palestinian public and the PLO that Saddam's cannon will save no one. Only by recognizing this will we be able to reestablish the mutual trust which can renew the dialogue and advance the peaceful resolution of the conflict.[17]

ICPME also undertook efforts to calm the atmosphere and convened a meeting of peace activists in Tel Aviv. Most of those who attended criticized Sarid's approach, and the prestigious writers Amos Oz, A. B. Yehoshua, and S. Izhar authored a petition, signed by all the participants, which proclaimed that "Israel is not required to educate the Palestinians but to reach an agreement with them." It reiterated the belief that "there is no connection between our feelings toward the PLO and the recognition of the necessary steps for peace. The road to peace requires negotiations between the state of Israel and the PLO."[18]

On September 26 Peace Now organized a public meeting with Faisal Husseini and Ghassan al-Khatib, a leader of the Palestinian Communist Party. The Palestinian leaders tried to explain the reasons for PLO's position on the Gulf crisis and called upon the Israeli public "not to put the Palestinians beyond the realm of international legitimacy because this will only push them to further despair and extremism."[19] In a letter sent by Peace Now to its supporters and colleagues in the United States, the movement stated that more than ever it felt

> the responsibility to stem the tide of despair . . . and to sound loud the bells of hope and reason once the storm in the Arabian desert will subside. . . . The Palestinian problem will remain with us whatever the outcome of the new crisis and we must not neglect to address it with foresight and compassion.[20]

Linkage

Even the more extreme factions within the peace movement were not immune to the anti-Saddam sentiments that swept Israel. However, their unconditional support for the Palestinian cause, and their strong links with the European and American peace movements, which opposed any military solution to the crisis, placed them in a special dilemma. Stanley Cohen, an American professor active in the radical left, observed:

> It is not enough to stay faithful to our two commitments: first, to social justice for the Palestinians, and second, to internationalism and our natural anti-war impulse. We also cannot be psychologically out of touch with Israeli society. Our position is analogous to someone who knows the social causes of and solutions to street crime, but is about to be mugged.[21]

Several activists on the left of Peace Now created a committee and prepared a petition titled "One Minute before the War."[22] Their demands echoed pleas heard throughout Europe and the United States not to resort to war, and to rely on diplomatic and economic pressures against Iraq. This position, however, did not receive a significant amount of support within Israel, even among the left. With Shamir's government on the sidelines of the conflict, Peace Now took the position that it was not its duty to give President Bush advice. On the personal level, many probably welcomed the prospect of Saddam receiving a crushing defeat at the hands of the U.S.-led coalition.[23]

The Iraqi crisis opened a schism between the mainstream peace groups and the more radical left with regard to the question of "linkage." In a desperate political maneuver designed to drive a wedge between the United States and its Arab allies, Saddam had tried to associate his retreat from Kuwait with an Israeli retreat from the occupied territories. The Palestinians, along with the extreme left in the Israeli peace movement, embraced this logic, but Peace Now did not endorse it despite the organization's long-standing support for an Israeli withdrawal. Peace Now maintained that these were separate issues and that Saddam's move was a political ploy aimed at justifying his aggression and mobilizing the Arab masses.[24]

Blood on the Holy Mount

The international tension caused by the Gulf crisis did not lessen the toll of the ongoing Intifada, nor diminish Israel's attempts to suppress it. On the contrary, during late fall 1990 acts of violence escalated on both sides. On October 8 violent clashes occurred between the Israeli police and thousands of Muslims gathered in the Haram al-Sharif, the site of the mosques on the Temple Mount in Jerusalem. The police panicked and lost control as the violence escalated. By the end of the day 21 Palestinians were dead and close to 200 wounded. Several Israeli policemen and civilians were also injured.[25]

A wave of attacks on Jewish civilians soon followed. Palestinian knife attacks against Jews increased, often with fatal results. On October 21 a young Palestinian construction worker, who was like many other Palestinians employed by a Jewish firm, fatally stabbed Iris Azouly, a young woman in her military service. While attempting to escape, the assailant killed two other Israelis. The assault took place in Bak'a, a partially gentrified quarter of south Jerusalem in which Mizrachi immigrants live alongside more affluent Israelis who moved into the area in the 1970s and 1980s. Many of the area's new residents were supporters of Peace Now, and the movement's main offices were located nearby.

The cycle of violence continued and several Palestinians were attacked as they passed through the neighborhood. Peace Now activists were also attacked by Jewish right-wing extremists, and the police were forced to disperse an angry crowd that attempted to storm the house of Amiram Goldblum, which stood not far from the site where Iris Azouly had been murdered. The crowd was shouting "Death to the Arabs!" and "Death to the Lovers of Arabs!"[26]

In response to earlier anti-Arab riots instigated by right-wing vigilantes, Peace Now organized "Groups for Peace and Good Neighborhoods." These squads were intended to rescue Palestinians under attack and to follow the perpetrators in order to identify them to the police and later testify against them in court.[27] In the wake of the assaults against fellow activists, the squads were renamed "Groups for the Defense of Democracy" and stationed near Peace Now's offices and the homes of its prominent members.[28]

The stabbings continued and the minister of defense ordered the occupied territories temporarily closed. As a consequence, 120,000 Palestinian laborers who earned their living inside Israel could not cross the Green Line and were left without an income for weeks at a time. This led to a debate within Israel concerning the desirability and practicability of permanent *hafrada* (separation) between Palestinians and Israelis. The left maintained that sealing the territories amounted to a tacit admission by the Shamir government that Israel ultimately had no choice but to withdraw from the territories. Likud was not persuaded by this argument, and eventually reopened the borders in response to pressure from Israeli employers, especially in the agriculture and construction sectors, who depended on Palestinian labor. Shamir viewed closure as a temporary collective punishment in no way connected to the question of the political future of the occupied territories.

Although Peace Now criticized the temporary closures—which were said to amount to "detaining the Palestinians in a ghetto from which they will be permitted to come out only by the whim of the occupier"— the peace activists maintained that political separation between Israelis and Palestinians was the ultimate objective of their struggle. Some within the movement called for an immediate political and economic separation between Israel and the territories to be achieved by massive investment in the Palestinian economy to increase employment for Palestinian workers, enhance Palestinian economic viability and independence, and form the economic base of the future Palestinian state.[29]

Olive Branches along Wadi Ara

Palestinian sympathy for Iraq placed the Arab citizens of Israel in an awkward position. Many of them viewed Iraq's invasion of Kuwait as a defiance of American intervention in the region and a challenge to the feudal rulers of the Arabian peninsula who hoarded the oil riches that rightfully belonged to the entire Arab nation.[30] Many Israeli Arabs may have initially questioned Iraq's invasion of Kuwait, but following the onset of Operation Desert Shield they adopted a more sympathetic attitude toward Saddam. Even so, the pro-Saddam rhetoric that appeared in Arabic newspapers published in Israel, and the symbolic acts of support staged in Arab communities,[31] did not approach the level of support for Iraq expressed by Palestinians in the occupied territories or in Jordan.

The Israeli right, especially the outspoken anti-Arab groups, interpreted such political expressions as treason. The atmosphere was further inflamed by the fact that recent attacks on Jews by Palestinians from the occupied territories had occurred in predominantly Jewish areas in which Israeli Arabs could move freely but were not easily distinguishable from Palestinians from the territories. An ugly wave of anti-Arab propaganda produced by racist elements within the Israeli right, who did not care to differentiate between Israeli Arab citizens and Palestinians from the occupied territories, was followed by a spate of retaliatory attacks against Israeli Arabs perpetrated by Israeli Jews.

At the end of 1990 Peace Now and ICPME initiated a dialogue with the Coordinating Committee of Arab Municipalities in Israel, which was headed by the mayor of Shfar'am, Ibrahim Nimr Hussein (affectionately known as Abu Hattem). A joint demonstration was organized along Wadi Ara, a densely populated area with several Palestinian villages alongside one of the main highways to the north, within the Green Line. On Saturday, January 12, 1991, thousands of Israeli Jews and Arabs linked hands in a human chain along the road. Slogans called for an end to the violence from all sides, and condemned racism and extremism. Each of the participants held an olive branch, and the main banner read, "Together We Shall Stop the Hatred!"[32]

A special feature of this demonstration was the participation of approximately five hundred new immigrants from the Soviet Union. Peace Now had made a special effort to reach out to these immigrants, who had arrived in the country in the 1990s and who were thought to be more liberal than the Soviet immigrants of the 1970s, who had tended to support right-wing policies. One of the recent immigrants who demonstrated at Wadi Ara told a journalist that "he and his friends felt a need to meet peace-loving Arabs."[33]

Into the Sealed Rooms

As the likelihood of war increased, Israelis responsible for civil defense began implementing measures to protect 'he population from threatened Iraqi missile attacks, including the possible use of chemical warheads. The IDF distributed gas masks to the population along with instructions that recommended sealing one room in every house or apartment against possible chemical contamination. This jolted the Israeli public into the realization that the danger of a missile attack was genuine, and the public watched in suspense as events unfolded in the Gulf.

Israeli apprehensions proved warranted. On the evening of January 17, Scud missiles began crashing into the suburbs of Tel Aviv. By the end of the forty-day U.S.-led air-and-land campaign against Iraq, forty-three missiles had hit Israel. Only one Israeli died as a direct result of a missile impact, and twenty were wounded, but twenty Israelis died as an indirect consequence and property damage was extensive, with hundreds of houses destroyed or severely damaged.

The primary effect of the missile attacks was psychological. Night after night for six weeks, millions of Israelis—Jews and Arabs alike—went to bed with the knowledge that they might be awakened by sirens signaling another missile attack, and that they would have only two or three minutes to reach their makeshift shelters.[34] Many opted to sleep in their sealed rooms, but they still had to put on their masks and place their babies in a plastic enclosure when the alarm sounded. In Tel Aviv and Haifa the explosions could be heard throughout the city. Thousands of Israelis left the urban centers and moved into hotels or the homes of friends in Jerusalem or Eilat, which were considered relatively safe. Many people, especially children, had to be treated for the psychological effects of fear and anxiety. Perhaps the most popular figure during these days was the military spokesmen Nahman Shai, who appeared on television and radio to announce that the danger had passed and people could leave the sealed rooms and return to their beds.

The feeling of vulnerability reminded many of the helplessness Jews had experienced during the Holocaust. One mother wrote:

Fear in the nights. Now also in our region. Shall I be able to defend my child if, God forbid, something really happens? Bad thoughts about help-lessness from other days come to the mind. Last night two alarms—who can have the power to continue this way? Does the baby still breathe? Did we remember to remove the cork from the filter? Will he come back safe from the kindergarten?[35]

Faced by these vicious attacks on the civilian population, the peace movement unequivocally condemned Saddam Hussein's aggression and expressed its hope for his quick and total defeat. On February 21, 1991, Peace Now issued a statement that noted that although in principle the movement preferred nonviolent solutions to international conflicts, "some threats can only be removed by eliminating their sources, if nec-essary by military means. The destruction of Saddam Hussein's power is a vital Israeli interest."[36] To a large degree this statement was intended as a response to appeals from European peace activists for their Israeli colleagues to join them in urging the United States to stop the destruc-tion of Iraq and to return to the negotiating table.[37]

The disagreement between the German and Israeli peace movements was especially pronounced. Several members and supporters of the German Green Party had arrived at the strange conclusion that if the Israeli government made an appeal to President Bush he might stop the attacks on Iraq. A small German delegation traveled to Jerusalem—ar-riving, as it happened, in the midst of a missile alarm—but most Israelis refused to meet with it. Before arriving in Israel, Hans Peter Stroeble, a senior member of the German Green Party, gave an interview in which he said that the Iraqi attacks on Israel "were the logical conclusion from the Israeli policy toward the Palestinian people and the Arab states, in-cluding Iraq." If the government of Israel did not appeal to President Bush for a cease-fire in the Gulf, said Stroeble, Israel would be "respon-sible for the continuation of the war."[38] Israelis were incensed and many could not help but discern strong anti-Semitic undertones in this outra-geous accusation, especially in light of the fact that the Israeli govern-ment had abstained from retaliating to the unprovoked missile attacks.[39]

Rather than boycotting the delegation Peace Now decided to con-front it. In a heated debate held in the Notre Dame Hotel on February 20, a leading figure in the movement, Menachem Brinker, told the delega-tion that "Israel is entitled to be the last country to call for a cease-fire in the Gulf, and has the right to be sorry if this war does not end in the total defeat of Saddam Hussein."[40] The German delegation left the country in haste the day after it arrived, and shortly thereafter Hans Peter Stroeble announced his resignation from the Green Party's leadership.[41]

The incident with the German peaceniks exposed a fundamental difference between the European and the Israeli peace movements. The majority of the European peace groups were motivated by a philosophical, perhaps even theological, opposition to war and violence. The majority of the Israeli peace activists approached the issue of peace in a different context. In general they did not address themselves to broad philosophical and ideological questions such as whether the use of violence to achieve political objectives is legitimate under any circumstances. Theirs was a narrower, pragmatic perspective. Although many within the movement were motivated by moral considerations, they were also committed to preserving Israel's security and the welfare of the state.

Peace Now, convinced that Israeli restraint was important from the perspective of the renewal of peace efforts once the war ended,[42] joined the overwhelming public support for the decision by the Shamir government to abstain from retaliating against Iraq.[43] This decision was made over the opposition of several hawkish strategists, who voiced concern that Israel's restraint might be misinterpreted by other potential adversaries as weakness in its deterrent posture.

Shamir had few options in light of the U.S. demand that Israel remain on the sidelines. The Americans wished to keep Israel out of the battle to avoid embarrassing their Arab allies. Furthermore, with the skies over Iraq swarming with U.S. and allied warplanes, for Israel to launch an air attack or to use its ground forces would have required prior coordination, which the Americans were unwilling to entertain. After considering the fact that Iraqi military forces and industrial centers were already being hard hit by allied bombing, Shamir decided to forgo Israel's one option of retaliating in kind with its own long-range missiles.[44]

Dancing on the Roofs

The similarity of opinions held by Peace Now and the Shamir government on Israel's military policy in the Gulf War did not squelch the movement's criticism of the government's handling of the Palestinian population during the crisis. When the missiles started to fall on Israel, Minister of Defense Moshe Arens placed the entire Palestinian population under a curfew. Most laborers who worked inside the Green Line had already been without an income for months, but now the Palestinians in the occupied territories were subjected to what practically amounted to collective house arrest. The curfew was lifted for only one or two hours every day to enable the population to buy food.[45]

Media reports of joyous Palestinian reactions to the missile attacks disturbed and angered many Israelis. It was reported that during the Scud attacks Palestinians in the territories climbed on their roofs to watch, cheering and dancing as the missiles passed overhead on their way to Tel Aviv. Some of these reports were indeed accurate, but the phenomenon was a good deal rarer than many journalists claimed.

Peace Now felt that the curfew was unwarranted and that the Israeli government was seeking "to manipulate the political mistakes which the Palestinians and the PLO have made in order to advance the policy of annexation." Peace Now claimed that even in the midst of the war, "there is no other option but to conduct a dialogue with them [the Palestinians] and thereby attempt to resolve the Israeli-Palestinian conflict."[46]

Peace Now's dialogue with Palestinian leaders continued during the war, despite the missile attacks. Activists used breaks in the curfew to visit their friends. Peace Now stressed the importance of countering the media image of Palestinians dancing on the roofs. Faisal Husseini tried to repair the damage caused by his earlier remarks, and publicly emphasized that he had never intended to give his blessing to the Scud attacks. He told an Israeli journalist that he had good friends in Tel Aviv for whose safety he was much concerned. He argued, however, that the long suffering of the Palestinians and their bitterness against Israel explained their apparent joy, "or shall we say satisfaction," at Israeli suffering, though he characterized this as a personal rather than a political reaction.[47] This equivocal clarification did not shield Husseini from the wrath of the Israeli right, or from the disappointment some on the Israeli left continued to feel.[48]

The weeks preceding the Gulf War and during the missile attacks were not propitious for peace activities. People's minds were preoccupied with the prospect of war, and the Palestinian "betrayal" brought the credibility of the peace movement's agenda into question.[49] Even the Women in Black disappeared from their regular sites, resuming their protests only when the war was practically over.[50]

The peace activists were encouraged, however, by the prospects for a renewal of the peace process once the war was ended. With the United States grateful both for the support of its Arab allies and for Israeli restraint, the Bush administration was widely expected to undertake a new Arab-Israeli peace initiative as soon the war was won. On February 24, 1991, in a "Letter to Our Friends in the USA," Peace Now wrote:

> The post-war period offers a unique historical opportunity for Israel to come to peace and understanding with its neighbors. The Arab partners in the

war coalition, Egypt, Syria, and Saudi Arabia, may show readiness to co-operate with the U.S. to find a solution to the conflict. . . . The U.S., in its desire to forge a new regional order, may also wish to put an end to this conflict. . . . The weakening of the PLO does not put an end to the need to solve the Palestinian problem. . . . It is an Israeli interest of the first order to find a way to discuss this matter with the Arab states and the accepted representatives of the Palestinians as soon as the war is over. . . . There exists a serious danger that the [Likud] government of Israel will try its best to torpedo peace talks in any form. . . . Therefore, we envisage a tough struggle which awaits the peace camp in Israel in its attempt to push on the beginning of negotiations.[51]

Baker's Shuttle Diplomacy

The Americans rejected any conditions on Iraq's withdrawal from Kuwait, and were not prepared to hand Saddam a political victory by accepting his notion of linkage. However, the Bush administration began to refer to a process that might be described as "sequential linkage." As early as October 1, 1990, in a speech to the UN General Assembly, President Bush had declared that "in the aftermath of Iraq's unconditional departure from Kuwait I truly believe there may be opportunities . . . for all states and people of the region to settle the conflicts that divide the Arabs from Israel."[52] This amounted to an American commitment to its Arab allies to undertake a new initiative in the Arab-Israeli peace process as soon as the Gulf crisis ended.

The White House lived up to its commitment. On March 6, 1991, less than a week after the guns in the Gulf went silent, the president told a joint session of Congress, "The time has come to put an end to the Arab-Israeli conflict. . . . The principles must be elaborated to provide for Israel's security and recognition, and at the same time for legitimate Palestinian political rights."[53] A few days later Secretary of State James Baker began shuttling between Middle Eastern capitals.

Like Henry Kissinger after the October War, Bush and Baker were convinced that the aftermath of war provided a window of opportunity for progress in the peace process. Within six months of the end of the Gulf crisis, Baker had made eight visits to the Middle East, logging hundreds of hours of negotiations with leaders in the region, including Palestinians in the occupied territories. The new formula for negotiations included two simultaneous bilateral tracks: one for Israel and the Palestinians, and one for Israel and the Arab states. However, the Palestinian representatives were required to remain formally a part of the Jordanian delegation. For many years Israel had insisted that the Arab-Israeli conflict had to be resolved by an agreement among sovereign states. The new formula managed to introduce the Palestinians into the process without requiring Israel to abandon this position. Israel also continued to insist that the PLO be excluded from the negotiations.

Its support for Saddam Hussein during the Gulf crisis cost the PLO dearly, both politically and financially. The Saudis, furious at the PLO, suspended their substantial financial support to the organization. His bargaining position weakened, Arafat accepted Baker's suggestion that the Palestinians be represented by an informal group from the occupied territories headed by leaders loyal to the PLO.[54] Arafat calculated correctly that he could influence the negotiations indirectly through such a Palestinian delegation.[55]

For a while Shamir tried to concentrate attention on the Syrian track. Some compared the process of making peace with Syria to the route traveled by Menachem Begin and Anwar Sadat a decade before. However, the drama of Sadat's trip to Israel and the vivid personalities of Begin and Sadat had given that event an atmosphere of warmth that was now absent. "This time the entire process is led by cold people like Baker and Assad," argued Tzali Reshef at a planning session of Peace Now's central forum. "Our job this time is much more difficult. We have to activate public opinion despite the absence of momentum."[56]

Syria's willingness to negotiate appeared lukewarm. Hafez Assad remained obstinate despite the fact that he had lost the political and military support of his former Soviet patron, and it soon became clear that the negotiations with Syria were not making the desired progress. This redirected attention to the core of the Arab-Israeli conflict: the future of the Palestinians.

The atmosphere in the territories was still inflamed.[57] The lifting of the curfew was followed by a renewed wave of stabbings and other attacks against Jews by Palestinian extremists.[58] The Israeli authorities responded by repeatedly closing the territories. An increasing number of Israelis could be heard calling for *hafrada*. Although support for such an idea sprang more from fear and anger than from any recognition of the political rights of the Palestinians, the growing acceptance of the idea of separation made the concept of a Palestinian state more palatable for many Israelis. Peace Now capitalized on this mood and came out with a new slogan, *"Lehipared Leshalom!"* (Let Us Separate in Peace).[59]

In May a new factor entered the negotiations. Israel had renewed its request for a $10 billion loan guarantee from the United States to be used for the absorption of Soviet immigrants.[60] As the summer of 1991 approached, this issue further strained relations between the two countries. Although Shamir sought to assure the Americans that his government would not proactively send Soviet immigrants to the occupied territories, the huge wave of subsidized housing construction, under the enthusiastic direction of Ariel Sharon (now minister of housing), made the assurance less than persuasive. Baker viewed this construction as an obstacle to his peace efforts. It was now the Americans who spoke in terms of "linkage," making the loan guarantees contingent upon a construction freeze in the occupied territories.[61] Early in September President Bush asked Congress to delay consideration of Israel's request for 120 days. Encountering congressional resistance, Bush decided to take his appeal to the court of U.S. public opinion, which is ordinarily negative toward foreign assistance. In a remarkably confrontational tone, Bush denounced Israel's settlement policy and the efforts of the Jewish lobby to influence U.S. foreign policy. Many within the Jewish community were disturbed by Bush's gambit, but it achieved its desired results, garnering substantial popular support for the president's tough position.[62]

Commando Informers

In spring 1991 Peace Now launched another effort to expose the development of new settlements. The movement believed that aggressive settlement policies endangered further immigration from the Soviet Union. These policies prevented Israel from receiving vital U.S. financial support, and recognition of that fact contributed to the growing awareness of Jews still in Russia and other former Soviet republics that Israel was having difficulty absorbing them. A joint advertisement by Peace Now and ICPME stated:

> The question is now clear and penetrating: immigrants or territories? Instead of investing in the creation of employment for the immigrants, the government invests its time and public funds in settlements and unnecessary provocations in the territories. We must tell the government: Immigrants—yes! Settlements—no![63]

Predictably, the government sought to disguise its settlement activities in the occupied territories. But Peace Now's Settlements Watch group renewed its efforts to publicize what the government was doing. Detailed reports were provided to the media and publicized in Israel and abroad,[64] on several occasions being intentionally released during

Baker's visits to the region.[65] These efforts incensed Sharon, who accused Peace Now of constituting a "commando unit of voluntary informants" in the service of the United States.[66] For its part, Peace Now demanded the suspension of Sharon's parliamentary immunity to enable the movement to pursue charges against him for incitement.[67]

Undeterred by Sharon's accusations, Settlements Watch continued its efforts, which included publicizing a claim that a new construction project in the northern West Bank would cost more than $1 billion to complete.[68] Peace Now appealed to the Supreme Court of Justice as part of an effort to challenge the legality of the new settlements.[69] The movement also petitioned for an injunction to "forbid . . . any new construction in the settlements which is not dictated by security considerations," as an interim measure pending the court's ruling, but this injunction was declined.[70]

During May seven leftist MKs visited the United States under the auspices of Peace Now to meet with Jewish leaders and government officials.[71] The delegation was criticized by conservative Jewish leaders, and MK Dov Shilansky, the Speaker of the Knesset and veteran activist on the right, felt that the delegation had acted inappropriately: "The opposition has to wage its struggles at home, not abroad." The delegation's spokesperson responded by explaining that its purpose was "to correct the wrong impression given by spokespersons from the right that the majority of the Israeli public supports the 'not an inch' policy."[72] Despite this clarification, the delegation found itself walking a political tightrope. It repeatedly had to respond to the accusation that it sought to encourage American pressure on Shamir to accept the proposed modalities for the peace process. Apologetically, the delegation stated its opposition to economic pressure or to "any cut in U.S. economic aid as a means to soften the government's position in the peace process."[73]

Who's Afraid of an International Conference?

During the summer of 1991 it appeared that Shamir's resistance to an international conference as a precursor to bilateral negotiations was weakening and that any additional pressure might tip the balance.[74] Indeed, after long and arduous negotiations Shamir finally conceded. This was a response not only to U.S. pressure but also to Israeli public opinion. After four years of the Intifada most Israelis had come to the conclusion that the uprising could not be suppressed.[75]

One of the thorny problems to be resolved was the issue of representation for the Palestinians. To avoid direct contact with the PLO, Secretary Baker had developed close relations with the political leadership of the Palestinians in the occupied territories, with whom he frequently met in Jerusalem. While all parties recognized that these people were loyal to, and received their instructions from, the PLO leadership in Tunis, they nevertheless emerged as a distinct group and gradually acquired legitimacy and prestige among the Americans, Israelis, and—no less significantly—the Palestinians themselves. This was the same group of leaders with whom Peace Now and other Israeli peace groups had developed close ties during the late 1980s and early 1990s.

Despite their hectic schedule of meetings with the Americans, the international media, and others, Faisal Husseini and his colleagues continued to meet often with members of the peace movement, whom they viewed as a barometer of Israeli public opinion. Peace Now's leaders urged their Palestinian counterparts not to miss the opportunity to participate in the proposed international conference, even if the conditions offered seemed less than ideal.[76]

Time for Peace Once More

During the summer of 1991 Peace Now's leaders focused their activities on four main areas: opposing expansion of settlements, encouraging the government to be flexible in the negotiations, increasing public support for the peace process, and persuading their Palestinian counterparts to be reasonable in their demands.

Peace Now also decided to reactivate "Time for Peace"—an organizational framework that had been developed during the previous year but which had been disrupted by the Gulf War. The movement now sought to build a large coalition, and solicited the support of the kibbutz movement as well as all the parliamentary groups on the left, including the Labor Party, which by this time had returned to the opposition.[77]

The Labor Party did not formally join the Time for Peace campaign despite the fact that Peace Now made an effort to formulate its approach in a manner that would be acceptable to Labor, using phrases such as "the right of the Palestinians to self-determination" and "territories for peace," both of which were consistent with previous Labor statements. No specific mention was made of the PLO or a Palestinian state.[78]

However, although the party decided not to join the effort officially, many individual Labor members participated in demonstrations organized under the Time for Peace framework.

Drawing on experience accumulated over a dozen years, and with a more stable and efficient organizational machinery than before, Peace Now organized an impressive array of activities. On October 16, 1991, a festive opening of the Time for Peace campaign was held in the Knesset. The following day a "peace convoy" traveled from Metulla, in northern Israel, to Jerusalem, stopping in towns and at road junctions on the way to hold impromptu gatherings. On October 18 a large demonstration was held in the town of Holon, and in Tel Aviv teams of activists organized a petition drive. On October 19 a march against the settlers was held in Hebron, and the next day a community event was organized in a Mizrachi neighborhood in Jerusalem. On October 21 activities were held in another neighborhood in Jerusalem and in Haifa. The announcement of these activities read, "Today peace is more possible and nearer than ever before. . . . This trip must end in peace! . . . This time we cannot miss peace!"[79]

A large demonstration had been planned for October 26 in the main square of Tel Aviv. The gathering seemed to have become superfluous, however, when on October 24 Shamir finally agreed to the convening of an international conference. Peace Now was thus surprised when two days later nearly 80,000 demonstrators showed up. A. B. Yehoshua sarcastically commented, "We have the unique opportunity to support Shamir and we cannot miss the pleasure." In a more serious tone he proclaimed, "We bless you Mr. Shamir from the bottom of our heart. . . . We are ready to forget all of your procrastinating. . . . Go in peace and come back with peace! . . . You may do it in your own way with your maneuvers, as long as you bring us peace now!"[80] The movement's veterans whispered among themselves, "If Shamir will bring us peace we might shut down this business. We are tired of demonstrations."[81]

Back to Madrid

On October 30, 1991, the international conference on the Middle East conflict convened in a royal palace in Madrid.[82] The opening session was an international media event of the first order. The proceedings were televised and the main actors were Hanan Ashrawi and Benjamin Netanyahu, the spokespersons of the Palestinian and Israeli delegations respectively. According to one observer, Ashrawi "presented a new image of the Palestinians—articulate, moderate, professional and persistent. . . . Palestinians in the refugee camps and in the occupied territories were enthralled with their newfound place in the world."[83] The presence of Presidents Bush and Gorbachev, in addition to representatives of the United Nations and the European Community, provided a dramatic validation of the seriousness of the conference.[84]

After months of hard bargaining and arm-twisting, James Baker had managed to wrangle major concessions from the Palestinians as well as the Israelis. Despite their long-standing objection, the Palestinians (with the behind-the-scenes acquiescence of the PLO) accepted a process that would initially address only a limited agenda—interim arrangements based on the concept of autonomy as incorporated in the Camp David Accords. For its part, Israel for the first time agreed to negotiate with a Palestinian delegation that was led, albeit unofficially, by a Palestinian from Jerusalem (Faisal Husseini), who received his orders from the PLO in Tunis. The controversy over the modalities of the international conference quickly became irrelevant because all parties soon recognized that the next step was to hold face-to-face bilateral negotiations.

There were few surprises in the opening statements of the conference. All sides seemed determined to make sure that no one forgot their grievances. "They abused history, abjured self-examination, wallowed in self-pity and preened in righteousness," observed one journalist. The proceedings were broadcast live throughout the Middle East, and it was transparently clear that the opening statements were primarily directed to domestic audiences rather than to the other side.[85]

The peace movement found some satisfaction in a few lines in the address by the official head of the Palestinian delegation, Haider Abdul-Shafi. Echoing what peace activists had for twenty years said to fellow Israelis about the costs of the occupation, Abdul-Shafi observed: "We have seen some of you at your best and at your worst, for the occupier can hide no secrets from the occupied, and we are witness to the toll that occupation has exacted from you and yours. . . . We have seen you look back in deepest sorrow at the tragedy of your past, and look on in horror at the disfigurement of the victims turned oppressors." Speaking to the peace movement, he said:

> We have responded with solemn appreciation to those of you who came to offer consolation to our bereaved, to give support to those whose homes were being demolished, and to extend encouragement and counsel to those detained behind barbed wire and iron bars. We have marched together, often

choking together in the nondiscriminating tear gas, all crying out in pain as clubs descended on both Palestinians and Israelis alike, for pain knows no national boundaries and no one can claim a monopoly on suffering.

He then referred to the Time of Peace demonstrations at the end of 1989: "We once formed a human chain around Jerusalem, joining hands and calling for peace. Let us today form a moral chain around Madrid and continue that noble effort for peace."[86] For the peace movement, Abdul-Shafi's words seemed to show that years of struggle had achieved positive results with Palestinians. It was now time to see if the efforts of the peaceniks had had a similar effect on Israelis.

14

A Handshake on the White House Lawn

Olive Branches, Not Stones

The convening of the Madrid Conference was an achievement of form rather than substance. As two astute observers noted:

> The Madrid Conference in and of itself was not a major historical event. It resolved no major problems, it reconciled no conflicting positions, it negotiated nothing of substance. . . . The really difficult steps are yet to be taken as the parties settle into bilateral negotiations that may require years to produce enduring peace accords . . . which necessarily will be a result of painful concessions and compromises and in the end may even seem more mundane than glorious. [Nevertheless] it was a significant first step in an historic effort to resolve Middle East conflicts: officials of embittered enemies actually sat at the same table and talked with one another.[1]

In the occupied territories Palestinians also participated in a new form of engagement. On October 29, 1991, the same youngsters who during the previous four years had regularly thrown stones at Israeli soldiers now handed them olive branches. Arafat's supporters in the Gaza Strip organized a peace demonstration, shook hands with their occupiers, and tied balloons to the soldiers' jeeps. When the Palestinian delegates to the Madrid Conference returned to the territories, they were greeted with a hero's welcome.[2]

On the Israeli side there was little public euphoria, but polls showed substantial support for the peace initiative. In one poll 92 percent supported Shamir's decision to go to Madrid, although only 56 percent expected that the conference would result in peace. The question of territorial compromise in exchange for peace still divided the nation into roughly equal halves, for and against. However, in a poll conducted in November 1991 the question "If the establishment of a Palestinian state turned out to be the last obstacle to peace, would you agree to concede?" produced an unprecedented 84 percent affirmative response.[3] Despite this growing support for compromise, most Israelis remained uncertain about the true meaning of Madrid. One observer noted, "Every Israeli has a Citizens Right Movement and a Likud party in his head. And now they can no longer ignore the debate between them."[4]

The Palestinian leaders in the occupied territories launched an effort to increase popular support for the peace process. Led by Sari Nusseibeh, apparently with the consent of PLO headquarters in Tunis, Fatah activists organized political action committees in a number of Palestinian towns and resumed their contacts with the Israeli peace movement. "These committees will lead to the creation of a stable, strong, and wide Palestinian peace movement. This is our Peace Now," declared Ziyad Abu-Zayyad.[5]

Peace Now sought to take advantage of the momentum created by the Madrid Conference, and during November organized a number of public meetings with Palestinians. On November 16 about fifty Israeli high school students met with fifty Palestinian students at Nahal Oz, a kibbutz just outside the Gaza Strip. On November 23 two other meetings took place in Ramallah and in the Reihan nature reserve in the northern region of the West Bank. The Palestinian participation in the meetings was sponsored by the Fatah committees, the Communist Party, and Fida (a splinter group of the DFLP that remained loyal to the PLO). The slogan used for this event was "Two Nations Talk Peace." Among the speakers was Hussein al-Sheikh, a Palestinian who had spent eleven years in Israeli jails.[6] After the meeting Tzali Reshef commented, "These young people constitute the buds of a large peace movement among the Palestinians. Like Peace Now they will now strive for coexistence with Israel and an independent life alongside Israel."[7] The warm atmosphere that prevailed in these meetings suggested that the wounds of the Gulf War had mostly healed.

Foot-Dragging in Washington

The euphoria did not last for long. Opposition to the peace process grew rapidly among the radical Palestinian and Islamic factions, which initiated a campaign of terror designed not only to inflict casualities on the Israelis but also to enrage them. In a classic tradition of terrorism, the attacks were intended to provoke draconian reactions from the Israelis, in turn eroding any popular support the peace process had initially received from the mainstream Palestinian community. Meanwhile Shamir repeatedly reminded all parties that his agreement to negotiate with the Arabs was not a softening of his opposition to any Israeli withdrawal from the occupied territories, or to the establishment of a Palestinian state.

Jewish settlers in the territories began pressuring the government to respond aggressively to the rising tide of attacks against them. The settlers feared that despite Shamir's tough talk, he might yield to international pressure and begin a process resulting in Palestinian independence. In winter 1992 demonstrations by the settlers and other extreme right-wing elements increased, as did retaliatory attacks by Jewish vigilantes against Palestinians. In a concession to the settlers Shamir permitted the establishment of a new settlement near the site where two settlers had been killed and announced the construction of 5,500 additional housing units in the existing settlements.[8]

During 1992 the bilateral negotiations between Israel and Syria, Lebanon, Jordan, and the Palestinians continued in Washington. Multilateral negotiations concerning such regional issues as water resources, arms control, refugees, the environment, and economic development took place at different locations around the world. These negotiations included representatives from Arab states such as Morocco and Saudi Arabia that did not share contiguous borders with Israel. Though the atmosphere was often friendly, limited progress was made in these multilateral discussions. Clearly, significant movement in these areas depended on tangible progress in the bilateral negotiations, but little could be discerned.[9]

The negotiations between Jordan and Israel progressed more smoothly. The issues to be negotiated included minor border adjustments, the allocation of water resources, and the return of the 1967 refugees. On these matters Israel was prepared to make significant concessions. However, due to his relatively weak political position, King Hussein could not afford to be perceived as cutting a separate deal with Israel ahead of the other Arab states and the Palestinians.

Lebanon, for its part, demanded that Israel withdraw from the security zone in southern Lebanon, but Israel conditioned such a withdrawal on the Lebanese government's ability to effectively control its territory. This implied the elimination of the threat posed by Hizbullah and other extreme groups. In any case, for all practical purposes Lebanon's affairs were now being directed from Damascus.

The bilateral negotiations between Syria and Israel experienced considerable difficulties. An impasse was soon reached when President Assad demanded Israeli commitment in advance to a full withdrawal from the Golan Heights. In response Israel demanded that Syria agree in principle to conclude a peace treaty and to begin full normalization of relations.

But perhaps the most frustrating negotiations were those between Israel and the Palestinians. The talks stalled following demands that each side must have recognized would be unacceptable to the other. The Palestinian delegation in Washington was comprised of Palestinians from the occupied territories, but regular contact between them and PLO headquarters in Tunis was assumed. Shamir's choice not to enforce the law that prohibited contact with the PLO demonstrated that even he recognized that Israel's negotiations with the Palestinians were in fact negotiations with the PLO. Although PLO representatives were not permitted to participate directly in the negotiations, Nabil Shaath, a senior member of the PLO establishment, and other PLO officials were in Washington to supervise the proceedings on Arafat's behalf. Telecommunications between Washington, Jerusalem, and Tunis became an hourly necessity, and the Palestinian delegates frequently traveled to Tunis on their way to and from Washington to report on their negotiations and to receive instructions from the PLO chairman.

Obviously this was a cumbersome process that impeded progress. As Shimon Peres later wrote, "Those who determined the course of the talks did not participate in them, whereas those who participated in the talks had no say in the course of the negotiations."[10]

By early spring 1992 progress in the peace process had evidently slowed and was being affected by a number of factors external to the negotiations. Knesset elections, scheduled for October, were advanced to June as a result of yet another parliamentary crisis, and the Israeli public shifted its attention to the campaign. Presidential elections were also approaching in the United States, and the Bush administration began redirecting its energies toward the domestic scene. Still, President Bush continued to uphold the linkage between the loan guarantees Israel requested and a freeze on settlements in the occupied territories.[11] Also, James Baker was reluctant to undertake any risky foreign policy initiatives, and appeared satisfied with merely avoiding a breakdown in the slow-moving negotiations.

A Flow of Peace Activities

During the first months of 1992 the peace movement's activities were limited. There were two reasons for this passivity. First, the government was finally negotiating with the "enemy," and there was little the movement could do at this point. The precise details of the negotiations in Washington were not known to the public, which made it difficult to assess the seriousness of the government's pursuit of peace and whether Shamir was being unnecessarily stubborn or a tough bargainer. Second, as Peace Now had discovered during previous campaigns, the months before an election are unfavorable for extraparliamentary activities.

Even so, by the spring of 1992 Peace Now began to intensify its activities once more. During 1991 Americans for Peace Now had continued to provide financial support to its colleagues in Israel, enabling Peace Now in Israel to pursue its activities even during bleak periods. Gavri Bar-Gil, the movement's executive director, approached his work with great energy and skill. A professional spokesperson, Eran Hayat, kept the media regularly informed of the movement's activities and its views on political events. Position papers and detailed activity proposals were prepared in advance of meetings, and news of the movement's decisions was quickly relayed to the press.[12]

The Settlements Watch group continued to monitor developments in the occupied territories and issued regular follow-up reports with details on new housing projects and their cost estimates.[13] Reports were also prepared concerning road construction, industrial investments, and infrastructure development.[14]

Several conferences were staged in development towns heavily populated by Mizrachim and Russian immigrants. Bus tours through the occupied territories were organized so that new immigrants could see for themselves how government resources were being used.[15]

Special attention was directed toward settlement activities within the Arab sections of Jerusalem. During the previous decade the settlers had sought to establish a Jewish presence in the Muslim and Christian quarters inside the Old City of Jerusalem.[16] The peace movement considered such activities provocative, and saw the settlers' real objective as the undermining of the tenuous but relatively peaceful coexistence between the three religious communities in the Holy City.

Early in 1992 settlers began occupying houses in the village of Silwan, a neighborhood just south of the Temple Mount where King David had established his capital three thousand years before. A number of Jewish families had lived in this area around the turn of the century, but since the 1920s the place had been inhabited exclusively by Palestinians. Settler groups began to purchase houses in this neighborhood and a number of Jews moved in; some Arab residents were intimidated and left their homes.

Peace Now provided legal help to the Palestinians and organized a demonstration against these activities. Teddy Kollek, the mayor of Jerusalem, participated in the demonstration along with Faisal Husseini. For several weeks the movement also organized an around-the-clock vigil in Silwan.[17]

Peace Now and the Consolidation of the Left

Peace Now was by now a veteran of Knesset election campaigns, and had developed something of a routine method of participating. However, the 1992 campaign was different in one important respect. Soon after the Knesset set the election date, the three parties most closely associated with the peace movement—Ratz, Mapam, and Shinui—decided to unite and form a parliamentary bloc. The coalition was called "Meretz" (Energy). For Peace Now this coalition posed a challenge of sorts insofar as Peace Now's constituency and the prospective constituency of Meretz widely overlapped, obliging the movement to articulate its unique role and specific policies in this new situation.[18]

Peace Now's first reaction was to propose the inclusion of two of its leaders on Meretz's list of candidates for seats in the Knesset,[19] arguing that Meretz would "not be complete without such an addition. The personal and electoral contribution of such central figures will be significant, since it is within their ability to energize Meretz and add a dimension which will make the list more than the sum of the parties which formed it."[20]

This appeal was unsuccessful, possibly due in part to the changing political culture, which was coming to look with disfavor on deal-making in the formation of election lists. Primary elections by the party membership were becoming the rule rather than the exception, leaving no room for individuals associated with Peace Now who were not previously active in one of the established parties.[21]

The unsuccessful outcome of this effort did not prevent the movement from developing a collective position that resembled policies adopted in previous campaigns. A consensus was soon reached that Peace Now would not affiliate with any political party, would remain active as an extraparliamentary entity and continue its own campaign to promote peace, but would support and coordinate with any party that endorsed its own positions on peace. Additionally, Peace Now would encourage its members to become active in political parties as individuals, while maintaining their participation in the movement's committees and councils.[22] Most of Peace Now's activists ultimately joined Meretz and actively campaigned for it.

The movement undertook two additional responsibilities. First, members urged Israeli Arabs to vote. Leaders from Peace Now met with Israeli-Arab leaders, including the Islamic fundamentalists, whose influence had grown inside Israel in recent years and who had won local elections in a few Arab municipalities. Some of these Arab leaders questioned the wisdom of participating in rather than boycotting the elections. The Jewish peaceniks argued that abstention would serve only the interests of the Israeli right, and urged the Arab leaders to encourage their constituents to participate.

The second effort was directed toward the Russian immigrants. Peace Now capitalized on contacts it had established with the immigrants and called on them to support the cause of peace at the polls.[23] During the campaign the movement published an advertisement that asked:

> What the Hell Are These Elections About? These elections are crucial for our future for a simple reason: If you vote for the settlements, you vote for economic depression and the cessation of further immigration. Those who want eternal rule over the territories will get knives, abominable murders and vigilante attacks [by settlers] which are no less abominable. . . . Without peace Israel is incomplete![24]

Rabin—A New Hope?

On June 23, 1992, the Labor Party won an impressive victory in the elections. Likud lost seven seats and Labor gained six. The new Meretz bloc received 12 seats (two more than the bloc's constituent parties had held before), and together with the Arab parties (the Communists and the Arab Democratic Party) the center-left bloc controlled 61 out of the 120 seats. It became inevitable that Yitzhak Rabin, who had replaced Shimon Peres as the head of the Labor Party, would form the new governing coalition.[25]

To avoid becoming too dependent on the votes of the Arab parties, Rabin invited Shas, the orthodox Mizrachi party, to join his coalition.

Rabin was committed to reviving the peace process, and in principle accepted the concept of territorial compromise in exchange for peace. He also promised a reordering of the nation's priorities, which meant among other things making dramatic cuts in the public financing of the settlers in the occupied territories. As far as the Washington bilateral negotiations were concerned, Rabin believed that the previously negotiated terms should not be altered. These terms, which were based on understandings known as the "Madrid formula" articulated in the letters of invitation to the Madrid Conference, excluded the PLO from participating directly in the negotiations and assured that at this stage only an interim agreement for Palestinian self-rule would be negotiated, leaving the ultimate solution for a later date.

Apparently Rabin still believed at this stage that he could avoid dealing with the PLO by empowering Palestinians in the occupied territories. He wanted the Palestinian representatives with whom Israel would negotiate to be chosen though democratic elections by the Palestinians in the West Bank and Gaza Strip. To the dismay of the Palestinians, Rabin kept Elyakim Rubinstein as the head of the delegation in the bilateral negotiations with the Palestinians and Jordanians. Rubinstein, a right-wing orthodox lawyer, was the only carryover from the Israeli delegation heads appointed by Shamir and represented in Palestinian eyes the rejectionist policies of his erstwhile boss.[26]

Despite these signs of continuity, there was in fact a fundamental difference between Rabin and Shamir in terms of their underlying assumptions and intentions. Shamir hoped that very little would come about as a result of the negotiations, and insisted that whatever the results Israel must maintain sovereignty and military control over the occupied territories. In contrast, Rabin sought significant results from the negotiations, including the beginning of Israel's retreat from the occupation, which he believed had become untenable. Rabin announced that within nine months an agreement on Palestinian self-rule would be achieved.[27]

Rabin's commitment to changing the nation's priorities produced immediate results. He halted spending on new settlements in the occupied territories and redirected resources to social and economic problems within the Green Line. This effectively froze many of the construction projects that Ariel Sharon had initiated after the National Unity Government collapsed in 1990. U.S. Secretary of State Baker applauded this move,[28] and President Bush was clearly interested in developing a good relationship with the new Israeli premier. Within weeks of Rabin's election Bush authorized the $10 billion loan guarantees that had been denied to the previous Israeli government. The peace process seemed to be reenergized.

For the peace movement these events appeared to represent the beginning of a new period in Israel's foreign and domestic policies.

> For many of us this was a turning point, a beginning of a new era, a new hope. . . . It became clear that the function of Peace Now had changed. After years of attempting to stop the downhill slide and offering an alternative path, our duty now was to be the voice reflecting public support for steps taken [by the government] that might advance peace.[29]

The presence of well-known peace activists in the new government, including Shulamit Aloni, Yair Tzaban, and Amnon Rubinstein, caused some within the peace movement to feel that extraparliamentary activities had lost their role in the pursuit of peace.

Polls conducted a few weeks after the establishment of the new government showed that public opinion was moving in the direction of compromise. The shift was especially noticeable with regard to the future of the Gaza Strip. In November 1992, 70 percent of those surveyed were prepared to return the entire Gaza Strip to Arab sovereignty, while only 14 percent believed that no part of Gaza should be returned. As far as the West Bank was concerned, 45 percent said that they were still not willing to relinquish any part of it. Despite this apparently high level of opposition to the idea of withdrawal from the West Bank, a gradual softening of attitudes was actually taking place. In similar polls conducted in the early 1970s, nearly 70 percent of those surveyed had rejected the notion of withdrawal. Between 1977 and 1992, when Likud had been in power, the average had consistently surpassed 50 percent.[30]

In polls taken during summer 1993, 71 percent of the Jewish respondents thought that freezing the settlements at that stage would help to advance the peace process, and 74 percent said that they could accept withdrawal from at least some of the territories in the West Bank and Gaza in exchange for peace. In comparison, only 21 percent thought no withdrawal should occur under any circumstances. A majority was still opposed to withdrawal from the Golan Heights.[31]

Revisiting the Territories

Following Labor's election victory most of the peace groups continued to function, but only in a limited capacity. Occasionally some of their leaders were invited by the media to comment on the peace process, but beyond this they were unable to sustain significant public initiatives. The women's groups continued their dialogues with Palestinian women, convening several small public meetings and publishing occasional papers and bulletins, but they too managed to attract only limited attention. As far as the peace process was concerned, attention was focused on the efforts of Rabin and his government.[32]

Nevertheless, in response to right-wing charges that Rabin did not have a "Jewish majority" behind him and therefore had no mandate to proceed with his peace efforts, Peace Now initiated a campaign under the slogan "There Is a Mandate for Peace." Peace Now leaders met with Rabin and urged him to pursue the process vigorously and be as flexible as possible. A meeting was also held with members of the Palestinian delegation to the Washington talks, in which Peace Now encouraged them to continue with the talks and to demonstrate flexibility.[33] During the new government's hundred-day grace period the movement offered "sweeping support for the peace process" and conducted a vigorous information campaign to "highlight the fact that compromises and concession are inevitable."[34]

The most important activities during the first months of Rabin's tenure were conducted by the Settlements Watch group under Amiram Goldblum. Following a review of all construction in the territories, the government decided that despite its intention to halt new construction a total freeze was financially and logistically impractical. Many of the projects reviewed were nearing completion and a decision to abandon them would have resulted in significant financial losses, a sharp increase in unemployment, and a crisis in the housing industry.[35]

The new minister of housing, Fuad Ben-Eliezer, issued orders to cease operations on 3,000 housing units on which the ground had not yet been broken, and on an additional 3,500 at the earth-removal stage. But in all cases in which foundation work had been completed and walls could already be seen above the ground, completion of the construction was permitted.[36] Settlements Watch published a report that showed that an additional 10,000 units were in various advanced stages, and if completed would eventually add 50,000 more settlers to the territories, a 40 percent increase in the settler population.[37]

A Peace Now delegation met with Ben-Eliezer and demanded a deeper freeze because the completion of a further 10,000 houses "would give cause to doubt the government's ability to change the nation's order of priorities." Ben-Eliezer refused the request but assured the group that he would eliminate most of the subsidies the settlers had been receiving.

Members of the delegation felt that despite their disagreement with the minister, "they liked the music of the new government and were impressed by the change of policy in principle."[38] To hold Ben-Eliezer to his promises, Amiram Goldblum prepared a detailed report on the various subsidies and incentives the settlers had been given by the Likud government, and initiated a lobbying effort in the Knesset to assure their cancellation.[39]

Toward the end of 1992 Peace Now published what it called the "Real Map," which identified all Jewish settlements and Palestinian population centers in the occupied territories.[40] At a press conference Peace Now explained that the goal of this publication was to dispel the notion perpetuated by the settler movement that the existing Jewish settlements in the occupied territories made territorial compromise unachievable. Goldblum pointed to the fact that "the settlers constitute no more than 6 percent of the population in the territories. . . . By the end of this year the entire Jewish population in the territories will reach 110,000, while more than two million Palestinians live there."[41] Gavri Bar-Gil argued that during the twenty-five years of occupation nearly $6 billion of public funds had been squandered in the territories. "Considering this enormous investment," Bar-Gil concluded, the settlers' movement had "failed miserably."[42]

The Hamas Deportations

By the end of 1992, a growing number of peace activists had become restless and expressed their concern that "although the new government honestly wants to see progress in the peace process, it fails to take the steps required for real success."[43] The Palestinian leaders also voiced growing disappointment in Rabin's premiership. They felt that Rabin adhered too rigidly to the Madrid formula, and believed that too little had been done to improve living conditions under the occupation.[44]

Attacks on Jews by Palestinian extremists, especially those associated with Izz al-Din al-Qassam, the military arm of Hamas, increased in frequency.[45] Rabin responded to public pressure and on December 17, 1992, following a particularly vicious murder of an Israeli soldier, he ordered the deportation to Lebanon of more than 400 Hamas leaders. According to accounts that leaked from the cabinet meeting in which this decision was reached, all the Meretz ministers supported Rabin's decision, although some expressed reservations.[46]

Feeling that their personal security was threatened by the Hamas attacks, a clear majority of Israelis supported the deportations.[47] They were, however, a blatant violation of international law and human rights. Rabin's decision also forced the PLO to publicly support its rival, Hamas, in the matter, and Arafat ordered the Palestinian delegation to return from Washington and to boycott the negotiations as long as the deportees remained stranded in southern Lebanon. After a while, a growing number of Israelis began to doubt if Israel's actions would actually lead to a reduction of violence, and domestic criticism of the deportations gradually increased. Within the ranks of Meretz, and especially in Ratz, a rebellion of sorts was under way against the party's representatives in the government. Shulamit Aloni publicly expressed regret for her initial support of Rabin's decision, and other leftist MKs voted against the measure when it came before the Knesset.

At first Peace Now was divided on the issue, and the organization's initial response was ambiguous. It published an advertisement titled "Peace Is the Best Punishment for Hamas," in which the movement contended that "a rapid breakthrough in the talks with the Palestinians, Mr. Prime Minister, will be a heavier blow to Hamas than the deportation of its leaders, who will be replaced by others soon."[48] Shortly thereafter a clear consensus of opinion was reached, opposing the deportations, and a demonstration was planned in Tel Aviv for December 26, 1992. The announcement summoning the faithful was headed, "Deportation—No! Talks with the PLO—Yes!" It went on to argue:

> The deportation of hundreds of Palestinians without trial, and therefore without conviction, constitutes a blow to the founding principles of the State of Israel and to basic human rights. The deportation is an act of political folly that may severely damage Israel in the long run. The deportation will not prevent bloodshed. Rather, it will deepen hostility and accelerate the conflict between the two peoples.[49]

On December 26, amid torrential rain, Tzali Reshef spoke to a relatively small gathering of demonstrators. "The deportation is a sin whether it is perpetrated by Shamir or by Rabin and our own friends. The mark of Cain was branded on our forehead. Our friends [in the government] betrayed the values we believe in."[50] The main purpose of the demonstration was to call on the government to cut its losses, return the deportees, and immediately resume the peace negotiations with the Palestinians, and Peace Now believed that this could best be achieved by opening a direct channel of communication with the PLO.[51]

The demonstration did not equal previous efforts in size or impact. Janet Aviad explained that "people from Meretz pressured us not to do it. There is no doubt that the bad weather contributed to the small turnout. But a more important factor was the reluctance of large numbers of people who opposed the deportation to come out and march against their own parties."[52]

Although lively debates within Peace Now were commonplace, they became more impassioned when representatives of the peace movement's own constituency served as ministers inside the government.[53] A meeting between Peace Now leaders and Meretz MKs witnessed heated exchanges, but both sides wanted to heal the rift created by the deportations as quickly as possible. A forum was established to facilitate ongoing consultations between the movement and those who served in the government and Knesset. Gavri Bar-Gil summarized the situation: "Like in a family we quarreled, but did not divorce."[54]

The movement now sought to regroup and develop a cohesive strategy for the months ahead, and on January 16, 1993, a general meeting of the active members convened at Kibbutz Ga'ash. The tenor of the debate indicated that the peace movement believed it still had an important role to play. Tzali Reshef pointed out:

> This may be the best government we can expect, but let them not think we are in their pockets. We shall judge them according to their actions, not by their ideological affiliation. . . . We have to function as the government's watchdog, and go out to the streets whenever we feel that the decision makers deviate from the road of peace.[55]

Janet Aviad told a journalist, "Our demonstration [against the deportation] was an important signal for those who did not understand our position; we are not dependent on anybody, we are committed to nobody but to the peace process."[56]

Palestinian leaders were initially shocked by the support for the deportations by members of Meretz. Shulamit Aloni, Dedi Zucker, and Yossi Sarid were closely associated with Peace Now, and the Palestinian leadership remained distant for a while.[57] But the critical position Peace Now eventually took toward the deportations helped to ease the tension.[58] A U.S.-mediated compromise was eventually reached, and Rabin announced that Israel would permit the return of some of the deportees immediately and that the others would be allowed to return at the end of the year.[59] Two months later, and after some additional symbolic concessions had been made, the PLO agreed to return to the peace talks at the end of April 1993.

But as soon as the delegations reconvened in Washington it became apparent that they remained at an impasse.[60] During April, May, and June 1993 Peace Now undertook a new public relations campaign. Called

"A New Peace Initiative Now!" this campaign was fired with a sense of urgency because the right wing, now in opposition for the first time in fifteen years, was organizing its own demonstrations, which spoke to the anger and fear felt by many Israelis as a result of Hamas's campaign of terror.[61] The Peace Now campaign aspired "to paint the country with peace." "Mandate for Peace" and other slogans were posted in cities and on highways; information tables were set up in town squares; and thousands of postcards bearing a picture of a dove were mailed to the prime minister, who was asked "to act without further delay to advance the peace process for which you have received a mandate, which includes the recognition that peace requires territorial concessions."

A "Peace Tent" was erected near the prime minister's residence in Jerusalem. Prominent personalities, including the prime minister himself, visited the tent. Rabin's visit gave the activists a sense of satisfaction and accomplishment. Despite its criticism of some of his policies, the movement recognized and applauded the prime minister's genuine desire to advance the peace process. For the activists, who for fifteen years had been called "traitors" and "deviants" by successive Likud governments and their supporters, the acceptance and legitimacy offered by the new government was a welcome change.

"A New Peace Initiative Now!" was launched with a march in Jerusalem and the publication of a new position paper.[62] The paper expressed the "feeling shared by a segment of the public, that looking back on the first ten months of Yitzhak Rabin's government a great opportunity might have been missed. . . . Rabin's promise to achieve an interim arrangement with the Palestinians within 6–9 months now seems to be a dream." The position paper also recommended that "Israel should negotiate with Palestinian representatives who are acceptable to all Palestinians, and lift its objection to the participation of PLO representatives in the talks."[63]

As of spring 1993 Rabin showed no sign of heeding any such advice. It was equally clear that Arafat too would not give the negotiators a green light to reach an agreement under the Madrid framework, instead repeatedly adding more conditions and demands that only impeded progress. The peace activists grew ever more frustrated. Despite the legitimacy accorded the movement by the new political establishment (and the fact that many of their friends were now serving in the government), the movement's influence on decision making apparently remained marginal. Peace Now began publicly to criticize Rabin for "adhering to an unnecessarily narrow interpretation of the Madrid formula.

[He] adheres to the positions previously held by Shamir, and does not dare to introduce new initiatives which could offer a chance for peace."[64] The movement did not know that even as it was chastising Rabin for his timidity another drama was unfolding that would yield results beyond the peace activists' wildest expectations.

A Second Track in Oslo

Early in December 1992 Yair Hirschfeld, a professor of Middle Eastern history at Haifa University, met in a London hotel with Ahmed Suleiman Karia, the head of the PLO Finance Department better known by his nom de guerre, Abu Alaa. The meeting was proposed by Hanan Ashrawi, then the spokeswoman of the Palestinian delegation to the Washington talks, and mediated by Terje Rød Larsen, a Norwegian scholar whom Hirschfeld had met the previous year when they were conducting research in the West Bank and Gaza. Hirschfeld and Abu Alaa agreed to try to formulate a declaration of principles that would be acceptable to both sides. Hirschfeld called on his friend Ron Pundik, a young historian at Tel Aviv University, to assist him.[65]

It was hard to believe that out of this meeting in London involving an academic and a relatively junior official on the Palestinian side something big would happen.[66] But Hirschfeld had three important advantages: he was a scholar with a fair knowledge of the political and psychological conditions of the peace process; he already had experience in dialogues with Palestinians; and he was well connected to the Israeli establishment. Hirschfeld was not a prominent leader in the peace movement, but he regularly attended Peace Now meetings and demonstrations. During the early 1990s he had become involved in IPCRI's Round Table Forum on Political Strategy, which was comprised of Palestinians and Israelis and produced papers intended to advance the peace process.[67]

The idea to formulate a mutually acceptable declaration of principles was not unprecedented. As far back as 1977 Herbert Kelman, Stephen P. Cohen, Issam Sartawi, and others had engaged in similar efforts,[68] and as recently as August 1990 eighteen members of the Knesset had signed a joint declaration with Palestinian leaders from the occupied territories.[69] In July 1991 Hanna Siniora and Moshe Amirav, at the time co-chairs of IPCRI, also signed a "Framework for a Public Peace Process" in a conference held at Stanford University's Center for Conflict Resolution.[70] However, whereas previous attempts had usually been undertaken by Israelis who opposed the ruling Likud government, Hirschfeld had close ties to official Israeli diplomacy.

Hirschfeld had been a member of the Labor Party for many years and was active in its different dovish circles. It was in these circles that he met Yossi Beilin, a confidant of Shimon Peres. Immediately after his meeting with Abu Alaa, Hirschfeld called Beilin, who happened to be in London at the time. Beilin encouraged him to continue to explore the new channel. But Beilin could not yet give him the authority to speak on behalf of the government of Israel.

Larsen was connected to Norway's Foreign Ministry through his wife, Mona Juul, a professional diplomat, and was thus able to obtain facilities away from the public eye in which the talks could take place. At this stage Johan Joergen Holst, Norway's minister of foreign affairs, took charge of planning fourteen additional meetings, which were held in various locations around Oslo over the next eight months. Some of the initial meetings took place at Borregard Manor, the summer lodge of Norwegian kings during the Middle Ages.

Prime Minister Rabin and Foreign Minister Peres were kept informed of the developments in the Oslo channel, and Hirschfeld regularly prepared written reports for Beilin.[71] After a couple of preparatory meetings between Hirschfeld, Pundik, and Abu Alaa (who was escorted by two other PLO officials from Tunis), the group began formulating a document. The fact that the Palestinians were willing to accept a gradual approach to self-rule—one that involved implementing the agreement in Gaza and Jericho first—appealed to Peres, who had spoken about "Gaza first" for some time.[72] It was also understood by all parties that the PLO was directly and officially involved in these negotiations. The Israelis were assured that Arafat personally had given Abu Alaa the green light to advance the negotiations.[73]

By the end of April 1993 the Oslo group produced a draft document that received enough interest in Jerusalem and Tunis to warrant the upgrading of their representation. "The role of those who started the Oslo link was that of a scout," Beilin recalled. "They had to test the seriousness of those who were sent to talk to them and the seriousness of those who had sent them. Once it became clear that the talks were turning into real negotiations, we had to send official negotiators."[74]

The preliminary stage handled by the freelance peace advocates was over. Uri Savir, the director general of the Ministry of Foreign Affairs and a seasoned diplomat, and Yoel Singer, a legal adviser to the ministry and a confidant of the prime minister, arrived in Oslo in early May to take over the negotiations. The PLO sent Abu Mazen, a close confidant of Arafat's, and senior members of its Executive Committee. The Oslo track had now become an official, albeit secret, diplomatic effort. The time had come for Arafat and Rabin to carefully examine the fine print being drafted in Oslo. At this stage, "legal details and technical minutiae of implementation became the main subject matter."[75]

Gush Shalom

The political atmosphere in the Middle East became strained just as the Oslo negotiations—still shrouded in total secrecy—were approaching a successful conclusion. Toward the end of July tensions along Israel's northern border heated up. In response to a number of attacks perpetrated by Hizbullah from Lebanon, the IDF initiated a campaign of artillery and aerial bombing of targets north of the "security belt." The operation was named "Din ve Heshbon" (Settling Accounts) and received widespread support from the Israeli public, fed up with the recurrent attacks by the various militant Shi'a groups operating in Lebanon. All the Meretz ministers in the cabinet voted in favor of the operation, though they cautioned against unwarranted escalation and the use of ground forces.

Thousands of artillery shells were fired north into villages under the control of Hizbullah, and Katyusha rockets were fired at Jewish settlements in northern Israel in response. Tens of thousands of Lebanese civilians fled to the north to escape the shelling. Israel threatened to continue the barrages unless Hizbullah and its Syrian hosts provided assurances that they would stop firing Katyusha rockets into Israel.[76]

The peace movement felt obliged to make a statement concerning the new circumstances. Characteristically, however, the leadership of Peace Now had difficulties achieving consensus and ultimately settled for an equivocal and ambiguous statement:

> Peace Now expresses its identification with those who live along the northern border. The movement calls on the government to do its utmost to assure their peace and security. Nevertheless, Peace Now warns [the government] against being dragged once again into the Lebanese quagmire, and states that true security for the northern border is linked to an eventual breakthrough in the peace negotiations with Syria.[77]

This lukewarm response left a number of people on the left dissatisfied—the same people, by and large, who had formed the various "committees" in previous years and who perceived themselves as the radical wing of the peace movement.[78] Uri Avneri, Matti Peled, Michel Warschawski, and other activists to the left of Peace Now, who had remained relatively quiet over the past two years, had recently organized a new group they called "Gush Shalom" (Peace Bloc). In their opinion Peace Now had been coopted by the Labor-Meretz coalition, and they saw the need for a genuinely independent peace lobby willing to criticize the Rabin government for its procrastination and provocations.

At a demonstration Gush Shalom organized early in June at the Erez checkpoint on the northern border of the Gaza Strip to protest the two-month closure of the territories, Uri Avneri told a journalist that "Gush Shalom was formed to put the peace movement back on the street and give the left a sense of direction." The journalist, though, reported that "the mood was far more like that of a reunion of old comrades from bygone struggles than the angry protest its organizers intended."[79]

On July 26, 1993, a small group of these activists demonstrated in front of the Press Club in Tel Aviv against the Israeli strikes in Lebanon. "The forty or so participants could hardly fill the cafeteria," observed a journalist. But they were the only group that publicly opposed the operation in Lebanon and that demanded a complete withdrawal of Israeli forces from Lebanon.[80] As the plight of tens of thousands of Lebanese civilians worsened, opposition within Peace Now also grew.

One week after the beginning of the Din ve Heshbon operation, Peace Now organized a vigil in front of the prime minister's residence in Jerusalem, distributing flyers that called for an end to the action in Lebanon. The language of this flyer was less ambivalent than the movement's earlier statement.

> Stop the Destruction, Renew the Momentum of Peace Now! The Northern settlements must be defended. The Galilee must be peaceful. But defense of the north does not mean expulsion of civilians from their homes. The defense of Kiryat Shmonah does not mean the destruction of Nabatiya. Scorched land and devastated villages will not guarantee a peace settlement. Expulsion will not bring peace. The key to the security of the Galilee lies in rapid progress towards a negotiated peace.[81]

Tears of Joy

By the middle of August the crisis had passed. Warren Christopher, the new U.S. secretary of state, mediated an agreement by which the Syrians agreed to restrain militias operating in territory under its control from attacking Israel proper and Israel agreed to cease its shelling.[82] With this agreement concluded, attention could now return to the peace process. On August 20, 1993, after numerous drafts and revisions, an agreed-upon version of the Declaration of Principles was initialed by Savir, Singer, and Abu Alaa in the presence of Shimon Peres and Abu Mazen in Oslo. Holst added his signature as a witness. The document was signed on the same table on which the document of Norway's separation from Sweden had been signed in 1905. A low-key but festive ceremony followed in the guest house of the Norwegian government. Mona Juul recalled, "All of us nearly cried. It was almost like living in a movie we had written ourselves."[83]

The time had come to bring the Americans into the game. Warren Christopher, who apparently had for some time known something of what was going on in Oslo, was fully briefed on August 27 by Peres and Holst.[84] President Bill Clinton gave the process his immediate support with the understanding that the formal accord would be signed in Washington. At the beginning of September the breakthrough was made public. For the first time the entire peace movement joined hands with the government in a major demonstration to celebrate peace. Peace Now, Gush Shalom, Meimad (the moderate orthodox party), Meretz, and the Labor Party planned a gala gathering to celebrate peace.

At this point the Oslo agreement was little more than a document with the potential to become an interim arrangement to facilitate the transfer of the Gaza Strip and Jericho to Palestinian self-rule, and to initiate a process leading to limited measures of self-rule for the Palestinians in the West Bank. It was hoped that this first step would be followed by additional negotiations and agreements in the future. For the Israeli public, however, these events signified the first steps on the road to reconciliation and peace. For the peace movement even this modest achievement appeared to be a messianic miracle. On September 4, 1993, a festive crowd poured into the Tel Aviv central square by the tens of thousands to celebrate.

The square in front of the Tel Aviv municipality, the traditional site of the peace movement's demonstrations and protests for the past fifteen years, now witnessed an entirely different event. "This was a real happiness. People cried of joy," wrote Yael Gvirtz, a journalist who had attended many of the peace movement's activities.

This was the biggest reunion the square ever witnessed. Those who were there fifteen years ago at the founding demonstration of Peace Now came back with their children. They came back from the places into which they had faded away in the course of these long years, dismayed, eroded, frightened by the bomb that killed Emil Gruenzweig. . . . This was not a demonstration of the left, nor was it a demonstration organized by professionals. . . . This was truly an eruption of joy of the young. It was an early peace festival which only the young, free from the burdens of historic experience, could afford. They danced for hours in mixed circles, joining hands and legs. . . . Many times in the past [the veteran activists] went through the lines of thugs who cursed them, spat at them, and threw rotten tomatoes and orange peels at them. This time they could stand there and watch their children dance.[85]

The ecstatic crowd cheered Minister Shulamit Aloni when she said, "No more parents will go weeping after the coffins of their sons." Amos Oz closed his remarks by saying, "And death shall rule no more.[86]

A Handshake After All

The key to understanding the success at Oslo must be found primarily in the shift of attitudes of both Yasser Arafat and Yitzhak Rabin. In the wake of the Gulf War and his pro-Saddam orientation, Arafat found himself and his organization facing apparently insurmountable political and financial problems. He had lost the political and financial support of many Arab states, most notably Saudi Arabia and the Gulf states, and the PLO was forced to dramatically reduce its expenditures. Many thought Arafat's tenure as the head of the PLO had finally come to an end. Arafat managed, however, to maintain the loyalty of the Palestinian leadership from the West Bank and Gaza Strip, and despite mounting challenges to his leadership from the radical left and the Islamic fundamentalists he remained the only one who could speak for his people.

Though the PLO was recognized by the United Nations and many other states as the representative of the Palestinian people, the United States and Israel had consistently refused to officially recognize it as such. In Oslo Israel offered Arafat this recognition in exchange for his agreement to most of Rabin's demands. Israel's recognition of the PLO was included in the Oslo draft, and was formally transmitted in an exchange of letters between Arafat and Rabin.[87]

For his part, Rabin had for years adamantly refused to provide Arafat and the PLO with the recognition they sought.[88] Through the Jordanian Option and later through his plan for general elections in the occupied territories, Rabin had repeatedly sought to exclude the PLO from the peace process. However, as the months passed without any tangible results at the negotiating table in Washington, Rabin accepted the fact that despite Arafat's political, economic, and military weakness he still held the keys to a Palestinian-Israeli peace. As the negotiations in Washington languished at the end of 1992 Shimon Peres admitted, "The bottom line was Arafat. If we did not make direct contact with Yasser Arafat the negotiations would remain at a standstill."[89]

In early 1993, when he first learned of the Oslo opening, Rabin was already considering a number of ways to establish a secret channel to the PLO.[90] He was now willing to offer the PLO an agreement based essentially upon the Madrid formula: a phased retreat of Israeli forces from the occupied territories, with a period of experimental autonomous rule implemented initially in the Gaza Strip and Jericho. This would give the PLO a chance to govern Palestinian affairs and reduce Palestinian terror, while building confidence between the parties that could contribute to a broader peace process. Rabin viewed a retreat from Gaza not as a concession to the Palestinians but as a positive advantage for Israel, which would no longer have to use its soldiers to police that unruly region. The success of this experiment was dependent on the ability of a Palestinian governing authority to effectively administer the affairs of Gaza after Israel withdrew. This included ensuring that order was maintained and no threat was posed to Israel's security. The PLO was the only partner that had the potential ability to accomplish this, and Arafat appeared willing to take over on Rabin's terms.

At the beginning of July 1993 Rabin still publicly rejected the proposal put forward by Meretz ministers to open a direct channel with the PLO. "Arafat is the only boss in the negotiations on behalf of the Palestinians," argued Yossi Sarid. "There is no sense in talking with the Palestinians unless we talk to Arafat."[91] Fuad Ben-Eliezer expressed in a cabinet meeting what Rabin and Peres had already realized: "I came to the conclusion that Arafat is the only source of authority [among the Palestinians]. He is the one who brakes the wheels, and he is the only one who can loosen them up and make them move again."[92] Less than two months later Rabin accepted these conclusions, and his subsequent actions permanently changed the course of Palestinian-Israeli relations.

Recognizing the PLO was one thing for Rabin; meeting Arafat face-to-face was something quite different. President Clinton wanted the formal signing ceremony to take place at the White House. Although they were excluded from the last chapter of the drama, the Americans had played a vital role in the search for peace over the previous five decades and remained vital to the process in the future. The White House staff wanted to

organize a grand ceremony similar to the one that was staged for the signing of the Camp David Accords. Rabin, however, preferred a far more modest
event. "There is no need for a demonstrative ceremony," insisted one of
Rabin's aides. But the drama of this moment could not be contained.[93]

On September 13, 1993, on the White House lawn, the letters expressing the mutual recognition of the State of Israel and the PLO were
exchanged. Shimon Peres and Mahmoud Abbas (a senior aide to Arafat
better known as Abu Mazen) signed the Declaration of Principles.[94]
Yitzhak Rabin, who had spent most of his life leading soldiers into battle,
and Yasser Arafat, who had spent most of his life sending guerrillas
against the State of Israel, stood side by side and shook hands. Rabin
seemed uncomfortable and uneasy about this gesture, while Arafat appeared to bask in the glory of the moment.

In terms of Israeli politics, Rabin had taken the greatest risks in reaching this point, and he would be the one to shoulder the responsibility for
better or worse. Shimon Peres had played a vital role in bringing the
Oslo negotiations to a successful conclusion, and he also deserved much
of the credit for this achievement. For the first time in twenty years
these two political rivals put their differences aside and worked together
for the purpose of peace. Israeli wits joked that the next handshake ceremony on the White House lawn would be between Peres and Rabin.

The White House ceremony marked a dramatic new beginning in the
Arab-Israeli conflict—or perhaps more accurately in its resolution. Both
the Palestinians and Israelis must have recognized that many more frustrating days of negotiations awaited them as they sought to implement
the Declaration of Principles. Even so, the relationship between Israelis
and Palestinians had clearly taken a radically new turn. Things could
never be the same again.

The founders and activists of Peace Now were pleased when both
Time and *Newsweek* printed a two-page spread featuring a photograph
of a huge banner from an earlier demonstration that read "Peace Now!"[95]
One journalist called it, "Peace Now's Golden Hour."[96] On September
13, Palestinian leaders and leaders from the Israeli peace movement
met in the same room in the American Colony Hotel in Jerusalem in
which they had held so many of their earlier dialogues to watch the
White House ceremony on television. Ziyad Abu-Zayyad, Hanna Siniora,
Uri Avneri, Dedi Zucker, Shlomo Elbaz, Latif Dori, Tzali Reshef, Janet
Aviad, and many others who reached out to each other a long time ago,
once again huddled in the ornate room. They could hear the jubilant

Palestinian crowds at the nearby Orient House, which unofficially became the seat of the Palestinian authority in Jerusalem.

Avishai Margalit said the event reminded him of November 29, 1947, when as a child he ran throughout the night with the blue-and-white flag that became the flag of the Jewish State. Dedi Zucker addressed the assembled Palestinians as the future members of a Palestinian parliament. "Who could believe that Palestinian children could run in the streets of Jerusalem with PLO flags without being attacked with tear gas by the Israeli police." A reporter who covered the event wrote:

> When Rabin shook Arafat's hand I thought for a minute that the ceiling in the room would blow up into the air from joy. Somebody opened a bottle of champagne and doused the sweating heads of those assembled with the sparkling liquid. It looked as if a genie was unleashed from his bottle and nobody knew what the genie might do next. . . . Many cried when they all sang 'We shall overcome.'[97]

Conclusion

Not an End

A few days after the handshake on the White House lawn, Peace Now announced a new initiative designed to counter the protests of Israeli right-wing groups bitterly opposed to the Oslo agreement. While the right has since sought to sabotage the peace efforts by different forms of protest and by further expansion of existing settlements, the peace camp on its part has insisted that sooner or later Jewish settlements will have to be cleared out from the areas designated for Palestinian self-rule. Some of the more extreme elements on the right tried to subvert the peace process by reverting to illegal activities, which climaxed in the assassination of Prime Minister Yitzhak Rabin on November 5, 1995, during a major peace rally assembled, as always, in the municipal square in Tel Aviv. As of the time of this writing—December 1995—despite the shock that engulfed the nation with the murder of Rabin, the strife between the peace groups and the settlers shows no signs of abating.

Since 1994, the radical left-wing group Gush Shalom has also intensified its activities. Gush Shalom harshly criticized the Rabin government for procrastinating in the talks on the implementation of the Declaration of Principles—which dragged on for eight months before the agreement on the evacuation of Gaza and Jericho was signed in Cairo in May 1994—and has denounced the delays in the implementation of the second stage agreed on in Oslo, by which the Israeli forces are to redeploy and retreat from all centers of Palestinian population to allow free and fair elections to the governing body of the Palestinian authority to take place. The senior reserve officers' Council for Peace and Security has also resumed its activities to support Rabin's peace efforts, seeking to counter an attempt by Likud and other right-wing parties to delegitimize the Oslo accord and undercut efforts to reach an agreement with Syria and Lebanon.

The peace treaty between Israel and Jordan, signed in October 1994 with great fanfare in the presence of President Clinton near Aqaba and Eilat, generated a few days of optimism and joy, but was soon overshadowed by increasing violence. During 1994 and 1995 the military arms of the two most radical Muslim fundamentalist Palestinian movements, Hamas and Jihad al-Islami, both of which continue to advocate armed struggle against Israel until its total liquidation, used young zealots as "human bombs." Carrying explosives, these suicide bombers detonated themselves in the midst of Israeli crowds, typically blowing up buses in the centers of cities populated by Jews. These acts of mass terror were countered by attacks perpetrated by Jewish vigilantes, the latter coming to an appalling head with the massacre on February 25, 1994, of some fifty Palestinians in the midst of their prayers in the Tomb of the Fathers in Hebron.

Nevertheless, after long delays and difficult negotiations, a further agreement between Israel and the Palestinian National Authority was reached. The new agreement, known as "Oslo B," was signed at the White House on September 27, 1995, two years after the first handshake between Rabin and Arafat. The new agreement defines in great detail the modalities of implementation of the second phase of the establishment of Palestinian self-rule, as agreed by the parties in Oslo and incorporated into the 1993 Declaration of Principles. These arrangements provide for the retreat of Israeli forces from most centers of Palestinian population in the West Bank, general elections for the council of the Palestinian Authority, and the establishment of self-rule. Despite its traumatic impact, the murder of Prime Minister Rabin has not disrupted the implementation of the Oslo B agreement. As these lines are written, the process has already started and the redeployment of Israeli forces in the West Bank is well under way. Yet, as agreed in Oslo, no Jewish settlers have been or will be removed from the occupied territories during this phase, and the complex negotiation of the final status of the Palestinian entity still lies ahead.

Clearly, the story of the Israeli peace movement is also far from complete. Nevertheless, several factors persuaded me to end this study with the Rabin-Arafat handshake in Washington, D.C. In the first place, subsequent events are too recent and the peace process too fluid and uncertain to permit even the limited analytical and historical perspective available to me for the period up to September 1993. Second, every book must of course end somewhere, and because the peace process may well take many more years to reach its conclusion, I decided to end at a point where, for the first time, some promising signs of an ending were visible.

A third rationale for my decision has to do with the nature of the peace process. The term "peace process" has often been used in the case of the Middle East conflict in a sweeping and undifferentiated fashion. However, when one looks at the cases of the peace treaty between Israel and Egypt and the agreement in principle between Israel and the Palestinians, three distinct phases can be seen. Although these phases certainly overlap, each has its own essential logic, method, and participants. In the first phase, despite a few secret, exploratory meetings by officials from both sides, no formal negotiations take place between the adversaries, and violence persists. During this stage reconciliation attempts are undertaken primarily by nongovernmental organizations and third-party mediators, frequently in opposition to the wishes of the political leadership of the antagonists.

In the second phase, official negotiations begin in which the principles that will govern the reconciliation process are negotiated by officials of the respective parties. These negotiations are accompanied by additional mediation efforts by third parties and further activities by nongovernmental groups, the latter aiming to create public support for the prospective conciliation and encouraging or criticizing the government as events warrant. This phase ends with some formal accord that requires more negotiations on the exact meaning of the principles agreed to and the modalities of their implementation.

In the third phase, implementation of earlier agreements begins to take shape on the ground. As this phase unfolds, the role of nongovernmental organizations and third-party mediators diminishes. Although peace groups continue to play an important function in fostering popular support for the process, the methods they employ are necessarily quite different from those used in the first and second phases, when street protests and parliamentary lobbying activities are the order of the day.

In the Egypt-Israel case the first phase ended with Sadat's visit to Jerusalem. The second phase ended with the Camp David Accords and the subsequent peace treaty signed in Washington in 1979. The implementation period lasted from 1978 to 1983, and ended with Israel's final withdrawal from the Sinai Peninsula. The peace movement was very busy during the first and second phases, but was not particularly active during the implementation. This can partially be attributed to the fact that at the implementation stage those who resisted the process had to confront the government rather than the peace movement. It seemed wiser to the peace

activists to let the rejectionists and the authorities battle between themselves, and to leave it to the government to enforce its own decisions and
international undertakings. The fact that the peace movement remained
on the sidelines during the evacuation of Yamit was not an accident.

Vis-à-vis the Palestinians, the process was more complex because
the formal recognition of the PLO as the legitimate partner for negotiations came only at a later stage. However, as far as Palestinian-autho-
rized delegates are concerned, the first phase ended in Madrid, where
the second phase was initiated and open negotiations between the official representatives of the parties were undertaken in bilateral talks in
Washington. The Oslo agreement and the signing of the Declaration of
Principles between the Israeli prime minister and the chairman of the
PLO have ushered in the third phase. The interim nature of the agreements reached so far, however, leaves much still to be negotiated. Negotiations on an ultimate settlement will not begin until 1996. Until this
happens the peace movement will certainly have an important role to
play in preparing public opinion for the painful concessions that will
surely be necessary. Meanwhile, the implementation of the agreements
already reached on full self-rule in Gaza and Jericho, and the more limited self-rule on the West Bank, is encountering many difficulties and
delays. Therefore, though the center stage at this third stage is occupied
by officials of the parties, nongovernmental groups remain active.

The intricate negotiations with the PLO on the implementation of the
Declaration of Principles have caused considerable debate within Israel
and among the Palestinians. The peace movement has participated actively in this debate, seeking to shape public opinion and encourage the
government to honor its commitments; nevertheless, with the government and a large part of the public supportive of ongoing peace efforts,
the movement's role has been significantly reduced and the methods available to it limited. Public energy for major demonstrations is largely absent, and shifting circumstances have necessitated constant reconsid-
eration of what messages the movement should broadcast. Despite its
many activities, the peace movement appears to the Israeli public, and
especially to the Palestinians, to lack resolve and clarity of purpose.[1]

A Quarter Century of the Struggle for Peace

How this new chapter in the story of the peace movement unfolds must
be left to future historians to describe and explain. Here, we must content

ourselves with the story so far. Though incomplete, it is already a long and complex tale, covering more than a quarter century and involving a large, colorful, and varied cast.

From its earliest beginnings, the Zionist movement hoped to achieve its goals without the use of violence, and Zionist leaders often spoke of peace and friendship with the Arab inhabitants of Palestine. Such peaceful protestations, though no doubt sincere, amounted to little more than pious hopes and wishful thinking, however. Because the Zionists never gave up their aspirations to concentrate millions of Jews in Palestine and to turn the country into a Jewish homeland, Palestinians understandably heard hypocrisy ringing in the Zionists' talk of peaceful coexistence.

Notwithstanding the efforts of a few brave but essentially marginal figures on the Israeli landscape in the first two decades of the State of Israel's existence, one can speak of a genuine peace movement in Israel only in the wake of the Six Day War. Not until 1967 did some segments of the Israeli public arrive at the conclusion that, at least in territorial terms, Israel had gained more than was wise to maintain and that land should now be traded for peace. We have seen how the Labor Party struggled with this issue in the years after 1967, how intellectuals working within the framework of the Movement for Peace and Security preached peace as the highest national priority, how individual crusaders such as Uri Avneri and Lova Eliav fought relentlessly to change the public mood. We have also noted how Arab intransigence, a growing Jewish territorial appetite, and a prevailing pessimism toward the prospects for peace made these gallant efforts futile.

Egypt, it seems, had first to regain its dignity by a daring crossing of the Suez Canal before it was able to dare another crossing of the lines of enmity. For Israelis, the arrival of President Sadat in Jerusalem demonstrated fully for the first time that peace was, after all, possible. The reaction to Sadat's visit gave birth to Peace Now and a mass peace movement in Israel. Despite its ups and downs, that movement was never to disappear from the Israeli political arena.

We have recorded three peaks in the development of the Israeli peace movement: the first, during 1978 and 1979, in which peace with Egypt was the focus; the second, during 1982 and 1983, in which protests at the Israeli military involvement in Lebanon took center stage; and the third, during 1988 and 1989, when the call for the recognition of the rights of the Palestinians to self-determination, for negotiations with the PLO, and for an end to the cruel suppression of the Intifada led a majority of Israelis to welcome the beginnings of a process of reconciliation.

Beginning in Madrid, that process then moved to Washington before finally arriving in Oslo.

We have seen how the peace movement fragmented along fault lines of ideology, temperament, tactics, and constituencies. We have also tried to show how the proliferation of groups and the growing variety of activities might have generated acrimony and rivalry but was vital to the larger movement's vibrancy, allowing diverse voices to join in their own key the chorus of protest. At its peaks of popularity, the movement managed to mobilize more than 200,000 participants—in Israeli terms, a most impressive number. In retrospect, Peace Now was clearly almost always the major player within the movement. Though harshly criticized from its left and right sides and often tormented by its own hesitancy, Peace Now's determination to remain inside the fort of Israeli society and pursue a moderate course gave it both its longevity and its ability to serve as the stage on which all other peace groups could meet. But while Peace Now was thus able to survive and often to prosper in terms of political stature, how far was it able to affect political reality?

The Effect of the Peace Movement

Did the peace movement have a significant impact on the peace process and on Israeli politics in general? The movement's veterans firmly believe this was the case and cite instances in which their influence was recognized. They point to the remarks made by Prime Minister Menachem Begin, who said that during the difficult negotiations at Camp David he remembered the large demonstration Peace Now organized to bid him farewell and encourage him to bring back peace. They recall the effects of the largest demonstration ever held in Israel, organized to protest Israel's involvement in the massacre at Sabra and Shatila, and a significant factor in the government's decision to establish the Kahan Commission of Inquiry that eventually led to the dismissal of Ariel Sharon as minister of defense.[2] Other veteran activists point to the restraining influence that B'tselem and other human rights organizations exerted on the conduct of the security agencies in the territories during the Intifada.[3] None of these assertions, however, can be proven conclusively, for other factors obviously influenced outcomes.

Begin's willingness to sign the Camp David Accords, for instance, was inspired not least by his personal desire to achieve peace with Israel's most powerful enemy. A withdrawal from Sinai, Begin may also have calculated, might be exchanged for a free hand in the remaining occupied territories. American pressure, the advice and pressure of Ezer Weizman and Moshe Dayan, and the fact that the Sinai was not viewed by Israelis as a part of the Holy Land were also significant factors in his decision. Nevertheless, it seems reasonable to conclude that at a minimum the peace movement's efforts influenced the environment in which these critical decisions were made.

Although the peace movement had little or no chance of shifting the opinions of diehard chauvinists and religiously motivated expansionists, it may well have influenced the less doctrinaire majority. Most Israelis were always divided in their own hearts, and kept swinging between a natural desire to end the conflict and disbelief in the possibility of achieving real reconciliation with the Palestinians. For this vast "middle," the fact that the peace movement continued to articulate the optimistic view and managed to mobilize many prominent Israelis who could not be dismissed as naive or disloyal helped many of these wavering Israelis to move toward the cause of peace once conditions permitted and political leaders dared to change their policies.

Hard political and military facts always had the lion's share in shaping public opinion. Thus, the cruel realization that the war of 1973 and the futile invasion of Lebanon in 1982 brought home to most Israelis—that even in winning a war Israel could lose, and that the broader conflict would endure—led many Israelis toward a more rational understanding of their situation. The Intifada and the inability of the Israeli forces to suppress it, together with the growing moral unease felt by many Israelis, were essential preconditions for the initiatives undertaken by Shamir in 1991 and by Rabin and Peres in 1993. Even so, the fact that the peace movement was always present to articulate in simple terms alternative peace policies made it easier for mainstream Israelis to move toward an acceptance of the need to negotiate and compromise with their Arab neighbors. In this way the peace movement had a far-reaching effect on public opinion, and through it on the decision-making elite. Since 1993, when peace activists listen to the radio or television and hear government leaders use the very same arguments they had for years rejected when propounded by the peace movement, the activists can surely feel a sense of satisfaction and reasonably claim to have had some effect on national policy.

The Israeli peace movement also played an important role in shaping the political and psychological conditions that prevailed on the Palestinian side. For many years, the Palestinians, like the Israelis, believed that there was "nobody to talk to." The intensive contacts that growing numbers of Palestinian peace seekers had with growing numbers of Zionist peaceniks changed this perception on both sides. As Haider Abdul-Shafi made clear in his remarks at the opening of the Madrid conference, such contacts opened the hearts and minds of many Palestinian leaders to the possibility—indeed the advisability—of a compromise solution. On the Israeli side, dialogue with the Palestinians helped the Israeli peace activists, and through them a growing segment of the Israeli public, to better understand the "enemy" and the inner workings of the Palestinian national movement.

While the peace movement thus exerted, albeit gradually and often indirectly, real influence on the Palestinian and Israeli publics at large, it should be pointed out that most peace activists were motivated less by pragmatic, political considerations than by their desire for personal fulfillment. One activist who on many occasions followed the movement into the hills of the West Bank and marched time and again through the streets of Tel Aviv and Jerusalem said, "I could never tell [if we made a difference]. But I never came out because of the effect it might have on the objective reality. I just could not sit back and do nothing. It helped change my own subjective reality."[4]

Perhaps this comment establishes some criteria by which the peace movement can be better understood. The movement's activities always primarily reflected the mood, values, and attitudes held by a significant minority within Israeli society, rather than a grand design for reshaping Israeli politics. Particular activities may have had specific policy objectives—and the movement's leadership definitely sought to influence Israel's policymaking—but a large number of protesters were motivated more by anger, frustration, and a personal sense of responsibility than by cold political calculations. Perhaps the simple fact that the movement allowed individual supporters to give vent to these emotions is itself sufficient reason to declare its efforts a success. And as one activist asked, "Could you imagine how Israel would have looked in these circumstances without so much as the voice of the peace movement pleading to resolve the conflict and put an end to the suppression of the Palestinians?"[5]

The Peace Movement and the Public

One of the most important struggles the peace movement undertook concerned popular perceptions and public discourse. As is well known, the art of politics entails the manipulation of language and symbols. The oft-cited example, "One man's terrorist is another man's freedom fighter" reminds us that conflicts might involve bullets, but they always involve words. This battle is waged not only between the antagonists, but also among the divergent groups within each nation.

The Israeli right, particularly under the leadership of Menachem Begin, was skillful in manipulating symbols and myths to serve its ends. For example, Begin always refused to use the term "occupied territories." For him, and for those who shared his vision, the West Bank was referred to by its biblical name, Judea and Samaria, and considered "liberated." Gradually an increasing number of Israelis began to employ these usages, which became an integral part of the political vocabulary. The peace movement can also claim important successes in this battle. The term "Palestinian" became the standard reference for the more than 2 million non-Jewish residents of the occupied territories, despite the efforts of the right to refer to them generically as "Arabs" in an effort to strip them of their particular identity. Also, "occupied" continues to be used instead of "liberated" or even "administered" (preferred by the right), to emphasize the hostile rather than benign nature of the Israeli presence in the territories.

The most significant accomplishment of the peace movement has been its ability to influence public opinion by broadening the scope of public debate. For a number of years, supporters of the peace movement (even the relatively moderate Peace Now, not to mention the more radical elements such as Yesh Gvul, the various "committees," and the Council for Palestine-Israel Peace) were viewed by a majority of Israelis as being on the fringes of Israeli society. Accusations of treason, collaboration, and subversion of the security and unity of the state were voiced not just by the extreme right but occasionally by mainstream figures. During most of the 1970s and 1980s positions advocated by the peace movement received no more than 20 percent of popular support. More radical demands, such as recognizing the PLO or retreating from the Golan, usually received only single-digit support.

To be sure, the battle for public opinion was sometimes counterproductive. The movement's slogan campaigns and mass demonstrations antagonized right-wing elements and alienated many Mizrachim. However, the insistent advocacy of the peace movement gradually led many people both in the center and on the left to modify their views and accept the need for mutual recognition and compromise. The idea that the occupation is a political, financial, and moral liability rather than a strategic asset and that Palestinian self-determination is inevitable gradually gained greater currency.

As one would expect, these arguments were more persuasive among those who already identified with the left. When Peace Now first launched its campaign in support of the peace treaty with Egypt in 1978, it was not yet viewed as a left-wing movement. But its relationship with the Likud government soon became adversarial. Following its opposition to the invasion of Lebanon in 1982, the divide between the peace movement and the Likud (and other groups on the right) widened considerably. With little hope of influencing people on the right of Israeli politics, the movement concentrated its efforts on influencing centrists and people with no strong political convictions. Of all the peace groups, Peace Now was especially active in targeting those who occupied the center of the broad spectrum of opinion within the Labor Party. Recent opinion surveys and policy preferences of the current Labor government strongly suggest that the movement was successful in gradually moving the "middle" toward compromise and reconciliation.

Motives

A perpetual debate within the peace movement was whether the movement should present itself as guided primarily by moral and humanitarian concerns or by the rational assessment of national interest. In other words, should the movement be motivated primarily by the plight of the Palestinians or by rational considerations of long-term Israeli interests?

The two approaches were never viewed as mutually exclusive and were always intertwined. However, at times this debate caused fragmentation and contributed to the creation of splinter groups.[6] Support for the national interest argument grew as one moved from the movement's center to its right, apparently offering mainstream Israelis a more persuasive rationale for supporting the cause of peace. In a protracted, violent struggle such as the Arab-Israeli conflict, sympathy and compassion for the enemy tend to be muted as a consequence of the psychological tendency to dehumanize the enemy. Thus, arguments couched in the terms, and within the context, of Israeli national self-interest tended be more persuasive than appeals to morality, especially when most Israelis saw the Palestinians as terrorists irrevocably committed to Israel's destruction.[7]

In contrast, the more one moved to the left within the movement, the greater the moral sensitivity to the suffering experienced by the Palestinians. These individuals identified with the Palestinians as victims and often felt a growing alienation from Israeli society that accentuated this sense of victimization. For them, the moral and ethical implications of Israel's responsibility demanded compassion and support for the other side.

Similarities can be found with the antiapartheid movement among South African whites and the anti–Vietnam War movement in the United States. In South Africa, the racial barriers and social distance between the victims and the victimizers made possible the dehumanization of blacks by Afrikaners and frustrated attempts to rouse whites to moral indignation at the evils of apartheid. In the case of the U.S. antiwar movement, the sheer physical distance from the Vietnamese, together with potent and pervasive anticommunist prejudices, created a similar moral distancing and made it extremely difficult for peace activists to counter the demonization of the Viet Cong.

Although the geographical distance between Israelis and Palestinians was negligible compared to that between Americans and Vietnamese, and though the racial divisions in Israel and the occupied territories were much less acute than in South Africa, prejudice and ethical distancing thrived among Israelis and Palestinians because of the sheer length of their conflict, the level of violence, and the incompatibility of their aspirations. In such circumstances, it was easy to depict the other side as killers, terrorists, or devious and unscrupulous conspirators undeserving of moral consideration, still less of sentimental compassion.

Nevertheless, the leaders of the Israeli peace movement consistently viewed moral concerns as an important component of its agenda, even though they recognized the greater persuasive appeal of the national interest argument. And moral sensitivity toward the "enemy" clearly did influence Israeli public opinion, as demonstrated by the significant impact of the Intifada on Israeli attitudes. As had been the case following the Sabra and Shatila massacres, many Israelis were profoundly disturbed by the widespread use of violence against an adversary who was generally unarmed. The gradual recognition that such conduct was eroding Israel's moral position was evidenced in the relative success enjoyed by the draft refusers of Yesh Gvul, the outcry of the parents of soldiers serving in Lebanon and in the occupied territories during the Intifada, and the somber silence of the Women in Black.

Friends or Adversaries?

In an interview he gave when the Gulf War ended, Faisal Husseini spoke of the damage done to the trust between the Israeli peace movement and the Palestinian leadership in the territories when the Palestinians voiced support for Saddam Hussein:

> Certain members of the peace camp [in Israel] confused Palestinians with allies. They no longer saw in us an adversary with whom they [would] have to make peace, but friends who were their allies. So they were shocked to realize that in certain circumstances and certain specific stages our views must diverge.[8]

Husseini was accurate in his observation that this distinction was overlooked by many Israeli peace activists, in terms both of their expectations of the other side and their view of themselves. In some respects the Israeli-Palestinian conflict is more of a civil dispute than an international conflict. Especially since 1967, the antagonists have not been separated by mine fields or barbed wire, and have in many instances experienced routine, daily contact. This enabled Israelis to associate with Palestinians, create true friendships across national demarcation lines, and personally witness the plight of the occupied. Some of them stopped viewing the conflict as two national movements pitted against each other in a struggle that for a long time was considered by both to be a zero-sum game. For these Israelis, the Palestinian was either a comrade or a victim, no longer an adversary.

The Palestinians, who understandably had exploited their status as victims of Zionist expansion to win international recognition and support, did not lose sight of their antagonism toward the existence of the Jewish state, even when they had no option other than to accept it as an irreversible reality.

Initially the PLO had sought not merely to liberate its people from the occupation of the West Bank and Gaza, but also to eliminate the State of Israel altogether. Even in 1988, when the mainstream of the Palestinian national movement accepted the two states solution, they did so in the name of pragmatism, not because they had abandoned their deep conviction that Zionism had perpetrated a gross injustice on their people.

Recognizing the suffering of, and seeking to correct the injustices done to, one's enemy should not blind us to the origins of the conflict. Genuine reconciliation is not the result of one side's surrendering its own perspective and identity. One should not patronize one's enemy by blurring the "uniqueness" of either side. When adversaries are willing to recognize each other as they are, rather than as they wish for them to be, the prospects for reconciliation improve. Only through mutual recognition of their diversity can adversaries achieve a better understanding of, and appreciation for, each other's interests and requirements.

A highly subjective and selective interpretation of the history of the conflict has posed a significant psychological obstacle to reconciliation. Recently several Israeli historians have reexamined this history in a more objective and self-critical manner;[9] such reassessments may help Israelis to better understand all sides' responsibility for the human tragedy of the Israeli-Palestinian conflict, and may contribute to efforts to achieve a judicious and mutually acceptable resolution of the strife. One hopes that a similar historical revision will soon occur on the Arab side as well.

Unity and Fragmentation

Israel's peace movement includes more than two dozen groups, institutions, and associations. As we have seen, at times there have been sharp differences over objectives, style, and strategies. Peace Now occasionally succeeded in briefly bringing the various factions of the movement together for a joint action, but for the most part the fragmentation was endemic. Why was this constant splintering unavoidable? Did it dissipate the movement's resources and impact?

Answers to these questions must be found in the complexity of the conflict, the diversity of the groups' constituencies, the wide range of methods available for protest, and the great variety of motives and reasons for participation. No single organization or association could have adequately addressed the variety of issues, represented the full spectrum of opinions, or satisfied the varied temperaments and goals of the people who wanted to participate in the struggle.

Fragmentation certainly constituted a significant disadvantage in financial terms. All peace groups suffered from inadequate funding, and had they pooled their resources they might have alleviated some of the problems caused by underfunding. Fragmentation was also counterproductive insofar as occasional squabbles within the movement, which always became public knowledge, may have fostered misleading stereotypes and damaged its public image. In the final analysis, however, fragmentation may have been more of a blessing than a curse. The numerous opinions voiced, and diverse activities undertaken, by the peace movement over the decades gave activists and supporters the opportunity to become involved in a manner that suited their personal preferences. The criticisms that splinter groups often voiced against other groups, especially against Peace Now, helped them to define their own idiosyncratic identities and justify their separate existence.

Another benefit of the movement's fragmentation was that it provided opportunities for many more people to become involved as activists and leaders. With the exception of occasional mass demonstrations, there is naturally a limit to the number of people any single organization can involve in its daily business. The Israeli peace movement soon recognized that it was impractical to try to include hundreds of activists in administrative meetings and daily consultations on operational details. The inner circle of activists in any given group—those who came to every lecture, vigil, and conference—never totaled more than a few hundred. But because of the proliferation of peace groups, this number was multiplied until it reached the thousands, thereby enhancing the strength of the movement as a whole.

The unsuccessful attempts to merge Peace Now with the International Center for Peace in the Middle East is a good illustration of the merits of diversity. The two groups held similar viewpoints on policy issues, and occasionally organized joint activities. However, they were significantly different in their structures, cultures, and methods. Peace Now was a mass movement that was popular primarily among younger people. It had the capacity to mobilize tens of thousands of its supporters when events warranted. However, organizational stability was not among Peace Now's strengths. ICPME, by contrast, was a well-established organization that recruited personalities directly from the leadership of the political parties, and undertook more consistent and longer-term endeavors. Although there was some duplication between them, both Peace Now and ICPME fulfilled important functions that the other could not have accomplished. A merger would have likely resulted in a decrease in the overall number of activities and a distortion of the peculiar style of one or the other or of both. This would not have served the best interests of the peace movement as a whole.

What of the Future?

What role will the peace movement play in the months and years ahead as the parties to the conflict continue to formulate and implement peace arrangements? Peace negotiations with Syria and Lebanon are still at their second stage and very far from closure. Syria has yet to fully recognize Israel's security requirements and the need to allow for full normalization of relations once peace is agreed, and Israel is still reluctant to accept that peace can be achieved only by surrendering full sovereignty over the entire Golan Heights. Although at this stage the main responsibility for moving the peace process ahead rests with official delegates of both sides, nongovernmental groups remain very active. Formidable opposition to concessions to Syria is being mounted by the almost 12,000 Jewish settlers in the Golan, by all the right-wing parties, and even by some elements within the Labor Party; recent public opinion polls also indicate that a large section of Israelis still reject the notion of yielding the entire Golan Heights to Syrian control. Such sentiments are all the more significant in light of the fact that the late Prime Minister Rabin promised to conclude no agreement with Syria before bringing the issue to a public referendum; his successor, Prime Minister Shimon Peres, may well feel obliged to honor Rabin's promise. In this area it seems that the peace movement still has much hard work to do in persuading Israelis to support whatever agreement can be secured in hard bargaining with Syria.

On the Palestinian track the problems are more immediate. Despite strong opposition to the Oslo and Cairo agreements mounted from the outset by Likud and, more violently, by the settlers and their supporters, the Labor-led government at first enjoyed the support of a clear majority of Israelis. Sadly, continuing terrorist attacks on Israelis by Palestinian Islamic groups since the signing of the agreements and the handing over of Gaza and Jericho to the Palestinian authorities have caused a sharp decline in Israeli support for the peace process. The shock and deep bereavement that engulfed the Israeli people after the assassination of Rabin, have tilted public opinion once again in favor of the peace process, and a clear majority of the Jewish population of Israel has expressed in recent polls its support for the declaration by Shimon Peres that the peace legacy of Rabin should not and cannot but be fulfilled. Nevertheless, the deep division that has haunted the Israelis since 1967 cannot be obliterated even by so traumatic an event, and the struggle for the future of the peace process will probably continue in full acrimony.

At the end of 1996 negotiations are scheduled to begin on the final status settlement with the Palestinians. While on the issue of interim arrangements the process has reached its third stage, on the final settlement the process still lingers at its second stage, and the principles governing the ultimate solution remaining undefined and must still be negotiated. These negotiations will include highly sensitive issues, such as whether a Palestinian state will emerge, the exact territorial boundaries of Palestinian sovereignty, the future of Jerusalem, the future of the Jewish settlements, and the fate of the millions of Palestinian refugees living elsewhere. On most of these matters, the level of resistance to compromise among Israelis is still high.

Clearly, this is no time for the peace movement to rest on its laurels. With the opposition to the peace process still bitter and vocal, with terrorist bombs wreaking carnage in Israeli streets, and with future negotiations riddled with ambiguities and real dangers, there is still much for the peace movement to do. As these lines go to print, peace activists in different groups are already busy consulting on measures to counter opposition to the peace process and to pressure the government to continue to implement the agreement reached with the Palestinians and to enter the final status negotiations with courage and resolve. Any slowing down or weakening of the peace process, the peaceniks claim, will be a prize given to terrorists and assassins.

A danger inherent in the Middle East peace process is that official treaties and commitments will remain tentative because of the heavy imprint of authoritarianism on the region's political culture. Some observers suggest that peace treaties concluded with authoritarian regimes are inherently unstable. However, the case of Egypt has demonstrated that peace treaties can endure, even after a sudden and violent change of regime. Israel can hardly wait for democracy to flourish in the region, nor should it delay its pursuit of peace in the hope that regimes will change. As in the Egyptian-Israeli Peace Treaty, security arrangements and verification procedures must be incorporated in peace agreements that will bolster the credibility and stability of those agreements. These mechanisms will help build confidence in the durability of such arrangements independent of a particular leader or regime.[10]

Those agreements that have already been achieved need nurturing. Increasing and consolidating popular support within Arab, Palestinian, and Israeli societies will help to solidify official treaties. Further dialogue toward this end might well be a task for which the peace movement is ideally suited.

If and when the Palestinians achieve sovereignty, it will be up to them to decide what kind of regime they will be governed by. Nonetheless, for two reasons the peace movement will be involved with this issue for a number of years to come. First, the close proximity of, and interaction between, Israeli and Palestinian societies make Israeli involvement in this question unavoidable. Second, Palestinian leaders who worked with the Israeli peace movement, as well as many of the grass-roots organizations in the occupied territories established during the occupation, are now looking to nongovernmental organizations for assistance. The peace movement must be careful not to impose itself on the Palestinians; it must be sensitive to their independence and renewed sense of pride and dignity. However, when called on for help it must be responsive and do whatever possible to assist the democratic forces within Palestinian society.

Finally, the Israeli peace movement should not lose sight of the fact that by the nature of its existence its ultimate goal must be to render itself obsolete. Should this occur, the members of the movement will be free to turn their energies to other priorities—nations at peace still provide many challenges for moral and conscientious people.

* * *

Moments before he was shot to death, Yitzhak Rabin stood on the dias of a peace rally and joined with the large crowd gathered in Tel Aviv's municipal square in singing the "Song of Peace." During his funeral, the head of the prime minister's bureau, Eitan Haber, told the mourners that as Rabin was singing the song, he folded a sheet of paper on which the lyrics were printed and put it in his vest pocket. The bullet that killed the prime minister pierced his heart through this sheet of paper, which was soaked with his blood.

Over the past two decades, the "Song of Peace" became a sort of anthem that was sung at the conclusion of each demonstration the Israeli peace movement staged. This song was commissioned not for the peace movement, however, but for one of the IDF's recreational music units shortly after the end of the Six Day War. This caused some controversy at the time, when one Israeli general prohibited the performance of the song before soldiers under his command, claiming that the song might subvert the morale and soften the hearts of his soldiers. The issue was brought before General Rabin, commander in chief of the IDF at the time. Rabin backed up his chief of education who argued that "Israel will never reach peace unless it has a strong army, but the army will not be strong unless its combatants are convinced that the ultimate goal of all their endeavors and sacrifices is to reach peace."[11]

Indeed, at the center of its consciousness the greater part of the Israeli peace movement always tried to balance both elements of this logic. Peace Now, the oldest and by far the largest group within the movement, was founded by reserve officers who made a significant contribution to the strength of the Israeli army and believed that a formidable military force was necessary not only for the defense of the State of Israel but also for the eventual attainment of peace. Yet their conviction that peace must be the ultimate goal of their efforts also led them, when they felt the time was ripe, to turn much of their energies to the struggle for peace. Their leaflets reading "No to Violence! Yes to Peace" are still floating in the streets of Israel as the last words of this book are being written.

Notes

Articles and books published in Hebrew are noted as such below, except in the case of the following journals and newspapers, which publish only in Hebrew: *Al Ha'mishmar, Davar, Dvar Hashavu'a, Ha'aretz, Hadashot, Harnizrach Hachadash, Hottam, Kol Ha'ir, Kol Yerushalaim, Koteret Rashit, Ma'ariv, Masa, Monitin, Nekuda, Tel Aviv,* and *Yediot Ahronot.*

Introduction

1. The three wars were the War of Attrition, 1968–70; the October War, 1973; and the Lebanon War, 1982. The Intifada erupted in the Gaza Strip on December 9, 1987.

2. Most of these works are mentioned in these notes. Worthy of special mention is the two-volume doctoral dissertation of Tamar Herman, completed at Tel Aviv University.

1. Zero Sum: The First Two Decades

1. UN General Assembly Resolution 181 (II), November 29, 1947. See Meron Medzini, ed., *Israel's Foreign Relations: Selected Documents, 1947–1974* (Jerusalem: Ministry for Foreign Affairs, 1976), doc. 8, 92–106.

2. In addition to the armies of Egypt, Syria, Jordan, and Lebanon, an Iraqi contingent also participated.

3. As a result of the war Jordan acquired and later annexed 2,200 square miles of territory that was supposed to be a part of the Arab state in Palestine. See Nadav Safran, *Israel the Embattled Ally* (Cambridge, Mass.: Harvard University Press, 1978), 60.

4. For details on these developments, see Netanel Lorch, *The Edge of the Sword: Israel's War of Independence, 1947–1949* (New York: Putnam, 1961), 321–438.

5. Moshe Dayan discusses this in his memoirs and quotes Ben-Gurion as saying, "Our primary aim is now peace; . . . immigration demands that there be an end to war." Moshe Dayan, *Story of My Life* (New York: William Morrow, 1976), 133.

6. In August 1949 the first public opinion survey was conducted in Israel by Louis Guttman. Eighty-one percent of the sample considered the armistice agreements a "political achievement" while only 19 percent opposed them. See Institute of Public Opinion Research, *Foreign Policy Problems in the Eyes of the Residents of Israel* (in Hebrew) (Institute of Public Opinion Research: Tel Aviv, 1949).

7. There are many accounts of the primacy given to achieving peace by Israel's leaders during 1949. See, for example, David Ben-Gurion's speech to the Knesset on the occasion of presenting the Security Service Law on August 8, 1949. David Ben-Gurion, "Army and Security" (in Hebrew) (Tel Aviv: Ma'arachot,1955), 102.

8. Moshe Sharett, "Israel and the Arabs: War and Peace" (in Hebrew), *Ot* (Tel Aviv) 1, no. 1 (September 1960).

9. United Nations Security Council, *Security Council Official Record (SCOR)*, 433d meeting, August 4, 1949.

10. Palestinian writers often refer to the 1948 war as their *Naqba*, a word they also use to describe the Jewish Holocaust during World War II. For a detailed treatment of the UN attempt to transform the armistice agreement into a full peace, see Ilan Pappe, *The Making of the Arab-Israeli Conflict, 1947–1951* (London: I. B. Tauris, 1994), chaps. 8 and 9.

11. For an extensive review of these efforts, see Saadia Touval, *The Peace Brokers* (Princeton: Princeton University Press, 1982). See also Mordechai Bar-On, *The Gates of Gaza: Israel's Road to Suez and Back, 1955–1957* (New York: St. Martin's, 1994), chaps. 7 and 8.

12. See especially Simcha Flapan, *The Birth of Israel: Myths and Realities* (New York: Pantheon, 1987), for one side and Conor Cruise O'Brien, *The Siege: The Saga of Israel and Zionism* (London: Weidenfeld and Nicolson, 1986), for the other.

13. See Itamar Rabinovich, *The Road Not Taken: Early Arab-Israeli Negotiations* (Oxford: Oxford University Press, 1991); and Avi Shlaim, *Collusion across the Jordan: King Abdullah, the Zionist Movement, and the Partition of Palestine* (New York: Columbia University Press, 1988). For a specific case, see Avi Shlaim, "Husni Zaim and the Plan to Resettle Palestinian Refugees in Syria," *Journal of Palestine Studies* 15, no. 4 (summer 1986): 68–80.

14. For a fuller treatment of this argument, see Mordechai Bar-On, "The Peace That Was Not" (in Hebrew), *Iunim* 2 (1992).

15. The main proponent of this argument was Kenneth Love, the correspondent of the *New York Times* in Cairo at the time. See his *Suez: The Twice Fought War* (New York: McGraw-Hill, 1969).

16. Quoted by Yehoshafat Harkabi, *Arab Attitudes to Israel* (Jerusalem: Israeli Universities Press, 1972), 187. Nasser told Egyptian soldiers some time later that "the Palestine battle was a smear on the entire Arab nation. No one can forget the shame brought by the battle of 1948. The rights of the Palestinian people must be restored." Reprinted in Walter Laqueur and Barry Rubin, eds., *The Israel-Arab Reader: A Documentary History of the Middle East Conflict* (London: Penguin, 1984), 140.

17. For a full report of the Anderson mission, see David Ben-Gurion, "The Secret Negotiations," *Ma'ariv*, July 2, 9, 16, and 23, 1971. Anderson reported on his mission to President Eisenhower and Secretary of State John Foster Dulles. The record of this conversation can be found in *Foreign Relations of the United States (FRUS) 1955–1957*, vol. 14 (Washington, D.C.: Government Printing Office), doc. 164, 302–307; doc.168, 310–314; doc.187, 342–343.

18. For a contemporary analysis of the 1949 Lausanne Conference, see Neil Caplan, *The Lausanne Conference, 1949: A Case Study in Middle East Peacemaking,*

Occasional Papers no. 113 (Tel Aviv: Moshe Dayan Center, 1993). A lengthy bibliography on the subject is included in this study.

19. For a detailed treatment of the struggle over the Negev, see Ilan Asia, *The Heart of the Conflict: The Struggle over the Negev, 1947–1956* (in Hebrew) (Jerusalem: 1994).

20. The documents are included in Yemima Resental, ed., *Documents on the Foreign Policy of the State of Israel*, vol. 4, *May–December 1949* (in Hebrew) (Jerusalem: Israel State Archives, 1991), 66–68.

21. For a different approach and critical interpretation, see Benny Morris, *Israel's Border Wars, 1949–1956* (Oxford: Clarendon, 1993).

22. On Soviet policies toward the Arab-Israeli conflict in the 1950s, see Yaacov Ro'i, *From Encroachment to Involvement* (Jerusalem: Israeli Universities Press, 1974). On the development of the Soviet-Egyptian arms deal, see Uri Ra'anan, *The USSR, Arms and the Third World* (Cambridge, Mass.: MIT Press, 1969).

23. For the shift in Israel's international orientation, see Uri Bialer, *Between East and West: Israel's Foreign Policy Orientation, 1948–1956* (Cambridge: Cambridge University Press, 1990).

24. Similar support for the Arab position on the blockade of the Strait of Aqaba was not forthcoming. In this case Egyptian policy clashed with the traditional Soviet position on freedom of navigation in international waterways. See Mordechai Bar-On, "The Soviet Position on the Issue of the Straits of Tiran" (in Hebrew), *Iunim* 1 (1991): 276–307.

25. For a full analysis of this war from the Israeli perspective, see Bar-On, *Gates of Gaza*. See also Motti Golani, "The Sinai Campaign, 1956: Military and Political Aspects" (Ph.D. diss., Haifa University, 1992).

26. Many books and memoirs have been written on the 1956 Suez crisis. The latest and most comprehensive is Keith Kyle, *Suez* (New York: St. Martin's, 1991).

27. See Mordechai Bar-On, *Challenge and Quarrel* (in Hebrew) (Sdeh Boker: Ben Gurion University Press, 1991), 286.

28. In 1954 Mapam split into two parties, but for a time both splinter groups remained active in the IPC. Most of this discussion on the IPC is based on the exhaustive treatment of the committee by Herman, "From the 'Peace Covenant' to 'Peace Now,'" 1:230–257.

29. The number of signatures reported by the movement was 312,000 in 1950, 401,000 in 1951, and 423,250 in 1954. Even if these figures were artificially inflated, the IPC's achievement was still impressive. See ibid., 235, 237, 242.

30. For a general description of Israel's political parties during this period, see Joseph Badi, *The Government of the State of Israel: A Critical Account of Its Parliament, Executive, and Judiciary* (New York: Twayne, 1963). An earlier account can be found in Marver Bernstein, *The Politics of Israel: The First Decade of Statehood* (Princeton: Princeton University Press, 1957). See also Leonard Fein, *Politics in Israel* (Boston: Little, Brown, 1967). For the role of the parties in foreign policy formulation, see Michael Brecher, *The Foreign Policy System of Israel: Setting, Images, Process* (New Haven: Yale University Press, 1972).

31. The Labor Party was then called Mapai, which is an acronym for the Workers' Party of Israel.

32. The most ardent proponent of this interpretation (beside Sharett's son, who published his diaries) is Gabriel Sheffer, whose biography of Sharett is forthcoming. See also Gabriel Sheffer, "Comprehensive Solution vis-à-vis Moderating the Arab-Israeli Conflict: The Clash between Moshe Sharett and Ben-Gurion Reconsidered," in Menachem Stern et al., eds., *Zionism and the Arab Question* (in Hebrew) (Jerusalem: Zalman Shazar Center, 1979).

33. Lecture to IDF officers, December 16, 1955, Letters and Meetings Files, Ben-Gurion Archives, Sdeh Boker.

34. Records of the Political Committee Meeting, Labor Party Archives, Beit Berl, Israel, March 28, 1953.

35. Record from a meeting at the Israeli embassy in Washington, D.C., April 14, 1953, Israel State Archives, Jerusalem, box 2382, file 22a. For a general discussion of these points, see Zaki Shalom, "The Opposition of Ben-Gurion and Sharett to the Territorial Demand on Israel 1949–1956" (in Hebrew), *Iunim* 2 (1992): 197–213.

36. Moshe Sharett, *Diary* (in Hebrew) (Tel Aviv: Ma'ariv Publications, 1978), 5:1385.

37. There are even indications that the rank and file of Mapam was closer to Ben-Gurion's views. See the testimony of a young officer from a Mapam kibbutz recorded during a study conducted by Major Yesha'aia Tadmor after the retaliation operation in Nuqieb in 1961, in "Morale and Leadership in the Nuqieb Raid" (in Hebrew) (issued by IDF Chief Education Officer, 1962).

38. For a general description of Jabotinsky's ideology and the development of the Revisionist Movement, see Yaacov Shavit, *Jabotinsky and the Revisionist Movement 1925–1948* (London: Frank Cass, 1988).

39. The quotation in English is taken from Lenni Brenner, *The Iron Wall: Zionist Revisionism from Jabotinsky to Shamir* (London: Zed Books, 1984), 74.

40. The full text of these famous articles was published by Joseph Nedava, ed., *The Road to Revisionist Zionism: Selected Articles from* Rasswiet *1923–1927* (in Hebrew) (Tel Aviv: Jabotinsky Archive Press, 1965).

41. For a history of the development of the Palestinian national movement in these years, see Yehoshua Porath, *The Emergence of the Palestinian-Arab National Movement, 1918–1929* (London: Frank Cass, 1974).

42. See Shlaim, *Collusion across the Jordan.*

43. On the intellectual struggle for self-identity among the Palestinians, see Pinhas Inbari, *The Palestine Option: PLO versus the Zionist Challenge* (in Hebrew) (Jerusalem: Carmel, 1989).

44. Dan Schueftan, *The Jordanian Option: The "Yishuv" and the State of Israel vis-à-vis the Hashemite Regime and the Palestinian National Movement* (in Hebrew) (Tel Aviv: Hakibbutz Hameuchad, 1986).

45. For more on these developments in Jordan and among the Palestinians in the 1950s, see Aqil Abidi, *Jordan: A Political Study 1948–1954* (London: Asia Publication House, 1965); and Amnon Cohen, *Political Parties in the West Bank under the Jordanian Regime, 1949–1967* (Ithaca, N.Y.: Cornell University Press, 1982).

46. See Malcolm Kerr, *The Arab Cold War, Gamal Abd al-Nasir and His Rivals, 1958–1970* (Oxford: Oxford University Press, 1971).

47. From the record of a meeting of Selwyn Lloyd, August 7, 1958, Public Record Office (PRO), London, file FO371/134348.

48. Uri Avneri, *My Friend the Enemy* (London: Zed Books, 1986), 15.

49. Avneri published a brochure in the name of his association entitled *War and Peace in the Semitic World* (in Hebrew) (Tel Aviv: Maavak Library, October

1947). A copy of an English summary was also published and may be found in Uri Avneri Private Archive.

50. For an excellent biography of Ratosh, see Yehoshua Porath, *A Poet and a Sword in His Hand* (in Hebrew) (Tel Aviv: Bitan Zmora Publishing, 1987).

51. Based on interviews conducted with Uri Avneri in Tel Aviv on July 23 and 29, 1992.

52. Uri Avneri, "The White General Staff," *Ha'olam Ha'zeh*, November 8, 1956.

53. Uri Avneri, "Who Actually Is the Enemy?" *Ha'olam Ha'zeh*, December 29, 1955. In fact no such "Liberation Movement" was involved because the riots were propagated in support of pan-Arabism, not a unique Palestinian interest.

54. The Stern Gang was a clandestine anti-British underground movement that was led, after the assassination of its founder Yair Stern, by a triumvirate composed of Nathan Yellin-Mor, Israel Eldad, and Yitzhak Shamir, who later became the prime minister of Israel.

55. Uri Avneri, "The Union of Jordan," *Ha'olam Ha'zeh*, June 2, 1957.

56. Uri Avneri, "The Third Round," *Ha'olam Ha'zeh*, December 22, 1955.

57. Avneri, "Who Actually Is the Enemy?"

58. Flapan presents these arguments in *The Birth of Israel*.

59. The term "Israeli Arabs" refers to the Palestinians who remained inside the boundaries of Israel at the end of 1948 and received Israeli citizenship.

60. Buber's best-known book is *I and Thou* (1923), a classic work of existentialist-dialogical philosophy.

61. For more on this group's activities during the 1950s, see Herman, "From 'Peace Covenant' to 'Peace Now,'" 1:197–213.

62. Victor Cygielman, interview by author, Jerusalem, August 16, 1992. Cygielman participated in the meeting with Buber along with Abdul Aziz Zuabi, the Arab member of the Knesset for Mapam, and the Marxist economist Darin-Drabkin. Yesha'aia Weinberg of the Holocaust Memorial Museum in Washington, D.C., confirmed much of this information in an interview on September 24, 1992. Weinberg was a member of the editorial board of *New Outlook* in the 1960s.

63. "Statement of Purpose," *New Outlook* 1, no. 1 (July 1957).

64. Curiel was eventually murdered under mysterious circumstances; the perpetrators were never identified. For more on Curiel, see chapter 9.

65. Among the participants were British MP Anthony Wedgwood-Benn, Bishop James A. Pike of California, and the prominent French journalist Claude Estier. A record of the conference was published in *New Outlook* 6, no. 2 (February 1963), and no. 3 (March–April 1963).

66. Two interviews with Sartre, one with the Egyptian paper *al-Ahram,* and the other with the Israeli paper *Al Ha'mishmar,* were published in *New Outlook* 9, no. 2 (February 1966) and no. 4 (May 1966).

67. Joseph Golan, interview by author, Jerusalem, August 12, 1992.

68. A similar affair occurred fifteen years later. See chapter 3.

69. On the origins of the conference, see Joseph Golan, "The Colloquium in Florence," *New Outlook* 3, no. 8 (July–August 1960): 34–36, 62.

70. Ibid.

71. Abdul Aziz Zuabi, who served at the time as deputy minister of health, attended the 1961 conference.

72. Among others, Shiloach had a meeting with Mehdi Ben Barka. For a record of the proceedings, see *New Outlook* 2, no. 3–4 (November–December 1958).

73. "Month by Month," ibid., 23.

74. Golan, interview.

75. "The Third Florence Colloquium," *New Outlook* 5, no. 7 (July 1961).

76. Detailed reports appeared daily in Israeli newspapers; some even sent special correspondents to the event. Summaries of the proceedings were written by Ada Luciano in *Ma'ariv,* October 19, 1960, and Israel Neuman in *Davar,* October 14, 1960.

77. Ben-Gurion's letter to La Pira dated October 17, 1960, in Golan's personal files, Jerusalem.

78. The third Florence conference was held in the summer of 1961 and was dedicated to a dialogue between Mediterranean and African states. A short evaluation of this conference is included in "The Third Florence Colloquium" (see note 75).

79. Golan, interview.

80. Some of the details of the Golan affair were kept secret at the time, even during a heated Knesset debate on the matter. On April 1, 1962, some of the information was revealed by Golan in an interview with Ada Luciano that appeared in *Ma'ariv,* May 4, 1962. A report on the incident was also written by Elkana Gali in *Yediot Ahronot,* March 6, 1962. On June 7, 1962, *Ha'aretz* published an editorial critical of the government's handling of the affair.

81. The phrase "no war, no peace" was coined in the early 1950s by Moshe Dayan. See "Military Operations in Time of Peace" (in Hebrew), *Ma'arachot,* no. 118–119 (May 1959).

82. Substantial Arabic literature exists that tries to explain the Arab defeat of 1948. For more on this see Harkabi, *Arab Attitudes to Israel*; and Avraham Sella, "The Arabs in the 1948 War" (in Hebrew) (Ph.D. diss., Hebrew University, Jerusalem, 1989).

83. See, for example, "Nasser Reveals Story of Operations and Secrets behind the Sinai Attack," *Egyptian Gazette,* December 6, 1956. See also Mohamed H. Heikal, *Cutting the Lion's Tail: Suez through Egyptian Eyes* (London: Andre Deutsch, 1986).

84. Quotation from a speech to his senior officers at Bir Gafgafa, in the Israel Military Intelligence Division's "Daily Summaries of Arab Media," May 23, 1967.

85. On the origins of the Palestine Liberation Organization and Fatah, see Helena Cobban, *The Palestinian Liberation Organization: People, Power and Politics* (Cambridge: Cambridge University Press, 1984). See also Ehud Ya'ari, *Fatah* (in Hebrew) (Tel Aviv: Schocken Books, 1970).

86. These figures were made public by Shimon Peres, then deputy minister of defense. See his *David's Sling* (New York: Random House, 1970).

87. Numerous works address the developments that led to the 1967 war. See, for example, Walter Laqueur, *The Road to War, 1967: The Origins of the Arab-Israeli Conflict* (London: Weidenfeld and Nicolson, 1969); and Nadav Safran, *From War to War: The Arab-Israeli Confrontation, 1948–1967* (New York: Pegasus, 1969).

2. The Debate over Peace Options in the Labor Party, 1967–70

1. There are many descriptions and analyses of this war. The official record of the Israeli side is in Mordechai Bar-On, *Six Days* (Tel Aviv: IDF Publications,

1968). A recent work is by Eric Hammel, *Six Days in June: How Israel Won the 1967 Arab-Israeli War* (New York: Scribner's, 1992)

2. The book was published in English under the title *The Seventh Day: Soldiers' Talk about the Six-Day War* (no editor mentioned) (London: Andre Deutsch, 1970), 177–178. For details of the riots that the Shelem brothers' father mentioned, see Howard Sachar, *A History of Israel* (New York: Knopf, 1986), 173–201.

3. Reprinted in Moshe Shamir, *Nathan Alterman: The Poet as a Leader* (in Hebrew) (Tel Aviv: Dvir, 1988), 107.

4. For more on this, from different standpoints, see Eliezer Schweid, "You Must Choose Life: The Holocaust in the Nation's Heart Search," *Kivunim*, no. 9 (fall 1980); and Mordechai Bar-On, "Zionist Lessons from the Holocaust" (in Hebrew), *Kivunim*, no. 11 (spring 1981). The heavy psychological baggage of the Holocaust reduces the willingness of Israelis to take risks with their security. Combined with the geographic and demographic circumstances of Israel's position in the Middle East, the Holocaust experience has led Israelis to require a wide margin of security for themselves and to look with skepticism at suggestions that that margin be narrowed. The language of Israeli political discourse on the Arab-Israeli conflict is saturated with allusions, symbolic catchwords, and metaphors borrowed from the collective memory of the trauma inflicted by the Nazis.

5. For example, the Iraqi premier spoke of "a rendezvous with our brothers in Tel Aviv," and Ahmad Shuqairi, the president of the Palestine Liberation Organization, declared: "There will be practically no Jewish survivors." See Jean Lacouture, *Nasser* (New York: Knopf, 1973).

6. The poet Nathan Alterman wrote of "the unparalleled transformation which turned the danger of annihilation into an unprecedented salvation." Nathan Alterman, *The Triangular Thread* (in Hebrew) (Tel Aviv: Hakibbutz Hameuchad, 1971), 38.

7. In 1967 Merkaz Ha'rav, the rabbinical school that in later years became a major center of right-wing messianism, published a book titled *The War of Salvation.* Religious nationalist circles tended to see the victory in terms of the great miracles that God has performed for the Jews in times of great peril.

8. This quotation is from a song that became very popular at the end of the Six Day War.

9. Shamir, *Nathan Alterman*, 111.

10. For more on the development of Israeli strategic doctrine, see Michael Handel, *Israel's Political-Military Doctrine*, Occasional Paper in International Affairs no. 30 (Cambridge, Mass.: Harvard University, 1973); and Avner Yaniv, *Deterrence without the Bomb: The Politics of Israeli Strategy* (Lexington, Mass.: Lexington Books, 1987).

11. This move was enacted through a bill (known as Municipalities Ordinance Law, no. 5727) proposed by the government and passed by the Knesset. The law empowered the minister of the interior to "enlarge, by proclamation, the area of a particular municipality through the inclusion of an area designated by order." On the following day Minister Haim Moshe Shapiro proclaimed the inclusion of East Jerusalem and some contiguous land in the Municipality of Jerusalem. Politically and practically this amounted to a unilateral annexation. The Knesset amendment is reprinted in John Norton Moore, *The Arab–Israeli Conflict: Readings and Documents* (Princeton: Princeton University Press, 1977), 1062–1063. The text of the proclamation was published as "Ordinance no. 2065, June 28, 1967," in State of Israel, *Government Ordinance Dockets* (Jerusalem, 1967), 3:2694–2695.

12. On July 4, 1967, the UN General Assembly resolved, almost unanimously, to consider the measures taken by Israel with regard to Jerusalem as invalid and called upon Israel "to rescind all measures already taken and to desist forthwith from taking any action which would alter the status of Jerusalem." UN General Assembly Resolution 2253 (ES-V), *General Assembly Official Record (GAOR)*, supp. 1, doc. A/6798 (1967).

13. Throughout the last twenty-eight years at least 70 percent, often as high as 95 percent, of Israeli Jews have supported the annexation of Jerusalem. Never were more than 8 percent ready to consider the return of the annexed part to Arab rule. Most of the survey figures in this and the following chapters are taken from the *Continuing Survey of Social Problem Indicators*, which was introduced in 1967 by Louis Guttman through the Israel Institute of Applied Social Research in Jerusalem. This survey uses an omnibus polling method, conducted at different intervals (though seldom less frequently than every other month) in which the attitudes of Israelis toward current political issues are measured. See also Russell A. Stone, *Social Change in Israel: Attitudes and Events 1967–1979* (New York: Praeger, 1982).

14. This decision was guarded as a secret at the time and was made public only several years later. A description of these events was published by Moshe Dayan, who at the time was minister of defense, in a number of articles in *Ma'ariv*, December 27, 1974, and May 30, 1975, and in *Yediot Ahronot*, February 28, 1975. The document has been referred to in many memoirs, but has not yet been officially released. Dayan paraphrased its content in the Hebrew edition of his memoirs *Avnei Derech* (Jerusalem: Idanim, 1976), 490–492. A more recent discussion can be found in Abba Eban, *Personal Witness: Israel through My Eyes* (New York: Putnam, 1992), 437.

15. Gahal was a bloc made up of Begin's own Herut party, the heir to Jabotinsky's Revisionist movement, and the centrist Liberals. In later years this bloc, with some small additions, was renamed and eventually forged into a unified party called Likud.

16. *Ma'ariv*, June 28, 1967.

17. The text is reprinted in Meron Medzini, ed., *Israel's Foreign Relations* (Jerusalem: Ministry for Foreign Affairs, 1976), 839–840.

18. I borrow the term from I. William Zartman's *Ripe for Resolution: Conflict and Intervention in Africa* (Oxford: Oxford University Press, 1985).

19. David A. Korn, who at the time was assigned to the political section of the U.S. embassy in Tel Aviv, quoted a former U.S. official who told him that on June 8, when the Sinai and the West Bank were already under Israeli control, Abba Eban (the Israeli minister of foreign affairs) assured Arthur Goldberg (the U.S. ambassador to the United Nations) that "Israel is not seeking territorial aggrandizement." While I could not find further confirmation of this testimony, it certainly concurs with the general attitude of the Israeli elite during those days. See David A. Korn, *Stalemate: The War of Attrition and Great Power Diplomacy in the Middle East 1967–1970* (Boulder, Colo.: Westview, 1992), 13.

20. Prime Minister Levi Eshkol declared: "I certainly hope that this was the last war in the region." He called on the Arab states to begin direct talks with Israel and expressed the opinion that "if and when peace comes—and now is the right time to advance toward it full steam—there is a great future for this area. . . . I think there has never been a more appropriate time than now to proceed and talk peace and development and progress." See interview with Prime Minister

Eshkol in "What's Next for Israel?" *U.S. News and World Report,* July 10, 1967. A speech made by Abba Eban at the UN General Assembly offered similar views. See *GAOR,* Fifth Emergency Special Session, 1,526th Plenary Meeting, New York, June 19, 1967, 7–16.

21. I could not find the source, but almost all Israeli books about this period quote him.

22. See "The Military Situation on the Suez Canal up to the Sinking of the Eilat," in Daniel Dishon, ed., *Middle East Record,* vol. 3 (Jerusalem: Israeli Universities Press, 1971), 296–301.

23. For the Israeli perspective on the events, see Dayan, *Story of My Life,* 444–446. See also Dishon, *Middle East Record,* 3:302–303.

24. On the War of Attrition along the Suez Canal, see Dan Schueftan, *Attrition: Egypt's Post-War Political Strategy 1967–1970* (in Hebrew) (Tel Aviv: Ma'arachot, 1989), chap. 5. See also Yaacov Bar-Siman-Tov, *The Israeli-Egyptian War of Attrition 1969–1970* (New York: Columbia University Press, 1980). For an Israeli military perspective, see General Itzhak Arad, ed., *The Thousand Days War* (in Hebrew) (Tel Aviv: Ma'arachot, 1971). The Egyptian perspective can be found in memoirs of the minister of war at the time, General Mahmoud Fawzi, *The Three Year War* (in Arabic) (Cairo: Dar al-Mustaqbal al-Arabi, 1984). See also Lieutenant Colonel Avraham Zohar, "The War of Attrition: Strategy and Tactics" (in Hebrew), *Ma'arachot,* no. 257 (August 1977).

25. Nasser's foreign minister stated that the president told the Soviets in July 1970 that he could have regained the Sinai by 1968, but that he could not accept a peaceful settlement and recognize Israel unless it withdrew from all occupied Arab territories and "implemented the UN resolutions on the rights of the Palestinians." See Mahmud Riad, *The Struggle for Peace in the Middle East* (London: Quartet Books, 1981), 143.

26. The term was first used by Nasser, but the Israelis adopted it because they believed that it would be the Egyptians who would suffer from attrition. See Schueftan, *Attrition,* 98, and note 3 on the same page.

27. For a detailed analysis of the Egyptian considerations and assessment, see Bar-Siman-Tov, *Israeli-Egyptian War of Attrition,* 43–59.

28. Nasser was rather skeptical as to the feasibility of the third phase but adopted the strategy nonetheless. A detailed report of the deliberations in the Egyptian High Command can be found in the memoirs of Mahmoud Fawzi. A detailed treatment of the considerations that led Nasser to begin the War of Attrition appears in Schueftan, *Attrition.* See also Mohamed Heikal, *Road to Ramadan,* 46.

29. The full text of the declaration is reprinted in Moore, *The Arab-Israeli Conflict,* doc. 38, 1084. See also Heikal, *Road to Ramadan,* 52–54.

30. *Al-Ahram,* January 3, 1969. Israeli military intelligence translated all of Heikal's articles, which were considered to be indicators of Nasser's views, and distributed them to many high-ranking officers.

31. On the development of the Palestinian Liberation Organization during the years after the 1967 war, see Cobban, *Palestine Liberation Organization,* chap. 3. See also Ehud Ya'ari, *Strike Terror: The Story of the Fateh* (New York: Sabra, 1970), 151–150, 350–383; and Arieh Yodfat and Yuval Arnon-Ohana, *PLO: Strategy and Tactics* (New York: St. Martin's, 1981), chap. 2. For an interesting, well-researched, though one-sided, book on these developments, see Gerard Chaliand, *The*

Palestinian Resistance (Middlesex, England: Penguin, 1972). On Israeli efforts to hamper the early efforts to stir up a revolt in the territories, see David Ronen, *The Year of the Shabak: The Deployment in Samaria and Judea—The First Year* (in Hebrew) (Tel Aviv: Ministry of Defense Publications, 1989).

32. For an Israeli description of this phase of the War of Attrition, see Mordechai Naor, *The War after the War* (Tel Aviv: Ministry of Defense Publications, n.d.) 17–21, 30–39.

33. Cobban, *Palestine Liberation Organization,* 41–42. Cobban uncritically accepts the Palestinian version of 15,000 Israeli soldiers participating in the battle. In fact not more than 1,500 Israelis crossed the Jordan. Her main source seems to be Abu Iyad and Eric Rouleau, *My Home, My Land: A Narrative of the Palestinian Struggle* (New York: Times Books, 1981), 57–60.

34. Iyad and Rouleau, *My Home, My Land.*

35. John Cooley may have additional sources, but they only corroborate the undisputed notion that Karameh was seen by the Palestinians as a major victory. See his *Green March, Black September* (London: Frank Cass, 1973).

36. On December 11, 1967, the Arab Nationalist Movement gave birth to its own guerrilla movement, the Popular Front for the Liberation of Palestine (PFLP). The text of its announcement is reprinted in *International Documents on Palestine, 1967* (Beirut: Palestine Studies Institute, 1968), 723–726. For a general description of the development of the PFLP, see Cobban, *Palestine Liberation Organization,* chap. 7. See also Rashid Hamid, "What Is the PLO?" *Journal of Palestine Studies* 5, no. 4 (summer 1975): 90–109; and Ya'ari, *Strike Terror,* 198–262.

37. The best critique of the postwar Arab world is in Fouad Ajami, *The Arab Predicament: Arab Political Thought and Practice since 1967* (Cambridge: Cambridge University Press, 1981).

38. For an analysis of the peripheralization of the West Bank Palestinians vis-à-vis Jordan, see Shmuel Sandler and Tuvia Frisch, *Israel, the Palestinians and the West Bank: A Study in Intercommunal Conflict* (Lexington, Mass.: Lexington Books, 1984). For a general analysis of Jordan's policies on the Palestinian issue, see Clinton Bailey, *Jordan's Palestinian Challenge 1948–1983* (Jerusalem: Leonard Davis Institute, 1984).

39. See Rosemary Sayigh, *Palestinians: From Peasants to Revolutionaries* (London: Zed Books, 1979).

40. The final takeover occurred at the Fifth Conference of the Palestine National Council, held in Cairo in February 1969, when Fatah and its supporters gained a virtual majority in the council and the executive committee and elected Yasser Arafat chairman. For a personal testimony of these events, see Iyad and Rouleau, *My Home, My Land,* 64–65. See also Chaliand, *Palestinian Resistance,* 56–58.

41. This document is sometimes referred to as the Palestinian Covenant.

42. The full text, with commentary, is in Yehoshafat Harkabi, *The Palestinian Covenant and Its Meaning* (London: Vallentine, Mitchell, 1975).

43. The first hijacking took place on July 22, 1968. An El-Al plane on its way from Rome to Tel Aviv was hijacked to Algeria. On the history of these attempts, see David Hirst, *The Gun and the Olive Branch: The Roots of Violence in the Middle East* (New York: Harcourt Brace Jovanovich, 1977), chap. 9. For a detailed description of the triple hijacking that eventually led to the civil war in Jordan in September 1970, see Peter Snow and David Phillips, *Leila's Hijack War* (London:

Pan Books, 1970). See also Leila Khaled, *My People Shall Live: The Autobiography of a Revolutionary*, ed. George Hajjar (London: Hodder and Stoughton, 1973).

44. Eshkol's response to the debate is in *Knesset Verbatim Record*, November 13, 1967, 50:120–122.

45. This shift in American policy may be partially explained by the fact that in 1956 Senate Majority Leader Lyndon Johnson strongly opposed the policies of President Eisenhower and Secretary of State Dulles, who pressured Israel into an unconditional unilateral retreat from the Sinai peninsula. The Soviet Union was determined to retain (and if possible expand) its regional influence, and subsequently intensified its involvement in the Arab-Israeli conflict. This inevitably led to greater American support for Israel. In a growing number of Washington circles Israel was viewed as an important strategic ally of the United States in containing Soviet influence in the Middle East. For a comprehensive analysis of U.S. policies in the Middle East, see Steven Spiegel, *The Other Arab-Israeli Conflict: Making America's Middle East Policy from Truman to Reagan* (Chicago: University of Chicago Press, 1985); and Bernard Reich, *Quest for Peace: United States-Israel Relations and the Arab-Israeli Conflict* (New Brunswick, N.J.: Transaction Books, 1977). For a general analysis of the Soviet role, see Walter Laqueur, *The Soviet Union and the Middle East* (New York: Praeger, 1969); and Galia Golan, *Soviet Policies in the Middle East from World War II to Gorbachev* (Cambridge: Cambridge University Press, 1990). For the military dimension, see Amnon Sella, *Soviet Political and Military Conduct in the Middle East* (New York: St. Martin's, 1981). On the involvement of the powers in the Middle East after the 1967 war, see Lawrence Whetten, *The Canal War: Four-Power Conflict in the Middle East* (Cambridge, Mass.: MIT Press, 1974).

46. The text of the president's address to the National Foreign Policy Conference of Educators was reprinted in U.S. House of Representatives Committee on Foreign Relations, *The Search for Peace in the Middle East, Documents and Statements, 1967–1988* (Washington, D.C.: Government Printing Office, 1989), 286–289.

47. United Nations Security Council, *SCOR*, Resolution 242, 1,382d meeting, November 22 1967.

48. Obviously this situation changed once Egypt was ready to sign a peace treaty, and later when other Arab states and even the PLO expressed readiness to negotiate on the basis of the principles enunciated in Resolution 242.

49. Sapir used the Hebrew word *chenek* (strangulation) in a cabinet debate on July 9, 1967. He quoted himself to this effect in a speech to the party's secretariat on November 9, 1972. See "Party Secretariat Meetings, Verbatim Record File, 1972," Labor Party Archives, Beit Berl.

50. Chaim Gouri, "A Chat with Pinhas Sapir" (in Hebrew), *Lamerchav*, January 3, 1969.

51. Yossi Sarid, interview by author, Tel Aviv, August 24, 1992. At the time, Sarid was Sapir's political adviser and confidant, as well as a member of the Knesset.

52. Speech to the party's secretariat, November 9, 1967.

53. The aging Ben-Gurion and a small number of his followers did not return to the Labor Party and preserved Rafi as a separate faction for a while. Ben-Gurion soon retired from politics altogether; the others eventually joined Likud. For a more detailed analysis of these developments, see Peter Medding, *Mapai in Israel* (Cambridge: Cambridge University Press, 1972).

54. To be sure, this expansionist approach was popular with the general public. Polls conducted in 1968 and 1969 showed that 68 percent of the public supported a hard line against the Arabs; only 12 percent were opposed. See Alan Arian, *Consensus in Israel* (New York: General Learning Press, 1971).

55. On March 27, 1949, General Yigal Allon, a Tabenkin loyalist, pleaded with Ben-Gurion to allow the IDF to complete the conquest of the West Bank, which could have been easily achieved. He wrote to the prime minister, "One cannot draw a line more solid than the Jordan River along the entire country." Quoted by Yeruham Cohen (who served as Allon's adjutant) in his book *In Daylight and in Darkness* (in Hebrew) (Tel Aviv: Hakibbutz Hameuchad, 1969), 272.

56. From a speech at the national convention of his party. Reprinted in Itzhak Tabenkin, *Party Issues* (in Hebrew) (Tel Aviv: n.p., 1951).

57. Speech reprinted in Itzhak Tabenkin, *The Lessons of the Six Day War: The Settling of the Undivided Land* (in Hebrew) (Tel Aviv: Hakibbutz Hameuchad, 1971), 11.

58. Yisrael Galili, "What Is the Main Question? An Open Letter to Prof. Jacob Talmon," reprinted in Yisrael Galili, ed., *A Continuous Struggle* (Tel Aviv: Hakibbutz Hameuchad, 1987), 13–28. For more on this exchange, see chapter 3.

59. Reprinted in Moshe Dayan, *A New Map: Different Relations* (in Hebrew) (Tel Aviv: Ma'ariv Publications, 1969), 30.

60. Voice of Israel radio broadcast, December 28, 1968. Reprinted in ibid., 138.

61. Ibid., 133.

62. Speech presented in Jerusalem, February 6, 1968. Reprinted in ibid., 177.

63. This lecture was given on August 1, 1968, on the occasion of the graduation ceremony of the IDF Staff and Command School. Reprinted in ibid., 19–29.

64. All quotations of Rupin are from his diaries, published as *Chapters of My Life,* and quoted by Dayan in his lecture, "The Reality of Non-Acceptance," in Dayan, *New Map,* 19–29. The Great Palestinian Revolt was the most significant attempt on the part of the Palestinian nationalists to stop further Zionist immigration and settlement of Palestine. It lasted in varying degrees of intensity from April 1936 until the outbreak of World War II in September 1939. It was ultimately crushed by the British forces.

65. Dayan was an amateur archaeologist and an avid collector of traces of the past. He wrote a book in which he described his attachment to the land of the Bible and its people, among whom he counted the Arab inhabitants. See *Living with the Bible* (New York: William Morrow, 1978). Dayan was far from being the only Israeli political figure whose views were colored by the Bible. For Ben-Gurion, like Dayan a secular Jew, the books of the Tanach (the Old Testament) "were the fruits and expressions of the political and ideological struggle of the people, who fought for their hold on the land, within the political and cultural environment in which they lived during the biblical period." See David Ben-Gurion, *Studies in the Tanach* (in Hebrew) (Tel Aviv: Ayanot), 48. For Ben-Gurion and most Israelis the Tanach has been the most important tool for political recruitment and national mobilization. As Uri Avneri observed: "The Bible is for Zionists . . . a book for today, not just a book of religion, literature or ancient history. This is a book of intense topical interest, a book of reference . . . dealing with the most immediate questions." See Uri Avneri, *Israel without Zionism: A Plan for Peace in the Middle East* (New York: Collier, 1971), 81. This sentimental attachment that many Israelis feel toward the land provides emotional support for the arguments in favor of absorbing the territories (particularly the West Bank) into Israel. It may also be noted that the Bible is to a large extent the story of the acquisition of the land of Canaan by the Israelites and their struggle to maintain that possession. It entails a continuous struggle against other nations living in the area.

66. Speech presented at the Mount of Olives cemetery. Dayan, *New Map,* 173.

67. After 1977 Dayan changed his mind and became a strong advocate of the peace process, which gained momentum with the arrival of President Sadat in Jerusalem. On this phase of his life, see Natan Yanai, ed., *Moshe Dayan on the Peace Process and the Future of Israel 1977–1981* (in Hebrew) (Tel Aviv: Ministry of Defense Publications, 1988).

68. Dayan, *New Map,* 142.

69. General Shlomo Gazit, a close confidant of the minister of defense, believed that Dayan's visit to Vietnam in 1966 made a great impression on him and influenced his view on the way Israel should handle the Palestinians. In a series of articles published simultaneously in the United States and Israel and subsequently compiled into a book, *The Vietnam Diaries* (in Hebrew) (Tel Aviv: Dvir, 1977), Dayan expressed harsh criticism of American policies in Vietnam. Dayan viewed the American management of the war as one that lacked an overriding strategy and clear objectives. Yet, in comparison, Gazit wrote that the Israeli policy "in the administered territories suffered from the same illness. . . . Dayan knew this and wanted to establish practical norms of behavior, on the tactical and operational levels, despite the lack of an overall strategy." See Gazit, *The Stick and the Carrot: The Israeli Administration in Judea and Samaria* (in Hebrew) (Tel Aviv: Bitan Zmora Publishers, 1985), 41.

70. The term "administered territories" was used in official documents as a compromise with the Likud members of the unity government, who claimed that the territories were "liberated" rather than "occupied." When Begin came to power in 1977, the biblical names Judea and Samaria became the official designation.

71. Gazit, *Stick and the Carrot,* 41–43; on the "open bridges" policy, see 204–222. A description of the new situation in the territories was offered by Dayan himself in *Life,* September 29, 1967. See also Shabtai Teveth, *The Cursed Blessing* (London: Weidenfeld and Nicolson, 1970).

72. From a lecture at the political conference of the National Religious Party in Tel Aviv, October 9, 1967. Reprinted in Dayan, *New Map,* 126.

73. Allon published a number of books on military affairs, two of which were published in English: *The Making of Israel's Army* (London: Vallentine, Mitchell, 1970), and *Shield of David: The Story of Israel's Armed Forces* (London: Weidenfeld and Nicolson, 1970).

74. Statement from a meeting with younger members of his kibbutz movement, quoted in Yeruham Cohen, *The Allon Plan* (in Hebrew) (Tel Aviv: Hakibbutz Hameuchad, 1973), 46.

75. From a written explanation Allon attached to his plan that was submitted to the cabinet on July 13, 1967. Reprinted in Yigal Allon, *The Hunt for Peace* (in Hebrew) (Tel Aviv: Hakibbutz Hameuchad, 1989), 17.

76. The plan was first written two weeks earlier, but Allon wanted to prepare the ground before formally proposing it to the government. He later revised his plan and submitted two more versions on February 27, 1968, October 12, 1968, and again on January 29, 1969. At first the government decided not to discuss the matter. Only on July 16, 1972, was it formally put on the agenda, but no decision was ever made. In June 1968 the Political Committee of the Labor Party discussed the plan, which was met with "great sympathy." See ibid., 15, 27. For the full story of the Allon Plan, see Cohen, *Allon Plan*. The text as originally proposed is reprinted in Allon, *The Hunt for Peace*, 16–27.

77. Allon was a staunch supporter of Tabenkin with respect to the necessity of land settlement for the fulfillment of Zionist goals. "Zionism's full implementation has always been and will remain based primarily on the settling of the land. . . . There is no goal more sacred than pioneer settlement of the land." See Yigal Allon, *A Curtain of Sand* (in Hebrew) (Tel Aviv: Hakibbutz Hameuchad, 1968).

78. Ibid., 29.

79. The term *defensible borders* became a common term in Israeli political discourse. Allon claimed that he was the first to use this term. See his article "Defensible Borders," in Yigal Allon, ed., *Communicating Vessels* (in Hebrew) (Tel Aviv: Hakibbutz Hameuchad, 1953), 127–139.

80. *Newsweek*, February 17, 1969, 49–54. The interview is reprinted in Ralph H. Magnus, ed., *Documents on the Middle East* (Washington, D.C.: American Enterprise Institute, 1969), doc. 86, 218–222.

81. Golda Meir, *My Life* (New York: Putnam, 1975), 370.

82. Meir was quite ill when the party called on her, but managed to carry the heavy strain of her responsibilities. Regarding the choice, she said, "I realized that unless I agreed, there would inevitably be a tremendous tug-of-war between Dayan and Allon." Ibid., 378.

83. Ibid., 367. The phrase "secure and recognized borders" is taken from UN Security Council Resolution 242.

84. Ibid., 273.

3. Professors for Peace

1. Avneri was a member of the Knesset in 1967. Interview, July 27, 1992.

2. Uri Avneri, "A Peace Plan," *Ha'olam Ha'zeh*, June 14, 1967, 4.

3. Eliav published a number of books about his adventures: *The Story of an "Illegal" Immigrants' Ship* (in Hebrew) (Jerusalem: World Zionist Organization, 1965); and *Between Hammer and Sickle* (Philadelphia: Jewish Publication Society, 1967). In the mid-1980s he published his autobiography, *Rings of Faith* (in Hebrew) (Tel Aviv: Am Oved, 1984).

4. Eliav, *Rings of Faith*, 288.

5. Ibid., 289–290.

6. Ibid., 291.

7. Arie Eliav, *New Goals for Israel* (in Hebrew) (Tel Aviv: Levin-Epstein, 1970).

8. Ibid., 16–22. This brochure was the first draft of a book that was published a few years later, *The Land of the Hart: Israelis, Arabs, the Territories and a Vision of the Future* (Philadelphia: Jewish Publication Society, 1974).

9. *Time*, January 26, 1970.

10. Eliav, interview by author, Tel Aviv, July 26 and August 2, 1992.

11. Eliav, *Rings of Faith*, 293–297.

12. The document was titled "The Palestinian Refugees and the Economic Development of the Administered Territories." A copy is in the private papers of the author. The main figures in the group were Professor Michael Feldman and Professor Shneor Lipson from the Weitzman Institute; Professor Ra'anan Weitz, the director of the Settlement Department of the Jewish Agency and a prominent expert in rural planning; Memmi de Shalit, the director general of the Ministry of Tourism; and Ehud Avriel, a member of a kibbutz who had served in many government positions, among them director general of the prime minister's office under Ben-Gurion.

13. Eliav, interview. Eliav said that he had met Robert McNamara, the head of the World Bank at the time, who encouraged him to start his project for refugee rehabilitation and reportedly told him, "Money is not the problem."

14. The figures are derived from the "Continuing Survey" of the Guttman Institute of Applied Social Research. See Stone, *Social Change in Israel*, fig. 1.1, 20.

15. Alterman, a devout supporter of David Ben-Gurion and Moshe Shamir, was a long-standing member of Mapam.

16. From an interview Tabenkin gave in January 1969 to *Yediot Ahronot*; reprinted in Itzhak Tabenkin, *The Lessons of the Six Days: The Settling of an Undivided Land* (in Hebrew) (Tel Aviv: Hakibbutz Hameuchad, 1970), 152.

17. The term "Greater Land of Israel" is an inexact translation of the Hebrew term *Eretz Yisrael Hashleima*, which literally means "The Land of Israel in Its Entirety." The description of the birth of the movement relies heavily on Shamir, *Poet as a Leader*, 125–141, 159–174.

18. Ibid., 130, 132, 134.

19. The manifesto is reprinted in ibid., 164. Tabenkin's two sons—Moshe, a poet, and Joseph, a commander of a famous brigade in the 1948 war—were among the founders. Both were members of their father's kibbutz. For a critique of the manifesto, see Dan Miron, "Analysis of the Manifesto of the Greater Land of Israel" (in Hebrew), *Politica* 16 (August 1987): 3–4.

20. Talmon's most noted work was on the totalitarian-democratic ideas of the French Revolution and the nineteenth century. See *The Origins of Totalitarian Democracy* (London: Secker and Warburg, 1955); *Romanticism and Revolt: Europe 1781–1848* (London: Thames and Hudson, 1967); and *Utopianism and Politics* (London: Conservative Political Center, 1957). Hourani is best known for his comprehensive study *A History of the Arab Peoples* (Cambridge, Mass.: Harvard University Press, 1991).

21. See *Observer* (London), September 10, 1967. The articles by Hourani and Talmon were reprinted under the title *Israel and the Arabs* (London: Wrens and Robins, 1967).

22. Jacob Talmon, "For Total Peace in the Middle East," a manuscript in the author's files.

23. Jacob Talmon, "An Open Letter to Minister Yisrael Galili," *Ma'ariv*, May 16, 1969. Because of Talmon's prominence, his letter to Galili aroused a public uproar and prompted numerous responses. See, for example, Shalom Rosenfeld, "A Palestinian Entity, the Ritual of Power and a Little Zionism," *Ma'ariv*, May 22, 1969. Galili also published a rebuttal in the same issue of *Ma'ariv*, which was reprinted in Israel. See Galili, *Continuous Struggle*, 13–28.

24. Yehoshua Arieli, "The Fate of Israel's Democracy Will Be Determined in the Territories," *Davar*, May 2, 9, 15, and 22, 1969.

25. Details about the development of the Movement for Peace and Security, unless otherwise noted, were provided by Arieli in an interview in Jerusalem on August 10, 1992. Arieli was active in a movement critical of Ben-Gurion in the early 1960s.

26. Gadi Yatziv, interview by author, Jerusalem, February 1, 1993. Some of the others who were involved included Professor Menachem Brinker, Dan Bitan, and Professor Jonathan Frankel.

27. In addition to Alterman, Shamir, Eldad, Greenberg, and others, the movement succeeded in gaining the endorsement of Shmuel Agnon, the only Hebrew novelist to receive the Nobel prize for literature (1966).

28. Yigal Eilam, interview by author, Tel Aviv, February 4, 1993.

29. A few settlements were created earlier on the Golan Heights and in the Gush Etzion area, but this one was more dramatic because it was situated in the middle of an Arab town. For the history of the early settlements in the occupied territories, see Peter Robert Demant, "Ploughshares into Swords: Israeli Settlement Policy in the Occupied Territories, 1967–1977" (Ph.D. diss., University of Amsterdam, 1988), 153–161. Rabbi Levinger describes the initial stages of his operation in an interview in *Davar*, September 5, 1975. For an analysis of the way the government handled these problems, see Yael Yishai, *Land or Peace: Whither Israel?* (Stanford: Stanford University Press, 1987), chap. 2.

30. The document is in Yehoshua Arieli's private files. The most prominent of the scholars who signed the manifesto were Professor Ernest Simon, the aging friend of Martin Buber, and Professor Yeshaia Leibovitch.

31. Yael Yishai offered the following critique: "Words were the only weapon wielded by the Peace and Security Movement and, more often than not, these words reached people who were already inclined to support the cause of peace." Yishai, *Land or Peace*, 144.

32. Mapam formally permitted its members to join the movement and provided it with some financial and logistical support, but the claim that it amounted to "Mapamization" of the movement is highly exaggerated. See ibid.

33. Yigal Eilam in letter to Gabriel Stein, May 26, 1968. Arieli files.

34. "An Israeli Peace Program Is Mandatory—Now," declaration of the Movement for Peace and Security made in May 1969. Arieli files.

35. The first National Unity Government was established on the eve of the 1967 war, with Levi Eshkol serving as prime minister. Golda Meir inherited the same coalition in 1969 and recreated it after the elections that were held in the fall of that year. This coalition included almost all of the political parties (supported by more than 80 percent of the members of the Knesset). The right-wing bloc headed by Menachem Begin resigned in August 1970 when Golda Meir consented to the cease-fire at the end of the War of Attrition. For more details, see David Shaham, *Israel: Forty Years* (in Hebrew) (Tel Aviv: Am Oved, 1991), chap. 15; and Howard Sachar, *A History of Israel: From the Rise of Zionism to Our Time* (New York: Knopf, 1979), 615–712.

36. See the article (in Hebrew) in the second bulletin of the Movement for Peace and Security, February 1969, 3. Arieli files.

37. From the May 1969 declaration and September 1969 manifesto. Arieli files.

38. The speech was first published by the movement in a brochure entitled *A Conference on Problems of Peace and Security*; it was later reprinted in Yehoshua Arieli, *History and Politics* (in Hebrew) (Tel Aviv: Am Oved, 1992), 412–423.

39. Among them were Robert Faloney, a member of the National Executive Committee of the Belgian Socialist Party; Claude Lanzman, the editor of *Temps Modernes* and a prominent French filmmaker; Giorgio La Pira, the mayor of Florence; British MP Maurice Orbach; and Nahum Goldmann, the president of the World Jewish Congress. The full proceedings were published in Simcha Flapan, ed., *To Make War or to Make Peace* (Tel Aviv: New Outlook, 1969).

40. Ibid., 8. Some Israeli Arabs participated, but none from the occupied territories or the Palestinian diaspora.

41. See chapter 10.

42. A debate followed the proposal to allow Mapam to join Labor in an electoral bloc. Dayan objected and declared that he was closer to Begin than to Ya'ari, the leader of Mapam. If this was not enough of a threat, Dayan appeared as a guest at the national conference of Herut, Begin's party. See Shaham, *Israel: Forty Years*, 307–309.

43. The four components of the Labor Alliance—Mapai, Tabenkin's group, Rafi, and Mapam—had 63 out of 120 seats in the Sixth Knesset and controlled a clear majority. The 1969 Knesset elections gave the alliance only 56 seats, which forced Golda Meir to form a coalition with other parties. Begin's Gahal alignment held 26 seats. A group that split from Herut and a group of Rafi veterans, which did not return to Labor, both leaning to the right, together gained seven seats. See Asher Arian, *Politics in Israel: The Second Generation* (Chatham, N.J.: Chatham House, 1989), 149. See also Herbert Smith, "Analysis of Voting," in Asher Arian, ed., *Elections in Israel, 1969* (Jerusalem: Jerusalem Academic Press, 1972), 63–80.

44. Some activists, led by Gadi Yatziv, in the Movement for Peace and Security tried but failed to organize a "peace list" to run in Knesset elections. Yatziv later claimed that they never assumed they could pass the minimum threshold necessary to win a Knesset seat; instead, they hoped to use the election campaign "to educate the people and attract their attention." Yishai, *Land or Peace*, 145. The Movement for Peace and Security quickly returned to its usual extraparliamentary role.

45. See U.S. House of Representatives Committee on Foreign Affairs, *The Search for Peace in the Middle East: Documents and Statements, 1967–1988* (Washington, D.C.: Government Printing Office, 1989), doc. 96, 292–300.

46. This story has been told by many authors. For example, see William Quandt, *Decade of Decisions: American Policy toward the Arab-Israeli Conflict 1967–1975* (Berkeley: University of California Press, 1977), 72–104.

47. The document is in the Arieli files.

48. "For an Israeli Peace Initiative," January 1970. Arieli files.

49. See *Ha'aretz*, March 10, 1970. In the event, the government did not make such an announcement, but Allon's statement was perceived as binding.

50. Arieli files. There were more signatures, but only the 150 most prominent ones appeared in the press.

51. Nahum Goldmann, "The Future of Israel," *Foreign Affairs* 48, no. 3 (April 1970): 443–459.

52. There was some controversy as to whether Nasser demanded governmental authorization or only knowledge. An apology for Meir's handling of the affair can be found in Mordechai Gazit, *The Peace Process 1969–1973* (Tel Aviv: Hakibbutz Hameuchad, 1984), 42–52. Gazit was Meir's chief of staff and main political adviser.

53. The Guttman survey (see note 14) showed a decline of twenty points in the "mood" indicators as well as in the "worry and happiness" indicators. See Stone, *Social Change in Israel*, figs. 4.1, 121, 4.2, 139.

54. The handwritten letter was sent by each of the seniors to Golda Meir on April 8, 1970. A few days later Uzi Benziman published in *Ha'aretz* a number of interviews with some members of the group. I received copies of the letter from Shmuel Shem-Tov, one of the leaders. See also Yael Gvirtz, "The Seniors Lost All Hope," *Yediot Ahronot,* October 2, 1992.

55. Copies of the advertisements are in the Arieli files.

56. See a detailed but apparently biased report in *Davar,* April 9, 1970.

57. These groups splintered in later years into different factions; some had Trotskyite inclinations, some favored Maoism. The groups never exceeded a few dozen members. On the history of Matzpen and its positions, see Nira Yovel-Davis, *Matzpen, the Socialist Organization in Israel* (Jerusalem: Hebrew University School of Economics and Political Science, 1977).

58. See letter from Uri Davis (of Matzpen) to Arieli, April 9, 1970, in the Arieli files. Davis was one of the few conscientious objectors in the 1960s.

59. See Bar-Siman-Tov, *Israeli-Egyptian War of Attrition.*

60. For the full text, see Medzini, *Israel's Foreign Relations,* doc.16, 913–914.

61. For a detailed analysis of Nasser's considerations, see Schueftan, *Attrition,* chap. 6. The main opposition came from Nasser's most loyal supporter, Mohamed Heikal.

62. The text is reprinted in Medzini, *Israel's Foreign Relations,* doc. 18, 915–916. The formal acceptance was sent to the United States on August 4, 1970. See ibid., doc. 19, 916–917.

63. Ibid., doc. 22, 921.

64. Ibid., doc. 23, 922–924.

65. The final expulsion of the Palestinian *fedayeen* from Jordan took place a year later, in July 1971, but during "Black September" the Jordanian army had effectively crushed their forces. For more details, see Bailey, *Jordan's Palestinian Challenge;* and Cobban, *Palestine Liberation Organization,* 48–52.

66. Arieli files.

67. "A Statement of the Mind or Stifling of the Mind?" (in Hebrew), August 25, 1970. Arieli files.

68. See the formal decision in Medzini, *Israel's Foreign Relations,* doc. 25, 930; see the text of Meir's announcement in the Knesset on December 29, 1970, in doc. 26, 930–935. For Jarring's report to the Security Council on these developments, see *SCOR,* Supplement for 1971, doc. S/10070, January 4, 1971.

69. This diplomatic step took the form of questions posed to both countries. The above is a summary of the most pertinent questions. See Medzini, *Israel's Foreign Relations,* doc. 28, 950–951.

70. In a book he wrote on the subject, Ya'acobi credits the initial idea to Colonel Yak Nevo, an Israeli Air Force pilot and senior officer who raised this suggestion as a result of his assessment that the Israeli Air Force would not be able to defeat the Soviet missiles. See Gad Ya'acobi, *On the Razor's Edge* (in Hebrew) (Jerusalem: Idanim, 1989). The story was told to the author in an interview with Ya'acobi in Tel Aviv on August 13, 1992. Early in February, Henry Kissinger, who served at that time as Nixon's national security adviser, discussed with the president his doubts as to the practicality of a comprehensive settlement and suggested for the first time his "step-by-step" approach. Because he was not in charge of the Middle East negotiations at the time, the idea was dropped. See Henry Kissinger, *White House Years* (Boston: Little, Brown, 1979), 582.

71. Gazit, *Peace Process*, 19–22. For the events in the United Nations in 1957, see Abba Eban, "The Political Struggle in the UN and the USA after the Sinai Campaign" (in Hebrew), an unpublished report written in Washington, D.C., in 1957. A copy can be found in the Israel National Archives.

72. Kissinger considered the State Department's search for a comprehensive settlement a mistake from the beginning of Nixon's presidency. He wrote later that he advised the president to focus "on a partial settlement, such as one with Jordan." Only later, as a result of the October War, did he start to focus on Egypt. See Kissinger, *White House Years*.

73. Ya'acobi, *Razor's Edge*, 57.

74. See Yehoshua Raviv, "Some Early Attempts at an Interim Settlement with Egypt 1971–1972" (in Hebrew), *Ma'arachot* nos. 243–244 (April–May 1975).

75. This was announced during a speech to the Egyptian National Assembly. Sadat discussed this in an interview in *Newsweek*, February 15, 1971.

76. For a detailed defense of Golda Meir's treatment of the interim arrangements in 1971–72, see Gazit, *Peace Process*, 97–130.

77. Professors' cable to Meir, December 25, 1971. Arieli files.

78. The appeal was sent as a cable to Meir and was simultaneously published in the press. See *Davar*, January 12, 1972.

79. Of all the signatories to the letter, Meir chose to answer Professor Dan Patenkin, a prominent economist at the Hebrew University in Jerusalem. Cable by Meir to Patenkin, December 27, 1971. Arieli files.

80. Interview with Patenkin in *Yediot Ahronot*, January 15, 1972.

81. There are many quotations to this effect. For example, in a cabinet session on July 25, 1971, Dayan stated that "a political deadlock . . . may lead to war in which the lives of many Israeli soldiers will be lost, even if Egypt will be defeated." Quoted in Ya'acobi, *Razor's Edge*, 147.

82. After the surprise and heavy losses incurred in the October 1973 war (the Yom Kippur War), the term "low probability" became a derogatory phrase to signify intelligence blunders and political blindness. See Shlomo Nakdimon, *Low Probability: A Narrative of the Dramatic Story Preceding the Yom Kippur War and of the Fateful Events Which Followed* (in Hebrew) (Tel Aviv: Revivim, 1982).

83. Ibid., 31.

84. On the expulsion of the Soviet military advisers from Egypt, see Ro'i, *From Encroachment to Involvement*, 569–577. For the Egyptian view on these events, see Heikal, *Road to Ramadan*, 160–184. For a general description of the events, see Golan, *Soviet Policies in the Middle East*, 77–90; and Robert O. Freedman, *Soviet Policy towards the Middle East since 1970* (New York: Praeger, 1975), 74–80, 93–104.

85. Golda Meir, speech in the Knesset, October 26, 1971. *Knesset Records.*

86. Nakdimon, *Low Probability*, 31.

87. Quoted by Abba Eban in *Ma'ariv*, September 29, 1989.

88. In the aftermath of the October War, in a debate in the Central Committee of the Labor Party, Golda Meir had to defend Galili and remind the participants that although the document carried Galili's name, it was Dayan who was responsible for its articulation. See *Verbatim Record of Proceedings of the Central Committee Debates,* December 5, 1973, Labor Party Archives, Beit Berl.

89. Dan Bitan, interview by author, Jerusalem, February 3, 1993.

90. The name was a reference to the biblical story of Balaam's ass. Interview with Yigal Eilam, Tel Aviv, February 4, 1993.

91. Eilam eventually published his ideas on Zionism in his book *An Introduction to Zionist History* (in Hebrew) (Tel Aviv: Levin-Epstein, 1972).

92. Eliav, *Rings of Faith,* 301.

93. For a full citation of the English version, see note 8.

94. Eliav, *Rings of Faith,* 314.

95. Eliav, *Land of the Hart,* 119, 120, 129. The book was published in Hebrew in 1972 in four consecutive editions by Am Oved, the Labor Party publishing house. It sold more than 15,000 copies, a very large number for nonfiction in Israel.

96. Ibid., 138. In later years Eliav developed a proposal to create a triple federation (which he called *Isfalur*) to include Israel, Jordan, and the Palestinian state. See Arie Lova Eliav, "Alternative to a Nightmare," *Jerusalem Post,* January 2, 1981.

97. Interview with Eliav, Tel Aviv, July 26, 1992.

98. Eliav, *Rings of Faith,* 316.

99. Ibid., 323–327.

100. The poem was published after the October War ended. See Lova Eliav, "The Seagull," *Davar,* November 8, 1973. It was published again, a week later, by Silvie Keshet in her column in *Yediot Ahronot,* November 16, 1973.

4. The October War and the End of Labor Supremacy, 1973–77

1. Quoted in Nakdimon, *Low Probability,* 135.

2. Quoted in Ze'ev Schiff, *October Earthquake* (Tel Aviv: University Publishing Project, 1974), 13. For a detailed, objective account of the war, see Trevor Dupuy, *Elusive War: The Arab-Israeli Wars 1947–1974* (New York: Harper and Row, 1978), 387–617. The chief of Israeli military intelligence, who was dismissed for the intelligence failure, recently published his own account of the war. See Eli Zeira, *The October 1973 War: Myth and Reality* (in Hebrew) (Tel Aviv: Yediot Ahronot Publications, 1993).

3. On the failed counteroffensive, see the testimony of the commander, General Avraham Adan (Bren), *On Both Banks of the Suez* (in Hebrew) (Jerusalem: Idanim, 1979). Good journalistic reports of the military events are provided in Dana Adams Schmidt, *Armageddon in the Middle East* (New York: John Day, 1974); and Insight Team of the *Sunday Times, Insight on the Middle East War* (London: Andre Deutsch, 1974).

4. See Edward N. Luttwak and Walter Laqueur, "Kissinger and the Yom Kippur War," *Commentary* 58, no. 3 (September 1974).

5. Data are taken from the regular surveys of the Israel Institute of Applied Social Research. The figures are for the question asked in general terms of "handling the problems of the present situation." When asked specifically on "security problems," the decline was worse and reached a low of 12 percent in March 1974.

6. In a survey Arian conducted in 1969 he found that only 37 percent of respondents mentioned the party's platform as the determining factor influencing their voting decision. See Alan Arian, *The Choosing People: Voting Behavior in Israel* (Cleveland, Ohio: Case Western University Press, 1973), 99.

7. See, for example, Yochanan Peres, Ephraim Yuchtman (Yaar), and Rivka Shafat, "Predicting and Explaining Voters' Behavior in Israel," in Alan Arian, ed., *The Elections in Israel, 1973* (Jerusalem: Jerusalem Academic Press, 1974).

8. The Israel Institute of Applied Social Research found a steep decline both in the morale of the Jewish population in Israel during the October War as well as in support for government policies, while indications of national unity rose significantly. See Stone, *Social Change in Israel*, figs. 4.1, 8.1, 11.1.

9. In his 1969 survey, Arian found that 84 percent of respondents listened to radio news regularly. See Arian, *Choosing People*. A 1970 survey showed that 77 percent of Israelis read at least one newspaper daily. See Eliahu Katz and Michael Gurevitz, *The Culture of Leisure in Israel* (in Hebrew) (Tel Aviv: Am Oved, 1973). Writing in the mid-1960s Leonard Fein observed that "there is an almost total absence of organizations with quasipolitical interests and other similar groups." See Leonard Fein, *Politics in Israel* (Boston: Little, Brown, 1967), 86.

10. See Eva Etzioni-Halevy, *Political Culture in Israel: Cleavage and Integration among Israeli Jews* (New York: Praeger, 1977), table 4.1, 70.

11. A heated debate on this issue took place in the Central Committee of the Labor Party on October 28, 1973, but a proposal to reopen the lists was defeated 256 to 107. Central Committee Debate Files, 1973, Labor Party Archives, Beit Berl.

12. On the disengagement negotiations and the special role Kissinger played in them, see Henry Kissinger, *Years of Upheaval* (Boston: Little, Brown, 1982), 450–666. See also Marvin Kalb and Bernard Kalb, *Kissinger* (Boston: Little, Brown, 1974), 500–542; and Quandt, *Decade of Decisions*. For a critical approach to Kissinger, see Matti Golan, *The Secret Conversations of Henry Kissinger: Step by Step Diplomacy in the Middle East* (New York: Quadrangle, 1976).

13. The figures are taken from Central Bureau of Statistics, *Israel Statistical Monthly Supplement* (Jerusalem: Central Bureau of Statistics, 1974). Further analysis of the 1973 elections can be found in Arian, *Elections in Israel, 1973*. A detailed analysis of Begin's rise to power can be found in Yonathan Shapiro, *Chosen to Command: The Road to Power of the Herut Party: A Socio-Political Interpretation* (Tel Aviv: Am Oved, 1989).

14. Asher Arian, *The Elections in Israel, 1977* (Jerusalem: Jerusalem Academic Press, 1978), 254.

15. David Nachmias, "Coalition, Myth and Reality," in Arian, *Elections in Israel, 1973*, 241–254.

16. In April 1971 *Time* published the results of a Louis Harris poll conducted in Israel in which 91 percent of the respondents (which included a representative sample of Israeli Arabs) believed that "Israel can triumph over the Arabs the fourth time around"; only 3 percent feared a possible defeat. *Time*, April 12, 1971, 32.

17. In the *Time* poll, Dayan received the highest popularity rating. Ninety-five percent of the respondents rated him as "excellent" or "pretty good."

18. The Hebrew term used was *Hamechdal*, which literally means "The Omission" and refers to the measures that could have been taken to avoid the war in the first place or at least avoid the initial setbacks once the war started. Interview with Motti Ashkenazi in Jerusalem, January 31, 1993. For a full treatment of the post–October War protest movement, see Moshe Livne, "Our Israel: The Rise and Fall of a Protest Movement" (M.A. thesis, Tel Aviv University, June 1977).

19. Ibid., endnote 42.

20. See Etzioni-Halevy, *Political Culture in Israel,* fig. 5.1, 100; fig. 9.1, 186.

21. Stone, *Social Change in Israel,* fig. 4.1, 139.

22. See Uri Bialer, *Between East and West: Israel's Foreign Policy Orientation 1948–1956* (Cambridge: Cambridge University Press, 1990), 9–53.

23. Sam Lehman-Wilzig, *Public Protest in Israel 1949–1992* (in Hebrew) (Ramat Gan, Israel: Bar Ilan University Press, 1992).

24. See Henriette Dahan-Kalev, "Self-Organizing Systems: Wadi Salib and the Black Panthers" (Ph.D. diss., Hebrew University, July 1991).

25. Erik Cohen, "The Black Panthers and Israeli Society," in E. Krausz, ed., *Studies in Israeli Society* (New York, 1980); and D. Bernstein, "Black Panthers: Conflict and Protest in Israeli Society" (in Hebrew), *Megamot* 25, no. 1 (September 1979).

26. Ehud Sprinzak, *The Buds of Delegitimization: Politics in Israel 1967–1972* (in Hebrew) (Jerusalem: Levi Eshkol Institute Publications, 1973).

27. Livne, *Our Israel,* 3.

28. Menachem Talmi, "From the Mango Groves to the Knesset Plaza," *Ma'ariv,* March 1, 1974.

29. Dayan, *Story of My Life,* 597.

30. The movement was never unified and remained a loose federation of both local groups and groups of reserve soldiers. The name "Our Israel" became a reference term for the media and the active participants.

31. *Yediot Ahronot,* February 17, 1974.

32. From a brochure labeled "Change," in the documents of Motti Ashkenazi released to the author (hereafter referred to as the Our Israel File).

33. Interview with Motti Ashkenazi, *Ma'ariv,* February 8, 1974.

34. *Ma'ariv,* March 4, 1974.

35. Ehud Sprinzak has identified three phases through which political protest movements progress on the slippery slope from legal behavior, based on an underlying acceptance of legitimacy of the system, to illegal behavior, based on the delegitimization of the political structures against which the protestors operate. The public behavior of Our Israel fits the phase described by him as a "confidence crisis," a situation in which groups of citizens raise a "fundamental critique of the regime and its accepted ideology and [do] not find a place in the regular power play of the parliamentary game." The protest movement that developed after the Yom Kippur War did not enter the second phase, labeled by Sprinzak as "conflict of legitimization," and certainly never reached the third phase in which groups employ illegal behavior and embrace an illegal symbolic discourse. See Sprinzak, *Buds of Delegitimization,* 5–6.

36. In the "organizational and functional framework" of the movement, the following item was included: "[The movement] will operate in every method which does not break the law." On one of the large demonstrations held in Jerusalem, Visnews reported that "the demonstrators broke up peacefully when their way to the Knesset building was blocked by riot police." Visnews production no.1617/74, Jerusalem, February 17, 1974. A written record of this production is included in the Peace Now Archive, Jerusalem, 1974 file.

37. Motti Ashkenazi, "Israeli Society in a Prolonged Confrontation," *Ma'ariv,* January 17, 1975. Iris Heinoch-Yaacobi reported from Haifa that many of the active people who belonged to the 1948 generation "did not give up the dream." Letter to Dalia, Yosi, and Motti Ashkenazi, April 28, 1974, in Our Israel File.

38. "Protocol of the Secretariat Meeting, April 28, 1974," Our Israel File.

39. Livne, *Our Israel,* endnote 61.

40. *The Agranat Committee Report* (Tel Aviv: Am Oved, 1975), 34–43.

41. See the protocol of the Independence Day Committee, April 9, 1974, Our Israel File.

42. Meir, *My Life,* 458.

43. On these developments, see Dayan, *Story of My Life,* 590–608.

44. "Agreement on Disengagement between Israeli and Syrian Forces," UN Security Council Document S/11302/Add. 1 Annex 1 (1974). Reprinted in Moore, *Arab-Israeli Conflict,* 1200–1202.

45. Livne, *Our Israel,* 21–23.

46. See, for example, Amnon Kapeliouk, *Not by Omission: The Policy That Led to War* (in Hebrew) (Tel Aviv: Amikam, 1975). The book was also published in French under the title *Israel: La Fin des Mythes.*

47. Dayan, *Story of My Life,* 598. One of the active members of the inner circle of the movement was Israel Harel, who later became a founder and leader of Gush Emunim.

48. Sam Lehman-Wilzig, "The Israeli Protester," *Jerusalem Quarterly* 26 (winter 1983). Lehman-Wilzig included in his research all forms of protest: political, economic, social, ethnic, religious, etc. His research showed that Israelis scored very high in their legitimization of extraparliamentary protest when compared to other Western societies, and showed an even higher propensity to participate in them personally (21.5 percent in Israel, as compared to 11 percent in the United States and only 6 percent in Austria, for example).

49. *Knesset Verbatim Record,* October 16, 1973, 68:4473–4495.

50. Her reference to this in her memoirs is quite moving. See Meir, *My Life,* 420.

51. Verbatim Record of the proceedings of the meeting on December 5, 1973, "Central Committee, Debate Verbatim Record File, 1973," Labor Party Archives, Beit Berl.

52. Kfar Etzion, a kibbutz between Bethlehem and Hebron, was demolished by the Jordanian Army in 1948 and was resettled by the children of the original members soon after the Six Day War.

53. On the tenth anniversary of Gush Emunim the entire issue of *Nekuda,* the magazine of the settlers in Samaria, Judea, and Gaza, was dedicated to the development of the movement. "Gush Emunim: The First Decade," *Nekuda,* February 3, 1984.

54. For analyses of the movement, its politics, institutions, and culture, see Ehud Sprinzak, *The Ascendance of Israel's Radical Right* (Oxford: Oxford University Press, 1991), 43–51; and Gideon Aran, "From Religious Zionism to Zionist Religion: The Origins and Culture of Gush Emunim, a Messianic Movement in Modern Israel" (in Hebrew) (Ph.D. diss., Hebrew University, 1987). A summary of this work in English can be found in Gideon Aran, "Jewish Zionist Fundamentalism: The Bloc of the Faithful in Israel," in Martin E. Marty and R. Scott Appleby, eds., *Fundamentalism Observed* (Chicago: University of Chicago Press,

1991), 197–264. See also Danny Rubinstein, *On the Lord's Side: Gush Emunim* (in Hebrew) (Tel Aviv: Hakibbutz Hameuchad, 1982); and Tzvi Ra'anan, *Gush Emunim* (in Hebrew) (Tel Aviv: Sifriat Poalim, 1980).

55. Gary S. Schiff, *Tradition and Politics: The Religious Parties in Israel* (Detroit: Wayne State University Press, 1977), 37–65. See also Stewart Reiser, *The Politics of Leverage: The National Religious Party of Israel and Its Influence on Foreign Policy* (Cambridge, Mass.: Harvard University Press, 1984).

56. See Lilly Weissbrod, "Gush Emunim Ideology: From Religious Doctrine to Political Action," *Middle Eastern Studies* 18, no. 3 (July 1982): 265–275. The teachings of Rabbi Kook can be found in Avraham Itzhak Hocohen Kook, *Orot* (in Hebrew) (Jerusalem: Kook Publications, 1950).

57. See Rubinstein, *On the Lord's Side,* 16–17.

58. Most of the "Black Hats" do not serve in the IDF because they are granted exempt status while studying in the *yeshivot* (rabbinical schools), which they often attend for many years.

59. The younger Kook was referred to by his first names in order to preserve and honor the memory of his father. Eliezer Don-Yehiya, an expert on the history and ideology of religious Zionism, described the differences between the two Kooks. While the father's messianism was primarily theological, the son translated his father's doctrine into "the level of operative attitudes." Holiness was perceived by the elder Kook as "potentially latent in the Jewish nation," whereas the son perceived holiness "not as an inner potential, but as a given fact," which he attached to the Jewish state and the Jewish army. See Don-Yehiya, "Jewish Messianism, Religious Zionism and Israeli Politics: The Impact and Origins of Gush Emunim," *Middle East Studies* 23, no. 2 (April 1987). An analysis of the elder Kook can be found in Kevin A. Avruch, "Gush Emunim: Politics, Religion, and Ideology in Israel," *Middle East Review* 11, no. 2 (winter, 1978–79): 26–31. Avruch referred to Kook's doctrine as the primary ideological alternative to the ideology of Labor Socialist Zionism.

60. According to Rabbi Kook, the entire Land of Israel included parts of Jordan east of the river, in which several of the twelve tribes of Israel lived in biblical times.

61. Quoted by Uriel Tal, "The Land and the State of Israel," in *Rabbinical Assembly Proceedings,* 1969, 38:9.

62. The full text is reprinted in Rubinstein, *On the Lord's Side,* appendix 1.

63. The early settlements on the Golan Heights were undertaken by disciples of Tabenkin from the secular kibbutz movement. On this story and the settling of Kfar Etzion, see Demant, "Ploughshares into Swords," 113–118.

64. See Rabbi Yehuda Amital, *Mamaalot Mimaamakim* (The Elevations from Depth), a brochure published in Hebrew by Yeshivat Har Etzion, Alon Shvut, 1974.

65. This step brought Gush Emunim great success even in terms of parliamentary representation. See David Newman, "Gush Emunim between Fundamentalism and Pragmatism," *Jerusalem Quarterly* 39 (1986): 33–43.

66. For students of religious institutions of holy learning one of the greatest sins is to waste time on activities other than the learning of the holy scriptures, but for this occasion the younger Rabbi Kook gave special permission to "close the books." See Rubinstein, *On the Lord's Side,* 48–50.

67. On these developments see Demant, "Ploughshares into Swords," chaps. 13, 14, 15.

68. Ibid., 289–291; and Rubinstein, *On the Lord's Side,* 51–57.

69. The holiday of Hanukkah commemorates the bravery of the Hasmoneans in their struggle in 166 B.C. to clear the temple of Hellenistic defiling. The holiday invokes strong nationalistic symbols. An hour-by-hour description of these events is in Demant, "Ploughshares into Swords," 381–435.

70. Meron Benvenisti, *The West Bank Data Project: A Survey of Israel's Policies* (Washington, D.C.: American Enterprise Institute, 1984), table 28, 61. Central Bureau of Statistics, *Statistical Abstract of Israel, 1978* (Jerusalem: Central Bureau of Statistics, 1979), table ii/4, 34, shows 4,400 Jewish settlers in Samaria and Judea at the end of 1977. This does not include Jerusalem. In 1977 the Arab population of the West Bank amounted to almost 700,000. See *Statistical Abstract of Israel, 1991*, table 27.2, 711. A summary of demographic developments in the occupied territories can be found in Yishai, *Land or Peace*, table 4, 35.

71. Rubinstein, *On the Lord's Side*, 63. On later developments in Gush Emunim, see David Newman, ed., *The Impact of Gush Emunim: Politics and Settlement in the West Bank* (New York: St. Martin's, 1985). For a review from within, see Yair Sheleg, "There Was Once a Movement," *Nekuda*, no. 114, October 1987. For a critique of Gush's ideology, see Amnon Rubinstein, *The Zionist Dream Revisited: From Herzl to Gush Emunim and Back* (New York: Schocken, 1984).

72. See Golan, *Secret Conversations of Henry Kissinger*. See also Edward R. F. Sheehan, *The Arabs, Israelis and Kissinger: A Secret History of American Diplomacy in the Middle East* (New York: Reader's Digest Press, 1976).

73. On these scandals, see Yitzhak Rabin, *The Rabin Memoirs* (Boston: Little, Brown, 1979), 304–314.

74. Prior to the 1981 elections Aloni added the word "peace" to the official name of her party. Shulamit Aloni, interview by author, Jerusalem, August 22, 1992.

75. Menachem Brinker, interview by author, Jerusalem, August 16, 1992. See also Nachmias, "Coalition, Myth and Reality."

76. A loosely organized movement developed in Israel in the early 1970s under the name of the Israeli New Left (the acronym in Hebrew was Siah). Gadi Yatziv, interview by author, Jerusalem, February 1, 1993.

77. As a matter of principle Rakach considered itself a mixed Jewish-Arab party; two of its four MKs were Jewish, but about 90 percent of its supporters were Arab. See Moshe Shokeid, "Strategy and Change in the Arab Vote: Observations in a Mixed Town," in Arian, *Elections in Israel, 1973*, 45–166.

78. Moked was 700 votes short of receiving a second seat and consequently lost about 10,000 votes. The 10,469 votes given to Uri Avneri were lost because he did not pass the 1 percent threshold.

79. Within the Labor Alliance there were also eight members of Mapam, but they were constrained by party discipline.

80. Uri Avneri unsuccessfully tried to create a unified peace movement in 1969. See M. Meisels, "The Efforts to Create a Broad 'Peace Front' Failed," *Ma'ariv*, September 24, 1969. In 1970 Avneri tried again and proposed to begin by establishing a "Coordination Forum," but nothing came out of this initiative either. Letter dated April 15, 1970, in Avneri's private archive.

81. Avneri founded a group with a similar name about a month earlier, but merged into the other group at its foundation. Interview with Avneri, Tel Aviv, July 23, 1992. See also *Ha'olam Ha'zeh*, December 17, 1975, 12–13. For more on these developments, see chapter 10.

82. The document is in Avneri's personal archive.

83. *Ma'ariv,* April 12, 1974.

84. *Ma'ariv,* May 16, 1974.

85. *Ma'ariv,* May 6, 1974.

86. *UN GAOR, 1975,* Supplementary Documents, Resolution 3375.

87. Ibid., Resolution 3376.

88. Ibid., Resolution 3379. The text is also reprinted in Medzini, *Israel's Foreign Relations,* doc. 128, 349–352.

89. Ibid., doc. 129, 353–359.

90. See Cobban, *Palestinian Liberation Organization,* 58–63. For the PNC document, see *International Documents on Palestine* (Beirut: Center for Palestine Studies, 1974), 411.

91. Yishai, *Land or Peace,* 146.

92. The monthly magazine of the right-wing settlers that began publication about the same time is called *Nekuda,* which also has a double meaning: a point of view, and a settlement.

93. The editorial board included many prominent peace activists such as MK Yossi Sarid, Yigal Eilam, A. B. Yehoshua, Raul Teitelbaum (from the Zionist splinter group of the Communist Party), and Saadia Marciano (of the Black Panthers).

94. Menachem Brinker, interview by author, Jerusalem, August 16, 1992.

95. Ibid. Brinker emphasizes the fact that Yuval Neria, who was a founder of Peace Now two years later, received valuable experience at *Emda.*

96. Ibid.

97. The editors regularly exchanged articles with *Nouvelle Observateur, The Statesman, Dissent, Ramparts,* and other magazines. They also published articles by Said Hammami and Walid Khalidi of the PLO.

98. This organization was a modest forerunner to B'tselem, the human rights watch group founded in Israel ten years later. See chapter 12.

99. For the Egyptian arrangement, see *SCOR,* Documents 1974, doc. S/1198/ rev. 1/ add 1. For the Syrian Agreement, see ibid., doc. S/11302/add. 1/ annex 1. Reprinted in Moore, *Arab-Israeli Conflict,* 1196–1202.

100. *SCOR* Documents 1973, doc. S/RES/338. See also Moore, *Arab-Israeli Conflict,* doc. 61, 1189.

101. Quandt, *Decade of Decisions,* 213.

102. Syria refused to attend and the PLO was not invited. Ibid., 218–224.

103. For Rabin's perception of these incidents, see his *Memoirs,* 253–275.

104. At the time there seemed to be a severe crisis in U.S.-Israel relations, but Gabriel Sheffer summarized the situation by saying that the "pattern of relations implied understanding on strategic issues and disagreement on tactical problems." See Gabriel Sheffer, *Patron and Client Relations: Israeli Dependence on the USA* (in Hebrew) (Jerusalem: Leonard Davis Institute, 1986), 21.

105. Golan, *Secret Conversations of Henry Kissinger,* 213–252.

106. See Quandt, *Decade of Decisions,* 260–281; and Moore, *Arab-Israeli Conflict,* doc. 68, 69, 70, 71, 1208–1227.

107. The full text is in Moore, *Arab-Israeli Conflict,* doc. 70, 1219–1223. See also Sheehan, *Arabs, Israelis and Kissinger,* 191, and appendix 8, 257. On the significance of this commitment in later years, see chapter 13.

108. Kissinger, *Years of Upheaval,* 1138–1142.

109. On the struggle between Hussein and the PLO, see Bailey, *Jordan's Palestinian Challenge,* 65–90.

110. Meetings with Hussein included at different times Rabin, Peres, and Allon, who was at this time the minister of foreign affairs. On these meetings, see Yossi Melman and Dan Raviv, *Behind the Uprising: Israelis, Jordanians, and Palestinians* (New York: Greenwood, 1989).

111. See Shaham, *Israel: Forty Years,* 372–373. On U.S. policy vis-à-vis the internal struggle in the Arab world, see Itamar Rabinovich, "The Challenge of Heterogeneity: U.S. Policy and the Intra-Arab Relations System, 1973–1977" (in Hebrew), in Itamar Rabinovich and Chaim Shaked, eds., *The Middle East and the USA* (Tel Aviv: Am Oved, 1980), 166–181.

5. Shalom Achshav—Peace Now

1. *Ma'ariv,* June 8, 1977.

2. See chapter 4, p. 83.

3. *Jerusalem Post,* September 12, 1977.

4. *Ha'aretz,* September 12, 1977. Asked by a journalist about the future status of the West Bank, Begin said, "You used the words West Bank, say Judea and Samaria, use these names always!" Quoted by Eric Silver, *Begin: The Haunted Prophet* (London: Weidenfeld and Nicolson, 1984), 160.

5. Quoted in Eitan Haber, *Menachem Begin: The Legend and the Man* (New York: Delacorte, 1978), 306.

6. On his own perceptions of these events, see Moshe Dayan, *Breakthrough: A Personal Account of the Egypt-Israel Peace Negotiations* (New York: Knopf, 1981), 1–54.

7. Arie Na'or, a close aide of Begin, wrote that prior to the elections Begin put peace as his main objective and started to inch away from his earlier doctrine. He quotes Begin as saying to his close aides during the election campaign, "Yes, we shall make peace! We shall make peace!" Arye Na'or, *Writing on the Wall* (in Hebrew) (Jerusalem: Edanim, 1988), 109–110.

8. Uzi Benziman, *Prime Minister under Siege* (Jerusalem: Adam Publishers, 1981), 12–13. This was also the main concern of the Carter administration. For a detailed analysis of U.S. policy toward the Middle East under Carter, see Spiegel, *The Other Arab-Israeli Conflict,* 315–340.

9. At least two more messages to this effect (in addition to what Dayan told al-Tuhami in Fez) were transmitted to Sadat by President Carter and by the Romanian president Ceaucescu, whom Begin had visited earlier that summer and whom Sadat visited at the end of October. See William Quandt, *Camp David: Peace Making and Politics* (Washington, D.C.: Brookings Institution, 1986), chap. 4; and Eitan Haber, Ze'ev Schiff, and Ehud Ya'ari, *The Year of the Dove* (New York: Bantam, 1979), chaps. 2 and 3. On the events around Sadat's visit to Romania, see Ismail Fahmy, *Negotiating for Peace in the Middle East* (Baltimore, Md.: Johns Hopkins University Press, 1983), 252–267.

10. Some commentators claimed that Sadat undertook his historic visit to Jerusalem on the assumption that Dayan had promised al-Tuhami that Israel would return the whole of Sinai. See Benziman, *Prime Minister under Siege,* 18. However, Dayan's disclaimer of such a promise seems to be credible. This is also the impression one gets from Ismail Fahmy's memoirs, *Negotiating for Peace,* 253–254.

11. During the late summer and early fall a flurry of activity in New York produced a joint statement by U.S. Secretary of State Cyrus Vance and Soviet foreign minister Andrei Gromyko that made both the Egyptians and the Israelis unhappy. See Quandt, *Camp David*, chap. 5. Only a few days before Sadat made his dramatic gesture, Carter advised him to adhere to the Geneva formula and told him that he, Carter, was making efforts "to recommend proposed procedures so that the Geneva conference can open soon." See Fahmy, *Negotiating for Peace*, 262–263. For more on these developments, see Spiegel, *The Other Arab-Israeli Conflict*, 329–340.

12. Sadat claimed that he made a similar offer "to go to any length to achieve [peace]" immediately upon assuming the presidency in September 1970. Anwar Sadat, *In Search of Identity: An Autobiography* (New York: Harper Colophon, 1979), 276.

13. *Ma'ariv* November 14, 1977. Some senior officers in the Israeli military and intelligence establishments suspected that this was a ploy to cover up preparations for a military offensive. See Benziman, *Prime Minister under Siege*, 35.

14. A lively description is found in Silver, *Begin*, 174–175.

15. For the official text of Sadat's, Begin's, and Peres's speeches, see *Knesset Verbatim Record*, November 21, 1977. The text of the two speeches are also reprinted in *Keesing's Contemporary Archives: Record of World Events* (London: Keesing's Publications, Longman, 1978), 29155 and 29158.

16. Sadat's memoirs, written shortly after his visit to Jerusalem, convey his original vision of peace. He wrote in unequivocal terms that "at the very heart of the [Middle East question] lies the Palestinian problem. . . . A peace agreement should [therefore] provide for the establishment of a Palestinian state on the West Bank of Jordan and the Gaza Strip, and Israel should withdraw from all territories occupied in 1967." Sadat, *In Search of Identity*, 297. At this stage Sadat also rejected Israel's demand for full normalization of bilateral relations. In his book he claims that these demands were only "a ruse to help [Israel] to gain time." Ibid., 299–300.

17. No record of these private discussions was kept other than the few details Begin reported to his colleagues.

18. Dayan, *Breakthrough*, 84–86.

19. Much of what follows draws on my earlier book, *Peace Now: The Portrait of a Movement* (in Hebrew) (Tel Aviv: Hakibbutz Hameuchad, 1985).

20. Interview with Lova Eliav.

21. Dayan, *Breakthrough*, 85–86.

22. According to Sadat, 5 million Egyptians participated in the demonstration.

23. The detailed plan was prepared by General Tamir, but the part on autonomy was Begin's creation. See Avraham Tamir, *A Soldier in Search of Peace: An Inside Look at Israel's Strategy* (London: Weidenfeld and Nicolson, 1988), 32–36; and Benziman, *Prime Minister under Siege*, 82–83. On the origins of the autonomy idea, see Na'or, *Writing on the Wall*, 112–117.

24. Steven Spiegel comments that Begin's choice to present his plan first to the U.S. president "revived active US involvement. A three-cornered relationship rapidly emerged." Spiegel, *The Other Arab-Israeli Conflict*, 342. See also Jimmy Carter, *Keeping Faith: Memoirs of a President* (New York: Bantam, 1982), 299–300.

25. The heads of the military committee were Ezer Weizman, the new minister of defense, and General Abd al-Ghani Gamasi, his Egyptian counterpart. Similarly, the political committee was chaired by the Egyptian and Israeli foreign ministers.

26. Haber, Schiff, and Ya'ari, *Year of the Dove,* 147–150. See also Mohamed Ibrahim Kamel, *The Camp David Accords: A Testimony* (London: KPI, 1986), 53–71.

27. See Carter, *Keeping Faith,* 303. From the outset of his presidency, Carter was convinced that a fair solution to the Palestinian problem was the key to peace in the Middle East. See, for example, Cyrus Vance, *Hard Choices: Critical Years in American Foreign Policy* (New York: Simon and Schuster, 1983), 164. Carter was impressed by a Brookings Institution report published in December 1975 that concluded that "there should be provision for Palestinian self-determination. . . . This might take the form either of a Palestinian state . . . or of a Palestinian entity voluntarily federated with Jordan but exercising extensive political autonomy." *Toward Peace in the Middle East* (Washington, D.C.: Brookings Institution, December 1975), 591–592.

28. Yael Gvirtz, "Signed: 348 Officers," interviews with the initiators fifteen years later published in *Yediot Ahronot,* April 2, 1993. See also Bar-On, *Peace Now,* 14–17.

29. Quoted by Phillip Gillon, "Anatomy of a Movement," *Jerusalem Post,* April 14, 1978. The list of signatures included two colonels, fifteen majors, six combat pilots, and several recipients of medals for combat distinction.

30. The letter is reprinted in Bar-On, *Peace Now,* 15–16.

31. See chapter 3, pp. 56–57.

32. Gvirtz, "Signed: 348 Officers."

33. Naftali Raz, interview by author, Mevaseret Yerushalayim, January 9, 1984.

34. The first book on Peace Now was written in the late 1970s by Arye Palgi, *Peace and Nothing More* (in Hebrew) (Tel Aviv: Sifriat Poalim, 1979).

35. These profiles are drawn from my personal impressions and interviews with members of the movement.

36. See Shulamit Hareven, *The Vocabulary of Peace* (San Francisco: Mercury House, 1995).

37. This last section does injustice to scores of people who made great contributions to the movement and who expended similar amounts of energy, talent, and dedication as those mentioned in the text. I apologize to those who were not included due to space constraints. The movement also made use of somewhat older and more prominent personalities such as Avishai Margalit, Menachem Brinker, Yehoshua Arieli, and Shaul Friedlander.

38. *Yediot Ahronot,* April 12, 1978.

39. Ezer Weizman, *The Battle for Peace* (New York: Bantam, 1981). The quotation appears on page 250 of the Hebrew edition but was deleted from the English edition.

40. This campaign was known as the Litani Operation. For more details, see Rafael Eitan and Dov Goldstein, *Story of a Soldier* (in Hebrew) (Tel Aviv: Ma'ariv Publications, 1985). For the political and strategic considerations, see Weizman, *Battle for Peace,* 269–281. For the Arab perspective, see Walid Khalidi, *Conflict and Violence in Lebanon: Confrontation in the Middle East* (Cambridge, Mass.: Harvard Center for International Affairs, 1979), 103–158.

41. Security Council Resolution 425. *SCOR,* Documents 1978, doc. S/INF/34. Reprinted in Moore, *Arab-Israeli Conflict,* vol. 4, part 1, doc. 19, 104. For more on UNIFIL, see John Mackinlay, *The Peacekeepers: An Assessment of Peacekeeping Operations in the Arab-Israeli Interface* (London: Unwin Hyman, 1989), 27–67; and Marianne Heiberg, "Peacekeeping and Local Populations: Some Comments on

UNIFIL," in Indar Jit Rikhye and Kjell Skjelsbaek, eds., *The United Nations and Peacekeeping* (London: Macmillan, 1990), 147–169. See also Indar Jit Rikhye, *The Theory and Practice of Peacekeeping* (London: C. Hurst, 1984), 100–113; United Nations, *The Blue Helmets: A Review of United Nations Peace-keeping,* 2d ed. (New York: United Nations, 1990), 111–152.

42. On the crisis in U.S.-Israeli relations during the spring of 1978, see Spiegel, *The Other Arab-Israeli Conflict,* 345–350; and Carter, *Keeping Faith,* 310–312.

43. I took the liberty to translate the first slogan liberally, not literally, because in Hebrew the words Peace (*Shalom*) and Entire (*Shalem*) make a good play. The term "Graves of the Fathers" referred to the Grave of the Patriarchs (Abraham, Isaac, and Jacob) in Hebron, and other holy shrines in the occupied territories cherished by the settlers.

44. Tzali Reshef, interview by author, Jerusalem, January 12, 1984. David Hall-Cathala, a sociologist from Lesotho who researched the Israeli peace movement, claims that this slogan was used earlier by a small group in Tel Aviv and was adopted by the movement later. See his *The Peace Movement in Israel 1967–1987* (New York: St. Martin's, 1990).

45. See Bar-On, *Peace Now,* 18–19.

46. The following description and analysis centers on the situation during the first five years of the movement (1978–83).

47. This is a large number in Israel, particularly when compared with the fact that in 1992–93 both Likud's and Labor's membership totals were less than this figure.

48. After the massacre in Sabra and Shatila in Lebanon in 1982, a demonstration organized by the movement attracted an all-time high of more than 250,000 participants. But this demonstration was organized by a coalition of Peace Now, the kibbutz movement, the Labor Party, and other parties on the left. For more on this, see chapter 7. The number of demonstrators always differed between what the movement reported, what the police reported (which was often 30 to 40 percent lower), and what the media reported (which was in the middle). For this study I generally used the police figures.

49. Janet Aviad, interview by author, Jerusalem, August 22, 1992. For more on the sociological composition of Peace Now, see chapter 8.

50. Some such activities were meant only to attract media attention as opposed to a large number of participants. For example, four academics stood vigil with placards on their chests and backs during rush hour in front of the homes of two cabinet members.

51. Interview with Naftali Raz, who was the head of the Operations Committee for many years.

52. Peace Now eventually took more specific positions on particular issues. These points were laid out in the first position paper the movement published at the end of May 1978. The original draft is in the private archive of Naftali Raz.

53. Many of the movement's leaders expressed their personal views in articles in the press, but these were not binding on the movement at large.

54. Interview with Jay Hurwitz, quoted in Hall-Cathala, *Peace Movement in Israel,* 45.

55. Professor Shaul Friedlander, for example, received the Israel Prize (the highest national award) in 1983. He arrived at the ceremony directly from a Peace Now demonstration.

56. The informal anthem of Peace Now was the "Song to Peace," which was originally performed in 1969 by an IDF chorus. The refrain reads, "Sing a song of love, not of war. Do not say the day will come, bring the day today." Both the music and the lyrics were inspired by the American song "Let the Sun Shine" from the antiwar musical *Hair.*

57. Reshef, interview.

58. Peace Now activists were also adept in manipulating headlines through the names they gave their activities. The operation on the road to Jerusalem was called "Prisat Shalom," which is a play on words meaning "Peace Greetings" and "Peace Deployment." See *Ha'aretz,* April 27, 1978.

59. "It was not difficult to grasp who was being held responsible for this change [in the atmosphere]," Dayan recorded in a meeting he held with Carter. See Dayan, *Breakthrough,* 123. He also observed that "though Carter spoke in a dull monotone voice there was fury in his cold blue eyes, and his glance was dagger-sharp." Ibid., 126.

60. Carter, *Keeping Faith,* 308.

61. Vance, *Hard Choices,* 215–216.

62. The problem of whether he had the authority to propose suggestions at his own initiative during meetings haunted Dayan throughout the entire process and occasionally created tension between Dayan and Begin. See Moshe Dayan, *Shall the Sword Devour Forever?* (in Hebrew) (Jerusalem: Edanim, 1981), 124–125.

63. The word *if* in Hebrew has two forms: *ilu* for the past and *im* for the future. Therefore, *ilu* refers more to an unrealistic contingency. Begin insisted on the use of *ilu.* Dayan, *Shall the Sword Devour Forever?* 147.

64. On the formation of this group that carried the code name "Zehava," see Weizman, *Battle for Peace,* 200–203.

65. On Begin's ambivalence, see Weizman, *Battle for Peace,* chap. 24.

66. Entry in Carter's diary of July 31, 1978, as quoted in Carter, *Keeping Faith,* 316.

67. *Ma'ariv,* June 20, 1978.

68. *Davar,* December 12, 1977; and *Ha'aretz,* December 19, 1977.

69. Zvi Shiloah, *The Guilt of Jerusalem* (in Hebrew) (Tel Aviv: Karni Publishing, 1989), 154–159.

70. Demant, *Ploughshares into Swords,* 539.

71. Raz, interview.

72. Reshef, interview.

73. Zbigniew Brzezinski, *Power and Principle: Memoirs of the National Security Adviser, 1977–1981* (New York: Farrar, Straus and Giroux, 1983), 234.

74. Ezer Weizman recalled, "Nobody said anything and nobody knew exactly what would happen at Camp David. We were moving in the dark." Weizman, *Battle for Peace* (Hebrew edition), 313.

75. Personal notes of Naftali Raz, Naftali Raz Personal Archive, Mevaseret Yerushalayim.

76. Reshef, interview.

77. The main sources are the participants themselves: Carter, *Keeping Faith,* 319–403; Vance, *Hard Choices,* 196–231; Dayan, *Breakthrough,* 149–190; Weizman, *Battle for Peace* (English edition), 340–377; Brzezinski, *Power and Principle,* 234–

288; Tamir, *Soldier in Search of Peace* (Hebrew edition), 48–52; Elyakim Rubinstein, *Paths of Peace* (in Hebrew) (Tel Aviv: Ministry of Defense Publications, 1992), 54–64; Quandt, *Camp David,* 206–258; and Kamel, *Camp David Accords,* 294–382. A revisionist description, based to a large degree on interviews with Egyptians and others who were critical of Sadat's handling of the negotiations, appears in Zahid Mahmood, "Sadat and Camp David Reappraised," *Journal of Palestine Studies* 15, no. 1 (fall 1985): 62–87.

78. See the description of the mood among the Egyptians before the final signing of the accords, in Kamel, *Camp David Accords,* 371–372. Kamel concludes that the worst development of the accords was the consecration of "Egypt's estrangement from the Palestinian cause."

79. Kamel, *Camp David Accords.* The full text is reprinted at 376–387, appendix G.

80. An interesting critique of the Camp David process and of Begin's performance during the discussions can be found in Sasson Sofer, *Menachem Begin in the Camp David Conference: A Chapter in the New Diplomacy* (in Hebrew), Policy Paper no. 15 (Jerusalem: Leonard Davis Institute, 1986). On the role of President Carter as a mediator and on the effects of mediation, see Saadia Touval, *The Peace Brokers: Mediation in the Arab-Israeli Conflict, 1948–1979* (Princeton: Princeton University Press, 1982), 284–320.

81. Tamir, *Soldier in Search of Peace,* 75.

82. For details on the military negotiations, see ibid., 75–81. On the political negotiations, see Dayan, *Breakthrough,* 199–258.

83. A summary of the political climate that surrounded the negotiations is in David Schoenbaum, *The United States and the State of Israel* (Oxford: Oxford University Press, 1993), 263–268.

84. This issue was deleted from the English edition of Dayan's book, but is included in the Hebrew original, *Halanetzah Tochal Herev* (Jerusalem: Wayrin, 1981), 151–156.

85. Bar-On, *Peace Now,* 34–35.

86. Dayan, *Breakthrough,* 259.

87. *Ma'ariv,* March 12, 1979.

88. Dayan, *Breakthrough,* 274. Carter commented on this occasion that "it was a shock to observe the degree of freedom permitted the members of the parliament to their relatively undisciplined exchanges." Jimmy Carter, *The Blood of Abraham: Insights into the Middle East* (Boston: Houghton Mifflin, 1985), 33.

89. Five Likud members voted against, two members abstained, and three declared themselves nonparticipants in the vote. Ariel Sharon voted against the agreement in the cabinet but voted in favor of it in the parliament. For the entire debate, see *Knesset Verbatim Record,* 85:1882-2088. The vote results are on 85:2088.

90. Carter, *Keeping Faith,* 428. At the end of May 1979 Sadat reciprocated by visiting Israel, this time Haifa and Be'er Sheva. Peace Now organized a welcome demonstration and held a brief meeting with the Egyptian president.

91. *Jerusalem Post,* June 14, 1979. It became known later that both Dayan and Weizman objected to these settlements. See Dayan's letter of resignation in *Shall the Sword Devour Forever?* 243; and Weizman, *Battle for Peace,* 366.

92. Raz, interview.

93. Bar-On, *Peace Now,* 35–36.

94. Joseph Burg, interview by author, Jerusalem, August 11, 1992.

95. Some of Begin's closest allies and friends were quite critical of his concessions. Shmuel Katz resigned from the party and publicly accused Begin of betraying the principles that they had cherished all their lives and of intentionally misleading the public as to the true meaning of the terms of the agreements. See Shmuel Katz, *No Courage and No Dignity* (in Hebrew) (Tel Aviv: Dvir, 1981), 200–221.

96. Carter concluded that Begin was "unwilling to carry out the more difficult commitments concerning full autonomy for the Palestinians and the withdrawal of Israeli military and civilian governments from the West Bank and Gaza." Carter, *Blood of Abraham*, 44.

97. Quoted in Benziman, *Prime Minister under Siege*, 262.

98. From the Naftali Raz Personal Archive. Reprinted in Bar-On, *Peace Now*, Appendix B, 130.

6. Consolidation, 1980–81

1. For their interpretation of these developments, see Dayan, *Shall the Sword Devour Forever?* 243–250; and Weizman, *Battle for Peace*, 363–370. An analysis of Begin's revisionist ethos can be found in Dan Horowitz, *The Heavens and the Earth: A Self-Portrait of the 1948 Generation* (in Hebrew) (Jerusalem: Keter Publishing, 1993), 55–58.

2. Basic Laws were designed by Israel's founders to be articles of a future constitution. This Basic Law was called "Jerusalem the Capital of Israel" and was passed on July 30, 1980. See State of Israel, *The Book of Laws*, no. 980, August 5, 1980, Jerusalem, 186. For the Knesset debate, see *Knesset Verbatim Record*, 89:4311–4325.

3. Technically this extended Israeli law and jurisdiction to the Golan Heights. It passed on December 14, 1981. "The Ramat Hagolan Law," in State of Israel, *The Book of Laws* no. 1034, December 15, 1981, Jerusalem, 6. For the debate in the Knesset, see *Knesset Verbatim Record*, 92:761–785.

4. Peace Now held a demonstration against this decision on August 3, 1980. See Bar-On, *Peace Now*, 150. Eventually, under U.S. pressure, the prime minister's office was not moved, although another government ministry was transferred to the new offices.

5. See Spiegel, *The Other Arab-Israeli Conflict*, 411. See also Alexander M. Haig Jr., *Caveat: Realism, Reagan and Foreign Policy* (New York: Macmillan, 1984), 329.

6. For a discussion of the U.S.-Israeli relationship during the Reagan administration, see Bernard Reich and Joseph Helman, *The United States-Israel Strategic Relationship in the Reagan Administration*, Institute of Jewish Affairs Research Reports no. 6 (London: Institute of Jewish Affairs, 1988). See also William B. Quandt, "American Policy toward the Arab-Israeli Conflict," in Thomas Naff, ed., *The Middle East Challenge 1980–1985* (Carbondale: Southern Illinois University Press, 1981), 40–49.

7. For more on this, see Helena Cobban, *The Superpowers and the Syrian-Israeli Conflict* (New York: Praeger, 1991), 78–111.

8. On the legal and political intricacies of the autonomy talks, see Ruth Lapidoth, "The Autonomy Talks," *Jerusalem Quarterly* 24 (summer 1982): 99–113. See also Sheffer, *Patron and Client Relations*, 23–28.

9. In a futile attempt to persuade Begin to stop the settlements, Sadat offered to divert water from the Nile to the Negev for a massive resettlement project. On this and the full content of Sadat's last letters to Begin, see Raphael Israeli, ed., *The Public Diary of President Sadat* (Leiden: A. J. Brill, 1978), 250–252.

10. Interview with Naftali Raz.

11. See Dan Hurwitz, *Dust and Blue Skies* (in Hebrew) (Jerusalem: Keter Publishing, 1993).

12. This is discussed in greater detail in chapter 8.

13. See chapter 4.

14. For more on public attitudes toward trade-offs between social services and defense-related spending, see Ofira Seliktar, "The Cost of Vigilance in Israel: Linking the Economic and Social Costs of Defense," *Journal of Peace Research* 17, no. 4 (1980): 339–352.

15. This is the most important annual event for Jewish organizations in North America.

16. Interview with Janet Aviad.

17. On this affair, see "We Shall Die, but Not Leave!" *Ha'olam Ha'zeh,* May 19, 1982, 15.

18. Many of the future leaders of the Palestinians in the occupied territories became known to the Israeli public through such conferences. These included Faisal Husseini, Sari Nusseibeh, Ziyad Abu-Zayyad, Ghassan al-Khatib, Zahira Cammal, and Hanan Ashrawi. Most of these leaders later constituted the core of the Palestinian delegation to the peace talks that took place in Washington following the Madrid Conference in 1992. For their role in the Palestinian national movement, see John and Janet Wallach, *The New Palestinians: The Emerging Generation of Leaders* (Rocklin, Calif.: Prima, 1992).

19. *Ha'aretz,* October 11, 1979.

20. For more on the development of dialogues with the Palestinian leaders, see chapter 10.

21. The notable exceptions were Rashad Shawwa of Gaza and Elias Freij of Bethlehem, who remained loyal to King Hussein. However, following the Rabat decision of 1974, they also recognized the PLO as the "sole legitimate representative of the Palestinian people."

22. On this development, see Pinhas Inbari, *Triangle on the Jordan: Secret Contacts among the USA, Jordan, and the PLO* (in Hebrew) (Jerusalem: Kana, 1982), 22–53.

23. For more details, see chapter 10.

24. Zucker and Tamir were young Israeli-born intellectuals and founders of Peace Now. Zucker served as the assistant to the minister of education in the Labor government and later became a prominent member of the Knesset. Tamir was a student at the Hebrew University at the time and later became a political science professor at Tel Aviv University and an important spokesperson for the Israeli women's peace network.

25. On some of the frustrations of the veteran activists regarding this incident, see Gvirtz, "Signed: 348 Officers," *Yediot Ahronot,* April 2, 1993, 28–31.

26. Shulamit Hareven, interview by author, Jerusalem, August 26, 1993.

27. Bar-On, *Peace Now,* 41.

28. Document in Naftali Raz's personal files.

29. For a biased but useful description of Sharon's record as minister of agriculture, see Uzi Benziman, *Sharon: An Israeli Caesar* (New York: Adama Books, 1985), 206–228.

30. In 1976 the Jewish population in the occupied territories (excluding Jerusalem) was 3,876; by the end of 1981 it had reached 17,000. A further increase occurred in 1984 when many of the housing projects begun by Sharon were completed. By the end of that year the population of settlers had reached 45,790. The statistics are taken from Ester Goldberg, *Jewish Settlements in the West Bank and the Gaza Strip: An Update, 1992* (Tel Aviv: International Center for Peace in the Middle East, 1993), chart no. 4.

31. See Meron Benvenisti, *The West Bank Data Project: A Survey of Israel's Policies* (Washington, D.C.: American Enterprise Institute, 1984), 19–36, especially table 7, 20. Also see Meron Benvenisti, *1986 Report: Demographic, Economic, Legal, Social and Political Developments in the West Bank* (Boulder, Colo.: Westview, 1986), 25–36.

32. The normalization was to a certain degree asymmetrical. Two years after the signing of the peace treaty Shimon Shamir (who later served as Israel's ambassador to Egypt) explained this asymmetry as a gap in perception in which the Egyptians continued to have ideological difficulties, especially in accepting the Zionist nature of Israel. Israelis faced difficulties on the utilitarian level, since they continued to question the practical value of the treaty and wondered whether peace would endure. See Shimon Shamir, *Two Years after Signing of the Peace Treaty between Israel and Egypt* (Tel Aviv: Tel Aviv University, May 20, 1981).

33. For a discussion of Sadat's motivations, see Israeli, *Public Diary of President Sadat,* 244–245.

34. For an analysis of the assassination, though critical of Sadat, see Mohamed Heikal, *Autumn of Fury: The Assassination of Sadat* (New York: Random House, 1983), 169–278.

35. Polls in September 1979 gave Likud only 20 percent of the votes, while Labor received 35 percent; the undecided vote remained quite large.

36. Sam Lehman-Wilzig, "Thunder before the Storm: Pre-Election Agitation and Post-Election Turmoil," in Asher Arian, ed., *Elections in Israel, 1981* (Tel Aviv: Ramot Publishing, 1984), 191. Lehman-Wilzig counted a significant rise in the number of violent events in the two-month pre-election period. See table 1, 194.

37. Zucker and Tamir were third and fourth on the list, respectively. Meron Benvenisti, a prominent researcher, was second on the list.

38. This is based on an interview with Amnon Sela in Jerusalem on August 18, 1992, and some archival material he provided to the author. See also a summary of the experiment by Baruch Knei-Paz, "Academics in Politics: An Israeli Experience," *Jerusalem Quarterly* 16 (summer 1980): 54–70. Miri Bitton also sent me important archival material. The Hebrew *Chug Avoda* may be understood as "Working Group" but can also mean "Labor Circle."

39. No date appears on the original letter, sent in August 1977. From the personal files of Amnon Sela.

40. Rabin resigned as prime minister after the media disclosed that his wife maintained a bank account in Washington, D.C., a violation of Israeli law.

41. Letter from Amnon Sela files.

42. These were Dan Hurwitz and Ze'ev Sternhal, both professors in the department of political science at the Hebrew University.

43. See the Circle 77 document, "Peace—Security—Borders: Guidelines and Positions for a Political Discussion" (in Hebrew), August 1980. This document was written by Dan Hurwitz and Amnon Sela. A copy of the original was provided to the author by Miri Bitton.

44. Raz, interview.

45. Knei-Paz, "Academics in Politics," 60.

46. For the Labor Party's approach to peacemaking in that period, see Shimon Peres, "A Strategy for Peace in the Middle East," *Foreign Affairs* 58, no. 4 (spring 1980): 887–901.

47. Their popular phrase was "Hold your nose and vote Labor!" Even the predominantly Arab Communist Party lost some of its votes for the same reason. In 1977 the Communist Party received 50 percent of the Arab vote; it received only 37 percent in 1981. See Avner Yaniv and Majid al-Hajj, "Uniformity or Diversity: A Reappraisal of the Voting Behavior of the Arab Minority in Israel, 1981," in Arian, *Elections in Israel, 1981,* 139–166.

48. By late 1979 some observers and even political allies considered Begin's health both mentally and physically impaired, and discussions about succession within Likud could be heard. See Amos Perlmutter, *The Life and Times of Menachem Begin* (New York: Doubleday, 1987), 360–362. Begin's deputy, Simcha Ehrlich, told his colleagues, "The Prime Minister is a sick and broken man, he is physically and mentally ill." Arie Avnery, *The Liberal Connection* (in Hebrew) (Tel Aviv: Zmora, 1983), 261.

49. Symbolically, Begin (who tended to be absentminded on occasions) entered the Knesset floor and instead of heading to the prime minister's seat went to the seat he had occupied for decades as head of the opposition. See *Davar,* December 22, 1979.

50. He also drastically reduced the taxes on imported cars. Within a month, Israelis had bought 8,000 new cars and 60,000 televisions. See Silver, *Begin,* 214–215.

51. See Itamar Rabinovich, *The War for Lebanon 1970–1985* (Ithaca: Cornell University Press, 1985), 114–119.

52. For details of the attack on the reactor, see Amos Perlmutter, Michael Handel, and Uri Bar-Yossef, *Two Minutes over Baghdad* (London: Corgi Books, 1982). The attack was undertaken with American-made aircraft. On the U.S. reaction, see Haig, *Caveat,* 180–184.

53. Begin's biographer wrote, "Begin approached the issue not only in practical terms, but from a passionately emotional and ideological stance." Perlmutter, *Life and Times of Menachem Begin,* 362. Some observers questioned whether Begin orchestrated the attack for political gains, and cited his disclosure of a personal letter Shimon Peres wrote shortly before the attack, warning Begin of the potential negative international repercussions of such a move. See *Ma'ariv,* June 9, 1981. The letter is quoted in Perlmutter, *Life and Times of Menachem Begin,* 364.

54. See Hanoch Smith, *The Israeli Elections: Significant Trends behind the Figures* (Jerusalem: American Jewish Committee Report, 1982).

55. The distribution was as follows: Tehiya, 3; Telem (Moshe Dayan's party), 2; Tami (a North African religious party), 3; the National Religious Party, 6; and the ultra-orthodox Agudat Yisrael, 4. For Knesset election results from 1949 to 1988, see Arian, *Politics in Israel*, 149. The difference between Likud and Labor was only 10,000 votes (718,941 for Likud, 708,536 for Labor). This pattern continued for the 1984 and 1988 elections. See Central Bureau of Statistics, *Statistical Abstract of Israel 1991* (Jerusalem: Central Bureau of Statistics, 1991), table 20.2, 550–551.

56. For a summary of the perspectives of the second Begin cabinet, see Bernard Reich, "Policy Perspectives of the Begin Government," *International Insight* 2, no. 1 (November/December 1981): 22–25.

57. Some accused the U.S. administration and American welfare organizations of promoting PLO interests in the occupied territories. See Inbari, *Triangle on the Jordan*, 45–56.

58. See Menachem Milson, "How to Make Peace with the Palestinians," *Commentary* 71, no. 5 (May 1981): 25–35.

59. In 1970 he advocated a "Palestinian solution," which he understood as "creating an Arab Palestinian state alongside Israel"; later, he apparently changed his mind. See Menachem Milson, "Our Attitude to the Arab Position" (lecture delivered in a conference on the Arab-Israeli Conflict, Van Leer Institute, Jerusalem, January 4, 1970; mimeographed copy in author's personal papers).

60. Milson, "How to Make Peace with the Palestinians."

61. Many Palestinians saw this new arrangement as an attempt to "unilaterally implement Israel's interpretation of the autonomy idea included in the Camp David Accords, give permanence to the changes Israel has introduced in the West Bank during the past fourteen years, and create a semblance of terminating the occupation and withdrawing the military government." See Raja Shehadeh and Jonathan Kuttab, Palestinian civil rights lawyers, as quoted by Geoffrey Aronson, *Creating Facts* (Washington, D.C.: Washington Institute for Palestine Studies, 1987), 254.

62. Quoted in Michael Palumbo, *Imperial Israel: The History of the Occupation of the West Bank and Gaza* (London: Bloomsbury, 1992), 158.

63. *BBC Survey of World Broadcasts,* Middle East, 6872/A11.

64. On November 17, Yusef Khatib, the head of the Ramallah-based Village League, and his son Kazim were shot at close range in their car on the way to their office. *Ha'aretz,* November 18, 1981. See also Aronson, *Creating Facts,* 260.

65. This group was led by several Peace Now veterans. See Bar-On, *Peace Now,* 48–49.

66. This did not include the Sonesta Hotel in Taba, which was evacuated a few years later as a result of international arbitration.

67. The best study on this movement to date is by Gideon Aran, *Eretz Israel: Between Politics and Religion* (Jerusalem: Jerusalem Institute for Israel Studies, 1985).

68. See Benziman, *Sharon,* 273.

69. Ian Lustick, "Israeli Politics and American Foreign Policy," *Foreign Affairs* 61, no. 2 (winter 1982): 386–387.

70. *Knesset Verbatim Record,* 93:2133–2135.

71. Aviad, interview.

7. War in the Land of Cedars

1. For a detailed description of this development, see Ze'ev Schiff and Ehud Ya'ari, *Israel's Lebanon War* (New York: Simon and Schuster, 1984), chap. 1. See also Dan Bavly and Eliahu Salpeter, *Fire in Beirut: Israel's War in Lebanon with the PLO* (New York: Stein and Day, 1984).

2. The Lebanese Forces (*Les Forces Libanais* in French) was a coalition of various Maronite militias dominated by the Gemayel family and their Phalange militia (*al-Kata'ib* in Arabic). In the late 1970s it was commanded by Bashir Gemayel. On the development of the Phalange, see Tawfik Khalaf, "The Phalange and the Maronite Community: From Lebanonism to Maronitism," in Roger Owen, ed., *Essays on the Crisis in Lebanon* (London: Ithaca Press, 1976), 43–57.

3. Haddad may have had the blessing of the Maronite leaders at the outset, but he gradually exerted his independence from them. Haddad told the author in 1976 that "when Lebanon will be liberated from the conquest of the Syrians and Palestinians it will become truly independent."

4. For the development of the contacts with Haddad, see Rafael Eitan, *A Soldier's Story: The Life and Times of an Israeli War Hero* (New York: Shapolsky Publishers, 1991), 186–193. On the "Good Fence," see Shimon Peres, *Tomorrow Is Now* (in Hebrew) (Jerusalem: Keter Publishing, 1978), 83–88.

5. For a general background on the formation of Lebanon and its internal fragmentation, see Meir Zamir, *The Formation of Modern Lebanon* (Ithaca: Cornell University Press, 1985). For a good summary of Lebanese history, see Kamal Salibi, *A House of Many Mansions: The History of Lebanon Reconsidered* (Berkeley: University of California Press, 1988). On the background to the civil war, see Kamal Salibi, *Crossroads to Civil War: Lebanon 1958–1976* (New York: Caravan, 1976); and Khalidi, *Conflict and Violence in Lebanon*. On the rise of the Shi'a, see Fouad Ajami, *The Vanished Imam: Musa Sadr and the Shi'a in Lebanon* (Ithaca, N.Y.: Cornell University Press, 1986); and Augustus Richard Norton, *Amal and the Shi'a: Struggle for the Soul of Lebanon* (Austin: University of Texas Press, 1987).

6. See Michael Hudson, "The Palestinian Factor in the Lebanese Civil War," *Middle East Journal* 32, no. 3 (summer 1978): 261–278; and Cobban, *Palestine Liberation Organization*, chap. 4. See also Hussein Sirriyyeh, "The Palestine Armed Presence in Lebanon since 1967," in Owen, *Essays on the Crisis in Lebanon*, 73–89.

7. Shimon Shiffer, *Snowball: The Story behind the Lebanon War* (in Hebrew) (Tel Aviv: Edanim, 1984), 22. For an in-depth discussion of Rabin's policy in Lebanon, see Tamir, *Soldier in Search of Peace*, 138–139.

8. See Eitan, *A Soldier's Story,* 189.

9. "We shall not let ourselves be drawn into a major war by the Christians," Weizman told the members of the Knesset Defense and Foreign Affairs Committee. Quoted in Shiffer, *Snowball,* 27. Early in his tenure Prime Minister Begin told Major Haddad, "Do not expect us to come fight your battles." Quoted in Eitan, *A Soldier's Story,* 195.

10. Schiff and Ya'ari, *Israel's Lebanon War,* 26.

11. Rashid Khalidi, *Under Siege: PLO Decision Making during the 1982 War* (New York: Columbia University Press, 1986), 28–36. See also Rashid Khalidi, "The Palestinians in Lebanon: Social Repercussions of Israel's Invasion," *Middle East Journal* 38, no. 2 (spring 1984): 225–266.

12. For a colorful description of the atmosphere around these developments, see Thomas Friedman, *From Beirut to Jerusalem* (New York: Farrar, Straus and Giroux, 1989), 119–131.

13. For a description of the PLO's military capabilities before the 1982 war, see Ze'ev Schiff's summary in *Ha'aretz*, July 18, 1982.

14. For more on U.S. policy in Lebanon during this period, see William Quandt, *Peace Process: American Diplomacy and the Arab-Israeli Conflict since 1967* (Berkeley: University of California Press, 1993), 335–382.

15. See Ze'ev Schiff, "The Military Balance in the North," *Ha'aretz*, July 27, 1981; Yoram Peri, "A Different War," *Davar*, July 24, 1981; and Eitan Haber, "The Problem of the Israeli Army," *Yediot Ahronot*, July 22, 1981. Ariel Sharon, who was about to assume his duties as minister of defense, objected to the cease-fire agreement. See his arguments in Ariel Sharon, *Warrior: An Autobiography* (New York: Simon and Schuster, 1989), 432–437.

16. Sharon, *Warrior,* 447.

17. Begin apparently did not share Sharon's aspiration to push the Syrians out of Lebanon, though he definitely agreed with the other parts of the plan and should have realized that such a plan would inevitably lead to a war with Syria. See Perlmutter, *Life and Times of Menachem Begin,* 375.

18. For a critical analysis of the Lebanon War, see Yitzhak Rabin, "Political Illusions and Their Price," in *The Lebanon War: Between Protest and Compliance* (in Hebrew) (Tel Aviv: Hakibbutz Hameuchad, 1983), 13–22. For a political critique, see Gadi Yatziv, "The War They Should Not Have Waged," in Ruvik Rosenthal, ed., *Lebanon: The Other War* (in Hebrew) (Tel Aviv: Sifriat Poalim, 1983), 91–112.

19. Quoted in Ehud Ya'ari and Ze'ev Schiff, *Milhemet Sholal* (the Hebrew edition of their book on the Lebanon War) (Tel Aviv: Schocken, 1984), 72. On the internal debates in the Israeli defense establishment, see Tamir, *Soldier in Search of Peace,* 144–160.

20. The PLO did not, however, abstain from action in other theaters of its guerrilla war. For instance, on January 28, 1982, a Fatah group crossed into Israel from Jordan, but was detected before it could launch its attack. See *Ma'ariv,* January 29, 1982.

21. Shiffer, *Snowball,* 87.

22. In November 1981 Yitzhak Rabin published a detailed analysis in which he emphasized the need for restraint because "any attempt to undertake far-reaching goals will bring about an Israeli failure." He supported meticulous adherence to the cease-fire agreement and, in the event of a Palestinian violation of it, the subjugation of only the areas from which the PLO was able to shell Israeli targets, which would subsequently be handed over to a UN peacekeeping force. See Yitzhak Rabin, "On Lebanon and Around It" (in Hebrew), *Mebafnim* 42, no. 3–4 (November 1981): 248–253.

23. Bar-On, *Peace Now,* 54.

24. Haig did not say that the United States objected to such a move, only that it would not support it, and that Israel might have to "move alone." See Haig, *Caveat.* See also Begin's remarks to Senator John Glenn, quoted in Shiffer, *Snowball,* 81.

25. For Sharon's version of his visit, see Sharon, *Warrior,* 450–451.

26. According to Raymond Tanter, a staff member of the National Security Council at the time, "It is clear that Haig provided Sharon with a go-ahead for a limited operation given a commensurate aggravation. There also is no doubt that Sharon had his forces speed through the green light before it could change colors." See Raymond Tanter, *Who's at the Helm? Lessons of Lebanon* (Boulder, Colo.: Westview, 1990), 111.

27. For details on Sharon's encounter with Haig, see Schiff and Ya'ari, *Israel's Lebanon War,* 72–77. See also Haig, *Caveat.* 330–335. In his memoirs, Haig tries to create the impression that he warned Israel against the attack, but the impression one gets from his own account is that he had at least a good measure of sympathy for the Israeli position.

28. Ya'ari and Schiff, *Milhemet Sholal,* 148.

29. On June 8, 1982, the Communist Party introduced a vote of no confidence in the Knesset. With the exception of Yossi Sarid and members of Mapam and Ratz, who abstained, all Labor and Likud MKs supported the government. See *Knesset Verbatim Record,* 94:2735–2747.

30. See the statements of soldiers who were mobilized before the troubles in the north broke out and were knowledgeable about the military preparations. Rosenthal, *Lebanon,* 17–88.

31. One of the first soldiers who died in battle was Major Guni Harnick, who commanded the unit that conquered a Palestinian stronghold entrenched in the Crusader's castle of Beaufort. Harnick was an outspoken sympathizer of Peace Now. The best treatment of this affair and the reaction of his parents is Ruvik Rosenthal, *The Beaufort Family* (in Hebrew) (Tel Aviv: Sifriat Poalim, 1989). For a short biography of Harnick, see Peter Hellman, *Heroes* (New York: Henry Holt, 1990), 153–193.

32. In a speech in the Knesset on the third day of the fighting, Begin said "When we shall reach the line of forty kilometers north of our northern border the job will be fulfilled and the fighting will cease." *Knesset Verbatim Record,* 94:2747. The editorials of most Israeli papers during the first three to four days also gave their support to the operation in its seemingly limited scope.

33. For a somewhat simplistic but interesting attempt to explain the psychological mechanisms that brought many to conform with this general mood, see Uri Leviatan, "Four Psychological Phenomena and the War in Lebanon" (in Hebrew), in Rosenthal, *Lebanon,* 145–154.

34. Interview with Naftali Raz.

35. Reuven Kaminer, interview by author, Jerusalem, August 20, 1992.

36. Judy Blank, interview by author, Jerusalem, August 16, 1992. In 1978 a "Committee against the Settling of Hebron" was formed. In the fall of 1981 a "Committee of Solidarity with Bir Zeit University" protested against the closure of the campus by Milson.

37. Some members of these committees were ideologically opposed to Zionism and were at different times connected with the anti-Zionist group Matzpen. The most prominent among them were Leah Tzemel, a lawyer who specialized in the legal defense of Palestinians, and her husband Michel Warschawski, better known by his nickname "Mikado."

38. Blank, interview. The most prominent Israeli Arabs in this group were Azmi Bishara and Jammal Zahalka. Both were teachers at Bir Zeit University and members of the Israeli Communist Party.

39. On the military developments of the Lebanon War, see Schiff and Ya'ari, *Israel's War in Lebanon,* chaps. 7, 8, 9, 10. See also Yair Evron, *War and Intervention in Lebanon: The Israeli-Syrian Deterrence Dialogue* (London: Croom Helm, 1987).

40. See Sharon, *Warrior,* 486–487.

41. Quotation in Schiff and Ya'ari, *Israel's War in Lebanon,* 187.

42. See soldiers' testimonies in Rosenthal, *Lebanon*, 27–29.

43. Claims about distortions in the media are included in Bavly and Salpeter, *Fire in Beirut*, 135–150. Bavly was in charge of the office of the Israeli military spokesman in Lebanon and had firsthand knowledge of the role of the media in the war. After the war, the Bertrand Russell Peace Foundation compiled a volume of personal testimonies, mostly from Europeans who were caught by the war on the Palestinian side. See Franklin P. Lamb, ed., *Israel's War in Lebanon: Eyewitness Chronicles of the Invasion and Occupation* (Nottingham, England: Spokesman, 1984).

44. Private archive of Naftali Raz.

45. *Yediot Ahronot,* June 27, 1982.

46. Professor Yehuda Meltzer, a philosopher who wrote his Ph.D. dissertation on the subject of morality and war, published a critique of the participation of Peace Now activists during the war in Lebanon. See his article "The Agonies of Peace Now" (in Hebrew), in Dina Menuchin and Ishai Menuchin, eds., *The Limits of Obedience* (Tel Aviv: Siman Kri'a Books, 1985), 151–159.

47. See Bar-On, *Peace Now,* 56.

48. On earlier conscientious objectors, see M. Blatt, U. Davis, and P. Kleinbaum, *Dissent and Ideology in Israel: Resistance to the Draft 1948–1973* (London: Ithaca, 1975). See also Penina Glazer-Migdal and Myron Glazer, "War Resisters in the Land of Battle," *Dissent* (summer 1977): 289–296. For an analysis of the phenomenon in terms of the psychology of morality, see Ruth Linn and Carol Gilligan, "One Action, Two Moral Orientations: The Tension between Justice and Care—Voices of Israel Selective Conscientious Objectors," *New Ideas in Psychology* 8, no. 2 (1990): 189–203.

49. The most prominent case involved Amnon Zichroni, who on May 28, 1954, went on a twenty-four-day hunger strike after being jailed for refusing to swear allegiance to the Israeli army and to handle weapons. The case was widely reported in the media, and Martin Buber and other prominent intellectuals called for clemency. Zichroni was eventually released and exempted from service. See *Davar,* June 20, 1954. Information was also provided in an interview with Zichroni, Tel Aviv, November 11, 1993. Another interview with Zichroni was published in *Ha'ir,* May 18, 1984. Zichroni became a successful civil rights lawyer and was involved in left-wing politics, most notably as the secretary of Uri Avneri's faction in the Knesset in the late 1960s. On this, see Amnon Zichroni, *1 against 119: Uri Avneri in the Sixth Knesset* (Tel Aviv: Dahaf Publications, 1969).

50. This outlook was well expressed in a letter an Israeli soldier wrote to his girlfriend after visiting a Holocaust museum in 1963: "I feel that out of all these atrocities and helplessness [of the Holocaust victims] a powerful urge to be strong is growing within me. I desire to be strong and sharp like a knife, strong and terrible. I want to know that never again will these eyes have to stare at me from behind the electrified barbed wires. We can only avoid it if I shall be strong. . . . Proud and strong Jews." Letter by Ofer Fenninger from Kibbutz Givat Haim, quoted in Avraham Shapira, ed., *Soldiers Chat* (in Hebrew) (Tel Aviv: private publication of several kibbutz members, 1968), 167.

51. On the philosophy of the issue, see Michael Walzer, "The Obligation to Disobey," in Michael Walzer, ed, *Obligations: Essays on Disobedience, War and Citizenship* (Cambridge, Mass.: Harvard University Press, 1970), 3–23. See also

Noam Chomsky, "The Obligation to Refuse," in Menuchin, *Limits of Obedience*, 82–88. On the psychological dimension, see Ruth Linn, "Conscientious Objection in Israel during the War in Lebanon," *Armed Forces and Society* 12, no. 4 (1986): 489–511.

52. Much of this information was gathered from an interview with Ishai Menuchin in Jerusalem on August 9 and 22, 1992.

53. The text is reprinted in Menuchin, *Limits of Obedience*, 175.

54. The first refuser was Sergeant Minski. See the list of the first 31 soldiers who were jailed for refusal to serve in Lebanon in *The Limits of Obedience and the Right to Refuse*, a brochure published in 1983 by Yesh Gvul (copy in the author's personal files). One of the early refusers was Danny Timmerman, the son of Jacobo, the Argentine Jewish writer and journalist who later published a harsh critique of the Israeli involvement in Lebanon. See Jacobo Timmerman, *The Longest War: Israel in Lebanon* (New York: Knopf, 1982).

55. According to Ruth Linn, who investigated the group, a total of 143 arrests for refusal were registered during 1982–85. "Hypothetical and Actual Moral Reasoning of Israeli Selective Conscientious Objectors during the War in Lebanon (1982–1985)," *Journal of Applied Developmental Psychology* 10, no. 1 (1989), 19–36.

56. General Dov Tamari, in a debate following the performance of a play called "The Refusal," as reported by Dani Tzidkoni in *Davar*, December 23, 1984.

57. Hanan Hever, "Poetry and Refusal in the Lebanese War," in Menuchin, *Limits of Obedience*, 149, 141. For a good review of these issues by another supporter of Yesh Gvul, see Gershon Weiler, *On War: A Philosophical Essay* (in Hebrew) (Tel Aviv: Hakibbutz Hameuchad), 1984.

58. A total of 15 out of 36 refusers whom Ruth Linn interviewed identified themselves with Peace Now; another 18 identified themselves as "Zionist Left." See her "Hypothetical and Actual Moral Reasoning," 22.

59. In the heat of some of the demonstrations, protestors occasionally clashed with the police and were detained for a few hours. At one point charges were filed against an activist who illegally pasted placards in places such as the marble wall in front of the prime minister's office. Some occasional property damage occurred during protests against settlements, but no Peace Now activist was ever indicted. Interview with Tzali Reshef.

60. See for example Yossi Sarid, "Gush Emunim Thanks Yesh Gvul," in *Ha'aretz*, January 2, 1986.

61. From the personal notes of the author.

62. See interview with Yitzhak Rabin reprinted in Yitzhak Rabin, *The War in Lebanon* (in Hebrew) (Tel Aviv: Am Oved, 1983), 19–31.

63. *Yediot Ahronot*, July 25, 1982.

64. Haig, *Caveat*, 343. By this time Haig's influence was on the wane. Raymond Tanter describes the controversies inside the Reagan administration on this issue between the regionalists, who were primarily concerned with U.S. standing among the Arab states (especially in the defense establishment), and the globalists, who were eager to weaken the Soviet proxies in the region, namely, the PLO and Syria. See Tanter, *Who's at the Helm?* 127–176.

65. See Khalidi, *Under Siege*, 116–129.

66. Schiff and Ya'ari, *Israel's Lebanon War*, 211–214. For Eitan's version, see his *Soldier's Story*, 307–309.

NOTES TO PAGES 150–153 / 375

67. See George P. Shultz, *Turmoil and Triumph: My Years As Secretary of State* (New York: Scribner's, 1993), 43–62.

68. On the debate among IDF commanders, see Schiff and Ya'ari, *Israel's Lebanon War,* 214–215.

69. Geva requested to remain with his brigade in some other capacity because, as he explained later, "I couldn't not be there, and I couldn't be there merely as an observer." Despite this request he was summarily discharged from military service. On this affair, see Schiff and Ya'ari, *Israel's Lebanon War,* 215–216. For the chief of staff's version, see Eitan, *Soldier's Story,* 321–334.

70. Schiff and Ya'ari, *Israel's Lebanon War,* 216.

71. The lecture appeared in *Ma'ariv,* August 20, 1982.

72. *Yediot Ahronot,* July 25, 1982.

73. Aharon Yariv, "War of Last Resort" (in Hebrew), in Aharon Yariv, ed., *War of Last Resort* (Tel Aviv: Jaffee Center for Strategic Studies, 1985), 15.

74. Ibid., 26. In his memoirs, Sharon claims that he intended to stop at the forty-kilometer line and abide by the cease-fire agreement, but the Palestinians continued to fight, which unintentionally led him to join with the Phalange in Ba'abda. This version of events seems to this author to be dishonest. See Sharon, *Warrior,* 470–478.

75. The quote is from a report on this development in Eli Shai and Ruthi Yovel, *Kol Ha'ir,* July 16, 1982.

76. Naomi Bentsur, interview by author, Jerusalem, November 7, 1993. Although the key figures were women, there were also men involved, so they preferred to be called "Parents" rather than "Mothers."

77. A brief description of this movement was published in *Newsweek,* June 10, 1985, 56. See also Lew Inbal, "The Voice of a Mother," *Koteret Rashit,* March 20, 1985, 12–13.

78. For a good analysis of the reasons why the relationship suffered, see Efraim Inbari, "Sources of Tension between Israel and the U.S.," *Conflict Resolution* 4, no. 2 (spring 1984): 56–65. On the evolution of the Reagan administration's Middle East policy, see Bernard Reich and Rosemary Hollis, "Peacemaking in the Reagan Administration," in Paul Marantz and Janice Gross Stein, eds., *Peace-Making in the Middle East* (Totowa, N.J.: Barnes and Noble, 1985), 133–155.

79. The PLO's conditions for their departure from Beirut were outlined on July 2, 1982, in the "Eleven Points" document. See Khalidi, *Under Siege,* 183–184.

80. The Palestinian forces were eventually spread throughout the Middle East, from Yemen to Algeria. The troops of the Palestine Liberation Army, which had been previously attached to some of the regular Arab armies, went back to their sponsors, including Syria, Iraq, and Jordan. The PLO headquarters was relocated in Tunis. For details, see Asher Susser, "The Palestine Liberation Organization," in Legum, Shaked, and Dishon, eds., *Middle East Contemporary Survey* (New York: Holmes and Meier, 1985), 7:278–324.

81. Shultz, *Turmoil and Triumph,* 78–84.

82. Sharon, *Warrior,* 495.

83. Schiff and Ya'ari, *Israel's War in Lebanon,* 229.

84. At the time, Israeli intelligence estimated that 2,000 armed Palestinian guerrillas and 7,000 armed members of the Murabitun (the Muslim leftist militia) remained in Beirut. These estimates were later found to be highly exaggerated.

85. For a detailed description of the assassination, see Friedman, *From Beirut to Jerusalem,* 157–160.

86. An authoritative summary of the following events is included in the *Report of the Inquiry Commission on the Events in the Beirut Refugee Camps in 1982* (in Hebrew) (Jerusalem: State of Israel Publication, 1983). This document is also known as the *Kahan Commission Report,* named after Chief Justice Yitzhak Kahan, who chaired the commission. A complete English version was published in Karz-Cohl, ed., *The Beirut Massacre: The Complete Kahan Commission Report* (Princeton: Princeton University Press), 1983.

87. Broadcast on Israeli radio on September 15, 1982, at 11 a.m., and published in the Israeli press the next day. For Sharon's version of these events, see *Warrior,* 500–504.

88. Eitan admits this much. For his version of events, see Eitan, *Soldier's Story,* 339–352.

89. The Phalange hoped for the opportunity to expel the Palestinians from Lebanon, by violent intimidation if necessary. These ideas were well known to the Israelis. See *Kahan Commission Report,* 14. This was also the assessment of General Eitan to the cabinet, as quoted by the report on page 32. For a harsh critique of the Kahan Commission recommendations, see Shimon Lerer, *The Missing Crucial Point* (in Hebrew) (Jerusalem: Amit Publications, 1983).

90. *Kahan Commission Report,* 35. Ze'ev Schiff received information about a massacre in the camps on the morning of September 17. He alerted General Tzipori, who at the time served in the cabinet as minister of communication. See Schiff and Ya'ari, *Israel's Lebanon War,* 266–269.

91. For a description of the events in Sabra and Shatila, I have relied heavily on the *Kahan Commission Report,* which seemed fair and accurate. Many writers, especially on the Palestinian side, portrayed the event as a premeditated conspiracy between the Israelis and the Maronites to liquidate the Palestinian presence from Beirut. For an example of this perspective, see Michael Jansen, *The Battle of Beirut: Why Israel Invaded Lebanon* (London: Zed Press, 1982), 91–110.

92. The exact number is disputed. The figures I use, cited by Israeli intelligence, are higher than the official figures of the Lebanese authorities and lower than the figures quoted by Palestinian sources. See *Kahan Commission Report,* 51–52. The Red Cross reported 460 dead, including 15 women and 20 children.

93. The Kahan Commission differentiated between "direct responsibility" (of which it cleared the Israelis involved) and "indirect responsibility" (for which it censured to different degrees a number of Israeli officers and ministers). The amount of prior knowledge Eitan and Sharon had regarding the Phalangists' intentions will never be known, though the overall evidence seems to point to a rather high level of complicity. See *Time,* September 27 and October 4, 1982; *Sunday Times* (London), September 26, 1982; and an article by Thomas Friedman (which won him the Pulitzer Prize) in the *New York Times,* September 26, 1982.

94. The testimonies included in Lamb, *Israel's War in Lebanon,* 537–632, seem to be grossly exaggerated. However, even considering exaggerations, they are still shocking.

95. See Schiff and Ya'ari, *Israel's War in Lebanon,* 281.

96. Quoted in *Kahan Commission Report,* 55.

97. Interview with Janet Aviad.

98. The organizers claimed the number of participants was 400,000, but I prefer to use the more conservative police estimate.

99. Sharon said this in the Knesset on September 22, 1982. He felt that captured PLO documents proved his contention. One of these documents reads, "The main thing now is to intensify the demonstrations [of Peace Now] everywhere in Israel." *Knesset Verbatim Record,* 94:3699. See also Sharon's view that "there were many people, perhaps most . . . who did not want this [inquiry] commission, who understood the danger of it, not only for Israel but for the Jewish people." Sharon, *Warrior,* 510.

100. "When gentiles kill gentiles." This phrase was reported by ministers as having been said, though it was never officially confirmed. See Schiff and Ya'ari, *Israel's Lebanon War,* 280.

101. *Ha'aretz,* September, 29, 1982.

102. On the deployment of the multinational peacekeeping forces, see Mackinlay, *Peacekeepers,* 68–118.

8. Peace and Ethnicity

1. See Shultz, *Turmoil and Triumph,* 85–89.

2. For a summary of U.S. policy in the Middle East in the wake of the Israeli invasion of Lebanon, see Barry Rubin, "The United States and the Middle East in 1983," in Legum, Shaked, and Dishon, *Middle East Contemporary Survey,* 7:21–29.

3. For the full text of the statement, see Moore, *The Arab-Israeli Conflict,* vol. 2, *The Difficult Search for Peace 1975–1988,* doc. 249, 1132–1137.

4. Attempts to resuscitate the peace process had already been undertaken by Secretary Haig in the spring of 1982. See Tanter, *Who's at the Helm?* 91. On the process of preparing the initiative, see Shultz, *Turmoil and Triumph,* 85–100.

5. This was a theme in his Senate confirmation testimony. See U.S. Senate, Committee on Foreign Relations, "Statement of the Secretary of State-Designate on the Nomination of George P. Shultz of California to be Secretary of State," *Hearings before the Committee on Foreign Relations,* 97th Cong., 2d sess., July 13–14, 1982.

6. In his memoirs, Reagan uses the term "self-determination" to mean measures of "self-rule." It is clear that he rejected the idea of a Palestinian state. See Ronald Reagan, *An American Life* (New York: Simon and Schuster, 1990), 430. Shultz considered "self-determination" a code word for a Palestinian state and would not use it affirmatively. See Shultz, *Turmoil and Triumph,* 88–89.

7. Perlmutter, *Life and Times of Menachem Begin,* 380–382.

8. See Shultz, *Turmoil and Triumph,* 94.

9. Moore, *Arab-Israeli Conflict,* 2:doc. 251, 1143–1145.

10. See parliamentary debate on September 8, 1982, *Knesset Verbatim Record,* 94:3641–3681.

11. Quoted in Bar-On, *Peace Now,* 61.

12. The Hebrew term *Mizrachi* (plural: *Mizrachim*) literally translates to "Easterner." I use it to designate Israelis who were born (or whose parents were born) in Islamic countries, from Morocco to Iran and from Turkey to Yemen. In official statistics of the State of Israel, such people are referred to as citizens of Afro-Asian origin. The term *Sepharadim,* which is often used, is archaic and erroneous, and the term "Oriental" (although etymologically the same as *Mizrachi*) may be misleading in English usage. As noted earlier in the text, the term *Ashkenazim* refers to Jews whose parents originated in Europe.

13. Colonel Reuven Gal, who served as the chief psychologist of the IDF, compared the ethnic backgrounds of soldiers who received medals of distinction in the conflicts of 1967, 1973, and 1982, and found a significant increase in the number and percentage of Mizrachim. Reuven Gal, telephone interview by author, November 5, 1993. See also Reuven Gal, *A Portrait of the Israeli Soldiers* (Westport, Conn.: Greenwood, 1986), 190–208.

14. In his memoirs, Sharon related how gratified he was by the support of his admirers, even as the cabinet discussed the recommendations of the Kahan report. See Sharon, *Warrior*, 519–521.

15. Shulamit Hareven, "A Testimony," *Yediot Ahronot,* February 14, 1983. All of the names mentioned in the text are Peace Now activists.

16. Among the wounded was Avraham Burg, the son of the minister of interior (who was at that moment sitting a few yards away in the cabinet meeting). Avraham Burg is currently a Labor MK and chairman of the Jewish Agency Executive Committee.

17. In 1933 Chaim Arlozorov, a leader of the Labor Movement, was murdered. Some considered it a political assassination, but this was never proved conclusively. In the 1920s a leader of an anti-Zionist ultra-orthodox faction was assassinated by the Zionist underground, and in the 1940s a member of the Stern group was apparently assassinated by his comrades for fear of treachery. The deep shock that engulfed the entire nation at the murder of Prime Minister Yitzhak Rabin on November 4, 1995, further testifies how out of tune with Israeli political culture such tragic events are.

18. The murderer was eventually apprehended and sentenced to a long prison term.

19. On the restraint of Peace Now leaders, see Lily Galili, "Peace Now—Now," *Ha'aretz,* February 18, 1983.

20. Amnon Dankner, "I Have No Sister!" *Ha'aretz,* February, 18, 1983.

21. The exact figure was 688,066. See *Statistical Abstract of Israel, 1991,* table 5.1, 164–165. Together with Mizrachim who lived in Palestine before the creation of Israel, and their offspring, they presently number more than 2 million, more then half the Jewish population of Israel.

22. These figures were derived from the *Statistical Abstract of Israel* series by Yochanan Peres. See his *Ethnic Relations in Israel* (in Hebrew) (Tel Aviv: Sifriat Poalim, 1977).

23. See, for example, Henriette Dahan-Kalev, "Israeli Identity between New Immigrants and Old-Timers" (in Hebrew) (paper read at a conference on immigration in the early years of the State of Israel, held in Jerusalem, March 1992; to be published by Yad Izhak Ben-Zvi Publications, Jerusalem). See also Virginia R. Dominguez, *People as Subject, People as Object: Selfhood and Peoplehood in Contemporary Israel* (Madison: University of Wisconsin Press, 1989). For a good literary work, see Eli Amir, *Scapegoat* (London: Weidenfeld and Nicolson, 1987). A marxist critique of the absorption process can be found in Shlomo Swirski, *Israel: The Oriental Majority* (London: Zed Books, 1989).

24. The first major ethnic riots occurred in Haifa's Wadi Salib district in 1958.

25. If the gross income per household of Ashkenazi Jews is indexed at 100, Mizrachim who immigrated to Israel between 1948 and 1954 had an average income level of 71.5 in 1965, and only 83.1 in 1980. Immigrants who came after 1955 trailed behind with an income of 75.8 in 1980. See *Statistical Abstract of Israel, 1981,* 293–294.

26. See Arian, *Elections in Israel, 1981.* On voting patterns of Mizrachi Jews before 1967, see Moshe Lissak, *Social Mobility in Israeli Society* (Jerusalem: Jerusalem Academic Press, 1969). See also Naomi Kies, "Constituency Support and the Israeli Party System," (Ph.D. diss., Massachusetts Institute of Technology, 1969); Avraham Diskin, "The Jewish Ethnic Vote: An Aggregate Perspective," in D. Caspi, A. Diskin, and E. Gutmann, eds., *The Roots of Begin's Success: The 1981 Israeli Elections* (London: Croom Helm, 1984).

27. Asher Arian, *Politics in Israel: The Second Generation* (Chatham, N.J.: Chatham House, 1989), table 8.4, 156.

28. For figures, see Hanoch Smith, *Israel's Knesset Elections: An Analysis of the Upset* (Jerusalem: American Jewish Committee, 1977); and Hanoch Smith, *Election Results 1977* (Jerusalem: Central Bureau of Statistics, 1977).

29. Michal Shamir and Asher Arian, "The Ethnic Vote in Israel's 1981 Elections," in Arian, *Elections in Israel, 1981,* 91–111.

30. Ofira Seliktar claims that "the impact of ethnicity, education and low socioeconomic status are highly interactive and reinforcing of each other." See her "Ethnic Stratification and Foreign Policy in Israel: The Attitudes of Oriental Jews towards the Arabs and the Arab-Israeli Conflict," *Middle East Journal* 38, no. 1 (winter 1984): 34–50.

31. A tendency among Mizrachim to be more hostile toward Arabs was found in surveys conducted in the 1960s, though anti-Arab prejudice was prevalent among Ashkenazim as well. See Yochanan Peres, "Ethnic Relations in Israel," *American Journal of Sociology* 76, no. 6 (May 1971): 1021–1047.

32. Abel Jacob, "Trends in Israeli Public Opinion on Issues Related to the Arab-Israeli Conflict, 1967-1972," *Jewish Journal of Sociology* 16 (December 1974): 187–208.

33. *Seker Dahaf* (in Hebrew), May 1984.

34. Shlomo Swirski quotes Yoel Marcus, a prominent journalist who attributed the success of Likud in the 1981 elections among the Mizrachim to Begin's ability to "appeal to the mentality of Orientals, in inflaming their national pride, in fanning their latent hatred against the Arabs." See Swirski, *Israel: The Oriental Majority,* 53.

35. This is demonstrated by the sensitivity expressed by Ben Dror Yemini, a Mizrachi peace activist, when he denies allegations published in the media concerning hatred toward Arabs by a group of Mizrachi youngsters from Tiberias. See his *A Political Punch* (in Hebrew) (Haifa: Mifras,1986), 61–62. On page 47 he states, "The most destructive and stupid myth is that of the Arab hatred of the Mizrachim born in the circles of the Israeli left." See also Eva Etzioni-Halevy (with Rina Shapira), *Political Culture in Israel: Cleavage and Integration among Israeli Jews* (New York: Praeger, 1977), 67–87. Some of the analysis of Mayseless and Gal also follows this line. See their *Hatred toward Arabs among Israeli High School Students: A Case of Prejudice* (Zichron Ya'akov, Israeli Center for Military Studies, May 1991).

36. These terms were coined by the Israeli sociologist Rivka Bar Yosef. See her article "Desocialization and Resocialization," in Moshe Lissak, O. Ben David, and

B. Mizrachi, eds., *Immigrants in Israel* (in Hebrew) (Jerusalem: Academon, 1969), 41–59.

37. Yochanan Peres, "Why Is It Difficult to Deal with Ethnic Pluralism in Israel?" in Alouf Hareven, ed., *Why Is It Difficult to Be an Israeli?* (Jerusalem: Van Leer Institute, 1986), 81.

38. Seliktar borrows the term *alienated identifiers* from Z. Ben-Sira, *Jewish Society in Israel: Ethnic Relations,* (Jerusalem: Israel Institute for Applied Social Research, 1983). See Ofira Seliktar, *New Zionism and the Foreign Policy System of Israel* (London: Croom Helm, 1986), 132–133. Another summary of some of these explanations can be found in Yael Yishai, "Israel's Right-Wing Jewish Proletariat," *Jewish Journal of Sociology* 14, no. 2 (December 1982). See also Ze'ev Ben-Sira, *Alienated Identification in Jewish Israeli Society* (in Hebrew) (Jerusalem: Magnes, 1988).

39. Louis Guttman, *The Continuing Survey, February-March 1972* (Jerusalem: Israel Institute for Applied Social Research [IISAR], April 1972), 48. Similar results were found with respect to attitudes toward Israeli Arabs.

40. See Yoram Peri and John Goldberg, *Are the Mizrachim More Hawkish?* (in Hebrew) (Tel Aviv: International Center for Peace in the Middle East, 1985), 18.

41. For an attempt at a comparative study of tolerance, see Michal Shamir and John Sullivan, "The Political Context of Tolerance: The U.S. and Israel," *American Political Science Review* 77, no. 4 (December 1983): 911–928. This may also explain why younger Israelis tend to favor more hawkish positions. See, for example, a summary of these findings in table 3.3 in Etzioni-Halevy, *Political Culture in Israel,* 55. While 22 to 25 percent of adults surveyed oriented themselves to the left, only 15 percent of youths did so; 36 percent of youths (as compared to 23 percent of adults) favored right-wing orientations. A survey taken among high school students in the summer of 1990 reported that 77 percent of respondents expressed negative attitudes toward Arabs. See *Ma'ariv,* August 8, 1990. See also Mayseless and Gal, *Hatred toward Arabs.*

42. For a review of the ethnic, social, economic, and educational composition of Israeli society, see U. O. Schmeltz, S. Dellapergola, and U. Avner, *Ethnic Differences among Israeli Jews: A New Look* (Jerusalem: Institute of Contemporary Jewry, 1991). On the level of education, see 60–78.

43. Amos Oz, *In the Land of Israel* (London: Flamingo, 1983), 35–36.

44. For an analysis of the rise of the movement and its ideology, see Etti Danino, "The Rise of Protest among Mizrachi Intelligentsia in Israeli Society: A Case Study of East for Peace" (master's thesis, Ben-Gurion University of the Negev, 1990).

45. The text of the group's "Statement of Purpose" and "East for Peace's Guiding Principles" are in the personal files of Shlomo Elbaz. An English version was published in *New Outlook* 27, nos. 3-4 (April 1984): 35.

46. Shlomo Elbaz, interview by author, Jerusalem, August 11, 1992. The first reports on the new movement were published by Lilly Galili in *Ha'aretz,* June 13, 1983, and by Daniel Gavron, "Smashing the Stereotype," *Jerusalem Post,* July 8, 1983.

47. Among the prominent intellectuals who supported the new movement were novelists A. B. Yehoshua, Sami Michael, and Shmuel Balas; the poet Erez Bitton; the literary critic Sasson Somech; and the physicist Henri Atlan. Shelley Elkayam, interview by author, Jerusalem, November 3, 1993.

48. Elbaz, interview. See also Ofra Yeshua-Leit, "The Gospel According to the East," *Ma'ariv,* July 29, 1983. Obviously the movement included many more personalities than can be mentioned here.

49. Elkayam, interview by author, Jerusalem, November 3, 1993. Her father's family originated in Morocco and immigrated to Palestine nine generations ago. Elkayam became an activist on behalf of East for Peace at the World Conference on Religion and Peace. For the proceedings of the fourth conference, held in Nairobi, Kenya, August 21–23, 1984, see John Taylor and Guenter Gebhardt, eds., *Religion for Human Dignity and World Peace* (Geneva: World Conference on Religion and Peace, 1986), 189–190. A more extended profile of Elkayam can be found in Abigail Pickus, "Where Words Are Sacred," *Jerusalem Post,* August 6, 1993.

50. Quoted in Hall-Cathala, *Peace Movement in Israel,* 84. *Tchach-tchach* is a derogatory reference to young Mizrachim.

51. This was not a new idea. The leaders of East for Peace acknowledged the important contribution of Eliahou Eliachar in this respect. For many years he was the president of the World Sephardi Federation, and represented this community in the Knesset. On his opinions concerning relations with the Palestinians, see Philip Gilon, *Israelis and Palestinians, Coexistence or . . . : The Credo of Elie Eliachar* (London: Collings, 1978). See also Eliahou Eliachar, *Living with Palestinians* (Jerusalem: Publications of the Sephardi Community of Jerusalem, 1975).

52. *Kol Ha'ir,* January 25, 1984.

53. For a presentation of new images of Judeo-Arab culture and history, see Ammiel Alcalay, *After Jews and Arabs: Remaking Levantine Culture* (Minneapolis: University of Minnesota Press, 1993).

54. Elbaz, interview. See also Yemini, *Political Punch,* 109–114.

55. Though Labor won a slight plurality over Likud in the 1984 election, the bulk of Likud's support still came from the Mizrachi population. See Paul Abramson, "Demographic Change and Partisan Support," in Asher Arian and Michal Shamir, eds., *The Elections in Israel, 1988* (Boulder, Colo.: Westview, 1990), 173–188. See especially fig. 10.3, 181.

56. Seadia Marciano, as quoted in Hall-Cathala, *Peace Movement in Israel,* 105. Elbaz claimed that their failure to attract more Mizrachim was due to lack of funds, but this seems to be a weak excuse.

57. Ibid., 105.

58. The term "orthodox" is used to identify the 20 percent of the Jewish population in Israel that adheres to traditional Jewish law. This sizable segment of Israeli society is divided between the ultra-orthodox and neoorthodox. Most ultra-orthodox are anti-Zionist or indifferent to Zionist ideology. The Ashkenazi-Mizrachi continuum cuts across the religious observance spectrum, though among strict orthodox (and especially among ultra-orthodox), there is a clear Ashkenazi majority. For more on this, see Samuel Heilman and Menachem Friedman, *The Haredim in Israel: Who Are They and What Do They Want?* (New York: American Jewish Committee, 1991).

59. Rabbi Eliezer Menachem Shach, considered the most influential man in the ultra-orthodox camp, declared, "The blood of Jewish children is more important than soil." See the anonymously edited *And the Sun Rose: The Founding of the Ultra Orthodox Association Degel Hatorah, and Its Ideology* (in Hebrew) (Bnei Brak, Israel: Institute for Historical Documentation, 1980), 136–237.

60. See Tamar Herman and David Newman, "The Dove and the Skull Cap: The Secular-Religious Divide in the Israeli Peace Movement" (in Hebrew), in Yeshaya Liebman, ed., *To Live Together: Secular-Religious Relations in Israeli Society* (Jerusalem: Keter Publishing, 1990), 133.

61. Much of the information included in this section was derived from an interview with Yehezkiel Landau, a leader of the orthodox peace movement, conducted in Jerusalem on August 26, 1992. See also David Newman, "Ideological and Political Attitudes of the Religious Peace Camp in Israel," *L'eyla, A Journal of Judaism Today* (spring 1991): 4–9.

62. The choice of the name is taken from the ending of the Kaddish, the most holy and frequently repeated Jewish prayer, "The Lord will bless His people with strength, the Lord will bless His people with peace."

63. *Violence and the Value of Life in Jewish Tradition* (Jerusalem: Oz ve Shalom Publications, 1984).

64. Ibid.

65. Over the years Professor Avi Ravitzki became a leading theologian and analyst of religious ideologies in Judaism. See his recent *Messianism, Zionism, and Jewish Religious Radicalism* (in Hebrew) (Tel Aviv: Am Oved, 1993); and his article "Peace" in Arthur Cohen and Paul Mendes-Flohr, eds., *Contemporary Religious Jewish Thought* (New York: Free Press, 1987), 685–702.

66. From *Torah, Zionism, Peace,* an anonymously edited work containing articles (in Hebrew) based on the lectures delivered at the founding conference of Netivot Shalom (Jerusalem: Netivot Shalom Publications, 1983).

67. Interview with Janet Aviad.

68. Tamar Herman and David Newman speak of alienation between secular and religious peaceniks based on the gap between the universalistic orientation of the secular and the particularistic inclination of the orthodox. See their "The Dove and the Skull Cap," 139.

69. A *succa* is a temporary structure used in the Jewish holiday of Succot. The term *succat shalom* is taken from the daily evening prayer. Ta'anit Esther is the day of mourning for Queen Esther, the Jewish wife of the Persian king. See Newman, "Ideological and Political Attitudes," 6.

70. The English publications of Oz ve Shalom continued into the late 1980s. The last English publication was "You Must Not Remain Indifferent," February 7, 1988. The last bulletin was no. 7–8, which appeared in the fall of 1986. The last Hebrew publication was "Be Separated from Me," issued in spring 1991.

71. "Statement of Principle," Oz ve Shalom/Netivot Shalom. For a detailed analysis of the movement's ideology, see Newman, "Ideological and Political Attitudes," 5–6.

72. Quoted in Myron Aronoff, *Israeli Visions and Divisions: Cultural Change and Political Conflict* (New Brunswick, N.J.: Transaction Books, 1989), 111.

73. Landau, interview. For a detailed description of the public activities of the movement, see Aronoff, *Israeli Visions and Divisions,* 112–117.

74. Herman and Newman, "The Dove and the Skull Cap," 134.

75. Quoted in ibid., 144.

9. Under the Shadow of National Unity, 1984–87

1. As noted in chapter 5, Begin apparently believed that he promised Carter only a three-month freeze, while Carter felt Begin had agreed to a much broader freeze. For a harsh critique of the Israeli settlement policies during this period, see Geoffrey Aronson, *Israel, Palestinians and the Intifada: Creating Facts on the West Bank* (New York: Kagan Paul International, 1990), especially 57–162.

2. On the development of the Jewish settlement in Hebron, see Ghazi Falah, "Recent Jewish Colonization in Hebron," in David Newman, ed., *The Impact of Gush Emunim: Politics and Settlement in the West Bank* (London: Croom Helm, 1985), 252–255.

3. Bar-On, *Peace Now,* 51.

4. For a summary of Israel's involvement in Lebanon during that period, see Itamar Rabinovich, "Israel and Lebanon in 1983," in Legum, Shaked, and Dishon, eds., *Middle East Contemporary Survey* 7:135–249. For a listing of violent incidents and Israeli casualties, see the chronology compiled by Moshe Gershovich, "Armed Operations," in ibid., 176–190.

5. For the internal developments in the Shi'a community in Lebanon during this period, see Norton, *Amal and the Shi'a.*

6. Linn and Gilligan, "One Action, Two Moral Orientations," 196.

7. According to Shultz, the main U.S. objective was to achieve the withdrawal of all foreign forces from Lebanon. See *Turmoil and Triumph,* 196. For a good critique of U.S. policy in Lebanon, see William Quandt, "Reagan's Lebanon Policy: Trial and Error," *Middle East Journal* 38, no. 2 (spring 1984): 237–254.

8. For detailed descriptions of these negotiations, see David Kimche, *The Last Option* (New York: Scribner's, 1991),162–181. See also Tamir, *Soldier in Search of Peace,* 181–223.

9. See Shultz, *Turmoil and Triumph,* 196–219.

10. For more on these developments, see Itamar Rabinovich, *The War for Lebanon 1970–1985* (Ithaca, N.Y.: Cornell University Press, 1984), 174–199.

11. Interview with Naftali Raz.

12. On the beginning of this movement, see chapter 7.

13. Interview with Naomi Bentsur.

14. Ibid.

15. For a strategic analysis of the Israeli deployment, see Avner Yaniv, *Dilemmas of Security: Politics, Strategy, and Israel's Experience in Lebanon* (Oxford: Oxford University Press, 1987), 148–215.

16. *Jerusalem Post,* August 29, 1983; and *Ha'aretz,* August 31, 1983.

17. In the early summer of 1983 a group of recently discharged soldiers organized a protest across the street from the prime minister's residence. They held a large poster with the number of Israelis killed in Lebanon to date. Arie Na'or, one of Begin's close aides, claimed that the daily reminder of the bloody price paid for the Lebanese adventure had a depressing impact on the prime minister. Raya Harnik, interview by author, Jerusalem, October 30, 1993.

18. See Mark Segal, "Begin's Bombshell," *Jerusalem Post,* August 29, 1983.

19. See the debate on the formation of the new government in the *Knesset Verbatim Record,* 97:3397–3455.

20. At the end of October 1983 a car bomb exploded at the Israeli base near the town of Tyre. The blast killed more than sixty people and wounded several dozen others. See *Jerusalem Post,* November 6, 1983.

21. For a description of the impact of extraparliamentary groups on the formulation of party election platforms, see Yael Yishai, "Drafting the Platform: The Territorial Clause," in Asher Arian and Michal Shamir, eds., *Elections in Israel, 1984* (Tel Aviv: Ramot Publishing, 1986), 235–250.

22. Taken from the personal archive of Naftali Raz. Reprinted in Bar-On, *Peace Now*, 143–145.

23. Ran Cohen and I were elected from Ratz; Yossi Sarid, Haim Ramon, and a few others returned on the Labor list; all Mapam members were identified with the movement, as were the three members of Shinui. In the Eleventh Knesset, Peace Now could count on the support of at least twenty MKs.

24. Labor (including Mapam, which later formed an independent faction) gained 44 seats, Likud 41. Shinui and Ratz gained three each; the Arab parties received six. On the right, Tečhiya gained five and Ometz one. See *Statistical Abstract of Israel, 1991*, table 20.3, 552. For analysis of the results, see Arian and Shamir, *Elections in Israel, 1984*.

25. This was assured by the right of both Likud and Labor to refer any controversial issue to the "inner cabinet," which was composed of five ministers from Likud and Labor each. Because a majority was required for any decision, both parties had virtual veto power. For a critique of the unity government, see Mordechai Bar-On, "Israel's National Unity Government, 1984–1986: A Retrospective," *Tikkun* 1, no. 2 (fall 1986): 65–69.

26. Jewish vigilantism increased in the territories in the early 1980s. It was ultimately exposed by the assistant attorney general, Judith Karp, in her "Investigation of Suspicions against Israelis in Judea and Samaria" (in Hebrew), in *A Report of the Monitoring Committee* (Jerusalem: Ministry of Justice, 1982). See also David Weisburd and Vered Vinitzky, "Vigilantism as Rational Social Control: The Case of the Gush Emunim Settlers," in Myron Aronoff, ed., *Cross-Currents in Israeli Culture and Politics* (New Brunswick, N.J.: Transaction Books, 1984), 80–81.

27. A third bomb, placed in the car of the mayor of El Bireh, was discovered in time. An Israeli policeman was permanently blinded trying to disarm it. See *Jerusalem Post*, June 4, 5, 6, 1981.

28. *Jerusalem Post*, July 27, 1983. At the time, the identities of the perpetrators were unknown. See *Ma'ariv*, July 27, 1983.

29. See Haggai Segal, *Dear Brothers* (in Hebrew) (Jerusalem: Keter Publishing, 1987); Naomi Gal-Or, *The Jewish Underground: Our Terrorism* (in Hebrew) (Tel Aviv: Hakibbutz Hameuchad, 1990); Ehud Sprinzak, *The Ascendance of Israel's Radical Right* (Oxford: Oxford University Press, 1991), 94–99; Ehud Sprinzak, *Fundamentalism, Terrorism and Democracy: The Case of Gush Emunim Underground*, Woodrow Wilson Occasional Papers (Washington, D.C.: Woodrow Wilson International Center for Scholars, 1987); and Yael Yishai, "The Jewish Terror Organization: Past or Future Danger?" *Conflict* 6, no. 4 (1986).

30. Ehud Spinzak, *Every Man Is Right in His Own Eyes: Illegalism in Israeli Society* (in Hebrew) (Tel Aviv: Sifriat Poalim, 1986), 121–146.

31. *Statistical Abstract of Israel, 1991*, table 20.2, 551. For a discussion of the rise of Kahane in socioeconomic terms, see Gershon Shafir and Yoav Peled, "Thorns in Your Eyes: The Socioeconomic Basis of the Kahane Vote," in Arian and Shamir, *Elections in Israel, 1984*, 189–206.

32. Ehud Sprinzak, "Kach and Kahane: The Emergence of Jewish Quasi-Fascism in Israel," in Arian and Shamir, *Elections in Israel, 1984*, 169–187.

33. For the story of the JDL as told by Meir Kahane, see his *The Story of the Jewish Defense League* (Radnor, Pa.: Chilton, 1975). For some of his ideological views, see Meir Kahane, *Never Again: A Program for Jewish Survival* (New York: Pyramid, 1972); and *The Jewish Idea* (Jerusalem: Institute of the Jewish Idea, 1974).

34. At first Kahane also used the name "Jewish Defense League" in Israel. He assumed the name Kach in 1975. In the wake of the 1973 war, and the establishment of Gush Emunim (which he refused to join), his own tactics became more radical. See Sprinzak, *Ascendance of Israel's Radical Right*, 80–87.

35. For critical biographies of Kahane, see Yair Kotler, *Heil Kahane!* (in Hebrew) (Tel Aviv: Modan, 1985); and Robert Friedman, *The False Prophet: Rabbi Meir Kahane, from FBI Informant to Knesset Member* (New York: Lawrence Hill, 1990).

36. Kahane was eventually acquitted due to a lack of evidence. See Friedman, *False Prophet*, 153.

37. Sprinzak, *Ascendance of Israel's Radical Right*, 83–84. Friedman quoted Kahane as having told him, "Begin's leaving was good for me," because many Mizrachim who had supported Begin now supported Kahane. See Friedman, *False Prophet*, 213.

38. An attempt to disqualify Kahane from running for the Knesset was blocked by the Supreme Court based on the argument that there was no specific law making racist propaganda criminal. The Supreme Court even challenged the Knesset to pass such a law. See Supreme Court Verdict no. Ein Bet 84/2 in *Piskei Din* (Verdicts), vol. 39, part 2 (Jerusalem: Ministry of Justice), 158 ff. For more on this, see chapter 10.

39. For more details, see David Hall-Cathala, *The Peace Movement in Israel 1967–1987* (New York: St. Martin's, 1990), 65–72.

40. Information on the history of Neveh Shalom can be found in *Neveh Shalom Newsletter*, Neveh Shalom Archive, and in Hall-Cathala, 126–131.

41. There is a wealth of details on these and similar groups in the archives of the New Israel Fund's Jerusalem and Washington offices. This organization is one of the main sponsors of such activities.

42. For a listing of these organizations, see Jay Rothman, *A Guide to Arab-Jewish Peacemaking Organizations in Israel* (Jerusalem: New Israel Fund, 1988).

43. The unique identities of the two kinds of Palestinians were brilliantly portrayed by David Grossman in *The Yellow Wind* (New York: Delta, 1988); and *Sleeping on a Wire: Conversations with Palestinians in Israel* (New York: Farrar, Straus and Giroux, 1993).

44. Interview with Janet Aviad.

45. For a list of these events during 1985, see Joshua Teitelbaum, "Armed Operations," in Itamar Rabinovich and Haim Shaked, eds., *Middle East Contemporary Survey*, vol. 11 (Tel Aviv: Moshe Dayan Center for Middle East and African Studies, 1987), 100–104.

46. *Ma'ariv*, September 26, 1985. In retaliation the Israeli air force bombed the PLO headquarters in Tunis on October 1. *Jerusalem Post*, October 3, 1985.

47. See Teitelbaum, "Armed Operations," 91–93.

48. *Jerusalem Post*, December 28, 1985.

49. Raz, interview.

50. See Peres's Knesset speech in which he presented his cabinet, and his response to the subsequent debate, *Knesset Verbatim Record*, 100:63–65, 108–112.

51. *Yediot Ahronot*, July 24, 1986.

52. For details of the economic austerity measures and their impact on the Israeli economy, see the *Statistical Abstract of Israel, 1991*, table 10.1, 275. A thorough analysis of the economic reform was written by Michael Bruno, who was at the time the chancellor of Israel's Central Bank. See his *Crisis Stabilization and Economic Reform: Therapy by Consensus* (Oxford: Clarendon, 1993). For a summary, see Michael Bruno and Liora Meridor, "The Costly Transition to Sustainable Growth," in Michael Bruno et al., eds., *Lessons of Economic Stabilization and Its Aftermath* (Cambridge, Mass.: MIT Press, 1991); Michael Bruno and Sylvia Piterman, "Israel's Stabilization: A Two-Year Review," in Michael Bruno et al., eds., *Inflation Stabilization* (Cambridge, Mass.: MIT Press, 1988).

53. For Israel's policies in Lebanon at the beginning of 1984, see Ze'ev Schiff, "Lebanon: Motivations and Interests in Israel's Policy," *Middle East Journal* 38, no. 2 (spring 1984): 220–227.

54. Bentsur, interview. See also an interview in *Newsweek*, June 10, 1985, 56.

55. For attempts at peace negotiations with Jordan in 1983 and 1984, see two articles by Mordechai Gazit, "The Middle East Peace Process," *Middle East Contemporary Survey* 7:150–171, 8:82–97.

56. On relations between West Bank Palestinians and the Hashemite regime after the 1967 war, see Clinton Bailey, "The Participation of the Palestinians in the Politics of Jordan" (Ph.D. diss., Columbia University, 1969). See also Clinton Bailey, "Changing Attitudes toward Jordan in the West Bank," *Middle East Journal* 32, no. 2 (spring 1978): 155–166; and Clinton Bailey, *Jordan's Palestinian Challenge 1948–1983* (Boulder, Colo.: Westview, 1984).

57. For an assessment of the PLO after the war in Lebanon, see Mordechai Bar-On, *Peace Politics in Israel from Sadat to Hussein* (Tel Aviv: International Center for Peace in the Middle East, 1986). On April 10, 1983, the king withdrew from playing an active role in promoting the Reagan plan as a result of his inability to convince the PLO of the advantages of his approach. See "Jordanian Cabinet Statement," *New York Times*, April 11, 1983.

58. Shultz, *Turmoil and Triumph*, 434–439.

59. Likud was adamantly opposed to the idea, and Peres delayed bringing the proposal to the cabinet as long as the Arab side was not yet ready. For a discussion of the secret diplomatic relations between Israel and Jordan, see Yossi Melman and Dan Raviv, *Behind the Uprising: Israelis, Jordanians, and Palestinians* (New York: Greenwood, 1989). For a summary of these developments between 1984 and 1987, see Adam Garfinkle, *Israel and Jordan in the Shadow of War: Functional Ties and Futile Diplomacy in a Small Place* (New York: St. Martin's, 1992), 99–144.

60. For an analysis of Jordan-PLO relations, see Menachem Klein, *Antagonistic Collaboration: PLO-Jordanian Dialogue 1985–1988* (in Hebrew), Policy Paper no. 27 (Jerusalem: Leonard Davis Institute, 1988).

61. The text of the agreement is reprinted in the *Journal of Palestine Studies* 14 (spring 1985): 206.

62. Asher Susser, "Jordan, the Palestinians and the Middle East Peace Process," in Itamar Rabinovich and Haim Shaked, eds., *Middle East Contemporary Survey*, vol. 9 (Tel Aviv: Tel Aviv University, 1985), 512–518.

63. For the text of the communique of the Executive Committee of the PLO on February 19, 1985, see Moore, *Arab-Israeli Conflict*, 4:doc. 337, 1589–1590.

64. Joshua Teitelbaum, "The Palestine Liberation Organization," in Itamar Rabinovich and Haim Shaked, eds., *Middle East Contemporary Survey*, vol. 10 (Boulder, Colo.: Westview 1986), 165–202.

65. The text of the Five-Year Development Plan of August 1986 is reprinted in the *Journal of Palestine Studies* 16 (fall 1986): 205. On April 19, 1987, the PLO officially rescinded the 1985 Amman Agreement. See *Journal of Palestine Studies* 17 (summer 1987): 195.

66. Mordechai Bar-On, "What Do I Want of the PLO?" *Ha'aretz*, October 24, 1984.

67. For a dissenting view, see Mordechai Bar-On, "The Israeli Rejection Front," *Al Ha'mishmar,* July 24, 1985. In this article I wrote: "Instead of reaching the Palestinians through Hussein, we should reach Hussein through the Palestinians."

68. According to some polls Shimon Peres achieved the highest popularity rating ever achieved by a prime minister. His approval rating was 85 percent. See Rephaella Bilski Ben-Hur, *With Shimon* (Tel Aviv: Dvir, 1992), 18.

69. David Shaham, interview by author, Tel Aviv, August 2, 1992.

70. "Statement of Purpose," ICPME Archive, Tel Aviv.

71. *Proceedings of the First World Conference* (Tel Aviv: International Center for Peace in the Middle East, 1983).

72. I informally represented Peace Now at the inauguration conference of ICPME, where I said: "For all the high degree of compatibility and closeness between Peace Now and the aims of the Center, the two organizations should maintain their autonomy." Ibid., 21. Attempts were made to merge the two organizations over the years, but all failed. See "Memorandum of Understanding," August 20, 1991, ICPME Archive.

73. Shaham, interview.

74. The parties included Shinui, Labor, Mapam, Ratz, and the Progressive List for Peace. The communists, who at that time were still closely affiliated with Moscow, did not participate.

75. Yossi Sarid, interview by author, Tel Aviv, August 24, 1992.

76. Mordechai Bar-On, "The Joy of Despair," *Yediot Ahronot,* February 24, 1986.

77. Meron Benvenisti, *The West Bank Data Base Project 1987 Report* (Jerusalem: Jerusalem Post Publications, 1987), especially 66–80. See also his *Conflicts and Contradictions* (New York: Willard Books, 1986).

78. This debate continues today. See Meron Benvenisti, *Shepherds' War* (Jerusalem: Jerusalem Post Publications, 1989); and his recent book in Hebrew, *Fatal Embrace* (Jerusalem: Keter Publishing, 1992).

79. The text of the London formula can be found in William Quandt, ed., *The Middle East: Ten Years after Camp David* (Washington, D.C.: Brookings Institution, 1988), 475–476.

80. The Van Leer group included Avishai Margalit, Itzhak Gal-Nur, and Galia Golan, all from the Hebrew University, and Yael Tamir from the political science department at Tel Aviv University.

81. Another important source of influence was the Frankfurt School. Hannan Hever, interview by author, Jerusalem, August 23, 1992.

82. Foucault's works published in English include, among others, *The Archaeology of Knowledge* (New York: Pantheon, 1972); *The Birth of the Clinic: An Archaeology of Medical Perception* (New York: Vintage, 1975); *Discipline and Punishment* (New York: Pantheon, 1977); *The History of Sexuality* (New York: Pantheon, 1978); *Madness and Civilization: A History of Insanity in the Age of Reason* (New York:

Vintage, 1975); and *The Order of Things: An Archaeology of Human Sciences* (New York: Vintage, 1973).

83. Hever, interview.

84. Ibid.

85. Ibid.

86. Adi Ofir, "My Brothers the Collaborators" (in Hebrew), *Politica* 14-15 (June 1987): 64–67.

87. From Adi Ofir's personal files.

88. Nurit Shleifman and Rachel Freudental, interview by author, Jerusalem, August 17, 1992.

89. Ofir, "My Brothers the Collaborators," 67.

90. Adi Ofir himself refused service in the occupied territories. See chapter 11.

10. The Israeli-Palestinian Dialogue

1. The full story of these relations goes beyond the scope of this study and has been covered by other scholars. See, for example, Menachem Stern et al., eds., *Zionism and the Arab Question: Collected Historical Studies* (in Hebrew) (Jerusalem: Zalman Shazar Center, 1979).

2. During this period intelligence gathering and political work were combined and coordinated by the Executive Committee of the World Zionist Organization. See the memoirs of Eliahu Sasson, *On the Road to Peace: Letters and Conversations* (in Hebrew) (Tel Aviv: Am Oved, 1978); and Ezra Danin, *Unconditionally a Zionist* (in Hebrew) (Jerusalem: Kidum, 1987).

3. During the early 1950s Gideon Raphael headed a special Middle East department in the foreign ministry that was responsible for secret diplomatic contacts. See his *Destination Peace: Three Decades of Israeli Foreign Policy* (New York: Stein and Day, 1981), 3–67.

4. Various individuals tried their hand in such dialogues. For instance, during the 1960s Nina Dinur held regular meetings in her home in Tel Aviv, and Simcha Flapan and Uri Avneri were consistently active in this field both in Israel and abroad. See Uri Avneri, *My Friend the Enemy* (London: Zed Books, 1986), 121–122.

5. Prior to 1967 the most significant contact between Israeli officials and Palestinian representatives took place during the UN-sponsored Palestine Conciliation Commission in Lausanne in the winter and spring of 1949. For more on this episode, see Ilan Pappe, "Moshe Sharett, David Ben-Gurion, and the Palestinian Option, 1848–1956," *Studies in Zionism* 7, no. 1 (1986): 77–97. On efforts at mediation between Israel and the Arab states, see Saadia Touval, *The Peace Brokers* (Princeton: Princeton University Press, 1982).

6. Amos Elon and Sana Hassan, *Between Enemies: A Compassionate Dialogue between an Israeli and an Arab* (New York: Random House, 1974).

7. She described her experiences in Israel and the Egyptian reactions in a memoir. See Sana Hassan, *Enemy in the Promised Land: An Egyptian Woman's Journey into Israel* (New York: Pantheon, 1986).

8. See Article 21 of the Palestine National Charter, reprinted and annotated in Yehoshafat Harkabi, *Palestinians and Israel* (Jerusalem: Keter Publishing, 1987). On the idea of the secular democratic state, see Alain Gresh, *The PLO: The Struggle Within* (London: Zed Books, 1988), 7–57.

9. Colin Legum, ed., *Middle East Contemporary Survey, 1976–1977,* (New York: Holmes and Meier, 1978), 206.

10. For such a position, see Isaac Deutscher, *Non-Jewish Jew and Other Essays* (Oxford: Oxford University Press, 1969).

11. For a discussion of the views of anti-Zionist Jews, see Noam Chomsky, *The Fateful Triangle: The United States, Israel, and the Palestinians* (Boston: South End Press, 1983).

12. The first attempt by a PLO leader to reach out to a larger Israeli audience was made on March 22, 1974, by Nayif Hawatmeh, the leader of the Marxist-Leninist Popular Democratic Front for the Liberation of Palestine (PDFLP), who agreed to be interviewed by Paul Jacobs, a radical American journalist, specifically for an Israeli newspaper. The attempt failed because Hawatmeh, bound by PLO doctrine, offered an ambiguous formula unacceptable even to "progressive" Israelis. See *Yediot Ahronot,* March 22, 1974. An English version was published in *New Outlook* 17, no. 3 (March 1974): 65–67.

13. The information in this section was derived from a document titled "Biography of Abe J. Nathan," which I received from Nathan's office in Tel Aviv, and from a telephone interview I held with him on January 22, 1994. Nathan has also been involved in helping people in disaster areas—victims of the civil war in Biafra, Cambodian refugees in Thailand, hunger-stricken Ethiopians, and earthquake survivors in the Nicaraguan capital Managua, and later in Guatemala.

14. In June 1968 the District Court in Tel Aviv gave him the choice between imprisonment or a fine. He chose to pay the amount of the fine as a personal contribution to a hospital and went to jail. In 1969 Nathan made two other attempts to fly to Cairo via commercial airlines to meet with Nasser, but failed.

15. "Biography of Abe J. Nathan," 2.

16. For more on this law, see pp. 213–216.

17. He had met Arafat once before in the summer of 1982 in Beirut. That meeting was part of a failed attempt to bring about the release of an Israeli pilot who had been captured by the PLO.

18. *Al Ha'mishmar,* October 11, 1991.

19. *Times* (London), November 16, 1973.

20. Ibid., December 17, 1973.

21. Only Hammami's second article was published in Hebrew, by *Ha'olam Ha'zeh,* January 16, 1974, 12, 20.

22. Avneri, *My Friend the Enemy,* 41. In 1968 Avneri wrote *Israel without Zionism: A Plan for Peace in the Middle East* (New York: Collier, 1971). This book, it should be noted, does not question Israel's continued existence as a state governed by Jews. Indeed, Avneri certainly could not be described as "struggling against Zionism as a doctrine and in practice"!

23. Avneri, *My Friend the Enemy,* 57.

24. Ibid., 53.

25. Ibid., 72.

26. *Jerusalem Post,* June 10, 1975.

27. Other prominent names included Amos Oz, A. B. Yehoshua, Yoram Kaniuk, and Simcha Flapan. See Arie Eliav, *Rings of Faith* (in Hebrew) (Tel Aviv: Am Oved), 240.

28. Interview with Matti Peled, Motza, January 20, 1994.

29. Ibid., and interview with Uri Avneri.

30. Shortly after the foundation of the Council for Israel-Palestine Peace, Uri Avneri was attacked by an assailant who repeatedly stabbed him. See *Ma'ariv*, December 19, 1975. For a detailed description of the event, see *Ha'olam Ha'zeh*, December 24, 1975, 16–17, 20–21, 28.

31. For details, see chapter 1, pp. 18–19.

32. Interviews with Eliav and Avneri.

33. Dani Amit, interview by author, Jerusalem, January 21, 1994. He recalled that on his return to Israel from the United States he stopped in London for a few days and happened to witness a group of Jews attacking a young Palestinian during a demonstration in Hyde Park. Amit felt obliged to come to the defense of the Palestinian, who later became a teacher at Bir Zeit University and subsequently introduced Amit to many of the faculty at that university. In the early 1980s Amit founded the Committee of Solidarity with Bir Zeit University. See chapter 6.

34. Ibid.

35. Peled, interview.

36. Eliav points out in his memoirs that the meeting was asymmetrical because Sartawi represented the Palestinian side whereas the Israelis did not represent Israel. Arafat tacitly supported Sartawi, but the meetings never received the official sanction of the PLO and most of the PLO establishment opposed the dialogue. See Eliav, *Rings of Faith*, 240.

37. Peled recalled that there was evidence of the great danger these meetings put Sartawi in. Another PLO official was killed in Paris after attending a press conference with Sartawi in 1982.

38. Interviews with Lova Eliav and David Shaham. A description of the first meeting with Issam Sartawi is in Eliav, *Rings of Faith*, 246–255.

39. The Israelis later introduced Sartawi to other international figures and some prominent progressive Jews, including Nahum Goldmann, the president of the World Jewish Congress; Austrian chancellor Bruno Kreisky; Willy Brandt, the secretary of the Socialist International and former chancellor of Germany; Leopold Sengor of Senegal; Houphouet-Boigny of the Ivory Coast; and Swedish prime minister Olaf Palme.

40. Matti Peled, quoted by Eliav in *Rings of Faith*, 256.

41. Alain Gresh maintained that Hammami was sidestepped because his main contacts continued to be the anti-Zionist group in London; Sartawi was able to transcend this phase and created contacts with Zionists who were closer to the Israeli establishment. This fact did not save Hammami, who was assassinated by the terrorist group Abu Nidal on January 4, 1978. See Avneri, *My Friend the Enemy*, 141.

42. See the front-page article by Shlomo Nakdimon in *Yediot Ahronot*, September 22, 1976.

43. See, for example, the comments of Chaim Tzadok, the minister of justice, in a Knesset debate on November 10, 1976. *Knesset Verbatim Record*, 78:261–262.

44. See the article by Ya'akov Caroz in *Yediot Ahronot*, January 7, 1977, 7. Rabin declared: "The terrorist organizations [the PLO] cannot serve as partners in a dialogue." *Yediot Ahronot*, March 18, 1977.

45. Peled, interview. See Peled's statement in the press conference in *Yediot Ahronot*, January 2, 1977.

46. Avneri, *My Friend the Enemy*, 155–156. For Qaddumi's denial, see *Yediot Ahronot*, January 3, 1977.

47. See chapter 6, pp. 124–125.

48. Peled, interview.

49. This was also the name of a much debated article published at the time by one of the most prestigious Palestinian intellectuals who came out in favor of a Palestinian state alongside Israel. See Walid Khalidi, "Thinking the Unthinkable: A Sovereign Palestinian State," *Foreign Affairs* 56, no. 4 (summer 1978): 695–713. Reprinted in Walid Khalidi, *Palestine Reborn* (London: I. B. Tauris, 1992), 82–104. Lova Eliav published a handsome tribute to Sartawi in the Israeli press, describing him as a "unique person, a refugee and exile, a fighter and physician who sacrificed on a platter of blood his soul and his body on an altar of peace." Reprinted in Eliav, *Rings of Faith,* 278–279.

50. Avneri, interview.

51. Gresh, *PLO,* 195.

52. One prominent case was the attempt in 1955 by Elmore Jackson. See his *Middle East Mission: The Story of a Major Bid for Peace in the Time of Nasser and Ben-Gurion* (New York: Norton, 1983).

53. One early workshop, organized by John Burton at the University of London in 1966, addressed the Greek-Turkish conflict in Cyprus. Another, organized by Leonard Doob in 1968 in Fermeda, South Tyrol, addressed the border disputes between Somalia, Ethiopia, and Kenya in the Horn of Africa. Kelman summarized the Burton and Doob experiments in "The Problem-Solving Workshop in Conflict Resolution," in Richard Merrit, ed., *Communication in International Politics* (Urbana: University of Illinois Press, 1972), 168–204.

54. Ibid., 186.

55. Stephen P. Cohen, et al., "Evolving Intergroup Techniques for Conflict Resolution: An Israeli-Palestinian Pilot Workshop," *Journal of Social Issues* 33, no. 1 (1977): 165–189.

56. These were Samir Anabtawy and Edward Azar, both political scientists, and Hussein Tuma, a clinical psychologist. See Herbert Kelman's summary of his work in "The Interactional Approach to Conflict Resolution and Its Application to Israeli-Palestinian Relations," *International Interaction* 6, no. 2 (1979): 99–122.

57. Herbert Kelman, "Coalition across Conflict Lines: The Interplay of Conflicts within and between the Israeli and Palestinian Communities," Working Paper no. 91-9, Harvard Center for International Affairs, Cambridge, Mass., 1992, 5.

58. The participants from the Israeli side were MK Yossi Sarid, MK Elazar Granot, MK Aharon Har'el, and MK Chaim Gil, all members of the Labor Alliance, and MK Mordechai Virshubski from Shinui. The participants from the Palestinian side were Walid Khalidi and Afif Safiyah, both members of the Palestine National Council, Sari Nusseibeh from Jerusalem, Rami Khouri from Amman, and Fouad Moughrabi from the United States. Herbert Kelman, interview by author, Boston, August 10, 1993.

59. Cohen et al., "Evolving Intergroup Techniques." These documents were in principle similar to the Declaration of Principles that was signed by Rabin and Arafat at the White House on September 13, 1993. See chapter 14.

60. "A Meeting of Minds on Middle East Peace," *New York Times,* March 9, 1984.

61. For example, four members of the Palestinian delegation to the negotiations held in Washington in 1992 and 1993 (after the Madrid Conference) had previously participated in these dialogues.

62. Kelman, interview.

63. Herbert Kelman, "Informal Mediation by the Scholar/Practitioner," in J. Bercovitch and J. Rubin, eds., *Mediation in International Relations: Multiple Approaches to Conflict Management* (New York: St. Martin's, 1992), 91–92. Professor Yari Hirschfeld, who initiated the Oslo talks in 1993, was a veteran of such dialogues.

64. The proliferation of these contacts was so widespread that it is impossible to cover all of them within the scope of this study. Interview with Amnon Zichroni, Tel Aviv.

65. This formula was officially accepted by the PLO only five years later. See chapter 11.

66. Both letters are in the author's personal files.

67. The effort was documented in a television program on public television in the United States. See "The Arab and the Israeli," *Frontline*, 1989, produced by York Associates Television, Washington, D.C. After his return to Amman, Milhem was elected to the Executive Committee of the PLO; I was elected to the Knesset.

68. Peled, Avneri, and Arnon were the Israelis present. Avneri, together with two staff members from his journal, also met Arafat during the siege in West Beirut, on July 3, 1982, but this was primarily a journalistic event. See Avneri, *My Friend the Enemy*, 3–14. See also *Ha'olam Ha'zeh*, July 7, 1982. For the full story of the Tunis meeting, see Avneri, *My Friend the Enemy*, 262–271. See also *Ha'olam Ha'zeh*, January 26, 1983.

69. The communiqué, brief and without substantive statements, confirmed that the meeting had been held and provided a list of participants. It included the statement, "Possibilities for a joint action to promote a just and lasting peace in the Middle East were explored."

70. For Israeli reactions, see *Ha'aretz*, January 23, 1983. Prime Minister Shamir defined the meeting as *shiflut* (base conduct).

71. Amnon Kapeliuk, an Israeli journalist, represented *Le Monde* at the conference and published a description of the events in *Yediot Ahronot*, February 15–17, 1983.

72. A full description of the event is in Avneri, *My Friend the Enemy*, 301–307.

73. Peace Now and ICPME declined an invitation to participate in the conference. Yossi Sarid called it "a staged and one-sided event. . . . A propaganda affair without a common base, and therefore without any positive purpose." *Ma'ariv*, August 14, 1983.

74. Avneri, *My Friend the Enemy*, 311–318. Avneri was again invited by Arafat three weeks later, but there was no substance to the meeting. Secrecy was required by Arafat, because by holding these meetings he violated the injunctions of the Palestine National Council. The drama faded, as Avneri noted: "Now our meetings with Arafat had become routine." *My Friend the Enemy*, 324.

75. Peled, interview.

76. See a summary of analysis made by Eliahu Katz and Chana Levinson in *Yediot Ahronot*, June 21, 1991. They found that during the 1980s the number of Israelis supporting negotiations with the PLO doubled, yet remained a minority by the beginning of the Intifada.

77. See *The Book of Laws*, no. 1191, 219. For the Knesset debate, see *Knesset Verbatim Record*, 105:4032–4052. For a critique of the law, see Baruch Bracha,

"Politicizing the Criminal Law: Criminalizing Politics," *New Outlook* 33, nos. 1–2 (January–February 1990): 12-13.

78. Interview with Tzali Reshef.

79. Gresh, *PLO,* 7–57.

80. The question of who was an indigenous Palestinian and who qualified to become a citizen of the new Palestine remained vague and was debated within the ranks of the PLO. See ibid., 30–33.

81. The formal name included the words "Founded by Israelis of Oriental Origin." Latif Dori, interview by author, Tel Aviv, January 23, 1994. A history of the activities of the Committee for Israeli-Palestinian Dialogue can be found in G. N. Giladi, *Discord in Zion: Conflict between Ashkenazi and Sephardi Jews in Israel* (London: Scorpion, 1990), 316–325.

82. The declaration is in the personal files of Latif Dori.

83. *Al-Fajr* (English edition), July, 25, 1986.

84. Hall-Cathala, *Peace Movement in Israel,* 114.

85. Interviews with Reuven Kaminer, Jerusalem, August 20, 1992, and Dori. A report from the Palestinian side was published by Ziyad al-Hayja in *Filastin al-Thawra,* November 15, 1986. It is quoted in Giladi, *Discord in Zion,* 320–321. See also the *New York Times,* March 22, 1987.

86. Although thirty-three delegates were at the airport, only twenty-two actually departed Israel. Dori, interview.

87. The other three were Reuven Kaminer, Yael Lotan, and Eliezer Feiler (who died of a heart attack during the trial). For more on the "Romanian Four," see Reuven Kaminer, "Challenging the Courts," *New Outlook* (January–February 1987): 13–15.

88. *Jerusalem Post,* June 23, 1993. Several months after the meeting in Romania, another group of Mizrachim, organized by the Israeli Communist Party and led by MK Charlie Biton, met a delegation of PLO officials headed by Mahmoud Abbas (Abu Mazin). This meeting took place in Budapest on June 9, 1987. Eight members of this delegation were eventually indicted. This case also dragged on for years. See the *Guardian* (London), June 15, 1987.

89. In most cases the police did not even bother to investigate media reports of meetings between Israeli members of the peace movement and PLO officials unless someone filed an official complaint. After a conference in Prague in December 1988 in which a number of senior PLO officials participated, a Likud MK filed a complaint against me and two other Israeli participants. The police conducted a brief investigation, but no charges were filed.

90. In response to a query, Yossi Beilin, the cabinet secretary, consulted with the attorney general and then officially informed Willy Gafni (of ICPME) that he could participate in an international conference with PLO officials provided he did not have personal contact with them. A copy of Beilin's letter, dated September 15, 1986, is in the personal files of the author.

91. Meetings of this nature were quite common during the late 1980s. A notable example was a successful conference that was jointly organized by the Israeli magazine *New Outlook* and the Palestinian *al-Fajr.* The conference was held on March 11–13, 1989, at Columbia University in New York City and was titled "The Road to Peace: Coexistence between Israelis and Palestinians." The conference was cosponsored by the American Friends of Peace Now and the American Council for Palestine Affairs, a new body of Palestinian academics living in the United States that supported the PLO. About twenty-five prominent politicians and academics from each side participated. Documents relating to this conference are in the personal files of the author in a file labeled "The Road to Peace."

92. For profiles of the new leaders, see John Wallach and Janet Wallach, *The New Palestinians: The Emerging Generation of Leaders* (Rocklin, Calif.: Prima, 1992). Shawwa was the mayor of Gaza, Khalaf of Ramallah, and Shak'a of Nablus.

93. In August 1988 Peace Now distributed a flyer featuring a drawing of two empty chairs with the caption "Is there somebody to talk to?" It also quoted conciliatory remarks made by these new Palestinian leaders, and posed the question of whether the Israeli side was ready for this. Peace Now Archive, 1988 file.

94. Peter Demant, "Israeli-Palestinian Dialogue: Pitfalls and Promises, the Jewish Side in the Gulf Crisis and Beyond" (paper presented at the annual meeting of the Association for Israel Studies, Jerusalem, 1991).

95. Aviad, interview.

96. Shaham, interview.

11. Intifada: The Palestinian Uprising, 1987–88

1. For a description of these events, see Ze'ev Schiff and Ehud Ya'ari, *Intifada: The Inside Story of the Palestinian Uprising* (New York: Touchstone, 1989), 17–23.

2. Ibid., 25–29.

3. The Palestinian journalist Daoud Kuttab wrote: "What was shaken up was the passivity and normality that had prevailed for most of the past twenty years." See Kuttab's "The Path of No Return: An Overview of the Intifada," in Jay Murphy, ed., *For Palestine* (New York: Writers and Readers, 1993), 90.

4. See Elie Rekhess, "The West Bank and the Gaza Strip," in Itamar Rabinovich and Haim Shaked, eds., *Middle East Contemporary Survey*, vol. 11, (Boulder, Colo.: Westview, 1989), 244–272. For the role of the PLO at the beginning of the Intifada, see Joshua Teitelbaum, "The Palestine Liberation Organization," 231–233, in the same volume.

5. Some Israelis claimed that the presence of the media often triggered violence. See Louis Rapoport, *Confrontations: Israeli Life in the Year of the Uprising* (Boston: Quinlan, 1988), 62–63. Regardless of the question of causation, it is widely agreed that the Palestinians learned how to use the media to their advantage.

6. In a cabinet meeting Rabin admitted that "the security forces did not foresee that the disturbances and public breach of the law would last so long and be so fierce." *Ha'aretz*, January 11, 1988. See Ze'ev Schiff's six-part series, "The Territories War: Lessons and Conclusions," *Ha'aretz*, February 7–12, 1988.

7. Schiff and Ya'ari, *Intifada*, 20.

8. *Ha'aretz*, December 29, 1987.

9. From an interview on Israeli television on January 13, as reported in *Davar*, January 14, 1988.

10. Ronni Talmor, ed., *B'tselem Annual Report 1989* (Jerusalem: B'tselem, December 1989). See also Schiff and Ya'ari, *Intifada*, 31.

11. *Ha'aretz*, January 20, 1988. The new orders were made public during a visit Rabin made to the West Bank. See *Yediot Ahronot* and *Ma'ariv*, January 20, 1988. In the wake of international and domestic criticism Rabin tried to explain his policy, but the damage was already done. See interview in *Davar*, February 12, 1988.

12. Israeli reactions to the Intifada are discussed in Rolly Rosen and Ilana Hammerman, *Soldiers in the Land of Ishmael: Stories and Documents* (in Hebrew) (Tel Aviv: Am Oved, 1990).

13. At the end of January 1988, Yossi Sarid and Dedi Zucker (MKs for the Movement of Citizens' Rights and Peace) sent a memorandum to the minister of defense in which they presented documented cases of abuses perpetrated by Israeli soldiers. Copies of the memo were distributed to other cabinet ministers, to members of the Knesset Committee on Foreign and Security Affairs, and to the media. *Ma'ariv*, January 25, 1988. The attorney general, Joseph Harish, sent a letter to Rabin in which he requested that Rabin issue clear regulations on the use of force and other guidelines to be followed by Israeli soldiers. These regulations were eventually published by the IDF's chief of education and the IDF's attorney general. See Mordechai Bar-On, "Israeli Reactions to the Uprising," *Journal of Palestine Studies* 17, no. 4 (summer 1988): 46–65.

14. On the development of the Intifada from a Palestinian perspective, see Hillel Frisch, "The Intifada from Spontaneous Disturbances to Organized Disobedience," in Ami Ayalon and Haim Shaked, eds., *Middle East Contemporary Survey*, vol. 12 (Boulder, Colo.: Westview, 1990), 284–287. See also Hillel Frisch, "From Armed Struggle to Political Mobilization" (in Hebrew), in Gad Gilbar and Asher Susser, eds., *At the Core of the Conflict: The Intifada* (Tel Aviv: Moshe Dayan Center for Middle East and African Studies, 1992), 40–67.

15. Ziyad Abu-Zayyad, interview by author, Jerusalem, August 15, 1992. See also Daoud Kuttab, "The Palestinian Uprising: The Second Phase, Self-Sufficiency," *Journal of Palestinian Studies* 17, no. 4 (summer 1988): 36–45. By the beginning of February 1988 Rabin admitted that a new situation had evolved and that Israel faced a true popular revolt. See report by Tali Zelinger in *Davar*, February 4, 1988.

16. See Salim Tamari, "Shopkeepers, Peddlers, and Urban Resistance in the Palestinian Uprising," in Takeshi Yukawa, ed., *Proceedings of the International Conference on Urbanism in Islam*, vol. 3 (Tokyo: Tokyo University, 1989).

17. On the way the Intifada was perceived by the Palestinians, see Daoud Kuttab, "A Profile of the Stonethrowers," *Journal of Palestinian Studies* 17, no. 3, (spring 1988): 14–23. In the same journal, see also Jonathan Kuttab, "The Children's Revolt," 26–35.

18. General Nehmia Dagan, the chief of education for the IDF, in a symposium on the limits of power, as quoted by *Voice of Jerusalem Radio* in a newscast on April 10, 1988.

19. Mikado's wife, Leah Tzemel, became a prominent lawyer who defended Palestinians in Israeli courts and who was active in the defense of civil and human rights in general. Much of the information in this section is derived from an interview with Michel Warschawski, Jerusalem, February 18, 1994.

20. At the time, most of these Palestinians were relatively unknown to the Israeli public, but later rose to positions of leadership in the Palestinian community. Mubarak Awad, a Palestinian-American, advocated nonviolent resistance and was deported by the Israeli authorities after the outbreak of the Intifada.

21. See Michel Warschawski, "The Committee against the Iron Fist: Prototype for Israeli-Palestinian Cooperation, 1985–1987," in Maxine Kaufman-Nunn, ed.,

Creative Resistance: Anecdotes of Nonviolent Action by Israeli-Based Groups (Jerusalem: Alternative Information Center, 1993), 81–84.

22. The Association for Civil Rights in Israel petitioned the case to the Supreme Court but was denied redress.

23. Warschawski, interview.

24. See Ian Lustick, *Arabs in a Jewish State: Israel's Control of a National Minority* (Austin: University of Texas Press, 1980). See also Elie Rekhess, "The Arabs in Israel and the Arabs of the Territories: Political Identification and National Solidarity, 1976–1988," *Hamizrach Hachadash*, nos. 125–128 (1989): 166–191. Mariam Mar'i, an Israeli-Palestinian activist, identified herself as "a Palestinian by nationality and Israeli by citizenship," *Israeli Democracy* (summer 1989): 15. For an analysis of the impact of the Intifada on Israeli Palestinians, see Elie Rekhess, "The Arabs of Israel and the Intifada" (in Hebrew), in Gilbar and Susser, *Core of the Conflict*, 99–127.

25. Warschawski, interview. On July 1, 1990, Mikado began serving a six-month prison term imposed by the Supreme Court, but this was not directly connected with his activities in Dai Lakibush. He was convicted of unwittingly working on behalf of a front organization for the Democratic Front of the Liberation of Palestine.

26. Lilly Galili, "I Am the Marker of the Borderline, the Marker of the Rift in the Society," interview with Adi Ofir, *Ha'aretz*, July 22, 1988.

27. Ibid.

28. Interview with Shleifman and Freudental. Some of these reports were made public by paid advertisements when finances allowed. See, for example, *Ha'aretz*, March 17 and March 24, 1988.

29. Shleifman and Freudental, interview.

30. For a description of the events, see *Jerusalem Post* and *Ma'ariv*, April 7, 1988.

31. *Ma'ariv*, April 10, 1988. On the following day the Supreme Court ordered the IDF to stop the demolition and allowed the villagers to appeal to the court. *Hadashot*, April 11, 1988. For a critique of the steps taken by the IDF, see Uriel Procaccia, "Another Look at the Houses of Beita," *Ha'aretz*, April 27, 1988.

32. Hannan Hever, interview by author, Jerusalem, August 23, 1992.

33. Shleifman, interview.

34. *Ha'aretz*, May 28, 1989; and *Ma'ariv*, May 30, 1989. On her experience in jail, see Dafna Golan's article in *Hadashot*, June 7, 1989.

35. Hever, interview.

36. Ibid.

37. On the beginnings of this movement, see chapter 7.

38. See Ishai Menuchin and Dina Menuchin, eds., *The Limits of Obedience* (in Hebrew) (Jerusalem: Siman Kria Books, 1985). For responses to the book, see Yossi Sarid, "Gush Emunim Thanks Yesh Gvul," *Ha'aretz*, January 2, 1986; Shlomo Avineri, "On the Obligation to Obey in a Democratic Regime," *Ha'aretz*, October 12, 1986; Yehuda Meltzer, "Ammunition for the Settlers?" *Al Ha'mishmar*, January 10, 1986; Haim Bar-Am, "Doubtful Pragmatism," *Ha'aretz*, January 7, 1986; Yehuda Meltzer, "The Philosopher in a Democratic Regime," *Ha'aretz*, October 19, 1986; and David Heid, "Socrates' Error," *Ha'aretz*, October 19, 1986.

39. A copy of the statement is in the files of Ishai Menuchin.

40. *Jerusalem Post*, January 19, 1988.

41. *Yediot Ahronot*, February 26, 1988.

42. The Kfar Kassem case occurred in October 1956 and involved the killing of approximately fifty Israeli Palestinians.

43. During the spring and summer of 1988 the Hebrew media carried many reports on the moral predicaments the IDF faced in confronting the Intifada. These included accounts of courts martial that resulted from abuses by soldiers. In one case two soldiers were brought to trial for trying to bury alive four Palestinian rioters near Nablus. See *Yediot Ahronot*, February 15, 1988. A CBS news team videotaped four soldiers beating two Palestinians after placing them under arrest. See *Ma'ariv*, March 18, 1988. Four soldiers of the Givati brigade were charged with beating to death a young Palestinian. See *Hadashot*, September 27, 1988; *Ma'ariv*, October 5, 1988; and *Ha'aretz*, December 2, 1988. Nearly two years after the events in question the Supreme Court ruled that Colonel Yehuda Meir would stand trial for ordering his soldiers to break the bones of a number of Palestinians in January 1988. See *Yediot Ahronot* and *Ha'aretz*, December 25, 1989.

44. *Davar*, July 5, 1988; and *Jerusalem Post*, July 7, 1988. For criticism, see Shulamit Aloni, "Mr. Attorney General!" *Yediot Ahronot*, July 10, 1988. See also Yitzhak Ben Nir, "Recognized and Secure Boundaries," *Davar*, January 8, 1989.

45. *Davar*, July 6, 1988. For a discussion of the legal aspects of conscientious objection, see Benny Morris (who was sentenced to prison for refusing to serve in Lebanon), "Serving Their Term," *Jerusalem Post*, June 3, 1988. See also Tzvi Singer, "An Attempt of Intimidation and Suppression of Opinions" (in Hebrew) in *Yerushalayim*, July 7, 1988. The protest against the police investigation was widespread and included prominent writers such as Amos Oz, A. B. Yehoshua, Yehuda Amichai, S. Izhar, and David Grossman. Most of these writers objected to the refusal in principle, but defended the right of the movement to express its opinions and to fight for its principles. *Ha'aretz*, January 6, 1989.

46. *Ha'aretz*, July 21, 1988. See also Reuven Yaron, "An Unwise Decision," *Ha'aretz*, July 26, 1988. Yishai Menuchin claimed that the feeble attempt to stop the activities of the movement achieved the opposite effect and gave the refusal a higher measure of legitimacy.

47. Rami Hasson served five prison terms of thirty-five days each; Angelu Heiden served four prison terms.

48. See Ariela Ringler-Hofman, "Grey Refusal," *Yediot Ahronot*, September 15, 1989. See also Yoram Peri, "Conscience above Duty," *Davar*, April 15, 1990. On the moral dilemmas facing the IDF during the Intifada, see "Israel's Troubled Army," *Newsweek*, May 1, 1989.

49. See "Do Not Touch the Protest!" *Ha'aretz*, January 17, 1989.

50. See *Knesset Verbatim Record*, January 11, 1989, 112:506.

51. *Ha'aretz*, July 27, 1990.

52. *Jerusalem Post*, July 30, 1990. For a more detailed account, see the article by Amnon Levi in *Hadashot*, July 30, 1990. See also Gideon Reicher's interview with Ornan Yekutieli in *Yediot Ahronot*, July 29, 1990. A similar debate took place in the General Council of the United kibbutz Movement. A draft resolution that criticized the refusal and established sanctions against refusers was defeated. A milder resolution was passed, expressing sentiments on the "negation of the refusal phenomenon and calling on members to continue their involvement with all security establishments." *Hadashot,* July 22, 1990. For a profile of an officer who was a member of a kibbutz and who spent time in jail for refusing to serve, see Ron'el Fisher, "Refuser No. 108," *Hadashot,* June 1, 1990.

53. This was the title of a book published in the early 1980s by the journalist Nahum Barnea. See his *They Shoot and Weep: On Politicians, Generals, Journalists, and Other People Who Love Themselves* (in Hebrew) (Tel Aviv: Bitan Publishers, 1981).

54. See letter from Tzali Reshef to the director of Kol Yisrael (the government radio station) in the Peace Now Archive, 1988 file. Two hundred thousand is one of the estimates of the number of people who signed the Peace Now petitions and attendance lists during this period.

55. See Ran Edelist, "Shalom Achshav," *Monitin* 86 (November 1985): 16–21, 84–86; and Shmuel Shem-Tov, "Let Us Meet in the Plaza" (in Hebrew), *Hagalil,* January 29, 1988.

56. For the process that led to the formation of the Unified Leadership, see Hillel Frisch, "The West Bank and the Gaza Strip: The Intifada from Spontaneous Disturbances to Organized Disobedience," in Ayalon and Shaked, *Middle East Contemporary Survey,* 12:277–305. On the emerging Palestinian leadership during the Intifada, see Meir Litvak, *Palestinian Leadership in the Territories* (Tel Aviv: Moshe Dayan Center for Middle East and African Studies, 1991).

57. For an analysis and Hebrew translation of the thirty-one leaflets the UNLU issued in the first twelve months of the Intifada, see Shaul Mishal and Reuben Aharoni, *Stones Are Not Everything: The Intifada and the Graffiti Weapon* (in Hebrew) (Tel Aviv: Hakibbutz Hameuchad, 1989). Other Palestinian groups also published leaflets, but only the Islamic Resistance Movement (Hamas) organized a leadership alternative to the PLO. During the first year of the Intifada Hamas published thirty-three leaflets.

58. Tzali Reshef, interview by author, Jerusalem, January 12, 1994.

59. *Jerusalem Post,* February 12, 1988.

60. *Jerusalem Post* and *Yediot Ahronot,* February 14, 1988.

61. For more on this development, see William Quandt, *Peace Process: American Diplomacy and the Arab-Israeli Conflict since 1967* (Berkeley: University of California Press, 1993), 359–363. On the peace movement's position toward these developments, see Bar-On, *Peace Politics in Israel.*

62. Shultz, *Turmoil and Triumph,* 1022. The initiative, outlined in a letter dated March 4, 1988, was delivered by Shultz to all concerned parties. The text of the letter is in *Turmoil and Triumph,* 1028–1029.

63. Abu Jihad (Khalil al-Wazir) directed Fatah activities in the territories. From PLO headquarters in Tunis he became the most influential leader of the Intifada. He was assassinated in April 1988 in Tunis by Israeli commandos. However, this assassination did not change the course of the Intifada. See Schiff and Ya'ari, *Intifada,* 45–49.

64. A public opinion poll conducted at the end of March showed that 60 percent of those polled supported the initiative. See *Jerusalem Post,* April 6, 1988.

65. *Jerusalem Post,* March 9, 1988.

66. *Yediot Ahronot,* March 13, 1988.

67. A copy of the document, dated January 14, 1988, and signed by "Palestinian nationalist institutions and personalities from the West Bank and Gaza," is in the author's personal files.

68. The full document is in the Peace Now Archive, 1988 file.

69. Moshe Amirav, interview by author, Jerusalem, February 13, 1994. Early in 1987 Amirav published a brochure for internal use in party circles entitled "A Peace Plan for the Integral Land of Israel," which caused some controversy among his colleagues. See Moshe Amirav, "Historical Revisionism as a Basis for a Peace Settlement," *Ma'ariv,* October 14, 1987; Moshe Ma'oz, "The Amirav Affair," *Yediot Ahronot,* September 28, 1987.

70. Ein Karem was a village deserted by its Arab residents in 1948 and inhabited by Jewish immigrants during the 1950s. It is located not far from the place where Faisal Husseini's father died in battle in the spring of 1948. See David Ish-Shalom, "If the Flame Caught the Cedars . . ." *Ha'aretz,* October 28, 1987.

71. In 1988 Sari Nusseibeh suggested that the Palestinians should demand the right to vote in Knesset elections. He argued that eventually they would become a majority in the state and change its character from within.

72. Amirav, interview. See also *Kol Ha'ir,* September 23, 1987.

73. For a summary, see "The Amirav Affair: A Retrospective," *Kol Ha'ir,* December 15, 1987.

74. Amirav, interview. Sharon said: "With such ideas he has no place in the Likud." *Hadashot,* January 17, 1988.

75. The English text, dated August 25, 1987, is in Moshe Amirav's personal files. The Hebrew text was published by Lilly Galili in her article, "Thus Shamir Brought the Story to an End," *Ha'aretz,* October 4, 1993.

76. See Ori Nir's article in *Ha'aretz,* September 23, 1987.

77. See Menachem Rahat's article in *Ma'ariv,* September 22, 1987; and Yossi Werter's article in *Hadashot,* January 17, 1987.

78. *Ha'aretz,* January 27, 1988. See also an interview with Amirav after the event in *Hottam,* January 29, 1988.

79. *Hadashot,* January 28, 1988.

80. Amirav participated in the "Road to Peace" conference at Columbia University and the "Give Peace a Chance" conference held in Brussels in 1988. See report by Victor Levi in *Hadashot,* March 22, 1988. Even Dai Lakibush invited him to speak at one of their conferences. See Lilly Galili's article in *Ha'aretz,* August 11, 1988.

81. At different times he served as the secretary of the Council for Peace and Security, as the secretary of Shinui, and as a member of the Municipal Council of Jerusalem for Meretz. He also was a cochair of IPCRI (see chapter 12).

82. For some of the controversies between Peace Now and the groups to its left, see Tova Tzimuki, "The Limits of Peace Now," *Ma'ariv,* January 22, 1988.

83. Dov Jeremiah, *My War Diary* (in Hebrew) (Nahariya: private publication, 1983).

84. See a summary of these activities in Daniel Ben-Simon, "Red Line," *Dvar Hashavu'a,* February 17, 1989.

85. Emil Habibi, interview by author, Jerusalem, March 23, 1992.

86. New Israel Fund, "Grants Committee Recommendation to the Board, January 1992" (New Israel Fund Archive, Jerusalem, 1992), 54–55; and "Grants Committee Recommendation to the Board, January 1994" (New Israel Fund Archive, Jerusalem, 1994), 59–61.

87. New Israel Fund, "Grants Authorized, July 1988–July 1989" (New Israel Fund Archive, Jerusalem, 1989), 186–187.

88. Imut file, New Israel Fund Archive, Jerusalem.

89. For a description of the efforts of Palestinian health care providers to improve medical services during the Intifada, see Mustafa Barghouti and Rita Giacaman, "The Emergence of an Infrastructure of Resistance: The Case of Health," in Jamal R. Nassar and Roger Heacock, eds., *Intifada: Palestine at the Crossroads* (New York: Praeger, 1990).

90. New Israel Fund, "Grants Committee Recommendation, January 1994," 54–56.

91. In the first Rabin government (1974) Yariv served as minister of information. He resigned in 1976 after a plan he developed with Victor Shem-Tov, a Mapam minister, was rejected by Rabin. The plan called on Israel to negotiate with any Palestinian organization (by implication including the PLO) that recognized Israel and renounced terrorism. For details on the Council for Peace and Security, see *Jerusalem Post Magazine,* March 27, 1992.

92. Council for Peace and Security, "Statement of Principles." Document in author's personal files.

93. Tamar Plesner-Liebes, interview by author, Jerusalem, February 14, 1994.

94. New Israel Fund, "Grants Authorized, July 1988–July 1989," 193–194. New Israel Fund referred to the group as "Parents against Demoralization." See also *Kol Ha'ir,* January 20, 1989.

95. A copy of the letter and its English translation are in the personal files of Tamar Plesner-Liebes. See also *Jerusalem Post,* May 2, 1989.

96. *Ma'ariv,* May 2, 1989; and *Davar,* May 16, 1989.

97. See letter to General Amnon Strasnoff, dated May 11, 1989, and his reply, dated May 17, 1989, in *Ma'ariv.* See also *Ha'aretz,* May 14, 1989.

98. *Yediot Ahronot,* May 28, 1989.

99. *Jerusalem Post,* June 12, 1989. The text of the captain's speech is in Danny Rubinstein, "Farewell to the Law of Dizengoff," *Ha'aretz,* June 13, 1989.

100. Orna Sasson-Levy, "The Problem of Gender in the Israeli Protest Movement: A Case Study" (paper presented at the annual meeting of the Association for Israel Studies, Milwaukee, Wisconsin, May 1992).

101. Judy Blank, "Israeli Women's Peace Movement," *Response* 24, no. 6 (June 1992). Also, interviews with Yvonne Deutsch, Jerusalem, August 17, 1992, and Gila Svirsky, Jerusalem, August 22, 1992.

102. Blank, "Israeli Women's Peace Movement." See also *Women in Black—National Newsletter* (in Hebrew and English), no. 1 (January 1992), no. 2 (spring 1992).

103. Sasson-Levy, "The Problem of Gender."

104. Gila Svirsky, "Women in Black," *Present Tense* 16, no. 4 (May–June 1989): 52–53.

105. Ibid. See also "The Mothers of Paris Plaza," *Davar,* November 11, 1988.

106. Gila Svirsky described some of these incidents in her article, "Women in Black Resist Violence," *Woman of Power,* no. 21 (fall 1991): 56–58.

107. Gila Svirsky, interview by author, Jerusalem, August 22, 1992. Rabbi Kahane's Kach group and members of the organization Parents of Victims of Arab Terror repeatedly tried to disrupt the vigil.

108. For a more detailed profile of Zahira Kamal, see John Wallach and Janet Wallach, *The New Palestinians: The Emerging Generation of Leaders* (Rocklin, Calif.: Prima, 1992), 101–120.

109. The group was called "Women for Women Political Prisoners," because the members also dealt with cases of Jewish women. See Blank, "Israeli Women's Peace Movement."

110. The quotation is from the Women and Peace information leaflet of June 1989, in the author's files.

111. Another group, Israeli Women against the Occupation (the Hebrew acronym was "Shani"), was organized in January 1988. Shani had a strong left-wing orientation on matters other than the issue of peace. See Katia Gibel-Azoulay, "Elitism in the Women's Peace Camp," *Jerusalem Post*, July 2, 1989.

112. Vivian Eden and Michal Sela, "Women's Groups March for Peace," *Jerusalem Post*, December 31, 1988. The gathering was addressed by Marsha Lubelski, the secretary general of Na'amat, the Labor-dominated Israeli women's organization; Professor Alice Shalvi, the chairwoman of the Israeli Women's Network; and Zahira Kamal.

113. *Yediot Ahronot*, December 31, 1988. The police estimated that the number of participants was 5,000. Some women were wounded and others were detained. See *Hadashot*, December 31, 1988. See also *New York Times*, December 30, 1988.

114. The Israeli delegation included MK Shulamit Aloni (Ratz), MK Nava Arad (Labor), Yael Dayan (the daughter of Moshe Dayan and an ardent peace activist and later an MK for Labor), Professor Galia Golan (Peace Now), Professor Naomi Chazan (Truman Peace Institute), and Chana Maron (the first lady of Israeli theater). Those who came from the occupied territories included Hanan Ashrawi, a literature professor from Bir Zeit University who later became the spokesperson for the Palestinian delegation to the Madrid and Washington peace negotiations; Suad Amiri, an architect and town planning teacher from Bir Zeit University who later served as a delegate to the peace talks; Rita Giacaman, a public health expert from Bir Zeit University; Mary Khass, an educator from the Gaza Strip; and Zahira Kamal. Leila Shahid, the PLO representative in Holland, also participated. A list of participants is in the author's files.

115. The groups connected to the PFLP abstained, but participated in some of the activities. Galit Hazan-Rokem, interview by author, Jerusalem, August 20, 1992.

116. The text of the declaration is in the author's personal files.

117. Galit Hazan-Rokem, interview by author, Jerusalem, August 20, 1992.

118. Izhar Be'er, interview by author, Jerusalem, February 18, 1994. Be'er was the executive director of B'tselem.

119. In one case the IDF chief of staff publicly challenged the numbers B'tselem reported on Palestinian casualties, and subsequently apologized when he learned that his figures were wrong and B'tselem's report was correct. In later years the military authorities often asked B'tselem to confirm their own information. Shirley Eran (a senior editor and researcher with B'tselem), interview by author, Jerusalem, February 21, 1994.

120. The first *Monthly Update* was published in May 1989. In July 1993 these reports were discontinued.

121. These reports included articles such as "The System of Taxation in the West Bank and the Gaza Strip As an Instrument for the Enforcement of Authority during the Uprising"; "The Military Judicial System in the West Bank"; "The Use of Firearms by the Security Forces in the Occupied Territories"; and "Detained without Trial: Administrative Detention in the Occupied Territories since the Beginning of the Intifada." All B'tselem publications are available in Hebrew and English in the B'tselem archives, Jerusalem.

122. Be'er, interview. See Stanley Cohen and Dafna Golan, *The Interrogation of Palestinians during the Intifada: Ill Treatment, "Moderate Physical Pressure," or Torture?* (Jerusalem: B'tselem, March 1991).

123. Eran, interview.

124. *New York Times,* August 1, 1988. A translation of the speech is in Menachem Klein, *Antagonistic Collaboration: PLO-Jordanian Dialogue 1985–1988,* Policy Paper no. 27 (Jerusalem: Leonard Davis Institute, 1988), 125–132.

125. Shultz wrote: "The King's decision appeared to mark the end of my initiative." See Shultz, *Turmoil and Triumph,* 1033.

126. This became known as the "Rabin initiative" and was formulated at the beginning of 1989. Rabin presented it in a speech at the meeting of the Labor caucus in the Knesset held on January 30, 1989. See Aryeh Shalev, *The Intifada: Causes and Effects* (Tel Aviv: Papyrus, 1990).

127. The term "inside" (*al-dakhil*) is used to signify the Palestinians in the occupied territories and their leaders; the term "outside" (*al-kharij*) refers to the Palestinians in the diaspora and the PLO leaders and their headquarters in Tunis. For a review of the role of the PLO in the Intifada, see Teitelbaum, "Palestine Liberation Organization," 229–276.

128. For an analysis of this debate, see Menachem Klein, *The PLO and the Intifada: Between Euphoria and Despair* (Tel Aviv: Moshe Dayan Center for Middle East and African Studies, 1991), 18–21.

129. The document was first distributed as an unofficial PLO paper at the Arab Summit Conference in Algiers in June 1988. An English version was published in the *Middle East Mirror* on June 2, 1988, and reprinted in the *Washington Post* on June 15, 1988.

130. The invitation to this meeting carried the caption "Is There Really No Partner?" Peace Now Archive, 1988 file.

131. *Jerusalem Post, Davar,* and *Ha'aretz,* July 28, 1988. Radwan Abu-Ayyash, the chairman of the Palestinian Journalists Union, participated in the meeting, as did Moshe Amirav, MK Ya'ir Tzaban (Mapam), and Itzhak Galnoor. The text of Husseini's speech is in the Peace Now Archive.

132. *Yediot Ahronot* and *Ma'ariv,* August 1, 1988. Husseini had been released from his first term of administrative detention only six weeks earlier.

133. *Jerusalem Post,* August 7, 1988. A spontaneous "teaser demonstration" took place near the prison in Jerusalem, where Husseini was held on the first day of his detention. See *Ma'ariv,* August 1, 1988. Peace Now requested an audience with Rabin, but this request was denied. See letter to Rabin, dated August 1, 1988, Peace Now Archive, 1988 file.

134. *Ha'aretz,* August 7, 1988. See also Jerome Segal, *Creating the Palestinian State: A Strategy for Peace* (Chicago: Lawrence Hill, 1989). The document found in Husseini's Center was written by Jerome Segal.

135. For a critique of Shamir's misunderstanding of the document, see Dan Margalit, "Yes to the Document!" *Ha'aretz,* August 9, 1988.

12. Time for Peace?

1. An English translation of the resolution is in *Journal of Palestine Studies* 18 (winter 1989): 213–223.

2. These preconditions included unconditional acceptance of UN Security Council Resolutions 242 and 338, unequivocal recognition of the State of Israel, and renunciation of terrorism.

3. Shultz, *Turmoil and Triumph*, 1037.

4. See the minutes of the meeting, Peace Now Archive, 1989 file. See also *Jerusalem Post,* December 1, 1988.

5. Peace Now Archive, 1989 file.

6. The quotation and a description of the internal transformation of the movement are in Ronit Antler, "Reorganization," *Hadashot,* December 1, 1988. On the Zucker-Tamir affair, see chapter 6.

7. On the negotiations that led to the establishment of the second National Unity Government, see Dan Korn, *Time in Gray* (in Hebrew) (Tel Aviv: Bitan Publishers, 1994), 206–226.

8. Shultz, *Turmoil and Triumph*, 1035. The metaphor used by Shultz clearly implies that the State Department recognized the need to deal with the PLO.

9. For more details on the U.S.-PLO negotiations, see Quandt, *Peace Process,* 367–375. Quandt was a member of the National Security Council under President Carter, and in 1988 was the key mediator from the American side. Mohamed Rabie, a Palestinian-American scholar, was active for the Palestinian side.

10. Drora Kass, interview with author, March 31, 1994. At the time Kass was the executive director of the U.S. section of ICPME and participated in the Stockholm meeting. See Quandt, *Peace Process,* 372–375.

11. See interview with Stanley Sheinbaum in "Stockholm Encounter," *New Outlook* 32, no. 3–4 (March–April 1989): 29–31.

12. The full text can be found in *Washington Post,* December 15, 1988.

13. See Shultz, *Turmoil and Triumph*, 1038–1045.

14. Andy Goldberg, "Peace Now Demo Calls for Talks with the PLO," *Jerusalem Post,* December 25, 1988.

15. *Yediot Ahronot,* December 23, 1988.

16. Joseph Alpher and Shai Feldman, eds., *The West Bank and Gaza: Israel's Options for Peace* (Tel Aviv: Jaffee Center for Strategic Studies, 1989), 2.

17. Ibid., 17.

18. Ibid., 7.

19. Ibid., 13.

20. Ibid., 115.

21. JCSS Study Group, *Israel, the West Bank and Gaza: Toward a Solution* (Tel Aviv: Jaffee Center for Strategic Studies, 1989), 7.

22. Ibid., 18–22.

23. Akiva Eldar, "A Proposal for a Settlement which Will Be a Best-seller," *Ha'aretz,* March 9, 1989.

24. See, for example, Faisal Husseini's reaction to the Jaffee Center report in minutes of a discussion activists held with Husseini in the Peace Now Archive, 1989 file.

25. Shmuel Toledano, interview by author, Jerusalem, July 12, 1992. In 1985 he was rather pessimistic: "Today and in the foreseeable future there are no options for peace." See his article "Goodbye to the Options," *Ha'aretz*, March 26, 1985.

26. A short document issued by the Council of Peace in Stages, in Shmuel Toledano's personal files.

27. Mina Tzemach, *Peace in Stages: Attitudes toward the Plan in 1992* (Tel Aviv: Dahaf, 1992). In January 1991 a third poll was taken with similar results.

28. Toledano, interview.

29. On January 24, 1990, *Filastin al-Thawrah* (the official paper of the PLO) published the plan and the Mina Tzemach polls. The DFLP's endorsement was published in *al-Quds* (an Arabic daily newspaper published in Jerusalem), on January 22, 1990.

30. In April 1992, Meretz, a newly formed coalition of three parties on the left, formally endorsed the Peace in Stages plan. Letter signed jointly by MK Shulamit Aloni, MK Ya'ir Tzaban, and MK Amnon Rubinstein, dated April 10, 1992, addressed to the "Council" in Toledano's personal files. The most prominent member of the executive committee was Shaul Rozolio, the retired chief police inspector who in the early 1980s served as Israel's ambassador to Mexico.

31. The following are just a few prominent examples: The Foundation for Peace in the Middle East sponsored Sari Nusseibeh and Mark Heller, *No Trumpets No Drums: A Two-State Settlement of the Israeli-Palestinian Conflict* (New York: Hill and Wang, 1991). The American Academy of Arts and Science convened a study group that published its report. See Ann Mosely Lesch, ed., *Transition to Palestinian Self-Government: Practical Steps toward Israeli-Palestinian Peace* (Bloomington: Indiana University Press, 1993). The International Security Studies Program of the American Academy of Arts and Sciences asked Naomi Chazan, Fouad Moughrabi, and Rashid Khalidi to present a paper, published as *Negotiating the Non-Negotiable: Jerusalem in the Framework of an Israeli-Palestinian Settlement* (Cambridge, Mass.: American Academy of Arts and Sciences, March 1991).

32. The project published more than two dozen working papers written by both Palestinian and Israeli scholars. See, for example, Hanna Siniora and Moshe Amirav, *Jerusalem: Resolving the Unresolvable*, IPCRI working paper no. 16 (Jerusalem: IPCRI, 1992).

33. Much of the information about IPCRI given here comes from an interview with Gershon Baskin, Jerusalem, March 14, 1994.

34. See "IPCRI Founding Proposal" in IPCRI Archive, Jerusalem, Proposals file, April 1988.

35. See "IPCRI Project Update," May 20, 1992, IPCRI Archive. See also *IPCRI News*, no. 4 (April 1992).

36. The proceedings were published in Gershon Baskin and Robin Twite, eds., *The Future of Jerusalem* (Jerusalem: IPCRI Publications, 1993).

37. Ibid., 273–296.

38. Baskin, interview. Some parts of the discussions were published in *Internal Security Issues and Interim Agreement*, IPCRI Publications 2, no. 1 (February 1993).

39. Professor Yair Hirschfeld, who later became a central figure in promoting the peace process in Oslo, was active in some of IPCRI's research projects. See chapter 14.

40. Baskin, interview. See also Gershon Baskin, *A Model Agreement for the Interim Period: Palestinian Self Rule.*, IPCRI Publications 1, no. 3 (January 1992).

41. See Asher Arian and Michal Shamir, eds., *Elections in Israel 1988,* (Boulder, Colo., Westview, 1990). Likud won forty seats and Labor thirty-nine; the pattern of ethnic voting was consistent, with Mizrachi support for Labor (and the left in general) at 25 to 27 percent. For more on the ethnic profiles of these elections, see Paul Abramson, "Demographic Change and Partisan Support," in ibid., 173–188. See also Yehuda Ben Meir, "Political Developments in Israel," in Shlomo Gazit, ed., *The Middle East Military Balance 1988–1989* (Boulder, Colo.: Westview, 1989), 50–63.

42. During the first year of the Intifada there was a shift in Israeli public opinion to the right, but this shift was more evident among Mizrachim. See Asher Arian and Raphael Ventura, *Public Opinion in Israel and the Intifada: Changes in Security Attitudes 1987–1988,* Memorandum no. 28 (Tel Aviv: Jaffee Center for Strategic Studies, 1989), 17–20.

43. Yossi Dahan, interview by author, Tel Aviv, July 19, 1992.

44. Ibid.

45. Forty-two and forty-four Palestinians were killed in March and April 1988, respectively. In 1989 and 1990 fatalities never reached that level, but in 1989 deaths still averaged more than twenty per month. According to a B'tselem report the total for that year was 293. See *B'tselem Annual Report 1989,* 13–23.

46. Ze'ev Schiff, "A War without an Exit," *Ha'aretz,* November 24, 1989.

47. The worst case occurred on October 30, 1988, when a civilian bus was attacked in Jericho and a Jewish woman and three of her children were burned to death. See *Jerusalem Post,* October 31, 1988.

48. During 1988 and 1989, Palestinians killed forty-six Israelis. Thirty-two of the Israelis were civilians; twenty-seven were killed inside the Green Line. See *B'tselem Annual Report 1989,* 23–25. Thirteen civilians were killed when a Palestinian from the Gaza Strip attacked a bus driver and caused the bus to crash into a ravine near Jerusalem. See *Jerusalem Post,* July 7, 1989.

49. Reuven Gal, ed., *The Seventh War: The Effects of the Intifada on Israeli Society* (Tel Aviv: Hakibbutz Hameuchad, 1990), 15.

50. Reuven Gal, "Psychological and Moral Aspects of the IDF Soldiers' Experience with the Intifada," in Gal, *Seventh War,* 135–147. Gal refers to experiments performed by G. Zimbardo in 1972 and S. Milgrom in 1974, and to the theory developed in the 1970s by M. P. Zeligman.

51. The most tragic aspect was the deaths of children under the age of sixteen, the number of which rose from forty-seven during the first year to seventy-four in the second year. See B'tselem, *Report 1990/1991.* General Matan Vilnai, commander of the Southern Command, told his officers, "Each child we kill is a catastrophe." See Ze'ev Schiff, "A War without Exit," *Ha'aretz,* November 24, 1989.

52. See Nili Mirski, "Another Planet," *Koteret Rashit,* January 13, 1988; Ya'ir Garbuz, "Here Are the Fire and the Tire," *Dvar Hashavu'a,* January 22, 1988; Ronit Matalon, "Black and White," *Ha'aretz,* January 15, 1988; Ilana Hammerman, "The Intellectual's Betrayal," and Ruth Yovel, "Twenty Minutes from the Armchair," *Kol Ha'ir,* January 15, 1988; Dalia Rabikovitch, "Gaza, the Children's Land," *Ma'ariv,* January 12, 1988; Mair Wisltier, "Abandon All Hope All Who Enter Here," *Hadashot* January 15, 1988; and Itzhak Ben-Ner, "With Clear Eyes in Gaza," *Davar,* January 10, 1988. All articles cited are in Hebrew.

53. Garbuz, "Here Are the Fire and the Tire."

54. Ben-Ner, "With Clear Eyes in Gaza."

55. *Dvar Hashavu'a,* January, 22, 1988.

56. Orly Lubin, "Fiction and Documentation: The Responsibility Dilemma," *Masa,* April 17, 1991.

57. Ilana Hammerman, interview by author, Jerusalem, March 15, 1994.

58. This is a translation of the Hebrew title. The English title is *Soldiers in the Land of Ishmael.* See chapter 11, note 12.

59. Ibid., 94–102. These lines are quoted from Walter Benjamin's essay on the nature of epic theater.

60. Ibid. There was a debate in the Hebrew media concerning the legitimacy of Hammerman's experiment. See Amnon Raz-Krakutchkin, "The Two Languages of Occupation," *Ha'aretz,* October 10, 1990; and Michael Handelsaltz, "The Corrupting Occupation," *Ha'aretz,* October 2, 1990.

61. Yitzhak Shamir, *Summing Up* (in Hebrew) (Tel Aviv: Edanim, 1994), 228.

62. Ibid., 236.

63. Ibid., 236–237. The full text of Shamir's peace initiative was endorsed by the government in the middle of May. See *Jerusalem Post,* May 15, 1989. For Rabin's proposals, see chapter 11.

64. One analyst noted that the "Shamir-Rabin initiative . . . resembled in many respects the program which the Labor Party presented in its election campaign in 1988." Korn, *Time in Gray,* 219.

65. *Ha'aretz,* April 7, 1989.

66. For policies suggested on the eve of the Bush administration, see Washington Institute Presidential Study Group, *Building for Peace: An American Strategy for the Middle East* (Washington, D.C.: Washington Institute for Near East Policy, 1988). For a background of the initial attitudes of Bush, Baker, and their teams, see Quandt, *Peace Process,* 383–391.

67. For the full text of the speech, see *Department of State Bulletin,* vol. 89 (Washington, D.C.: Government Printing Office, July 1989), 24.

68. Shamir, *Summing Up,* 245.

69. These decisions were known in Israeli parlance as *chishukim* (barrel hoops), because they were meant to circumscribe the government's freedom of action. On the internal development of Likud, see Korn, *Time in Gray,* 220–223.

70. *Hadashot,* July 9, 1989.

71. Baker's "Five Points" were made public by Thomas Friedman in the *New York Times,* December 7, 1989.

72. Shamir also linked his rejection of Baker's proposal to a remark made by President Bush, which for the first time explicitly included East Jerusalem in the areas where Israel should stop its settlement activities. See David Makovsky, "Anatomy of a Break Down," *Jerusalem Post* (international edition), March 24, 1990.

73. Interview with Tzali Reshef, January 12, 1984.

74. In September 1989 President Mubarak produced a "Ten-Points Initiative" that was designed to build on the Shamir peace initiative. The movement urged the government not to reject it. See article by Lilli Galili in *Ha'aretz,* September 25, 1989. On September 25, 1989, a group from Peace Now met with Mohamed Bassiuni, Egypt's ambassador to Israel, to express its appreciation and support of President Mubarak's mediation efforts. Peace Now press release, September 24, 1989, Peace Now Archive, 1989 file.

75. Reported by the *Jerusalem Post,* October 8, 1989.

76. The support given to Israeli peace groups from the Jewish diaspora requires considerable elaboration and cannot be adequately addressed in the framework of this study.

77. See "Progress Report of Project Majority," November 1989, Peace Now Archive, 1989 file.

78. Reuven Kaminer, interview by author, August 20, 1992. Michel Warschawski remarked that the activities of Dai Lakibush declined as a result of its members forming specialized groups, especially women's groups such as Women in Black and Shani. Michel Warschawski, interview by author, Jerusalem, February 18, 1994.

79. *Jerusalem Post,* December 12, 1989.

80. Peace Now insisted that it would be the sole sponsor from the Israeli side, although all the other peace groups would be invited. See letters dated October 2, 1989, sent by Janet Aviad to Jean-Marie Lambert in Paris; a letter dated October 12, 1989, to Mikko Lohikovski in Helsinki; and a letter to Chiara Ingrass of Rome dated November 2, 1989. All letters are in the Peace Now Archive, 1989 file.

81. "The True Story," an official report in Peace Now Archive, 1990 file.

82. Author's personal notes.

83. See Michal Sela, "Sixity Hurt at Peace Now Rally," *Jerusalem Post*, December 31, 1989. See also *New York Times*, December 31, 1989.

84. "Investigation of Peace Now Events, December 30, 1989" (in Hebrew), Peace Now Archive, 1990 file.

85. On the measures taken by the police, see article by Yoram Bar, *Jerusalem Post,* April 15, 1990. Peace Now considered the measures taken against the area commander to be unjustified. See *Hadashot* and *Yediot Ahronot,* April 18, 1990.

86. The rate of Soviet immigration to Israel jumped from 2,300 in 1988 to 13,000 in 1989, and 185,000 in 1990. See *Statistical Abstract of Israel, 1989,* table 5.4, 170; *Statistical Abstract of Israel, 1990,* table 5.4, 175; and *Statistical Abstract of Israel, 1991,* table 5.4, 168.

87. Shamir was reported to have said, "A great immigration requires a great Israel."

88. Shamir, *Summing Up,* 254–255.

89. See Makovsky, "Anatomy of a Break Down."

90. For the full story of the coalition formation process in the spring of 1990, see Korn, *Time in Gray,* 227–246.

91. On the suspension of the U.S.-PLO dialogue, see *New York Times,* June 21, 1990.

92. *Knesset Verbatim Record,* 117:3863–3886.

93. Peace Now recommended to the Palestinian leaders that they concentrate their activities against settlements in the occupied territories and not condemn the immigration from the Soviet Union. The PLO subsequently announced that it would not denounce immigration in general. See Lilly Galili's article in *Ha'aretz,* January 31, 1990.

94. Amiram Goldblum, interview by author, Jerusalem, March 12, 1994.

95. "Peace Now Press Release," January 30, 1990, Peace Now Archive, 1990 file.

96. See "Settlement Reports," Peace Now Archive, 1990 file.

97. See "Peace Now Press Release," October 31, 1990, Peace Now Archive, 1990 file.

98. "Letter to the Prime Minister," August 2, 1990, Peace Now Archive, 1990 file.

99. See Lilly Galili, "The Supreme Court on Appeal by Peace Now," *Ha'aretz,* May 4, 1990.

100. *Yediot Ahronot,* May 4, 1990.

101. A semiannual bulletin published in May 1990 listed twenty-five different public activities organized by the movement during the first half of 1990. See "Update from Israel," issued by Friends of Peace Now (New York), April 6, 1990, and "Project Majority Progress Report, March 1990," both in the Peace Now Archive, 1990 file.

102. Letter of the Local Council of Elkana," Peace Now Archive, 1990 file. The passage is from the King James translation of Isaiah 57:20.

103. See Yehudit Greenblat, "'It Is Good He Killed Them': A Kahane Supporter in a Rally," *Ha'aretz,* May 22, 1990.

104. *Jerusalem Post,* June 8, 1990.

105. The demonstration was held in response to the murders of seven Palestinians in Rishon le Tzion, but was actually directed against the policies of Shamir toward the peace process in general. See article by Yehudit Greenblat, *Ha'aretz,* May 27, 1990. The media reported that the demonstration attracted 50,000 people.

106. The full text can be found in the report, "Peace Now Rally in the Kings of Israel Square," May 26, 1990, in the Peace Now Archive, 1990 file.

107. Nathan Alterman, "The Plagues of Egypt," in *Old Poems* (in Hebrew) (Tel Aviv: Hakibbutz Hameuchad, 1971), 233–234.

13. From Sealed Rooms to Madrid

1. *Yediot Ahronot,* April 3, 1990.

2. See Shamir, *Summing Up,* 264.

3. Adel Safty, *From Camp David to the Gulf* (Montreal: Black Rose, 1992), 179.

4. Many books have been written on the political and military aspects of Iraq's invasion of Kuwait. Among others, see Bob Woodward, *The Commanders* (New York: Simon and Schuster, 1991); Rick Atkinson, *Crusade: The Untold Story of the Persian Gulf War* (Boston: Houghton Mifflin, 1993); and Micah Sifry and Christopher Cerf, *The Gulf War Reader: History, Documents, Opinions* (New York: Random House, 1991).

5. For an analysis of the reactions of the Arab states to the crisis, see Walid Khalidi, "Why Some Arabs Supported Saddam?" in *The Gulf Crisis: Origins and Consequences* (Washington, D.C.: Institute for Palestine Studies, 1991). See also Amatzia Baram and Barry Rubin, eds., *Iraq's Road to War* (New York: St. Martin's, 1993).

6. In what became known as "The Mother of All Battles" speech, Saddam spoke of the eventual victory of Iraqi forces that would open the doors "for the liberation of the beloved Palestine, Lebanon, and Golan. Then Jerusalem and the Dome of the Rock will be released from bondage." See Sifry and Cerf, *Gulf War Reader,* 315–316.

7. For discussions of Palestinian support for Saddam, see Ibrahim Abu-Lughod, "The Politics of Linkage: The Arab-Israeli Conflict in the Gulf War," and Hanan Ashrawi, "The Other Occupation: The Palestinian Response," in Phyllis Bennis and Michel Moushabeck, eds., *Beyond the Storm: A Gulf Crisis Reader* (New York: Olive Branch Press, 1991). See also George Abed, "The Palestinians and the Gulf Crisis," *Journal of Palestine Studies* 20, no. 2 (winter 1991): 29–42; and Norman Finkelstein, "Palestinian Attitudes during the Gulf War," *Journal of Palestine Studies* 21, no. 3 (spring 1992): 54–70.

8. See Izhar Be'er, *Ha'aretz,* August 12, 13, 15, 1990. The Mufti of Jerusalem, Sheikh Sa'ad ad-Din Alami, sent a cable to Saddam Hussein and pleaded with him to "liberate the holy place of Islam from the Americans and others."

9. *Ha'aretz,* August 17, 1990.

10. Aviva Shabi, "The Left: A Rupture with the Palestinians," *Yediot Ahronot,* August 17, 1990.

11. Yaron London, "Good-bye Husseini, Good-bye Nusseibeh," *Yediot Ahronot,* August 14, 1990.

12. Shabi, "The Left."

13. Ibid. See also remarks of Yossi Sarid and Yaron London in David Grossman, "Ye Peace Pursuers, Raise Your Voices!" *Yediot Ahronot,* August 24, 1990; Yael Dayan, "You Threw the Baby Out with the Bath Water," *Yediot Ahronot,* August 21, 1990; and Uri Avneri, "The Left Hand and the Right Voice," *Ha'aretz,* August 21, 1990.

14. Palestinian Politics after the Gulf War: An Interview with Faisal Husseini," *Journal of Palestine Studies* 20, no. 4 (summer 1991): 99–108.

15. Interview with Janet Aviad. See also Izhar Be'er in *Ha'aretz,* August 17, 1990. The account Stanley Cohen gives of these events and his critique of Peace Now are biased. The movement was shaken but never "collapsed." See Cohen's "From the Sealed Room: Israel's Peace Movement during the Gulf War," in Bennis and Moushabeck, *Beyond the Storm,* 205–214.

16. Peace Now Archive, 1990 file.

17. The full text is in *Jerusalem Post,* August 17, 1990.

18. Shlomo Slutzki, "Sarid Did Not Show Up," *Hadashot,* August, 31, 1990.

19. Lilly Galili, *Ha'aretz,* September 27, 1990.

20. See the letter sent by the author to the American Friends of Peace Now, August 13, 1990. Peace Now Archive, 1990 file. For more on these developments, see Don Peretz, "The Impact of the Gulf War on Israeli and Palestinian Political Attitudes," *Journal of Palestine Studies* 21, no. 1 (fall 1991): 17–35.

21. Cohen, "From the Sealed Room," 210.

22. After the war started, the committee changed its name to "An End to the War," or simply "Dai!" (Enough!).

23. Interview with Menachem Brinker.

24. For the logic of linkage, see Safty, *From Camp David,* 229–236.

25. For a detailed account, see B'tselem, *Loss of Control: The Temple Mount Event—Preliminary Investigation* (Jerusalem: B'tselem, October 14, 1990)

26. Amiram Goldblum, interview by author, Jerusalem, August 18, 1992. The riots were partially spontaneous, but agents of Kahane's movement took advantage of the mood and led attacks against the Arabs as well as the peaceniks.

27. Doron Meiri, "Left Volunteers," *Hadashot*, August 31, 1990.

28. See Daniel Williams, "Israel Peace Activists Forced to Retreat," *Los Angeles Times*, October 23, 1990; and Anthony Lewis, "A Broken Dream," *New York Times*, December 7, 1990.

29. See *Peace Now Newsletter* (in Hebrew), no. 3 (January 1991). This document also lists the movement's activities during the second half of 1990.

30. Daher Zeidani, interview by author, Jerusalem, August 22, 1992. In the middle of August Mahmud Shibli-Zahalka conducted a telephone survey among Israeli Arabs and discovered that 69 percent of those called considered Saddam Hussein an "Arab national hero." Zahalka felt that the results reflected appreciation for Saddam among Palestinians "for his courage, persistence, pan-Arab, and anti-American policies." See Izhar Be'er, *Ha'aretz*, August 9, 1990. See also Sara Ozacky-Lazar and As'ad Ghanem, *The Arabs in Israel under the Shadow of the War in the Gulf* (Giv'at Haviva, Israel: Center for Arab Studies, 1991).

31. Ilan Pappe, "A Modus Vivendi Challenged: The Arabs in Israel," in Baram and Rubin, *Iraq's Road to War*, 168.

32. *Davar*, January 13, 1991.

33. *Peace Now Newsletter* (in Hebrew), no. 4 (March 1991).

34. Ilan Pappe described the attitudes of the Israeli Arabs threatened by the missiles. See Pappe, "Modus Vivendi." The Palestinian writer Emil Habibi said: "Every household in this country, both Jewish and Arab, must be made aware of the perception that we all share a common fate." *Davar*, January 23, 1991.

35. Reprinted in *Peace Now Newsletter* (in Hebrew), no. 4 (March 1991).

36. *Yediot Ahronot*, February 21, 1991. Reprinted in English in *New Outlook* 34, no. 2 (February–March 1991): 16–19.

37. See Lilly Galili, "Peace Now against the European Peace Movement," *Ha'aretz*, January 30, 1991.

38. *Ha'aretz*, February 22, 1991.

39. Joern Boehme, "Friedenskräfte in Israel: Ein Historischer Überblick," in Joern Boehme and Christian Stezing, eds., *Friedenskräfte in Israel* (Frankfurt: Haag and Herchen, 1992), 11–67.

40. Galili, "Peace Now."

41. See Gabi Bron, *Yediot Ahronot*, February 22, 1991.

42. See the editorial article in *Peace Now Newsletter* (in Hebrew), no. 4 (March 1991). See also Ruvik Rosental, "The Peace Camp Will React in the Place and at the Time Which Will Suit It," *Hadashot*, February 8, 1991.

43. Polls taken during the Scud attacks showed that 80 percent of those surveyed supported the "restraint/nonretaliation" policy. See Elihu Katz and Hanna Levinson, "Public Opinion in Wartime" (report of Israel Institute of Applied Social Research, Jerusalem, February 20, 1991).

44. It is likely that some threshold, in terms of damage and casualties, existed beyond which Israeli decision makers would have considered retaliation necessary. The general public believed that Israel would retaliate massively if Saddam were to use chemical warheads. A government spokesman unofficially told an American researcher at the time that if Iraq attacked Israel with chemical weapons, "Baghdad will be no more." Quoted to the author by his research assistant at the United States Institute of Peace, Joseph Helman.

45. B'tselem Information Sheet, *Human Rights in the Occupied Territories during the War in the Persian Gulf* (Jerusalem: B'tselem, January-February 1991).

46. "Our Policy on the Gulf War" (internal discussion paper, n.d.), Peace Now Archive, 1991 file. See also interview with Tzali Reshef in *Ha'aretz*, February 8, 1991.

47. Nahum Barnea, "Faisal Does Not Climb on His Roof," *Yediot Ahronot*, January 28, 1991.

48. Teddy Kollek, the mayor of Jerusalem, sent Husseini a letter warning him that "those who bless the enemies of Israel should not be surprised when the war is over that their words bear bitter results." *Ha'aretz*, January 28, 1991.

49. Polls taken in 1990 showed a decline in the support for negotiations with the PLO, from a high of 37 percent in April to 22 percent in August, and 24 percent in November and December. See Elihu Katz, Hanna Levinson, and Majid al-Hajj, "Attitudes of Israelis (Jew and Arabs) toward Current Affairs" (report of Israel Institute of Applied Social Research, Jerusalem, January 10, 1991).

50. *Jerusalem Report*, March 7, 1991, 16.

51. "Letter to Our Friends in the USA," Peace Now Archive, 1991 file.

52. UN General Assembly Provisional Record, 45th Session, Plenary Meeting 14, October 5, 1990 (A/45/PV/90), 62–75. Reprinted in *New York Times*, October 6, 1990.

53. *Washington Post*, March 7, 1991. The full text is reprinted in Quandt, *Peace Process*, appendix L, 495–496.

54. See Brewster Grace, "A Middle East Peace Conference: The Window of Opportunity, Half Open or Half Closed?" (a report of the Quaker Middle East Representatives, Amman, June 1991).

55. See Quandt, *Peace Process*, 396–406.

56. *Ha'aretz*, October 12, 1991.

57. See Mordechai Bar-On, "Israel and the Gulf War: A View from the Israeli Peace Movement," in Bennis and Moushabeck, *Beyond the Storm*, 205–214.

58. By October 1991 the number of Israelis stabbed by Palestinians had risen to twenty-two. See B'tselem Report, "Violation of Human Rights in the Occupied Territories 1990/1991," 20. A detailed analysis of the impact of the closure of the territories on the Palestinian population is given in B'tselem Information Sheet, "The Closure of the West Bank and Gaza Strip: Human Rights, Violations against Residents of the Occupied Territories, Jerusalem," April 1993.

59. *Peace Now Newsletter*, no. 4 (March 1991), Peace Now Archive, 1991 file.

60. For a report on Israel's intention to ask for the guarantees, see Joel Esteron, *Hadashot*, February 8, 1991. See also Ori Nir, *Ha'aretz*, May 24, 1991.

61. Thomas Friedman, "Baker Cites Israel for Settlements," *New York Times*, May 23, 1991.

62. See *New York Times*, September 13, 1991.

63. Copy in Peace Now Archive, 1991 file.

64. See *Settlement Watch Report no. 1: Governmental Investments in the Territories* (May 1991); and *Settlement Watch Report no. 2: Road Paving for Settlements* (July 1991). Both documents are in the Peace Now Archive, 1991 file. See also Lilly Galili, *Ha'aretz*, July 18, 1991.

65. Goldblum, interview.

66. *Hadashot,* May 6, 1991. See also Dan Izenberg, "Sharon Grist for Knesset Mill," *Jerusalem Post,* May 7, 1991.

67. See Peace Now letter (dated May 7, 1991) to the attorney general, Peace Now Archive, 1991 file.

68. See Lilly Galili and Eitan Rabin, *Ha'aretz,* September 25, 1991; and Lilly Galili and Gideon Alon, *Ha'aretz,* October 6, 1991.

69. See Michal Goldberg, *Yediot Ahronot,* July 17, 1991. The full brief is in the Peace Now Archive, 1991 file.

70. See Peace Now announcement to the press, October 13, 1991, Peace Now Archive, 1991 file.

71. The delegation included members of Ratz, Mapam, and Shinui, and Lova Eliav and Yossi Beilin from the Labor Party. See *Ma'ariv,* May 6, 1991.

72. See *Jerusalem Post,* May 6, 1991.

73. Ori Nir and Shlomo Shamir, *Ha'aretz,* May 7, 1991. For a critical essay, see the editorial "Is This Trip Necessary?" *Jerusalem Post,* May 6, 1991.

74. See letter from Janet Aviad to Micha Harish, the secretary general of the Labor Party, October 15, 1991. Peace Now Archive, 1991 file.

75. See Elihu Katz and Hanna Levinson, "What Israelis Agree About," a paper prepared by the Israel Institute of Applied Social Research and published in *Yediot Ahronot,* June 21, 1991. The headline stated: "Polls: 75 Percent Support Returning Territories in Exchange for a Peace Agreement." The researchers concluded that the Intifada did not dramatically change the attitudes of Israelis toward specific aspects of the peace process. However, they noted that a majority (80 percent) considered the status quo as unacceptable. See Hanna Levinson and Elihu Katz, "The Intifada Is Not a War: Jewish Public Opinion on the Israeli-Arab Conflict," in A. A. Cohen and Gadi Wolfsfeld, eds., *Framing the Intifada: People and Media* (Norwood, N.J.: Ablex, 1993).

76. Aviad, interview.

77. See letter from Aviad to Harish.

78. Menachem Sheizaf, "Peace Changes Colors," *Yerushalayim,* May 24, 1991.

79. *Ha'aretz,* October 18, 1991.

80. Quoted by Tamar Tablusi, *Yediot Ahronot,* October 27, 1991. Polls taken at the time showed overwhelming support for Shamir's decision: 91 percent favored Israel's participation in the conference, but only 37 percent expressed the belief that the conference would yield practical results. See *Yediot Ahronot,* October 29, 1991.

81. Orit Galili, *Ha'aretz,* October 27, 1991.

82. Ironically this was one year prior to the 500th anniversary of the expulsion of the Arab and Jewish communities from Spain. Some observers noted that Spain was chosen as the venue for the conference because for both Arabs and Jews it was a homecoming of sorts to a "golden age." See Milton Viorst, "Report from Madrid," *New Yorker,* December 9, 1991, 58.

83. Brewster Grace and Ann Grace, "The Madrid Conference: Foundations for Arab-Israeli Peace Negotiations" (a report of the Quaker Middle East Representatives, Amman, March 1992).

84. More than 5,300 journalists from around the world were accorded credentials to cover the event. See Viorst, "Report from Madrid."

85. Viorst, "Report from Madrid," 64. See also Shamir, *Summing Up,* 284–291.

86. *Ha'aretz*, November 1, 1991.

14. A Handshake on the White House Lawn

1. Grace and Grace, "Madrid Conference."

2. *Jerusalem Post*, November 1, 1991.

3. *Yediot Ahronot*, November 29, 1991. Another poll taken a few weeks earlier reported that although only 32 percent believed that the Madrid Conference would bring peace, more than 60 percent were in favor of a freeze on settlements during the negotiations. *Hadashot*, November 1, 1991. According to another poll, 71 percent favored a freeze. *Yediot Ahronot*, November 8, 1991.

4. Professor Yaron Ezrahi, quoted in the *Washington Post*, December 24, 1991.

5. *Yediot Ahronot*, November 11, 1991.

6. Hanan Shlein and Meir Reuveni, *Ma'ariv*; and Yossi Torpstein, *Yediot Ahronot*, November 24, 1991.

7. Betzal'el Amikam, *Al Ha'mishmar*, November 24, 1991.

8. Jackson Diehl, "Radicalizing of the West Bank," *Washington Post*, January 13, 1992.

9. Shimon Peres, *The New Middle East* (New York: Henry Holt, 1993), 7–10. For more details, see Quandt, *Peace Process*, 404–405.

10. Peres, *New Middle East*, 7.

11. Leslie Gelb, "Bush's Ultimatum to Shamir," *New York Times*, January 17, 1992; Thomas Friedman, "US Detailed Terms Israel Must Meet for Deal on Loans," *New York Times*, February 25, 1992; and Thomas Friedman, "Bush Rejects Israel Loan Guarantees," *New York Times*, March, 18, 1992.

12. The 1992 and 1993 files in the Peace Now Archive are rich with documentation. See, for example, "Summary of Proceedings of the Central Forum," January 27, March 9, March 23, April 6, May 25, July 14, July 27, 1992.

13. See, for example, the report of April 14, 1992, which includes a table with all "Construction Starts and Ground Preparation in the Settlements January to March 1992." Peace Now Archive, 1992 file.

14. The reports were published in Hebrew and English. See "Comprehensive Report on Settlements, January 1992"; "Who Is Worth More? Report on Investment in Industry in the Settlements of the West Bank and Gaza Strip, for the Period of January–June 1991"; and "Report on Building in Settlements in the West Bank and Gaza, July 1992": all are in the Peace Now Archive, 1992 file. ICPME also joined this struggle and commissioned a study that provides a summary of the situation of Jewish settler activities in the occupied territories. See Esther Goldberg, *Jewish Settlement in the West Bank and Gaza Strip: Profile—1992* (Tel Aviv: International Center for Peace in the Middle East, 1993). In a press conference on January 22, 1992, a Peace Now spokesperson reported that during the previous year the Shamir government had spent more than $1 billion in the occupied territories. Arie Bender, *Ha'aretz*, January 23, 1992. This figure seems to be exaggerated. Ariel Sharon retorted by saying that he wished he had such an amount to spend.

15. "Summary of Main Activities, July 1991–June 1992," June 17, 1992, Peace Now Archive, 1992 file.

16. These endeavors were led by a number of Orthodox *yeshivot*, particularly one called Ateret Cohanim. Ariel Sharon supported these ventures and early in

1988 he symbolically established his residence in the middle of the Muslim quarter in Jerusalem.

17. "Summary of Main Activities, July 1991–June 1992."

18. For a discussion of the formation of Meretz, see editorial and interview with MK Shulamit Aloni, *New Outlook* 35, no.2 (April 1992): 5, 20–21.

19. Janet Aviad and Tzali Reshef were suggested as candidates.

20. Letters to Shulamit Aloni, Yair Tzaban, and Amnon Rubinstein, February 27, 1992, Peace Now Archive, 1992 file. See also Yehuda Litani, "New Faces in the Mirror," *Al Ha'mishmar,* February 23, 1992.

21. Lilly Galili, *Ha'aretz,* February 27, 1992. After the 1992 election Tzali Reshef became an active member of the Labor Party and Janet Aviad became a member of the Central Council of Ratz.

22. See a paper by Brinker, Galnoor, Margalit, and Peri (not dated); a paper by Amiram Goldblum (not dated); a paper by Tzali Reshef, January 19, 1992; a paper by Yuli Tamir (not dated); and two undated and unsigned papers titled "Shalom Achshav and the Elections" (all in Hebrew), Peace Now Archive, 1992 file. See also "Time to Vote Peace: Peace Now Deployment during the Election Period" (in Hebrew), March 17, 1992, Peace Now Archive, 1992 file.

23. Two public meetings were organized specifically for Russian immigrants in Jerusalem and Tel Aviv. See "Summary of Main Activities, July 1991–June 1992."

24. The last sentence was a play on words in Hebrew: *Yisrael lo shlema bli shalom!* See *Ha'aretz,* June 1, 1992.

25. For an analysis of the 1992 elections, see Sammy Smooha and Don Peretz, "Israel's 1992 Knesset Elections: Are They Critical?" *Middle East Journal* 47, no. 3 (summer 1993): 444–463.

26. See Avinoam Bar-Yossef and Oded Shorer, *Ma'ariv,* August 24, 1992; and Shimon Shiffer, *Yediot Ahronot,* August 25, 1992.

27. In his first meeting with President Bush, Rabin proposed a detailed timetable in which elections to the Palestinian Council in the occupied territories would take place in April 1993. *Ha'aretz,* August 14, 1992.

28. Clyde Haberman, "Settlements Put on Hold in Israel," *New York Times,* July 20, 1992.

29. Editorial in *Peace Now Newsletter* (in Hebrew), no. 5 (March 1993), Peace Now Archive, 1993 file.

30. Elihu Katz and Hanna Levinson, *Territories for Peace? Depends Which, Depends When?* (Jerusalem: Guttman Institute for Applied Social Research, 1992).

31. Polls taken by Geocartographia: The Institute for Spatial Analysis (n.d.). Copy in the author's files.

32. Organizations for human rights such as B'tselem, the Hot Line, and the Center for Alternative Information continued to function because in most cases they had the financial support of foundations, a permanent staff, and an agenda that was not necessarily influenced by day-to-day politics.

33. "Summary of the Proceedings of the Central Forum," November 30, 1992, Peace Now Archive, 1992 file. For a summary of the meetings, see the letter from Gavri Bar-Gil to "Our Friends in Europe and Canada," December 10, 1992, Peace Now Archive, 1992 file.

34. "Summary of the Proceedings of the Central Forum," November 2, 1992, Peace Now Archive, 1992 file.

35. Daniel Williams, "Roofless Houses Reveal Predicament for Rabin," *Los Angeles Times,* July 24, 1992; and David Hoffman, "No Letup in Construction at West Bank Settlement," *Washington Post,* July 24, 1992. Officials in the treasury department and the heads of the construction union warned that 15,000 workers would have to be dismissed. See Eli Danon and Esther Goldbresht, *Ma'ariv,* July 23, 1992.

36. The cabinet canceled the establishment of thirteen new settlements approved by Shamir's government. See Nadav Shragai and Yerah Tal, *Ha'aretz,* July 21, 1992.

37. "Report on the Current Situation of Construction in Settlements in the West Bank and Gaza," Peace Now Settlements Watch, July 1992, Peace Now Archive, 1992/1993 file. See also Nadav Shragai, *Ha'aretz,* July 23, 1992.

38. See Lilly Galili and Yerah Tal, *Ha'aretz,* August 17, 1992; Dani Kipper, *Yediot Ahronot,* July 17, 1992; and Dan Izenberg, *Jerusalem Post,* July 17, 1992.

39. Amiram Goldblum, "Canceling All Preferential Treatment of the Settlers: Issues to Be Discussed and Handled," August 1992, Peace Now Archive, 1992/1993 file.

40. The map was published in Hebrew in October, and in English in November, 1992. The English version was titled "The Real Map: A Demographic and Geographic Analysis of the Population of the West Bank and the Gaza Strip." Peace Now Archive, 1992/1993 file.

41. Hannan Shlein and Yossi Levi, *Ma'ariv,* December 1, 1992.

42. Ibid. See Tzvi Singer, *Yediot Ahronot;* and Lilly Galili, *Ha'aretz,* December 1, 1992. The settlers challenged the accuracy of Peace Now data and claimed that the number of settlers had reached 125,000. See Michal Sela, *Davar,* December 1, 1992.

43. *Peace Now Newsletter* (in Hebrew), no. 5 (March 1993). For a critique of Rabin's early days, see Yossi Werter, "And If It Does Not Succeed," *Hadashot,* November 27, 1992.

44. Lilly Galili, *Ha'aretz,* February 1, 1993.

45. Late in October 1992 the cabinet was informed that forty-six Israelis had been killed in acts of terror since the beginning of the year. See Avinoam Bar-Yossef, *Ma'ariv,* October 21, 1992.

46. On the method Rabin used to persuade Meretz ministers to support his decision, see Orly Azulai-Katz, "Rabin Sold Everybody," *Yediot Ahronot,* December 20, 1992. For a survey of opinions of the ministers, taken a few days after the decision, see *Ma'ariv,* December 22, 1992. The minister of justice was apparently the only member of the cabinet to vote against the deportations.

47. Polls taken early in the crisis showed 91 percent support for the deportations.

48. *Ha'aretz,* December 17, 1992. See also Vered Levi, "Self-Protest," *Tel Aviv,* January 1, 1993, 59–61.

49. *Jerusalem Post,* December 23, 1992.

50. Avi Peled, *Ma'ariv,* December 27, 1992.

51. *Peace Now Bulletin* (in Hebrew), no. 5 (March 1993): 4. Media reports of the demonstration are in *Yediot Ahronot, Ha'aretz, Hadashot,* and *Jerusalem Post,* December 27, 1992.

52. See letter from Janet Aviad to Jerry Bubis, December 28, 1992, Peace Now Archive, 1992/93 file. See also Lilly Galili, "Too Attentive to the Voice of the People," *Ha'aretz,* December 29, 1992.

53. "The main problem the movement faces today," commented Tzali Reshef, "is how to function in the Rabin era. How can we be an active extraparliamentary movement when the political conditions dictate passivity and consent with a sympathetic government?" *Peace Now Bulletin* (in Hebrew), no. 5 (March 1993): 11.

54. Quoted in *Hottam*, January 1, 1993. See report of a discussion between Zucker, Aviad, and Goldblum, "Let's Talk about It," *Hadashot*, December 25, 1992.

55. "Let's Talk about It."

56. Ibid.

57. *Ha'aretz*, February 14, 1993. During this temporary disenchantment Lilly Galili wrote an article titled "Difficult to Get By" in which she suggested that the Palestinians abstain from meetings with Peace Now. However, because meetings actually never stopped, it seems that she overestimated the level of their alienation. For the different meetings in January, see Gavri Bar-Gil, "A Letter to Members of the Central Forum," January 11, 1993, Peace Now Archive, 1993 file.

58. See "Summary of Meeting with Hanan Ashrawi, Ghassan el Khatib, and Faisal Husseini at the Orient House, March 5, 1993," Peace Now Archive, 1993 file.

59. The deportation was originally meant to last two years. Hamas declined the offer to return some of the deportees; they all returned at the end of the year.

60. On the resumption of the Washington talks, see Oded Shorer, *Ma'ariv*, April 28, 1993. See also the editorial "A New Beginning," *Ha'aretz*, April 23, 1993.

61. For the planning of this campaign, see "Summary of the Proceedings of the Central Forum," March 22 and April 27, 1993, Peace Now Archive, 1993 file.

62. The Hebrew term *emdatenu* (our position) was used by Peace Now in the title of a document outlining the movement's position. See drafts of position papers in Peace Now Archive, 1993 file.

63. "Emdatenu: A New Peace Initiative Now," Peace Now Archive, 1993 file.

64. Yehuda Tzur, *Al Ha'mishmar*, April 7, 1993.

65. Much of the following information is taken from Amos Elon, "The Peacemakers," *New Yorker*, December 20, 1993, 77–85. Elon interviewed Hirschfeld and Pundik, whom he called "two obscure freelance Israeli peaceniks." Pundik also gave his story in an interview with Itzhak Livni in a broadcast on Israel Radio on December 12, 1993. A shorter version was published as "The Oslo Diary" (in Hebrew), *Politica*, no. 51 (November 1993). See also Yossi Beillin, *Israel—40 Plus: A Political Profile of Israel's Society in the 1990s* (in Hebrew) (Tel Aviv: Yediot Ahronot Publications, 1994); and Jane Corbin, *Gaza First: The Secret Norway Channel to Peace between Israel and the PLO* (London: Bloomsbury, 1994).

66. See Kevin Fedarko, "Swimming the Oslo Channel," *Time*, September 13, 1993.

67. Gershon Baskin, interview by author, Jerusalem, March 14, 1994. On IPCRI, see chapter 12.

68. See chapter 10, pp. 205–208.

69. Izhar Be'er, *Ha'aretz*, August 3, 6, 1990.

70. *IPCRI News*, no. 3 (October 1991).

71. Mordechai Nessiahu claims that Rabin knew about the Oslo channel long before Peres became privy to the secret, but this is questionable. See M. Nessiahu, Meir Stiglitz, and Ziv Tamir, eds., *Time of Peace: Facts and Thoughts on the Oslo Track* (in Hebrew) (Tel Aviv: privately printed by the editors, 1994).

72. Peres, *New Middle East*, 20.

73. See Fedarko, "Swimming the Oslo Channel."

74. Beilin, *Israel—40 Plus.*

75. Elon, "Peacemakers," 84–85.

76. A senior Israeli army officer told journalists that the IDF would, "erase those villages from the earth unless their villagers put pressure on the Lebanese government to stop Hizbullah's activities." *Yediot Ahronot,* July 29, 1993. Reports from Lebanon occupied much of the Israeli media during the operation. See, for example, *Ma'ariv,* July 27, 1993.

77. Quoted in Vered Levi, *Jerusalem,* July 30, 1993, 29. The movement published an advertisement in which it appealed to the government to "do what is necessary to advance the peace talks and exercise the force you possess with the utmost care." Peace Now Archive, 1993 file.

78. Michel Warschawski, interview by author, Jerusalem, February 18, 1994.

79. Michael Parks, "Israel's Left Wonders If It Has Lost Its Voice," *Los Angeles Times,* June 14, 1993.

80. Vered Levi, *Jerusalem,* July 30, 1993.

81. Peace Now Archive, 1993 file.

82. The agreement excluded attacks inside the security belt. See Ze'ev Schiff, "In Place of a Military Summary," *Ha'aretz,* August 6, 1993.

83. Elon, "Peacemakers," 85.

84. Peres, *New Middle East,* 29–30.

85. Yael Gvirtz, "A True Joy with Tears," *Yediot Ahronot,* September 5, 1993.

86. Quoted in Lilly Galili, *Ha'aretz,* September 5, 1993. Her report, while not highly animated, provides a detailed description of the demonstration. See also Raine Marcus in the *Jerusalem Post* of the same day.

87. For the centrality of mutual recognition in the entire process, see Beilin, *Israel—40 Plus.*

88. Yossi Beilin related in his book that as early as 1980 Peres admitted to him privately that Israel would eventually have to negotiate with the PLO; however, Peres also said that the Israeli public was not ready for it. In regard to the PLO, there was little outward difference between the approaches of Peres and Rabin. See ibid.

89. Peres, *New Middle East,* 16–18.

90. See Amnon Barzilai, "On a Bright Day Rabin Can See Tunis," *Hadashot,* November 27, 1992. The article followed news that Rabin had met with MK Abedel Wahab Darawshe, who had just met with Arafat in Tunis.

91. See *Ha'aretz,* July 5, 1993.

92. Ibid.

93. See *Yediot Ahronot,* September 5, 1993.

94. The text of the Declaration of Principles and the other documents signed in Washington were reprinted in *Declaration of Principles on Interim Self-Government Arrangements* (Jerusalem: Ministry of Foreign Affairs,1993).

95. *Time,* September 13, 1993; and *Newsweek,* September 20, 1993.

96. Akiva Eldar, *Ha'aretz,* September 10, 1993.

97. Igal Sarna, "Their November 29th," *Hadashot,* September 14, 1993.

Conclusion

1. For instance, on April 4, 1995, the renowned writer David Grossman called on Peace Now to awaken and resume its mass activities. See his article "Bekotzer Yedchem," *Ha'aretz*, 4 April, 1995.

2. Yossi Ben-Artzi, interview by author, Haifa, May 5, 1994.

3. Izhar Be'er, interview by author, Jerusalem, February 18, 1994.

4. Interview with Nurit Shleifman.

5. Interview with Janet Aviad.

6. Ilan Pappe, a historian and activist on the Israeli left, told the author that he could never become unequivocally active in Peace Now because he detested the argument often used by the movement that the occupation was corrupting Israelis. "The victims were not the Israelis but the Palestinians. I could never forget for a moment that the main evil of the occupation is the killing and wounding of Palestinians." Interview by author, Haifa, July 20, 1994.

7. Seeking to capitalize on anti-Arab sentiment and defame the peace movement, the Israeli right frequently described the peace movement as "Arab lovers."

8. Faisal Husseini, "Palestinian Politics after the Gulf War (An Interview)," *Journal of Palestine Studies* 20, no. 4 (summer 1991): 99–108.

9. See, for example, Benni Morris, *The Birth of the Palestinian Refugee Problem* (Cambridge: Cambridge University Press, 1989).

10. For a detailed discussion of this issue, see Mordechai Bar-On, *Past Lessons and Future Logic: Security Requirements of Peace Making in the Middle East* (College Park, Md.: Center for International Development and Conflict Resolution, University of Maryland, 1994).

11. Quotation taken from the personal notes of the author.

Select Bibliography

Primary Sources

Archives
Israel State Archives, Jerusalem.
Jaffee Center for Strategic Studies, Clippings Archive, Tel Aviv.
Peace Now Archive, Jerusalem.
Labor Party Archives, Beit Berl.

Personal Archives
Arieli, Yehoshua, Jerusalem.
Aviad, Janet, Jerusalem.
Avneri, Uri, Tel Aviv.
Menuchin, Yishai, Jerusalem (the main archive of Yesh Gvul).
Raz, Naftali, Mevaseret Yerushalayim.

Interviews
Aloni, Shulamit (Jerusalem, August 22, 1992).
Amirav, Moshe (Jerusalem, February 13, 1994).
Amit, Dani (Jerusalem, January 21, 1994).
Arieli, Yehoshua (Jerusalem, August 10, 1992).
Ashkenazi, Motti (Jerusalem, January 31, 1993).
Aviad, Janet (Jerusalem, January 5, 1984, and July 27, 1992).
Avneri, Uri (Tel Aviv, July 23 and 29, 1992).
Baskin, Gershon (Jerusalem, March 14, 1994).
Be'er, Izhar (Jerusalem, February 18, 1994).
Ben-Artzi, Yossi (Haifa, May 3, 1994).
Bentsur, Naomi (Jerusalem, November 7, 1993).

Bitan, Dan (Jerusalem, February 3, 1993).

Blank, Judy (Jerusalem, August, 16, 1992).

Brinker, Menachem (Jerusalem, August 7 and 16, 1992).

Burg, Joseph (Jerusalem, August 11, 1992).

Cygielman, Victor (by telephone, August 16, 1992).

Dahan, Yossi (Tel Aviv, July 29, 1992).

Deutsch, Yvonne (Jerusalem, August 17, 1992).

Dori, Latif (Tel Aviv, November 3, 1993).

Eilam, Yigal (Tel Aviv, February 4, 1993).

Elbaz, Shlomo (Jerusalem, August 11, 1992).

Eliav, Arie (Lova) (Tel Aviv, July 26 and August 2, 1992).

Elkayam, Sheli (Jerusalem, November 3, 1993).

Eran, Shirley (Jerusalem, August 12, 1992).

Golan, Joseph (Jerusalem, August 12, 1992).

Goldblum, Amiram (Jerusalem, August 18, 1992).

Habibi, Emil (Jerusalem, March 23, 1992).

Hammerman, Ilana (Jerusalem, March 15, 1994).

Hareven, Shulamit (Jerusalem, August 26, 1993).

Harnik, Raya (Jerusalem, October 30, 1993).

Hazan-Rokem, Galit (Jerusalem, August 20, 1992).

Hever, Hanan (Jerusalem, August 23, 1992).

Kaminer, Reuven (Jerusalem, August 20, 1992).

Kelman, Herbert (Boston, August 10, 1993).

Kesse, Tzvi (Tel Aviv, August 2 and 13, 1992).

Landau, Yehezkiel (Jerusalem, August 26, 1992).

Menuchin, Yishai (Jerusalem, August 9 and 22, 1992).

Nathan, Abe J. (by telephone, January 22, 1994).

Pappe, Ilan (Haifa, July 20, 1994).

Peled, Matti (Motza, January 20, 1994).

Plesner-Liebes, Tamar (Jerusalem, February 14, 1994).

Raz, Naftali (Mevaseret Yerushalayim, January 7, 8, and 9, 1984).

Reshef, Tzali (Jerusalem, January 12, 1984).

Sarid, Yossi (Tel Aviv, August 24, 1992).

Sela, Amnon (Jerusalem, August 18, 1992).

Shaham, David (Tel Aviv, August 2, 1992).

Shueftan, Dan (Ramat Gan, July 23 and 29, 1992).

Shleifman, Nurit, and Freudental, Rachel (jointly, Jerusalem, August 17, 1992).

Swirski, Shlomo (Tel Aviv, August 13, 1992).

Swirski, Gilla (Jerusalem, August 22, 1992).

Tamir, Yael (Jerusalem, February 3, 1993).

Toledano, Shmuel (Jerusalem, July 12, 1992).

Warschawski, Michel (Jerusalem, February 18, 1994).

Weinberg, Yesha'aia (Washington, D.C., September 24, 1992).
Ya'akobi, Gad (Tel Aviv, August 13, 1992).
Yakobson, Dan (Tel Aviv, February 4, 1993).
Yatziv, Gadi (Jerusalem, February 1, 1993).
Zeidani, Daher (Jerusalem, August 22, 1992)
Zichroni, Amnon (Tel Aviv, November 11, 1993).

Israeli Newspapers and Journals

Emda (monthly magazine, in Hebrew)
Ha'aretz (daily newspaper, in Hebrew)
Al Ha'mishmar (daily newspaper, in Hebrew)
Ha'olam Ha'zeh (weekly magazine, in Hebrew)
Jerusalem Post (weekly newspaper, in English)
Ma'arachot (IDF monthly magazine)
Ma'ariv (daily newspaper, in Hebrew)
Nekuda (monthly magazine of the settlers' movement, in Hebrew)
New Outlook (monthly journal, in English)
Yediot Ahronot (daily newspaper, in Hebrew)

Published Documents

Medzini, Meron, *Israel's Foreign Relations: Selected Documents, 1947–1974.* 2 vols. Jerusalem: Ministry for Foreign Affairs, 1976.

Moore, John Norton, ed. *The Arab-Israeli Conflict,* 4 vols. Princeton: Princeton University Press, 1974–91.

U.S. House of Representatives Committee on Foreign Relations. *The Search for Peace in the Middle East: Documents and Statements, 1967–1979.* Washington, D.C.: Government Printing Office.

Memoirs

Brzezinski, Zbigniew. *Power and Principle: Memoirs of the National Security Adviser, 1977–1981.* New York: Farrar, Straus, and Giroux, 1983.

Carter, Jimmy. *Keeping Faith: Memoirs of a President.* New York: Bantam, 1982.

Dayan, Moshe. *Story of My Life.* New York: William Morrow, 1976.

Eban, Abba. *Personal Witness: Israel through My Eyes.* New York: Putnam, 1992.

Eitan, Rafael. *A Soldier's Story: The Life and Times of an Israeli War Hero.* New York: Shapolsky, 1991.

Haig, Alexander M. *Caveat: Realism, Reagan, and Foreign Policy.* New York: Macmillan, 1984.

Rabin, Yitzhak. *The Rabin Memoirs.* Boston: Little, Brown, 1979.

Reagan, Ronald. *An American Life.* New York: Simon and Schuster, 1990.

Sadat, Anwar. *In Search of Identity: An Autobiography.* New York: Harper Colophon, 1979.

Shamir, Yitzhak. *Summing Up.* Tel Aviv: Edanim, 1994.

Sharon, Ariel. *Warrior: An Autobiography.* New York: Simon and Schuster, 1989.

Sharett, Moshe. *Diary.* Tel Aviv: Ma'ariv Publications, 1978.

Shultz, George P. *Turmoil and Triumph: My Years as Secretary of State.* New York: Scribner's, 1993.

Vance, Cyrus. *Hard Choices: Critical Years in America's Foreign Policy.* New York: Simon and Schuster, 1983.

Secondary Sources

Books

Ajami, Fouad. *The Arab Predicament: Arab Political Thought and Practice since 1967.* Cambridge: Cambridge University Press, 1981.

Alpher, Joseph, and Shai Feldman, eds. *Israel, the West Bank and Gaza: Toward a Solution.* Tel Aviv: Jaffee Center for Strategic Studies, 1989.

———. *The West Bank and Gaza: Israel's Options for Peace.* Tel Aviv: Jaffee Center for Strategic Studies, 1989.

Arian, Asher, ed. *Elections in Israel, 1981.* Tel Aviv: Ramot Publishing, 1983.

———. *Politics in Israel: The Second Generation.* Chatham, N.J.: Chatham House, 1989.

Arian, Asher, and Michal Shamir. *Elections in Israel, 1988.* Boulder, Colo.: Westview, 1990.

Aronoff, Myron. *Israeli Visions and Divisions: Cultural Change and Political Conflict.* New Brunswick, N.J.: Transaction Books, 1989.

Aronson, Geoffrey. *Israel, Palestinians and the Intifada: Creating Facts on the West Bank.* New York: Kegan Paul International, 1990.

Atkinson, Rick. *Crusade: The Untold Story of the Persian Gulf War.* Boston: Houghton Mifflin, 1993.

Avineri, Shlomo. *The Making of Modern Zionism: The Intellectual Origins of the Jewish State.* New York: Basic Books, 1981.

Avneri, Uri. *Israel Without Zionism: A Plan for Peace in the Middle East.* New York: Collier, 1971.

———. *My Friend the Enemy.* London: Zed Books, 1986.

Bailey, Clinton. *Jordan's Palestinian Challenge 1948–1983.* Boulder, Colo.: Westview, 1984.

Baram, Amatzia, and Barry Rubin, eds. *Iraq's Road to War.* New York: St. Martin's, 1993.

Bar-On, Mordechai. *The Gates of Gaza: Israel's Road to Suez and Back, 1955–1957.* New York: St. Martin's, 1994.

Bar-Siman-Tov, Yaacov. *The Israeli-Egyptian War of Attrition 1969–1970.* New York: Columbia University Press, 1980.

Bennis, Phyllis, and Michel Moushabeck. *Beyond the Storm: A Gulf Crisis Reader.* New York: Olive Branch Press, 1991.

Benvenisti, Meron. *Conflicts and Contradictions.* New York: Willard Books, 1986.

Bialer, Uri. *Between East and West: Israel's Foreign Policy Orientation 1948–1956.* Cambridge: Cambridge University Press, 1990.

Brecher, Michael. *The Foreign Policy System of Israel: Setting, Images, Process.* New Haven: Yale University Press, 1972.

Brenner, Lenni. *The Iron Wall: Zionist Revisionism from Jabotinsky to Shamir.* London: Zed Books, 1984.

Chomsky, Noam. *The Fateful Triangle: The United States, Israel and the Palestinians.* Boston: South End Press, 1983.

Cobban, Helena. *The Palestinian Liberation Organization: People, Power and Politics.* Cambridge: Cambridge University Press, 1984.

———. *The Superpowers and the Syrian-Israeli Conflict.* New York: Praeger, 1991.

Cohen, A. A., and Gadi Wolfsfeld, eds. *Framing the Intifada: People and Media.* Norwood, N.J.: Ablex Publishing, 1993.

Cohen, Amnon. *Political Parties in the West Bank under the Jordanian Regime, 1949–1967.* Ithaca, N.Y.: Cornell University Press, 1982.

Corbin, Jane. *Gaza First: The Secret Norway Channel to Peace between Israel and the PLO.* London: Bloomsbury, 1994.

Dayan, Moshe. *Breakthrough: A Personal Account of the Egypt-Israel Peace Negotiations.* New York: Knopf, 1981.

Diskin, Avraham, and Emmanuel Gutmann. *The Roots of Begin's Success: The 1981 Israeli Elections.* London: Croom Helm, 1984.

Dupuy, Trevor. *Elusive War: The Arab-Israeli Wars, 1947–1974.* New York: Harper and Row, 1978.

Eliav, Arie. *Land of the Hart: Israelis, Arabs, the Territories and a Vision of the Future.* Philadelphia: Jewish Publication Society, 1974.

Elon, Amos, and Sana Hassan. *Between Enemies: A Compassionate Dialogue between an Israeli and an Arab.* New York: Random House, 1974.

Esco Foundation for Palestine. *Palestine: A Study of Jewish, Arab, and British Policies.* New Haven: Yale University Press, 1947.

Etzioni-Halevy, Eva (with Rina Shapira). *Political Culture in Israel: Cleavage and Integration among Israeli Jews.* New York: Praeger, 1977.

Fahmi, Ismail. *Negotiating for Peace in the Middle East.* Baltimore: Johns Hopkins University Press, 1983.

Fein, Leonard. *Politics in Israel.* Boston: Little, Brown, 1967.

Flapan, Simcha. *The Birth of Israel: Myths and Realities.* New York: Pantheon, 1987.

Friedman, Thomas. *From Beirut to Jerusalem.* New York: Farrar, Straus, and Giroux, 1989.

Gal-Nur, Itzhak. *Steering the Polity: Communication and Politics in Israel.* Beverly Hills: Sage, 1982.

Garfinkle, Adam. *Israel and Jordan in the Shadow of War: Functional Ties and Futile Diplomacy in a Small Place.* New York, St. Martin's, 1992.

Gazit, Shlomo, and Ze'ev Eytan, eds. *The Middle East Military Balance 1988–1989.* Boulder, Colo., Westview, 1989.

Giladi, G. N. *Discord in Zion: Conflict between Ashkenazi and Sephardi Jews in Israel.* London: Scorpion, 1990.

Golan, Galia. *Soviet Policies in the Middle East from World War II to Gorbachev.* Cambridge: Cambridge University Press, 1990.

Grossman, David. *The Smile of the Lamb*. New York: Farrar, Straus, and Giroux, 1990.

———. *The Yellow Wind*. New York: Farrar, Straus, and Giroux, 1988.

Haber, Eitan. *Menachem Begin: The Legend and the Man*. New York: Delacorte, 1978.

Haber, Eitan; Ze'ev Schiff; and Ehud Ya'ari. *The Year of the Dove*. New York: Bantam, 1979.

Hammel, Eric. *Six Days in June: How Israel Won the 1967 Arab-Israeli War*. New York: Scribner's, 1992.

Harkabi, Yehoshafat. *Arab Attitudes to Israel*. Jerusalem: Israeli Universities Press, 1972.

Hassan, Sana. *Enemy in the Promised Land: An Egyptian Woman's Journey into Israel*. New York: Pantheon, 1986.

Hertzberg, Arthur. *The Zionist Idea: A Historical Analysis and Reader*. New York: Doubleday, 1959.

Hirst, David. *The Gun and the Olive Branch: The Roots of Violence in the Middle East*. New York: Harcourt Brace Jovanovich, 1977.

Horowitz, Dan, and Moshe Lissak. *Trouble in Utopia: The Overburdened Polity of Israel*. Albany: State University of New York Press, 1989.

Hurwits, Dina, ed. *Walking the Red Line*. Philadelphia: New Society Publishers, 1992.

Iyad, Abu, and Eric Rouleau. *My Home, My Land: A Narrative of the Palestinian Struggle*. New York: Times Books, 1981.

Jackson, Elmore. *Middle East Mission: The Story of a Major Bid for Peace in the Time of Nasser and Ben-Gurion*. New York: Norton, 1983.

Kamel, Mohamed Ibrahim. *The Camp David Accords: A Testimony*. London: KPI, 1986.

Kerr, Malcolm. *The Arab Cold War, Gamal Abd al-Nasir and His Rivals, 1958–1970*. Oxford: Oxford University Press, 1971.

Khalidi, Rashid. *Under Siege: PLO Decision Making during the 1982 War*. New York: Columbia University Press, 1986.

Khalidi, Walid. *Palestine Reborn*. London: I. B. Tauris, 1992.

Kimche, David. *The Last Option*. New York: Scribner's, 1991.

Klein, Menachem. *Antagonistic Collaboration: PLO-Jordanian Dialogue 1985–1988*. Policy Paper no. 27. Jerusalem: Leonard Davis Institute, 1988.

Laqueur, Walter. *The Road to War, 1967: The Origins of the Arab-Israeli Conflict*. London: Weidenfeld and Nicolson, 1969.

———. *The Soviet Union and the Middle East*. New York: Praeger, 1969.

Laqueur, Walter, and Barry Rubin, eds. *The Israel-Arab Reader: A Documentary History of the Middle East Conflict*. London: Penguin, 1984.

Lissak, Moshe. *Social Mobility in Israeli Society*. Jerusalem: Jerusalem Academic Press, 1969.

Lorch, Netanel. *The Edge of the Sword: Israel's War of Independence, 1947–1949*. New York: Putnam, 1961.

Lustick, Ian. *Arabs in a Jewish State: Israel's Control of a National Minority*. Austin: University of Texas Press, 1980.

Mackinlay, John. *The Peacekeepers: An Assessment of Peacekeeping Operations at the Arab-Israeli Interface*. London: Unwin Hyman, 1989

Melman, Yossi, and Dan Raviv. *Behind the Uprising: Israelis, Jordanians, and Palestinians*. Westport, Conn.: Greenwood, 1989.

Morris, Benny. *Israel's Border Wars, 1949–1956*. Oxford: Clarendon, 1993.

Murphy, Jay. *For Palestine*. New York: Writers and Readers, 1993.

Nassar, Jamal R., and Roger Heacock, eds. *Intifada: Palestine at the Crossroads*. New York: Praeger, 1990.

Newman, David, ed. *The Impact of Gush Emunim: Politics and Settlement in the West Bank*. London: Croom Helm, 1985.

Norton, Augustus Richard. *Amal and the Shi'a: Struggle for the Soul of Lebanon*. Austin: University of Texas Press, 1987.

Nusseibeh, Sari, and Mark Heller. *No Trumpets No Drums: A Two-State Settlement of the Israeli-Palestinian Conflict*. New York: Hill and Wang, 1991.

O'Brien, Conor Cruise. *The Siege: The Saga of Israel and Zionism*. London: Weidenfeld and Nicolson, 1986.

Oz, Amos. *In the Land of Israel*. London: Flamingo, 1983.

Peres, Shimon. *The New Middle East*. New York: Henry Holt, 1993.

Perlmutter, Amos. *The Life and Times of Menachem Begin*. New York: Doubleday, 1987.

Porath, Yehoshua. *The Emergence of the Palestinian-Arab National Movement, 1918–1929*. London: Frank Cass, 1974.

Quandt, William. *Camp David: Peace Making and Politics*. Washington, D.C.: Brookings Institution, 1986.

———. *Decade of Decisions: American Policy toward the Arab-Israeli Conflict, 1967–75*. Berkeley, Calif.: University of California Press, 1977.

———. *Peace Process: American Diplomacy and the Arab-Israeli Conflict since 1967*. Berkeley, Calif.: University of California Press, 1993.

———, ed. *The Middle East: Ten Years after Camp David*. Washington, D.C.: Brookings Institution, 1988.

Ra'anan, Uri. *The USSR, Arms and the Third World*. Cambridge, Mass.: MIT Press, 1969.

Rabinovich, Itamar. *The Road Not Taken: Early Arab-Israeli Negotiations*. Oxford: Oxford University Press, 1991.

———. *The War for Lebanon 1970–1985*. Ithaca: Cornell University Press, 1984.

Raphael, Gideon. *Destination Peace: Three Decades of Israeli Foreign Policy*. New York: Stein and Day, 1981.

Rapoport, Louis. *Confrontations: Israeli Life in the Year of the Uprising*. Boston: Quinlan, 1988.

Reich, Bernard. *Quest for Peace: United States-Israel Relations and the Arab-Israeli Conflict*. New Brunswick, N.J.: Transaction Books, 1977.

Reiser, Stewart. *The Politics of Leverage: The National Religious Party of Israel and Its Influence on Foreign Policy*. Cambridge, Mass.: Harvard University Press, 1984.

Riad, Mahmud. *The Struggle for Peace in the Middle East*. London: Quartet Books, 1981.

Rikhye, Indar Jit. *The Theory and Practice of Peacekeeping*. London: C. Hurst, 1984.

Ro'i, Yaacov. *From Encroachment to Involvement*. Jerusalem: Israeli Universities Press, 1974.

Rubinstein, Amnon. *The Zionist Dream Revisited: From Herzl to Gush Emunim and Back*. New York: Schocken, 1984.

Sachar, Howard. *A History of Israel*. New York: Knopf, 1986.

———. *A History of Israel: From the Rise of Zionism to Our Time*. New York: Knopf, 1979.

Safran, Nadav. *From War to War: The Arab-Israeli Confrontation, 1948–1967*. New York: Pegasus, 1969.

———. *Israel the Embattled Ally*. Cambridge, Mass.: Harvard University Press, 1978.

Safty, Adel. *From Camp David to the Gulf*. Montreal: Black Rose Books, 1992.

Said, Edward. *The Question of Palestine*. New York: Vintage, 1979.

Sandler, Shmuel, and Tuvia Frisch. *Israel, the Palestinians, and the West Bank: A Study in Intercommunal Conflict*. Lexington, Mass.: Lexington Books, 1984.

Sayigh, Rosemary. *Palestinians: From Peasants to Revolutionaries*. London: Zed Books, 1979.

Schiff, Gary S. *Tradition and Politics: The Religious Parties in Israel*. Detroit: Wayne State University Press, 1977.

Schiff, Ze'ev, and Ehud Ya'ari. *Israel's Lebanon War*. Ed. and trans., Ina Friedman. New York: Simon and Schuster, 1984.

Schoenbaum, David. *The United States and the State of Israel*. Oxford: Oxford University Press, 1993.

Segal, Jerome. *Creating the Palestinian State: A Strategy for Peace*. Chicago: Lawrence Hill Books, 1989.

Segev, Tom. *The First Israelis, 1949*. New York: Free Press, 1986.

Seliktar, Ofira. *New Zionism and the Foreign Policy System of Israel*. London: Croom Helm, 1986.

Shaham, David. *Israel: Forty Years*. Tel Aviv: Am Oved, 1991.

Shavit, Yaacov. *Jabotinsky and the Revisionist Movement 1925–1948*. London: Frank Cass, 1988.

Shlaim, Avi. *Collusion across the Jordan: King Abdullah, the Zionist Movement, and the Partition of Palestine*. Oxford: Clarendon, 1988.

Sifry, Micah, and Christopher Cerf. *The Gulf War Reader: History, Documents, and Opinions*. New York: Random House, 1991.

Silberstein, Laurence, ed. *New Perspectives on Israeli History: The Early Years of the State*. New York: New York University Press, 1991.

Silver, Eric. *Begin: The Haunted Prophet*. London: Weidenfeld and Nicolson, 1984.

Smooha, Sammy. *Israel: Pluralism and Conflict*. Berkeley, Calif.: University of California Press, 1978.

Spiegel, Steven. *The Other Arab-Israeli Conflict: Making America's Middle East Policy from Truman to Reagan*. Chicago: University of Chicago Press, 1985.

Sprinzak, Ehud. *The Ascendance of Israel's Radical Right*. Oxford: Oxford University Press, 1991.

Stone, Russell A. *Social Change in Israel: Attitudes and Events, 1967–1979*. New York: Praeger, 1982.

Teveth, Shabtai. *The Cursed Blessing*. London: Weidenfeld and Nicolson, 1970.

Touval, Saadia. *The Peace Brokers: Mediation in the Arab-Israeli Conflict*. Princeton: Princeton University Press, 1982.

Wallach, John, and Janet Wallach. *The New Palestinians: The Emerging Generation of Leaders*. Rocklin, Calif.: Prima Publishing, 1992.

Weizman, Ezer. *The Battle for Peace*. New York: Bantam, 1981.

Wolfsfeld, Gadi. *The Politics of Provocation: Participation and Protest in Israel*. Albany: State University of New York Press, 1988.

Woodward, Bob. *The Commanders*. New York: Simon and Schuster, 1991.

Ya'ari, Ehud. *Strike Terror: The Story of the Fateh.* New York: Sabra, 1970.

Yishai, Yael. *Land or Peace: Whither Israel?* Stanford: Stanford University Press, 1987.

Articles

Abed, George. "The Palestinians and the Gulf Crisis." *Journal of Palestine Studies* 20, no. 2 (winter 1991): 29–42.

Arian, Asher. "Elections 1981: Competitiveness and Polarization." *Jerusalem Quarterly* 21 (fall 1981).

Avruch, Kevin A. "Gush Emunim: Politics, Religion, and Ideology in Israel." *Middle East Review* 11, no. 2 (winter 1978–79).

Bailey, Clinton. "Changing Attitudes toward Jordan in the West Bank." *Middle East Journal* 32, no. 2 (spring 1978).

Bar-On, Mordechai. "Israeli Reactions to the Uprising." *Journal of Palestine Studies* 17, no. 4 (summer 1988): 46–65.

———. "Israel's National Unity Government, 1984–1986: A Retrospective." *Tikkun* 1, no. 2 (fall 1986).

———. "Trends in the Political Psychology of Israeli Jews." *Journal of Palestine Studies* 17, no. 1 (fall 1987): 21–36.

Blank, Judy. "The Israeli Women's Peace Movement." *Response* [United Methodist Women's magazine] 24, no. 6 (June 1992).

Cohen, Stephen P., et al. "Evolving Intergroup Techniques for Conflict Resolution: An Israeli-Palestinian Pilot Workshop." *Journal of Social Issues* 33, no. 1 (1977).

Don-Yehiya, Eliezer. "Jewish Messianism, Religious Zionism and Israeli Politics: The Impact and Origins of Gush Emunim." *Middle Eastern Studies* 23, no. 2 (April 1987).

Finkelstein, Norman. "Palestinian Attitudes during the Gulf War." *Journal of Palestine Studies* 21, no. 3 (spring 1992): 54–70.

Glazer-Migdal, Penina, and Myron Glazer. "War Resisters in the Land of Battle." *Dissent* (summer 1977): 289–296.

Goldmann, Nahum. "The Future of Israel." *Foreign Affairs.* 48, no. 3 (April 1970).

Herman, S. N. "In the Shadow of the Holocaust." *Jerusalem Quarterly* 3 (1977).

Hudson, Michael. "The Palestinian Factor in the Lebanese Civil War." *Middle East Journal* 32, no. 3 (summer 1978).

Husseini, Faisal. "Palestinian Politics after the Gulf War." *Journal of Palestine Studies.* 20, no. 4 (summer 1991).

Inbari, Efraim. "Sources of Tension between Israel and the United States." *Conflict Resolution* 4, no. 2 (spring 1984).

Jacob, Abel. "Trends in Israeli Public Opinion on Issues Related to the Arab-Israeli Conflict 1967–1972." *Jewish Journal of Sociology* 16 (December 1974).

Kelman, Herbert. "The Interactional Approach to Conflict Resolution and Its Application to Israeli-Palestinian Relations." *International Interaction* 6, no. 2 (1979).

———. "Israelis and Palestinians: Psychological Prerequisites for Mutual Acceptance." *International Security* 3, no.1 (summer 1978).

———. "The Palestinization of the Arab-Israeli Conflict." *Jerusalem Quarterly* 46 (spring 1988).

Khalidi, Walid. "Thinking the Unthinkable: A Sovereign Palestinian State." *Foreign Affairs* 56, no. 4 (summer 1978).

———. "Why Some Arabs Supported Saddam." In *The Gulf Crisis: Origins and Consequences*, Institute for Palestine Studies occasional paper. Washington, D.C.: Institute for Palestine Studies, 1991.

Knei-Paz, Baruch. "Academics in Politics: An Israeli Experience." *Jerusalem Quarterly* 16 (summer 1980).

Kuttab, Daoud. "The Palestinian Uprising: The Second Phase, Self-Sufficiency." *Journal of Palestine Studies* 17, no. 4 (summer 1988): 36–45.

———. "A Profile of the Stonethrowers." *Journal of Palestine Studies* 17, no. 3 (spring 1988): 14–23.

Lapidoth, Ruth. "The Autonomy Talks." *Jerusalem Quarterly* 24 (summer 1982).

Lehman-Wilzig, Sam. "The Israeli Protester." *Jerusalem Quarterly* 26 (winter 1983).

Liebes, Tamar. "Decoding Television News: The Political Discourse of Israeli Hawks and Doves." *Theory and Society* 21 (1992).

Linn, Ruth. "Conscientious Objection in Israel during the War in Lebanon." *Armed Forces and Society* 12, no. 4 (1986): 489–511.

Linn, Ruth, and Carol Gilligan. "One Action, Two Moral Orientations—The Tension between Justice and Care: Voices in Israel Selective Conscientious Objectors." *New Ideas in Psychology* 8, no. 2 (1990).

Lustick, Ian. "Israeli Politics and American Foreign Policy." *Foreign Affairs* 61, no. 2 (winter 1982): 379–399.

Luttwak, Edward N., and Walter Laqueur. "Kissinger and the Yom Kippur War." *Commentary* 58, no. 3 (September 1974).

Mahmood, Zahid. "Sadat and Camp David Reappraised." *Journal of Palestine Studies* 15, no. 1 (fall 1985): 62–87.

Milson, Menachem. "How to Make Peace with the Palestinians." *Commentary* 71, no. 5 (May 1981): 25–35.

Newman, David. "Gush Emunim between Fundamentalism and Pragmatism." *Jerusalem Quarterly* 39 (1986): 33–43.

Pappe, Ilan. "Moshe Sharett, David Ben-Gurion, and the 'Palestinian Option,' 1848–1956." *Studies in Zionism* 7, no. 1 (1986): 77–96.

Peres, Shimon. "A Strategy for Peace in the Middle East." *Foreign Affairs* 58, no. 4 (spring 1980).

Peres, Yochanan. "Ethnic Relations in Israel." *American Journal of Sociology* 76, no. 6 (May 1971).

Peretz, Don. "The Impact of the Gulf War on Israeli and Palestinian Political Attitudes." *Journal of Palestine Studies* 21, no. 1 (fall 1991): 17–35.

Quandt, William. "Reagan's Lebanon Policy: Trial and Error." *Middle East Journal* 38, no. 2 (spring 1984): 237–254.

Schiff, Ze'ev. "The Green Light." *Foreign Policy* 50 (spring 1982): 73–85.

———. "Lebanon: Motivations and Interests in Israel's Policy." *Middle East Journal* 38, no. 2 (spring 1984): 220–227.

Seliktar, Ofira. "The Cost of Vigilance in Israel: Linking the Economic and Social Costs of Defense." *Journal of Peace Research* 17, no. 4 (1980): 339–355.

————. "Ethnic Stratification and Foreign Policy in Israel: The Attitudes of Oriental Jews towards the Arabs and the Arab-Israeli Conflict." *Middle East Journal* 38, no. 1 (winter 1984): 34–50.

Shlaim, Avi. "Husni Zaim and the Plan to Resettle Palestinian Refugees in Syria." *Journal of Palestine Studies* 15, no. 4 (summer 1986): 68–80.

Smooha, Sammy, and Don Peretz. "Israel's 1992 Knesset Elections: Are They Critical?" *Middle East Journal* 47, no. 3 (summer 1993): 444–463.

Swirski, Gilla. "Women in Black." *Present Tense* 16, no. 4 (May/June 1989).

Swirski, Shlomo. "The Oriental Jews in Israel: Why Many Tilted toward Begin." *Dissent* 31, no. 1 (winter 1984): 77–91.

Weissbrod, Lilly. "Gush Emunim Ideology: From Religious Doctrine to Political Action." *Middle Eastern Studies* 18, no. 3 (July 1982): 265–275.

Yishai, Yael. "Israel's Right-Wing Jewish Proletariat." *Jewish Journal of Sociology* 24, no. 2 (December 1982).

Index

Jennings Randolph Program for International Peace

As part of the statute establishing the United States Institute of Peace, Congress envisioned a fellowship program that would appoint "scholars and leaders of peace from the United States and abroad to pursue scholarly inquiry and other appropriate forms of communication on international peace and conflict resolution." The program was named after Senator Jennings Randolph of West Virginia, whose efforts over four decades helped to establish the Institute.

Since it began in 1987, the Jennings Randolph Program has played a key role in the Institute's effort to build a national center of research, dialogue, and education on critical problems of conflict and peace. Through a rigorous annual competition, outstanding men and women from diverse nations and fields are selected to carry out projects designed to expand and disseminate knowledge on violent international conflict and the wide range of ways it can be peacefully managed or resolved.

The Institute's Distinguished Fellows and Peace Fellows are individuals from a wide variety of academic and other professional backgrounds who work at the Institute on research and education projects they have proposed and participate in the Institute's collegial and public outreach activities. The Institute's Peace Scholars are doctoral candidates at American universities who are working on their dissertations.

Institute fellows and scholars have worked on such varied subjects as international negotiation, regional security arrangements, conflict resolution techniques, international legal systems, ethnic and religious conflict, arms control, and the protection of human rights, and these issues have been examined in settings throughout the world.

As part of its effort to disseminate original and useful analyses of peace and conflict to policymakers and the public, the Institute publishes book manuscripts and other written products that result from the fellowship work and meet the Institute's high standards of quality.

Joseph Klaits

Director

In Pursuit of
PEACE

This book is set in ITC Leawood; the display type is Helvetica Condensed. Cover design by Marie Marr; interior design by Joan Engelhardt and Day W. Dosch. Page makeup by Day W. Dosch. Editing by Nigel Quinney, Priscilla Jensen, and Wesley Palmer. Indexing by Elinor Lindheimer.